Global Water Resources

This is a Festschrift in honour of Professor Asit K. Biswas, for his manifold contributions to water resources policy and management and his extensive efforts over six decades to generate, synthetize, apply, and disseminate knowledge at national and global levels.

Global Water Resources: Festschrift in Honour of Asit K. Biswas includes invited contributions on global water issues from 23 globally renown leaders in the public and private sectors, as well as academia, who have made significant contributions to the field of water resources policy, management, development, and governance. The vision and expertise of this distinguished group of experts provides a unique focus on unfolding water issues and their bearing on world development.

This book will be of great value to scholars, students, and policymakers interested in water resource governance, sustainable development, and climate change.

The chapters in this book were originally published as a special issue of the *International Journal of Water Resources Development*.

Cecilia Tortajada is Professor at the School of Interdisciplinary Studies, College of Social Sciences, University of Glasgow. She has been an advisor to major international institutions like FAO, UNDP, JICA, ADB, OECD, IDRC and GIZ, and has worked in numerous countries in Africa, Asia, North and South America and Europe on water and natural resources management and environment policies. She is a member of the OECD Initiative on Water Governance and recipient of the prestigious Crystal Drop Award of the International Water Resources Association.

Eduardo Araral is Associate Professor at the Lee Kuan Yew School of Public Policy, National University of Singapore. He is the Co-Director of the Institute of Water Policy, Vice Chairman of the Asia Pacific Water Forum and Associate Editor of the Oxford University Press book series on water governance.

Routledge Special Issues on Water Policy and Governance

Edited by:
Cecilia Tortajada (IJWRD) – Institute of Water Policy, Lee Kuan Yew School of Public Policy, NUS, Singapore
James Nickum (WI) – International Water Resources Association, France

Most of the world's water problems, and their solutions, are directly related to policies and governance, both specific to water and in general. Two of the world's leading journals in this area, the *International Journal of Water Resources Development* and *Water International* (the official journal of the International Water Resources Association), contribute to this special issues series, aimed at disseminating new knowledge on the policy and governance of water resources to a very broad and diverse readership all over the world. The series should be of direct interest to all policy makers, professionals and lay readers concerned with obtaining the latest perspectives on addressing the world's many water issues.

Legal Perspectives on Bridging Science and Policy
Edited by Mara Tignino, Raya Marina Stephan, Renée Martin-Nagle and Owen McIntyre

Virtual Water
Implications for Agriculture and Trade
Edited by Chittaranjan Ray, David McInnes and Matthew R. Sanderson

Flood Resilience of Private Properties
Edited by Thomas Hartmann, Willemijn van Doorn-Hoekveld, Helena F.M.W. van Rijswick and Tejo Spit

A River Flows Through It
A Comparative Study of Transboundary Water Disputes and Cooperation in Asia
Edited by Selina Ho

Putting Water Security to Work
Addressing Global Sustainable Development Challenges
Edited by Chad Staddon and Christopher A. Scott

Global Water Resources
Festschrift in Honour of Asit K. Biswas
Edited by Cecilia Tortajada and Eduardo Araral

For more information about this series, please visit: https://www.routledge.com/series/WATER

Global Water Resources

Festschrift in Honour of Asit K. Biswas

Edited by
Cecilia Tortajada and Eduardo Araral

Routledge
Taylor & Francis Group
LONDON AND NEW YORK

THIRD WORLD CENTRE FOR WATER MANAGEMENT

First published 2022
by Routledge
2 Park Square, Milton Park, Abingdon, Oxon, OX14 4RN

and by Routledge
605 Third Avenue, New York, NY 10158

Routledge is an imprint of the Taylor & Francis Group, an informa business

British Library Cataloguing-in-Publication Data
A catalogue record for this book is available from the British Library

ISBN13: 978-1-032-01662-7 (hbk)
ISBN13: 978-1-032-01664-1 (pbk)
ISBN13: 978-1-003-17949-8 (ebk)

DOI: 10.4324/9781003179498

Typeset in Myriad Pro
by codeMantra

Publisher's Note
The publisher accepts responsibility for any inconsistencies that may have arisen during the conversion of this book from journal articles to book chapters, namely the inclusion of journal terminology.

Contents

Citation Information

The chapters in this book were originally published in the *International Journal of Water Resources Development*, volume 36, issue 2–3 (2020). When citing this material, please use the original page numbering for each article, as follows:

Foreword
Masagos Zulkifli
International Journal of Water Resources Development, volume 36, issue 2–3 (March-May 2020, Special issue) pp. 223–225

Introduction
Festschrift
Cecilia Tortajada and Eduardo Araral
International Journal of Water Resources Development, volume 36, issue 2–3 (March-May 2020, Special issue) pp. 226–228

Chapter 1
A decade of work on water governance at the OECD: what have we learnt?
Angel Gurría
International Journal of Water Resources Development, volume 36, issue 2–3 (March-May 2020, Special issue) pp. 229–234

Chapter 2
The knowledge economy in the twenty-first century: a modest proposal
Annie Callanan
International Journal of Water Resources Development, volume 36, issue 2–3 (March-May 2020, Special issue) pp. 235–238

Chapter 3
Scotland: a world-leading Hydro Nation
Anton Muscatelli, Erin McKee and Sean McGivern
International Journal of Water Resources Development, volume 36, issue 2–3 (March-May 2020, Special issue) pp. 239–244

Chapter 4
Nestlé's corporate water strategy over time: a backward- and forward-looking view
Paul Bulcke, Samuel Vionnet, Christian Vousvouras and Ghislaine Weder
International Journal of Water Resources Development, volume 36, issue 2–3 (March-May 2020, Special issue) pp. 245–257

Chapter 5

Scarcity of water or scarcity of management?
David Molden
International Journal of Water Resources Development, volume 36, issue 2–3 (March-May 2020, Special issue) pp. 258–268

Chapter 6

Singapore's water challenges past to present
Peter Joo Hee Ng and Celine Teo
International Journal of Water Resources Development, volume 36, issue 2–3 (March-May 2020, Special issue) pp. 269–277

Chapter 7

Facing the challenge of extreme climate: the case of Metropolitan Sao Paulo
Benedito P.F. Braga and J. Kelman
International Journal of Water Resources Development, volume 36, issue 2–3 (March-May 2020, Special issue) pp. 278–291

Chapter 8

China's achievements of water governance over the past seven decades
Shaofeng Jia and Wenbin Zhu
International Journal of Water Resources Development, volume 36, issue 2–3 (March-May 2020, Special issue) pp. 292–310

Chapter 9

Some reflections on water for residential uses in developed countries
Francisco González-Gómez, Miguel Á. García-Rubio and Jorge Guardiola
International Journal of Water Resources Development, volume 36, issue 2–3 (March-May 2020, Special issue) pp. 311–324

Chapter 10

Can water professionals do more?
Michael Rouse
International Journal of Water Resources Development, volume 36, issue 2–3 (March-May 2020, Special issue) pp. 325–337

Chapter 11

Reflections on flood control in Japan and recommendations for developing countries
Yutaka Takahasi, Kimio Takeya, Miki Inaoka, Wataru Ono and Kaoru Sasaoka
International Journal of Water Resources Development, volume 36, issue 2–3 (March-May 2020, Special issue) pp. 338–350

Chapter 12

A retrospective analysis of Laos's Nam Theun 2 Dam
Thayer Scudder
International Journal of Water Resources Development, volume 36, issue 2–3 (March-May 2020, Special issue) pp. 351–370

Chapter 13

What I learned from Asit Biswas about transboundary water, ethics, mentoring and, in general, how to be a better human being
Aaron T. Wolf
International Journal of Water Resources Development, volume 36, issue 2–3 (March-May 2020, Special issue) pp. 371–376

Chapter 14

Water resilience and human life support - global outlook for the next half century
Malin Falkenmark
International Journal of Water Resources Development, volume 36, issue 2–3 (March-May 2020, Special issue) pp. 377–396

Chapter 15

Adaptive and sustainable water management: from improved conceptual foundations to transformative change
Claudia Pahl-Wostl
International Journal of Water Resources Development, volume 36, issue 2–3 (March-May 2020, Special issue) pp. 397–415

Chapter 16

Economically challenged and water scarce: identification of global populations most vulnerable to water crises
Taikan Oki and Rose E. Quiocho
International Journal of Water Resources Development, volume 36, issue 2–3 (March-May 2020, Special issue) pp. 416–428

Chapter 17

The status of the UN Watercourses Convention: does it still hold water?
Gabriel Eckstein
International Journal of Water Resources Development, volume 36, issue 2–3 (March-May 2020, Special issue) pp. 429–461

Chapter 18

Australian water decision making: are politicians performing?
James Horne
International Journal of Water Resources Development, volume 36, issue 2–3 (March-May 2020, Special issue) pp. 462–483

Chapter 19

Rent-seeking behaviour and regulatory capture in the Murray-Darling Basin, Australia
R. Quentin Grafton and John Williams
International Journal of Water Resources Development, volume 36, issue 2–3 (March-May 2020, Special issue) pp. 484–504

Chapter 20

Quenching the thirst of rapidly growing and water-insecure cities in sub-Saharan Africa
Madiodio Niasse and Olli Varis
International Journal of Water Resources Development, volume 36, issue 2–3 (March-May 2020, Special issue) pp. 505–527

Chapter 21

Sustainability of water and energy use for food production based on optimal allocation of agricultural irrigation water
Mo Li and Vijay P. Singh
International Journal of Water Resources Development, volume 36, issue 2–3 (March-May 2020, Special issue) pp. 528–546

Chapter 22

Rethinking on the methodology for assessing global water and food challenges
M. Dinesh Kumar, Nitin Bassi and O. P. Singh
International Journal of Water Resources Development, volume 36, issue 2–3 (March-May 2020, Special issue) pp. 547–564

Contributors

Eduardo Araral Institute of Water Policy, Lee Kuan Yew School of Public Policy, National University of Singapore, Singapore.

Nitin Bassi Institute for Resource Analysis and Policy Liaison Office, New Delhi, India.

Benedito P.F. Braga Universidade de São Paulo (USP), Escola Politécnica – Departamento de Engenharia Hidráulica e Ambiental, São Paulo, Brazil.

Paul Bulcke Nestlé SA, Vevey, Switzerland.

Annie Callanan Chief Executive, Taylor & Francis Group, Abingdon, UK.

M. Dinesh Kumar Institute for Resource Analysis and Policy, Hyderabad, India.

Gabriel Eckstein Texas A&M University School of Law, Fort Worth, USA.

Malin Falkenmark Stockholm Resilience Centre, Sweden.

Miguel Á. García-Rubio Department of Applied Economics, University of Granada, Spain Water Institute, Granada, Spain.

Francisco González-Gómez Department of Applied Economics, University of Granada, Spain Water Institute, Granada, Spain.

R. Quentin Grafton Crawford School of Public Policy, Australian National University, Canberra.

Jorge Guardiola Department of Applied Economics, University of Granada, Spain.

Angel Gurría Secretary-General, Organisation for Economic Co-operation and Development (OECD), Paris, France.

Peter Joo Hee Ng PUB, Singapore's National Water Agency, Singapore.

James Horne James Horne and Associates, Canberra, Australia.

Miki Inaoka Global Environment Department, Japan International Cooperation Agency, Tokyo.

Shaofeng Jia Key Laboratory of Water Cycle and Related Land Process/Institute of Geographic Sciences and Natural Resources Research, Chinese Academy of Sciences, Beijing, China.

J. Kelman Universidade Federal do Rio de Janeiro (UFRJ), Instituto Alberto Luiz Coimbra de Pós-Graduação e Pesquisa de Engenharia (Coppe), Rio de Janeiro, Brazil.

Mo Li School of Water Conservancy & Civil Engineering, Northeast Agricultural University, Harbin, China.

Sean McGivern University of Glasgow, UK.

Erin McKee University of Glasgow, UK.

David Molden Director General, International Centre for Integrated Mountain Development (ICIMOD), Lalitpur, Nepal.

Anton Muscatelli Principal, University of Glasgow, UK.

Madiodio Niasse Land, Water and Environmental Governance Expert, Ngaparou, Senegal.

Taikan Oki United Nations University, Tokyo, Japan. Institute for Future Initiatives, University of Tokyo, Japan.

Wataru Ono Global Environment Department, Japan. International Cooperation Agency, Tokyo.

Claudia Pahl-Wostl Institute of Environmental Systems Research, University of Osnabrück, Germany.

Rose E. Quiocho Graduate School of Engineering, University of Tokyo, Japan.

Michael Rouse Department of Geography and Environment, University of Oxford, Oxford, UK and International Advisor.

Kaoru Sasaoka Global Environment Department, Japan. International Cooperation Agency, Tokyo.

Thayer Scudder Department of Humanities and Social Sciences, California Institute of Technology, Pasadena, USA.

O. P. Singh Department of Agricultural Economics, Banaras Hindu University, Varanasi, India.

Vijay P. Singh Department of Biological and Agricultural Engineering & Zachry Department of Civil and Engineering, Texas A&M University, College Station, USA. National Water Center, UAE University, Al Ain, United Arab Emirates.

Yutaka Takahasi Professor Emeritus, Tokyo University, Japan.

Kimio Takeya Distinguished Technical Advisor to the President, Japan International Cooperation Agency, Tokyo, Japan.

Celine Teo PUB, Singapore's National Water Agency, Singapore.

Cecilia Tortajada School of Interdisciplinary Studies, College of Social Sciences, University of Glasgow, UK. Editor-in-Chief, International Journal of Water Resources Development.

Olli Varis Water and Development Group, Aalto University, Espoo, Finland.

Samuel Vionnet Valuing Nature, Antigua, Guatemala.

Christian Vousvouras Nestlé SA, Vevey, Switzerland.

Ghislaine Weder Nestlé SA, Vevey, Switzerland.

John Williams Crawford School of Public Policy, Australian National University, Canberra.

Aaron T. Wolf Oregon State University, Corvallis, USA.

Wenbin Zhu Key Laboratory of Water Cycle and Related Land Process/Institute of Geographic Sciences and Natural Resources Research, Chinese Academy of Sciences, Beijing, China.

Masagos Zulkifli Minister for the Environment and Water Resources, Government of Singapore, Singapore.

Foreword

Masagos Zulkifli

Water is essential for life. Without water, there would be no life on Earth.

Today, one in 10 people – more than 700 million – lack access to a basic drinking water service. One of the Sustainable Development Goals of the United Nations is universal and equitable access to safe and affordable drinking water by 2030.

With expanding global population and agricultural and industrial needs, the demand for clean water is ever increasing. The challenges of water security are compounded by climate change, which will bring more frequent and intense droughts and floods, affecting the availability and distribution of water resources.

To ensure water security in a changing climate, good water management and governance are critical. Good policies need to be backed by effective implementation. Strong support from public agencies, businesses, non-governmental organizations and members of the public is also needed to successfully implement such plans. Everyone needs to work together to tackle our water challenges.

As a small, highly urbanized island state in South-East Asia, Singapore has embraced a holistic approach to water security. One of the most water-stressed countries in the world, Singapore has developed a diversified water supply with its Four National Taps: water from the local catchment, imported water, high-grade reclaimed water (known as NEWater) and desalinated water.

Our water journey began in the early days of independence, over 50 years ago. Our founding Prime Minister, Mr Lee Kuan Yew, recognized that water security was key to Singapore's survival, and famously declared, 'Every other policy had to bend at the knees for our water survival.' He tasked PUB, Singapore's National Water Agency, to collect every drop of water and make it potable.

To realize our first National Tap, Mr Lee called for the clean-up of all rivers and streams in Singapore, including the Singapore River. The massive clean-up operations, which involved resettlement of many homes and businesses, took a decade to transform the Singapore River from an open sewer into a beautiful waterway. These clean-up efforts paved the way for the creation of Marina Reservoir in 2008, an iconic reservoir in the heart of our city. The Marina Reservoir has made Singapore one of the few countries in the world to tap urban stormwater for its water supply. Overall, two-thirds of our island serves as a water catchment.

PUB began researching water reclamation and desalination in the early 1970s. Although the production process was initially expensive and unstable, PUB persisted over several decades and eventually successfully added NEWater and desalinated water as National Taps in 2003 and 2005, when technological breakthroughs made these economically viable and reliable. With the successful recycling of used water, Singapore is one of the few countries to have closed the entire water loop, embracing a circular economy approach.

These efforts to enhance our water supply must be complemented by good water demand management. Water needs to be priced right to reflect the latest cost of water supply and its scarcity value. At the same time, PUB has consistently promoted water conservation through the years and encouraged homes and industry to use more efficient water fittings, equipment and processes. Household water consumption per capita has fallen from 165 litres per day in 2003 to 141 in 2018, and is targeted to fall further to 130 by 2030.

We are leveraging technology to manage water demand. PUB is rolling out the first phase of its Smart Water Meter Programme, which will see the installation of 300,000 automated water meters by 2023. Customers will be able to monitor their daily water usage and receive high usage notifications, to encourage them to conserve water.

Our water infrastructure must be continuously maintained and upgraded. To reduce water losses during transmission, PUB regularly replaces older pipes and uses the latest resilient materials to increase the durability of pipes. Last year, we completed the upgrading of one of Singapore's oldest water treatment plants, at Choa Chu Kang, with advanced and efficient treatment processes, such as ceramic filtration membrane and ozone-biological activated carbon treatment.

To help us tackle the water challenges arising from climate change, we will continue to invest heavily in research and development. PUB is working with partners on electro-deionization technology and biomimicry, which could halve the energy required for water desalination. PUB is also deploying data analytics and sensors to identify and anticipate issues ranging from transmission losses to flash floods. These investments have catalyzed a thriving water industry, turning Singapore into a major hydro-hub for the testing and implementation of new technologies.

Looking ahead, Singapore will harness synergies across water and other sectors such as waste, energy and food. When completed in 2027, Tuas Nexus will be the world's first greenfield development to integrate a water reclamation plant and an incineration plant. Tuas Nexus will co-digest used water sludge and food waste into biogas, which in turn will help power the plant. By expanding our circular economy approach, we hope to maximize Singapore's resource resilience and contribute to a sustainable future.

This Festschrift or special issue of the *International Journal of Water Resources Development*, prepared by Dr Cecilia Tortajada and Professor Eduardo Araral, commemorates the 80th birthday of Professor Asit Biswas. Professor Biswas is well respected internationally and one of the world's leading water experts. He founded this journal in 1985 and was its Editor-in-Chief for 29 years; currently, he serves as Editor. Professor Biswas is strongly committed to achieving a water-secure world and has advised many policy makers, including those in Singapore. In recognition of his contributions over several decades, he was awarded the prestigious Stockholm Water Prize in 2006.

Professor Biswas is a valued friend of Singapore and has been advising the Singapore International Water Week, a global platform to share and co-create innovative water solutions, since its inception in 2008. Over the years, he has helped garner strong participation in the Water Week to foster productive discussions of our water challenges.

In honour of Professor Biswas's outstanding and inspiring work, more than 20 prominent leaders of water utilities and the public and private sectors, as well as outstanding academics, have contributed to this Festschrift. This issue will be a valuable resource in humanity's journey to achieve water security, and it is a fitting tribute to Professor Biswas on this auspicious occasion.

INTRODUCTION

Festschrift

This Festschrift is a tribute to Professor Asit K. Biswas on his 80th birthday, for his manifold contributions to water resources policy and management and his extensive efforts to synthetize, apply and disseminate knowledge at the global level. His contributions, spanning more than five decades, have had enormous impacts on the lives of millions of people all over the world.

Professor Biswas is considered one of the leading water and environment experts globally. He has worked and taught in universities in Asia, Africa, Europe, North America and South America and lived for prolonged periods in cities on all the continents.

Professor Biswas has been a policy and strategic advisor to 19 governments at prime ministerial and ministerial levels, six heads of UN agencies, two secretaries-general of the OECD, two heads of the World Bank, five CEOs of major multinational corporations on the *Fortune* 500 list, several heads of bilateral and multilateral aid organizations and numerous national and international water, environment and development institutions.

He has been a very successful bridge-builder between the North and the South, scientists and policy makers, governments and NGOs, academics and practitioners, and media and the general public. Through his advisory work to governments, the public sector and businesses, and mentorship of students from all over the world, as well as his technical books and papers in 41 languages, and hundreds of media articles and interviews, his footprint on environmental and water management has been very substantial.

One of his major contributions has been in institution building. He actively participated in the establishment of the Canadian Ministry of the Environment, the United Nations Environment Programme, United Nations University, the Institute for Water, Environment and Health in Canada, the Third World Centre for Water Management in Mexico, the International Centre for Water and Environment in Spain, and the Institute of Water Policy in Singapore. On the professional side, he has been the co-founder of the International Water Resources Association, the International Society for Ecological Modelling, and the World Water Council. He helped with the idea of establishing the Intergovernmental Panel on Climate Change. He is also one of the prime movers behind the Stockholm Water Symposium, which later became Stockholm World Water Week, and Singapore International Water Week.

Professor Biswas has also been directly associated with a large number of universities and research institutions all over the world. Among these institutions are the University of Oxford, University of Loughborough, University of Glasgow and University of Strathclyde in the UK; Queen's University, University of Ottawa and University of Alberta in Canada; the International Institute for Applied Systems Analysis in Austria; the University of Lund and the Royal Institute of Technology in Sweden; Aalto University in Finland; Mexico National Autonomous University, Metropolitan Autonomous University and National Polytechnic Institute in Mexico; University of Tokyo and Shibaura Institute of Technology in Japan; Asian Institute of Technology in Thailand; University of Wuhan, Tsinghua University and

Chinese Academy of Sciences in China; and the Indian Institute of Technology (Bhubaneswar and Kharagpur). In the last 10 years, he has been at the Institute of Water Policy of the Lee Kuan Yew School of Public Policy, National University of Singapore.

Throughout his career, Professor Biswas' work has focused on all four aspects of water and environment-based knowledge: generation, synthesis, application and dissemination. A strong advocate of policy- and practice-oriented research, he has constantly challenged prevailing wisdom with the objective of advancing knowledge and its application. He has encouraged thinkers and practitioners alike to look beyond what is apparent, in the search for broader, creative and multifaceted alternatives. He has eschewed linear alternatives, since, as he would say, they do not work in the real world.

Professor Biswas has been a strong proponent of ideas that result in tangible solutions rather than poor adaptions that would not render the necessary benefits for which they were intended.

'Knowledge does not advance by consensus' is one of the phrases he uses the most. Thus, throughout his life, he has worked only with persons with vision, foresight and broad mindsets. This has allowed him to develop a wide network composed of the brightest minds, many of whom are generously contributing to this Festschrift.

A true visionary, he has championed ideas that have often been 20 or 30 years ahead of their time. For instance, already in the late 1960s, he advocated a new social, economic, political and environmental framework for water management which would enable effective translation of scientific (both natural and social) and technical advances into meaningful policy measures. In 1969, he was one of the pioneers who proposed the use of mathematical models for planning and management of river basins. He applied this concept for the first time to the Saint John River basin in Canada.

He is the 'father' of the concept of the International Water Supply and Sanitation Decade (1981–1990) and worked tirelessly to get it approved unanimously by the UN General Assembly. His contributions to formulating the Decade were explicitly noted by the Assistant Secretary General during the UN Assembly debate. Because of this Decade, hundreds of millions of people in the developing world received access to clean water and adequate sanitation.

Professor Biswas has been a science-driven, fact-based policy advocate. His role for over five decades as a global facilitator of international and regional platforms, where governments, organizations and individuals meet, discuss and take concrete actions on environment and water-related issues, has taken many forms. For instance, as an eminent world expert and firm believer that water is a source of collaboration and not conflict, he was invited to chair the Middle East Water Commission (1993–1997). He successfully involved high-level personalities from the region to discuss water problems face to face in several neutral locations. Because of his work through this commission, some of the actual treaties on water issues between the countries of the region were agreed to.

For his international contributions and reputation, he was awarded the 2006 Stockholm Water Prize. He has also been awarded the Person of the Year Award by the Canadian prime minister, the Walter Huber Award from the American Society of Civil Engineers, the Crystal Drop and the Ven Te Chow and Millennium awards from the International Water Resources Association, and the Aragon Environment Prize from Spain. He holds honorary doctorates from seven of the world's leading universities. Reuters named him one of the top 10 water trailblazers of the world; *Impeller* magazine identified him as a 'true global hero'; and the readers of *Water & Wastewater International* named him the world's second-most influential industry leader.

He has mentored young scholars and students from many different geographies, opening and many times creating doors for them. Being concerned that potential water leaders of the next generation were not being heard at major international fora, Professor Biswas initiated a one-year programme to select and mentor 15 potential young global water leaders from all over the world. He mentored them regularly over a four-year period, including a meeting every year where he invited very well-established water leaders to interact with the next generation of leaders. All 15 are now leading global water personalities, including the current director of the Postdam Institute for Climate Impact Research.

In Singapore, at both the Institute of Water Policy, Lee Kuan Yew School of Public Policy, and PUB, National Water Agency, Professor Biswas has found a very enabling and stimulating environment for intellectual discussions. This has strongly underpinned his latest work in various aspects of water management from multidisciplinary, multisectoral and multi-issue perspectives.

This Festschrift, sponsored by the Institute of Water Policy at the Lee Kuan Yew School of Public Policy, includes contributions from 23 globally renowned leading personalities from academia, national and international organizations, and businesses, who have had close working relationships with Professor Biswas, in many cases over several decades. At the Institute of Water Policy, we truly appreciate the time and effort that went into these insightful analyses.

Under the umbrella of the Institute of Water Policy, we are confident that this Festschrift will become an important contribution to the literature.

Cecilia Tortajada

http://orcid.org/0000-0001-6308-4924

Eduardo Araral

http://orcid.org/0000-0001-7665-616X

A decade of work on water governance at the OECD: what have we learnt?

Angel Gurría

ABSTRACT
Our societies, economic systems and collective well-being depend on water security and access to water services. Yet, megatrends related to climate change, urbanization and demography are likely to generate more uncertainty about water availability and demand. Responding to these threats will require sharp actions to ensure universal access to drinking water and sanitation. Simultaneous action is also needed to invest in infrastructure and better articulate who does what, how, at which scale, and why. This article explores a decade of work on water governance at the OECD, providing key observations and lessons learnt.

A shared conviction that water security is key to sustainable development

In 2010, in their landmark book *Future water governance: problems and perspectives*, Professor Asit Biswas and co-author Cecilia Tortajada warned:

> One development can be predicted with complete certainty; the world in 2030 will be significantly different from what it is in 2010.... Water governance may have to change more during the next 20 years compared to the past 2000 years, if societal expectations are to be successfully met.

Fully in line with this statement, when I campaigned to become secretary-general of the OECD in 2006, I proposed water as one of my three priorities (together with migration and health) to support better policies for better lives. At the time, there was a striking lack of awareness of the water challenge world-wide.

From my earlier experience as minister of finance and public credit in Mexico, I was convinced that water was a critical driver for sustainable growth. This is why I set up and chaired the Water Financing Taskforce during the 6th World Water Forum (Mexico, 2006), actively contributed to the Camdessus report (World Panel on Financing Water Infrastructure, 2003) and joined the United Nations Secretary-General's Advisory Board on Water and Sanitation to send a wake-up call to decision makers.

On many occasions, Professor Biswas and I joined forces to insist that greater solidarity and inclusion are essential to water security and climate justice and that public policies should support fair distribution of the socio-economic benefits of water and secure human health, environmental sustainability and income opportunities. We have also

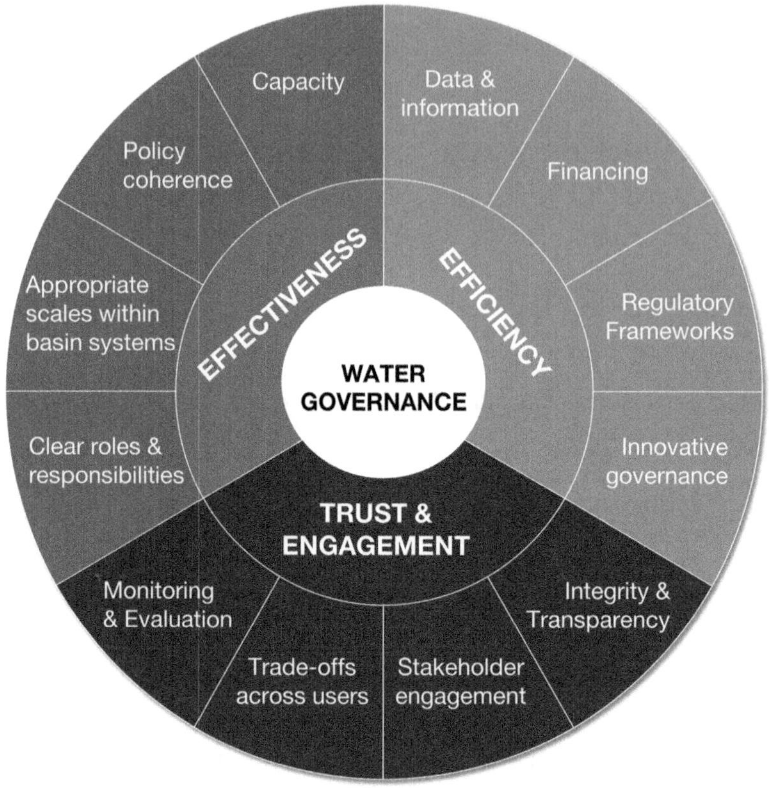

Figure 1. Overview of the OECD principles on water governance. Source: OECD (2015).

repeatedly warned that no country should take current levels of water security or service delivery for granted, and that serious action is needed in *all* countries, be they developed, emerging, or developing.

Today, the economics and governance of water security are finally seen as integral parts of how societies can better achieve and sustain socio-economic development, inclusive growth and environmental sustainability at all levels. The acknowledgement of water as a dedicated goal in the 2030 Agenda for Sustainable Development is a testament to this recognition.

A gloomy outlook that requires urgent action

What on Earth is not driven by water? Our entire society, economic systems, and collective well-being depend on water security and access to water services. We cannot afford to ignore the severity of the crisis any longer.

Today, nearly 200 million people per year are affected or killed by floods, droughts and other water-related disasters. By 2050, water demand will increase by 55%, over 40% of the world's population will live under severe water stress, and the number of people exposed to flood risk will rise from 1.2 billion now to 1.6 billion, 20% of the global population (OECD, 2012). Continued intense groundwater depletion threatens food security in several regions of the world. And more than 2 billion people do not have access to safe drinking water, while even more lack access to sanitation (WHO/UNICEF, 2017).

Megatrends related to climate change, urbanization and demography will be compounding factors and will continue to exacerbate tensions, generating more uncertainty about water availability and demand. Responding to these threats will require sharp actions and ambitious reforms to concurrently manage the risks of 'too much', 'too little', and 'too polluted' water while ensuring universal access to drinking water and sanitation and reducing the disruption of our freshwater systems.

Designing and implementing such reforms using evidence-based public policies requires acknowledging that the solutions to water challenges cut across sectors (e.g., environment, agriculture, health, land use and spatial planning) and depend on a coordinated approach by governments. They also require significant investment: projections of global financing needs for water infrastructure range from USD 6.7 trillion by 2030 to USD 22.6 trillion by 2050.

Yet, investing in infrastructure is not enough. Simultaneous action is needed to improve governance arrangements: setting the right incentives, managing complexity, and better articulating who does what, how, at which scale, and why. Fundamentally, effective governance is at the heart of finding sustainable solutions to this water crisis.

From vision to action

When I joined the OECD, I set up a multidisciplinary water team tasked to engage different policy communities, including environment, public governance, territorial development, agriculture, financial affairs and development cooperation. By mainstreaming the water challenge into the OECD inclusive growth agenda, we have contributed to improving awareness, providing evidence and supporting ambitious reforms through benchmarks, standards and experience sharing. Our achievements include a wealth of groundbreaking economic analyses, solid policy recommendations and direct support to countries' reforms on the ground. Also, because we firmly believe that 'governance' is not only about 'governments' and that meeting the water challenge is a much broader shared responsibility, we make sure that stakeholders are engaged alongside policy makers.

A decade of OECD work on water governance has taught us that the cross-cutting nature of water policy requires a whole-of-government, multilevel and multi-stakeholder approach to manage trade-offs across siloes and to ensure that decisions made in any related policy area are water-wise. Health, environment, agriculture, energy, spatial planning, regional development, gender equality and poverty alleviation are all directly related to water. This is why governing water is first and foremost about managing a complex system of responsible authorities, scale, stakeholders and priorities.

The OECD's achievements and legacy to improve water policies for better lives were crystallized in the *OECD Council recommendation on water* (2016), a concise legal instrument common to the 36 OECD countries that is a unique source of coherent, evidence-based guidance on water quality, water quantity, water-related risks and disasters, water governance, and water pricing and financing. A cornerstone of its development was the *OECD principles on water governance* (2015), which provide the 12 essential actions in relation to water governance frameworks, institutions and instruments.

Since their adoption, the principles have also been endorsed by non-OECD countries, including China, Brazil, South Africa and Morocco, and over 140 stakeholder groups, who are using them as a tool for dialogue, self-assessment and collective action. The principles are built around three mutually reinforcing blocks of water governance:

- *Effectiveness* is about defining clear, sustainable water policy goals and targets at all levels of government, to implement those policy goals and to meet expected targets.
- *Efficiency* is about maximizing the benefits of sustainable water management and welfare at the least cost to society.
- *Trust and engagement* is about building public confidence and ensuring inclusiveness of stakeholders from across society.

The evidence base from more than a decade advising governments

While supporting water reforms in developed and developing countries, we strived to raise the water profile in local and national agendas with a range of tools and frameworks for action. Actions included:

- Our '3 Ts' called for combining taxes, tariffs and transfers to finance access to water services, changing the conventional wisdom from full to sustainable cost recovery.
- Our Checklist for Private-Sector Participation contributed to dispelling myths about the role of the private sector in water and clarifying how to make the best use of private operators.
- Our Water Security Framework provided a methodology to 'know', 'target' and 'manage' water risks, recalling that related decisions remain essentially political.
- Our work on water governance in cities showed that ageing infrastructure, tighter public budgets and megatrends are generating serious threats for OECD city dwellers.
- Our work on water pollution explored innovative ways to tackle emerging pollutants, which raise emerging concerns globally, although we know little about their harmful effects overall.

What we have learned about governance from supporting water reforms at all levels

Coping with current and future challenges requires robust public policies, targeting measurable objectives at the right time and on the appropriate scale, clear roles and responsibilities for relevant authorities, and regular monitoring and evaluation. Water governance can greatly contribute to the design and implementation of such policies, with shared responsibility across levels of government and the broader range of stakeholders (e.g., civil society, business) who have an important role to play to reap the economic, social and environmental benefits of good water governance.

The water sector has intrinsic characteristics that make it highly sensitive to and dependent on multilevel governance. Water connects across sectors, places and people, as well as across geographic and temporal scales. In most cases, hydrological boundaries and administrative perimeters do not coincide. Freshwater management is both a global and a local concern, and involves a plethora of public, private and non-profit stakeholders in the decision-making, policy and project cycles. Water is also a highly capital-intensive and monopolistic sector, with important market failures where coordination is essential. To varying degrees, countries have allocated increasingly complex and resource-intensive responsibilities to sub-national governments, resulting in interdependencies across levels of government that require coordination to mitigate fragmentation. Finally, the governance landscape for freshwater management has changed in the last 25 years. Information flows more easily and potentially sheds greater light on malpractices and failures.

OECD evidence shows that there is not a one-size-fits-all solution to water challenges worldwide, but rather a large diversity of situations within and across countries. Governance responses should therefore be adapted to territorial specificities to fit water policies to places. In short, governance is *good* if it can help solve key water challenges using a combination of bottom-up and top-down processes while fostering constructive state–society relations. It is *bad* if it generates undue transaction costs and does not respond to place-based needs. Water governance systems (whether they are more or less formal, complex, or costly) should be designed according to the challenges they are required to address. This problem-solving approach means that the *forms* of water governance should follow the *functions* of water governance. Governance should always remain a means to an end and never become a self-serving goal. Structuring, institutionalizing and/or formalizing institutions should not distract policy makers from the ultimate objective of delivering sufficient water of good quality, while maintaining or improving the ecological integrity of water bodies.

There is now greater recognition that bottom-up and inclusive decision making is key to effective water policies. In addition, a number of legal frameworks have triggered major evolutions in water policy, including the EU Water Framework Directive, the UN General Assembly's resolution on the 'Human Right to Water and Sanitation', and more recently, the Sustainable Development Goals. The Integrated Water Resources Management concept has had uneven results within and across countries; it underwent some rejuvenating calls for operationalization frameworks that consider the issue in a consistent and sustainable way. However, in many places implementation is lagging. Regardless of a country's development level or exposure to water risks, there are common governance challenges: fragmented roles and responsibilities, unclear allocation of tasks, patchy financial management, lack of long-term strategic planning, data and information gaps, corruption, and weak capacity, monitoring and stakeholder engagement.

Despite persistent challenges, many OECD and partner countries have made significant efforts to improve coordination. Better coordination across different policy areas took place in Mexico through action on energy subsidies that exacerbated groundwater depletion. Better engagement across levels of government happened in Brazil, where an ambitious Water Pact set the right political and financial incentives to work together in strengthening state and federal water resources management systems. While the functional autonomy of the regional water boards was preserved in the Netherlands, efforts to use economic incentives more systematically and improve the transparency of information on water costs are currently underway.

In a global context where water resources are already overused or overallocated, we need partnerships between institutions and spatial planners, greater representation of vulnerable groups, and better data and monitoring. Transparency and accountability are also essential to ensure customers access high-quality services, at the least cost to society. A resilient economy shouldn't focus on crisis management and short-term fixes but seek risk management and prevention through long-term strategies and political commitment.

We live in a world facing striking challenges: from climate change and economic crises to demographic shifts. Our water resources are finite and can be a source of prosperity or distress when water disasters damage goods and harm people. However, each crisis is an opportunity for change. The importance of water has gained increasing prominence on policy agendas globally, but we should all continue to support ambitious and collective action towards better water policies for better lives.[1]

Note

1. The opinions expressed and arguments employed herein do not necessarily reflect the official views of the member countries of the OECD.

Disclosure statement

No potential conflict of interest was reported by the author.

References

OECD. (2012). *OECD environmental outlook to 2050: The consequences of inaction*. Paris: OECD Publishing. Retrieved from https://doi.org/10.1787/9789264122246-en

OECD. (2015). *Principles on water governance*. Retrieved from: https://www.oecd.org/cfe/regionalpolicy/OECD-Principles-on-Water-Governance.pdf

OECD. (2016). *OECD Council recommendation on water*. Retrieved from https://www.oecd.org/water/recommendation/

WHO/UNICEF. (2017). *Progress on drinking water, sanitation and hygiene: 2017 update and SDG baselines*. Retrieved from http://www.who.int/mediacentre/news/releases/2017/water-sanitation-hygiene/en/

World Panel on Financing Water Infrastructure. (2003). *Financing water for all*. Retrieved from https://www.worldwatercouncil.org/fileadmin/world_water_council/documents_old/Library/Publications_and_reports/CamdessusReport.pdf

The knowledge economy in the twenty-first century: a modest proposal

Annie Callanan

I was honoured to be invited to contribute to this Festschrift special issue to celebrate the 80th birthday of Professor Asit K. Biswas, editor of the *International Journal of Water Resources Development*. What follows are some reflections based on the 'modest proposal' that, as newly appointed CEO of academic publishing group Taylor & Francis, I presented to a forum of experts in scholarly publishing and communications. Since Professor Biswas is not only a highly respected editor and distinguished expert in water resources but he has also been tireless in extending the reach of scientific research and policy making far beyond their usual audiences, the following remarks focus on how we must harness today's technologies to make knowledge a truly global resource.

I respect expertise and am conscious that the rapid innovations taking place in my own industry must work hand-in-glove with scholars to maximize the potential of their work. The way we use new media to build better platforms to share knowledge more effectively will impact on all our futures.

Sometimes new and different can be insightful. My own world view has been shaped by different dimensions and acronyms, all on a mission to disrupt the competitive advantages and big dreams of others. Here I attempt to share my early observations, first by outlining a modest perspective on the current state of academic publishing, followed by an even more modest proposal formed from an outsider's view looking in.

As an American I consider myself an expert disruptor. It's sort of what we do. Americans respect disruption because it fixes stuff that ultimately breaks and progresses (things) along, even for those whose historical bias favours continuity (or at least used to). In our micro-moment, today's disruption is digital. And if disruption spells progress, lots of progress is coming our way. Long-standing traditional centres of gravity are shifting – rapidly.

English language pre-eminence in knowledge dissemination will soon share a stage with China and any other funding sources serious about solving twenty-first-century problems. By that, I mean not just intellectually stimulating theoretical problems, or 'dead ends', or 'won't be solved for centuries' problems, but today's real-world problems – those perhaps less reputationally rewarding but no less impactful. So how will disruptive forces play out in the current publishing ecosystem? This is one newcomer's view.

Technology will soon dissolve barriers, across languages and cultures. In 2007 it cost $1 million to translate 1 million English words into Chinese. Today's cost is $30 for the same translation. Tomorrow's cost will be $0. Instantaneous translation will soon enable knowledge sharing across diverse borders and cultures. The good news: scholarship that crosses stubborn boundaries of language, culture and discipline will improve outputs. Crossing boundaries fosters diversity of thought, which ironically is increasingly at risk in the twenty-first century.

Cross-*disciplinary* collaborations that engineer scientific pursuits, with explicit societal aspirations and impacts, will further amplify the practical applicability and long-term viability of research.

Crude definitions of quality will no longer hold up under the scrutiny and precision of twenty-first-century technology. How we measure will matter. Looking at the total research output for 2016, for example, we know that by 2021, over 40% of that output will remain uncited (Van Noorden, 2017; wizdom.ai, 2017). Does that render 2016 a success or failure in terms of outcomes from the investments made?

Using a twentieth-century artefact to measure quality will not answer that question. Citations can be pragmatic for tracking iterative research, i.e., for those working on small fragments of *big* problems. But a multidisciplinary approach and new success criteria will be required for more practical problems, like this one, where only collaboration across diverse disciplines will drive a solution.

Too many of today's real-world problems don't secure funding due to 'one size fits all' quality benchmarks. But technology will soon enable more impactful funding decisions. Funding has typically rewarded citations and those who have perfected the art of grant writing. To illustrate the current imbalance, look at the funding for Alzheimer's research, one of those 'won't be solved for centuries' problems.

Someone in the world develops dementia every three minutes (Alzheimer's Society, 2019). Between 2014 and 2016, thousands of articles were published in the top journals. But right now, 50 million people are struggling to live with the disease. They, and millions more who serve as their caregivers, need assistive technologies, technologies that might solve many small problems quickly, but which won't accrue citations. Out of the sum total, only 704 articles focused on helping those living with the disease (Web of Science, 2018). Practical value and human impact are attributes of measurement, and important success factors that will advance the higher human purpose science and technology are trying to serve, and not just the science itself.

Many attributes along the continuum of our knowledge endowment seem dated, and very twentieth-century. More and more of our global youth are being left behind – by schools that appear designed to enable nineteenth-century factory work rather than the mitigation of rapid skills obsolescence, and by the growing challenge of accessing critical twenty-first-century knowledge no longer on shelves – critical knowledge and skills that would have otherwise secured a sustainable future. There will be real-world consequences if we fail to educate new generations with the competencies they need to participate and thrive in modern life.

Even ignoring for a moment those not privileged enough to afford a higher education, recent studies from the US indicate that despite four years of academic rigour in leading academic institutions, even privileged graduating students, also known as future researchers, demonstrate little to no improvement in critical thinking and therefore don't become better problem solvers (Belkin, 2017, p. 2).

Moreover, despite a massive investment and years of debt, 50% of employers say graduates, a.k.a. recent consumers of today's corpus of scholarly communication, are not ready for the workplace, mostly due to poor critical reasoning skills, and increasingly the absence of those *very skills* demanded by our modern world (Belkin, 2017, p. 2).

Academic institutions are failing at a time when our collective imperative for learning has never been greater. Human knowledge now doubles every 13 months, soon to be every 12 hours (Schilling, 2013). Ninety per cent of all data in the world was created just in the past two years. The total collective knowledge in circulation by 2020 will be *21 million times* greater than all knowledge currently housed in all academic research libraries combined (Ranking Web of Universities, 2018).

Even in a fully open world, the human brain can absorb only a small fraction of that data set. As the supply of new knowledge accelerates, so does the obsolescence rate of existing knowledge. Fifty per cent of a first year's college curriculum in the US is obsolete by the time a student graduates. In the twenty-first century the need to learn is no longer episodic but continuous. Unless you are living off a trust fund or endowment, knowledge over centuries has served two human imperatives: professional advancement and economic sustainability. Increasingly, these goals are unattainable except for a privileged few. Why? Because academic institutions, with the complicity of publishers, are still largely delivering twentieth-century product to a generation trying to successfully meet twenty-first-century demands.

To those in academia considering the notion of relevancy I humbly say: Professional rewards and recognition for researchers, faculty and the institution *are important*; but of even greater importance right now is impact!

To my fellow publishing colleagues contemplating relevancy in an age of disruption, I say, there *is demand* for designed knowledge artefacts that meet the needs of twenty-first-century learners. And I don't mean young learners, but rather those for whom a 'higher' education will be continuous, not episodic. Learners who will build the twenty-first-century economy. Those committed to addressing real-world problems, not just theories. Those passionate about collective health for both our planet and our people. Those striving for sustainable relevance irrespective of age or credentials. And those in desperate need of an economic lifeline. Learners all over the world are asking for help!

Let's not dismiss the proof or assume libraries will keep up with the fiscal demands of an exponentially growing corpus. The twenty-first is our social century. As publishers, we have the opportunity to be listening directly and *responding* to twenty-first-century knowledge demand, demand which will sound very different from twentieth-century demand.

Academic institutions are not adapting fast enough. Technology will enable publishers to become better digital listeners, and therefore better enablers, developers and amplifiers of the knowledge most relevant to solving twenty-first-century problems.

There are 7.6 billion people in the world. Six billion of them, and counting, have mobile phones, a.k.a. learning devices, a.k.a. no need for global travel or fancy academic settings or mastery of the English language or thousands of dollars in pursuit of too much information from the past, and too little knowledge for the future (Belkin, 2017). Today's generation of learners are tuned in. We just have to bring knowledge *to them*, in the bite-size nodes they are accustomed to.

Whether researching knowledge or learning from it, the pursuit of its bounty is one connected continuum, a continuum that is *collectively* failing. We must all shoulder some blame. 'Open' science feels like a rallying cry, from a generation no longer advancing and not understanding why. But 'open' is also an expression of the *collective failure* of an *entire ecosystem*, so let's not allow ourselves to be casually defined, notwithstanding the importance or intent. Insufficient access to information is hardly our planet's most pressing collective problem. 'Free' already exists in excess of what learners can practically find, access, comprehend and derive tangible value from.

Seeking relevancy in an age of technological and scientific disruption will necessitate applying a humanities filter to steer wisdom's higher purpose. Only by doing so will we continue to endow far more to the world in terms of meaningful human advancement. By becoming practical and perceptive listeners, technology will enable us to curate knowledge that is precisely the wisdom required for a new generation to advance, find relevancy, and sustain a respectable place in the modern world.

I promised you a 'modest proposal'. Here it is. As the world's pre-eminent knowledge suppliers, let's develop and advance twenty-first-century knowledge artefacts with a better blend of science *and* humanities to solve our most pressing social problems:

- collective health – which should include extending the quality of life and not just its duration;
- sustainability through modern skills and competencies, and not just theoretical knowledge for knowledge's sake;
- and finally, true knowledge democratization, where any child born anywhere in the world in this century has the opportunity to self-serve with small but steady bites from the world's knowledge corpus to lift themselves out of a life of poverty and subjugation.

For this next generation, let's open the on-ramp to every motivated knowledge seeker. Collectively we can do this. Eighty-five per cent of the jobs that will exist in 2030 have not even been invented yet. The pursuit of twenty-first-century knowledge *must not* be for the privileged few.

Disclosure statement

No potential conflict of interest was reported by the author.

References

Alzheimer's Society. (2019). *Facts for the media*. Retrieved from https://www.alzheimers.org.uk/about-us/news-and-media/facts-media

Belkin, D. (2017, June 5). Exclusive test data: Many colleges fail to improve critical thinking skills. *Wall Street Journal.*

Clarivate Analytics. (2018). *Web of Science.*

Ranking Web of Universities. (2018, July). *Countries arranged by number of universities in top ranks.* Author. Retrieved from https://www.webometrics.info/en

Schilling, D. R. (2013, April 13). Knowledge doubling every 12 months. *Industry Tap into News.*

Van Noorden, R. (2017, December 3). The science that's never been cited. *Nature, 552*, 162–164. doi:10.1038/d41586-017-08404-0

wizdom.ai. (2017, November). Retrieved from https://www.wizdom.ai/

Scotland: a world-leading Hydro Nation

Anton Muscatelli, Erin McKee and Sean McGivern

ABSTARCT
We are facing a global crisis and the status quo must change if we want to preserve our planet for future generations. The University of Glasgow was the first in Scotland to declare a climate emergency and as a progressive Scottish institution, it is our responsibility to lead the way in promoting sustainable practice. This paper looks at some key examples that provide a model for other nations to adapt their own practices for water and wastewater management. It discusses why Scotland has chosen to view water as a major financial resource for the country and how public-sector bodies collaborate effectively with communities to ensure the people of Scotland reap the benefits of green water management.

Clean water is essential to human lives: we bathe in it, drink it, cook with it, cultivate with it, clean with it and use it for sanitation purposes. We often have the luxury in the developed world of forgetting how much we rely on safe, clean and sustainable sources of water.

As sea levels rise and nations are hit by drought, it is more important than ever that we prioritize green water management and work towards a wider goal of sustainability as part of addressing the climate emergency we are faced with today.

The United Nations has declared 2018–2028 the Water Action Decade, with the primary aim to avert a global water crisis and protect our most important natural resource. This will require us to be innovative and research-driven and to learn from those who are spearheading environmental change. My own home country of Scotland is one of these environmental pioneers.

Scotland may only be home to 5.4 million people, but we have around 19,000 km of coastline, which makes up approximately 8% of Europe's coast. Our rivers and lochs hold 90% of the UK's surface freshwater but cover only 2% of our land area. We have some of the world's cleanest drinking water, with 99.1% of public drinking water of a high quality, one of the highest rates in the world.

Not only are we rich in water, but our overall natural capital is worth £273 billion. Our water is not just of great importance to our natural heritage, but also a precious economic resource, and this has not gone unnoticed by the Scottish government.

Scotland was one of the first countries to sign up to the UN's Sustainable Development Global Goals in 2015, and the Scottish government has set its own ambitious, but achievable, sustainability targets. The Climate Change (Scotland) Act 2009 developed a framework for reducing greenhouse gas emissions by at least 42% by 2020, and at least 80% by 2050.

The Scottish government also oversees the Climate Challenge Fund, a funding programme which supports initiatives tackling climate change, and since its introduction in 2008, 622 communities across Scotland have received grants worth over £85.8 million. Through this community work, around 27,000 tonnes of waste have been recycled. For example, in 2016, a partnership between my institution, the University of Glasgow, and the Scottish government saw the development of a food waste project called Don't Waste Our Future. This initiative raised awareness of food waste and involved schools, students and teachers from across seven European countries.

Whilst the Scottish government has continued to develop its policies on climate change and sustainability over the years, the importance of incorporating water management strategies in these policies has simultaneously increased. There now exists a web of policies on the economy, health, social well-being, culture and the environment which are woven together by an underlying objective to ensure that the most sustainable choices are being made.

Projects, such as Hydro Nation, which seek to use Scotland's expertise and knowledge of water to benefit the economy through innovative management practices, can provide a template for other nations to follow and combine diverse policy areas to achieve sustainability targets.

To see how Scotland does this so effectively, we must look at it nationally, internationally and on a more local level – looking at the work the Scottish government is doing domestically with several organizations and why it is choosing to collaborate; how Scotland is participating internationally and how it has learned from global partners; and finally how individual institutions such as my own, the University of Glasgow, are playing a part in the fight against climate change and contributing to sustainable water management at a local level in Scotland.

To begin, it is important to focus on the key public-sector organizations the Scottish government works with domestically towards its targets for water sustainability. Water management is the responsibility of the cabinet secretary for environment, climate change and land reform, and beneath this level there are several public-sector bodies that answer to the Scottish government and have their priorities set by the cabinet secretary.

First, Scottish Water is the body 'responsible for providing water and waste water services' across Scotland (Audit Scotland, 2005, p. 5, exhibit 1). Scottish Water is tasked with protecting and improving the quality of drinking water in Scotland. It does this through sustainable land and water management practices and by incorporating climate change policy in everything it does. For example, the Scottish government has set targets for reducing carbon emissions, and thus Scottish Water has incorporated this in its water treatment activities. One of the largest solar panel schemes in Scotland was commissioned by Scottish Water in Speyside in north-eastern Scotland, with 80% of the energy generated to be used to take the water from a nearby river to be pumped to water treatment works. Eleven other photovoltaic schemes are now operational across Scotland at different water treatment works.

Moreover, the Scottish government is a signatory to the Ellen MacArthur Foundation's New Plastics Economy, a global commitment to end plastic pollution. To coordinate with this, in 2018 Scottish Water introduced the Your Water, Your Life campaign, which encourages people to make tapwater their first choice and carry a refillable bottle rather than buy plastic bottles of water. This campaign aimed to highlight the benefits of tapwater not only for the environment but also for health and economic reasons. Scottish Water also works with academic institutions in research on plastics in our wastewater systems and is raising awareness of the inappropriate disposal of plastic products.

In these instances, different sectors of the Scottish government and its policies are being coordinated within Scottish Water's activities to support sustainable water management. This approach is effective because all of these coordinated projects between Scottish Water and Scottish government policies will contribute to the government's overall goals for climate change and sustainability.

Another body which works on Scotland's water management is the Scottish Environment Protection Agency (SEPA). SEPA's overarching goal is to protect the environment, but a major strand of this focuses on sustainable water management.

SEPA's One Planet Prosperity strategy ensures that compliance with environmental regulation is non-negotiable. It works with businesses and communities to deliver projects which tackle climate change, many of which are related to water management. For example, river restoration across Scotland has been a priority for SEPA, as will this not only improve water sustainability but also have economic and social benefits. In the River Garry in Perthshire, SEPA delivered a project in 2017 to improve the ecological quality of the water and get enough water flowing to allow salmon to return. The work included the removal of an old weir, which was a barrier to migrating salmon, and this now allows a sustainable volume of water to flow for the first time in over 60 years. Since the salmon have returned, the number of anglers in the area has increased, making the river a tourist destination, and the natural flow of sediment is improving the ecological health of the river. This illustrates how the coordination of sustainable water management with environmental policies can reap both environmental and economic rewards for communities.

The final public body with a major interest in sustainable water management in Scotland is Scottish Canals. The historic significance of Scotland's canals is immense: they were instrumental in the industrial evolution of Scotland and shaped communities across the country, particularly in Glasgow. Former staff member of the University of Glasgow and inventor of the steam engine, James Watt, assisted in the widening of the River Clyde and the construction of the Forth and Clyde and the Caledonian Canals back in the 1700s, and today these canals are still being reimagined to bring sustainable benefits for the people of Scotland.

Around 332 million litres of water are used each day to run Scotland's canals, but initiatives by Scottish Canals are ensuring that this water is not going to waste. Canal water has a lower carbon footprint than drinking water, as it is gravity fed and is arguably a greener way of providing water for recreational activities, such as the Falkirk Wheel (a major Scottish tourist attraction), and for industry.

Scottish Canals are also exploring the potential for renewable energy generation from canal water and reusing dredged sediments as new materials for road surfaces and bricks. Emphasis has also been placed on the cultural benefits of Scotland's canals. For example, efforts to create nature reserves on the canals, the cultural and musical Glasgow Canal Festival and sporting competitions on canals have seen local communities take ownership of sustainability projects because they now place value on protecting and preserving clean and healthy canals.

There are also redevelopment works happening along canal pathways to encourage more people to walk and cycle rather than use their car. Glasgow's Smart Canal combines 200-year-old canals with modern-day digital surface water technology to make Glasgow a 'sponge city'. The Smart Canal will allow the north of the city to 'passively absorb, clean and use rainfall intelligently. Advanced warning of heavy rainfall will automatically trigger a lowering of the canal water level to create capacity for surface water run-off' (Glasgow City Region, n.d.). This project has significant environmental benefits through the use of green infrastructure and will avoid the need for excavation and subsequent pollution from construction activities. It will also help in flood prevention across Glasgow at a time when water levels are rising and our weather is becoming even more unpredictable.

Thanks to these initiatives, there is a clear public desire to maintain the health and sustainability of our canals. People are keen to preserve the heritage and advantages surrounding their local canals, and consequently the Scottish government's overall goals to reduce emissions and pollution and to tackle climate change are being addressed too.

All of these public bodies work collaboratively on many projects across Scotland, along with the Scottish government as a whole and other public and private-sector organizations. For example, Scottish Water and SEPA signed a sustainable growth agreement to recover value from waste and make Scotland more resistant to climate change. This cooperative and interdisciplinary approach enables complex issues, which are too large for any one organization to tackle effectively, to be more suitably managed.

Ensuring collaboration across the board is undoubtedly a difficult task. Scotland's involvement in projects such as the Hydro Nation Forum is important in bringing together all of the different bodies and factions working on sustainable water management and getting them all on the same page. Scotland is working to become the first Hydro Nation and aims to make Glasgow a global knowledge hub for research, teaching and technological innovation for water-related issues.

Becoming a Hydro Nation and encouraging different bodies to work together is to the greater good of the environment, which should be enough of a prize, considering the climate emergency our planet faces. However, an additional incentive is the economic benefits such an approach can bring.

One of the underpinning themes of Scotland's Economic Strategy is the 'circular economy' approach. In a circular economy, efficiency is increased and waste is reduced because every possible avenue to reuse and recycle an amenity is explored. This is illustrated in the work of Scottish public-sector bodies dealing with water management because Scotland is extracting the maximum value possible from its water through river restoration schemes, renewable energy initiatives, cultural projects, and so on.

Scotland's water sector is worth an estimated £1.8 billion to the economy, thus there is an economic incentive in ensuring the sustainability of the nation's water management systems. Although the driving force for some may be financial gain, the resulting initiatives ultimately have a positive impact on the environment and are helping shape Scotland as a sustainable nation.

And it is not only Scotland's work at home where lessons can be learnt. The work Scotland does abroad and in collaboration with international partners is also an area of real success. The European INTERREG funding stream granted funding to Scottish Water, Scottish Canals and five other partner organizations to establish the SURICATES northwest European network of water and wastewater test facilities. The partnership will support innovation and encourage cooperation with small and medium-sized enterprises in the recycling of wastewater and flood control measures. The consortium consists of partners from Belgium, Germany, France and beyond, whilst the public bodies in Scotland act as leads for the project.

In its European engagement, Scotland has arguably taken a leading role in sustainable water management measures and has been open and cooperative in sharing knowledge with its European neighbours. Yet, Scotland is not only working with European partners, it also has a variety of international water management projects underway. In fact, sustainable water management has been incorporated in Scotland's own international development policy and in its interactions with developing nations.

For example, the Scottish government funded the Water Futures Project in Malawi, which will help provide an open data resource to evaluate the risks facing water sources and help address water gaps for the Malawian population. The government also signed a memorandum of understanding at the Commonwealth Heads of Government meeting in 2018 on the Indian Mission for Clean Ganga (the River Ganges).

Scotland was also a key player in the 2015 Global Goals for Sustainable Development of the UN, which put sustainable water management at the top of a list of global priorities. Therefore, just as sustainable water management is linked with a number of domestic policies, so too is it linked with the Scottish government's international engagement.

At a local level there are also key lessons for how Scotland is succeeding in water management and sustainability. Specific community projects such as those I have mentioned are contributing to meeting Scotland's environmental goals and targets. However, it is also important to mention the work of researchers and universities in Scotland, as we are helping shape the minds of the future generation, who will inherit these global environmental challenges. We are also playing our part in the discovery of practices and innovation in technology which are improving efficiency and sustainability in Scotland and across the world. To give an insight into some of the work of my own institution, the University of Glasgow, I will mention two projects which are benefitting not only Scotland but the global community too.

The University of Glasgow took part in the Eurolakes project with several other EU academic institutions. It focussed on water resource management for important deep European lakes and their catchment areas. The project was successful in producing affordable and integrated water management strategies to control pollution and advise EU policymakers.

An ongoing cross-border project known as Aquasense has seen the University of Glasgow receive over €900,000 to help support an innovative network for training in water monitoring using sensors, big data and artificial intelligence. These projects are benefitting local communities in Scotland whilst also helping to form the global approach to sustainable water management. It is this synergy between local activity and wider national and international objectives which puts Scotland at the forefront of green water management and the sustainability agenda as a whole.

Scotland's water is a huge part of our geography but also our economy and our everyday lives, and if we did not put such great emphasis on incorporating water management in policies and activities across the country then we would arguably not be as successful at achieving our climate change goals as we are currently.

There are undeniably lessons which Scotland must learn too, from our own domestic experts and from the general public, but also from other international leaders in water management. These lessons will only be learnt from the sharing of best practices and from the prioritization of water in future discussions and policies at the global level.

Yet, overall, Scotland is still making real headway as a global leader in green water management and sustainability. By viewing water as a major financial resource which can be reused and repurposed for economic, health and cultural benefits, Scotland is reaping environmental benefits.

The circular economy approach sees less waste and more efficiency in Scotland's water management systems, which is helpful for the Scottish government's environmental and financial goals. Moreover, a joint approach to water sustainability practices sees Scottish public-sector bodies collaborate together and with communities. It also sees Scotland collaborating with international partners, and local Scottish institutions cooperating with their counterparts across borders. Scotland is taking a globalized approach to sustainable water management, and in an increasingly isolationist climate, this should be commended.

Glasgow's and Scotland's commitment to sustainability was highlighted recently with the announcement that we would host the major climate change conference, COP26, in 2020. This will be a fascinating opportunity to highlight some of the successes we have had in our efforts to tackle climate change, water management and sustainability.

Water is a human right; indeed it is one of key building blocks of human life. By taking this seriously and putting it front and centre in our policy agenda, Scotland has reaped many benefits and is working to leave a cleaner, more sustainable world for future generations.

If we are serious about achieving global development goals, reversing some of the damage we have already done to our planet and tackling the climate emergency, it is vital not only that Scotland build on its existing progress but also that other nations follow Scotland's lead.

Disclosure statement

No potential conflict of interest was reported by the authors.

ORCID

Anton Muscatelli http://orcid.org/0000-0003-3001-0640

References

Audit Scotland. (2005). Overview of the water industry in scotland. Retrieved from https://www.audit-scotland.gov.uk/docs/central/2005/nr_051013_water_overview.pdf

Glasgow City Region. (n.d.). Pioneering new digital surface water drainage system. Retrieved from http://www.glasgowcityregion.co.uk/article/9857/Pioneering-new-digital-surface-water-drainage-system

Nestlé's corporate water strategy over time: a backward- and forward-looking view

Paul Bulcke, Samuel Vionnet, Christian Vousvouras and Ghislaine Weder

ABSTRACT
Water is essential for the food industry, including sourcing, production, distribution and consumption. This article documents the journey taken by Nestlé with regard to water since the early 2000s. We take a deeper dive into its most recent corporate initiative, Caring for Water, and make a first attempt to quantify the impact of this initiative on the business and society, within a mindset of creating shared value. The article concludes by trying to draw out some general lessons that may be further explored to strengthen future corporate initiatives. The overall importance of collaboration is highlighted as a critical ingredient.

Introduction

Water is vital to life: it is essential for individuals, society, nature, and economic prosperity. Yet, despite this vital role, water is widely mismanaged, resulting in strained supply in many locations around the world, and affecting, in turn, socio-economic well-being and stability. Looking ahead, water resources are likely to be stretched even further as the global population grows, economic activity increases, and incomes rise. It is expected that, by 2030, annual demand for renewable freshwater resources will exceed sustainable supply by 40% (2030 Water Resources Group, 2009).

From the specific perspective of a food company, water is probably its most strategic resource. Water touches every link in the food value chain. It is an essential input in growing the necessary raw materials, i.e. agriculture. It is an essential resource for food processing. And it is an essential element for consumers in preparing their meals and staying healthily hydrated.

It is clear, then, that growing challenges around water, including shortages stemming from overuse, rising political and social tensions around water access and use, rising risks to the water supply security of private firms, and the deterioration of water infrastructure (municipal and other) due to insufficient investment, will increasingly impact firms in the food and beverage industry (Bulcke, 2018).

Given the societal and firm context, and in line with Nestlé's purpose, 'enhancing quality of life and contributing to a healthier future' (https://www.nestle.com/sites/default/files/asset-library/documents/library/documents/corporate_social_responsibility/nestle-csv-full-report-2016-en.pdf) and Nestlé's mindset for doing business, 'creating shared value', the focus on water as a priority issue for the company is well placed. Through the mindset of creating shared value, Nestlé seeks to move beyond corporate social responsibility to create value, through its core business, for both shareholders and for society.

This article seeks to address how Nestlé has approached the challenges around water since the turn of the century. It is structured as follows. We first document Nestlé's journey with respect to water, especially how Nestlé has sought to engage on water in society and help frame a discussion at the highest level of policy making. We then describe the current company-wide flagship initiative, Caring for Water (https://www.nestle.com/sites/default/files/asset-library/documents/library/documents/corporate_social_responsibility/creating-shared-value-report-2018-en.pdf), which operationalizes and systematically drives the water agenda throughout the company. We then take a novel step by exploring how and to what extent Caring for Water might contribute to creating business and also societal value, using a methodology called impact valuation. Impact valuation develops and analyzes impact pathways originating from the direct activities of the company in terms of output, outcome, and ultimately, impact. More specifically, it uses economic valuation techniques to obtain results in monetary units that can be easily assimilated by a wide range of stakeholders and that can moreover be used to compare impacts across various activities, eventually helping prioritize more relevant and meaningful activities.

We seek to contribute to a better understanding of how firms can make water a priority among their leadership, along their value chain and across stakeholders, but also, thanks to the use of impact valuation methodology, to highlight quantitatively and in detail how this strategy can contribute to creating shared value.

Nestlé's approach to global water mega-trends

Water as an essential resource for Nestlé

Water is essential for Nestlé. The ingredients Nestlé uses need water to grow. Nestlé needs water to run its factories and manufacture its products, and Nestlé's employees need water to be productive. Nestlé's consumers also need water to prepare and use many of the food and beverage products.

Indeed, from the very start of Nestlé's industrial activities, 150 years ago, the centrality of water to the company was explicitly recognized (Bulcke, 2018). The company's first factory, a milk powder factory, was built in 1865 in Vevey, Switzerland, right next to the local river, and since then, for the most part, all major factories of the Nestlé Group have been located next to water sources (rivers, canals, underground aquifers), typically within a water-rail-road triangle.

Nestlé's first wastewater treatment plant became operational as early as the 1930s, highlighting the company's recognition of the importance not just of water quantity but also of water quality, for itself but also for the local environment. Today, across all of Nestlé's global operations, wastewater is treated, even where this might be difficult to ensure. The first acquisition of a bottled water company in the 1970s added a new dimension to Nestlé's approach. Steps to protect the quality of groundwater became an integral part of the Nestlé philosophy.

Currently, more than 35% of Nestlé's production sites and a significant number of the sourcing areas around its factories are in regions of water stress. Moreover, several ingredients in Nestlé's supply chain, including dairy, sugar, cereals and meat, rely on irrigation water (Galli &

Vousvouras, 2019). In line with this, in a 'materiality' analysis undertaken by the company in 2018, water was highlighted as one of the most important issues for the company, in terms of both importance to stakeholders and impact on Nestlé's immediate and long-term success (see Figure 1A in the online supplemental material, at https://doi.org/10.1080/07900627.2020.1712193).

Nestlé's company and societal engagement on water

Around 2000, it became clear to the company that water was going to become a significant global challenge. At its annual strategic retreat in 2002, the executive board initiated a discussion on the terms of reference for a new and more comprehensive approach to water. As one outcome of this discussion, the factual base for Nestlé's strategy on water was elaborated, resulting in a new positioning and new actions for the company to take to address water efficiency and scarcity. The company leadership agreed that water would become a high priority for the company, and that the chairman would take the lead, given the strategic nature of the challenge and the need for high visibility and advocacy.

In 2008, water became one of the three pillars of Nestlé's fundamental guiding principle on how to do business responsibly, namely creating shared value, and the first Nestlé report in this mindset, 'Meeting the Global Water Challenge' (published in 2012 alongside Nestlé's 2011 annual report) focused entirely on water. 'Creating shared value' encapsulates a fundamental belief held by the company that businesses are successful and create value for shareholders over time only if they simultaneously create value for society.

Also in 2008, a small group of like-minded manufacturers came together, along with the International Finance Corporation and the McKinsey Group, to informally create the 2030 Water Resources Group (2030 WRG) as an ad hoc platform focused on tackling the challenge of water overuse. In November 2009, the group published a seminal report, 'Charting Our Water Future' (2030 WRG, 2009), which highlighted the need for action but also what kinds of actions might be needed. Focusing on individual watersheds, this report outlined analytical and other tools to draw out cost-effective and relevant actions that could be taken by policy makers and stakeholders together to address the widening water supply–demand gap.

By January 2010, the 2030 WRG was formally established, with the World Economic Forum as its host. In 2012, the group moved its operations to sit within the International Finance Corporation (part of the World Bank Group). The 2030 WRG was and is an important initiative for Nestlé, which has chaired or co-chaired its governing council since establishment.

Setting up the 2030 WRG was a strong and early recognition by Nestlé and its partners of the crucial need for a very broad and high-level perspective when addressing the global water challenge, as well as solutions that are comprehensive, credible and disruptive. Today, the group is operational in 11 countries and three sub-national states across Asia, Africa and South America.

In 2011, Nestlé received the Stockholm Industry Water Award for driving water efficiency across its operations. In 2012, Nestlé published its first set of commitments to creating shared value (https://www.nestle.com/sites/default/files/asset-library/documents/library/documents/corporate_social_responsibility/nestle-csv-full-report-2012-en.pdf), including reducing direct water withdrawal per ton of product by 40% between 2005 and 2015. In 2014, this objective became a firm part of Nestlé's commitment to Water Stewardship. Having achieved the 2015 target, the company elaborated further targets in 2016, in line with the development of its commitments for 2020. These included reducing direct water withdrawals per ton of product by 35% between 2010 and 2020. While still an ambitious target, compared with the 2013 target, it reflected the decreasing return on factory water efficiency investments. Indeed, over time, Nestlé factories around the world have become best in class in internal water management.

Nestlé also took a renewed look at its overall corporate water strategy in 2016, with an eye on mitigating operational and reputational risks and acting where it really matters. This resulted in the development of a comprehensive water stewardship approach called Caring for Water (Galli & Vousvouras, 2019), which became the flagship initiative in Nestlé's Purpose and Values Framework (Figure 2A) and which was formally launched in 2018. Its implementation quickly became mandatory in every market in which Nestlé operates.

Valuing the impact of Caring for Water

The Caring for Water initiative

The cost of additional water made available (through water efficiency projects at factories for instance) increases very sharply when only looking at solutions within the boundaries of Nestlé operations (Figure 1). However, when this boundary is extended to the catchment level or a level that involves other stakeholders, the cost is much lower, and can make much higher volumes of water available. This cost curve was created based on a review of selected investments of Nestlé using the Water Stewardship Benefit Accounting Method, published in 2019 (Reig, Larson, Vionnet, & Bayart, 2019). This methodology allows quantifying the benefit of investment in water stewardship in volumetric units (m^3).

The insight from this figure is that Nestlé's strategy cannot rely only on actions at the factory level to reduce its exposure to water-related issues. It needs to act at a wider scale, at the catchment level, for instance. It also requires looking at the supply chain and not only at operations, 35 times as much water is used to produce crops as is used to process them in factories (in the specific case of Nestlé). For this reason, Nestlé had to extend its corporate water stewardship strategy, in turn leading to the launch of the Caring for Water initiative.

Water is a collective resource, and as such it can only be managed sustainably if water users and other relevant stakeholders agree on caring for it collectively. Also, water challenges are local, in the sense that they vary from watershed to watershed. This spirit of acting where it matters and focusing on actions beyond the factory fence is reflected in Caring for Water.

The Caring for Water initiative rests on four pillars, comprising factories, watersheds, agriculture and communities, each reflecting a specific rationale.

- *Operations*. As a private-sector operator, Nestlé must first look for ways to mitigate the direct risks to the company from water shortages and quality failures and to protect its operations at the relevant levels: factories, sales, and so on. This is achieved by steadily reducing water requirements and extending wastewater treatment (in quantity and quality), as well as reuse.
- *Catchment*. Nestlé must then commit to acting and investing strategically in resources outside its factories through collective action. This implies advocating and helping to develop, collectively, comprehensive solutions to water challenges within watersheds.

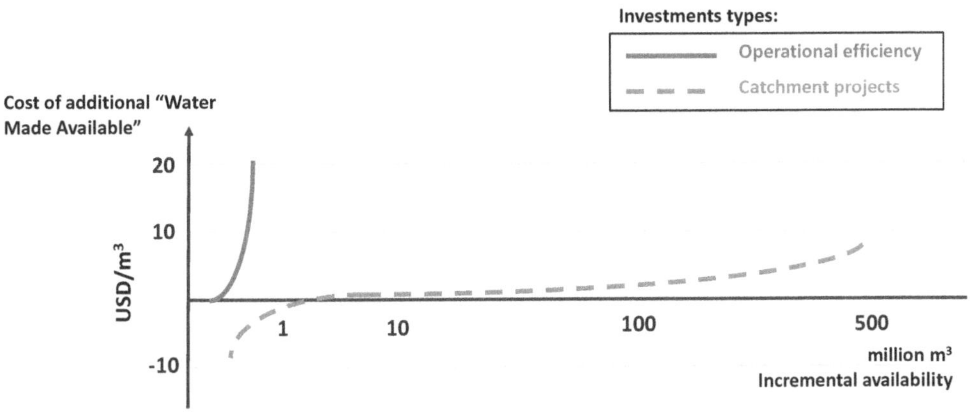

Figure 1. Cost curve (USD per m^3 made available) for activities within (inside factories) and outside (at catchment level) the operations of Nestlé.

- *Agriculture supply chain.* Focus must be extended to Nestlé's supply chain, that is, agriculture. Agriculture is a large user of water, and more efficient use of water resources in the agricultural supply chain is necessary to make this more resilient.
- *Community.* Finally, Nestlé must invest in communities, notably the immediate communities surrounding its operations, but also along the entire value chain, because healthy communities are the basis of sustainable economic and social development.

To operationalize the Caring for Water initiative, the company currently uses the principles and approach of the Alliance for Water Stewardship (AWS) Standard (https://a4ws.org/the-aws-standard-2-0/download-the-aws-standard-2-0/). The standard was developed through a multi-stakeholder process and helps organizations implement water stewardship in five steps:

- *Gather and understand.* Collect and consolidate factory and catchment data; understand the context and existing water-related challenges.
- *Commit and plan.* Commit publicly to the AWS principles and set a comprehensive water stewardship plan.
- *Implement.* Work in collaboration with key stakeholders to address shared water challenges.
- *Evaluate.* Assess the progress and results from implementing the plan; review and set corrective action points if needed.
- *Communicate and disclose.* Communicate transparently with various stakeholders and disclose related issues and achievements.

With this standard, the AWS provides a common language for those willing to be proactive in water stewardship activities through an eye-opening implementation approach and a credible external auditing/certification process. The AWS guides companies in assessing risks and needs, and in focusing efforts where it matters most and for the benefit of all.

Nestlé also supported the deployment of this strategy by investing in developing a set of collaboration, tools and initiatives. These include:

- The Water Stewardship Benefit Accounting Method (developed with a consortium of other firms, consultants and NGOs) is allowing companies to quantify in volumetric terms their contribution to solving water-related issues.
- The Cost of Water Stewardship method enables understanding the cost of a wide range of solutions for water-related issues, and provides a global estimate broken down per country and catchment. This is key information to drive action by companies and other stakeholders.
- **The impact valuation** methodology was developed based on the natural capital protocol and the human and social capital protocol (about which more below). It uses economic valuation techniques to assess the value of impacts on society and businesses. The tool allows us to comprehensively capture all the impacts of an organization and express them in units close to the economy or the business, which simplifies interpretation and comparison, as well as communication.

Impact valuation

A mindset of creating shared value is not exclusive to Nestlé. Across the world, corporations are beginning to embrace competitive strategies built on positive social and environmental impact, addressing societal needs in ways that also improve their bottom line. But measuring this impact, either for society or for the business, is one of the biggest challenges faced by firms engaged in creating shared value (Vionnet & Couture, 2015). Thus, developing new tools and metrics to understand, measure and ultimately manage socio-environmental impacts is important. Comprehensive and standardized tools and metrics would allow companies to mitigate risk, enhance performance, reduce their footprint, identify new opportunities and increase the return on their investments (Vionnet & Couture, 2015). To this end, for several years, Nestlé has engaged, alone but also with others, in pioneering research to improve our understanding of the methodological approaches to valuing impact. For example, the Impact Valuation Roundtable was initiated based on the input of Nestlé and other companies willing to exchange knowledge and develop operational approaches to impact valuation.

The practice of impact valuation remains in an early stage, even if more and more companies are beginning to explore it. As such, and given the important complexity involved, there are many valuation approaches and methodologies.

A new trend has emerged in the field of impact valuation, based on the full accounting of impact across types of capital (human, social and natural). The World Business Council for Sustainable Development and the Natural Capital Coalition have supported the development of standards that allow organizations to assess or measure their impact on society or on the business itself, depending on the impact pathway chosen. Nestlé has pioneered a study using these standards, together with alternative methodologies and data, to assess the societal and business impact of its Caring for Water initiative.

Methodology

General framework

Impact valuation at Nestlé relies on two high-level protocols: the human and social capital protocol and the natural capital protocol. These were developed in 2017 to support the private sector, in particular in assessing its impacts and dependencies on human, social and natural capital. They provide a general guideline for impact valuation, which is framed as having four steps: framing the study (including setting the objectives); defining the scope (including the types of impact pathways to be assessed); measuring and valuing; and applying and interpreting the results (Figure 3A).

These protocols do not provide the data, nor do they help identify the most applicable methods to value different pathways and topics. A range of methodologies were thus used to value the impact of the Caring for Water initiative, including the social return on investment method and life cycle assessment (ISO 14044). For each activity in the initiative, theoretical impact pathways were developed (Figure 4A), one for value for society and the other focused on the value for the business. Outcomes and impacts were clearly defined in each case.

Scoping the Caring for Water initiative

Given the complexity of the activities of the Caring for Water initiative, the scope of the impact valuation analysis was simplified to cover a selection of representative investments in water efficiency in operations, water in agriculture, investments in relevant catchment areas, and investments in communities (in particular water, sanitation and hygiene [WASH] projects). The results were then scaled to the level of spending or global activity communicated by Nestlé. The investments carried out under Nestlé's WASH activities were assessed using a country-level model and statistics. The projects covered are listed schematically in Figure 5A and described more fully in the Appendix.

Business value

Business value impact pathways have generally been less studied than societal impact pathways, particularly when it comes to intangibles such as reputation. The methods are thus not fully mature. Nonetheless, a broad set of topics were defined, comprising direct costs and two sets of topics related to Nestlé's reputation, namely stakeholder preferences and disruption (Figure 2).

Direct costs are relatively straightforward to delineate, while reputational topics are more complex. Two pathways were thus chosen, one positive (preference for Nestlé) and one negative (disruption).

In doing the analysis, it was observed that the greater the impact of an activity and the smaller its probability, the harder it was to identify the business value. The uncertainty of the result appears to increase with greater potential impact and smaller probability of occurrence (Figure 3). Looking at impact pathways, it was observed that they were more complex, longer and more indirect for activities with large impact and small probability, making them trickier to assess with certainty and metrics that are close enough to business metrics (such as profit).

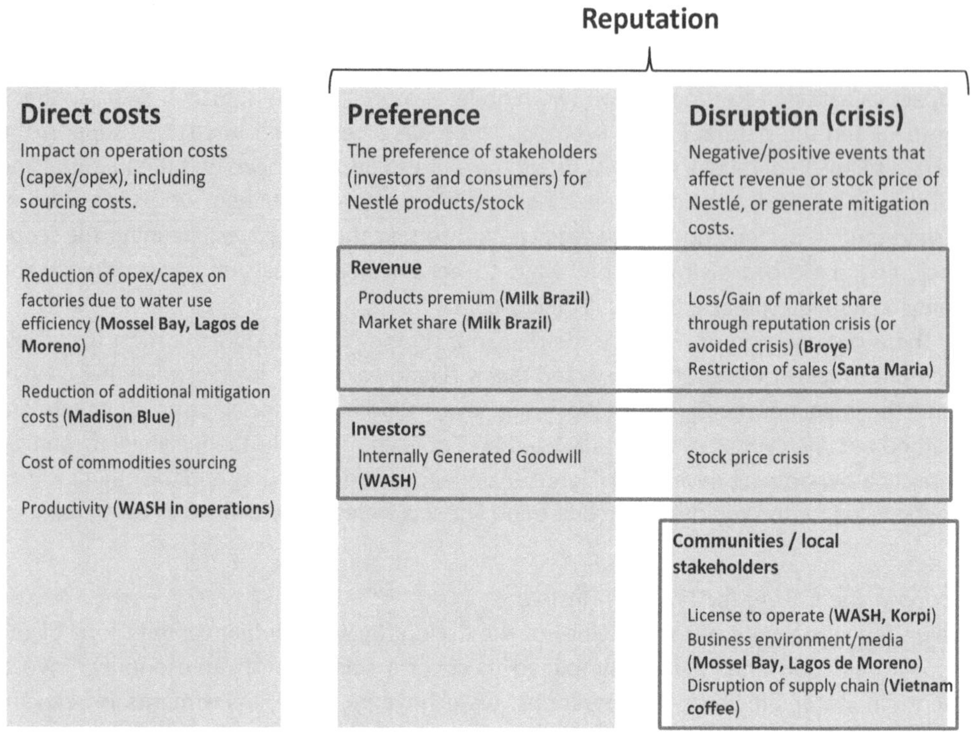

Figure 2. Three pillars model for business value impact valuation.

Data

Data were collected from Nestlé and its partners to the extent possible. Due to substantial data gaps, however, secondary data sources were also used. The data covered activities between 2017 and 2019. The reference year is 2018, unless otherwise specified.

Results

The Caring for Water initiative was calculated to have generated a societal return on investment (SROI) of 12.5, ranging from 0.4 to 80. The business return on investment (ROI) was calculated to be 1, ranging from 0.4 to 4.5 (Table 1). For the latter, elements of reputation and avoided risks were not fully accounted for due to lack of data and methodology issues, leading to a lower return on investment than might have been expected.

The results were split into internal (activities within the operational boundaries of Nestlé) and external (outside Nestlé). This split shows that the best return on investment, for *both* Nestlé and society, occurs when investments are made outside Nestlé's factory walls (ROI 2.6/SROI 76.9, versus ROI 0.7/SROI 0.5). This may be because Nestlé has already invested significantly, as outlined above, to increase the efficiency of its operations, and because operations represent only a small fraction of the entire water use in the Nestlé value chain.

Figure 6A provides insight into the distribution of value created for the business and for society, beyond ROI or SROI. As expected for societal value, operations efficiency does not represent a big contribution. WASH in operations is limited too, because Nestlé employees without access to WASH are not numerous, compared to WASH investments outside the

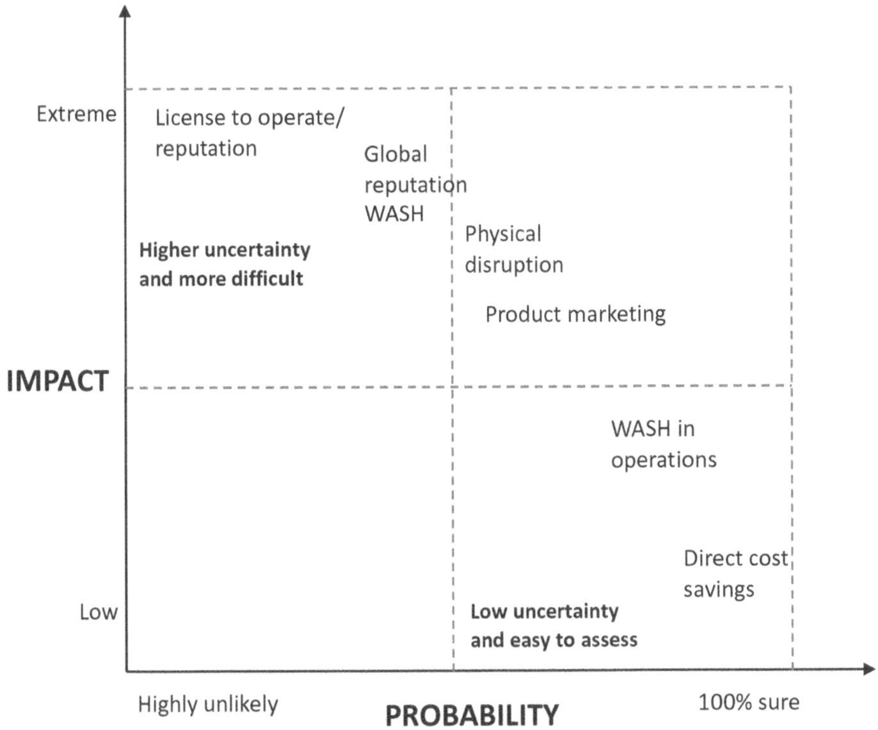

Figure 3. Illustration of the impact valuation techniques classified along the probability of occurrence and their potential impact on the business.

Table 1. Overview of results from Caring for Water.

	Nestlé's return on investment	Society's return on investment
Total	1 (range 0.4–4.5)	12.5 (range 0.4–80)
Internal	0.7	0.5
- Operations efficiency		
- Water, sanitation and hygiene in operations		
External	2.6	76.9
- Catchment investments		
- Agriculture		
- Water, sanitation and hygiene outside operations		

operations of Nestlé, which contribute a third of the total societal value. Agriculture and catchment investments almost account for the other two-thirds. For business value, operations efficiency represents an important value in absolute terms, given that this has been an important focus of past investments, despite lower returns more recently. Catchment investments and agriculture show an important contribution, mostly through indirect cost benefits (e.g. reputation and avoided risk). Despite its high societal value, WASH is not currently contributing significantly to business value, partly due to the lack of methodology and data to account for it.

Figure 4 provides detailed results for business value, including direct costs, media coverage (as a proxy for reputation), risk avoidance (shown by reputational events such as reduced sales or licence-to-operate issues), consumer preferences (proxied by the premium paid by consumers for Nestlé milk in Brazil) and integrated generated goodwill.

Limitations

The analysis encountered several limitations which would need to be further addressed in future analytical work of this kind.

First, several aspects of the impact on society and business were difficult to account for and were left out of the study. Reputation value in particular was difficult to assess, given the poor maturity of current methods, as well as data gaps and complex impact pathways. The results are thus subject to significant uncertainty.

Second, and critically, availability of and access to data for all activities remains poor, and data gaps are thus significant. Going forward, significant effort would be needed to support this type of methodological approach.

Insights for Nestlé

The impact valuation confirms the strategic direction of the Caring for Water initiative, focusing on water stewardship activities beyond the factory walls. In recent decades, Nestlé has developed water management within factories to a level of excellence at which more investment in water infrastructure delivers only small returns, from both a business and a societal point of view. Today, most water-related issues are outside Nestlé's operational

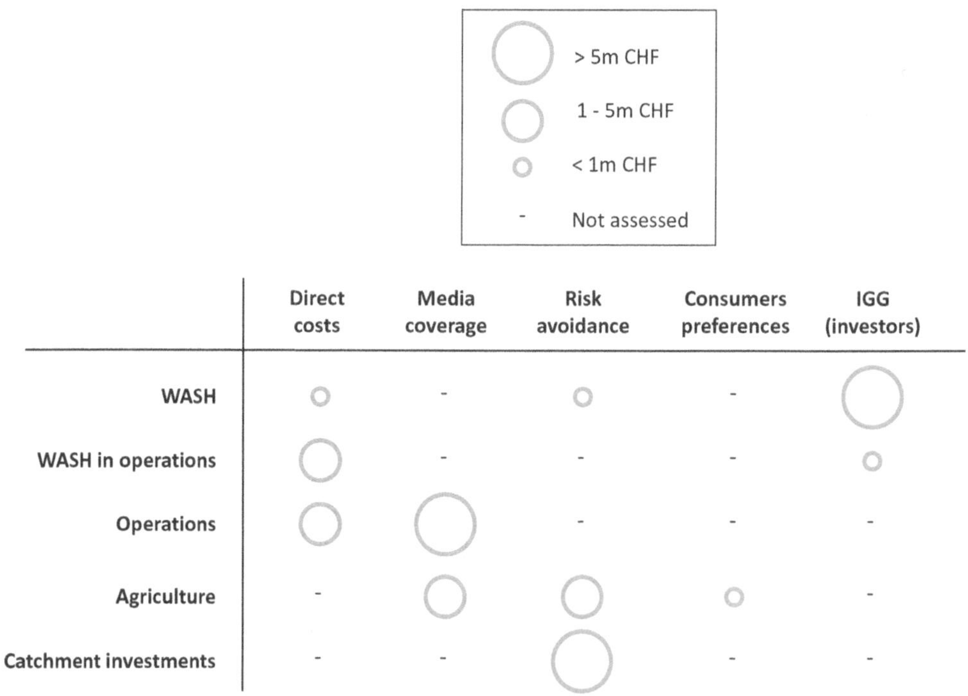

Figure 4. Detailed results for business value of Caring for Water.
Notes: IGG, Internally generated goodwill; WASH, Water, sanitation and hygiene

scope. Investments in watersheds, in agriculture and in communities address a much bigger fraction of water issues and have a higher return for the society and for the business.

As the company increasingly moves from inside to outside investments, the impact valuation shows significant potential to improve the focus, the set-up and the execution of water stewardship projects to deliver higher business and societal returns. Projects partners involved in collective action should clearly define the results and the impacts they are working towards, including the business value the projects are expected to generate. Research conducted in the scope of the impact valuation shows that very often water stewardship projects do not deliver clear business value (e.g. sourcing costs, consumer value, or media coverage), as they were neither set up nor executed for this purpose. The methodology of the impact valuation presented here can help align water stewardship projects with the societal and business priorities of the company and maximize the overall impacts of a project. Eventually, with good design, there is a positive role for all four impact areas of the Caring for Water initiative: factories, watersheds, agriculture and communities.

Conclusions

Water is one of the most critical challenges facing the environment, society and business today. Water is essential to life, but it is in short supply in many places around the world. Looking to the future, as populations and consumption grow, the world's already strained water resources will be stretched even further to secure the food and sanitation society demands. More broadly, water scarcity could have a significant negative impact on economic growth and societal prosperity, with all the implications this entails. Indeed, the World Economic Forum Global Risks Report has identified water as one of the top five global risks for eight consecutive years (since 2012).

For Nestlé, water has always been a high-priority issue. Nestlé's journey towards sustainability has included the establishment of the 2030 WRG, which works with like-minded stakeholders to find comprehensive and systemic solutions to close the water supply–demand gap, and the development of corporate flagship initiatives, such as Caring for Water, that bring value to both society and its shareholders. The potential to deliver even more value in the future is real, and decision making can be improved by evidence and facts, including those that may be provided through impact valuation.

Clearly, water-related challenges and risks cannot be addressed by Nestlé alone. Collaboration is needed, very much in the sense articulated by UN Sustainable Development Goal 17. Such collaboration is already happening for investments at the catchment and supply chain levels, but this will need to be scaled. Collaboration with the public sector and legislators will be also required, to bring about systemic change while maintaining the viability of our society and economy. Nestlé is already playing a role in influencing the global dialogue on water and collaborating with governments and other stakeholders, but again, most of the changes remain ahead of us.

Disclosure statement

No potential conflict of interest was reported by the authors.

References

2030 Water Resources Group. (2009). *Charting our water future: Economic frameworks to inform decision making*. New Delhi: 2030 Water Resources Group.

Bulcke, P. (2018). Nestlé and its response to megatrends in water. In A. Biswas, C. Tortajada, & P. Rohner (Eds.), Assessing *global water megatrends* (pp. 231–244). Singapore: Springer.

Clasen, T. F., Alexander, K. T., Sinclair, D., Boisson, S., Peletz, R., Chang, H. H., ... Cairncross, S. (2015). Interventions to improve water quality for preventing diarrhea (review). *Cochrane Collaboration*, 10. doi: 10.1002/14651858.CD004794.pub3

Dicker, D., Nguyen, G., Abate, D., Abate, K. H., Abay, S. M., Abbafati, C., ... Abdelalim, A. (2018). Global, regional, and national age-sex-specific mortality and life expectancy, 1950–2017: A systemic analysis for the global burden of disease study 2017. *The Lancet*, *392*(10159), 1684–1735.

Fewtrell, L., Kaufmann, R. B., Kay, D., Enanoria, W., Haller, L., & Colford, J. M. (2005). Water Sanitation, and hygiene interventions to reduce diarrhea in less developed countries: A systematic review and meta-analysis. *Lancet Infectious Diseases*, *5*, 42–52. doi:10.1016/S1473-3099(04)01253-8

Galli, C., & Vousvouras, C. (2019). Nestlé caring for water. Internal document. Nestlé SA, Vevey, Switzerland.

Prüss-Ustün, A., Bartram, J., Clasen, T., Colford, J. M., Cumming, O., Curtis, V., ... Cairncross, S. (2014). Burden of disease from inadequate water, sanitation and hygiene in low- and middle-income settings: A retrospective analysis of data from 145 countries. *Tropical Medicine and International Health*, *19*(8), 894–905. doi:10.1111/tmi.2014.19.issue-8

Reig, P., Larson, W., Vionnet, S., & Bayart, J.-B. (2019, August). *Volumetric Water Benefit Accounting (VWBA): A method for implementing and valuing water stewardship activities* (Working Paper). Washington DC: World Resources Institute.

Vionnet, S., & Couture, J.-M. (2015). Measuring value: Towards new metrics and methods. Retrieved from https://www.nestle.com/sites/default/files/asset-library/documents/creating-shared-value/nestle-measuring-value-2015.pdf

Waddington, H., & Snilstveit, B. (2009). Effectiveness and sustainability of water, sanitation, and hygiene interventions in combating diarrhea. *Journal of Development Effectiveness*, *1*(3), 295–335. doi:10.1080/19439340903141175

Appendix

The approaches to societal and business value are outlined here. Note: WASH = water, sanitation and hygiene.

	Societal value: summary of valuation approach
WASH and WASH in operations	WASH interventions were based on a country model which accounted for the potential reduction of diarrhoeal diseases. Statistics from the World Health Organization (Global Burden of Diseases, Dicker et al., 2018) were used to regionalize the model, and relevant literature (Clasen et al., 2015, Fewtrell et al., 2005, Prüss-Ustün et al., 2014, Waddington & Snilstveit, 2009) was then used to link the different interventions to an increase in well-being. This was calculated using disability-adjusted life years and valued using the productive value of life, using OECD average GDP per capita (https://data.oecd.org/gdp/gross-domestic-product-gdp.htm).
Water in operations	The cases of Lagos de Moreno (Mexico) and Mossel Bay (South Africa) were used to scale the benefits calculated to cover all investments in operations. The benefits were based on the shadow price of water, provided the Natural Capital Finance Alliance tool. This includes the potential avoided impact on agriculture, domestic supply, human health and the environment (ecosystem services).
Water in agriculture	The valuations were based on the shadow price provided by the Natural Capital Finance Alliance tool (when more information was not available). For Vietnam, lower production cost, leading to higher income for farmers, was accounted for. These estimates were scaled to the total impact using the total investments in this area.
Catchment investments	The valuation of selected projects (Broye, Madison Blue, Santa Maria, Cucomanga and Korpi) was based on the shadow price provided by the Natural Capital Finance Alliance tool (when more information was not available). This was the case for Broye and Korpi, where custom benefit assessments were done. These assessments were based on avoided costs for the community, increased ecosystem services, and jobs created.
	Business value: summary of valuation approach
WASH	The internally generated goodwill allocated to WASH was accounted for based on the presence of the topic in the annual report compared to other sustainability topics. We assumed that 5% of the internally generated goodwill is related to sustainability topics. On top of this, the potential avoided risk of disruption of licence to operate due to local community pressure was accounted for. The potential reduction in sourcing cost from Côte d'Ivoire in particular was also addressed as a test.
WASH in operations	Increased productivity was accounted for through the linkage to reduced diseases that would result from the lack of WASH services. Most developed countries did not see a benefit, as WASH issues are rare there.
Water in operations	The business benefits were assessed in terms of lower operations costs and earned media coverage.
Water in agriculture	Both the Brazil milk sourcing project and the Vietnam coffee sourcing projects were assessed. The Brazil business benefit was based on the potential premium paid by consumers for the brand of Nestlé being linked to better sustainability. For Vietnam, the earned media benefit was accounted for, as well as the avoided risk of supply disruption due to water scarcity, which would lead to higher cost of sourcing.
Catchment investments	All catchment investments were valued in term of avoided risks. Broye investments avoided the drilling of a new well for Nestlé. Cucamonga did not have any identified benefit. Madison Blue investments avoided the operational cost of additional treatment of water that would have been required. Santa Maria and Korpi business benefits were based on avoided reputational risks that would reduce sales and profit. Korpi business benefit also accounted for the avoided increased cost of water licence for wells.

Scarcity of water or scarcity of management?

David Molden

ABSTRACT
This article investigates the relation between water scarcity and water management. There are many different perceptions of water scarcity, which can include the conditions of arid environments, a general lack of access to water, insufficient water at a basin scale, or difficulty in meeting competing needs. All these issues will intensify with greater consumption and climate change. Asit Biswas reminds us that the root cause of scarcity is the way water is managed. Following this wisdom, I examine different contexts of scarcity I have encountered in my work and reflect on the management challenges which drive and transform water scarcity.

Introduction

'There is no scarcity of water, only a scarcity of management.' I have heard this provocative comment several times from renowned water leader, Prof. Asit Biswas. I knew of Asit Biswas when I was a graduate student at Colorado State University, but had a chance to meet him through the International Water Management Institute, where I worked. Since then we have met frequently, and recently I had the privilege of working with him and Cecilia Tortajada to produce special issues for the *International Journal of Water Resources Development*. Both Asit and Cecilia have been tremendously supportive of the work of the International Centre for Integrated Mountain Development (ICIMOD) and its work on water management.

In the 20 years I have known him, Asit has always been someone who makes me critically examine my work. When I first heard the statement above, I thought that surely there are a lot of cases of water scarcity, such as in very arid environments where there is a physical lack of water. Then again, when water is well managed it is possible to thrive in difficult environments; and even in wet environments people may struggle with water scarcity. To elaborate on Asit's point I draw on personal and professional experiences in Southern California, Egypt, Lesotho and the Himalayas. I will start where the inspiration for my career began: Southern California and the Mountain Kingdom of Lesotho.

Los Angeles

When I was growing up in a suburb of the city of Los Angeles in the 1960s, I thought water was plentiful. Our neighbourhood was a delightful green space with grass, trees, gardens and sprinklers. As a water user, I could turn on the tap and not worry about quality or quantity. I did not know where the water came from.

Later, I learned about Los Angeles' hydraulic infrastructure, which was developed to source water from great distances through pipes and channels. That infrastructure diverts water from the Colorado River and fertile irrigated areas, like the Owens Valley. The book *Cadillac Desert* (Reisner, 1993) recounts the hydraulic development of the Western US. Los Angeles's mega-infrastructure project, aimed at promoting growth and development, did not recognize the limits of water resources development, at a time when supply from distant sources seemed plentiful. As the movie *Chinatown* can attest, the hydraulic project of Southern California has always been controversial.

As Los Angeles grew, surrounded by profitable agriculture, failures of that large-scale hydraulic infrastructure and increasing competition for regional water supplies brought to light the important question of management over scarcity. The recent California drought, for example, shows not only that we have reached water limits, but also that such scarcity is driven by poor planning and management.

Lesotho

My first postgraduate job was at Butha Buthe High School in Lesotho, teaching mathematics, science and English to a very energetic group of youths from Lesotho and South Africa. I had the opportunity of living in the wonderful village of Tlokoeng, which in many ways was as far away as possible from where I grew up in Los Angeles.

While the village had no shortage of joy and friendship, there was no electricity, nor any running water. My neighbour and friend 'Me Masebabatso offered to carry a bucket of water of about 25 litres to the roundhouse or *rondaaval* where my wife, Karen, and I made our home. That water came from a local spring, which was also a social gathering place for the village women, and it was about a 30-minute walk away. We would use 25 litres for a day or two, saving enough water after cooking for a nice bucket bath and reusing it for our vegetable garden. Unfortunately, both of us came down with typhoid fever, probably because the source of water was not protected well enough.

My first experience with water management was to help instal a well for the village. The villagers organized to make a request and copayment, and fortunately, there was a project that could fill the demand. To my delight, they named the well Sediba sa David (David's well). The handpump made a big difference in both the amount and the quality of water that could be obtained and in the lives of people. But even with the handpump, the women still had to carry buckets of water on their heads, and for some, the distance was still far. This was a life-changing event: I changed my career course and went back to university to learn more about water.

Lesson 1: There are many different views of water scarcity

While 'water scarcity' is a common term, it has different meanings in different contexts. There are physically water-scarce environments, such as the deserts of Egypt or the Kalahari Desert (where I worked finding water wells). In these arid environments, the lack of rainfall makes water use a key concern. I will refer to this as physical water scarcity. However, if I hear that someone is struggling to acquire enough water, I understand that often this is more an issue of access. In this article, I will call this use scarcity. As described in this article, the reasons for use scarcity are many, and it is ultimately this type of scarcity that humanity must overcome. Another type of scarcity emerges at the basin level when it becomes difficult to allocate the existing supply to all users and uses. This is the situation in Los Angeles and many other areas of the world, such as Egypt's Nile Valley, and I will call it basin scarcity. Much of my career has been aimed at understanding scarcity (Seckler, Amarasinghe, Molden, De Silva, & Barker, 1998) and how to deal with it (Molden, 1997).

Egypt

Egyptians proudly say that their country is a gift of the Nile. My family had the fortunate experience of living in Cairo, and I did field research for my PhD in Upper Egypt. We also lived in Alexandria, where I worked in the Nile Delta area on irrigation rehabilitation. We then moved back to Cairo, where I conducted strategic research on the long-term usage of Nile River water in Egypt.

At the edge of the Nile Delta, one can easily see the contrast between the sandy, barren desert and the rich green fields of the Nile Valley. This is an area of intense irrigation, as well as a large, dense and thirsty population. In fact, the water is so intensively used that very little flows to the sea – a sign that the limits are being reached, or more likely breached. It is an area that has received huge investments in hydraulic infrastructure development, with a major step being the creation of the High Aswan Dam in the 1960s, and the expansion of irrigation in the Nile Delta.

The critical question, 'How far can the Nile water be stretched to feed the need of burgeoning cities and the growing demand for food?' was one of my tasks when I worked in Egypt in the early 1990s. Working on the entire Nile River basin 10 years later, it became clear to me that upstream countries also needed water for their people, food and energy. Today, management of this transboundary river basin remains an issue to be addressed (Awulachew, Smakhtin, Molden, & Peden, 2012; Conniff, Molden, Peden, & Awulachew, 2012).

In this situation where water limits are reached, there is apparently no water for additional uses, so that an increase in use, say by cities, typically means that water gets reallocated and shifted from one use to another. Even saving water in agriculture is not as easy as it seemed (Seckler, 1996). Water management issues become much more complex as a change in use by one user can readily impact other users: the different water use sectors are closely connected.

Cities, agriculture, industry and water must be managed with a holistic basin approach. Equity becomes a concern, as water is often allocated away from those with less wealth and power. Issues of pollution, water reuse, and enough water for navigation all become interrelated, and variability in supply can really challenge water managers. Unsustainable practices arise when people try to obtain more water from declining groundwater tables, or tap too much from river systems, such that not enough environmental flows remain. Water management agencies set up to expand irrigation or manage city water alone are not geared up to solve these issues. The Nile River is also shared between many countries, raising difficult political issues. Such issues of 'over-development' and allocation emerge over and over in many river basins throughout the world (Falkenmark and Molden, 2008).

Lesson 2: Development can solve water scarcity, but also create water scarcity

The situations in California and Egypt, in contrast to Lesotho, offer different insights. Clearly in Lesotho water was a scarce commodity. People really had to struggle for a few drops. In spite of water in springs and in the river valley, access to water was a real issue. Infrastructure investments are often intended to ease scarcity at the user level. In the Lesotho, case, the pump eased access and brought relief to households. In Southern California, huge investments were made in hydraulic infrastructure to support and expand a growing economy. And in Egypt, dams, barrages and canals were built to expand and control the water supply so that more people could have more access to water for household uses and irrigation, not to mention the industries and economies this supported.

Another type of scarcity occurs when societies reach the physical limits of water availability. In Los Angeles, the solution was to go farther afield and tap water from distant sources. In Egypt there are limited options, as the upstream countries are demanding more. With too many demands on rivers countries over-rely on groundwater, which has its long-term limits and remains a serious water challenge. Water users become interconnected sometimes in direct ways and other times in subtle ways, and the complexity of management increases many times.

As the cases of Egypt and Southern California illustrate, the expansion of irrigated agriculture is a major driver of basin-level scarcity. With its high consumptive use of water, growing food takes a lot of water. Expanding irrigated agriculture in Egypt and California is a major factor in driving up basin water use to the limits and thus to basin scarcity. This is because of the high consumptive water use by irrigation, or liquid water being converted to evaporation and transpiration that is not available for reuse.

The politically more difficult question is when, where and by how much to limit irrigated agriculture. Reducing agriculture in Egypt or California could free up water. I remember hearing Tony Allan (1994) talk in the early 1990s about how trade could free up water in Egypt. On the one hand, a growing, wealthier population will require more food, and more water to grow the food (Molden, 2007). On the other hand, where and how should the food be grown is an important global question. This also brings to mind the relationship between what we eat and how much food we waste. Food habits and the relation of food and water remain important considerations for individual users, cities and nations (Lundqvist et al., 2008).

There are patterns of water use and development which seem to be common across the globe and can be thought of in terms of trajectories of water basin development (Keller, Keller, & Davids, 1998; Molden, Sakthivadivel, Samad, & Burton, 2005; Molle & Wester, 2009). To overcome problems of scarcity at the user level, hydraulic infrastructure is built to supply more water to various uses, for example by putting in water pumps in Lesotho, or building dams and canals in Egypt. With increasing demands and more and more expectations for water to support expanding agriculture, more water is removed from its natural system and diverted to meet various needs. However, there is a point when hydrologic limits are reached, and if it is technically too difficult or expensive to get more water, or water rights become a concern, societies have to learn to live with what is available, and deal with the natural variability of water cycles. As these limits are reached, there is much more concern about ecosystem functions, and the struggle is how to reallocate precious water amongst various users – environment, agriculture, industry, drinking, energy and more. When this upper limit is reached, when there is no additional water in natural systems to be tapped, there is human-made scarcity. There is not enough water for all the apparent needs, and the question of who gets water, and whether there is enough for the environment, remains a real issue. So we see a shift from dealing with scarcity at a local level to an overall induced scarcity at river basin and larger scales, which may again cause use-level scarcity if not managed well.

Kathmandu Valley

I now live in a ring of hills (in other countries they would call them mountains) surrounding the Kathmandu Valley, near the hill called Phulchowki (2780 m). Our house is at the head end of one of the valley's water systems. Fortunately, we have a good water supply: a village district committee-run water system that is fed by a forest spring. However, moving down the hill towards the main city of Kathmandu, the situation becomes worse and worse. It is quite common to see leaky pipes spilling water on the ground, and many water tankers on the road, delivering water to water-starved Kathmandu.

There are several streams and springs flowing down from Phulchowki Hill. Beautiful ancient temples, ponds and stone spouts show the importance of and reverence for water since ancient times. The streams support rich wildlife and are a favourite place for Karen to photograph dragonflies and birds. But many of them are now dry for most of the year.

When looking for birds and dragonflies, Karen and I notice a water management issue similar to that of the Nile basin but on a much smaller scale. Curious about why these streams are dry except when it rains, we explored upstream. There is a surprising network of pipes tapping into the water to feed nearby downstream urban settlements. In one of our favourite biodiversity habitats, water developers built a water harvesting bund to capture water and to deliver it downstream and to the water tankers that deliver water into Kathmandu. With all the pipes in place, the streams below have dried up for most of the year, a clear case of breach of environmental flows.

Just as in the case of the Nile, the use of these small streams has already reached a limit, and the management issues become more complex as users become more interconnected. When people walk upstream they see the stream flowing and assume that by tapping it they can add more water to their system. The reality is that they are simply taking water from other users downstream – including the traditional ponds and systems that have served the area for hundreds of years. There is significant damage to the aquatic ecosystem. But when you point this out to water developers, they simply state that people need water and such development is necessary. Yet, I sincerely doubt that such planners conducted or took heed of hydrologic analysis and water accounting. With better planning, management and foresight, the same amount of water could be delivered to the city without damaging such important ecosystems.

Lesson 3: Institutions are more important than infrastructure in overcoming scarcity

People and politicians often view hydraulic infrastructure as a quick fix to water problems, whether it be major dams, or developers tapping into more supplies upstream in the Kathmandu Valley. There is no doubt that water infrastructure is a necessity worldwide, but the key lesson is that infrastructure development must go hand in hand with institutional development. In managing water there is often a complex web of institutions responsible for water management, and understanding institutional needs is often beyond the engineering training that many water managers receive.

The Kathmandu Valley, like so many other places I have witnessed, struggles to meet growing multiple demands on water resources. Kathmandu's irrigated agriculture is declining, but even that does not free up water for the sprawling city. Planners and managers have just not been able to keep up, and mismanagement exacerbates both use and basin-level scarcity.

I would say that in terms of river basin trajectories, Kathmandu lies midway between the Lesotho village situation and the Los Angeles or Egypt water case. The city population is burgeoning, with more than 3 million inhabitants, up from the 1 million when I lived there in the 1990s and was working on irrigation in Nepal. Agricultural fields are rapidly turning into urban landscapes. The Kathmandu Valley receives about two metres of rainfall, and heavy monsoons; it is the source of the Bagmati River and has a significant aquifer system. It seems like nature supplies enough water for the inhabitants, yet most people in Kathmandu lack adequate clean drinking water. People ultimately learn how to fill the gap. The situation is well described by my daughter, who studied the situation in depth (Molden, Griffin, & Meehan, 2016; Molden, Khanal, & Pradhan, 2018). Her studies showed the dire consequences of water mismanagement as women, men and recent migrants spend inordinate amounts of time, money and energy on accessing and saving water. They also showed the ingenuity in how groups organized to overcome difficulties. Several user groups in the Patan area overcame scarcity by working together to operate their own groundwater systems and revitalize ancient water systems.

During my stay in the Kathmandu Valley in the early 1990s, the Melamchi water project was designed to bring water in from sources north of the valley, through a tunnel. This large hydraulic infrastructure for trans-basin river diversion was seen as the way to provide adequate access to water for the citizens. Remarkably, the project is not yet complete, nearly 30 years later. My sense is that even if the project comes, it will not solve the water problems. There are a plethora of water management issues, from inequitable distribution of water to lack of maintenance, and a very weak institutional infrastructure. Until these are addressed, there will still be water problems, and water scarcity will be a reality.

The mountains

Mountain areas are referred to as water towers, or sources of water for river and groundwater systems. The hills and mountains of Lesotho and the Hindu Kush Himalaya (HKH) are home to some of the poorest people on earth, with little investment in water infrastructure to benefit the local people. Population densities in mountains are typically much lower than in the surrounding plains, and typically there is a high flow in rivers, supporting a small population, so water availability per capita can be very high, suggesting no scarcity (water availability in Lesotho is 2599 cubic metres per capita per year; in Nepal, 7366; in Egypt, 20; and overall in India, 1116). So from the perspective of water availability, the impression is that mountain areas should not be water-scarce at all. Yet, experience in the Himalayas and in Lesotho shows that people in the hills and mountains indeed struggle a lot to get adequate supplies of water for drinking, sanitation and agriculture. What is happening?

The basic physical challenge in hills and mountains is to overcome gravity. Villages and towns are often on the top of hills or on the slopes, and one reason for this is to avoid floods. The town of Cherapunjee has some of the highest recorded rainfall values on earth, with an average annual rainfall of over 11 m, but paradoxically it is known as a wet desert, because the water quickly flows downhill. The rivers are down in the valley, so to use river water, people have to work against gravity. The traditional solution is to capture water before it runs downslope to the rivers. Springs are an important source. People also try to store water in the soil, as well as ponds and reservoirs.

As a result, for much of the year, people in the hills and mountains suffer from severe use-level water scarcity. Women spend much of their day fetching water from springs, and each drop is precious. There are examples of excellent water management in the hills, where farmers have organized to capture streams or springs on the slopes of hills and divert it to irrigation. People have marvelled at these traditional systems, and the management system for resource mobilization, operation and maintenance (Ostrom, 1990; Pradhan, 1989). In a world full of water mismanagement, experiencing these can really be a positive experience, showing hope for the future.

Lesotho is also known in water circles for the Lesotho Highland Development Project, a massive undertaking begun in 1986 to supply water and electricity to Lesotho and South Africa (Keketso, 2003). So there is investment in water, and this was also meant for the overall economic development of the country. My initial stay in Lesotho from 1977 to 1979 was before the project was built, and I remember that people talked about the project, how it would bring water and electricity to light up villages. I visited again many years later, in 2007, when the project was complete. The dam and reservoir were strikingly beautiful, and a mark of great engineering. However, when I visited the village of Tlokoeng, where I had lived, water access was still an issue, although the scarcity had been reduced with more wells. During my visit, Tlokoeng received an electric connection for the first time – 10 years after completion of the first phase of the Highland Development Project. Most of the water and electricity are flowing into South Africa. The question of *who benefits* from water development remains one of the key water management issues we have to face.

Climate change

I joined ICIMOD in 2011. It is ideally placed to address the issue of sustainable development in mountains, as it covers the mountains and hills in the eight countries of the HKH: Afghanistan, Bangladesh, Bhutan, China, India, Myanmar, Nepal and Pakistan. Ten major river basins, home to about 2 billion people, have their sources in the HKH. Clearly the governments and people are concerned about what is happening in the mountains and how it will impact their river systems. Downstream of the HKH, water from the mountains serves over half the irrigated area on earth, and there are huge cities such as Delhi, Lahore, Dhaka and Chengdu. Seven of these 10 rivers are transboundary, and in almost all the basins, water managers struggle to provide enough water for everyone. Disasters from floods and droughts are on the rise; water pollution is already high; and ecosystem services from rivers are diminishing – all symptoms of poor water management.

And what will happen with climate change? There was a striking lack of data and research in the mountains in spite of their importance as the water towers of Asia. But, fortunately, over the last 10 years there have been robust scientific studies on the HKH cryosphere and its changes and subsequent impact downstream; these are synthesized in the HIMAP report (Bolch et al., 2019; Wester, Mishra, Mukherji, & Shrestha, 2019).

Overall studies show that most glaciers across the HKH are thinning and retreating rapidly. In the short term, over say 10 to 40 years, melting glaciers and snow will add more water to the rivers, but there will be a turning point ('peak water') when it starts decreasing.

In the long term, most climate models point to more rain in the region. The overall result is that the overall annual volume of water in the main rivers may not decrease by 2100, but hydrologic patterns will change, and variability in flows will increase. This points to lower flows in the lean season, and higher flows in the flooding season. For people in the mountains who live close to the glaciers and who are well adapted to glaciers and snow, less water from melting will have its impacts. In other words, water managers will have to face more uncertainty and more variability. Given the water management regimes that already struggle with existing supplies, this will certainly be a challenge for Asia, and indeed segments of society could suffer from water scarcity. China Water Risk (Hu & Tan, 2018) estimates that US$ 4 trillion of business assets are at stake from climate change and water management in these river basins.

During my time with ICIMOD, we have been trying to understand the impacts of climate change on the cryosphere – the snow, glaciers and permafrost – and thus on downstream river systems. In 2014, I had the good fortune to visit the mountainous areas of Pakistan to understand what was happening to the glaciers and its impact on the Indus River. What was striking during that visit was the melting glaciers, but also the difficulty of getting good measurements. I was impressed by the green agricultural fields and fruit orchards, and the irrigation systems built and managed to supply water equitably to villagers. But what struck me most was the voice of the mountain community. We were warmly welcomed in village after village. Villagers explained to us their problems with water. They were losing their water source because of retreating glaciers, and they were in danger of floods from glacier lakes and storms. They even asked what methods they could use to stop glaciers from retreating. While there was plenty of water in the rivers, it was very silty, and not seen as a potential source of water because of the silt and difficult access. There was a plea for help, and we tried to respond with some interventions, such as solar pumps to tap the rivers and early flood warning systems aimed at adapting to climate change. I returned five years later and was proud to learn that some of these interventions were successful – but some were not, in this very difficult environment. It really made me reflect on our global systems, where the people who contribute so little to climate change are its biggest victims.

Lesson 4: Realizing the human right to water is a growing concern and needs targeted approaches

I have learned that while mountains are isolated, and sometimes at the back of people's thoughts, they are also our early warning signal on how humanity is dealing with sustainable development. Climate change is already real for many mountain people, and challenging their resilience. Global management of our resources impacts people at the local level, and indeed adds to water management challenges.

In the future, more demand for water from a larger, wealthier population will require additional water for cities and agriculture than supplied at present. Then there is the gap between rich and poor, with people being left behind in water development. It is already a struggle to keep enough water for ecosystems to support biodiversity. Then on top of that is the uncertainty and shifting hydrologic patterns that will arise from climate change. If we as a global community do not do better at managing our water resources, many people will experience scarcity. And unfortunately those who have less of a political voice, or less money, will be more at risk.

Asit Biswas invited me to a seminar hosted by the Pontifical Academy of Sciences, where we discussed the human right to water. There was a wide recognition that inequalities exist, and that water is a main concern for the poor and marginalized. It was also clear in the meeting that water access is related to complex societal issues and power relations between communities and people that need to be addressed at the same time. This will require targeted approaches with an understanding of social and political issues as well as water issues. This is very apparent in the hills and mountains of Lesotho and the HKH, and even more urgent in view of the disproportionate impacts of climate change.

Conclusions: reflections on water scarcity

A simple way to think about water scarcity is that it is a situation where there is not enough water to meet essential needs, like drinking or growing food. When water scarcity hits, supply is less than demand or expectations, and when it is poorly managed, people spend a lot of time and money to get water. This can happen at different scales, and with interactions across scales. Most water users in the Kathmandu Valley face immense problems getting enough water due to failures in water governance. In many mountain and hill villages, including my village in Lesotho, people spend an inordinate amount of energy fetching water.

At a larger scale, supply has to meet competing and growing demands. With population growth, situations can change from where there was enough water to meet everyone's demands, to a situation where there is not enough to go around. Allocation decisions are made that can force scarcity at the use scale. This is certainly the case in Egypt and in California: there is not enough water to go around for the various demands. Societies tend to not recognize the limits of water supplies, and they tend to focus on acquiring additional supplies rather than managing existing supplies. In so many places, like Egypt, there is a misdirected sense that more irrigation can be done, in spite of a limited water supply. This is repeated in many basins around the world. Because we overbuild and expect too much, we arrive at a situation where there is not enough water to go around, and when water is reallocated it tends to meet the needs of wealthier and more powerful people, rather than the poor or marginalized.

We do have cases of good water management, where the supply of water closely meets demand. Where water is managed well, scarcity can be overcome, but when there is mismanagement, scarcity can be devastating. Water managers in farmer-managed systems in Nepal have demonstrated the ability to share a limited supply equitably amongst users. However, in many irrigation systems across Asia, mismanagement is pervasive, and the head–tail problem is common, where those near the source of water get more than those downstream. In the Kathmandu Valley, some users have a plentiful supply, but most suffer.

With high levels of basin scarcity, the water management challenges are daunting. Growth in demand, and rapidly changing societal demands, and mechanisms to fairly allocate water in ways that best support economies, are a challenge. Pollution issues exacerbate the problems of water use and reuse. People tend to look for other sources of water, but that is not always the solution either, as it might take away water from other uses – essentially robbing Peter to pay Paul. On top of this, we will have to face the challenge of climate change and even greater variability in water supplies. With growing demands for water superimposed on poor water management regimes, and the challenges of climate change, we have some daunting challenges ahead. Water scarcity will still be an issue, even though there is enough water, and enough money.

We need another way of looking at water, and we need to take some brave steps. Politicians need to be involved, and to look beyond easy and short-term fixes, and somehow society will have to be educated to demand this. Unfortunately, water management can be an incredibly complex issue, with intersecting issues of governance, and different positions in society – rich and poor, men and women, powerful and marginalized. Water also crosses sectoral interests, such as environment, energy and food. We will need more water managers and people engaged in water who are trained to be able to take a more holistic view of water, and who can understand not only the complexities of hydrology but also the social sciences. If we are to realize the dream of a human right to water, we have to be able to focus on the issues of the poor and marginalized. We will need more and better investments in water, and in the human capacity to manage water.

Let us go back to the original statement by Asit Biswas: we don't have a scarcity of water, but a scarcity of management. Clearly a major cause of scarcity is mismanagement, and unfortunately this abounds across the world. It is true in areas of high development of water resources. There are also places where access to enough water remains an issue, for example in the hills and mountains of the HKH and Nepal. In the world there is plenty of water, and also plenty of financial resources. The question is whether we are adequately managing our financial, human, and natural resources so that water flows to the places it is most needed.

Acknowledgments

I would like to thank my daughter Olivia Molden and my wife Karen Conniff for their insights, as well as critical and careful review. We have gone through these experiences and learned a lot together. ICIMOD gratefully acknowledges the support of its core donors: the governments of Afghanistan, Australia, Austria, Bangladesh, Bhutan, China, India, Myanmar, Nepal, Norway, Pakistan, Sweden and Switzerland.

Disclosure statement

No potential conflict of interest was reported by the author.

Funding

This work was supported by the governments of Afghanistan, Australia, Austria, Bangladesh, Bhutan, China, India, Myanmar, Nepal, Norway, Pakistan, Sweden and Switzerland.

ORCID

David Molden http://orcid.org/0000-0003-3201-9518

References

Allan, T. (1994). Economic and political adjustments to scarce water in the Middle East. *Studies in Environmental Science, 58*, 375–388.

Awulachew, S. B., Smakhtin, V., Molden, D., & Peden, D. (Eds.). (2012). *The Nile River Basin: Water, agriculture, governance and livelihoods*. Abingdon, UK: Routledge - Earthscan.

Bolch, T., Shea, J., Liu, S., Azam, M. F., Gao, Y., Gruber, S., ... Racoviteanu, A. (2019). Status and change of the cryosphere in the Extended Hindu Kush Himalaya Region. In P. Wester, A. Mishra, A. Mukherji, A. Shrestha (Eds.), *The Hindu Kush Himalaya assessment* (pp. 209–255). Cham: Springer.

Conniff, K., Molden, D., Peden, D., & Awulachew, S. B. (2012). Nile water and agriculture: Past, present and future. In *The Nile River Basin: Water, agriculture, governance and livelihoods* (pp. 27–51). Abingdon, UK: Routledge.

Falkenmark, M., & Molden, D. J. (2008). Wake up to realities of river basin closure. *International Journal of Water Resources Development, 24*(2), 201–215. doi:10.1080/07900620701723570

Hu, F., & Tan, D. (2018). *No water, no growth: Does Asia have enough water to develop?* Hong Kong: China Water Risk.

Keketso, L. (2003). The mixed blessings of the Lesotho Highlands Water Project: An assessment based on local perspectives. *Mountain Research and Development, 23*(1), 7–10. doi:10.1659/0276-4741(2003)023[0007:TMBOTL]2.0.CO;2

Keller, J., Keller, A., & Davids, G. (1998). River basin development phases and implications of closure. *Journal of Applied Irrigation Science, 33*(2), 145–164. doi:10.1.1.485.4832

Lundqvist, J., de Fraiture, C., Molden, D., Berndes, G., Berntell, A., Falkenmark, M., ... Lannerstad, M. (2008, May). *Saving water: From field to fork: Curbing losses and wastage in the food chain.* Stockholm, Sweden: Stockholm Environment Institute. (SIWI Paper 13) Prepared for the Commission on Sustainable Development.

Molden, D. (1997). *Accounting for water use and productivity* (SWIM Paper 1). Colombo, Sri Lanka: International Irrigation Management Institute.

Molden, D. (Ed.). (2007). *Water for food, water for life: A comprehensive assessment of water management in agriculture.* London: Earthscan; Colombo: International Water Management Institute.

Molden, D., Sakthivadivel, R., Samad, M., & Burton, M. (2005). Phases of river basin development: The need for adaptive institutions. In M. Svendsen (Ed.), *Irrigation and river basin management: Options for governance and institutions* (pp. 19–29). Wallingford: CABI.

Molden, O., Griffin, N., & Meehan, K. (2016). The cultural dimensions of household water security: The case of Kathmandu's stone spout systems. *Water International, 41*(7), 982–997. doi:10.1080/02508060.2016.1251677

Molden, O. C., Khanal, A., & Pradhan, N. (2018). The pain of water: A household perspective of water insecurity and inequity in the Kathmandu Valley. *Water Policy*, 1–16. doi:10.2166/wp.2018.116

Molle, F., & Wester, P. (Eds.). (2009). *River basin trajectories: Societies, environments and development.* Wallingford, UK: CABI.

Ostrom, E. (1990). *Governing the commons: The evolution of institutions for collective action.* Cambridge, UK: Cambridge University Press.

Pradhan, P. (1989). *Patterns of irrigation organization in Nepal: A comparative study of 21 farmer-managed irrigation systems in Nepal* (IIMI Country Paper Nepal 1). Colombo, Sri Lanka: International Irrigation Management Institute (IIMI).

Reisner, M. (1993). *Cadillac desert: The American West and its disappearing water.* New York: Penguin Books.

Seckler, D. (1996). *The new era of water resources management: From "dry" to "wet" water savings.* Research Report 001/IIMI Research. Colombo, Sri Lanka: International Irrigation Management Institute.

Seckler, D., Amarasinghe, U., Molden, D., De Silva, R., & Barker, R. (1998). World water demand and supply, 1990 to 2025: Scenarios and issues. *Water Management, 19*, 50. doi:10.3910/2009.019

Wester, P., Mishra, A., Mukherji, A., & Shrestha, A. (Eds). (2019). *The Hindu Kush Himalaya assessment.* Cham: Springer.

Singapore's water challenges past to present

Peter Joo Hee Ng and Celine Teo

ABSTRACT

Problems with drought, floods and public sanitation are commonplace for any developing country. The manner in which Singapore has overcome these difficulties, however, may well be exceptional. Water scarcity was, is, and remains a trial for Singapore's decision makers. Singapore's water management method is distinguished by three qualities: integration, circularity and the taking of an uncommonly long view. Thus, despite nature's poor endowment, today's Singapore is not short of water. This is possible only because it has been realistic about its circumstances, and has used its intellect and imagination, researching continuously, and continues to muster the will to pursue hard-nosed water policies.

Introduction

In its 2015 report, the World Resources Institute declared Singapore to be at the highest risk of becoming severely water stressed by the year 2040, out of the 167 territories it surveyed. That Singapore, in the tropics and the regular recipient of 2400 mm of rainfall a year, should become short of water might be surprising, but is no less true. The lack of land, rather than of rain, is the prime element constraining water sufficiency in Singapore.

Tropical rain poses another challenge. It is intense and often comes all at once. Any failure to convey runoff away quickly enough means extensive flooding. Taming and storing all that rainfall will require extensive drainage and many large reservoirs.

In addition to providing an adequate water supply to its populace and dealing with frequent inundation, administrators of early Singapore also had to contend with the lack of public sanitation. How modern Singapore was able to overcome this trio of water challenges and become a master of water management is instructive in many ways. It is a story that bears recounting in some detail, not least to learn the many lessons contained within of how a poorly endowed city-state could eventually achieve enduring water security.

Singapore's early water systems

It is apt and useful, in this 200th year since its founding, to pause and take a backward glance at how Singapore's water system developed and advanced along the way. What becomes immediately apparent is that even from its early days, Singapore's water system has always been intricately tied to the city's growth. As Singapore grew and transformed, from the sleepy fishing village at the time of Raffles's arrival to the glittering metropolis of the present day, its water system was continuously shaped by engineers, city planners and even physicians. We see that the need to improve public health was the primary motivation behind the construction of its first drainage and sewerage systems; and that ever-increasing urbanization drove the creation of Singapore's first water supply scheme.

First drains and sewers

It was Malcom Watson, the chief medical officer, who, in 1914, conceived of Singapore's first drains – as a means of malaria prevention. He had observed that Telok Blangah was the 'most malarious district in Singapore' (Watson, 1921), and decided to build drains there to remove stagnant water and eliminate mosquito breeding places. On the completion of the scheme, which consisted of earth drains, brick drains and subsoil pipes, malaria rates dropped dramatically. From then, drainage systems were deemed effective measures against malaria and promptly replicated in other districts.

In a similar fashion, it was concern about poor public health that triggered the first sewers to be built in Singapore. Throughout the 1800s, domestic sewage management was rudimentary and certainly unsanitary. Raw sewage was removed and disposed of by night soil men (Yeoh, 2003), who then sent some of the collected excreta to small plantation owners to be used as fertilizer. However, the bulk of it was either buried or landfilled (Tan, 1972). Worsening odour issues led the municipal government to study various other options for disposal. In 1911, the municipal engineer, Robert Pierce, proposed that a shallow network of sewers be constructed, which would connect to pumping stations and a disposal works. For the purpose of public sanitation, the main Singapore town area was divided into three zones, with the southern zone draining into the Park Road pumping station, zone 1 in the north draining into the River Valley pumping station, and northern zone 2 into the Albert Street pumping station. Three trunk sewers then pumped sewage to the Alexandra Road Disposal Works, and effluent was later released into the Singapore River. Records show that the Alexandra Road Disposal Works became operational in 1915 (Tan, 1972).

By conveying waste through subterranean lines, sewage was swiftly removed and the smell nuisance greatly reduced. It was reported that by the early 1930s, 100,000 persons enjoyed modern sanitation, while another 165,000 continued to rely on the night soil men. Singapore's early sewerage system continued to expand, such that by 1971, 1,1180,000 persons (57% of the population) were served by flushing toilets, 340,000 remained on the night soil scheme, and the other 360,000 continued to depend on outdoor latrines or other means of sewage disposal (Tan, 1972). Today, Singapore is, of course, 100% sewered up, and has progressed to become the operator of the world's most extensive deep tunnel sewerage system.

The first water supply system

A ready water supply was an essential facilitator of Singapore's economic development, in addition to satisfying a growing urban population which could no longer depend on groundwater wells. It was British resident John Crawford who proposed, in 1823, that a reservoir and waterworks be built to cater to the needs of the Singapore port (Yeoh, 2003). Later, in 1852, John Turnbull Thomson, the government surveyor, carried out the first water demand study and pushed for a water supply system in downtown Singapore consisting of a storage reservoir, a service reservoir at Fort Canning (originally Government's Hill), and water pipelines and distribution cisterns (Thomson, 1852). However, these early proposals were not implemented, due to lack of government and public interest (Yeoh, 2003).

It was not until 1868 that the first reservoir and waterworks were completed. Water was abstracted from Thomson Road Reservoir (today's MacRitchie Reservoir), piped to waterworks for treatment, and then distributed to people living near the Singapore River. Back then, piped water supply was limited to 12 hours a day and had to be stopped during the dry season (Yeoh, 2003). The first service reservoir was subsequently built in 1902 on Pearl's Hill to serve the residents of nearby Chinatown.

Even as the municipal government continued to expand Singapore's water supply infrastructure, it was never quite enough. As early as 1903, municipal engineer Robert Peirce assessed that even if all potential water resources in Singapore were to be fully developed and utilized, water supply would still not be able to keep up with growing population into the 1920s (Yeoh, 2003).

The water agreements

Hence, Singapore looked to Malaysia for water.

In 1927, Johor's Sultan Ibrahim and Singapore's municipal commissioners agreed that Singapore could lease the Gunung Pulai catchment area for raw water supply. In 1929 the Sultan Ibrahim Reservoir at Gunung Pulai was completed and officially opened by Hugh Clifford, governor of the Straits Settlements (Remembering Singapore, 2018; Tan, 2016).

When two new water agreements were signed in 1961 and 1962 between Johor State and Singapore's City Council, the 1927 agreement was voided. The 1961 agreement allowed Singapore to tap water resources from Johor's Tebrau and Skudai Rivers. The 1962 agreement allowed Singapore to extract water from the Johor River, up to 250 million gallons per day, for 99 years. Both countries agreed to abide by the 1961 and 1962 water agreements, even after Singapore achieved independence from Malaysia in 1965. A supplementary agreement in 1990 allowed PUB to construct and operate the Linggiu Reservoir in Johor (Remembering Singapore, 2018).

Arguing with the neighbours

At the point of independence, Singapore's leaders intentionally pressed for the two water agreements to be incorporated into the Singapore-Malaysia Separation Agreement of 1965 (Ministry of Information, Communications and the Arts, 2003; Mohamad, 2015; Tan, 2016). The Separation Agreement was in turn enacted into the Malaysian Constitution and registered with the United Nations. But this did not deter Tunku Abdul Rahman, Malaysia's prime minister, from telling British high commissioner Anthony Head on the day of Singapore's independence (9 August 1965) that Malaysia could always pressure Singapore by turning off the water, should Singapore not comply with Malaysian wishes or if its foreign policy was prejudicial to Malaysia's interests (Kwa, 2002; Tan, 2016).

Threats to like effect were to be repeated by different Malaysian officials on several later occasions. One such instance was in 2002, during a period of contentious negotiation on water pricing. The Malaysian minister for law, Rais Yatim, was quoted in newspapers as saying that Malaysia could easily enact legislation to declare the 1961 and 1962 water agreements null and void (Mohamad, 2015). This eventually led Singapore's prime minister, Goh Chok Tong, to inform Malaysia's prime minister, Mahathir Mohamad, that because of Malaysia's scare tactics and threats of cutting water supplies, Singapore planned to produce as much desalinated and recycled water as it could, and let the 1961 agreement lapse (Ministry of Information, Communications and the Arts, 2003; Mohamad, 2015).

Modernity and closing the water loop

Looking back, Robert Pierce's appraisal of Singapore's fundamental water scarcity could not have been more prescient. Scarcity of water supply was, is, and will surely remain a trial for Singapore's decision makers and water planners. Unquestionably, it was this realization that led Singapore to ceaselessly search for means to overcome water scarcity, and to make its next innovation. Safeguarding water security has always loomed large in the minds of Singapore's leaders and the calculations of Singaporean administrators. The late Lee Kuan Yew, Singapore's first prime minister, knew that his city-state's growth and prosperity were directly contingent on water security. He worked tirelessly throughout his life to secure Singapore's water future, and had famously said that 'water dominated every other policy. Every other policy had to bend at the knees for water survival' (Ng, 2018).

The water system in present-day Singapore and the way it is managed is the culmination of a decades-long quest by Singaporean water engineers for alternative water sources. The Singapore method is distinguished by three qualities: integration, circularity and reuse.

The recovery and reclamation of wastewater, and its subsequent recycling for potable use, follow a geometric progression. Even at 50% recovery losses, continuous reuse effectively doubles the available supply. This was to be a key insight for Singapore's water planners. And as soon as reuse technology became viable, at the turn of the millennium, PUB adopted it with great zeal. From 2003, it started to produce NEWater – its brand of ultra-high-quality recycled water – on an industrial scale. At the same time, the water supply, sewerage and sanitation, and drainage systems, previously operating independently, were brought together and operated as one whole. This necessitated the reconstitution of PUB as Singapore's sole water agency, with responsibility for overseeing an integrated national water infrastructure.

The idea starts with rain. Rain falls and becomes stormwater. Stormwater is collected in drains, channelled to reservoirs and stored. Stored rainwater is treated to become potable water, which is supplied to people, commerce and industry. As PUB supplies good water, water that has been used is returned to it. That used water is collected, treated and turned into good water again, to be supplied for human use or stored in reservoirs. At the same time, seawater is desalted, turned into good water and fed as another stream into the loop.

The 'water loop' is simple enough, but in most parts of the world it is still managed in separate pieces. In most places, the water economy is a linear one: good water is taken from nature, and used just once by humans, and then the wastewater is simply thrown away. In many places, the water department is separate from the sewerage department, which is separate again from the drainage department. And invariably, all three will work at cross purposes. Hence, Singapore's closing of the water loop proved to be a stroke of administrative and operational genius.

Singapore's secret for a sustainable water supply was to manage the entire water system as one whole. In this way, the Singapore water economy became a fully circular one, long before it was fashionable to speak of circularity. For PUB, supplying good water, reclaiming used water and taming stormwater are the three legs that hold up a unitary mission.

Singapore's water strategy

Despite nature's severely poor endowment, today's Singapore is not short of water, and is confident that it will continue to enjoy water security in the long term.

Singapore's water strategy has three parts. First, it does all it can to maximize natural yield, striving to collect every drop of rain that falls on the island and channelling the stormwater into storage reservoirs. Two-thirds of Singapore is water catchment and a watershed for capturing rainfall that will eventually end up as drinking water. Maximizing catchment yield is not trivial, as it entails acute trade-offs *vis-à-vis* alternative land use, as well as a willingness to invest heavily in drainage and storage infrastructure.

As Singapore progressively urbanized, it became unavoidable that zoning land as water catchment would ultimately compete directly with residential and industrial use. In 1983, to meet residential land needs, the Singapore government decided that water catchment land outside the central nature reserve would no longer be protected but could be exploited for non-polluting use, with overall urbanization capped at 34.1%. Later, in 1991, to open up even more residential land, the cap was removed entirely and, as mitigation, water treatment works upgraded to handle stormwater water of a lower quality. Today, residential and commercial development is unrestricted within water catchment, although more polluting industries are still prohibited. Singapore remains one of very few places in the world where the drinking water supply is sourced from urbanized runoff.

To capture the very last drop of rainfall, every one of Singapore's 17 reservoirs had to be connected up. This was a large investment in its own right. Once interlinked, lesser reservoirs no longer have to spill, while greater ones can offer additional storage capacity. Reservoir integration, facilitated by pipelines and pumping stations, makes stormwater husbandry far more efficient and has the effect of increasing overall system yield.

The second part of Singapore's water strategy required nothing less than a fundamental shift in mindset. More than anywhere else in the world, Singapore thinks of water as an endlessly reusable resource. In the Singaporean mind, the H_2O molecule is never lost. The country has been long convinced that water can always be reclaimed and retreated so that it can be drunk again. PUB is a world leader in this and has been producing NEWater from treated sewage effluent for the last 16 years. PUB's NEWater easily surpasses every World Health Organisation (2017) guideline for drinking water quality. Presently, PUB has enough NEWater capacity to meet half of Singapore's water demand, and aims for it to meet 55% of demand by 2060 (PUB, 2019).

Singapore's success with potable reuse can be attributed to the combination of three factors: technological expertise, government support and public acceptance (Lee & Tan, 2016). Technical know-how in reuse accumulated gradually over time. PUB began exploring reuse treatment technologies from 1972, as part of the Water Master Plan, 30 years before NEWater became a practical reality. Cost remained a hurdle until well into the 1990s. Improving technology led to a demonstration plant being built in 2000, which offered the opportunity for production-scale testing of treatment processes to suit local climate and effluent quality, and, at the same time, for acquiring hands-on operational familiarity. PUB also took pains to convene an international panel of experts, tasked with independent assessment of this new venture. The panel concluded that NEWater was wholly safe for potable use (Tan, Lee, & Tan, 2009).

Public acceptance of NEWater has been high in Singapore, bolstered by both people's awareness of the country's water-stress situation and proactive government support. Singapore's government went out its way to build public confidence and to show that NEWater was perfectly safe to drink. Perhaps most memorable was when then prime minister Goh Chok Tong toasted the nation by downing a bottle of it at the National Day Parade in 2002. This gesture, witnessed by tens of thousands and relayed live on national television, was highly symbolic and greatly reassuring. To keep up momentum, PUB fashioned a spiffy visitor centre inside its Bedok NEWater Factory and diligently brought school and community groups through it daily so that the science and technology behind wastewater reclamation could be explained to the man on the street.

Third and no less important, Singapore's water strategy embraced seawater desalination. When membrane separation technology made desalination economically feasible, Singapore took it up in a big way. PUB currently operates some of the largest and most advanced desalination plants in the world.

As with NEWater, Singapore's desalination journey was kick-started by the 1972 Water Master Plan, which recommended investigating and experimenting with unconventional water sources. However, the prevalent flash distillation technology was found to be too energy-intensive and unreliable (Tan et al., 2009). After 26 years, and several feasibility and consultancy studies, a decision was made in 1998 to implement reserve-osmosis (RO) desalination. The intent then was for seawater desalination (NEWater came later, in 2003) to replace water imported under the 1961 Water Agreement after it expired in 2011. SingSpring, Singapore's first desalination plant, with a capacity of 30 million gallons per day, was eventually commissioned and became operational in 2005. The three RO desalination plants Singapore currently possesses have a combined capacity that can meet up 30% of its daily water demand (PUB, 2019). Two more plants are under construction and expected to be ready in 2020.

Challenges remain

Of course, Singapore's strategy – constructed around getting the most out of local rains, endless recycling of wastewater for potable use and the desalting of seawater – even if perfectly executed, only guarantees the availability of water. The necessary corollary must be to use this water in the most efficient and productive fashion. Every day, about 430 million gallons of water is consumed in Singapore. That is almost equivalent to 800 Olympic-sized pools of water. Non-domestic use, by commerce and industry, already accounts for more than half of total daily demand. And Singapore's demand for water can only grow, increasing in tandem with population and economic growth.

Singapore's domestic water consumption – 141 litres per person per day at the time of writing (Ministry for the Environment and Water Resources, 2019) – although low by international standards, is still deemed to be wasteful. Singapore's populace is perennially challenged to be even more frugal and to use water ever more judiciously. Much of the water consumed by industry is used for cooling and processing. Much of it is only used once, and then either lost to the atmosphere or discarded. This is profligate, and has to be continually curtailed through better engineering and substitution.

Then there is the question of energy. Rain is free, and making it drinkable is fairly cheap. Desalination and NEWater are far more expensive ways of producing potable water. It takes just 0.2kWh of energy to treat a cubic metre of rainwater, compared to 1 kWh/m^3 to turn sewage effluent into NEWater and a whopping 3.5 kWh/m^3 to make seawater drinkable (PUB, 2018). Obviously, the latter two 'manufactured' sources of water supply, although weather-resistant, require more capital and energy and are correspondingly costlier. Even so, Singapore's water future lies, without a doubt, with reuse and desalination. Together, NEWater and desalination will have to meet 85% of Singapore's water needs by 2061, when the 1962 Water Agreement ends, imports cease, and demand is expected to be twice today's (PUB, 2019).

What once was scarce has been turned into plenty; so what is costly can surely also be made inexpensive. PUB's current annual energy use is about 1000 GWh. Assuming a doubling of water demand and no change in operations, PUB would need 4000 GWh/y, a quadrupling, to power its operations in 2060 (PUB, 2018). Clearly, business as usual is not sustainable, and PUB has every incentive to dramatically reduce the energy required for its treatment processes.

PUB has high ambitions in this regard and fully intends to more than halve the current 3.5 kWh/m^3 for seawater desalination, to 1.5 kWh/m^3 in the interim and then to 1 kWh/m^3 in the long run (PUB, 2018). It thinks this can be achieved though electro-deionization and biomimicry technologies or a combination of both. PUB has successfully tested electro-deionization at pilot scale and is preparing for full-scale deployment, in 2020, in a process train at the new Tuas Desalination Plant. At the same time, research into biomimicry has yielded encouraging results and is informing PUB's ongoing efforts to develop low-energy ultrapermeable membranes.

PUB expects to increase NEWater recovery rates by another 15%, to 90%. It is also hopeful that the electrodialysis reversal / RO technology it has been trying out at Ulu Pandan Water Reclamation Plant will allow it to halve the energy required for the RO process in NEWater production, and be subsequently scaled up at its upcoming Tuas Water Reclamation Plant (PUB, 2018). Indeed, PUB deems that its water reclamation plants could be entirely energy self-sufficient in the future, and is actively enhancing liquids treatment and boosting biogas production.

Given their large expanse of water surface, PUB's reservoirs have considerable solar potential. It recently announced that it will procure and instal what will be the world's single largest floating solar photovoltaic system on its Tengeh Reservoir. Rated at 50 MW peak, the Tengeh system, when completed in 2021, will generate enough energy to power the equivalent of 13,500 apartments (Liu, 2019) and significantly reduce PUB's reliance on fossil fuels for water treatment.

Climate change

Resource conservation and energy efficiency are challenging, but they do not by themselves pose existential threats to Singapore's water system. The effects of climate change, however, could be catastrophic, and if not prepared for, they will certainly devastate the water infrastructure that has been carefully built up over the years. At the 2019 National Day Rally, prime minister Lee Hsien Loong declared the threat of climate change to be one that endangers Singapore's very survival: 'The SAF [Singapore Armed Forces] and climate change defences are existential for Singapore. These are life and death matters. Everything else must bend at the knee to safeguard the existence of our island nation' (Ministry of Communications and Information, 2019).

When the National Climate Change Secretariat (2018) applied the findings of the International Panel for Climate Change Fifth Assessment Report to Singapore, it found that sea levels were likely to rise one metre by 2100, and rainfall would increase by 25% for the 2070–2099 period. Thus, since 2017, PUB has adopted both greater rainfall intensity and higher sea levels as design parameters for future drainage projects. Upcoming critical infrastructure like the Tuas Mega Port and Changi Airport Terminal 5 are being built at significantly higher platform levels.

Conclusion

Singapore's early water challenges were not unique. Problems with drought, floods and public sanitation are commonplace for any developing country. However, the manner in which Singapore overcame these difficulties may well be exceptional.

Because it is deemed unthinkable for Singapore to be short of water, or to have overflowing sewage, or to endure widespread flooding, it plans for an uncommonly long time horizon. The aim is to ensure that Singapore's water system will be adequate, resilient and sustainable, all at once (Ng, 2018). It was this mindset that drove Singapore to decide that potable reuse and advanced seawater desalination would be key to its water future.

Although severely water-stressed due to its small physical size, modern-day Singapore is far from water crisis. This is so only because as a country, it has been coldly realistic about its circumstances; it has deployed its collective intellect and imagination to constantly research and test new technologies; and it remains determined to pursue and to implement hard-nosed water policies (Ng, 2018). To provide enough water for its people and industry, Singapore's method is to remain highly pragmatic, plan well in advance, and then conscientiously execute its plans over a sustained period. It is this very strategy that has let it turn a disadvantage into a strength, and what seems an unsurmountable vulnerability into endless opportunity (Ng, 2018).

Disclosure statement

No potential conflict of interest was reported by the authors.

ORCID

Celine Teo http://orcid.org/0000-0002-8425-3851

References

Kwa, C. G. (2002). Introduction: Making the supply of water from Johor to Singapore into a security issue. In Y. C. Kog, I. F. J. Lim, J. S. R. Long, & C. G. Kwa eds. *Beyond vulnerability? Water in Singapore-Malaysia relations. IDSS monograph* (pp 1–13). Singapore: Institute of Defence and Strategic Studies.

Lee, H., & Tan, T. P. (2016). Singapore's experience with reclaimed water: NEWater. *International Journal of Water Resources Development*, *32*(4),611–621. doi:10.1080/07900627.2015.1120188

Liu, V. (2019, June 7). PUB plans massive floating solar panel system in reservoir. *Straits Times*. Retrieved from https://www.straitstimes.com/singapore/environment/pub-plans-massive-floating-solar-panel-system-in-reservoir

Ministry for the Environment and Water Resources. (2019, March 7). Speech by Mr Masagos Zulkifli, minister for the environment and water resources, at the committee of supply debate 2019, on 7 March 2019. Retrieved from https://www.mewr.gov.sg/news/speech-by-mr-masagos-zulkifli–minister-for-the-environment-and-water-resources–at-the-committee-of-supply-debate-2019–on-7-march-2019

Ministry of Communications and Information. (2019, August 18). National Day Rally 2019 (English Speech). Retrieved from https://www.gov.sg/microsites/ndr2019/press-room/news/content/ndr2019-eng

Ministry of Information, Communications and the Arts. (2003, March 4). Water talks? If only it could. Retrieved from https://www.mfa.gov.sg/-/media/Images/MFA/Water-Talks_-If-Only-It-Could.pdf.

Mohamad, K. (2015). *Malaysia Singapore fifty years of contentions 1965–2015*. Malaysia: Other Press.

National Climate Change Secretariat. (2018, February 20). Impact of climate change on Singapore. Retrieved from https://www.ncsc.gov.sg/climate-change-and-singapore/national-circumstances/impact-of-climate-change-on-singapore

Ng, P. J. H. (2018). Chapter 10, Singapore: Transforming water scarcity into a virtue. In A. K. Biswas, C. Tortajada, & P. Rohner, eds. *Assessing global water megatrends* (pp 179–186). Singapore: Springer-Nature.

PUB, The National Water Agency. (2018, July 4). PUB pushes the frontier of water technology to reach future energy and sludge reduction targets. Retrieved from http://www.nas.gov.sg/archivesonline/data/pdfdoc/20180704002/Press%20Release_PUB%20RD%20blueprint.pdf.

PUB, The National Water Agency. (2019). Singapore water story. Retrieved from https://www.pub.gov.sg/watersupply/singaporewaterstory.

Remembering Singapore. (2018, May 28). *Gunung pulai and its links to Singapore*. Retrieved from https://rememberingsingapore.org/gunung-pulai-singapore-links/

Tan, G. P. (2016). *Singapore chronicles: Water*. Singapore: Institute of Policy Studies, Straits Times Press.

Tan, T. H. (1972, March). Sewerage, sewerage treatment and disposal in Singapore. In *Regional workshop on water resources, environment and national development, Singapore* (pp. 143–180). Washington, DC: National Academy of Sciences.

Tan, Y. S., Lee, T. J., & Tan, K. (2009). *Clean, green and blue: Singapore's journey towards environmental and water sustainability*. Singapore: ISEAS.

Thomson, J. T. (1852). *Report on the projected water-works for the supply of Singapore town*. Singapore: Singapore Free Press Office. Retrieved from National Library Board Singapore, Digitised Images.

Watson, M. (1921). *The prevention of malaria in federated Malay states: A record of twenty years' progress*. University of Waterloo.

World Health Organisation. (2017). Guidelines for drinking-water quality. Retrieved from https://www.who.int/water_sanitation_health/publications/drinking-water-quality-guidelines-4-including-1st-addendum/en/

World Resources Institute. (2015). Ranking the world's most water-stressed countries in 2040. Retrieved from http://wri.org/blog/2015/08/ranking-world-s-most-water-stressed-countries-2040

Yeoh, B. S. A. (2003). *Contesting space in colonial Singapore: Power relations and the built environment*. Singapore: NUS Press.

Facing the challenge of extreme climate: the case of Metropolitan Sao Paulo

Benedito P.F. Braga and J. Kelman

ABSTRACT

This article describes the hydrologic conditions that resulted in the most severe drought ever experienced in Metropolitan São Paulo (2014–2015). The dramatic situation was tackled by structural and non-structural initiatives by water authorities to avoid social chaos in a region home to more than 21 million people. The article also considers the post-crisis scenario when, in 2018, the metropolis was hit by another serious drought. Due to more rational consumption, a better prepared water system and the start-up of two major water transfer structures, which added new contributions from nearby basins, the critical situation was not perceived by the population.

Introduction

Water availability, in both quantitative and qualitative terms, is one of the major concerns of both the business community and government authorities worldwide. Water is a fundamental element of food, energy and health security. Water is also the engine for socio-economic development. In September 2015 the United Nations General Assembly passed Resolution 70/1, 'Transforming Our World: The 2030 Agenda for Sustainable Development', in which a standalone target for water was approved. A 2012 report by the US National Intelligence Council claimed that 'water may become a more significant source of contention than energy or minerals out to 2030 at both the intrastate and interstate levels'.

Given the importance of water in the global scene and understanding that peoples' concerns about climate are not climate per se but the consequences of too much or too little water due to climate change, we must increase our resilience to climate variability. By and large, all the impacts of climate variability are manifested through, by and with water, whether it is impacts on ecosystems or hydrological extremes.

Hydrologic extremes have recently manifested themselves in different parts of the planet. It is salient the states of California, Texas and Arizona in the United States since 2013; Australia went through the Millennium Drought in 2000–2010; and in South Africa in 2017, the government announced the possibility of the Day Zero, when dam levels would not be able to supply Cape Town. Fortunately, this did not occur. Some years earlier, in 2013, Singapore faced unexpected climate challenges, just to name some of many situations around the world. In all these cases, we note the importance of water infrastructure and demand management to face the challenge.

In 2014 and 2015, the state of São Paulo, in South-East Brazil, had the most severe water crisis in its 125-year hydrologic record. Was this extreme drought as an outlier, or must we consider it in planning, as an event that will recur in the coming years?

This article describes the hydrologic conditions in the most severe drought experienced by the state and the structural and non-structural initiatives by water authorities to avoid social chaos in the São Paulo Metropolitan Region (SPMR).

The physical and hydrologic context

Figure A1 shows the 12 hydrographic regions of Brazil and their correspondent freshwater availability, in terms of average annual yield. (Figures A1–A26 are in the online supplementary data, at https://doi.org/10.1080/07900627.2019.1698412). Brazil has 12% of the world's freshwater resources, but most (70%) of this water is concentrated in the Amazon basin, which hosts only 7% of the Brazilian population. South-East Brazil, which is the focus of this article, is in the Paraná basin, which has the third-largest average availability (361 km^3/y).

There are three states in South-East Brazil: São Paulo, Minas Gerais and Rio de Janeiro. The population of São Paulo is 43 million, which corresponds to 21% of the Brazilian population (Brazilian Institute of Geography and Statistics, 2019), and 32% of GDP (Investment Promotion Agency, 2019).

A 2015 report from the National Water Agency (ANA) indicated that in 2014 South-East Brazil experienced anomalous precipitation patterns. Figure A2 shows the rainfall amounts and the return periods during the rainy season (January to March) in 2012–2014. Warmer colours represent drier climate (red means a return interval longer than 100 years). The exceptionality of the 2014 drought can be appreciated for a large extent in central and eastern São Paulo State. Figure A3 shows the average annual rainfall distribution in the state for 1979–2013, and Figure A4 shows the contrast with what happened in 2014.

During the drought, most of the northern and eastern parts of the state had less than 900 mm of annual rainfall, though the average is more than 1200 mm. This situation led the Water Resources Department of the State of São Paulo (DAEE) to issue new water permits exclusively for the water supply of the population.

Many municipalities in these areas passed municipal decrees of state of public calamity, giving them access to state and federal funds and expedited bidding processes for emergency civil works. Figure A5 shows the water resources management regions affected and the respective municipalities.

SPMR

SPMR is in the upstream reach of the Tiete River, a tributary of the Parana River (Figure A6). It is the most active economic region of Brazil (18% of Brazilian GDP and 54% of São Paulo state GDP), and its 21 million people (São Paulo Company for Metropolitan Planning, 2019), makes it one of the world's most densely populated. The combination of its dense urban concentration and its location at the furthest edge of the Alto Tietê basin makes it a region of very low per capita water availability, even under normal climate conditions. The situation is similar to that experienced in semi-arid regions.

Eight water treatment plants (Figure A6) operated by Sabesp (Water and Sanitation Company of the State of São Paulo) provide all the potable water for SPMR (São Lourenço, the ninth metropolitan water production system, started operation in April 2018, after the water crisis). In 2014, their joint maximum production capability was almost 73 m^3/s. Based solely on the hydrologic record available before the 2014–2015 drought, the firm yield from the rivers and reservoirs feeding these water treatment plants would roughly match the maximum production capability. However, if the full hydrologic record is used, including 2014–2015, the firm water yield shrinks to less than 52 m^3/s. This 31% drop is the most vivid expression of the severity of the drought.

SPMR draws most of its water from the neighbouring Piracicaba River basin, through the Cantareira system (Figure A6). Water travels 80 km through a set of interconnected reservoirs, tunnels, channels and pumping stations (Figure A7), comprising one of the largest water supply schemes in the world, with a nominal capacity of 33 m^3/s (Barros and Netto, 2010). Figure A8 shows the monthly inflows to the Cantareira system. The magnitude of the drought experienced by this system, which provides almost 50% of the supply, is such that the 2014 inflow to Cantareira was roughly 50% of the all-time low discharge in 83 years of records, which had occurred in 1953.

As a result, in January 2015, the Cantareira system storage was less than 5% of maximum, including dead storage (technical reserve), and the water level was several metres below the intake elevation. Since May 2014, water had been pumped out of the dead storage.

Table 1 compares the potable water production in February 2014, just before the adoption of anti-crisis measures (described later), with production in April 2015, when these measures were in place.

The water supply system operated by Sabesp serves practically the entire population of the formally urbanized area of SPMR, where one can find meters in virtually all households. But this is not the case in many of the informal settlements, where roughly 10% of the metropolitan population lives (Brazilian Institute of Geography and Statistics, 2013). Most people living in the informal settlements have illegal and unpaid access to potable water through precarious and wasteful distribution systems formed by a bundle of small-diameter plastic tubes connected to the mains (Figure A9).

Several barriers impede the water utility from entering these irregular settlements to provide regular services. Some relate to judicial disputes over land ownership (people

Table 1. Potable water production before and during the water crisis (m^3/s).

System	February 2014	April 2015	Difference
Cantareira	31.77	13.48	−18.29
Guarapiranga	13.77	15.05	+1.28
Alto Tietê	14.97	12.25	−2.72
Rio Grande	4.94	5.09	+0.15
Rio Claro	3.83	3.87	+0.04
Alto Cotia	1.16	0.76	−0.40
Baixo Cotia	0.88	1.01	+0.13
Ribeirão da Estiva	0.096	0.086	−0.01
São Paulo Metropolitan Area total	**71.42**	**51.60**	**−19.82**

have invaded private property), others to environmental restrictions (people have invaded protected areas), and still others – most of them – to the impossibility of installing water supply and sewage collection systems in neighbourhoods where there are no streets to bury the pipes under. This unorganized urbanization process began in the 1950s, when only 30% of the Brazilian population lived in the cities, and has grown worse, especially in the early 1970s, with the intensification of the industrialization process.

In a few years, the urban population swelled to 70% of the national population, but the infrastructure growth was much slower, resulting in several problems. For one, a large quantity of untreated sewage is dumped into the local water bodies, impelling the search for new water supply sources far away from the demand centre (Braga, Porto, & Silva, 2006). But in spite of difficulties, practically everyone living in SPMR has access to potable water in their household, through either formal or informal connections.

Facing the challenge of the 2014–2015 drought

The strategy adopted by the state government and Sabesp to face a potential social disaster included the implementation of structural measures (emergency construction works that were implemented from the very first signs of the crisis, which reinforced the infrastructure and gave the different supply systems more resilience) and non-structural measures (demand management via economic instruments and raising public awareness) (Figure A10).

Infrastructure development

Emergency civil works

When the water level was approaching the minimum elevation necessary for the free flow through the intake of the upstream Jaguari Reservoir (Figure A11), Sabesp installed a set of floating pumps and built channels and coffer dams to pump water from the dead storage to a provisional upper pond built adjacent to the intake (Figure A12).

This simple engineering solution stirred a public debate, fuelled by the media, about alleged health hazards for the people that would drink water from the 'dead' storage. It was a false problem, because for many years a bottom gate had been continuously releasing water from the reservoir to the downstream to ensure the minimum environmental flow along the natural waterway. Nevertheless, a serious media campaign was set up to explain that there was no risk to health, using the term 'technical reserve' instead of 'dead storage'.

Interbasin transfers and interconnection of production systems

Many construction works were performed in the distribution network in 2014 and 2015 to increase the operational flexibility of the eight producing systems of SPMR. Structural integration, extending the system to sectors belonging to other water sources, was made possible by a series of operations, mainly refurbishing water mains and pumping stations and also replacing or adapting boosters.

In this way, sectors that before the crisis were only supplied with water from the Cantareira system began to receive water from other, better-stocked producing systems. Some 3.5 million people stopped consuming water from Cantareira, and instead received water from the Guarapiranga, Alto Tiete and Rio Grande systems (Figure A13).

Since April 2015, the Rio Grande system has also been a new source for 250,000 people who were previously served by the Guarapiranga system. This was achieved by installing 2.1 km of water mains to carry the water to the southern part of the city. The surplus water from Guarapiranga was redirected to areas previously served by the Cantareira system. At the end of May 2015, it was the Claro River system's turn to boost its contribution to the area previously attended by the Cantareira, with the construction of a new link between two water mains in the eastern part of São Paulo.

Pumping stations and mains that had been decommissioned due to excessive leakage were refurbished. For the Franca Pinto pumping station and main, this required the injection of high-density polyethylene piping into 550 m of the 6600 m water main. This allowed an additional supply from Guarapiranga to help the sector served by the Cantareira system.

The steps taken in 2014 and 2015 to increase the operational flexibility of water production and distribution relieved the water sources most affected by the drought. The swap of the source of supply of the Paulista Avenue region, located at one of the highest spots of São Paulo City (at an altitude of about 830 m), is an example of this flexibility increment. Previously supplied by the Cantareira system, because of its favourable topography for water distribution, the region was now also supplied by the Guarapiranga system, which is in the southern part of the city at a lower altitude.

The overall result was an increase in the capacity to transfer flows between the production systems by 6.6 m^3/s. This meant that 3.5 million people that previously received water exclusively from the Cantareira could also receive water from other systems (Figure 1).

An important initiative undertaken in 2015 was the constructions of the pipelines to interlink different bulk water sources. First, 9 km of water mains and a pumping station were installed to transfer water from the Guaió River, in Suzano Municipality, to the Taiaçupeba

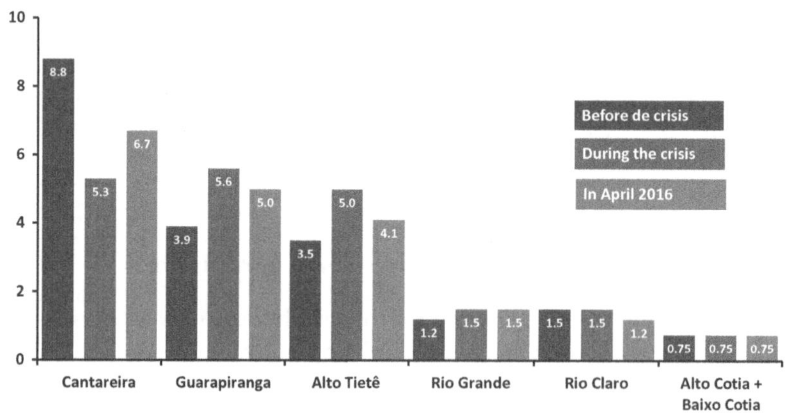

Figure 1. Interconnection of sources and population served (in millions).

reservoir in the Alto Tietê system. This took four months to be built and added 1 m^3/s of water to the SPMR integrated supply system. Next, the Rio Grande and the Alto Tiete systems were interconnected by two parallel water mains made of high-density polyethylene, with a flow capacity of 4 m^3/s over a distance of 10.5 km (Figure A14). This construction work also stirred much public debate, mostly fuelled by the press, and litigation in the judiciary. Some feared that this arrangement would jeopardize the quality of the drinking water. Others were concerned about impacts on the environment. Still others used the debate as a political weapon to blame the government for poor planning. It was necessary to launch a difficult battle at the public opinion front.

Once the links were in place for redistributing areas of the city from one production system to another, the next step was to increase the water treatment capacity and to build new water storage within the distribution system.

These were made possible by the technological advantages of ultrafiltration membranes: quicker filtration, less space needed for the equipment, fully automatic functioning and fewer chemicals. Two modules of ultrafiltration membranes (1 m^3/s each) were installed in the Guarapiranga system, increasing its production capacity from 14 m^3/s to 16 m^3/s.

Twenty-two steel storage reservoirs, with a storage capacity of 147,000 m^3, were installed in different sectors of the city. They provide a reserve of treated water and uninterrupted supply to districts far from the principal water mains. This was an efficient option for making the distribution system more secure and flexible. Besides expanding storage capacity and using strategic locations, closer to the region served, some reservoirs can receive water from more than one production system.

Demand management

Pressure relief valves and water loss reduction

SPMR's distribution system is divided into sectors for better management. Boosters pump the water to serve regions at a higher altitude, and pressure relief valves (PRVs) at lower levels alleviate leaks and eventual damage to the pipes and other structures. PRV technology is used in the best systems worldwide and has been used in SPMR since the 1990s. PRVs are also used for remote control of pressure at times of low demand, such as the early hours of the morning, when there is more pressure in the networks. Starting in October 2014, with the worsening of the drought, the water loss due to leakages decreased 7.6 m^3/s, which corresponds to around 42% of the total water savings during the crisis, thanks to the pressure reduction in the distribution system, which was extended to time intervals beyond the early hours of the morning. This policy proved more effective than the traditional method of rotating shutdowns among sectors.

At the start of 2016, the periods of pressure reduction returned to normal, that is, were restricted to night-time. Currently there are 1303 PRVs operating in SPMR. During the crisis, many were installed, today representing coverage of 55% of the distribution network, which consists of 33,000 km of secondary pipes and 1200 km of water mains.

Reducing water losses has been a priority of the water supply sector in the state of São Paulo for more than two decades. In 2009, Sabesp introduced the Corporate Loss Reduction Programme, in technical partnership with the Japan International Cooperation Agency, with forecasted investment cash flow until 2020 of R$ 5.5 billion. The objective is to reduce unaccounted-for water to 18%. In 2015 it was 27%, including 18% due to leakage (Figure A15).

Reducing leakage requires the installation of PRVs, substitution of mains, acoustic sweeps to locate leaks (so far, more than 87,000 repairs) and substitution of connection pipes to households (so far, more than 280,000 branches). Limiting non-physical losses due to illegal connections or fraud, as well as inaccurate metering, demand anti-fraud patrols and the replacement of meters, respectively. In 2015 alone, 3.7 billion litres of illegal consumption was identified, and more than 255,000 water meters were replaced.

Economic instruments: bonuses and fines

Bonuses for those who reduce water consumption, and a contingency tariff for those who waste water, were strategic measures to restrain demand. Starting in February 2014, at the beginning of the crisis, a discount on the water bill (bonus) was granted to water savers – those who reduced their water consumption by at least 20%, compared to their own average. This programme had the support of most families. More than 80% of consumers reduced their consumption, and 49% received discounts in 2014 and 70% in 2015.

The net effect was a lumped reduction of 3.5 m^3/s in potable water production, or around 19% of the total water savings during the crisis (Figure A16). Starting in January 2015, a penalty was imposed on those who did not understand the severity of the crisis and increased their consumption. Some 19% of consumers were in this situation, but 8% were exempt from the charge because they did not use more than 10 m^3 per month.

Communication campaigns

The government of the state of São Paulo and Sabesp encouraged conscientious use of water through visits, lectures and the distribution of posters and leaflets at condominiums, schools, commercial establishments and homes, making people aware of the importance of economizing water. Concurrently with the growing press coverage, widespread advertising/awareness campaigns were carried out in 2014, with over 3000 TV insertions and 13,000 radio insertions, besides publications in newspapers and magazines; it is estimated that each citizen was reached at least 40 times by water-saving messages.

In February 2015, the state government began another campaign called Every Drop Counts, promoting the importance of water rational use. More than 20 million printed materials were distributed by the Water Guardian team. Campaign teams made almost 74,000 visits in 2015. Two million people were approached directly, and almost 20 million indirectly. It was also necessary to launch a publicity campaign of print, radio and television advertisements.

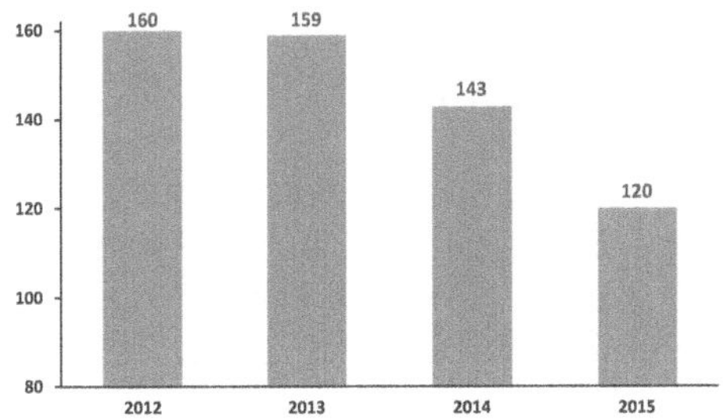

Figure 2. Impact of non-structural measures on per capita consumption (household clients, litres per person per day) in the São Paulo Metropolitan Area, 2012–2015.

Figure 2 shows the combined effect of economic incentives and communication campaigns on the water consumption of SPMR. Prevailing per capita household water consumption was reduced by 20%.

Reduction in water supply production of the Cantareira system

Figure A17 synthesizes the overall result of all these actions: it was possible to reduce potable water production in the Cantareira system from approximately 32 m^3/s to 13 m^3/s. The breakdown of different actions shows that this enormous saving was due to PRV/leakage reductions (7.7 m^3/s), interconnection of systems (6.6 m^3/s), economic incentives (3.4 m^3/s), and reduced supply to partner utilities in SPMR (0.8 m^3/s). This reduction of almost 60% was essential to keep the Cantareira storage from running out, which would have brought a major collapse in the water supply system of SPMR (Figure 3).

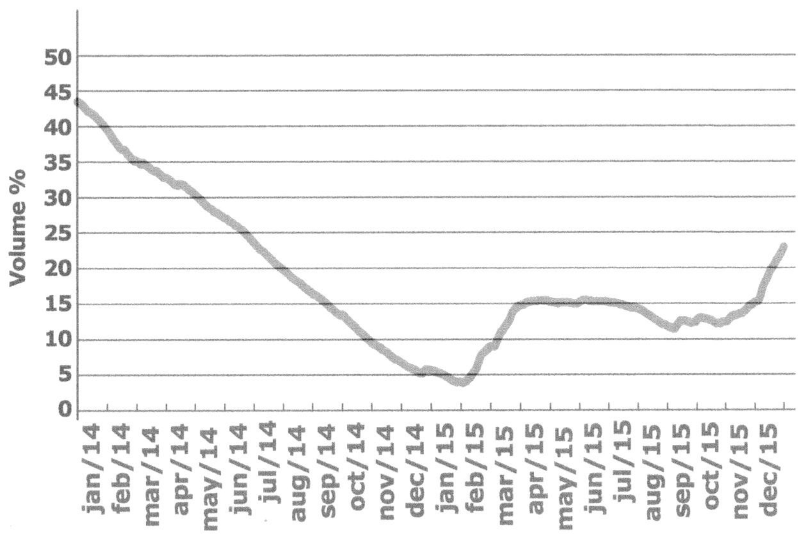

Figure 3. Depletion of storage in the Cantareira system during the 2014–2015 crisis (% of operational volume, including technical reserve).

Post-crisis scenario

SPMR faces a new challenge in 2018

After the driest period (2014–2015), the next two years (2016–2017) saw the recovery of the main systems that supply SPMR. But in 2018, there was another very dry period. The Cantareira system did not record significant rainfall (over 10 mm) for 71 days. The Guarapiranga system faced the same situation for 117 days, and the Alto Tietê system had six months of almost no rain. Together, these three metropolitan reservoirs supply about 16 million people. This situation adversely affected the metropolitan system as a whole (Figure A18), with natural contributions well below the historical average (Figure A19). The Cantareira system was also severely impacted (Figure 4).

Nonetheless, in 31 December 2018, the cumulative overall volume of the water sources was 916.8 million m^3. This is slightly more than the amount registered on the same date in 2017, but 7% more than the total in December 2013, just before the water crisis (Figure 5).

Though the Cantareira water level has dropped in 2018 (in September 2018 the system registered only 33% of storage, against the post-crisis peak of 68%, reached 14 months earlier, in July 2018), a range of factors has helped keep the total water storage at comfortable levels.

The adoption and incorporation of rational consumption habits acquired during the water crisis, in particular by domestic consumers, who use more than 80% of the water (Figure A20), contributed significantly. Thus, water production in 2018 maintained an average of 60.9 m^3/s to supply SPMR, 15% less than the 69.1 m^3/s average production in 2013, before the water crisis (Figure A21).

Average per capita domestic consumption in these three post-crisis years was 129 litres per day, 24% less than the 169 litres per day in 2013, before the crisis. In 2014–2015, it was even lower: 123 litres per day (Figure A22).

Combined with rational water consumption, the higher transfer capacity between water systems, higher water treatment capacity, new water sources and the lowered pressure in the distribution system (retained after crisis in the night-time) enabled Sabesp to maintain the reduced use of the Cantareira system. In February 2016, the better conditions of the water sources also resulted in an expansion in the authorization for

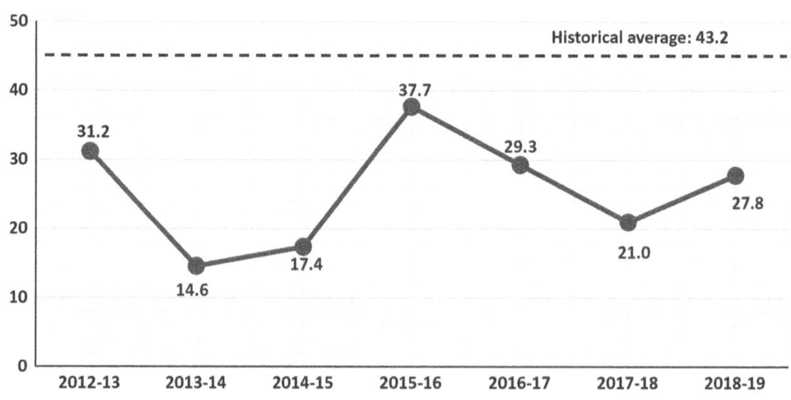

Figure 4. Natural inflow (m^3/s) in the Cantareira system per hydrological year (October–September), 2012–2019. In the 2017–2018 hydrological year, the inflow was again far below the historical average.

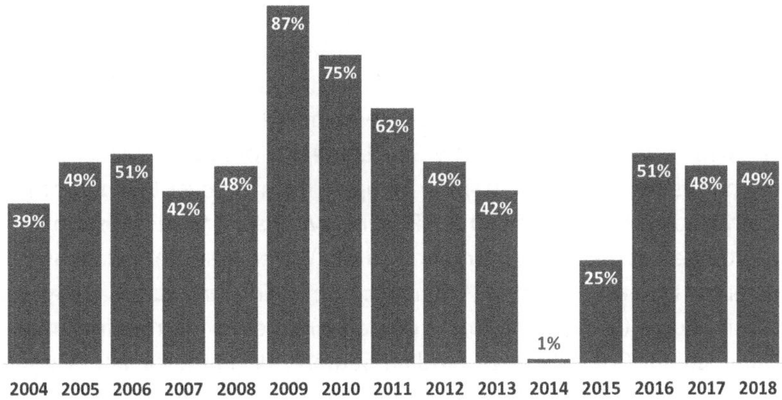

Figure 5. Total water storage in São Paulo Metropolitan Area reservoirs, 2004–2018 (%).

Sabesp to withdraw water from the Cantareira system, which had been granted by ANA and DAEE starting in 2013.

Based on the behaviour of the rainfall, water inflows and the level of the water sources, Sabesp was authorized to extract up to 23 m^3/s, a significant increase over the 13.5 m^3/s authorized in 2015. Later in 2016 (September–November), withdrawal of up to 25 m^3/s was authorized. In December 2016, uptake of up to 31 m^3/s was granted – still less than the 33 m^3/s permitted before the crisis.

In July 2018, as the level of reservoir water fell to less than 40%, the maximum allowed withdrawal from the Cantareira was reduced from 31 m^3/s to 27 m^3/s. But most of the time since the outbreak of the crisis, withdrawal has remained below the granted volume (Sabesp, 2019) (Figure A23). The Cantareira system reached the end of 2018 on an upward trend (Figure A24).

Particularly from the first half of 2018, the circumstances that enabled less dependence on the Cantareira water for SPMR supply was also made possible by two major construction projects, providing interbasin transfers from the Ribeira River basin (6.4 m^3/s) and the Paraíba do Sul River basin (8.5 m^3/s), and adding new sources of water to the SPMR integrated supply system.

The 19.6 km Jaguari–Atibainha interconnection was started in March 2018. Some 13.2 km of pipeline and 6.4 km of pipeline tunnel make it possible to transfer an average flow of 5.13 m^3/s and a maximum of 8.5 m^3/s of raw water from the Jaguari dam in the Paraíba do Sul basin to the Atibainha dam in the Cantareira system. This means that when the Paraíba River is in normal conditions, with the greater part of its waters flowing into the Atlantic in the state of Rio de Janeiro, part of this flow can be stored in the Cantareira system.

It also allows a reverse flow (Atibainha to Jaguari) of up to 12.2 m^3/s, so the Cantareira system can also serve as a water tank to supply the Paraíba do Sul basin in times of drought in that basin. It increases the water reserve and security for the population of both basins (Figure A25).

This interbasin transfer stirred a debate between the São Paulo and Rio de Janeiro metropolitan regions which ended up in the Federal Supreme Court. Eventually, an agreement made by the states involved in this issue established technical rules and priorities for the water sharing among all users. Although São Paulo and Rio de Janeiro are 400 km apart, both regions fetch water from the same river, which runs for roughly 1000 km and crosses three Brazilian states (Kelman, 2015).

In April 2018 it was the turn of the São Lourenço producer system to be put into operation. The system allows the transfer of up to 6.4 m^3/s over 82 km, from the uptake point at Cachoeira do França dam (in the Ribeira River basin) to the western part of SPMR. The water is treated at the Vargem Grande Paulista Water Treatment Plant and the system also has reservoirs capable of storing 125 million litres. The structure is ready to supply up to two million people (today's and future demands) in seven metropolitan municipalities: Barueri, Carapicuíba, Cotia, Itapevi, Jandira, Santana de Parnaíba and Vargem Grande Paulista (which were partly supplied by the Cantareira system). Since Sabesp's water supply system in SPMR is integrated, the increase in water availability indirectly benefits the entire metropolitan population (Figure A26). A third interbasin transfer, of up to 2.5 m^3/s from the Itapanhau River basin, is under environmental impact assessment.

With the operational start-up of these two major construction works, the transfer capacity of the SPMR water production systems was increased from 3 m^3/s in 2013 (before the water crisis) to 12 m^3/s in 2018. Without them, the water storage in the Cantareira system and therefore in the SPMR integrated system would be much smaller (Figure A27).

Lessons learned

The worst drought in the history of SPMR could have led to social unrest. The storage level in the most important water source system fell to less than 5%. A combination of structural and non-structural measures, including an important collaboration from the population in using water more efficiently, were essential in facing this challenge. And much emergency water infrastructure was implemented in record time, allowing more flexible use of the nine reservoir systems in the region.

Today, SPMR is far better prepared to face much worse droughts than those foreseen in the various water resources plans produced since the 1960s. Based on a long time series and assuming stationary conditions, the 2014–2015 is such a rare event that one is tempted to consider it an outlier, with little relevance to planning. However, the prudent decision maker has to consider that the stationary hypothesis may be wrong, due to climate and land use changes, and that the wise attitude is to be prepared for the recurrence of similar events (the 'firm yield' criterion). For this reason, the government of the state of São Paulo and Sabesp have decided to invest heavily in new strategic infrastructure to secure a normal water supply even if the water scarcity of 2014–2015 returns.

Facilities such as the Rio Grande– AltoTietê and Jaguari–Atibainha interconnections have brought greater water security than we had before. These works will remain on stand-by most of the time, but can be triggered at any time when necessary.

Together with the strengthening of water infrastructure, reducing waste is another fundamental task to guarantee supplies. In the last 20 years, the state government has made major efforts in this direction, building infrastructure at a cost of more than US$

2.5 billion (partly financed by the Inter-American Development Bank). But much more needs to be done.

A key initiative is being launched by the state government for demand management, to include subsidies to help the poor instal water-efficient appliances; low-interest loans to help apartment owners instal individual metering; and regulations on non-potable water reuse. Sabesp is working to eliminate the maze of pipes scattered along the alleyways of the irregular but irreversibly established settlements. This of course requires articulation with city councils and the Public Attorney's Office. The Catholic Church, which included sanitation as a theme of its 2016 Fraternity Campaign, is another important partner.

Giving priority to work to underpin water security means, inescapably, that other equally important but less urgent investments have to be postponed. But it does not change the permanent goal of providing sewage collection and treatment services for everyone.

Another important lesson learned from the water crisis is that there is an urgent need to review how water supply and sanitation tariffs are established. When customers become more parsimonious in their water use, water utilities make less money. Sabesp relies solely on revenues from consumers for operation and expansion of the system supply. No subsidies from taxpayers are provided.

Society and the courts also need to understand that the purpose of sanitation is to maximize social well-being using the resources that are available, with water treatment and distribution having first priority, followed by sewage collection, and then sewage treatment. In other words, Brazil has to follow the example of developed countries: put people's health above any other consideration. It makes little sense, therefore, to divert the scarce financial resources of the water companies to 'environmental compensation' fees, which are intended to punish companies for polluting rivers or the ocean during the period that sewage is collected but not treated. Such punitive measures eliminate resources that are necessary for the expansion and improvement of the utilities' services.

Conclusions

The water crisis SPMR suffered in 2014 and 2015 is an example of the impacts of climate variability and land use change being felt in the water sector. These impacts were magnified by the fact that the drought hit a densely populated area. The consequences could have been catastrophic if structural and non-structural measures were not timely implemented.

Tapping water from the dead volume of the largest reservoir in the Cantareira system through the construction of coffer dams and the use of floating pumps was essential in this crisis. The interlinking of storage reservoirs was fundamental to provide flexibility in the joint operation of the three major water sources in the region. Structural integration, in the form of extending the system to sectors belonging to other water sources, was made possible by a series of operations, such as refurbishing the water mains and the pumping stations, and replacing or adapting boosters. Membrane filtration technology was used to increase water treatment capacity. The stock of treated water at strategic points was increased through the construction of sector reservoirs, minimizing interruptions in supply. Large investments were necessary to reduce physical and commercial water loss by replacing networks, branch lines and water meters, and by strict measures to control fraud.

Demand management was also fundamental in facing this crisis. More than ever we all feel how important water is. The debate on the subject has taken hold of society and those who make decisions in the political-governmental sphere. The adherence of more than 80% of the population of Greater São Paulo to the water rationalization attitude, as stimulated by the educational campaigns carried out by the state government and Sabesp, represents a great success. It was also made possible by the economic incentives imposed by the water utility, which significantly reduced consumption.

The contingency tariffs, with reductions for those saving water and increases for those using too much, worked admirably. However, the extension of these incentives for more than a year depressed the income of the water utility. Sabesp had to adjust its budget to anticipate investments in water infrastructure to improve water security, at a time when revenues were very low due to less water being sold, and at a lower price. The unavoidable result was a temporary slowdown in initiatives already underway to expand sewage collection and treatment.

As the Chinese saying goes, every crisis represents an opportunity - to innovate, to change paradigms, and above all, to implement sustainable long-term solutions. After two years of intense challenges and much hard work, the population and the political class are much more aware of the importance of water security. That daily per capita consumption (household use) remains lower than it was before the crisis shows that the behavioural change is here to stay.

The lesson learned is that in the future we need to be more resilient to the vagaries of climate, as we experienced again in 2018, when the metropolitan region was hit by another serious drought, just three years after the 2014–2015 crisis. This time, though, the critical situation was not noticed by population. This experience shows that good adaptation to climate change implies more infrastructure and good governance through strong public institutions, efficient regulatory agencies, adequate legal frameworks and the understanding of the population to use water parsimoniously and efficiently.

Disclosure statement

No potential conflict of interest was reported by the authors.

References

Barros, L. A. A. B., & Netto, N. P. (2010). *Uma história visual da construção do sistema cantareira*. São Paulo: Editora Autor.

Braga, B., Porto, M. F. A., & Silva, R. T. (2006). Water management in metropolitan São Paulo. In C. Tortajada, O. Varis, J. Lundqvist, & A. K. Biswas (Eds.), *Water management for large cities* (pp. 151–166). Abingdon: Routledge.

Brazilian Institute of Geography and Statistics. (2013). *Censo Demográfico 2010: Aglomerados Subnormais. Informações Territoriais* [2010 Brazilian demographic census: Informal settlements.

Territorial information]. Retrieved from https://biblioteca.ibge.gov.br/visualizacao/periodicos/552/cd_2010_agsn_if.pdf

Brazilian Institute of Geography and Statistics. (2019). *População Brasileira* [Brazilian population]. Retrieved from www.ibge.gov.br/apps/populacao/projecao/

Investment Promotion Agency. (2019). São Paulo GDP. Retrieved from https://www.en.investe.sp.gov.br/why-sao-paulo/diversified-economy/gdp/

Kelman, J. (2015). Water supply to the two largest Brazilian metropolitan regions. *Aquatic Procedia, 5*, 13–21. doi:10.1016/j.aqpro.2015.10.004

National Water Agency (ANA). (2015). *Conjuntura dos Recursos Hídricos no Brasil: Edição Especial Crise Hídrica de 2014* [Brazilian water resources report: 2014 water crisis special edition], p. 13.

Sabesp. (2019). Sabesp's 2018 sustainability report (pp. 24–25). Retrieved from http://site.sabesp.com.br/site/uploads/file/relatorios_sustentabilidade/sabesp_rs_2018_english.pdf

São Paulo Company for Metropolitan Planning. (2019). Região Metropolitana de São Paulo [São Paulo metropolitan region]. Retrieved from http://emplasa.sp.gov.br/RMSP

United Nations General Assembly. (2015). *Transforming our world: The 2030 Agenda for sustainable development* (70th General Assembly Resolution A/70/L.1). New York: UN.

US National Intelligence Council. (2012). *Global trends 2030: Alternative worlds*. Washington, DC: Central Intelligence Agency.

China's achievements of water governance over the past seven decades

Shaofeng Jia and Wenbin Zhu

ABSTRACT
Since the founding of the People's Republic of China in 1949, great achievements have been made by China in all aspects of water governance. Besides water conservancy projects, a water resources management system with Chinese characteristics has also been completed. In this article, we summarize the achievements of the past 70 years in flood control, soil and water conservation and water supply, and introduce the water governance institutions of China that sustain those achievements. This provides valuable experience and ideas for other countries that are suffering from similar water issues.

Introduction

Situated in the south-east of Eurasia, China's climate is significantly influenced by East Asian monsoon circulation. Due to the strong variability of monsoon climate, the spatial and temporal distribution of precipitation in China is extremely uneven, which leads to frequent floods and droughts. Take the Yellow River, the mother river of the Chinese nation, as an example. From the seventh century to the twentieth century, the Yellow River basin experienced 110 catastrophic floods and 95 times of severe drought. Thus, on average, such a natural calamity occurs every 6.8 years (Pan, 2002). Consequently, all dynasties and generations in Chinese history attached great importance to water governance. The earliest water governance in China can be tracked back to more than 4000 years ago, when King Yu tamed flooding in the Xia dynasty. Special geographical conditions mean that China is a country with frequent floods and droughts. Meanwhile, rivers are the birthplace of Chinese civilization. Chinese people have long regarded water governance as an important part of governing and prospering the country (Li, 1992; Liu & Yang, 2012).

These 4000-plus years of development history brought China rich experience in water governance. However, due to the constraints of science and technology in ancient times and destruction by war in modern history, China's capabilities in water governance were not greatly improved for long time. For example, in the early days of the People's Republic of China (PRC), flood control capability was still very weak. On average, all seven of the major rivers (Yangtze, Yellow, Pearl, Haihe, Huaihe, Liaohe and Songhua) experienced a moderate flood every two years and severe flood disaster every three years. Therefore, after the founding of the PRC in 1949, the central government initiated massive water governance projects in the seven major rivers, although numerous issues waited to be taken up and the country's financial resources were limited. Persistent efforts were also made in soil and water conservation, water supply, hydropower development, water pollution control, and water ecological restoration to cope with different challenges in water governance emerging with social economy development (Liu et al., 2013).

2019 marked the 70th anniversary of the founding of New China. The objective of this study is to systematically summarize the development process of New China's water governance as well as the corresponding achievements of these 70 years. On the one hand, this study is an attempt to clarify the development path and evolution process of water governance in China. On the other hand, it hopes to provide other countries with valuable experience and ideas when tackling water issues.

The article is in four parts. The first part is the introduction about the background and significance of this research. The second summarizes the great achievements of water governance of China in the fields of flood control, water supply, soil and water conservation and so on. The third summarizes the general evolution and the advantages of New China's water governance. The last part summarizes the difficulties that China is still facing in water governance, and points the way to the future of China's water governance.

Representative achievements in water governance

Flood control

The spatial-temporal distribution of China's rainfall is quite uneven due to the influence of the East Asian monsoon climate. Around 60–80% of the annual rainfall occurs from June to September. For this reason, two-thirds of the country's land is threatened by flood disasters to varying degrees. According to the Ministry of Water Resources of the PRC (MWR, 2018b), economic losses from flood disasters can reach 100 billion yuan every year, the worst of all natural hazards (Kundzewicz et al., 2019). Therefore, flood prevention and control is a long-term task of water governance in China.

The development of New China's flood control strategy has had three stages. First, from the establishment of the PRC to the reform and opening up, China focused on the construction of water conservancy projects, including reservoirs, dikes, flood storage areas and channel improvements (Table 1). In 1949, China only had six large and 17 medium-sized reservoirs. And none of them had flood control capabilities except for the three large reservoirs in the Song-Liao River basin. By 1978, 84,000 reservoirs had been built in China, including 311 large ones, with total storage capacity of 400 km^3. A preliminary flood-control engineering system for major rivers was formed (Wang & Liu,

Table 1. Reservoir number and dike length in different years (Ministry of Water Resources, 2018c).

Year	Reservoirs	Large reservoirs	Medium-sized reservoirs	Total storage capacity (km^3)	Dike length (km)
1949	1,200	6	17	20	42,000
1979	86,000	319	2,252	408.1	168,000
1989	83,000	358	2,480	450.3	217,000
1999	85,000	400	2,681	449.9	266,000
2009	87,000	544	3,259	706.4	291,000
2017	99,000	732	3,934	903.5	306,000

2009). China now has more reservoirs than any other country, and accounts for about half of the world's total (FAO, 2011). Table 1 shows that 1949 to 1979 was a critical period for the construction of China's reservoir projects. About 75% of China's large reservoirs, 66% of its medium-sized reservoirs and 90% of its small reservoirs were built between 1957 and 1977 (Liu & Zhang, 1999).

Second, from the reform and opening up to the early twenty-first century, China's main strategy against flood disasters was to build a flood control and drought relief system by combining project measures with non-project measures. On the one hand, it aimed to overcome the defects of existing flood control systems through continuing project construction. For example, the world-renowned Three Gorges Reservoir on the Yangtze River and the Xiaolangdi Reservoir on the Yellow River were built during this period. On the other hand, it set out to establish and improve non-project measures, including regulations and precaution systems, to strengthen flood control capability through management, monitoring and early warning. Table 2 shows China's flood-control-related laws and regulations in different periods. These laws and regulations, which provide legal, administrative, enforceable and technical evidence, assure the standardization and normalization of China's flood control work. The enacting and implementation of the Law on Flood Control is of groundbreaking significance and shows that China has entered into a new stage of controlling flood by law. In terms of the precaution system for flood control, China mainly introduced the following measures: built a network of hydrological stations for flood monitoring and a system for information transmission and forecasting; established a flood control system for emergency communication, decision making, flood warning and information feedback; and improved the flood prevention planning system for emergency response, safeguard and aftermath work. An emergency response mechanism with unified command, quick reaction, coordinated processing and efficient operation was thus set up (Shi, Shen, & Yu, 2010).

Since the beginning of the twenty-first century, with the rapid social and economic development, the problem of water shortage in China has been increasingly obvious. Many experts and scholars have put forward the idea of converting floodwater into resources (Zhang et al., 2018). The achievements of the above two stages have also laid indispensable project and non-project foundations for floodwater utilization. Since 2007, with sustainable development in mind, the State Council has been underlining the role of floodwater in the relocation of regional water resources when approving flood control planning for major rivers. In this stage, China's main strategy has been shifted from

Table 2. The main laws and regulations related to flood control enacted in different years.

Law or regulation	Year enacted
Catastrophic Flood Control Plan for Yellow River, Yangtze River, Huaihe River, Yongding River	1985
Catastrophic Flood Control Plan for Haihe River Basin	1986
Guidance for Safe Construction in Flood-Storage and Retarding Basin	1988
Regulation of the People's Republic of China on the Administration of River Courses	1988
Water Law of the People's Republic of China	1988
Advice of State Flood Control and Drought Relief Headquarters on Normalized and Standardized Construction in Flood Control and Drought Relief	1991
Flood Control and Regulation of the People's Republic of China	1991
Regulation on the Administration of Reservoir Dam Safety	1991
Flood Control Law of the People's Republic of China	1997
Suggestions on Enhancing Construction and Management in Flood-Storage and Retarding Basin	2006

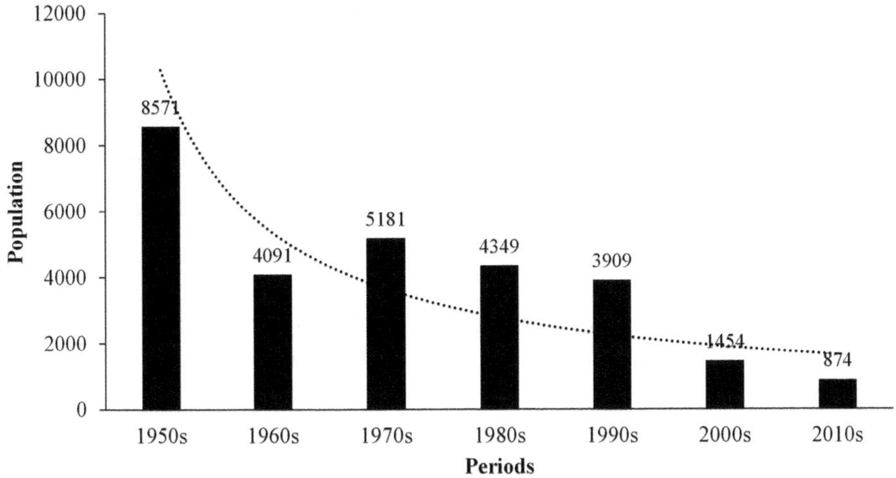

Figure 1. Deaths from flood disasters in China in different periods (Ding, Li, & Guo, 2016).

controlling floods to managing floods (Fu, 2009). To ensure safety, maximally impound floodwater to steadily supply water for rural and urban residents and to meet the water demand for agricultural irrigation. There are three ways to utilize floodwater as a resource: by dredging the underlying land surface and altering the hydrological features to hold more floodwater for a longer period, to allow ecological restoration of rivers and groundwater recharge; by interconnecting river systems and transferring water across regions to optimize the allocation of floodwater, to resolve the uneven spatial distribution of water resources; and by integrating flood forecasting into the optimal regulation and storage of reservoirs to relocate the flood flow in time and space, thereby impounding floodwater, reducing peak flood and storing floodwater for water conservancy (Qi, 2015).

Through its efforts in the seven decades since the establishment of the PRC, China has made historic achievements in dealing with flood disasters. The standard for flood control in seven major rivers has been improved significantly. Table S1 (in the online supplemental data, at https://doi.org/10.1080/07900627.2019.1709422) shows the flood control standards for some key sections of the seven major rivers. Flood control standards in cities have also seen obvious improvement. Of the 639 cities assigned flood control tasks, 207 are up to the standard (Urban Flood Prevention Research Group, 2001). Beijing, Tianjin, Guangzhou and Shanghai are armed with flood control standards that enable them to prevent a catastrophic flood that might occur every 200 years. The standard for some key capital cities, including Shijiazhuang, Harbin, Shenyang and Lanzhou, can ensure the city's safety from a flood that might occur every 100-plus years. Medium-sized cities have a standard effective against a flood with a 20-to-50-year recurrence period (Liu, 2009a). Figure 1 shows the trend in deaths from flood disasters over different periods in China (Ding, Li, & Guo, 2016).

Soil and water conservation

Soil and water loss (SWL) is a problem in both developing and developed nations. China is one of the countries suffering the most from this problem. The total SWL-stricken area has reached up to 3.56 million km^2 across the whole country, accounting for 37.1% of its territorial area (Zhang, Gao, & Peng, 2008). The Yellow River basin is the most affected region. With the annual average soil erosion modulus as high as 3700 t/km^2, the situation in the Loess Plateau, where the Yellow River passes through, is the worst in the world. To be specific, about 1.6 billion tons of sediment was being transferred annually from the Loess Plateau to the lower reaches of the Yellow River. The height of the river bed increased by 10 cm every year as a result of sediment deposition, forming a 'suspended river' in the downstream region (Jiang, Zhang, et al., 2019). This posed a threat to the life and property of over 100 million people who live in the areas along the Yellow River banks (Hou, Zhang, & Wang, 2003).

Soil and water conservation (SWC) refers to preventive and rehabilitative measures against SWL caused by either natural factors or human activities (Chen, Wei, Fu, & Lv, 2007). Since the founding of the PRC in 1949, great importance has been attached to SWC by the government. Through establishing administrative authorities and research institutions in central and local governments, sets of conservation measures tailored to local conditions have been explored, and a series of conservation policies have been developed. These efforts have forged a comprehensive governance system against SWL with Chinese characteristics. Specifically, during the agricultural cooperation movement in the 1950s, the government attempted to improve the situation by incorporating SWC into the campaign, resulting in a nationwide upsurge of afforestation in mountain areas and SWC in concerned regions. In the early 1960s, the focus was moved to the key governance of the most SWL-stricken areas, mainly in the middle reaches of the Yellow River (Zhai, 2010). After the Agricultural Meeting in Northern China in 1970, the authority explored new ways to conserve soil and water in conjunction with the construction of basic farmlands, and carried out large-scale farmland infrastructure construction throughout the country. In 1980, a pilot project of comprehensive rehabilitation of small river basins was launched in different SWL-stricken areas, aiming to integrate the SWC governance work with local economic development, and transform the process of SWC in small river basins into a process of economy development in these areas. In 1982, the State Council issued the Regulations on Soil and Water Conservation Work and launched the first national specially funded key management project focused on governing the eight areas where SWL was the most severe at the time. From then on, China started to tackle SWL problems in contiguous regions over small watersheds along major rivers. After 1989, China successively identified several key headwaters and the regions around the major headwaters as targeted SWC areas. A new prospect of SWL governance over the upper reaches of the seven major rivers was opened up (Duan, 1994). Table 3 shows the laws and regulations related to SWC formulated by the Chinese government in different periods. Importantly,

Table 3. Main laws and regulations related to soil and water conservation enacted in different years.

Law or regulation	Year enacted
Interim Outline of Soil and Water Conservation of the People's Republic of China	1957
Decisions on the Conservation of Soil and Water in the Middle Reaches of the Yellow River	1964
Measures for Soil and Water Conservation in Small River Basin	1980
Regulations on Soil and Water Conservation	1982
Law of the People's Republic of China on Soil and Water Conservation	1991
Outline of Prevention and Inspection on Soil and Water Conservation (2004–2015)	2004
Law of the People's Republic of China on Soil and Water Conservation (Revised)	2010
National Plan for Soil and Water Conservation (2015–2030)	2015

the Law on Soil and Water Conservation, enacted in 1991, defined SWC as a basic state policy. Since then China has officially adopted a rule-of-law approach to SWC.

In the twenty-first century, ecological rehabilitation projects for SWC have been carried forward. Through closing hillside farmlands and prohibiting grazing in ecologically fragile areas, China has made great efforts to reduce SWL caused by human activities so that ecosystem rehabilitation and restoration can be achieved. This has facilitated harmonization between the ecological environment and farming and animal husbandry. In 2005, the MWR officially initiated the revision work on the Soil and Water Conservation Law. The Standing Committee of the National People's Congress solicited more than 8000 public opinions, and passed through the revision in 2010 (MWR, 2006). The promulgation and implementation of the new law on SWC in 2011 eased the intensification of SWL caused by massive production and construction activities. The key SWC projects in river basins have forged ahead steadily; a pilot project for comprehensive SWL rehabilitation of side slopes has been carried out effectively; and the construction of warping dams against SWL has continued (MWR, 2011). In 2015, China's first National Soil and Water Conservation Plan (2015–2030) was formulated by the MWR, which defined stage objectives and key tasks for SWC, deployed key projects to comprehensively prevent and control SWL, initiated special inspection of the enforcement of the SWC law, and established effective supervision systems for implementation planning (MWR, 2016). The Measures for the Administration of the Soil and Water Conservation Eco-environment Monitoring Network and their implementation plan were issued in 2018, which not only fostered the setting up of state-level, river-basin-level, provincial-level and city-and-country-level monitoring organizations for SWC, but also facilitated the establishment and development of a collaborative monitoring mechanism (Wu, Wang, Li, & Sun, 2019).

After 70 years of continuous exploration, remarkable achievements in comprehensive SWL prevention and control have been made by the public sector under the leadership of the central government. The statistics show that 1,271,800 km^2 of the land area suffering from SWL has been brought under control since the reform and opening up. From 1950 to 1985, China's total SWL rehabilitation area was 338,400 km^2, with an annual control of 9400 km^2 (Hu, 2010). From 1986 to 2018, 933,400 km^2 of land hit by SWL was rehabilitated, so up to 28,300 km^2 was brought under control each year (MWR, 2019). The annual average rehabilitation was three times as fast compared to that in the 1950–1985 period. The nationwide SWC work produced outstanding achievements. In particular, the runoff and sediment condition in the Yellow River and the ecological status in the Loess Plateau entered into a new stage. The sediment discharge of the Yellow River has decreased from an 1.6 billion tons (annual average) to less than 100 million tons in recent years (Figure 2). Thirty years ago, almost no one would have predicted that the sediment discharge of the Yellow River could decrease to the current level. This dramatic change challenges the conventional thinking on SWL rehabilitation, and the success of the SWC work in the Yellow River basin has caught the attention of the world (Wang, et al., 2016).

Water supply

China's annual average total volume of freshwater resources is about 2800 km^3, the sixth-largest in the world. But this is only 2220 m^3 per capita, 28% of the world average, and average water resources for cultivation are around 1400 m^3 per mu, only half the world

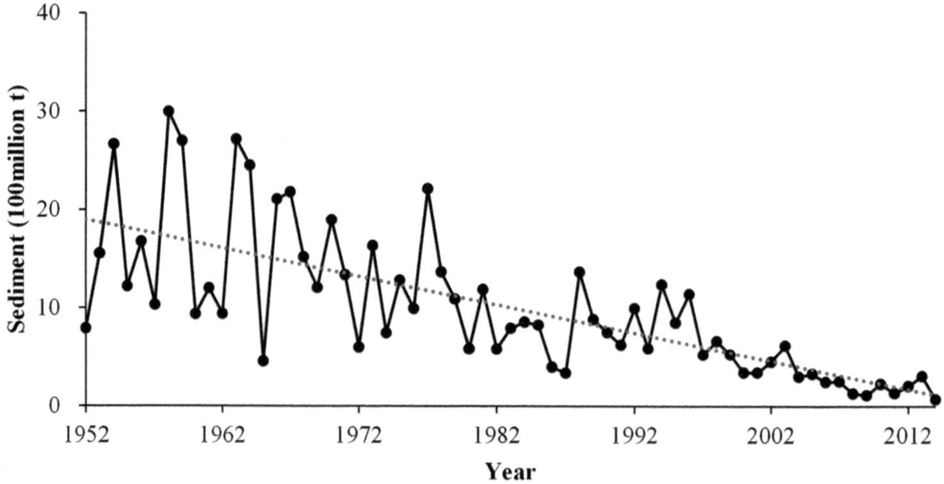

Figure 2. Trend in annual sediment discharge of the Yellow River, measured at Tongguan hydrologic station (Mu, Hu, Gao, Wang, & Zhao, 2017).

average. Thus, China is listed by the United Nations as one of the 13 most water-scarce countries (Zhang, Li, & Tang, 2012). The lack of water resources is aggravated by the spatial mismatch between water resources and the distribution of population and cultivated land: 46% of the population and 60% of the cultivated land are in the north of China, but this region only has 19% of the nation's water resources. Therefore, per capita water resources are less than a quarter of those in the south, and average water resources per mu are less than 15% of those in the south (Wang et al., 2014). This mismatch is a worldwide concern: how to feed 20% of the world's population and meet their development needs with only 7% of the world's freshwater resources (Shao, Tang, Zhang, & Li, 2006).

Since the founding of the PRC, great achievements have been made in water conservancy infrastructure construction and water supply capacity improvement. At the very beginning, regarded as the main water supply facilities, there were only 23 large and medium-sized reservoirs and 72 waterworks throughout the country. Of the 23 reservoirs, six had a capacity over 100 million m^3, and 17 had 100,000 m^3 to 100 million m^3. Water supply facilities have evolved from conventional water supply projects to combinations with unconventional water supply projects, and multiple types of facilities working together can improve efficiency. Besides reservoirs, electromechanical wells and pumping stations have been added to the conventional water supply system. By 2018, the country had 98,795 reservoirs, 2,360 waterworks, 4.96 million electromechanical wells and 95,077 pumping stations for water supply (MWR, 2018b). As a result, 233.78 km^3 water can be delivered from reservoirs, and the water supply capacity of pumping stations and electromechanical wells is up to 307.17 km^3. In the 1950s, water diversion projects were initiated to address the uneven spatial distribution of water resources. A total of 137 water diversion projects have been built or are under construction (Gao, Yao, Chen, & Chen, 2018). Such projects can now distribute 263.31 km^3 of water. Since the 2013 launch of the South-to-North Water Diversion Project, for example, 25 km^3 of water has been transmitted cumulatively, benefiting more than 100 million people along the route (MWR, 2018b).

In the early days of New China, water supply in rural areas relied heavily on self-built wells, water cellars and rivers. The total length of the water transmission and distribution pipeline was only 6589 km, with the total water supply capacity of 103.1 km^3 nationwide (Ministry of Water Resources and Electric Power, 1984). Later on, domestic water supply was converted into tap-water supply through the construction of water transmission and distribution pipelines that expanded from urban to rural areas. Currently, the total length of the national water supply pipeline is 1,682,000 km, of which 797,000 km is in urban areas, with total water supply of 59.38 km^3; 235,000 km is in counties, with total water supply of 11.3 km^3; 533,000 km covers towns and delivers 13.19 km^3 of water in total; and 117,000 km is distributed in rural areas, with water supply capacity of 1.26 km^3 (Ministry of Housing and Urban-Rural Development, 2018). To alleviate water shortages and improve the recycling rate, China has also made great progress in unconventional water resources utilization. Unconventional water supply projects include sewage treatment and reuse, rainfall collection, and seawater desalination. Nearly 4000 sewage treatment plants and 136 seawater desalination projects have been set up across the country. The total water supply resulting from sewage treatment, rainfall collection and seawater desalination has increased to 16.5 km^3, from 11.1 km^3 in 1997 (Compilation Committee of 50 Glorious Years of Water Conservancy, 1999; MWR, 2018a). The urban sewage reuse rate has risen to 15% (Yan, 2018), and the volume of seawater desalination has increased from 200 m^3 per day in 1981 to 1,189,100 m^3 per day (Zhu, Xue, & Xu, 2014).

The combination of these types of water supply infrastructure increased the nation's water supply capacity to 856.24 km^3 by 2018. Figure 3 shows China's water supply development over the past 70 years. From 1949 to 1995, water supply volume surged due to rapid population growth and improvement of water supply capacity. In contrast, the water supply from 2008 to 2018 was relatively stable and fluctuated around 601.55 km^3 (MWR, 2018b). The stability of the water supply over this period indicates that insufficient water supply in China ended in 2008. China's achievements in water supply can be further elaborated in domestic water supply, industrial water supply and

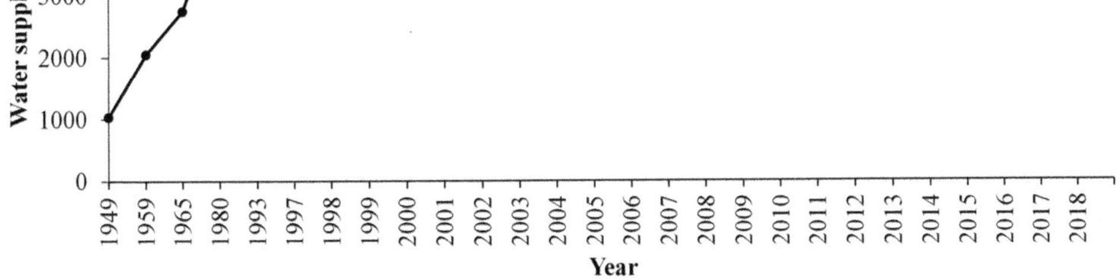

Figure 3. Water supply variations from 1949 to 2018 (Ministry of Water Resources and Electric Power, 1984; Ministry of Water Resources, 2018c).

Table 4. Comparison of water supply between 1949 and 2018 (Compilation Committee of 50 Glorious Years of Water Conservancy, 1999; Ministry of Water Resources, 2018b; Zhao, 1999).

Year	1949	2018
Reservoirs	23	98,795
Waterworks	72	2360
Water pipeline length (km)	6,589	1,682,000
Water supply capability (100 million m^3)	1,031	8,562.4
Annual per capita water consumption (m^3)	187	436
Domestic water supply (100 million m^3)	6	838.1
Population (100 million)	5.42	13.95
Water supply penetration rate (%)	42	90
Agricultural water supply (100 million m^3)	1,001	3,766.4
Farmland irrigation area (100 million mu)	2.4	10.17
Industrial water supply (100 million m^3)	20	1277

agricultural water supply (Table 4). In 1949, the domestic water supply was only 600 million m^3, urban water consumption was 38.2 litres per capita per day (Hong, Lu, & He, 2006) and the penetration rate of urban water supply was 42% (Zhao, 1999). Industrial water supply was 2 km^3, and agricultural water supply totalled 11.1 km^3 (Ministry of Water Resources and Electric Power, 1984).There were only a few hundred irrigation areas over 10,000 mu (Lin, 1989). The total irrigated farmland was 240 million mu, accounting for 16.3% of the total cultivated land at that time (Compilation Committee of 50 Glorious Years of Water Conservancy, 1999). As of this writing, total domestic water supply has reached 838.1 km^3. In urban areas, water consumption is 178.9 litres per capita per day, and the water supply penetration rate is 98.3%. In rural areas, water consumption is 120.2 litres per capita per day, and the water supply penetration rate is 92.87%.

In addition to increasing water supply capacity, China has attached great importance to water saving and water reuse to ensure water supply security. In industry, 82.12 km^3 of water is reused, with a recycling rate of 89.53%, and in rural areas, 1.8 km^3 is reused, with a recycling rate of 62.88% (Ministry of Housing and Urban-Rural Development, 2018). In agriculture, techniques such as micro-irrigation and drip irrigation have been widely deployed. Water-saving irrigation area has increased from 228 million mu in 1998 to 515 million mu in 2018, and the irrigation water use efficiency has increased from 0.51 in 2011 to 0.554 in 2018 (MWR, 2018b).

The evolution and advantages of China's water governance

The evolution of China's water governance institutions

The key to overcoming water challenges and realizing sustainable utilization of water resources is to strengthen water resources management (Jiang, Lei, & Tang, 2005). Since the establishment of the PRC, China's water resources management has experienced constant development and improvement to cope with the challenges of socio-economic development. In the 1950s and 1960s, flood disaster prevention and control was the first priority. In the 1970s and 1980s, water supply became the first priority. In the 1990s and 2000s, water pollution control became the first priority. In the 2010s, more integrated ecological civilization construction became the requirement. The evolution of China's water resources management can be divided into three stages: from decentralized management to integrated management, and then gradually to stringent management at both basin and administrative scales (Jiang, Geng, Xu, & Huang, 2011).

From 1949 to 1987, the management of China's water resources was decentralized (Long, Cheng, Fan, & Zhou, 2001; Tian & Hu, 2018; Wang, 2010). Water-related responsibilities were scattered among multiple departments. The Water Resources Department was only in charge of flood control and water conservancy construction for inter-basin water transfers (Jia & Zhang, 2011). China did not have an independent department to focus on water environment protection and water pollution control. In 1974, pollution in Beijing's Guanting Reservoir prompted the State Council to set up an environmental protection leading group, so an official organization working on water environment protection was established in China. In 1982, the State Council set up the Ministry of Urban-Rural Development and Environmental Protection, with an internal body, the State Bureau of Environmental Protection (SBEP). In the same year, the Regulations on Water Resources Management in Shanxi Province were issued, officially declaring for the first time in China that water abstraction must be licensed by the government. Per the Regulations, Shanxi Province started to collect water resources fees (Li, 2013). Other provinces then followed this example, with different measures to collect water resources fees. In 1984, the State Council made the Ministry of Water Resources and Electric Power responsible for water-resources-related issues. The Law on the Prevention and Control of Water Pollution came out in the same year to establish a management system for water pollution prevention and control across different regions and departments.

China's water resources management stepped into a brand new stage in 1988 with the promulgation of the Water Law (Shen, 2014). The law introduced a water resources management system that combines integrated management with administration across different levels and departments, especially the combination of basin management through basin commissions and regional management through local governments. The law also underlined that the MWR was in charge of integrated water resources management throughout the county. In the same year, the SBEP became a deputy-ministerial-level administration under the direct leadership of the State Council, and acted as the department in charge of the comprehensive administration of environmental protection. Along with the subsequent institutional reforms of the State Council, Integrated Water Resources Management was increasingly strengthened (Yu, Edmunds, Lora-Wainwright, & Thomas, 2016). A revised Law on the Prevention and Control of Water Pollution in 1996 specified that the SBEP was the authority to carry out integrated supervision of water pollution prevention and control. In 1998, the SBEP was upgraded to the ministerial-level State Environmental Protection Administration. In the same year, the State Council declared that the authority over urban flood control and groundwater management were transferred to the MWR (Gao & Liu, 2008). Thus, China gradually realized the integrated management of water resources from 1988 to 2002. The MWR is in charge of most water-related management, although during this period water resources protection at the basin scale was led by both the MWR and the State Environmental Protection Administration.

With the new Water Law of 2002, China's water resources management evolved gradually into stringent management. In 2011 the Central Document No.1 of the central government stated that China would adhere to 'the most stringent water resources management system'. The system was specified the Three Red Lines, which set clear goals for total water consumption, water use efficiency and water environment restoration in both basins and administrative regions at all levels (Global Water Partnership, 2015; Tao et al., 2012). At the end of 2016, to carry out and enforce the Three Red Lines, the Chinese leadership decided to implement the river chief system in the whole country. The river chief system, in which local leaders assume overall responsibility for river and lake management, links environmental protection to the performance evaluation of top officials (Dai, 2014; Jia, 2017). It has not only further strengthened integrated water resources management but also significantly reduced the squabbling and wrangling caused by sectoral segmentation, which hampered the implementation of the most stringent water resources management system. Nowadays, China has completely entered the stage of the most stringent water resources management. Since the 18th National Congress of the Communist Party of China (CPC), the central government has regarded the construction of ecological civilization as a matter of fundamental importance for the future of the Chinese nation (Gu, Hu, & Zhou, 2013; Zhao, Huang, & Ma, 2016). It has set forth that social and economic development must be in line with local water resources carrying capacity, and that any development leading to the overexploitation of water resources, the pollution of water environment or the degradation of water ecology must be prohibited (Ren, Guo, Li, & Li, 2016; Wang, Jiang, Xiao, Chen, & Hu, 2017).

The characteristics and advantages of China's water governance

Important leaders give high priority to water governance

China is a country with a unitary form of government, and the CPC takes the leading role, so the top leaders' attitude towards water governance is very important. Since the founding of the PRC, every generation of top leaders of China has given high priority to water governance.

Mao Zedong, the first-generation leader of the CPC, was determined to tackle flood disasters. He personally inspected the four major water conservancy projects and helped form the basic principle for China's water governance in the early days of the PRC. First, in response to the severe floods in the Huaihe River in 1950, Mao Zedong made an important instruction, 'We must restore the Huaihe River [一定要把淮河修好]', invited experts to discuss emergency rescue and flood control strategies and urged that the Huaihe River governance project start as soon as possible. In the same year, the State Council issued the Decision on Governing the Huaihe River, which introduced a policy of 'storage and discharge' according to the different situations in the upper, middle and lower reaches and initiated the first large-scale project for water conservancy in New China (Liu, 2009b).

Second, the section of the Jingjiang River in the middle reaches of the Yangtze River has been the most severely flooded place on the Yangtze River. In 1952, leaders of the State Council and water conservancy experts drafted and issued the State Council Regulations on the Jingjiang River Flood Diversion Project. Mao Zedong wrote the inscription: 'For the benefit of the people, fight for the victory of Jingjiang project [为广大人民的利益,争取荆江分洪工程的胜利].' In an amazing 75 days, 300,000 people completed the main project of the Jingjiang River flood diversion area, with a flood storage capacity of 5.4 km^3.

Third, the Yellow River is the mother river of the Chinese nation, but it was also frequently stricken by floods. In 1952, Mao Zedong inspected the Yellow River and made a famous instruction, 'We must govern the Yellow River well [一定要把黄河的事情办好].' After that, Mao Zedong visited the Yellow River with water conservancy experts three times, in 1953, 1954 and 1955. In 1955, he approved the Plan on Comprehensive Utilization and Governance of the Yellow River. A series of projects were started, including repairing dams, building reservoirs and setting up flood detention areas. These projects formed a downstream flood control system featuring 'water interception in the upper reaches, water drainage in the lower reaches and water detention on both banks', which completely changed the Yellow River's situation, which had seen 'three levee breaches in two years and drastically re-routing in every century' (Zhang & Li, 2018).

Fourth, in 1963, the Haihe River suffered the worst flood disaster since the founding of the PRC. Mao Zedong immediately pronounced, 'We must effect a radical cure of the Haihe River [我们一定要根治海河].' According to his instructions, the MWR, the Hebei Provincial government and other relevant departments, together with experts in different disciplines, designed and put forward a set of water governance schemes that could fundamentally solve the flood problems in the Haihe River: 'impounding water in the upper reaches, dredging water in the middle reaches, draining off water in the lower reaches, and retaining water appropriately' (Liu, 2007). These schemes established a preliminary flood control infrastructure system for the Haihe River basin, and a flood control pattern was formed in which floods from different branches are discharged to the sea through different channels.

Since the reform and opening up, China's water governance has made substantial progress in regularization, modernization and legalization. From 1979, under the guidance of Deng Xiaoping and other party and state leaders, the CPC's Central Committee began to adjust the policy on water governance and gradually shifted the focus from engineering construction to engineering management and improving economic benefits. This was an important transformation towards a modern water governance system. In 1981, the Central Committee held the first conference on water governance at the national level since the founding of the PRC, and proposed a new policy for water conservancy: 'to shift the focus of water conservancy work to management and strengthen management in all aspects'. Deng Xiaoping also attaches great importance to hydropower development. When he heard the report from experts on the preparations for the Three Gorges Project, he firmly stated, 'Be determined and never bog down!' Supported by Deng Xiaoping and other party and state leaders, the Yangtze River Basin Planning Office submitted the Report on Building the Three Gorges Water Project at the end of 1981. In March 1983, the Yangtze River Basin Planning Office finished the Feasibility Study Report of the Three Gorges Water Project. In response to the different opinions on the Three Gorges Project at home and abroad since 1985, Deng Xiaoping several times invited experts from various parties to demonstrate the necessity and feasibility of the project. Finally, the Three Gorges Project officially started on 14 December 1994 and was completed on May 2006. After the disastrous floods in the Yangtze River and Songhua River basins in 1998, president Jiang Zemin called for a serious reflection on the causes of the floods and put in place the principle of 'closing hillsides for reforestation, returning farmland to woodlands and lakes, removing barriers for flood diversion, strengthening dykes and dams, and dredging river channels' (Jiang, Wang, & Xiang, 2019). Facing various water governance challenges caused by socio-economic development, President Jiang Zemin made overall plans and adjusted the water governance policy and strategy to 'reasonable exploitation, efficient utilization, optimal allocation, all-round conservation, effective protection, and comprehensive governance' (Zhang, 2002).

Since the beginning of the twenty-first century, China's socio-economic development and improvement of people's lives have put forward new requirements for water governance (Xie, Zhou, Zhen, Lu, & Xiao, 2005). During this period, the policy of water governance was gradually adjusted. The design of the water governance policy had more theory support and became more practical and time-oriented. Decision-making on water governance was also more scientific and democratic. In 2011, the No. 1 Document of the Central Committee was the Decision on Accelerating Water Conservancy Reform and Development, which is the first comprehensive policy document of the Central Committee on water governance since the founding of the PRC. It stated clearly that water governance is of great strategic importance and is crucial to people's welfare, economic security, ecological security and national security. In this document, water governance is brought to a very high strategic position and the development goals of water governance for the next decade are set. In the Report to the Eighteenth National Congress of the Communist Party of China of 2012, president Hu Jintao clearly stated:

We should vigorously promote ecological civilization construction, accelerate the construction of water conservancy projects, improve the system for preventing and mitigating natural disasters, take integrated steps to control water and soil erosion, put in place the most stringent water resource management, strengthen the protection of water sources and the control of water utilization, and build a water-saving society.

In 2014, president Xi Jinping further summarized the water governance policy as 'taking water conservation as a priority, striking a spatial balance, adopting systematic thinking on water governance, and giving full play to both the government and the market'. He also proposed the river chief system for water administrative management and the idea that 'lucid waters and lush mountains are invaluable assets' to guide economic development. President Xi's thoughts on development have become important guidelines for China's water governance in the new era. He has emphasized that water governance should adopt systematic thinking to coordinate all factors and distinguish the primary, secondary and causal relationships. The key at present is water conservation, and water conservation must be the priority in all aspects of water governance. 'Spatial balance' refers to striking a balance between 'resources and environment' and 'population and economy' to foster harmony between man and nature. In water governance we should strengthen water demand management and regard the carrying capacity of water resources, aquatic ecology and water environment as rigid constraints on socio-economic development (Wu, Gao, & Li, 2018). 'Systematic governance' refers to regarding mountains, water, woodlands, farmlands, lakes and grasslands as a community of shared destiny. It requires coordinating all elements of the natural ecology and adopting a systemic approach. 'Implementing hard measures at both ends' means properly handling the roles of government and the market in water governance. President Xi emphasized that to establish a reasonable and effective water governance system, we must give full play to both the market and the government and clearly identify what the government should do versus what can be solved through market mechanisms.

Strong execution system of central decision

Because of the unitary system and the leading role of CPC, when the top leaders of China make a decision, the execution force of the governance system is very strong. Not only will the government's organizational system but also the party's organizational system will implement the decision from top to bottom and layer by layer. The strict cadre assessment system enables every cadre to fulfil his duties according to the requirements of the Central Committee.

Routine rules of expert assessment and public participation

In China, experts have a very important role in the governance system. Almost every research, planning, or design project must pass the assessment of an expert team from related professional fields. There are very tight contacts and cooperation between decision makers, scientists and engineers.

There are also regulations for public participation in water governance. The working out of any policy involving the daily life of people must include a hearing. And the environment impact assessment report of all engineering projects (except those involving state secrets) must be given public notice for some period and accept public comments. The public can also participate in the various processes of water governance, from the formulation of laws and policies to the construction and operation of the project. A recent example is the ability to monitor and report on black and odorous water bodies through a smartphone app.

Challenges and the way forward

Since the founding of New China 70 years ago, China has made remarkable achievements in various aspects of water governance, such as flood control, water supply, soil and water conservation and water resources management. However, there is still a significant gap between China and the developed countries in all these regards. In addition, new challenges constantly spring up with the rapid socioeconomic development. First, 'ecological civilization' construction has a prominent position in China's future development. Due to provision for ecological water use, any increase in socio-economic water consumption will not be easy in the future. Consequently, water shortage will continue to be one of the most stringent constraints on China's socio-economic development (Liu, Dong, & Li, 2011). Across the country, low water-use efficiency and uneven spatial distribution of water resources are important causes of shortage (Deng, Li, & Song, 2016; Wang, Jiang, Wang, Huang, & Deng, 2019). But the causes of water shortage at the regional scale are much more complex. In most regions in the south, water shortage is mainly caused by water pollution and seasonal drought, while in the north insufficient rainfall plays a bigger role. Also, natural conditions in parts of the south-western river basins make the construction of water conservancy facilities very difficult (Tong, Zhou, & Peng, 2016).

Second, in the past, China's extensive exploitation of water resources neglected the protection of natural ecosystems, resulting in serious shortages of water for environmental conservation (Liu & Speed, 2009). The exploitation of surface water severely squeezed the ecological water use of most rivers, and the over-exploitation of groundwater caused serious funnels in the north of China (Cheng, Li, Yue, & Huang, 2019). A preliminary estimate is that for the major rivers in China up to 13.2 km^3 of ecological water has been occupied by human activities, and the amount of groundwater overexploitation is as high as 21.5 km^3 (Wang, Wang, & Wang, 2011). This has not only caused shrinkage of water bodies but also reduced their capacity for self-purification.

Third, with the urbanization of China, impervious areas in cities are expanding rapidly. In many cities, the volume of urban stormwater has exceeded the drainage capacity of the sewer system. As a result, waterlogging has become one of the most urgent flood problems (Dai, van Rijswick, Driessen, & Keessen, 2017; Jia et al., 2019; Zhang, Miao, Li, Liu, & Fang, 2019). From 2010 to 2016, more than 180 cities in China had flooding or waterlogging every year (MWR, 2017a). From 2007 to 2015, more than 360 cities across the country suffered waterlogging, and of these one-sixth were flooded for more than 12 hours, with depth of flooding exceeding half a metre (Ministry of Housing and Urban-Rural Development, 2018).

Confronting these challenges, China's central government has put forward the policy of giving priority to water conservation; keeping water consumption, population growth, economic development and ecological conservation in balance; combining water governance with the management of mountain, forest, farmland and grassland; giving equal emphasis to the roles of administrative management and market mechanism in water governance.

Under the guidance of this policy, the focus of China's current water governance work has shifted to improving the defects of water conservancy projects and strengthening the supervision of the water conservancy industry. Also, based on the concept of ecological civilization construction, green development strategy with focus on resource conservation, environmental protection and ecological conservation is becoming more and more important to cope with various water-related challenges. Besides traditional water governance policies, policies on the adjustment of industrial structure and the optimization of economic development are playing a bigger role to keep socio-economic development in line with local water resources carrying capability. With water conservation, China will make sure that socio-economic development is in harmony with water resources utilization, that the connections between water and other key elements of ecosystems are sound, and that the relationship between the government and the market is well managed, so as to drive forward the reform of China's water governance in the new era.

Disclosure statement

No potential conflict of interest was reported by the authors.

Funding

This research was funded by the Strategic Priority Research Programme of the Chinese Academy of Sciences [XDA20010201].

References

Chen, L., Wei, W., Fu, B., & Lv, Y. H. (2007). Soil and water conservation on the Loess Plateau in China: Review and perspective. *Progress in Physical Geography, 31*(4), 389–403. doi:10.1177/0309133307081290

Cheng, B., Li, H., Yue, S., & Huang, K. (2019). A conceptual decision-making for the ecological base flow of rivers considering the economic value of ecosystem services of rivers in water shortage area of Northwest China. *Journal of Hydrology, 578,* 124126. doi:10.1016/j.jhydrol.2019.124126

Compilation Committee of 50 Glorious Years of Water Conservancy. (1999). *Water conservancy brilliant 50 years.* Beijing: China Water & Power Press.

Dai, L. P. (2014). A new perspective on water governance in China: Captain of the river. *Water International, 40*(1), 87–99. doi:10.1080/02508060.2014.986702

Dai, L. P., van Rijswick, H. F. M. W., Driessen, P. P. J., & Keessen, A. M. (2017). Governance of the sponge city programme in China with Wuhan as a case study. *International Journal of Water Resources Development, 34*(4), 578–596. doi:10.1080/07900627.2017.1373637

Deng, G., Li, L., & Song, Y. (2016). Provincial water use efficiency measurement and factor analysis in China: Based on SBM-DEA model. *Ecological Indicators, 69,* 12–18. doi:10.1016/j.ecolind.2016.03.052

Ding, L. Q., Li, N., & Guo, L. (2016). Drainage capacity of flood control and need to be strengthened. *China Water Resources, 15,* 10-11+14. doi:10.3969/j.issn.1000-1123.2016.15.005

Duan, Q. P. (1994). Review of China's 45 years of soil and water conservation work: Obvious benefits, heavy task and long road to go. *Soil and Water Conservation in China, 10,* 6-10+59. doi:10.14123/j.cnki.swcc.1994.10.003

FAO. (2011). *FAOSTAT: FAO statistical databases.* Rome: Food and Agriculture Organization of the United Nations.

Fu, Z. C. (2009). Celebrate the 60th anniversary of the new China. *China Flood & Drought Management, 19*(5), 1. doi:10.15920/j.cnki.22-1179/tv.2015.06.010

Gao, X. P., & Liu, Y. H. (2008). A comparative study of the three-dimensional regulations on organizational reform of the State Council of 1998 and 2008 based on the perspective of the conversion of government functions. *Jiangsu Social Sciences, 6,* 12–15. doi:10.3969/j.issn.1003-8671.2008.06.003

Gao, Y. Y., Yao, J. W., Chen, G. F., & Chen, W. Y. (2018). Current situation and prospects of water diversion schemes in China. *China Water Resource, 4,* 49–51.

Global Water Partnership. (2015). China's water resources management challenges: The 'Three Red Lines'. Retrieved from www.gwp.org

Gu, S., Hu, Y., & Zhou, H. (2013). Ecological civilization construction: Scientific connotation and basic paths. *Resources Science, 35*(1), 2–13. doi:1007-7588□2013□01-0002-12

Hong, J. M., Lu, K. M., & He, S. P.(2006). The 5th World Water Conference of International Water Association, organized and compiled by the Science and Technology Department of the Ministry of Construction. *China urban water supply technology development manual.* Beijing: China Architecture & Building Press.

Hou, C. B., Zhang, J. M., & Wang, S. Z. (2003). Several key technologies in water and sediment regulation of the Yellow River. *Water Resources Development Research, 3*(3), 19–21. doi:10.13928/j.cnki.wrdr.2003.03.005

Hu, S. M. (2010). Achievements and benefits of soil and water loss governance in China. *Journal of Economics of Water Resources, 28*(1), 19-23+76. doi:10.3969/j.issn.1003-9511.2010.01.006

Jia, S. F. (2017). The river chief system should really realize the 'Chief responsibility system'. *China Water Resources, 2,* 11–12. doi:10.3969/j.issn.1000-1123.2017.02.006

Jia, S. F., Li, Y. Y., Lv, A. F., Liu, W. H., Zhu, W. B., Yan, J. B., ... Guan, Z. L. (2019). City-storm-flood events in China, 1984–2015. *International Journal of Water Resources Development, 35*(4), 605–618. doi:10.1080/07900627.2018.1513830

Jia, S. F., & Zhang, J. (2011). Institutional reform of water resources management in China. *China Population, Resources and Environment, 21*(10), 102–106. doi:10.3969/j.issn.1002-2104.2011.10.016

Jiang, B. L., Geng, L. H., Xu, P. B., & Huang, C. S. (2011). A tentative analysis of water resource management practice and development tendency of the water resource management mode. *China Rural Water and Hydropower, 10,* 66–69. doi:1007-2284(2011)10-0066-04

Jiang, C., Zhang, H., Wang, X., Feng, Y., & Labzovskii, L. (2019). Challenging the land degradation in China's Loess Plateau: Benefits, limitations, sustainability, and adaptive strategies of soil and water conservation. *Ecological Engineering, 127,* 135–150. doi:10.1016/j.ecoleng.2018.11.018

Jiang, W. L., Lei, B., & Tang, Q. (2005). Water resources management and its research progress. *Resources Science, 27*(1), 153–157. doi:10.3321/j.issn:1007-7588.2005.01.025

Jiang, X., Wang, Y., & Xiang, L. (2019). Construction and achievements of flood prevention and disaster reduction systems in China. *China Flood & Drought Management, 29*(10), 6–9. doi:10.16867/j.issn.1673-9264.2019170

Kundzewicz, Z. W., Su, B., Wang, Y., Xia, J., Huang, J., & Jiang, T. (2019). Flood risk and its reduction in China. *Advances in Water Resources, 130*, 37–45. doi:10.1016/j.advwatres.2019.05.020

Li, R. S. (2013). Development and evolution of water resources fees in China and current situation of collection and management. *Knowledge Economy, 5*, 55. doi:10.15880/j.cnki.zsjj.2013.05.019

Li, Y. (1992). Opening up various capital channels and establishing a stable new mechanism of water conservancy investment. *Journal of Economics of Water Resources, 3*, 51–54.

Lin, S. G. (1989). The development and achievement of irrigation science and technology in our country. *Journal of Irrigation and Drainage, 1*, 1–5. doi:13522/j.cnki.ggps.1989.01.001

Liu, B., & Speed, R. (2009). Water resources management in the People's Republic of China. *Water Resources Management, 25*(2), 193–208. doi:10.1080/07900620902868596

Liu, B. J., & Zhang, J. H. (1999). Reservoir construction and flood control in China. *Yangtze River, S1*, 1-3+10. doi:10.16867/j.cnki.cfdm.2009.05.001

Liu, H. S. (2007). On the experience and lessons in the movement to bring the Haibe River under permanent control in Hebei Province. *Contemporary China History Studies, 3*, 105-111+128. doi:10.3969/j.issn.1005-4952.2007.03.019

Liu, J., & Yang, W. (2012). Water sustainability for China and beyond. *Science, 337*(6095), 649–650. doi:10.1126/science.1219471

Liu, J., Zang, C., Tian, S., Liu, J., Yang, H., Jia, S., … Zhang, M. (2013). Water conservancy projects in China: Achievements, challenges and way forward. *Global Environmental Change, 23*, 633–643. doi:10.1016/j.gloenvcha.2013.02.002

Liu, J. J., Dong, L. C., & Li, Z. H. (2011). Comprehensive evaluation of China's water resources carrying capacity. *Journal of Natural Resources, 26*(2), 258–269. doi:CNKI:SUN:ZRZX.0.2011-02-008

Liu, N. (2009a). Consideration on flood control and drought relief for Haihe River Basin. *Water Resources and Hydropower Engineering, 40*(8), 4–8. doi:10.3969/j.issn.1000-0860.2009.08.003

Liu, Y. N. (2009b). Overall planning and coordination for further harnessing the Huaihe River. *China Water Resources, 12*, 10–11. doi:10.3969/j.issn.1000-1123.2009.12.006

Long, A. H., Cheng, G. D., Fan, S. Y., & Zhou, L. H. (2001). Administrative separatist problems and countermeasures on China's water resource management. *China Soft Science, 8*, 17–21. doi:10.3969/j.issn.1002-9753.2001.08.005

Ministry of Housing and Urban-Rural Development. (2018). *Statistical yearbook of urban and rural construction in China 2017*. Beijing: China Statistics Press.

Ministry of Water Resources and Electric Power. (1984). *Modern water conservancy construction in China*. Beijing: Water Resources and Electric Power Press.

Ministry of Water Resources. (2006). *China water resources yearbook 2006*. Beijing: China Water & Power Press.

Ministry of Water Resources. (2011). *China water resources yearbook 2011*. Beijing: China Water & Power Press.

Ministry of Water Resources. (2016). *China water resources yearbook 2016*. Beijing: China Water & Power Press.

Ministry of Water Resources. (2017a). *China water resources yearbook 2017*. Beijing: China Water & Power Press.

Ministry of Water Resources. (2017b). *China water resources yearbook 2016*. Beijing: China Water & Power Press.

Ministry of Water Resources. (2018a). *China soil and water conservation bulletin 2018*. Beijing: China Water & Power Press.

Ministry of Water Resources. (2018b). *China water resources yearbook 2018*. Beijing: China Water & Power Press.

Ministry of Water Resources. (2018c). *National statistical bulletin on water resources development in 2017*. Beijing: China Water & Power Press.

Ministry of Water Resources. (2019). *Chinese Journal of Soil and Water Conservation: 70 years of soil and water conservation*. Retrieved from http://swcc.mwr.gov.cn/stbcsbyw/201910/t20191021_1365672.html

Mu, X. M., Hu, C. H., Gao, P., Wang, F., & Zhao, G. (2017). Key issues and reflections of research on sediment flux of the Yellow River. *Yellow River, 39*(8), 1-4+48. doi:10.3969/j.issn.1000-1379.2017.08.001

Pan, J. Z. (2002). Achievements, problems and prospects in China's water conservancy construction. *Engineering Sciences, 4*(2), 42–51. doi:10.3969/j.issn.1009-1742.2002.02.007.

Qi, Y. C. (2015). Review of flood resources research under changing environment. *Jilin Water Resources, 6*, 34-37+41. doi:10.3969/j.issn.1009-2846.2015.06.011

Ren, C., Guo, P., Li, M., & Li, R. (2016). An innovative method for water resources carrying capacity research: Metabolic theory of regional water resources. *Journal of Environmental Management, 167*, 139–146. doi:10.1016/j.jenvman.2015.11.033

Shao, M., Tang, X., Zhang, Y., & Li, W. (2006). City clusters in China: Air and surface water pollution. *Frontiers in Ecology and the Environment, 4*, 353–361. doi:10.1890/1540-9295(2006)004[0353:CCICAA]2.0.CO;2

Shen, D. (2014). Post-1980 water policy in China. *International Journal of Water Resources Development, 30*(4), 714–727. doi:10.1080/07900627.2014.909310

Shi, G. Q., Shen, H. Z., & Yu, J. J. (2010). Review and prospect of 60-year flood control and drought fighting in Yangtze River basin. *Yangtze River, 41*(4), 9-13+45. doi:10.3969/j.issn.1001-4179.2010.04.004

Tao, J., Zuo, Q. T., Xue, H. L., Dou, M., Liang, S. K., & Mao, C. C. (2012). Control indicators and determination methods of 'Three Red Lines' of the strictest water resources management system. *Water Saving Irrigation, 4*, 64–67. doi:1007-4929(2012)04-0064-04

Tian, G. L., & Hu, Y. C. (2018). The course, evolution and development of China's water price reform since reform and opening up. *Price: Theory & Practice, 11*, 8–13.

Tong, S., Zhou, Z., & Peng, H. (2016). Spatial patterns of scarcity of water and its shortage types in China. *Ecological Economy, 32*(7), 168–173. doi:10.3969/j.issn.1671-4407.2016.07.035

Urban Flood Prevention Research Group. (2001). Urbanization process and urban flood control planning in China. *Water Resources Planning and Design, 3*, 4–11. doi:CNKI:SUN:SLGH.0.2001-03-001

Wang, D., Wang, J., & Wang, J. (2011). Rational water resources development and water use amount control. *China Water Resources, 23*, 59–63. doi: CNKI:SUN:SLZG.0.2011-23-012

Wang, H. (2010). *Research on water resources problem and sustainable development strategy in China*. Beijing: China Electric Power Press.

Wang, J., Jiang, D., Xiao, W., Chen, Y., & Hu, P. (2017). Study on theoretical analysis of water resources carrying capacity: Definition and scientific topics. *Journal of Hydraulic Engineering, 48*(12), 1399–1409. doi:10.13243/j.cnki.slxb.20170651

Wang, J. X., Jiang, Y. T., Wang, H. M., Huang, Q. Q., & Deng, H. B. (2019). Groundwater irrigation and management in northern China: Status, trends, and challenges. *International Journal of Water Resources Development*. doi:10.1080/07900627.2019.1584094

Wang, S., Fu, B., Piao, S., Lv, Y., Ciais, P., Feng, X., & Wang, Y. (2016). Reduced sediment transport in the Yellow River due to anthropogenic changes. *Nature Geoscience, 9*, 38–41. doi:10.1038/ngeo2602

Wang, X., & Liu, H. X. (2009). New China development strategy of flood control and drought. *China Flood & Drought Management, 19*(S1), 1–5. doi:10.16867/j.cnki.cfdm.2009.s1.002

Wang, Y. J., Gao, C., Wang, A. Q., Wang, Y. Y., Zhang, F. Y., Zhuo, J. Q., … Su, B. D. (2014). Temporal and spatial variation of exposure and vulnerability of flood disaster in China. *Climate Change Research, 10*(6), 391–398. doi:CNKI:SUN:QHBH.0.2014-06-001

Wu, N. D., Wang, J. P., Li, F. P., & Sun, J. (2019). Current situation, problems and countermeasure suggestions on the construction of soil and water conservation law system. *Soil and Water Conservation in China, 445*(4), 29–33. doi:10.14123/j.cnki.swcc.2019.0065

Wu, Q., Gao, L., & Li, M. (2018). Spatial equilibrium: The principle of balancing population economy and resources and environment must be established. *Water Resources Development Research, 18* (9), 17–24. doi:10.13928/j.cnki.wrdr.2018.09.003

Xie, G. D., Zhou, H. L., Zhen, L., Lu, C. X., & Xiao, Y. (2005). Carrying capacity of water resources for China's development. *Resources Science, 4*, 2–7. doi:10.3321/j.issn:1007-7588.2005.04.001

Yan, D. Y. (2018). Research progress of urban waste water reuse technology. *China Resources Comprehensive Utilization, 36*, 99–101. doi:1008-9500(2018)01-0099-03

Yu, H. H., Edmunds, M., Lora-Wainwright, A., & Thomas, D. (2016). Governance of the irrigation commons under integrated water resources management: A comparative study in contemporary rural China. *Environmental Science & Policy, 55*(1), 65–74. doi:10.1016/j.envsci.2015.08.001

Zhai, J. (2010). On soil and water conservation of Sanchuanhe River basin in Shanxi Province during the period of agricultural cooperation. *Journal of Jin Zhong University, 27*(4), 85–88. doi:10.3969/j.issn.1673-1808.2010.04.023

Zhang, H. W., & Li, Z. S. (2018). Study on river course and beach management in the lower Yellow River. *Chinese Journal of Environmental Management, 10*(01), 99–100. doi:10.3321/j.issn:1007-7588.2005.04.001

Zhang, J. H., Li, J., & Tang, Y. (2012). Analysis of the spatio-temporal matching of water resource and economic development factors in China. *Resources Science, 34*, 1546–1555. doi:1007-7588 (2012) 08-1546-10

Zhang, J. Y. (2002). Taking sustainable utilization of water resources as the goal, we should make great efforts to work out the comprehensive planning of water resources in China. *China Water Resources, 5*, 11–16. doi:10.3969/j.issn.1000-1123.2002.05.002

Zhang, J. Z., Yu, Z. Q., Yu, T. F., Si, J. H., Feng, Q., & Cao, S. X. (2018). Transforming flash floods into resources in arid China. *Land Use Policy, 76*, 746–753. doi:10.1016/j.landusepol.2018.03.002

Zhang, X. C., Gao, Z. L., & Peng, K. S. (2008). Success and treatment measures of soil and water conservation with Chinese character. *Chinese Journal of Nature, 30*(1), 17–22. doi:10.3969/j.issn.0253-9608.2008.01.004

Zhang, Z., Miao, Y., Li, J., Liu, D., & Fang, X. (2019). Improvement effect of rainfall source control facilities on urban drainage capacity in different regions of China. *Journal of Hydrology, 579*, 124127. doi:10.1016/j.jhydrol.2019.124127

Zhao, H. Z. (1999). Fifty glorious years of urban construction in china. *Urban and Rural Development, 10*, 6–7.

Zhao, Q. G., Huang, G. Q., & Ma, Y. Q. (2016). The ecological environment conditions and construction of an ecological civilization in China. *Acta Ecologica Sinica, 36*(19), 6328–6335. doi:10.5846/stxb201410081968

Zhu, S. F., Xue, L. B., & Xu, Z. D. (2014). The development history and an analysis of status of desalination at home and abroad. *Technology of Water Treatment, 40*, 12-15+23. doi:10.16796/j.cnki.1000-3770.2014.07.004

Some reflections on water for residential uses in developed countries

Francisco González-Gómez, Miguel Á. García-Rubio and Jorge Guardiola

ABSTRACT

Although the major challenges concerning access to water are found in developing countries, the problems affecting developed countries should not be overlooked. These include non-universal access for the poorest households, deterioration in the quality of water resources, and in some cases, reluctance to accept non-conventional sources of water. Faced with this situation, it is reasonable to ask whether sufficient, appropriate efforts are being made to prevent a decline in the well-being of a growing share of the population. Finding a solution to these challenges requires a holistic approach.

Introduction

The major global challenges related to water are concentrated in developing countries, as shown by the statistics provided by the WHO/UNICEF Joint Monitoring Programme for Water Supply, Sanitation and Hygiene (WHO and UNICEF, 2017). But we should be wary of complacency regarding the situation in developed countries. On the one hand, the real situation is more complex than that reported by WHO/UNICEF (Guardiola, Gonzalez-Gomez, & Grajales, 2010; Martínez-Santos, 2017); on the other hand, it is difficult to determine the extent to which water meets human needs when the way of meeting these needs depends on the context, including cultural aspects. The relationship between water and human beings is shaped not only by facts but also by perceptions.

Therefore, this article discusses some problems that affect developed countries (though not only those): non-universal access for groups at risk of poverty and social exclusion; deterioration in the quality of water resources for numerous reasons – one of them, the emergence of non-traditional pollutants; and low public acceptance of non-conventional water resources as a way of addressing problems of scarcity. Taken together, all these problems represent a crucial challenge that needs to be tackled more decisively in the water policies of developed countries.

From this perspective, we outline the past challenges, questioning whether the decisions made to address them are good enough. Bad or inappropriate decisions may mean that people's needs regarding access to water are not being met satisfactorily in developed countries. It is essential to gain a real understanding of the challenges presented here and to propose appropriate solutions. There are two clear messages we wish to convey in this article: first, that developed countries also face challenges regarding better access to clean water for residential uses; second, that the problems identified should be addressed through well-informed and participatory processes, rather than exclusively through bureaucratic, technological approaches.

Are there really no problems of access to water in developed countries?

On 28 July 2010, the United Nations recognized drinking water and sanitation as human rights. The indicator used to measure progress in this regard is the percentage of the population with access to water for personal and domestic uses that is sufficient, safe, acceptable, physically accessible and affordable.

In developed countries, water affordability is regarded as an insignificant problem. This is at least partly because there are no statistics on affordability and water cut-offs in developed countries such as Spain. According to Jones and Moulton (2016), the lack of information on the problem of water affordability in developed countries means that it remains hidden from the public; it can thus be thought of as an invisible crisis. With limited data scattered among different institutions or simply non-existent, the problems remain unseen and are consequently difficult to address (Josset et al., 2019).

Nevertheless, there is a real problem of access to water in developed countries. The data on *average* access to water can mask affordability issues for substantial portions of the low-income groups (Martins, Quintal, Cruz, & Barata, 2016). Studies have examined this issue in developed countries, including the United States (Mack & Wrase, 2017; Teodoro, 2019), England and Wales (Bradshaw & Huby, 2013; Zetland, 2016), Belgium (Vanhille, Goedemé, Penne, Van Thielen, & Storms, 2018), Portugal (Martins, Quintal, & Antunes, 2019; Martins et al., 2016) and Spain (López-Ruiz, Tortajada, & González-Gómez, 2020; Yoon, Saurí, & Domene, 2019).

Water security can be defined as reliable access to clean water with these characteristics: access without the threat of water cut-offs; being able to pay the water bill without having to give up other basic goods; subsidized access to water in times of economic shock or prolonged financial distress; and public participation and administrative transparency at the system level. The threat of cutting off the supply might ensure the payment of those who can afford to pay their bill, but it may not be the most appropriate procedure for low-income consumers. Beyond their responsibility for service delivery, governments and water companies have an ethical duty to support their more vulnerable customers. While it is right to expect consumers to pay for the services they use, payment should not take priority over personal well-being.

In the US, with the reduction of federal funds for essential infrastructure investments, water and wastewater utilities rely more heavily on consumer revenues to finance their investments. This has recently led to 'water crises' in cities such as Baltimore and Detroit (Qureshi, 2018; Rahman, 2018), where residents unable to pay rising bills have been disconnected from water services. If water rates rise by the projected amounts over the coming years, conservative estimates predict that the percentage of US households who will not be able to pay their water bill could triple, from 11.9% to 35.6% (Mack & Wrase, 2017).

In Europe, disconnecting domestic customers from the water supply is generally allowed if they do not pay their bills. Only a few countries (Austria, France, Hungary, Ireland and the UK) prohibit the disconnection of water for main residences, hospitals and schools (EurEau, 2016). In some countries – Finland, for example – customers can also be disconnected from the network for wastewater and stormwater; however, because of environmental problems and risks, this measure is not normally implemented.

In England and Wales, the economic regulator of the water sector, Ofwat (2015), reported a 56% increase since 2012 in the number of people needing help to pay their water bills. As of the end of 2017, a total of 260,540 customers were receiving support through water companies' social tariffs. That is, about 1% of customers benefit from social tariffs, far fewer than the 12% who find their bills unaffordable (Money Advice Trust, 2018). There is an ongoing debate about the effects of the privatization of urban water services that started in the 1980s. For some authors, the introduction of privatization and greater reliance on market mechanisms has not been detrimental in terms of access to water for low-income households (Graham, 2006). For others, the result has been upward pressure on prices and restructuring of services, in ways that disadvantage the poorest in society (Bayliss & Mattioli, 2018). A similar debate is currently going on in other countries, such as Spain, where public and private management of urban water services coexist (García-Rubio, López-Ruiz, & González-Gómez, 2019; López-Ruiz et al., 2020).

Although not many countries have regulations which protect the human right to water or access to safe water for low-income families, many have assistance programmes that have proven to be effective. There are two types of measure aimed at facilitating access to safe water for low-income families (OECD, 2009): income support measures and tariff-related measures. Income support measures address the individual consumer's ability to pay from the income side, through income assistance, water services vouchers, tariff rebates and discounts, bill re-phasing and easier payment plans, and arrears forgiveness; tariff-related measures keep the size of the water bill low for certain groups, e.g. with refinement of increasing-block tariffs, tariff choice and tariff capping (OECD, 2002). Another important element is that the measures are designed to prevent the consumer from being disconnecting from an essential service.

Consumers living in extreme poverty can face significant psychological barriers to identifying themselves as being in need of social assistance (poor psychological health, isolation and shame). In such cases, they tend to favour individualistic strategies for reducing other spending and making payments on their water bills, even when this may jeopardize their ability to afford other essential goods (Ali, Bourova, & Ramsay, 2016). To more successfully tackle affordability problems, special tariff schemes should consider household income, family size and family composition (number of children) (Arbués & Barberán, 2012; Barberán & Arbués, 2009; Wichelns, 2013).

While recognizing the efforts that governments are making to ensure access to water for low-income families, an important question needs to be raised. How should we consider access to the vital minimum amount of water? As a human right, as recognized in 2010 by the United Nations (some countries accepted, some did not, and others abstained)? Or as a public benefit programme? We believe this question should be approached from different perspectives. First of all, we need transparent, reliable statistics to understand the scale of the problem in developed countries. It is reasonable to ask whether the different assistance mechanisms implemented in these countries are really reaching all the families that need them, but we simply do not have the information to answer this question. Second, it is necessary to agree how much water per person per day should be guaranteed to low-income families. Third, to comply with the United Nations' declaration of water as a human right, countries that have not yet done so must urgently incorporate this right into their national legislation. Finally, a decision must be made on how to finance water consumption for low-income families.

On this last issue, it is worth emphasizing that if consumers want good service, the water utilities must, at the very least, be able to cover the costs of the service. Universal access to water must therefore be guaranteed through public solidarity from the rest of the population.

Is the water safe to drink?

Although it mostly affects developing countries, another important challenge in developed countries relates to contaminants such as micropollutants, including microplastics and pharmaceuticals. The most worrying thing is that we cannot avoid their ingestion when we drink the water.

Since the 1970s, detailed information has been reported on the presence of microplastics in the marine environment (Carpenter, Anderson, Harvey, Miklas, & Peck, 1972; Colton, Burns, & Knapp, 1974; Gregory, 1977). The term 'microplastic' applies to a particles with an upper size limit of 5 mm and without a specified lower limit. The most abundant types are polypropylene, nylon, polystyrene, polyethylene, polycarbonate, polyvinyl chloride and polyethylene terephthalate, but acrylates, polyurethane, ethyl-vinyl acetate and polyamides have recently been found (Simon, van Alst, & Vollertsen, 2018). As research has focused on the issue more intensively since the early 2000s, microplastics are considered an emerging pollution concern; a recent study indicates that plastics can be cytotoxic to human cells (Schirinzi et al., 2017). Particles less than 130 μm in size can be translocated into human tissues, trigger a localized immune response, and release constituent monomers, toxic chemicals added during plastic production, and pollutants absorbed from the environment, including heavy metals and persistent organic pollutants like PCBs and DDT (Cox et al., 2019). The ubiquity of microplastics across ecosystems has been demonstrated by recent monitoring studies, which have established that, in addition to marine environments, microplastics are found in a variety of surface freshwater bodies throughout the world, e.g. in Asia (Di & Wang, 2018; Free et al., 2014; Su et al., 2016; Wang, Ndungu, Li, & Wang, 2017; Zhang, Gong, Lv, Xiong, & Wu, 2015; Zhao, Zhu, & Li, 2015; Zhao, Zhu, Wang, & Li, 2014), Europe (Dris et al., 2015; Faure, Corbaz, Baecher, Neuhaus, & de Alencastro, 2012; Fischer, Paglialonga, Czech, & Tamminga, 2016; Lechner et al., 2014; Leslie, Brandsma, Van Velzen, & Vethaak, 2017; Mani, Hauk, Walter, & Burkhardt-Holm, 2015; Sadri & Thompson, 2014), America (Anderson et al., 2017; Baldwin, Corsi, & Mason, 2016; Eriksen et al., 2013; Lima, Costa, & Barletta, 2014; McCormick, Hoellein, Mason, Schluep, & Kelly, 2014; Moore, Lattin, & Zellers, 2011) and Africa (Naidoo, Glassom, & Smit, 2015).

Thus, urban water supplies using surface water as a raw water resource can be affected by the presence of microplastic particles. Although this has not been widely studied, there is evidence of microplastic contamination of tap water in both developing countries (Cuba, Ecuador, India, Indonesia, Lebanon, Uganda) and developed countries (England, France, Germany, Ireland, Italy, Slovakia, Switzerland, US) (Kosuth, Mason, & Wattenberg, 2018). Nor does bottled mineral water appear to be a safer alternative (Mason, Welch, & Neratko, 2018; Oßmann et al., 2018; Schymanski, Goldbeck, Humpf, & Fürst, 2018); in fact, Cox et al. (2019) estimate that people whose water intake comes exclusively from bottled water can ingest about 90,000 microplastic particles per year, compared to 4000 particles ingested by those who consume only tap water.

More studies are needed of the changes in microplastics during drinking water treatment and of their possible appearance in tap water. Microplastics in water is an emerging area of concern; it is thus necessary to establish a research agenda that includes a review of the available evidence and agrees on analytical methods that are sufficiently sensitive to nanoplastics (those in the range of 1 to 300 μm). In addition, a more exhaustive assessment of the risk to human health is required, including the development of analytical methods to identify the exact composition of the microplastics detected in drinking water. Without such measures, it will not be possible to properly manage and control the associated chemical and toxicological effects.

Water pollution by pharmaceuticals (mainly analgesics, antipyretics, psychiatric drugs, antibiotics, lipid regulators and antineoplastics) has also been acknowledged as an environmental problem (WHO, 2012). Effluent from sewage treatment plants is the predominant pathway through which pharmaceuticals enter surface water and accumulate in aquatic environments (Luo et al., 2014).

Many pharmaceuticals are not effectively removed by conventional water treatment. Although higher removal rates (above 99%) can be achieved through more advanced processes for treating water intended for human consumption, including granular activated carbon, membrane technologies, ozonation and ultraviolet radiation, some compounds are not completely eliminated by these processes (Jones, Lester, & Voulvoulis, 2005).

Despite assurances from the WHO (2012) that trace concentrations of pharmaceuticals in drinking water are very unlikely to pose risks to human health, knowledge gaps exist in terms of the risks of long-term exposure to low concentrations of pharmaceuticals and the combined effects of mixtures of pharmaceuticals. A growing number of new chemicals is being introduced annually, making water quality management extremely difficult (Biswas & Tortajada, 2019).

Technologies currently used in wastewater treatment plants are not entirely capable of removing micropollutants (Browne, Galloway, & Thompson, 2007), so they end up in the aquatic environment. The preferred solution, and the most sustainable one, is to prevent them from entering the water cycle in the first place. Legislation should be implemented based on the source control approach and the precautionary principle. Therefore, there is a need to address two fundamental challenges concerning the quality of the water consumed in developed countries. First, we need to know exactly what substances we are ingesting with our drinking water. Monitoring is costly and not always carried out as often as desirable; nor are measurements taken of all the parameters laid down in the respective regulations. And national regulations may fail to address important health-related parameters. Second, we must accurately determine the long-term health risks of consuming certain substances that are not eliminated by the current processes of raw water purification, wastewater treatment and production of reclaimed water.

Are non-conventional sources of water really a panacea?

Water stress occurs in many developed countries, including Australia, the southern US, Spain, Italy and Greece (Gassert, Luck, Landis, Reig, & Shiao, 2014; Mekonnen & Hoekstra, 2016). There are numerous strategies for alleviating water stress. In general, one option is through measures that promote a more efficient and sustainable use of water. Non-tariff measures are more efficient in terms of water conservation and face less public opposition than tariff measures (Garcia-Valiñas, Martínez-Espiñeira, & To, 2015; Tortajada, González-Gómez, Biswas, & Buurman, 2019; Wichman, Taylor, & Von Haefen, 2016). A newer alternative is the use of non-conventional water sources: desalination, reclaimed water and rainwater.

We question whether desalination and reclaimed water are good solutions to satisfy human needs. Some studies have found that desalinated water and reclaimed water are not a perfect substitute for the current tap water supply (Hurlimann & Dolnicar, 2016; Schmid & Bogner, 2018). Drinking, cooking and personal hygiene are considered the least desirable end-uses for desalinated and reclaimed water; and these are precisely the uses for which water is a basic good (Dolnicar & Hurlimann, 2010; Hui & Cain, 2018). In general, the use of desalinated and reclaimed water is more widely accepted when there is no bodily contact or ingestion involved (Dolnicar & Hurlimann, 2010; Hui & Cain, 2018).

The lower acceptance of these sources of water has practical consequences: people rejecting the use of reclaimed water (Fielding, Dolnicar, & Schultz, 2019; Hurlimann & Dolnicar, 2010) and resorting to strategies such as drinking bottled water (Fragkou & McEvoy, 2016); and desalination plants with excess capacity (Green & Bell, 2019; Turner et al., 2016). Bottled water enjoys greater acceptance than desalinated water and reclaimed water (Dolnicar & Schäfer, 2009), and demand for it increases when the population perceives the tap water as unsafe (Javidi & Pierce, 2018; Johnstone & Serret, 2012).

There may also be risks associated with non-conventional sources of water, including desalinated water and reclaimed water. The first is a financial risk. Although the cost of reverse osmosis continues to drop, the production costs are still quite high (Bell, 2015; Bhojwani, Topolski, Mukherjee, Sengupta, & El-Halwagi, 2019). Moreover, since consumers do not accept water that is sold at a higher price and also perceived by some to be of poorer quality, not enough income is always generated to cover the costs. The situation is critical when facilities have large excess capacity, at times as much as 100% (García-Rubio & Guardiola, 2012; Green & Bell, 2019; March, 2015; Turner et al., 2016).

When wastewater has not been treated properly, there are also environmental risks. The production of water by osmosis, the least harmful desalination and reclamation technology in environmental terms, entails high energy consumption and release of CO_2, the highest of the different alternative water supply systems (Bhojwani et al., 2019; Raluy, Serra, & Uche, 2005). Desalination also generates brine as a waste product (Jones, Qadir, van Vliet, Smakhtin, & Kang, 2019; Petersen, Frank, Paytan, & Bar-Zeev, 2018).[1] There are also risks related to bottled water. There is no assurance that it is completely safe, as it is not always regulated. And its production may have a larger carbon footprint than centralized drinking water supply systems (Godskesen, Meron, & Rygaard, 2018).

Although the United Nations (2017) advocates the provision of reclaimed water for drinking uses, this option is less widespread today. The first experiences were in Windhoek, where reclaimed water is already a standard practice. Regarding desalination, there is a growing number of plants in many parts of the world, including Australia, Israel, the United States and Spain. Although it is true that desalination plays an important role in water security during drought in Australia and Spain, the situation is somewhat paradoxical. Even though it is a less preferred source of water, with high financial and environmental costs, different actors and forces are driving the construction of new desalination plants.

First, large companies have legitimate interests in the sector. They have developed the required technology and know-how, and have already consolidated their position in the water treatment and purification industry. Desalination is an industry with high profitability for construction companies, and currently has a global production capacity of 97.4 million m^3 of water per day (Global Water Intelligence and International Desalination Association, 2018). The desalination lobby has been very effective in its advocacy and promotion, including in Australia and Spain (Fuenfschilling & Truffer, 2016; Tal, 2011). Second, there may be political interests at work. Political actors act rationally when they deliberately pursue electoral advantages (Dowding, 2019). The politician may prefer to develop desalination plants involving a 'ribbon cutting' (Kingdom, Liemberger, & Marin, 2006) over other actions, such as restricting water for non-residential uses or engaging in efforts to reduce unregistered water use in supply networks (González-Gómez, García-Rubio, & Guardiola, 2011; Kingdom et al., 2006).

It is essential to conduct public consultations on acceptance of reclaimed or desalinated water before project development (Marks, 2006; Russell & Hampton, 2006). The public may prefer measures for saving water and using it efficiently, which would mean consuming their same tap water. Possible measures include a change in consumption habits and the use of domestic water-saving technologies, which could be continually incentivized through awareness-raising campaigns. They could also entail investment to reduce leakage from the public water networks and reduce apparent losses. When available, various rainwater harvesting techniques may help delay the need for other, less accepted water supply options (Steffen, Jensen, Pomeroy, & Burian, 2013).

Summary and conclusions

There are a number of global challenges concerning water, including issues related to safety, access, availability and sustainability. Regarding residential uses, the challenges are undoubtedly more apparent in developing countries. However, there are also challenges in developed countries. This article provides a reflection on three specific issues there: access to safe water for low-income families; protecting human health by ensuring a supply of safe water; and desalinated and reclaimed water as non-conventional sources aimed at guaranteeing domestic water supply.

In developed countries, a primary challenge is to ensure universal access to adequate quantities of safe water. Despite international recognition of the human right to water, affordability problems clearly still afflict populations at risk of poverty and social exclusion in developed countries, including Spain. In fact, the 2008 global financial crisis dramatically increased the percentage of the population in a situation of vulnerability. It is paradoxical that a globalized human society declaring equality of rights is facing growing social and geographic polarization, with part of that society lacking basic resources for survival, such as water.

Ultimately, the lack of global embodiment of the human right to water in national legislation makes it difficult for the most vulnerable populations to defend this right; nor are there any widespread, standardized mechanisms of social action to reduce problems of affordability. The most dramatic breaches of the human right to water can be seen in cases where water supply is cut off due to non-payment, with only a few countries legally prohibiting disconnection or establishing a necessary minimum amount of water for domestic use. If a developed country does not guarantee the right of access to water for its population, is it really a developed country?

And the water supply not only has to be affordable, it must also meet quality conditions. In this regard, the contamination of water by emerging micropollutants is becoming an ever-greater challenge, in a context where treatment processes are not equipped with the technologies required to eliminate these new forms of pollution. In any case, the type and the extent of the problem we are facing remain unclear. For more clarity on this issue, more widespread analyses of pollutants are needed, as well as a determination of the long-term health effects of many of the substances found in water which are not currently eliminated by the usual treatment processes. This is a growing problem, as there are more and more substances being produced that degrade the quality of water. However, countries are generally more concerned about water quantity than quality.

One more challenge is to respond to the growing problem of water stress. There is a growing tendency to resort to technological solutions to alleviate this problem, such as desalination or reclamation. Public acceptance of these types of sources, low in some places at present, and their high costs, make them less feasible for wide-scale use. The public prefer water from conventional sources and even harvested rainwater. The supply of desalinated and reclaimed water when not strictly necessary, resulting from decisions that do not take into account the opinion of all the actors involved, can cause preventable environmental impacts and inefficient allocation of resources. Although desalination and reclamation plants consider efficiency and conservation measures, other alternatives may be more appropriate in terms of efficiency and conservation of water resources and protection of the environment.

We are not disparaging the idea of finding a solution to the problem of water stress through technological ingenuity, but we do wish to underline that it is sometimes necessary to seek out other types of solutions. In addition, decision-making processes and water supply policies must always take into account the public interest. Therefore, public behaviour that serves private or business interests must be constrained. This is fundamental in contexts where there is increasing pressure on available water, and financial resources are limited.

Finally, we emphasize the importance of a more holistic approach to the various problems related to water availability. Policy, managerial, technical and sociological perspectives should be considered, and when making decisions it should be borne in mind that access to high-quality water is a universal right.

Note

1. Brine is also produced in normal wastewater treatments, although in smaller amounts.

Acknowledgments

We thank Cecilia Tortajada and Asit Biswas for their comments on various versions of this research. Of course, all possible mistakes are the responsibility of the authors.

Disclosure statement

No potential conflict of interest was reported by the authors.

Funding

This work was supported by the the Spanish Agencia Estatal de Investigación and the European Regional Development Fund (project ECO2017-86822-R); the Regional Government of Andalusia (project B-SEJ-018-UGR18) and the University of Granada (Plan Propio. Unidad Científica de Excelencia: Desigualdad, Derechos Humanos y Sostenibilidad -DEHUSO-).

ORCID

Francisco González-Gómez http://orcid.org/0000-0002-9800-4944
Miguel Á. García-Rubio http://orcid.org/0000-0002-2546-7163
Jorge Guardiola http://orcid.org/0000-0002-3594-9756

References

Ali, P., Bourova, E., & Ramsay, I. (2016). The role of legal hardship protections in coping with debt problems: Insights from a survey of consumers. *Competition and Consumer Law Journal, 24*(2), 77–100.

Anderson, P. J., Warrack, S., Langen, V., Challis, J. K., Hanson, M. L., & Rennie, M. D. (2017). Microplastic contamination in Lake Winnipeg, Canada. *Environmental Pollution, 225*, 223–231. doi:10.1016/j.envpol.2017.02.072

Arbués, F., & Barberán, R. (2012). Tariffs for urban water services in Spain: Household size and equity. *International Journal of Water Resources Development, 28*(1), 123–140. doi:10.1080/07900627.2012.642235

Baldwin, A. K., Corsi, S. R., & Mason, S. A. (2016). Plastic debris in 29 Great Lakes tributaries: Relations to watershed attributes and hydrology. *Environmental Science & Technology, 50*(19), 10377–10385. doi:10.1021/acs.est.6b02917

Barberán, R., & Arbués, F. (2009). Equity in domestic water rates design. *Water Resources Management, 23*(10), 2101. doi:10.1007/s11269-008-9372-3

Bayliss, K., & Mattioli, G. (2018). *Privatisation, inequality and poverty in the UK: Briefing prepared for UN Rapporteur on extreme poverty and human rights* (Sustainability Research Institute Papers No. 116). Leeds, UK: University of Leeds.

Bell, S. (2015). Renegotiating urban water. *Progress in Planning, 96*, 1–28. doi:10.1016/j.progress.2013.09.001

Bhojwani, S., Topolski, K., Mukherjee, R., Sengupta, D., & El-Halwagi, M. M. (2019). Technology review and data analysis for cost assessment of water treatment systems. *Science of the Total Environment, 651*, 2749–2761. doi:10.1016/j.scitotenv.2018.09.363

Biswas, A. K., & Tortajada, C. (2019). Water quality management: A globally neglected issue. *International Journal of Water Resources Development, 35*(6), 913–916. doi:10.1080/07900627.2019.1670506

Bradshaw, J., & Huby, M. (2013). Water poverty in England and Wales. *Journal of Poverty and Social Justice, 21*(2), 137–148. doi:10.1332/175982713X669835

Browne, M. A., Galloway, T., & Thompson, R. (2007). Microplastic: An emerging contaminant of potential concern? *Integrated Environmental Assessment and Management: An International Journal, 3*(4), 559–561. doi:10.1002/ieam.5630030412

Carpenter, E. J., Anderson, S. J., Harvey, G. R., Miklas, H. P., & Peck, B. B. (1972). Polystyrene spherules in coastal waters. *Science, 178*(4062), 749–750. doi:10.1126/science.178.4062.749

Colton, J. B., Burns, B. R., & Knapp, F. D. (1974). Plastic particles in surface water of the northwestern Atlantic. *Science, 185*(4150), 491–497. doi:10.1126/science.185.4150.491

Cox, K. D., Covernton, G. A., Davies, H. L., Dower, J. F., Juanes, F., & Dudas, S. E. (2019). Human consumption of microplastics. *Environmental Science & Technology, 53*(12), 7068–7074. doi:10.1021/acs.est.9b01517

Di, M., & Wang, J. (2018). Microplastics in surface waters and sediments of the Three Gorges Reservoir, China. *Science of the Total Environment, 616*, 1620–1627. doi:10.1016/j.scitotenv.2017.10.150

Dolnicar, S., & Hurlimann, A. (2010). Desalinated versus recycled water: What does the public think? *Sustainability Science and Engineering, 2*, 375–388.

Dolnicar, S., & Schäfer, A. I. (2009). Desalinated versus recycled water: Public perceptions and profiles of the accepters. *Journal of Environmental Management, 90*(2), 888–900. doi:10.1016/j.jenvman.2008.02.003

Dowding, K. (2019). *Rational choice and political power*. UK: Bristol University Press.

Dris, R., Gasperi, J., Rocher, V., Saad, M., Renault, N., & Tassin, B. (2015). Microplastic contamination in an urban area: A case study in Greater Paris. *Environmental Chemistry, 12*(5), 592–599. doi:10.1071/EN14167

Eriksen, M., Mason, S., Wilson, S., Box, C., Zellers, A., Edwards, W., … Amato, S. (2013). Microplastic pollution in the surface waters of the Laurentian Great Lakes. *Marine Pollution Bulletin, 77*(1–2), 177–182. doi:10.1016/j.marpolbul.2013.10.007

EurEau. (2016, August 26). *Access to water and measures in case of non-payment* (Briefing note). Brussels: European Federation of National Associations of Water and Wastewater Services.

Faure, F., Corbaz, M., Baecher, H., Neuhaus, V., & de Alencastro, L. (2012). Pollution due to plastics and microplastics in Lake Geneva and in the Mediterranean Sea. *Archives des Sciences, 65*, 157–164.

Fielding, K. S., Dolnicar, S., & Schultz, T. (2019). Public acceptance of recycled water. *International Journal of Water Resources Development, 35*(4), 551–586. doi:10.1080/07900627.2017.1419125

Fischer, E. K., Paglialonga, L., Czech, E., & Tamminga, M. (2016). Microplastic pollution in lakes and lake shoreline sediments: A case study on Lake Bolsena and Lake Chiusi (central Italy). *Environmental Pollution, 213*, 648–657. doi:10.1016/j.envpol.2016.03.012

Fragkou, M. C., & McEvoy, J. (2016). Trust matters: Why augmenting water supplies via desalination may not overcome perceptual water scarcity. *Desalination, 397*, 1–8. doi:10.1016/j.desal.2016.06.007

Free, C. M., Jensen, O. P., Mason, S. A., Eriksen, M., Williamson, N. J., & Boldgiv, B. (2014). High-levels of microplastics pollution in a large, remote, mountain lake. *Marine Pollution Bulletin, 85*(1), 156–163. doi:10.1016/j.marpolbul.2014.06.001

Fuenfschilling, L., & Truffer, B. (2016). The interplay of institutions, actors and technologies in socio-technical systems: An analysis of transformations in the Australian urban water sector. *Technological Forecasting and Social Change, 103*, 298–312. doi:10.1016/j.techfore.2015.11.023

García-Rubio, M. A., & Guardiola, J. (2012). Desalination in Spain: A growing alternative for water supply. *International Journal of Water Resources Development, 28*(1), 171–186. doi:10.1080/07900627.2012.642245

García-Rubio, M. A., López-Ruiz, S., & González-Gómez, F. (2019). Derechos humanos en España: Protección del derecho al agua en familias con problemas de asequibilidad por riesgo de pobreza y exclusión social. Análisis crítico para una reforma legal. *Agua y Territorio, 13*, 103–114. doi:10.17561/at.13.4381

Garcia-Valiñas, M. A., Martínez-Espiñeira, R., & To, H. (2015). The use of non-pricing instruments to manage residential water demand: What have we learned? In Q. Grafton, K. A. Daniell, C. Nauges, J. D. Rinaudo, & N. W. W. Chan (Eds.), *Understanding and managing urban water in transition* (pp. 269–281). Dordrecht: Springer.

Gassert, F., Luck, M., Landis, M., Reig, P., & Shiao, T. (2014). *Aqueduct global maps 2.1: Constructing decision-relevant global water risk indicators* (Working Paper). Washington, DC: World Resources Institute. Retrieved from http://www.wri.org/publication/aqueduct-globalmaps-21-indicators

Global Water Intelligence and International Desalination Association. (2018). *31st worldwide desalting plant inventory*. UK: GWI and IDA.

Godskesen, B., Meron, N., & Rygaard, M. (2018). LCA of drinking water supply. In M. Z. Hauschild, R. K. Rosenbaum, & S. I. Olsen (Eds.), *Life cycle assessment* (pp. 835–860). Cham: Springer.

González-Gómez, F., García-Rubio, M. A., & Guardiola, J. (2011). Why is non-revenue water so high in so many cities? *International Journal of Water Resources Development, 27*(2), 345–360. doi:10.1080/07900627.2010.548317

Graham, C. (2006). The politics of necessity: Electricity and water in Great Britain. *Journal of Consumer Policy, 29*(4), 435–448. doi:10.1007/s10603-006-9020-3

Green, A., & Bell, S. (2019). Neo-hydraulic water management: An international comparison of idle desalination plants. *Urban Water Journal, 16*, 125–135. doi:10.1080/1573062X.2019.1637003

Gregory, M. R. (1977). Plastic pellets on New Zealand beaches. *Marine Pollution Bulletin, 8*(4), 82–84. doi:10.1016/0025-326X(77)90193-X

Guardiola, J., Gonzalez-Gomez, F., & Grajales, A. L. (2010). Is access to water as good as the data claim? Case study of Yucatán. *International Journal of Water Resources Development, 26*(2), 219–233. doi:10.1080/07900621003655692

Hui, I., & Cain, B. E. (2018). Overcoming psychological resistance toward using recycled water in California. *Water and Environment Journal, 32*(1), 17–25. doi:10.1111/wej.2018.32.issue-1

Hurlimann, A., & Dolnicar, S. (2010). When public opposition defeats alternative water projects: The case of Toowoomba Australia. *Water Research, 44*(1), 287–297. doi:10.1016/j.watres.2009.09.020

Hurlimann, A., & Dolnicar, S. (2016). Public acceptance and perceptions of alternative water sources: A comparative study in nine locations. *International Journal of Water Resources Development, 32*(4), 650–673. doi:10.1080/07900627.2016.1143350

Javidi, A., & Pierce, G. (2018). US households' perception of drinking water as unsafe and its consequences: Examining alternative choices to the tap. *Water Resources Research, 54*(9), 6100–6113. doi:10.1029/2017WR022186

Johnstone, N., & Serret, Y. (2012). Determinants of bottled and purified water consumption: Results based on an OECD survey. *Water Policy, 14*(4), 668–679. doi:10.2166/wp.2011.048

Jones, E., Qadir, M., van Vliet, M. T., Smakhtin, V., & Kang, S. M. (2019). The state of desalination and brine production: A global outlook. *Science of the Total Environment, 657*(20), 1343–1356. doi:10.1016/j.scitotenv.2018.12.076

Jones, O. A., Lester, J. N., & Voulvoulis, N. (2005). Pharmaceuticals: A threat to drinking water? *TRENDS in Biotechnology, 23*(4), 163–167. doi:10.1016/j.tibtech.2005.02.001

Jones, P. A., & Moulton, A. (2016). *The invisible crisis: Water unaffordability in the United States* (Vol. 6). Cambridge, MA: Unitarian Universalist Service Committee.

Josset, L., Allaire, M., Hayek, C., Rising, J., Thomas, C., & Lall, U. (2019). The US water data gap: A survey of state-level water data platforms to inform the development of a national water portal. *Earth's Future, 7*(4), 433–449. doi:10.1029/2018EF001063

Kingdom, B., Liemberger, R., & Marin, P. (2006). *The challenge of reducing non-revenue water in developing countries: How the private sector can help: A look at performance-based service contracting* (Water Supply and Sanitation Board Discussion Paper No. 8). Washington, DC: World Bank.

Kosuth, M., Mason, S. A., & Wattenberg, E. V. (2018). Anthropogenic contamination of tap water, beer, and sea salt. *PloS ONE, 13*(4), e0194970. doi:10.1371/journal.pone.0194970

Lechner, A., Keckeis, H., Lumesberger-Loisl, F., Zens, B., Krusch, R., Tritthart, M., … Schludermann, E. (2014). The Danube so colourful: A potpourri of plastic litter outnumbers fish larvae in Europe's second largest river. *Environmental Pollution, 188*, 177–181. doi:10.1016/j.envpol.2014.02.006

Leslie, H. A., Brandsma, S. H., Van Velzen, M. J. M., & Vethaak, A. D. (2017). Microplastics en route: Field measurements in the Dutch river delta and Amsterdam canals, wastewater treatment plants, North Sea sediments and biota. *Environment International, 101*, 133–142. doi:10.1016/j.envint.2017.01.018

Lima, A. R. A., Costa, M. F., & Barletta, M. (2014). Distribution patterns of microplastics within the plankton of a tropical estuary. *Environmental Research, 132*, 146–155. doi:10.1016/j.envres.2014.03.031

López-Ruiz, S., Tortajada, C., & González-Gómez, J. (2020). Is the human right to water sufficiently protected in Spain? Affordability and governance concerns. *Utilities Policy*. 63, 101003. doi:10.1016/j.jup.2019.101003

Luo, Y., Guo, W., Ngo, H. H., Nghiem, L. D., Hai, F. I., Zhang, J., … Wang, X. C. (2014). A review on the occurrence of micropollutants in the aquatic environment and their fate and removal during wastewater treatment. *Science of the Total Environment, 473–474*, 619–641. doi:10.1016/j.scitotenv.2013.12.065

Mack, E. A., & Wrase, S. (2017). Correction: A burgeoning crisis? A nationwide assessment of the geography of water affordability in the United States. *PloS ONE, 12*(4), e0176645. doi:10.1371/journal.pone.0176645

Mani, T., Hauk, A., Walter, U., & Burkhardt-Holm, P. (2015). Microplastics profile along the Rhine River. *Scientific Reports, 5*, 17988. doi:10.1038/srep17988

March, H. (2015). The politics, geography, and economics of desalination: A critical review. *Wiley Interdisciplinary Reviews: Water, 2*(3), 231–243. doi:10.1002/wat2.1073

Marks, J. S. (2006). Taking the public seriously: The case of potable and non potable reuse. *Desalination, 187*, 137–147. doi:10.1016/j.desal.2005.04.074

Martínez-Santos, P. (2017). Does 91% of the world's population really have 'sustainable access to safe drinking water'? *International Journal of Water Resources Development, 33*(4), 514–533. doi:10.1080/07900627.2017.1298517

Martins, R., Quintal, C., & Antunes, M. (2019). Making ends meet: Actual versus potential joint affordability of utility services. *Utilities Policy, 56*, 120–126. doi:10.1016/j.jup.2018.12.002

Martins, R., Quintal, C., Cruz, L., & Barata, E. (2016). Water affordability issues in developed countries: The relevance of micro approaches. *Utilities Policy, 43*(Part A), 117–123. doi:10.1016/j.jup.2016.04.012

Mason, S. A., Welch, V. G., & Neratko, J. (2018). Synthetic polymer contamination in bottled water. *Frontiers in Chemistry, 6*(407). doi:10.3389/fchem.2018.00407

McCormick, A., Hoellein, T. J., Mason, S. A., Schluep, J., & Kelly, J. J. (2014). Microplastic is an abundant and distinct microbial habitat in an urban river. *Environmental Science & Technology, 48*(20), 11863–11871. doi:10.1021/es503610r

Mekonnen, M. M., & Hoekstra, A. Y. (2016). Four billion people facing severe water scarcity. *Science Advances, 2*(2), e1500323. doi:10.1126/sciadv.1500323

Money Advice Trust. (2018). *A decade in debt: How the UK's debt landscape has changed from 2008 to 2018, as seen at National Debtline*. London, UK: Author.

Moore, C. J., Lattin, G. L., & Zellers, A. F. (2011). Quantity and type of plastic debris flowing from two urban rivers to coastal waters and beaches of Southern California. *Revista de Gestão Costeira Integrada / Journal of Integrated Coastal Zone Management, 11*(1), 65–73. doi:10.5894/rgci194

Naidoo, T., Glassom, D., & Smit, A. J. (2015). Plastic pollution in five urban estuaries of KwaZulu-Natal, South Africa. *Marine Pollution Bulletin, 101*(1), 473–480. doi:10.1016/j.marpolbul.2015.09.044

OECD. (2002). *Social issues in the provision and pricing of water services*. Paris: Author.

OECD. (2009). *Managing water for all: An OECD perspective on pricing and financing: Key messages for policy makers*. Paris: Author.

Ofwat. (2015). *Affordability and debt 2014–2015*. Birmingham, UK: Water Services Regulation Authority.

Oßmann, B. E., Sarau, G., Holtmannspötter, H., Pischetsrieder, M., Christiansen, S. H., & Dicke, W. (2018). Small-sized microplastics and pigmented particles in bottled mineral water. *Water Research, 141*, 307–316. doi:10.1016/j.watres.2018.05.027

Petersen, K. L., Frank, H., Paytan, A., & Bar-Zeev, E. (2018). Impacts of seawater desalination on coastal environments. In G. Gude (Ed.), *Sustainable desalination handbook* (pp. 437–463).

Qureshi, H. N. (2018). *Binding civil and civic infrastructure: The need for transparency and accountability in Baltimore's water crisis* (Thesis). M.C.P., Department of Urban Studies and Planning, Massachusetts Institute of Technology, Cambridge, MA.

Rahman, K. S. (2018). Infrastructural exclusion and the fight for the city: Power, democracy, and the case of America's water crisis. *Harvard Civil Rights-Civil Liberties Law Review, 53*(1), 533–562.

Raluy, R. G., Serra, L., & Uche, J. (2005). Life cycle assessment of water production technologies, Part 1: Life cycle assessment of different commercial desalination technologies (MSF, MED, RO). *International Journal of Life Cycle Assessment*, *10*(4), 285–293. doi:10.1065/lca2004.09.179.1

Russell, S., & Hampton, G. (2006). Challenges in understanding public responses and providing effective public consultation on water reuse. *Desalination*, *187*(1–3), 215–227. doi:10.1016/j.desal.2005.04.081

Sadri, S. S., & Thompson, R. C. (2014). On the quantity and composition of floating plastic debris entering and leaving the Tamar Estuary, Southwest England. *Marine Pollution Bulletin*, *81*(1), 55–60. doi:10.1016/j.marpolbul.2014.02.020

Schirinzi, G. F., Pérez-Pomeda, I., Sanchís, J., Rossini, C., Farré, M., & Barceló, D. (2017). Cytotoxic effects of commonly used nanomaterials and microplastics on cerebral and epithelial human cells. *Environmental Research*, *159*, 579–587. doi:10.1016/j.envres.2017.08.043

Schmid, S., & Bogner, F. (2018). What Germany's university beginners think about water reuse. *Water*, *10*(6), 731. doi:10.3390/w10060731

Schymanski, D., Goldbeck, C., Humpf, H. U., & Fürst, P. (2018). Analysis of microplastics in water by micro-Raman spectroscopy: Release of plastic particles from different packaging into mineral water. *Water Research*, *129*(1), 154–162. doi:10.1016/j.watres.2017.11.011

Simon, M., van Alst, N., & Vollertsen, J. (2018). Quantification of microplastic mass and removal rates at wastewater treatment plants applying Focal Plane Array (FPA)-based Fourier Transform Infrared (FT-IR) imaging. *Water Research*, *142*, 1–9. doi:10.1016/j.watres.2018.05.019

Steffen, J., Jensen, M., Pomeroy, C. A., & Burian, S. J. (2013). Water supply and stormwater management benefits of residential rainwater harvesting in US cities. *Journal of the American Water Resources Association*, *49*(4), 810–824. doi:10.1111/jawr.12038

Su, L., Xue, Y., Li, L., Yang, D., Kolandhasamy, P., Li, D., & Shi, H. (2016). Microplastics in Taihu Lake, China. *Environmental Pollution*, *216*, 711–719. doi:10.1016/j.envpol.2016.06.036

Tal, A. (2011). The desalination debate: Lessons learned thus far. *Environment: Science and Policy for Sustainable Development*, *53*(5), 34–48.

Teodoro, M. P. (2019). Water and sewer affordability in the United States. *AWWA Water Science*, *1*(2), e1129. doi:10.1002/aws2.v1.2

Tortajada, C., González-Gómez, F., Biswas, A. K., & Buurman, J. (2019). Water demand management strategies for water-scarce cities: The case of Spain. *Sustainable Cities and Society*, *45*, 649–656. doi:10.1016/j.scs.2018.11.044

Turner, A., White, S., Chong, J., Dickinson, M., Cooley, H., & Donnelly, K. (2016). *Managing drought: Learning from Australia. Some very large plants*. Sydney: Institute for Sustainable Futures, University of Technology.

United Nations. (2010, July). *Resolution A/RES/64/292*. New York: Author.

United Nations. (2017). *The United Nations world water development report 2017. Wastewater: The untapped resource*. United Nations World Water Assessment Programme. Paris: UNESCO.

Vanhille, J., Goedemé, T., Penne, T., Van Thielen, L., & Storms, B. (2018). Measuring water affordability in developed economies: The added value of a needs-based approach. *Journal of Environmental Management*, *217*, 611–620. doi:10.1016/j.jenvman.2018.03.106

Wang, W., Ndungu, A. W., Li, Z., & Wang, J. (2017). Microplastics pollution in inland freshwaters of China: A case study in urban surface waters of Wuhan, China. *Science of the Total Environment*, *575*(1), 1369–1374. doi:10.1016/j.scitotenv.2016.09.213

WHO. (2012). *Pharmaceuticals in drinking-water*. Geneva: World Health Organization.

WHO and UNICEF. (2017). *Progress on drinking water, sanitation and hygiene: 2017 update and SDG baselines*. Geneva: World Health Organization and United Nations Children's Fund.

Wichelns, D. (2013). Enhancing the performance of water prices and tariff structures in achieving socially desirable outcomes. *International Journal of Water Resources Development*, *29*(3), 310–326. doi:10.1080/07900627.2012.721675

Wichman, C. J., Taylor, L. O., & Von Haefen, R. H. (2016). Conservation policies: Who responds to price and who responds to prescription? *Journal of Environmental Economics and Management*, *79*, 114–134. doi:10.1016/j.jeem.2016.07.001

Yoon, H., Saurí, D., & Domene, E. (2019). The water-energy vulnerability in the Barcelona Metropolitan Area. *Energy and Buildings, 199*, 176–189. In Press. doi:10.1016/j.enbuild.2019.06.039

Zetland, D. (2016). The struggle for residential water metering in England and Wales. *Water Alternatives, 9*(1), 120–138.

Zhang, K., Gong, W., Lv, J., Xiong, X., & Wu, C. (2015). Accumulation of floating microplastics behind the Three Gorges Dam. *Environmental Pollution, 204*, 117–123. doi:10.1016/j.envpol.2015.04.023

Zhao, S., Zhu, L., & Li, D. (2015). Microplastic in three urban estuaries, China. *Environmental Pollution, 206*, 597–604. doi:10.1016/j.envpol.2015.08.027

Zhao, S., Zhu, L., Wang, T., & Li, D. (2014). Suspended microplastics in the surface water of the Yangtze Estuary System, China: First observations on occurrence, distribution. *Marine Pollution Bulletin, 86*(1–2), 562–568. doi:10.1016/j.marpolbul.2014.06.032

Can water professionals do more?

Michael Rouse

ABSTRACT

Based on case studies, the author identifies some critical elements for successful water services. The article reviews some policy aspects, namely the need for sustainable cost recovery, that piped supply is the best option in urban areas, and that there is no viable alternative to continuous (24/7) water supply for achieving sustainable services. Although water professionals are justified in having promoted, and in continuing to promote, these policies, they have failed to communicate these critical elements to government decision makers. The author suggests a possible route to correcting this failure.

Introduction

In celebrating a major milestone in the life of Asit Biswas, a great thinker who has always challenged 'established wisdom', it is appropriate to consider whether we water professionals are making a difference. All of us at one time or another have believed that we know what needs to be done to achieve universal access to sustainable water and sanitation services. Equally, we all have had times when we have been frustrated by lack of progress 'on the ground'. We might think 'if only the politicians would focus on the steps necessary for reform'; or 'if only the donors would provide more support to capacity building'; or 'if only the academics would give more attention to the application of their research'; or 'if only the operational managers were prepared to adopt new thinking'; or this or that. It is always 'they' who need to do something. Do we as individuals stop to consider whether we are pursuing the right approach, or if is there anything else we might be doing? Do we give enough attention to what works and why, and equally important, go beyond our preconceived ideas to really understand why there is a lack of progress?

Where should we start on this professional self-assessment? There have been good intentions in the form of international initiatives and targets, beginning in the 1960s and through the Water Decade, the Millennium Development Goals (MDGs) and currently the Sustainable Development Goals. We know that in spite of these commendable attempts to bring focus to needs (Rouse & El Achi, 2019), the 'holy grail' of universal access is still a long way away.

This article considers what has been achieved and the associated success factors. It looks at the challenges ahead and whether more of the same will be sufficient. Are there alternative approaches, and in particular, what else should water professionals do? Due to rapid urbanization, the high cost of infrastructure and the poverty and slum challenge in developing countries, the focus is on urban systems. The discussion centres around water supply and not sanitation. However, some parallels with wastewater are mentioned.

Measures of improvement

The Joint Monitoring Programme's (2017) report on the MDGs concluded that the goal of halving the population without a sustainable water supply had been met, although there had been less success with sanitation. There were wide variations in access improvement, with lower success in parts of Africa. There were inaccuracies in reporting, and it was recognized that the quality of monitoring of drinking water quality was not reliable and that the JMP report undercounted the people without access to safe drinking water (Bartram et al., 2014). The metrics have been improved (Bain et al., 2018) for Sustainable Development Goal (SDG) 6.1, which followed the MDGs and which aims for universal access by 2030. Achieving true sustainability, with continuity of supply for generations following 2030, also needs to be considered. There is limited information on the success factors associated with the MDG results, other than political commitment, so it is necessary to consider case-study experience.

Some case studies

Management-driven successes

Phnom Penh

The management example most quoted, and for good reason, is the success of Ek Sonn Chan in Phnom Penh, in which he demonstrated that it is possible to achieve universal access and continuous supply in a low-income country (Chan, 2009). Initially, he was given both financial and technical support, but he demonstrated that an exceptionally managed water service provider can become self-sufficient. Critically, he received continuous political support, without interference in management. Unfortunately, the Ek Sonn Chan experience is rare in developing countries, with many barriers to successful public service management, including poor remuneration, compared with the private sector (as discussed later in the article). In the absence of management driven progress, there is the option of sound service delivery policies and processes, which have to come from the top down in a regulatory environment.

Uganda

In Uganda, the National Water and Sewerage Corporation was formed in 1973 as the beginning of integration in the country. Due to difficult political climates, including the Amin period, in which management did not have the freedom to manage, limited progress was made. In 1998 a new board was formed and a new chief executive appointed (Muhairwe, 2009) with the freedom to introduce effective management practices, such that today, the corporation provides good service to most areas in Uganda.

Regulation-driven successes

Regulation largely came in with privatization, or corporatization. It was seen as necessary in both cases. With privatization in the UK it provided oversight on investment and tariffs. In corporatization it was introduced to achieve separation between the politics of government and the service provider's management. This has brought some objectivity in planning and tariff setting in the developed world, but it has not eliminated political interference in some developing countries (Jamison & Castaneda, 2014), where often service provider managers are political appointees.

An excellent example of successful regulation-led reform is Malaysia. There were major problems with water services, partly due to failing public–private partnership contracts. Successful reform was achieved by the vision and dedication of the minister of energy, water and communications, Y. B. Dato' Sri Dr Lim Keng Yaik. Having sought good advice, he was able to get the Constitution changed to make water a joint federal/state responsibility, and on 1 January 2008 the regulator, the National Water Services Commission (SPAN), began operations. The state water authorities became state-owned corporatized-public companies regulated by SPAN. The law establishing SPAN also set up a Water Asset Management Company (PAAB), which with government backing was able to obtain long-term low-interest loans on the international money market. This money finances infrastructure approved by SPAN in each of the state water company's five-year delivery plans. For each constructed asset there is a 40-year leasing arrangement between PAAB and the water company, at an affordable leasing charge approved by SPAN, after which the asset is owned by the water company. Another important initiative was the establishment of formal water consumer consultative groups in each state. The Malaysian model, which to a certain extent was based on the system in operation in England and Wales, has been very successful in achieving sustainable water services.

Ghana, Kenya and Zambia are good examples of countries in Africa which have pursued a regulator-based approach. In Kenya a highly experienced and competent team is able to influence policies and development decisions. The regulator's influence is limited by not having the authority to require action by the service providers. Ghana on paper has an ideal regulatory structure, but regulator-approved programmes and associated tariffs are not ratified by the government, and subsidies are insufficient to implement the necessary reforms.

Zambia, through the introduction of regulation by the National Water Supply & Sanitation Council (NWASCO), is an example of effective reform and development. The increase in service coverage is shown in Table 1. NWASCO's (2018) report projects that SDG 6.1 (universal coverage) will be achieved by 2030.

Table 1. Progress in Zambia, 2004–2018.

Performance Aspect	2004 (%)	2018 (%)
Water service coverage	66	88
Sanitation coverage	27	63
Costs covered by collection	89	104
Metering ratio	36	81
Non-revenue water	48	49

Source: NWASCO's (2018) annual report (approximate percentages from diagram 10.3, p. 99).

Exceptional management is rare in the public water sector in developing countries, and it is unlikely to ever be sufficiently available to provide independent direction and action. Regulation, if reasonably independent of government, has been shown to provide the direction and capacity building to achieve progress. Both management and regulator approaches require governments able to develop sound policies, and able to allow managers to manage and regulators to regulate.

What are the factors of success?

In 'A Road Map to Sustainable Urban Water Supply', Rouse & El Achi (2019) consider successful countries and the common factors for success. They are:

- As reform takes several decades, government policies must be consistent across jurisdictions.
- Water and city planning should be integrated. This is essential where there is rapid urbanization.
- Water distribution systems, both existing and new, will be the major cost of achieving SDG 6.1 (but see the section below on piped systems).
- Sustainable water services cannot be achieved without continuous (24/7) supply.
- It is rarely recognized, but there is a requirement for investment to obtain good data, to develop network models, to extend the systems to unserved areas, and to deal with leakage.
- The governance structure must make provision for delivery plans (typically five years). These are hard-nosed business plans to deliver defined customer service objectives stage by stage towards the long-term strategic directives. These plans must be fully costed, with committed finance, and must be verifiable, monitored and enforced.
- Recruitment of skilled and committed staff is vital. Currently most public workers are poorly paid compared with the private sector, so the best people leave for better remuneration. Staff remuneration and conditions which are comparable with the private sector, with incentives to reward improved performance, should be introduced.
- Subsidies should be targeted to assist the poor. General government subsidies aimed at helping the poor actually give the most benefit to the more wealthy, as they consume more water. Also, they are a disincentive for water service management to be more efficient, and they reduce the opportunity for increased investment in poor areas.
- There must be sustainable cost recovery for at least operating costs and maintenance to achieve sufficient income to maintain systems, and to gain the creditworthiness necessary to attract private finance. The success in Phnom Penh has shown that it can be achieved in a very poor country.
- In poor water service situations there is likely to be little willingness to pay, partly because 'why pay for bad service' but also because the cost of seeking water elsewhere reduces people's ability to pay.

What are the reasons for insufficient progress?

In simple terms it is the lack of the above, although some aspects such as good management and staff are critical because they can manage round deficiencies such as poor subsidy policies. But good managers are unlikely to wish to work for very long in a governance environment which is not conducive to progress. But even with good management and good cost recovery from charges (the latter being unlikely given the last item in the list above), there is the question of availability of sufficient additional funding to make the necessary improvements. Are there ways of reducing the capital required? Can we question accepted approaches?

Given the importance of and the publicity around climate change, water resources seem to attract political attention, together with the issues of water allocation to cities and agriculture and the need for water conservation measures. The increased number of extreme events, resulting in more prolonged dry periods and more intense rainfall and flooding, are bringing focus to runoff controls, improved water storage and conservation measures to use water more wisely. To a certain extent, due to publicized water and health issues and the severe pollution of rivers, there is awareness of the need to invest in treatment processes, with donors willing to help.

In comparison, the distribution of water and the collection of wastewater receive scant attention. Why is it that the items in the supply chain which constitute the largest cost elements and require the greatest investment are least understood and do not receive the required attention from governments? Is it because they are the least pictorial, and don't offer compelling publicity images? Is it because the research is less sexy? Or is it because water professionals are failing to communicate their importance in the level of service that can be provided and in sustainability of services? There is also the question as to whether water professionals agree on approaches and solutions.

It is important to consider three questions which have major implications for investment and affordability: In urban areas, are pipe systems the best way of distributing water? With pipe systems, is rationing by intermittent supply really sustainable? And is full cost recovery necessary for sustainability?

Piped system supply

Water is heavy, and with the quantities required (even at the bottom end of access service) of 25 litres per person per day – for 1000 people this is 25 m^3 per day, weighing 25 tonnes – what are the options? Piped supply has become the accepted norm, but what of other distribution options? Is it feasible to consider tanker distribution systems with associated local storage? To supply the 1000 people would require two or three water tanker trucks suitable for local transport. Depending on distance, each tanker could perhaps make three trips per day, serving 3000 people. A town of 100,000 people would require a fleet of between 66 and 99 tankers. Such tankers might have a life of 20 years. There would also be a requirement for local storage. Other than for the wealthy, there would have to be communal systems from which water would be collected, similar to water collection from wells in rural systems. There would be consideration of how many storage tanks of what size at what average distance from consumers, suitable locations for tanks and the supervision and charging regimes of the systems.

An alternative is distribution of water in jerry cans of say 20 litres capacity which would be used also for storage. These could be distributed on trucks in larger numbers or by motorcycles in smaller quantities. Trucks might have a capacity of 50 jerry cans; with three journeys a day this would require about eight trucks for 1000 people. A population of 100,000 would require around 270 trucks. Either road tanker or truck/jerry can distribution is logistically challenging and expensive. Bottled water is an option for water to be consumed, but the cost is the highest per litre and a supply of water for other purposes is still necessary. The cost of vendor charges depends on the method and distance from supply. All the prices are greater than for piped water supply (see the example in Tables 2 and 3).

Another critical factor is water quality and the relationship between levels of safety and health, which then brings in other considerations, including education, less capacity for economic development, and other coping costs. A full discussion of quality issues is outside the scope of this article. The WHO classification of 'safely managed service' supply (Figure 1) is valuable in comparing the distribution options.

Table 2. Complimentary water systems in Dar es Salaam.

Source	Price/payment	Shillings/ litre	US$/m^3
Own connection	Monthly lump sum, flat rate, based on:	0.27	0.34
Neighbour's tap/water kiosk	20 shillings per 20-litre container	1	1.25
Pushcart water vendor	70–200 shillings per 20-litre container	3.50–10	4.38–12.50
Tanker truck (10,000 litres)	60,000–80,000 shillings per truckload	6–8	7.50–10.00

Source: Kjellen (2000).

Table 3. Comparison of water supply options.

Water supply option	Cost to consumer (US$/m^3)	Cost to consumer relative to HH connection	Net benefit to utility per m^3 relative to HH connection
Meter cluster	0.73	80%	−0.4
Water tanker with communal standpost operator	4.55	500%	0.7
Individual household connection	0.90	100%	1.0
Utility-staffed kiosks	3.93	440%	125
Prepaid metered standpost	3.93	440%	180

Source: Adapted from Water & Sanitation for the Urban Poor (2014).

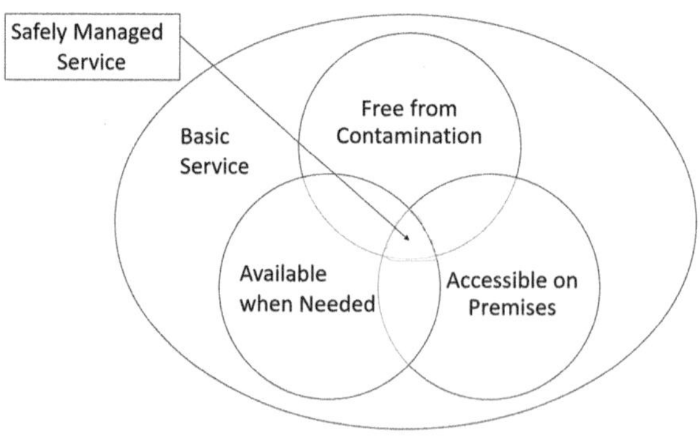

Figure 1. Safely managed service.
Source: World Health Organisation (2017).

Table 4. Comparison of four water distribution options.

Factor	Pipe network	Road tanker (10,000 L)	Truck jerry cans (1000 L)	Bicycle or hand-cart (100 L)
Public or private	Public	Generally private, some public	Private	Private
Lifetime cost	Cost C/litre used here for comparison	10–20 times C. See Table 2		
Costs over time	High initial capital cost, low operating cost	Initial investment in vehicles and storage followed by largely fuel costs	Initial investment in vehicles and jerry cans followed by largely fuel costs	Minimal set-up costs, then operator time costs
Volume of water delivered	Greatest, not a limiting factor	Limited by carrying capacity for most consumers	Limited by consumer jerry can storage	Limited to basic needs of drinking and cooking
Complexity	Highest	Requires local storage and payment systems	Jerry can filling logistics	Lowest
Quality Regulated	Yes	Not normally		
Time to begin providing supply	Slowest due to capital cost design, planning approval and construction	Depends on time to purchase vehicles and storage, and to arrange access to filling points		Immediate
Continuous (24/7) supply	Yes, with good maintenance; commonly no, because of lack of maintenance	No, for most people water would have to be collected	Yes, if jerry cans provide enough storage, but not continuous on tap	No
Water losses	Can be high; see intermittent supply, below	None, other than at storage tank taps	None, other than household spillage	Virtually none
Environmental factors	Disturbance during construction; energy for pumping	Emission of vehicles, depending on fuel requirements; for cost reasons, old vehicles often used in developing countries; impact on traffic congestion		None

Source: The Author.

Table 4 compares a pipe network and tanker, truck and bicycle water distribution.

Well-managed pipeline distribution (i.e., with 24/7 supply) emerges as the preferred option in all respects except the initial high capital cost and the time to begin operations. The current dilapidated state of most distribution systems in developing countries raises the question as to whether piped systems can be a viable approach in the short SDG timeframe of 2030. This is discussed in the next section.

Even if pipeline systems can be made viable for many supply areas, due to lack of access currently, and a backlog of investment in existing systems, tanker and other private vendor supplies would be essential in what would be a substantial transitional period. However, such short-term measures are likely to be regarded as 'job done', with loss of incentive to achieve sustainable pipeline systems.

There are many other combinations of piped and tankered systems. A study in Ghana (Frances & Nokes, 2014) provides a valuable comparison of the cost per litre of options to the consumer and the benefits to the utility compared with a household piped supply. Meter clusters reduce the price for consumers, but the water has to be carried to the point of consumption. That is also true of utility-operated kiosks and prepaid metered stand-posts (in which payments have to be made before water can be taken), but the water is much more expensive. However, there could be a policy of subsidizing the prepaid meter option. All of the piped supply options are subject to the problems of intermittent supply.

All the above options have their place in making progress in the short term. They all rely on either piped supply or road transport. But for future sustainable safe water supply of an acceptable daily quantity of 25 litres per person per day or more, the aim in densely populated areas has to be piped distribution systems with individual building connections and 24/7 supply. The challenge is how to finance the systems and how to achieve cost recovery.

Continuous (24/7) or intermittent supply

Based on its success in achieving safe, continuous water supply, pipeline distribution became regarded as the standard for urban areas, and systems were installed widely during the colonial period and promoted by developed countries' consultants. Almost universally, insufficient attention was given to the maintenance and refurbishment of these systems. Initially, deterioration was slow, and the problems of neglect did not appear, until leakage levels began to reduce the ability to maintain supply, and major investment in refurbishment was required. In parallel, tariffs had not kept pace with operational needs, and governments were reluctant to approve the necessary investment in the water systems and indeed in other public service infrastructure. Although the focus of this article is on developing countries, it is instructive to mention first some developed-country experience. In the UK, in which there was rapid urbanization with the industrial revolution, systems became 'old' earlier than in most countries, and there were wake-up calls in the 1980s from major pipe bursts and collapsing sewers. There were national reviews resulting in publications such as *Taken for Granted* (1970) and *A National Assessment* (Department of the Environment/National Water Council, 1977). These works, which highlighted the major problems with underground assets, are now 40–50 years old, but it is important to mention them, as this was only a 'wake-up call', and it took many more years for serious investment to be made. However, the reports did stimulate major activity of investigation. In 1980 the Water Research Centre set up a new laboratory to study, measure and find solutions to the problems of deteriorated water mains and sewers (Water Research Centre, 1989, 2001) Technology and techniques have developed since the publication of the rehabilitation manuals, but they provided the framework for addressing the problems of neglected systems. Good progress has now been made in the UK on the backlog of refurbishment, although there is more to be done. Many other European countries have taken steps to invest in water networks, but in many cities in the US (for example), the deterioration has reached a crisis level (Cohen, 2018; Folkman, 2018; Brodine, 2017). One reason for the difference between Europe and the US is that US water tariffs are very low (Swain, Lazar, & Pine, 2005), one-third to one-half of those in European countries. Another reason is that there was much greater institutional reform in Europe, with small service operations integrated to a scale at which good management and scientific services are affordable (Rouse, 2013).

In many developing countries, system deterioration has resulted in rapid leakage. Where measured, typically more than 60% of the water put into the supply system leaks out, resulting in low pressure and intermittent supply. Consequently, systems have to be operated in turn to provide each area some water. As each pressure loss and repressurization causes further deterioration of pipes and joints, the situation becomes worse and worse, with many people receiving water only a few hours a day or a few hours a week. At that point, it is very difficult to repair leaks faster than they appear. Is there now greater awareness that rationing by intermittent supply is not sustainable, as it creates a downward spiral of decline, and that political buy-in is needed for action to be taken?

Where there are accurate network maps it is possible to model systems such that distribution zones can be designed so that investment can be made in each zone in turn to achieve continuous supply (Rouse & El Achi, 2019). However, in many cities, investment is required to locate pipes and prepare network maps before network analysis is possible. Currently there is not sufficient political awareness of the large investment requirement for information and refurbishment, and donors seem to prefer to fund new systems. How is it possible to achieve political buy-in for action to be taken?

Affordability and full cost recovery

There are many issues around the question of cost recovery: unwillingness of politicians to raise tariffs, especially close to elections; general subsidies being unreliable, insufficient, time-consuming to manage, disincentivizing efficient operations, and benefitting the wealthy, who consume more water to the detriment of the poor; unwillingness of consumers to pay for a poor service; and opportunities for government to interfere in utility operations. Many of these factors contribute to the vicious circles of decline (Rouse, 2013); see Figure 2.

I believe that the premise that water should be free is no longer being promoted, especially as the UN Resolution on Water and Sanitation as a Human Right (Aulbuquerque, 2014) states clearly that water should be affordable, not free. There is still the view that tariffs based on full cost recovery are not affordable for the poor. What is not generally recognized is that many of the poor pay much more for water from vendors than they would from access to the public supply (Figure 3). Although the original Arthur McIntosh (2003) diagram was based on data collected in Asia prior to 2003, it is still generally applicable. The argument is that public water supply can be made affordable for all if the wealthier consumers pay tariffs which reflect costs and are in line with full cost recovery. The use of subsidies targeted to instal systems to reach the poor areas is critical to begin that transition. However, for the piped public supply to be affordable, it has to be reliable, because the poor cannot pay for both the public service and additional water from vendors. This is one of the main reasons for the failure of general subsidies. They discourage service providers from being efficient, because they can rely on the subsidy, but also there is no incentive for consumers to use water wisely (Rouse, 2013).

Targeted subsidies are essential, not only to assist the poor directly, but specifically to build the water mains to serve the poor areas. The challenge is how to persuade governments to change from general subsidies to full cost recovery from realistic tariffs and targeted subsidies for the poor. There are questions on how to manage the transition, the timeframe, and how to establish the necessary public consultation.

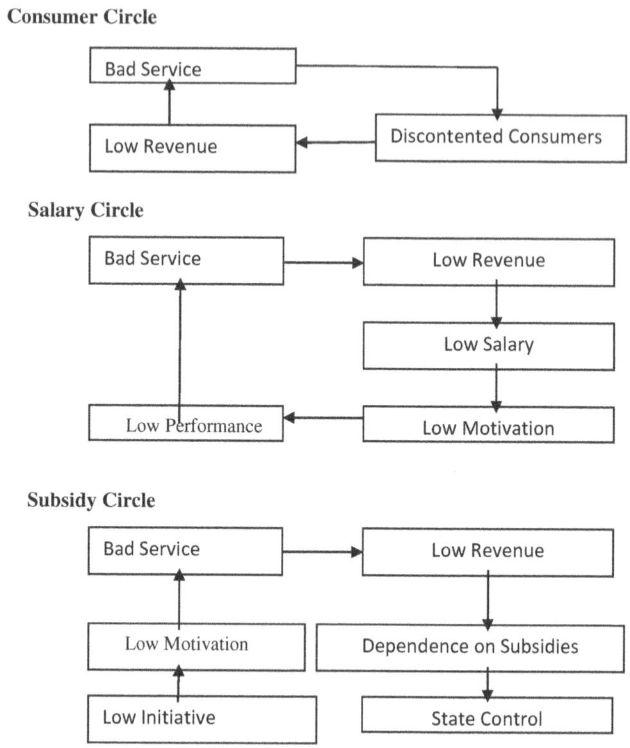

Figure 2. The vicious circles of water service decline.

Source: Presentation by Eero Kontula, Finnida, at World Bank/WaterAid Workshop, London, August 2004, taken from Rouse (2013).

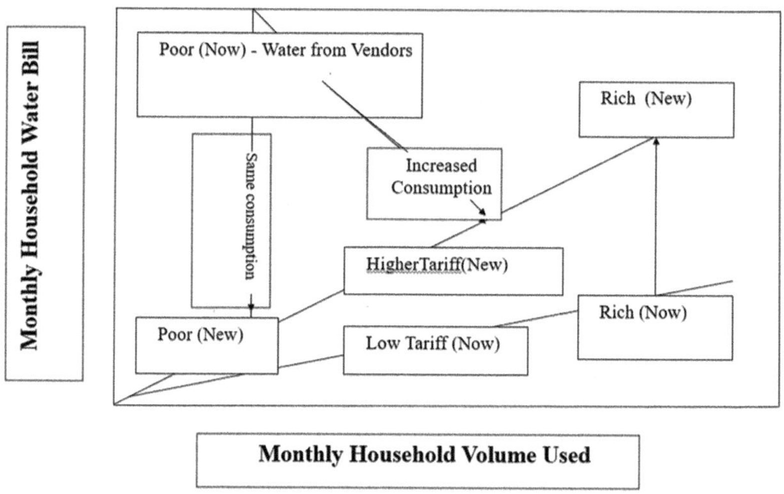

Figure 3. Increase tariffs to help the poor. Source: adapted from McIntosh (2003).

Importantly, full cost recovery from tariffs is essential for the long-term sustainability of services. It is also essential as part of the creditworthiness of service providers, in giving donors the confidence to support capital developments.

So what to do?

None of the above reviews has identified any shortcuts to universal and sustainable water service. It requires good information, recognition of the scale of investment needed, good planning, and capacity building, all of which require political commitment. But it would be wrong to say that no progress can be made without investment in information on current operations and infrastructure. There is some 'low-hanging fruit', such as repair of large, obvious leaks and replacement of old, inefficient pumps. These actions should be taken while planning for the periods of development leading to universal access.

So the requirements for success have been identified and quantified; and technically and operationally, water professionals have got it right. Then why is the goal of universal access so far away? Where have water professionals failed? Success depends on every sector, with government officials, service providers, consultants, academia and donors using the same language, with the same understanding, working together. This may seem simple and obvious, but all three of those things – language, understanding and cooperation – are very complex. Part of the problem is that groups of water professionals tend to operate in their own silos and within their own peer groups. They attend different meetings and events. Their papers are written for their own peer groups. Academic papers have to go through refereeing and satisfy the publishing industry that the research is robust. For career advancement, the priority is to impress one's peers, not to pave the way for implementation or development of better operations. Operational managers have little time to write papers, and it is not generally helpful for their careers. Consultants tend to produce glossy reports, often in the form of impressive PowerPoint presentations, which for business reasons have to match their clients' expectations. Donors are generally in the business of lending money, so funding proposals are infrastructure-led rather than service-improvement-led. Government papers have to satisfy political agendas. There are of course exceptions to all these generalizations, but often the various factions are not 'on the same page'.

Events such as the annual World Water Week in Stockholm, and Singapore International Water Week, do bring together water professionals with representatives from high-level international organizations and some government ministers. These events have influenced the UN and other agencies, resulting in the Millennium Development Goals, the Sustainable Development Goals and the UN Resolution on Water and Sanitation as a Human Right. These initiatives are vital, but for some reason(s) the goals and the various publications do not penetrate into the decision-making mechanisms of governments. There may be a level of awareness, but it does not get translated into the necessary actions on the ground. It does not get through the 'all too difficult' barrier. Communication between governments and water professionals needs to be rethought.

For governments' attention and action is it a matter of the 'messenger' having local credibility? Is it a matter of acceptable messengers being able to take the important messages on policy and practice and relay them in 'local' language (related to both mother tongue and local circumstances)? The credible messengers could come from any sector of water professionals (university professors, utility directors, well-known individual consultants or heads of NGOS) but they must be sufficiently influential and senior to gain access to the decision makers. The initiative, say based on SDG 6, might be for national water associations to form a small group of 'messengers' and give them a checklist of well-defined action-based messages which together would provide the material for policy implementation. The list of messages would cover governance, planning, finance, and technical and operational matters. Perhaps the International Water Association would be the appropriate organization to prepare the message material and to communicate such a campaign through the national water associations, or other local bodies. With its wide membership and expert groups, the association could prepare relevant sets of information, including covering the subjects discussed in this article, and other important aspects such as South-to-South technology transfer.

Conclusion

Review of some key issues related to universal and sustainable water services in urban areas has shown that important policies on such aspects as pipeline distribution, continuous supply and cost recovery are vindicated. But water professionals have failed in communication with government officials. The solution may lie in harnessing influential local water professionals who have access to decision makers and providing them with well-defined action messages. Returning to the title of this article, 'Can water professionals do more?' – yes, they can.

Disclosure statement

No potential conflict of interest was reported by the author.

References

Aulbuquerque, C. de, et al. (2014). *Realizing the human rights to water and sanitation: A handbook.* Geneva: OCHR.

Bain, R., Johnston, R., Mitis, F., Chatterley, C., & Slaymaker, T. (2018). Establishing sustainable development goal baselines for household drinking water, sanitation and hygiene services. *Water, 10*(12), 1711. doi:10.3390/w10121711

Bartram, J., Luyendijk, R., Hossain, R., Fisher, M., Gordon, B., Wardlaw, T., & Brocklehurst, C. (2014). Global monitoring of water supply and sanitation: History, methods and future challenges. *International Journal of Environmental Research and Public Health, 11*, 8137–8165. doi:10.3390/ijerph110808137

Brodine, M. (2017). Buried no longer: Confronting America's water infrastructure challenge. *Urban Water Learning Network*. Retrieved from http://www.urbanwaterslearningnetwork.org/resources/awwa-confronting-americas-water-infrastructure-challenge2017

Chan, E. S. (2009). Bringing safe water to Phnom Penh's City. *International Journal of Water Resources Development, 24*(4), 597–609. doi:10.1080/07900620903306323

Cohen, B. (2018). US drinking water supply is at risk from deteriorating pipes. *Washington Examiner.* Retrieved from https://www.washingtonexaminer.com/opinion/op-eds/us-drinking-water-supply-is-at-risk-from-deteriorating-pipes

Department of the Environment/National Water Council. (1977). *Sewers and water mains – A national assessment*. NWC/DoE Standing Technical Committee Report no. 4. London: HMSO.
Folkman, S. (2018, March). *Water main break rates in the USA and Canada. A comprehensive study*. Utah State University. Retrieved from https://digitalcommons.usu.edu›cgi›viewcontent
Frances, R., & Nokes, C. (2014). *Urban water supply guide. Service delivery options for low-income communities*. London: Water & Sanitation for the Urban Poor.
Jamison, M., & Castaneda, A. (2014). *Addressing improper political interference* (PURC Working Paper). University of Florida. Retrieved from https://www.regulationbodyofknowledge.org›faq›how-can-persons-performing-reg-8483aja
Joint Monitoring Programme. (2017). Progress on drinking water, sanitation and hygiene: 2017. Retrieved from https://www.who.int/mediacentre/news/releases/2017/launch-version-report-jmp-water-sanitation-hygiene.pdf
Kjellen, M. (2000). Complementary water systems in Dar es Salaam, Tanzania: the case of water vending. *Water Resources Development, 16*(1).
McIntosh, A. C. (2003). *Asian water supplies: Reaching the urban poor*. Manila: Asian Development Bank.
Muhairwe, W. T. (2009). *Making public enterprises work; From despair to promise: A turn around account*. London: IWA.
NWASCO. (2018). Urban and peri-urban water supply and sanitation sector report 2018. Retrieved from http://www.nwasco.org.zm/index.php/media-center/publications/annual-reports/send/6-annual-reports/66-nwasco-2018-sector-report
Rouse, M., & El Achi, N. (2019). A road map to sustainable urban water supply. In S. J. Dadson, D. E. Garrick, E. C. Penning-Rowsell, J. W. Hall, R. Hope, & J. Hughes (Eds.), *Water science, policy and management: A global challenge* (pp. 309–328). Chichester, UK: John Wiley & Sons Ltd.
Rouse, M. J. (2013). *Institutional governance and regulation of water service* (2nd ed.). London: IWA Publishing..
Swain, H., Lazar, F., & Pine, J. (2005). *Watertight: The case for change in Ontario's water and wastewater sector*. Toronto: Expert Panel on Water and Wastewater Strategy, Government of Ontario.
Taken for Granted. (1970). *Report of the working party on sewage disposal*. London: HMSO.
Water & Sanitation for the Urban Poor. 2014. *Urban water supply guide*. Retrieved from https://www.wsup.com/insights/the-urban-water-supply-guide-service-delivery-options-for-low-income-communities/
Water Research Centre. (1989). *Water mains rehabilitation manual*. Swindon, UK: Author.
Water Research Centre. (2001). *Sewerage rehabilitation manual* (4th ed.). Swindon: Author.
World Health Organisation. (2017). Progress on drinking water, sanitation and hygiene: Joint Monitoring Programme update 2017. Retrieved from https://www.who.int/water_sanitation_health/monitoring/coverage/indicator-6-1-1-safely-managed-drinking-water.pdf

Reflections on flood control in Japan and recommendations for developing countries

Yutaka Takahasi, Kimio Takeya, Miki Inaoka, Wataru Ono and Kaoru Sasaoka

ABSTRACT
This paper describes the discussions on flood control in Japan, recently adding climate change, and the activities of the Japan International Cooperation Agency for disaster risk reduction. JICA led the negotiations of the UN Sendai Framework for Disaster Risk Reduction 2015–2030, as a main member of the government of Japan. The Sustainable Development Goals' demand to 'leave no one behind' requires that the social system protect even the poorest people who live in disaster-prone areas. Local disaster risk reduction planning plays an indispensable role; and JICA wrote an eight-step methodology to formulate these plans. The emphasis in each country needs to shift from planning to implementation.

Review of flood control in Japan and challenges for the future[1]

Flood control policy in Japan is shifting from reliance on structural measures to integrated flood management, seeking the best combination of structural and non-structural measures, and adding consideration of extreme weather events that exceed the design level of existing structures.

The socio-economic development in Japan in the twentieth century resulted in urbanization and development of paddy fields into residential and commercial areas. The more the value of land increased, the more determined the government became to avoid any future inundation in the basins. The basic concept of flood control in Japan was to drain the flow to the river mouth and to the sea as soon as possible, with no overflow at dikes or levees. The construction of huge levees and dikes in the plains reduced flood damage substantially. But now the rainfall that used to stay temporarily in the basin would rush to the waterway, increasing the peak flow. As more development occurred, flood management became more crucial in the basins. The more flood management works were constructed, the greater was the peak flow in the mid- and downstream, necessitating even more flood management works. This cycle resulted in extreme floods that exceeded the design level of existing structures.

The twentieth-century engineers tended to prioritize and valorize the construction of massive structures and facilities. But dams and levees are only one of the many options to control flooding, and could never have been the ultimate solution by themselves. For example, dams were indispensable in the reconstruction of Japan after the war, through large-scale water resource development and flood control. On the other hand, sedimentation in upstream dams reduced the supply of sand in the downstream, causing riverbank and coastal erosion, and reducing water quality. Dams were not the perfect solution, and the rivers seemed to reject the flood control approach that tries to prevent overflows. Areas at risk should not be developed. But when dams and levees are built, the area *appears* to be safe, which encourages development, making the area (paradoxically) less safe. Thus, a focus on structural flood measures may leave a legacy of risk. Takahashi mentions in his interview (Sugimoto, 2010) that one of the reasons for this was the incorrect approach of bureaucrats who only focused on immediate flood measures, and who also neglected the limitations of structural measures in protecting against extreme floods.

The most efficient approach is now recognized to be integrated flood management, which is a combination of measures in each basin. This is a paradigm shift – from depending solely on structural measures to prevent the overflow of even a drop of water, to allowing overflow in the case of an extreme flood, and using a combination of other measures to mitigate the damage. Some examples of traditional and primitive but practical and successful technologies are ponds to retain the overflow, and elevated roads along levees. Underground retaining facilities can delay the peak flow, and non-structural measures such as hazard maps can warn people of locations of potential inundation. Land use control can restrict development in flood-prone areas. Dependency on structural measures needs to shift to sharing damage mitigation tasks among multiple measures.

Takahasi wrote in 1971 that the concept of flood control needs to shift from structural measures to non-structural measures such as land use control and collaboration with the community. Takahasi also proposed underground retaining facilities and the development of hazard maps. But these activities were long limited to specific cities and to small and medium-sized rivers, on which dams were not effective. It took until 2000 for the approach to be applied to all rivers in Japan.

To achieve integrated flood management, all concerned ministries need to work together, overcoming silos. Community participation is also important. People with interest in the community or the river itself have a right to express their opinion on the future of river. Integrated flood management implies various measures throughout the watershed. The number of community members affected will therefore be far greater than the stakeholders in a dam project.

Experience shows that flood control requires a range of measures, including structural measures, land use control, and cooperation with the community. In the twentieth century, Japan depended too much on imported technology. Technology is only one approach, and flood control needs to understand and cooperate with the nature and history of the watershed.

Japanese experience of investment in disaster risk reduction measures

The government of Japan has made continued efforts to reduce disaster risk by investing in mitigation measures under disaster-related domestic policy. The UN International

Strategy for Disaster Reduction (2015, p. 125) introduced this as a good practice, and commented that 'In Japan ... continued investment in flood protection – together with regulation – has resulted in a dramatic reduction in the areas flooded and in mortality.'

In 1959, disasters in Japan (mainly Typhoon Vera) caused 5565 deaths or missing persons. The efforts of the government have successfully reduced the deaths attributable to flooding to one-hundredth of previous levels (Japan International Cooperation Agency, 2016).

Figure 1 shows the change in fatalities from floods, compared to cumulative government spending on flood management. The number of lives lost to floods fell drastically in the initial stage of flood control efforts. This shows that investment in disaster risk reduction (DRR) is necessary to protect lives and to support socio-economic development in a country that faces frequent disasters. Figure 2 shows the trend of the annual budget for disaster prevention in Japan. In the period of rapid economic growth from 1960 to 1980 (when GDP per capita was still below USD 10,000), spending on disaster prevention was as high as 7% of the national budget, on average.

Trend in disaster-related international aid

In general, individuals and governments react to disasters after they occur, rather than preparing for them or trying to limit their effects before they happen. Every time a disaster hits, it harms the people and the economy in the region, and the central and local governments conduct rescue activities and recovery work. In the two decades from 1991 to 2010, disaster-related aid accounted for only 3.5% (US$ 106.7 billion) of all international development aid (ODI and Global Facility, 2013). This means that international aid had not recognized disasters as a priority. Moreover, in disaster-related aid, 65.5% is for emergency response, and 21.8% is for reconstruction and rehabilitation. Thus,

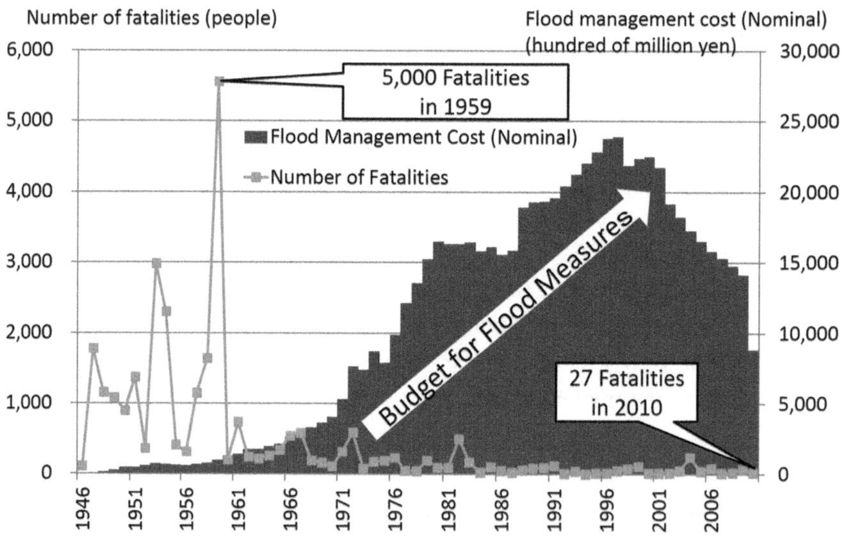

Figure 1. Cumulative flood management cost and change in fatalities.
Source: Inaoka, Takeya, & Akiyama (2018).

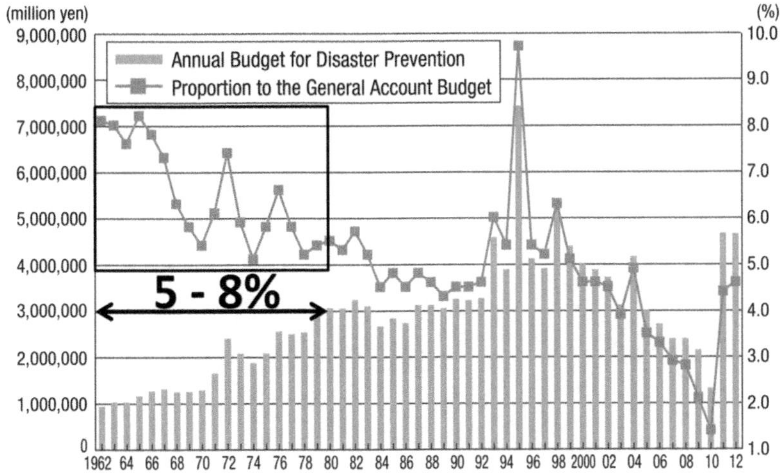

Figure 2. Trend in annual budget for disaster prevention in Japan.
Source: Inaoka et al. (2018).

aid focuses on post-disaster response, or in other words, humanitarian aspects. Aid for DRR, which focuses on investment in countermeasures *before* disaster occurs, has accounted for only 12.7% of disaster-related aid, and only 0.4% of all development aid (ODI and Global Facility, 2013).

Figure 3 shows the trend in disaster-related international aid in those same two decades. The total amount of aid has dramatically increased after catastrophes, such as the Indian Ocean Tsunami of 2004. Even then, the international community still tends to focus on humanitarian and post-disaster aid – emergency response, or reconstruction and rehabilitation. But these disasters did prompt greater pre-investment in DRR.

In many developing countries, investments in DRR are limited, and expenditures mostly go to responses after a disaster. In short, this is a 'crisis control' situation, and disaster risks are not reduced. Hence, every time a disaster occurs, the country takes damages. In this situation, only the wealthy can protect themselves through self-help measures. And that does not correspond to the Sustainable Development Goals, which require that no one be left behind (UNGA, 2015, p. 3).

The Japan International Cooperation Agency (JICA), which implements overseas development assistance based on Japanese experiences, has been emphasizing DRR. Figure 4 shows the trend in JICA's DRR cooperation based on the five priority actions of the Hyogo Framework for Action (UN Office for Disaster Risk Reduction, 2005). Projects have concentrated on Priority Action 4, 'Reduce the underlying risk factors', which is the only priority action consistent with investment in DRR. Moreover, the Report by ODI and the World Bank lists JICA as one of the top donors, and a champion donor among bilateral donors that provide DRR cooperation (ODI and Global Facility, 2013; Department for International Development, Environmental Resources Management, 2005). The experiences and views of Japan on investment in DRR strongly affect the strategy of other donors with regard to disaster-related aid to developing countries.

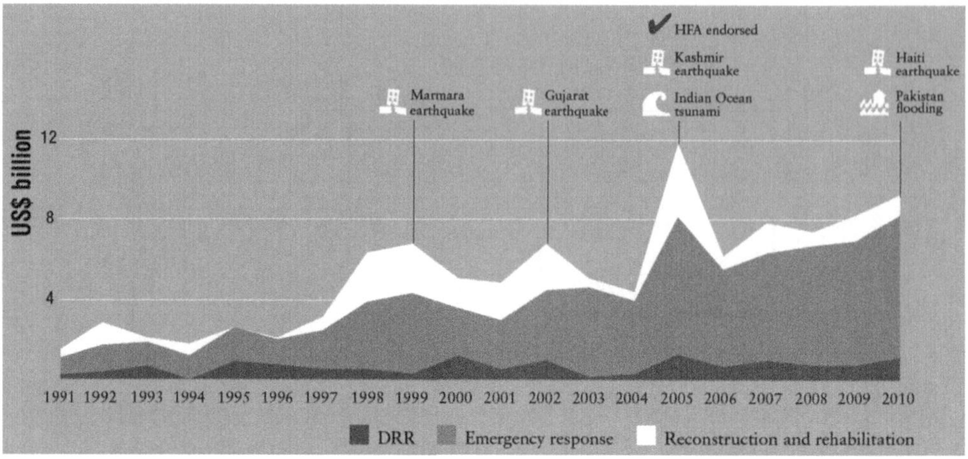

Figure 3. Disaster-related financing, 1991–2010.
Source: ODI and Global Facility (2013).

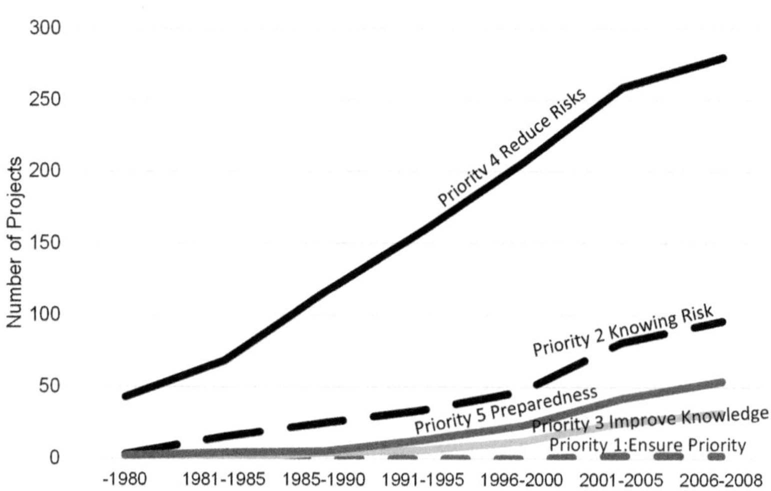

Figure 4. Trend in projects by Hyogo Framework for Action priorities.
Source: Japan International Cooperation Agency (2015).

The UN International Strategy for Disaster Reduction (2015, Part I, Chapter5) recognized a unique macro-economic growth model, DR^{2}AD (Disaster Risk Reduction Investment Accounts for Development), which JICA developed to enable policy makers to assess the impacts of DRR policies and measures. The DR^{2}AD model emphasizes the effectiveness of investment in DRR and encourages such investment, especially in developing countries. This was one of the lobbying activities by JICA and the government of Japan towards the 3rd World Conference on Disaster Risk Reduction (WCDRR), held in Sendai in March 2015, which gradually achieved international recognition of the importance of investment in DRR.

Incorporation of Japanese experiences in the Sendai Framework

JICA, with the government of Japan, communicated its experiences to the international community in preparation for the 3rd WCDRR. The aim was to internationally standardize the concept, emphasizing three points: pre-investment in DRR measures, strengthening the capacity of central governments for DRR, and 'Build Back Better'. The UN Office for Disaster Risk Reduction (UNDRR, 2017) defines 'Build Back Better' as the use of the recovery, rehabilitation and reconstruction phases after a disaster to increase the resilience of nations and communities through integrating disaster risk reduction measures into the restoration of physical infrastructure and societal systems, and into the revitalization of livelihoods, economies and the environment.

The year 2015 also produced essential world frameworks such as the Sustainable Development Goals and COP21 (the Paris Agreement), which strongly influenced the development strategies of countries and organizations. The international community recognized DRR as critical for development. Both DRR and humanitarian aid were integrated into development policies.

DRR and 'Build Back Better' were included in the Priorities for Action of the Sendai Framework for Disaster Risk Reduction 2015–2030 (United Nations, 2015b), which was adopted at the 3rd WCDRR (Figure 5). In the Sendai Framework, seven targets (four output targets and three input targets) were established as monitoring tools to measure progresses in each country.

Figure 6 shows how the seven global targets of the Sendai Framework relate to each other. Three of the targets (*e, f* and *g*) aim to increase input to the DRR sector. There is a nested relation among the other four targets: as the DRR sector gains maturity in each country, targets also evolve from minimum protection of human lives (a humanitarian issue, in which the needs and challenges are smaller and can be solved by early-warning systems, etc.) to protecting the economy (a development issue, in which the needs and challenges are larger, since they require prevention measures). In other words, JICA believes that target *d* covers all the included targets, and even in countries with primitive DRR, where it still has to focus on reduction of mortality, the government always needs a broader vision, aiming to ensure sustainable development. JICA carefully examines the situation of each recipient country and decides the best balance of measures to be developed.

The seven global targets of the Sendai Framework have two deadlines: 2020 and 2030 (Figure 7). Target *e* is to formulate national and local DRR strategies by 2020, whereas the other targets aim at 2030. This is because the plans and strategies are the base of any actual activities, so for the first five years the Sendai Framework needs to focus on implementation plans, followed by implementation based on these plans in the remaining 10 years. At present, the most urgently required action is for each state to prepare practical local DRR plans.

The local DRR plans defined in the Sendai Framework aim to reduce disaster risks. For example, the national government contributes to reducing risks by constructing reservoirs and embankments. Local governments contribute to reducing risks by regulating land use and managing reservoirs (public aid). Communities conduct mutual-aid and self-help activities such as evacuation drills and confirming evacuation routes.

Priority for Action

Priority 1: Understanding disaster risk.
Priority 2: Strengthening disaster risk governance to manage disaster risk.
Priority 3: Investing in disaster risk reduction for resilience.
Priority 4: Enhancing disaster preparedness for effective response, and to «Build Back Better» in recovery, rehabilitation and reconstruction.

Target

a) Substantially reduce global disaster mortality by 2030, aiming to lower the average per 100,000 global mortality rate in the decade 2020–2030 compared to the period 2005–2015;
b) Substantially reduce number of affected people globally by 2030, aiming to lower the average global figure per 100,000 in the decade 2020–2030 compared to the period 2005–2015;
c) Reduce direct disaster economic loss in relation to global gross domestic product (GDP) by 2030;
d) Substantially reduce disaster damage to critical infrastructure and disruption of basic services, among them health and educational facilities, including through developing their resilience by 2030;
e) Substantially increase the number of countries with national and local disaster risk reduction strategies by 2020;
f) Substantially enhance international cooperation to developing countries through adequate and sustainable support to complement their national actions for implementation of the present Framework by 2030;
g) Substantially increase the availability of and access to multi-hazard early warning systems and disaster risk information and assessments to people by 2030.

Figure 5. Sendai Framework for Disaster Risk Reduction 2015–2030.
Source: United Nations (2015b).

Natural disasters worldwide

The situation of natural disasters differs among countries and regions, for example in frequency of occurrence, number of affected people, number of deaths, and economic damage.

Figures A1 to A5 (see supplemental online material) use data from EM-DAT, the Emergency Events Database (Université catholique de Louvain – CRED, n.d.). The occurrence of incidents depends on climate and topography, with the greatest incidence in Asia (Figure A1). The number of people affected depends not only on occurrence but also on population density, and so again is much greater in Asia than in all other continents (Figure A2). The number of deaths tends to be highest in Africa, in contrast to occurrence and population density (Figure A3). The causes of deaths in Africa are mainly droughts and biological causes – Africa embodies complex issues that also connect with food and nutrition issues, or health services.

The total economic damage caused by disasters (Figure A4) depends strongly on the assets that existed before the disaster. Given the socio-economic situation, countries and people in Africa have limited assets to lose in the first place. These countries will need to build up their socio-economic assets before DRR can gain recognition. Meanwhile, mainstreaming DRR in economic development activities will be the most important aspect in these countries. Any development projects, such as roads or power supply, will need to consider DRR in their design.

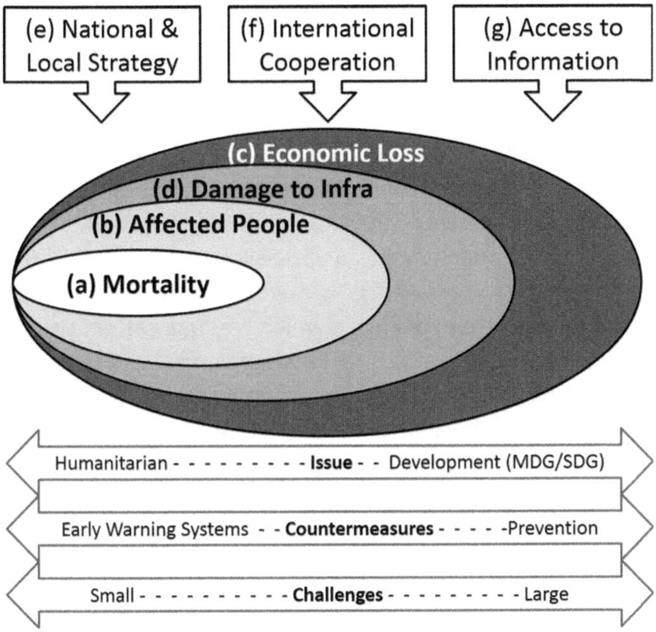

Figure 6. Relations among global targets.
Source: Inaoka et al. (2018).

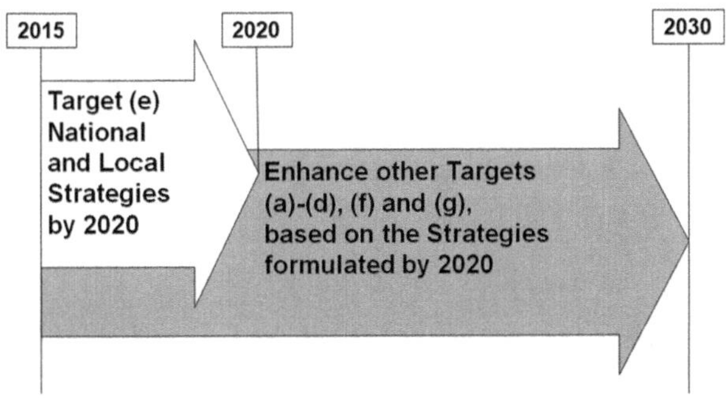

Figure 7. Target year of global targets.
Adapted from United Nations (2015b).

These figures are evidence of how diverse the situations are in different countries; DRR plans need to be carefully tailored to suit each country. But given that Asia appears to be at higher risk, and that Japan is one of the most developed countries in Asia, there is no doubt that the experiences of Japan in DRR will be useful to other countries.

Local disaster risk reduction plans

The Sendai Framework mentions both national and local DRR plans in target *e*, whereas JICA has specifically emphasized local DRR plans. There are two reasons for this. First, local DRR plans are still in development. Many countries have already developed national DRR plans during the era of the Hyogo Framework for Action. National DRR plans serve to show the general and overall idea of DRR in a country. These ideas have to be practically shaped into local DRR plans. Second, existing local DRR plans are mostly response plans only, and so they do not actually reduce disaster risk. Based on the Sendai Framework, JICA defines local DRR plans as 'holistic investment plans to reduce disaster risks in an area'. To reduce disaster risks in an area, the local DRR plans are where the local context can be and needs to be taken into account. This is why JICA has been emphasizing development of local DRR plans.

The most effective way to reduce risk is investment in DRR led by public aid, and focusing on tackling the residual risks which remain after and during the risk reduction measures of the national and local governments (Figure A5). Local DRR plans which work as investment plans are effective, since this kind of plan reduces disaster risks. Communities must respond to the residual risks. These efforts reduce disaster risks (mitigation) and contribute to quick response (preparedness), leaving no one behind.

Consideration of time scale is important in local DRR plans. The hazards and risks in an area change over time. For example, the population may increase or decrease. There may be industrial development in a particular area. Embankments and dams may be constructed, as a part of structural measures by the national government. Moreover, it takes time for reservoirs and embankments to be completed. This means that risks will remain until construction is complete. Local DRR plans should adjust to reduce those risks, which change from time to time.

Land use regulations also should be considered for high-risk areas to prevent unplanned industrialization. Measures should also be considered for areas where risks will remain after construction of reservoirs and embankments.

JICA has defined eight steps to develop an ideal local DRR plan, which will be explained in detail in the next section. By following these steps, the following contents necessary for local DRR plans can be obtained:

- Hazard map
- Risk map
- List of existing/planned countermeasures
- Time line of residual risks
- List of countermeasures based on residual risks
- List of prioritized countermeasures
- Budget allocation plan
- Implementation/monitoring plans.

These are example contents of local DRR plans. The local DRR plan should follow the disaster management cycle, and if a response plan already exists or is preferred to be included, it can also be added as a part of the local DRR plan. JICA does not lay out strict and solid contents of local DRR plans, because from JICA's perspective, plans must be flexible, depending for instance on disaster types in the area.

JICA's eight steps for developing a local DRR plan

In November 2017, JICA held a meeting with representatives from eight countries to discuss experiences and opinions on developing local DRR plans. The participants were from Bangladesh (Ministry of General Planning), Indonesia (National Development Planning Agency), Iran (National Disaster Management Organization), Mongolia (National Emergency Management Agency), Myanmar (Ministry of Social Welfare Relief and Resettlement), Nepal (Ministry of Home Affairs), the Philippines (selected cities) and Sri Lanka (Disaster Management Centre).

JICA compiled the outputs of the meeting to produce a guide describing eight steps to develop a local DRR plan.

(1) Collect local hazard information.
This step is preparatory to identifying risk areas, since these are where hazard and exposure (such as where people live and where critical infrastructures are located) overlap. The output of this step is to add hazard areas to the base map.

(2) Identify local disaster risks.
Risk areas can be identified based on the result of Step 1 and by confirming exposure. Information on land use, city development plans, etc., are useful to confirm exposure. Risk areas are the areas which should be protected. As the output from this step, risk areas (where hazards and exposures overlap) are added to the base map. Risk areas are the target areas for DRR.

(3) Confirm DRR plans with national and concerned authorities.
In Step 2, areas which should be protected were identified. The next stage is to consider countermeasures for these areas. National and concerned authorities may already have plans to reduce risks. In this step, these plans are confirmed. From this step, a list of existing/planned countermeasures is obtained.

(4) Identify residual risks, considering progress over time.
The steps and time span of the plans of the national and concerned authorities need to be checked. Risks will decline as countermeasures are taken, but some risks will remain while countermeasures are being applied, and even after they are completed. They also may be unexpected disasters, which occur once in 1000 years or so. These are the residual risks the local DRR plan should focus on. In this step, it is recommended to draw a time line of existing and planned countermeasures so that it will be easier to visualize what kind of risks remain and when.

(5) List all necessary DRR measures for local governments.

(6) Prioritize DRR measures.
Based on the list created in Step 5, the best mixture of countermeasures is considered, and they are prioritized.

(7) Arrange for budget allocation at the necessary level.
Budget allocation is critical for a practical and ideal local DRR plan, since the prioritized measures should actually be implemented. In this step, concerned parties are listed, and budget allocations among those parties are considered and agreed.

(8) Implement DRR measures, with periodic review. Situations and contexts in the target area will change over time. Centres of population will move, and even the location of critical infrastructure can change. Thus, a practical and ideal local DRR plan includes a schedule for monitoring and adjustment.

These eight steps will enable the development of a practical, ideal and effective plan to reduce local risks. National and local governments should develop local DRR plans together. It is also important to include all relevant stakeholders, because otherwise implementation will be jeopardized.

Given that 2020, the target year for target *e* (national and local strategy), is so close, three aspects should be considered: locations, disaster types, and investments in DRR. The areas at the greatest risk should prepare their DRR plans first. Protection from the disasters with the greatest potential impact should be prioritized. The investment plan will depend on the type of disaster. And although local DRR plans may include emergency response plans, plans to *reduce risks* should be written first.

Challenges of assistance and ways forward

Once the DRR plans are prepared (hopefully by 2020), emphasis will need to shift to implementation. Three elements are critical in the implementation of DRR: government leadership, allocation of funds, and the capacity of agencies for punctual implementation of budget and plans.

First, there are indispensable roles for both the central and the local government. The local government needs to: (a) identify what the central government plans for their district, and prepare how to reduce the residual risks; (b) regulate to prevent creation of future risks through inappropriate land use planning or development; and (c) prepare for disaster response activities for which the sole responsibility to secure the lives of the people lies in the local government. Some important tasks of the central government are: (a) submitting DRR laws to the parliament; (b) establishing regulations to prevent investment and development activities to cause new and unexpected risks; and (c) convincing the treasury that predisaster investment is more economically efficient than post-disaster recovery or lost opportunity costs; and leading local governments to make their own efforts to prevent risks.

Second, without funding, no DRR plan can be implemented. As mentioned in the previous section on flood control, Japan spent more than 5% of its budget on DRR for several decades after World War II. The government of the Philippines decided to spend no less than 5% for the same purpose (Lawphil, 2010). Other countries are trying to make decisions to spend 2–5%, but this is still not common.

Finally, capacity development is critical for both the central government and local governments. Most local governments do not have the capacity to produce hazard maps. Support from the central government is important and needs to be increased. The character of natural hazards determines the difficulty of risk mapping. For example, local people are already aware of the historical flood area, and that information is useful for initial mapping. For earthquakes, science such as geology and earthquake magnitude are important, but vulnerability depends more strongly on the quality of houses and other structures, so the risk also depends on social aspects and the capacity of the local people to understand their risks.

JICA continues to put its greatest focus on reducing disaster risks in the period of the Sendai Framework (2015–2030). JICA hopes to encourage developing countries to follow the experience of Japan in investment in DRR, at the same time keeping in mind the emerging issues Japan is facing. A shrinking population will change the location of residential areas at risk; greater longevity will make evacuation harder. Climate change will also cause extreme weather events that exceed the design level of existing structures.

Conclusion

Recent discussions of flood control in Japan incorporate the effects of climate change, and the activities of JICA to enhance DRR. JICA, as a main member of the government of Japan, led the negotiation of the UN Sendai Framework for Disaster Risk Reduction 2015–2030, and succeeded in incorporating Japanese experience and knowledge in the Sendai Framework. Local DRR plans are indispensable in ensuring a social system to protect even the poorest people who live in disaster-prone areas. This is also in line with the mandate of the Sustainable Development Goals to 'leave no one behind'. JICA has written an eight-step methodology to formulate local DRR plans. The emphasis in every country needs to shift from planning to implementation. Three elements are critical in the implementation of DRR: government leadership, allocation of funds, and the capacity of agencies for punctual implementation of budget and plans. JICA will continue its assistance to encourage developing countries to follow the experience of Japan in investment in DRR, at the same time keeping in mind the emerging issues Japan is currently facing.

Note

1. The views in this document are those of the authors and do not necessarily represent the views of Tokyo University, Japan International Cooperation Agency or its partners.

Disclosure statement

No potential conflict of interest was reported by the authors.

ORCID

Miki Inaoka http://orcid.org/0000-0003-4874-9224

References

Department for International Development, Environmental Resources Management. (2005, December). *Natural disaster and disaster risk reduction measures: A desk review of costs and benefits, draft final report*. UN Office for Disaster Risk Reduction. Retrieved from http://www.unisdr.org/files/1071_disasterriskreductionstudy.pdf

Inaoka, M., Takeya, K., & Akiyama, S. (2018). JICA's policies, experiences and lessons learned on impacts of urban floods in Asia. *International Journal of Water Resources Development*, *35*(2), 343–363. doi:10.1080/07900627.2018.1444980

Japan International Cooperation Agency. (2015, March). JICA's cooperation on disaster management toward mainstreaming disaster risk reduction: Building disaster resilient societies. Retrieved from http://gwweb.jica.go.jp/km/FSubject0301.nsf/ff4eb182720efa0f49256bc20018fd25/3958a0a725aba98549257a7900124f29/$FILE/E.pdf

Japan International Cooperation Agency. (2016, January). Japan brand ODA (DRR). Author. Retrieved from https://www.jica.go.jp/english/publications/brochures/c8h0vm0000avs7w2-att/japan_brand_04.pdf

Lawphil. (2010, May 27). Republic act no. 10121 Philippine disaster risk reduction and management act of 2010. Author. Retrieved from https://www.lawphil.net/statutes/repacts/ra2010/ra_10121_2010.html

ODI and Global Facility for Disaster Reduction and Recovery at the World Bank. (2013, December). Financing disaster risk reduction: A 20-year story of international aid. ODI. Retrieved from https://www.odi.org/sites/odi.org.uk/files/odi-assets/publications-opinion-files/8574.pdf

Sugimoto, H. (2010, January 10). Opinion: Prof Yutaka Takahasi, Professor Emeritus Tokyo University [オピニオン：ダムやめて治水どうする　東大名誉教授　高橋裕さん]. *Asahi Shimbun*, p. 9.

Takahasi, Y. (1971). Transformation of National Land and Floods [国土の変貌と水害]. Tokyo: Iwanami Shinsho.

UN International Strategy for Disaster Reduction. (2015). Global assessment report on disaster risk reduction 2015. PreventionWeb. Retrieved from https://www.preventionweb.net/english/hyogo/gar/2015/en/home/GAR_2015/GAR_2015_127.html

UN Office for Disaster Risk Reduction. (2005). Hyogo framework for action (HFA). Author. Retrieved from https://www.unisdr.org/we/coordinate/hfa

UNDRR. (2017, February 2). Terminology. Retrieved from https://www.unisdr.org/we/inform/terminology#letter-b

UNGA. (2015, October 21). Resolution adopted by the General Assembly on 25 September 2015. United Nations. Retrieved from https://www.un.org/ga/search/view_doc.asp?symbol=A/RES/70/1&Lang=E

United Nations. (2015a, October 21). A/RES/70/1: Resolution adopted by the General Assembly on 25 September 2015. Author. Retrieved from https://www.un.org/ga/search/view_doc.asp?symbol=A/RES/70/1&Lang=E

United Nations. (2015b, March 18). Sendai Framework for Disaster Risk Reduction 2015–2030. UN Office for Disaster Risk Reduction. Retrieved from https://www.unisdr.org/files/43291_sendaiframeworkfordrren.pdf

Université catholique de Louvain - CRED. (n.d.). EM-DAT: The emergency events database. Retrieved from http://emdat.be/

A retrospective analysis of Laos's Nam Theun 2 Dam

Thayer Scudder

ABSTRACT

I was appointed in 1997 at the start of the World Bank's independent International Environmental and Social Panel of Experts for the Nam Theun 2 Dam. I made over 20 visits to Laos to carry out our analyses, before resigning in March 2014. This article concentrates on the Nakai Plateau resettlement and, where relevant, the dam's Watershed Management and Protection Area, which included a large area between the future reservoir and the Vietnam border. It includes what I consider the main mistakes that were made during the resettlement process on the Nakai Plateau.

Introduction

In the late 1990s and at the turn of the century my viewpoint on the long-term acceptability of large dams had become increasing sceptical (Scudder, 2019). However, as Jacques Leslie (2014) put it in his book *Large Dams*, I was still looking for the one good large dam! That dam, I thought, was Laos's Nam Theun 2 Dam (NT2).

In 1997, the World Bank had asked me to join their independent panel of experts (POE) on the environmental and social impacts of NT2, along with Lee Talbot and T. C. Whitmore. The bank had institutionalized such panels in the 1980s to deal with their most difficult large projects.

Joining the panel was a major mistake on my part. My reason for joining was too influenced by recent emphasis in the World Bank on the need for host countries and engineering companies to pay more attention to environmental and social issues when planning, implementing and monitoring large dams. This increased emphasis was largely due to Robert Goodland, the bank's senior environmental officer, and Michael Cernea, senior social scientist and adviser, who in the 1980s had pioneered the bank's first required environmental and social guidelines. Goodland would be spending quite a bit of his time in Laos actually monitoring the environmental guidelines' implementation in the NT2 case.

In addition, I was very impressed with the scientists, Lee Talbot and T. C. Whitmore, with whom I would be working. Talbot had been environmental adviser for several US presidents, as well as a director-general of the International Union for the Conservation of Nature and Natural Resources (IUCN), while Whitmore, with close associations with

Cambridge University and Oxford, was the premier expert on tropical forests. When illness forced him to resign from the panel, he was replaced by David McDowell, also a former director-general of IUCN, as well as former ambassador of New Zealand to the United Nations. Such colleagues definitely influenced me to join the panel as well as remain on it as long as I did.

Another pioneering aspect associated with NT2 was a four-volume concession agreement (Nam Theun 2 Hydroelectric Power Project Concession Agreement, 2005) the government of Laos signed in 2003 and the World Bank signed in 2005. Pioneered for the NT2 project, the agreement required the project 'to materially improve resettler livelihoods on a sustainable basis' (p. 4, Schedule 4, Part 1 in Vol. 2A), rather than just restore them as required by the bank's own resettlement guidelines.

That pioneering fact alone had encouraged me to join the panel. Our first visit to Laos happened to coincide with the latter part of the 1990s. An Asian economic crisis caused major changes in the final structure of the Nam Theun Power Company (NTPC), of which the most important was the dominance of Electricité du France.

One other general point is important before commencing a detailed analysis of the specifics of why I resigned from the POE. The construction of large dams is seldom, if ever, based on a detailed process of options assessment. Certainly, that is the case with all of the large dam projects that I have evaluated since 1956. As far back as 1966, the US National Academy of Sciences, National Research Council (1966, p. 60), with Gilbert White as chair, emphasized in their report, *Alternatives in Water Management,*that 'there may be many alternatives to water development for promoting regional growth'. Where mega-dams are involved, the stage of options assessment has been bypassed, because the decision to proceed has been made by the head of state or by a country's political elite.

Such political decision making can also jeopardize a project when a change of government or party politics occurs, as in Sri Lanka. Seeing the minister of Mahaweli development as his main rival, the new president tried to marginalize him by downgrading the Mahaweli Project at the very time that additional finance and effort were needed to complete the country's largest project.

Another political factor weakening mega-dams for regional development was the opposition of national and/or state ministries to a single organization taking over functions that they considered their own. In regard to the Tennessee Valley Authority, I remember Gilbert White explaining that the authority's formation created sufficient resistance from both the private sector and other government agencies that the United States never supported another such regional authority.

A similar situation caused the demise of the Bandama Valley Authority in the Ivory Coast. The successor to the first head, who did not have similar support from the president, was unable to resist those ministries that wished to restrict the authority's functions to relocation of project-affected people, and to divide rehabilitation activities like agriculture, fisheries and education among themselves.

Laos's Nam Theun 2 project

The POE first arrived in Laos in January 1997, which was during the severe South East Asian economic crisis, which temporarily reduced Thailand's demand for electricity from

Laos. In 2002 the original consortium collapsed, with Electricité du France becoming the main partner, with 35% of the investment in the NTPC. Laos is the second-largest investor. After 15 years, Laos has the option of increasing its share to 40%, with full ownership transferred at no cost to Laos at the end of the 25-year concession period (for details, see Shoemaker & Robichaud, 2018).

NT2 was a huge project for Laos. It involved two major tributaries of the Mekong River: the Nam Theun and the Xe Bang Fai. The dam was to be built on the Nakai Plateau just before the Nam Theun entered a series of gorges. (An overview of the project is given by World Bank, 2018.)

The Nakai Plateau

Before joining the panel, I should have looked more carefully at the capacity of the resettlement area and of the Lao government to improve the living standards of the large majority of resettlers and their descendants, as well as the interest of the government of Laos and Electricité du France in implementing such a policy effectively. The area available for resettlement once the reservoir was full was only about 40% of the area the villagers had previously used. Further back from the Nam Theun River after reservoir filling, that land for resettlement was also inadequate because of low soil quality, and inadequate availability of timber and other non-timber forest products.

Furthermore, while there was no significant rural host population to compete for resettlement land, most of the over 4500 resettlers belonged to poorly educated and politically weak ethnic minorities unable to compete for natural resources in surrounding areas with relatively recent migrants into some of the local villages.

A new village, Nong Boua Kham, had been built for 57 soldiers brought to the Nakai Plateau to herd cattle for the military. Some of them married women from other villages. Better educated and financed, they were equipped to make the most of the opportunities the project offered. Other competitors for local resources were better educated and politically powerful residents in the small town of Oudomsouk, which also served as the Nakai district centre. As for the nation of Laos, although most of the national population, as on the Nakai Plateau, belonged to ethnic minorities that were protected in the constitution, government policies largely ignored them.

Once the dam was built, reservoir water would be channelled to the southern edge of the plateau, where it would flow down the escarpment in a tunnel to the power complex and via a reservoir and a 25 km concrete channel into the Xe Bang Fai on route to the Mekong. Before the decision to build the NT2 dam, the watershed had been controlled and logged by one of the three military agencies that controlled the long border between Laos and Vietnam. In spite of the large-scale logging and poaching, the watershed was still a magnificent mountain rainforest with a wide range of wildlife, including elephants and the recently discovered Saola, a new genus of large mammals, as well as other mammals and plants yet to be identified. POE visits, largely on foot, to the watershed emphasized both the natural environment (not stressed in this article) and the 4959 villagers who lived along the upper Nam Theun and four watershed tributaries that joined the Nam Theun where it crossed the Nakai Plateau.

The villagers belonged to over 20 ethnic groups in three ethno-linguistic groupings, of which the Vietic-speakers were considered the oldest residents in the watershed. Some had been migratory hunter-gatherers in recent times. As elsewhere, the government had forcibly resettled them in a few of the watershed villages. The largest group were the Brou, who visit with, and are closely related to, the Brou on the Nakai Plateau.

The POE was especially concerned about the villagers' 2% yearly population increase. For that reason, the POE's first emphasis on the need for family planning within the NT2 project dealt with the watershed population, whose women were eager for family planning contraceptive devices and drugs regularly brought to their village by trained personnel.

To increase contact with the Nakai Plateau and the district town and headquarters, the POE emphasized the need to reduce contact with the large town of Lak Xao and Khamkeut District by downgrading the connecting road into a narrow track only for two-wheel tractors.

The government had no intention of turning the watershed villagers (aside from the Vietic-speakers) into resettlers. Two Lao NGOs, with World Bank, IUCN and other financial aid, were involved in providing aid and advice to some of the villages, while an agricultural officer from the Nakai District headquarters was stationed in the watershed. A programme of the Watershed Management and Protection Authority (WMPA) was to train the villagers to patrol for poachers, while the POE wanted selected villages eventually to become involved in assisting biological and social research, and eventually ecotourism, although two villages had already requested that their village get a field research station, which they would build.

Unfortunately, the government had little interest in the cultures of the 20 different ethno-linguistic groups of resettlers on the Nakai Plateau and in the watershed villages. According to Chamberlain (2002, p. 10), one Viet, one Brou and one Sek-speaking community in the watershed should have been identified for three-to-six-month ethnographic studies. The results would become 'the primary reference point for development work that ensues'. His advice was ignored by the government and the project.

Such research would have been essential to correct government policies and actions. Shifting cultivation would have been an excellent example. In the watershed, villagers had learned that when yields in their fields began to decline, the land should be fallowed for at least 10 years before being cultivated again. Not only did the government allow only a three-year fallow, but if the owner failed to cultivate, ownership would be lost.

The Xe Bang Fai component of the NT2 project

The NT2 project is just too complicated to include a detailed discussion of the very different environmental and social impacts along the Xe Bang Fai than on the Nakai Plateau and in the watershed. It was a positive move for the project to include most downstream villages in the development work. But the programme was not comprehensive, nor was it completed, for lack of adequate funding from the beginning.

Project impacts on the 218 Xe Bang Fai villages (reduced, for unexplained reasons, to 158 in later studies) were serious but required very little resettlement. For that reason, not only did the project authorities pay less attention to the Xe Bang Fai than to the Nakai Plateau and the watershed, but where negative impacts occurred, a replacement policy was followed rather than an improvement one.

Project authorities argued over financial responsibilities, with NTPC initially refusing to provide over US$ 16 million, which the POE believed was insufficient; we were proved right in due course. Furthermore, when fiscal responsibility was handed over to the provinces involved, none of them had the funds or the capacity to take over their responsibilities to Xe Bang Fai downstream villages, to mitigate adverse back water effects on villages upstream from the canal exiting from the reservoir below the power station, and to help affected villages along the lower reaches of Xe Bang Fai tributaries.

This situation, along with unacceptable project delays in planning and initiating an effective development programme, was most unfortunate, as the government lost the opportunity to design and implement an effective development programme to serve as a pilot project for communities living downstream from future dams in Laos.

NT2 and the World Bank

At the time of our panel's first visit to Laos in 1997, the World Bank had yet to decide whether to finance the NT2 project. The Bank's initial intention was to help the government of Laos improve its capacity to host the planning, construction and monitoring of the NT2 dam's budgeting, and supervision of construction, as well as dealing with environmental and resettlement issues, with the knowledge gained to be applied also to other large dams in Laos. While over the long term such an approach made sense, it had serious costs for the NT2 dam, which the government planned to build with or without World Bank involvement.

The restructured and renamed Department of Energy Business in the restructured Ministry of Energy and Mines had been actively involved from the start in NT2 planning. The prime minister had an active interest, with the POE working directly with the senior deputy prime minister. Several international agencies had been involved in environmental and social planning well before the POE's arrival. CARE, for example, was largely responsible for baseline analysis of and planning for the approximately 4500 resettlers, and IUCN and the Wildlife Conservation Society were dealing with environmental and social issues, with special attention to the watershed.

During the panel's second visit in 1997, two smaller dams were visited in southern Laos. In both cases, the inability of the government to deal with environmental and resettlement issues was obvious.

The World Bank continued to have an inadequate staff at their Lao headquarters. It fielded its own small, relatively inexperienced teams to deal with various anticipated problems poorly articulated to other donors, and was providing some unreliable finance to IUCN's watershed work, with gaps in World Bank funding interfering with continuity and schedules.

The major ongoing POE concern during the panel's initial visits between 1997 and 2005 continued to be the bank's indecision as to whether or not to finance the NT2 project. We doubted that the bank was aware of the damage resulting from its failure to sign the concession agreement until 2005. The POE's third report (Scudder, Talbot, & Whitmore, 1998) was very critical of such delays, which had 'caused serious breaks in the continuity of funding both for conservation planning and the implementation' of important livelihood projects, such as the project's demonstration farm for small scale resettler irrigation. Funding discontinuity by the bank has also interrupted work by other international agencies. Such discontinuity is especially harmful in a country like Laos with inadequate budgets and capacity of its own. It also undermines the trust and enthusiasm of affected people.

The problem was especially serious where the bank's initial emphasis was on its own small-scale projects, without linkage with the inadequately financed ongoing projects of other agencies, like IUCN, when bank funding stopped. In its fifth report (Scudder, Talbot, & Whitmore, 2001) the POE recommended that the bank 'recognize that further delay in initiating pre-appraisal studies can be expected to make implementation of the resettlement program more difficult', for resettlers were becoming impatient and sceptical about the implementation of the resettlement process.

On 11 April 2002, the Lao National Assembly endorsed the NT2 project as an essential development initiative. On 3 October 2003, the concession agreement was signed by the government. Though the World Bank had yet to agree to fund the project, international interest increased in 2002, when the Asian Development Bank showed an interest in possible NT2 involvement.

The POE's sixth report (Scudder & Talbot, 2003) returned to the risks associated with the World Bank's delayed appraisal of the NT2 project. Further delays had occurred since the fifth report, as had further village impoverishment, simply because households were hesitant to make new livelihood investments.

Without a doubt, the implementation delays increased resettler anxieties and lowered their living standards, which were dependent on NTPC stipends. The situation was eloquently presented to the POE by the representative of the Lao Women's Union at a January 2003 meeting at the Nakai District headquarters. 'People would become poorer as they wait for the project', she said. 'They want to grow fruit trees, but have to wait for the project; they want to open paddy fields but they have to wait for the project.'

The POE has also been critical of the bank's lack of staff continuity in assessing the NT2 project and lack of flexibility in applying the bank's safety net resettlement guidelines. Fortunately, the bank combined its project pre-appraisal and appraisal assessments and agreed in 2004 to finance NT2 with the concession agreement, with the government finally signing in April 2005.

The POE's eight report was submitted in February 2005 (Scudder & Talbot, 2005), three months before the bank signed the concession agreement with the government. While the agreement strengthened the POE's position and emphasized that the POE was to exist throughout the project, at one point some bank officials wanted to deemphasize the POE's role. But the government and NTPC wanted the POE to remain with the project until it was handed over to the government. Apparently, the company at that time believed that the POE's international standing and public reports were in NTPC's interest.

The POE's ninth report (McDowell, Scudder, & Talbot, 2006a) followed the World Bank's signing of the concession agreement (which strengthened the POE's position by strengthening POE responsibilities). The tenth report (McDowell, Scudder, & Talbot, 2006b) followed the ninth report by only nine months due to the seriousness of a range of environmental and resettlement issues.

Government policies

Government resettlement policies, as elsewhere in Laos, were to aggregate the 4500 resettlers residing in 22 Nakai Plateau communities (to be called hamlets in the future) into larger multicultural settlements, at the expense of their cultural independence, of the influence of the weaker communities, and of access to sufficient land for agriculture and livestock management, as well as of the hunting and gathering interests of the weaker ethnic groups.

Two economic models that would require less land were under consideration: agroforestry and more intensive irrigated crop agriculture, which initially involved three households on the demonstration farm (the POE recommended, without effect, that the number be increased to at least 10 households so that community formation experiments could also be included). Furthermore, resettlement livelihood activities were being delayed due to the initial interest of resettlers in the development of new homes with schools, and access to roads to the district headquarters and stores, and to the outside world.

Lao government policies

Following the prime minister's Decree 193, of December 2000, which established the boundaries of the NT2 watershed, Decree 25, of 26 February 2001, specified the objectives and activities of the WMPA. NTPC agreed to release initial funds for the authority in April 2003.

On the Nakai Plateau, Decree 37, of April 22, authorized and pioneered letting resettler communities undertake 'sustainable forestry business activities', including felling and sale of timber, and a regulation from the provincial governor established a financially independent Nakai Plateau Village Forestry Association.

A major accomplishment during the past few years has been to establish NT2 as the lead and most complex project in Laos's economic development, which included important linkages between the watershed villages and villagers on the Nakai Plateau. Attention should be paid to the cultures and economies of the various ethnic groups in both zones, as recommended by Laos-based anthropologist James Chamberlain, a recommendation that the government and donors ignored. The POE did not have the time on its short missions to deal with that fault, although we did try to return to the same families in carefully selected Nakai Plateau villages.

Impact of the NT2 dam on the resettlers' natural resources

Perhaps the panel's largest single mistake was to underestimate the adverse effect that the NT2 dam would have on the resettlers' natural resource base. The resettlers lost to the future reservoir approximately 45,000 hectares (ha) of highly productive crop and grazing land, plus valuable timber and non-timber forest products, in return for only 20,000 ha of low-quality land further inland from the Nam Theun River, which would have to support a denser and larger population due to government policies, especially village consolidation and allowed immigration policies.

Village consolidation

The POE had little success in convincing the government not to apply the national policy to consolidate resettler villages into larger communities and to combine ethnic groups. Certainly, that would reduce costs of providing schools and clinics. It would also integrate the various ethnic groups with the Lao-speaking majority at the expense of their languages and cultures. Furthermore, consolidation on the Nakai Plateau would adversely affect economic access to land for agriculture and grazing, and for trees and other natural resources. Consolidation would especially lead to the exploitation of the Vietic population, who were formerly hunter-gatherers, as well as of other cultures.

Immigrants

In the NT2 case there have been three kinds of immigrants taking up residence in resettler villages. Least culturally and economically intrusive are the relatives and households of similar cultural background who choose, for a variety of reasons, to join a resettled village, especially from the watershed, and were allowed to by the government of Laos.

Then there are two categories of better educated Lao-speakers who choose to move into several Nakai plateau villages. Seeking employment, one category included men (with and without families) who came from the Lak Xao area or neighbouring districts between Lak Xao and the Nakai Plateau during a period of major pre-dam logging by two large companies. They tended to settle in resettler villages. The second category were soldiers that the military sent to the Nakai Plateau to herd cattle for the army. They were given their own village (Nong Boua Kham) by the government, to which they brought women they married from various resettler villages.

When the dam was built, and immigrants from Lak Xao and surrounding areas preferred to return to where they came from following resettlement, NTPC provided funds to prepare a small irrigated area (Nam Pan) in their homeland to which they were willing to move. But that scheme was a fiasco for several reasons. The two most important were that the farmland available would be inadequate to support married children, and that the water for irrigation from a small stream had been contaminated by an illegal Army gold mine near the top of a steep ridge above Nam Pan.

When I visited the mine, I was served brandy by the welcoming Vietnamese workers, who pointed out that the mine would be extended over a large area. The NT2 project solution was to integrate the disappointed immigrants into the already overpopulated northernmost Nakai Plateau resettlement cluster, which contained more households than the central or southern cluster. As for the 57 soldiers and their families, the army, having backed down on initial plans to move them off the Nakai Plateau, resettled them in their own village in the overcrowded northern cluster.

A former protected area of several thousand hectares across the Nam Theun from land under the jurisdiction of the WMPA was made available. The POE was unable to convince the government to further extend the northern resettlement area with land controlled by the army further downstream.

Another major example where a POE recommendation for benefiting resettlers was ignored was the refusal of the company and the government to hire a senior social scientist to deal with major social issues, and other social scientists to deal with social issues as they arise. Instead, the company hired two engineers as senior staff to deal with the major economic and social issues in resettled villages. Like other officials in the field, they complained of micromanagement by the company's senior official (who was based in the capitol and would not let senior staff in the field to do their jobs), insufficient funds, and insufficient junior extension workers (especially livelihood assistants, who should be based in villages), whose number was reduced through time.

Also rejected was the POE recommendation that the project encourage a few students at the National University of Laos to do their senior thesis on relevant NT2 resettlement topics, and that other students (including resettlers) be trained for employment.

Participatory family planning

Far too little attention was paid by project authorities to family planning, though early on two non-government organizations not only emphasized its importance but also emphasized that village women wanted not only family planning assistance but also reliable access to birth control medicine on a three-month basis. The POE recommended a mobile clinic that would make preannounced visits to every village.

The POE followed up by recommending (in its seventh report) that participatory family planning in the context of health and livelihood improvement must be a NT2 priority issue. Ten years later (in 2014), when I resigned from the panel (I was replaced by Elizabeth Mann, who joined David McDowell and Lee Talbot), the government had still not implemented an effective family planning programme – a failure that will have large economic and social costs.

Family planning must be included because of the limited land available for future generations. The second-generation problem had already become one of the project's most serious problems.

The second-generation problem

It was already apparent by 2006. In the pilot village (Nong Boua), new marriages involving children had already occurred, with up to three families living in a single house or a new house being built on a plot meant for a single household. Greater pressure on the limited arable land resources can be anticipated, especially in the northernmost resettlement cluster, where consolidation of six villages into one area and major road construction have significantly reduced the availability of arable land. NTPC has made the second-generation problem more severe through more emphasis on village construction rather than on the economic development of the households living in those villages.

In its 18th report, based on a visit in early 2010 (McDowell, Scudder, & Talbot, 2010), the POE noted that livelihood activities should be emphasized before the second-generation problem emerged. Unfortunately, not only does the second-generation problem already exist but the various project agencies appear to be unaware of its threat to livelihood development goals for resettlers of the first, second and all future generations. Furthermore, to the best of my knowledge, only the government of Laos has emphasized the importance of secondary school education and training for second-generation children, so that they could become school teachers and extension staff for village development activities.

Need for a Vietic and other ethnic villages

A Vietic village

Also ignored by the government was the POE and World Bank–supported request of the small Vietic population to have their own village in their own spirit territory. Instead, they were resettled in two of the large consolidated villages.

In both of those villages the POE found that consolidated Vietic households were not only exploited by other villagers but also given inadequate livelihood opportunities and health care (especially in regard to drug abuse, with exploited Vietic labourers sometimes paid in drugs). The project also ignored the request by both the World Bank and the POE that an appropriate NGO be hired to work with Vietic and other ethnic households.

Pakatan

Pakatan culture is related to Vietic culture. When the POE learned that a Pakatan village was to be integrated with two large Hmong villages, we urged the deputy prime minister to make an exception to government policy by allowing Pakatan to remain a geographically separate village, as opposed to a weak hamlet in a consolidated village. Though he agreed to this one exception, politically Pakatan was integrated with two Hmong villages, while the new Hmong-dominated Village Development Committee gained access to the Pakatans' former land.

Nong Boua

Nong Boua was the first ethnic village to which the POE made frequent visits. In my last visit to Laos, we sat for over an hour one rainy evening with the former headman and his wife. Their village had been incorporated as a hamlet into one of the three most powerful resettler villages. When I asked whether that had caused them any problems, they answered: when jobs became available, their hamlet never received any.

Resettler livelihood

Some NTPC personnel saw NT2 as only a hydro project, even after the official name was changed in 2007 to the Nam Theun 2 Multipurpose Project. Though it was especially true of NTPC dam construction personnel, even road and village construction were given priority over livelihoods.

Monitoring

The major international agencies involved in the NT2 project funded their own monitoring systems. Initially the World Bank funded two such systems; one was the independent POE. The other reported directly to the president of the bank. Because it was duplicating the activities of the POE, the bank's system was eventually terminated.

The POE was appalled by the inability of the NT2 project agencies to design and use a satisfactory monitoring system prior to the 9 December 2008 inauguration of the dam:

> The October 1998 Census and Socio-Economic Survey on the Nakai Plateau provided a starting point for implementing a statistical analysis of changes and continuities of resettler livelihood throughout the Resettlement Implementation Period. Rejecting that approach, NT2 Project agencies attempted to monitor resettlement impacts on every household. Such an approach is 'neither feasible or practical' as the POE stated in its first report (February 1997) for providing the type of data and analysis needed for adaptive management purposes. (McDowell et al., 2010, p. 10)

Though by 2010 the project's Monitoring and Evaluation Unit was finally designing, and preparing to implement, a more appropriate system, the POE has had to rely on its own interviewing to explore living standard and income trends. During our February 2010 visit, our concern had increased that resettler incomes might be dropping in a significant number of households. Further data collected in October 2010 in a small number of households and from officials did suggest that over the past three years, the income of a significant number of previously non-vulnerable households had begun to drop, while debt loads were increasing.

The POE recommended 'that the Monitoring and Evaluation Unit promptly check the POE findings on debt and income trends and that the NTPC gender specialist and the social scientist be included in the survey team' (pp. 10–12).

The five livelihood pillars

The information that follows is based on my own knowledge until March 2014, complemented by information from the POE's most recent report (McDowell, Mann, & Talbot, 2018b).

The fisheries pillar

This pillar reminded me of the days when I was the senior sociology consultant for the Fisheries Division of the UN's Food and Agriculture Organization (Scudder & Conelly, 1985). Of the five pillars, fisheries were the most reliable resource the NT2 project created for the resettlers.

Throughout the tropics, the productivity of a fishery increases during the first few years as fish feed on the organic material that has been inundated. Once that material has been consumed or dispersed, productivity drops to the reservoir's carrying capacity.

Fish catches in the Nakai Reservoir have followed that classic pattern. After relatively high yields following dam closure, the catch more or less stabilized at a lower level. The NTPC Fishery Research Unit reported that the catch had remained relatively similar for roughly four years, up to 2013, the last years for which they had data prior to my departure.

Unfortunately, the resettlers lost access to a significant portion of fish during the best years of fishing when the government allowed a politically influential timber company to contract for the removal of rosewood and conifers from the reservoir. Barges were hired; the POE counted at least 12 operating on the reservoir at one time. On another occasion, 25 barges were moored on the shore, and their employees continued to fish; some were professional fishers from the Nan Ngum Reservoir in northern Laos.

While the reservoir was restricted to the resettlers, and approximately 300 Oudomsouk residents, for an initial 10 years and then 20 years by the prime minister's decrees, the barge workers fished during the best years. Unfair competition also came from the Oudomsouk fishers, who could afford more effective equipment.

Both female and male resettlers fished, with women subsequently learning how to process and cook fish for marketing.

The success of the fisheries pillar was also limited by other factors. One that most village fishers emphasized was competition from outsiders (like the barge labourers) illegally fishing the reservoir. Actually, there were two types of illegal fishing. One was the villagers themselves, some fishing in protected areas reserved for reproduction, and some selling their catch to outside traders, thus avoiding the 7% tax on catches that would otherwise go to the village fishing association. The other type of illegal fishing was by outsiders. The POE's concern was that such illegal fishing steals resources from the resettlers, undermining the sustainability of their most reliable livelihood pillar.

What is required is more effective law enforcement on the reservoir, with village fishery associations and the WMPA patrolling by boat to deter illegal fishing. For years there has been friction between the village fishing associations and the WMPA, due to the WMPA's inability to use its authority to patrol protected areas of the reservoir over which it has responsibility or to cooperate with the resettlers. This is particularly a problem where the WMPA controls a key section of the reservoir north of the Thalang Bridge and upstream from the dam that falls in another district between the bridge and the dam, which is where most of the illegal fishing and marketing takes place, but where the WMPA does not allow resettler patrolling or trading. Some co-patrols with the WMPA and the village fishing associations have been undertaken in these areas, and these are a welcome but still exceptional development.

There is an urgent need to give the resettler fishers a feeling of ownership of the fish resource and recognition of their self-interested responsibility to watch for and report or apprehend those conducting illegal activities that undermine their fishery livelihood. One problem is that most resettlers still have not even registered their own boats or become active supporters of their village fishing associations.

The POE's 28th report noted that a priority review of the fisheries pillar had yet to be completed. 'Any real improvements in the effectiveness of enforcement have been, at least anecdotally, purely temporary – illegal fishing and trading remain a problem. Many boats are unregistered and even fewer fishers carry licenses' (McDowell et al., 2018b, p. 14).

Forestry pillar

The forestry pillar was unique in Laos, as it was the first time that the central government gave a rural population control over the forests adjacent to their villages. Expectations for the pillar were high, since it was expected to provide a third of the income for each resettler village. Since joining the POE, David McDowell has taken over responsibility for the forestry pillar, so my assessment of its history is based largely on his knowledge and on the last report of the POE (McDowell et al., 2018b).

To summarize, no dividends were paid to resettlers between April 2012 and my departure in 2014; the inventorizing, protection and management of the forest resource have been minimal; the harvesting and use of the timber have been deficient, to a level which has produced serious waste; marketing has been inadequate, and the endeavours to meet market demands seriously flawed; and there has been little success in the few attempts to begin the process of fostering regeneration and forestation of degraded or cleared forest land.

The size of the forest estate has been reduced by encroachments, the largest being the conversion of some of the land to additional agricultural land, which has been distributed to resettlers and often burned off for shifting cultivation without the considerable timber resources being harvested beforehand. When logs were removed ahead of the burning, they were seldom processed but only abandoned in log yards or ponds. One assessment is that shifting cultivation, mainly for rice, had cleared around 700 ha of community forests in 2013, which would amount to 4–5% of the hamlet forests.

Looking to the future, the initial and inclusive Village Forestry Management Committee failed the resettlers. According to the POE's July 2018 report (McDowell et al., 2018b), resettlers have received no income from the forestry pillar for four years. Sixteen hamlet forestry management plans have been completed, with sufficient resettler participation, but implementation has yet to occur.

Agriculture pillar

As late as March and April 2008, no full-time national and international marketing experts had been recruited, not just to cover the resettlers but for farmers in all project areas. In its 15th Report (30 April 2009), the POE's recommendation on this matter was one of the most important, because project efforts to commercialize agriculture and livestock require that marketing receive equal importance with production. Though a suitable national expert was recruited, he resigned because marketing had yet to be properly integrated within the livelihood programme.

Each resettler household received one 0.66 ha plot and one 0.22 ha plot, an area for a household garden, as well as access to irrigation, reservoir and island drawdown areas, and gully dams. In the POE's opinion the results from these resources nowhere near justify the work put into them. The reasons are various. The soils are seldom fertile in the resettlement area; the pumped irrigation and intensive farming practices systems are a new and poorly implemented technology; the two larger projects on the 0.66 ha farms are too complex.

Agriculture received a major setback in 1973 when NTPC brought in a French couple from Madagascar who stopped what agriculture had been accomplished, especially in Nong Boua, where the resettlers had established irrigated agriculture and the first water user association. Mushrooms were grown, and several other crops, which women had begun to market in Oudomsouk. The French couple stopped all such agricultural development to concentrate on pasture development. Their pasture ideas were good, but should not have been encouraged at the expense of other agricultural development underway at the time. It took NTPC over a year to realize their mistake and to end the French couple's contract.

Not only had a year been lost, but when I resigned in 2014 no water user associations had been formed to service the irrigation that the concession agreement required to be initiated on the bottom portion of the resettlers' 0.66 ha field. In spite of the investment of time and energy by the resettlers, the government and the company, agriculture was still a disappointing sector at the time of my departure in March 2014. Remunerative and usually less labour-intensive pursuits existed, like fishing and timber poaching.

I collaborated with David McDowell on the agricultural pillar sections that follow. Many of the statistics make for discouraging reading. In spite of a range of options being offered, resettlers use of the largest allocation of land to them (the 0.66 ha plot per household) was declining, not growing. Agro-forestry, pasture development and industrial crop cultivation (e.g. cassava) were offered, but only agro-forestry has been taken up with any enthusiasm or significant results.

Agro-forestry is the bright spot on the agricultural front. The area devoted to it has been growing. This is clearly a growth area, and plans are afoot to expand the sector accordingly. At the time of my departure, about a third of households were receiving seeds for planting, a proportion which should be expanded as rapidly as possible.

Likewise, an intensified programme aimed and designed largely for the second-generation families should be initiated to take up the opportunities offered by the idle irrigation systems set up by the company. Only 31 are currently being used. At least another 50 are apparently repairable. They should be repaired, and associated 0.22 ha plots should be reassigned to hand-picked second-generation families to develop the unutilized irrigation systems. Though NTPC was critical of contract farming, that was another option to be considered by the second generation.

Is a substantial intensification and acceleration of the use of the 0.66 ha plots realistic? We spent time with a hard-working woman, employing two or three others. Two-thirds of her fully developed plot, accessing water for irrigation from a nearby tank, was planted in vigorously growing pineapple plants. Under three long seedling and plant shelters, she was producing scores of vegetables and hundreds of plant seedlings for sale. There was not a plough in sight. Each cabbage or chilli plant was in its own carefully dug round hole, filled with ground-up soil fertilized with home-made organic matter (derived from rice husks, a vegetable oil additive and decayed vegetable materials) and watered on a daily basis. She makes a good living from her labours and enterprise. Replicated many times over, with a variety of products to head off over-production for the limited local market, this operation could make the resettlement agricultural sector look healthier. This is the beginnings of a farmer-to-farmer exercise being set up, and already this woman is showing others how she manages. More such exercises must be undertaken, with the village extension workers mobilized to foster them. Farmer-to-farmer programmes are working well in the Xe Bang Fai downstream area.

Good progress is being made in increasing the percentage of resettlers growing products for their own use in home gardens.

There also is a need to set targets and timelines regarding the use of reservoir margins for gully dams and the reservoir and islands for drawdown agriculture, which has a long history among the resettlers. In the past, practically every village had access to a small Nam Theun tributary where a gully dam could be built. One such dam was built by the demonstration farm, which provided enough water to irrigate the crops of the three resident families.

The potential of drawdown agriculture along the shores of islands in a hamlet's territory or the shore of the reservoir has often been mentioned by both the company and the POE for growing varieties of rice and, more likely, for creating pasture for cattle and buffalo. Major complementary problems are the shallowness of the reservoir and climate change, which together could cause unexpected flooding and flood recession, which have destroyed different varieties of rice in the past.

The comments on agriculture in the POE's 28th report (July 2018)[1] refer to the planning process rather than to plan implementation, since agricultural development has not met expectations. The necessary agriculture planning will be incorporated in the Nakai Plateau Livestock, Agriculture and Fisheries Project. Led by the District Agriculture and Forestry Office, this plan 'should be the basis of a new agricultural development plan to meet the requirements of the concession agreement and ... its funding and technical support should be fully integrated into overall development planning for the resettlement villages' (McDowell et al., 2018b, p. 11).

Livestock pillar

Livestock is a livelihood pillar that is assuming greater importance for the resettlers. It includes pigs, goats, ducks, chickens, and, especially important, large stock, including cattle and buffalo. Because of their potential contribution to the livelihood of the resettlers, large livestock are of primary concern in the livestock pillar.

In 2013 buffalo were starving in large numbers because of lack of grazing area – a serious problem that resettlers said never happened when they lived at their old village sites. Since this starvation was due to the project, the POE recommended that the company provide compensation for the thousands of buffalo that had died since October 2007. As the POE explained to NTPC management, some resettlers have lost over 50% of their buffalo, while others had to sell emaciated buffalo at half price. Some resettlers solved their problem by illegally allowing some of their buffalo to run wild across the Nam Theun in the watershed. The POE visited one family that had managed to keep a small herd together there by giving them a salt lick during regular visits.

Over the years the POE has emphasized the need to vaccinate buffalos and cattle to protect them from epidemic diseases such as foot and mouth disease and haemorrhagic septicaemia, which might be introduced from the watershed and Khamkeut District, where the diseases have been reported and rates of vaccination were low. An ongoing, comprehensive vaccination programme is now being carried out on the Nakai Plateau by village veterinarians and village extension workers, with support of the company. The first comprehensive round was completed by the end of July 2014, and good progress has been reported, although the totals remain low by international standards.

While both buffalo and cattle provide sources of cash in emergencies, in recent years, it appears to us that a shift is occurring to raise cattle for income, with people in several villages reporting to us that they were shifting from buffalo to cattle ownership. For example, in Ban Done Village, we were told that many villagers increasingly prefer cattle to buffalo. They felt that the cattle were more disease resistant, but significantly, they reported that their cows could expect a calf a year, which, after three years, could be sold for LAK 2.5 to 2.8 million. Buffalo are less prolific. Another example is Nakai Village, where people were shifting rapidly from buffalo to cattle and noting that the cattle provided 'a stable income'. These are two of the largest villages on the plateau, so the livestock situation there may be a significant indicator of trends in other villages also.

Most of the buffalo and cattle owned by the resettlers feed on rather sparse grasses and other vegetation, often in the degraded forest areas. They have adapted to this rather rough diet, and they show moderate productivity on it. However, if the livestock are to be managed for maximum profit, they require substantially more nutritious fodder. For higher productivity, they need to form more project-encouraged production groups and require better managed pasture development, better livestock feeding practices and better animal husbandry. Pasture improvement will require application of fertilizers, active management of the livestock, and probably more nutritious feed species. Above all, it will require understanding by the villagers of the importance of livestock development. Such expenditures are totally foreign to most resettlers, and achieving their active cooperation and participation would require a significant educational effort.

Such education has not occurred. According to the POE report of 2018, 'we once again drew attention to the continued rapid growth in numbers of large livestock reported by farmers well above the assessed carrying capacity of the plateau based on existing practices of open grazing.... One reason there has been no crisis yet is that possibly a fifth or more of these animals – at least 1000 by the village reports we received on this mission – have in fact have been turned loose to graze in the protected area where they do considerable damage, and the WMPA wants them out' (McDowell et al., 2018a, p. 12).

Off-farm pillar

The concession agreement places considerable emphasis on 'training on other income generating activities and technical support' and 'that two types of training ... are conducted' (10.4 and 10.4.1). One type deals with the first four pillars. The other type emphasizes training and extension programmes aimed at, for example,

> involving villagers in the defining and planning and implementation of education and training components of the resettlement program which will be directed towards improving the standard of living; helping adapt and upgrade the skills of the villagers to facilitate the adoption of the practices proposed under the livelihood model ... ; [and] providing supporting health, nutrition and vocational education for the successful adoption of new livelihood systems across and between communities.

According to POE Report 21B,

> the Off-Farm Pillar has yet to attract the attention paid to the other four pillars. More attention is needed now for further education and especially vocational training for second generation students who are interested in careers as members of Nakai District's team of development workers. (McDowell, Scudder, & Talbot, 2013)

While the POE is pleased to note more emphasis on training the second generation as electricians and mechanics, training as masons, carpenters and in other skilled professions is also needed to maintain resettler villages and provide employment opportunities elsewhere. According to POE Report 22,

> The proliferation of off-farm activities has happened only slowly, with resettlers inclined to engage in pursuits that they are familiar with or in more immediately remunerative activities like rosewood gathering and selling activities. It has to be said that until recently here has been a lack of dynamism in the area of capacity building in general. (McDowell & Talbot, 2014)

According to the POE's latest report (McDowell et al., 2018b), Nakai District now has four staff members working full-time on off-farm programmes, three of whom are from the district. An initial monitoring survey in April, 2018, shows

> growth within both small businesses and employment since 2016. A total of 62 people attended training courses from 2015 until 2018. Of these, 34 found a job of which 20 were in a field related to their training. It isn't possible to attribute all this activity to NTPC programmes, but the results are encouraging. (p. 15)

Key NTPC issues

Between 1997 and 2014, when I resigned from the POE, NTPC had given environmental and social issues significantly less standing than construction. Four-to-six-month resettlement delays had occurred. A major problem was that NTPC's head contractor operates essentially independently, with little consultation with any other teams. For example, too many labourers at the dam site would have a negative impact on the surrounding environment and at the expense of a future programme on eco-tourism. When we discussed the size of the dam site labour camp during our January 2006 mission, we were assured by the head contractor that the camp would hold a maximum of 650 workers and that sewage and other environmental safeguards were taken. Just prior to our next visit, we learned that the head contractor had increased the labour force during the 2006 dry season to about 1100 and that more labourers were expected during the next dry season. Clearly, the head contractor went ahead with this breach of agreement with no further consultation.

During the POE's next visit, the POE required, first, that the head contractor produce a specific environmental assessment and protection plan for the dam labour site, including sewage disposal. Second, the plan must be agreed on by the NTPC teams, and the POE must be given adequate proof of implementation. Third, there must be a written agreement from the head contractor that the agreed-on figure cannot be exceeded without the concurrence of NTPC and the POE. Only then will the POE approve a specified increase in the number of labourers at the camp above the originally agreed 650.

I recall another high NTPC official who was convinced that the company would find it much easier to get future contracts in Laos for hydro projects as opposed to multipurpose ones. He stated that conviction at the ceremony for initial power generation. He referred to NT2 as a hydro project, though its official title at the ceremony now was as a multipurpose project.

As another arbitrary and environmentally destructive example, the well-built and attractive labour camp at the dam site, with kitchen and dining area overlooking the reservoir, which could have played an important role in developing an eco-tourism programme, was totally removed when the dam was completed. The engineers were also unaware that illegal and environmentally destructive logging was going on less than 300 yards from the labour camp entrance. Very destructive to the resettlement programme, totally inadequate attention was paid to the adverse impacts of the coffer dam on resettlement villages and fields for grazing and cultivation of rice further up the watershed side of the Nam Theun, as well as along a major watershed tributary. This affected the agriculture and housing of at least seven villages, whose resettlers had to be shifted to temporary housing before the next wet season.

The POE also found that reservoir water backed up behind the NT2 dam had flooded approximately 80 ha of rainfed rice along the Nam Sot, which entered the reservoir from the watershed. Careful hydrological surveys completed on the resettler (south) side of the reservoir had not been completed by the company on the watershed side. The negative impact on the Nam Sot also brought attention to at least one village that was negatively affected by flooding. As a result, it was forcibly integrated into upstream Nam Sot villages, all of which were then consolidated into one village.

Project road contractors tended to ignore resettlement and forest issues in the alignment of major and minor roads. It was apparent that one subcontractor at least had only limited experience in how to use the natural contours of the land in a high-rainfall area to lessen erosion and subsidence, or how to build effective lateral drainage systems to lessen the impact on slopes of large volumes of runoff, or how to use the forest cover as protection from the impact of downpours.

Government officials were unaware of the ability of outsiders to bypass the main gate and checkpoint when taking illegally purchased fish for sale in the city of Lak Xao. The checkpoint was located where the roads from the reservoir, the NT2 dam and a large Hmong village joined. Behind that village, the POE found that a rough track had been built though Hmong gardens which allowed illegal fish traders and other thieves to drive around and behind the checkpoint gate and back to the main road.

The future of Laos

A long thin country, with a mountainous border mainly with Vietnam, Laos's many Mekong tributaries running the width of the country are well suited for dams, whose hydropower is expected to make Laos the 'energy battery' for the surrounding countries. 'As of May 2019, the Lao government reported having 63 operational hydropower plants ... an additional 112 under construction ... and a further 340 planned' (International Rivers Network, 2019, p. 8). What those figures indicate is that every Mekong tributary in the country will eventually be compromised by one or more dams. Based on my experience with dams since 1956, flows in those tributaries will be conserved and regularized to generate as much hydropower as possible.

The situation in Laos at the beginning of the 2019 rainy season is that the Mekong in effect ceased flowing in central Laos, primarily because dams in both China and Laos are retaining in their reservoirs all the rainfall that is occurring. The situation is complex and appears to involve, according to concerned experts, the interplay of El Niño, climate change, and especially, in my opinion, the increasing number of dams in China and Laos.

China is the dominant player among all the countries along the Mekong River. China's 11 operating dams

> have a total electricity generating capacity of 21,300 megawatts – more than the installed capacity of all the downriver countries combined. For starters, by reducing the flow of fresh water and nutrient-rich sediment from the Himalayas into the sea, these mega-dams are causing a retreat of the Mekong Delta in southern Vietnam. The resulting sea water intrusion is forcing rice farmers to switch to shrimp farming or growing reeds. (Chellaney, 2019, p. 1)

China's maintenance work on the Jinghong River in the summer of 2019

> resulted in the release of torrents of water. The resulting floods in Thailand and Laos destroyed crops and disrupted fish. Damaging local people's livelihood, China then refilled the Jinghong Dam using Mekong water. The drop in downstream levels compounded water-scarce conditions, the result of a 40% shortfall in monsoon rains in June and July instead of overflowing during the summer, the Mekong River Commission reports, the river reached record low levels, depleting fish stocks and setting back rice production.... Despite all this, China has shown no sign that its dam-building frenzy is abating. (p. 2)

In Laos, initially reduced 2019 flows from its depleted reservoirs are also playing a role in lowering the Mekong. The Mekong in Laos in June and July is now so low that some types of aquatic life are dying. Meanwhile, the environmental and socio-economic impact of Laos's dams on Laos's river basin population can be expected to worsen over the length of the dammed tributaries. Road construction to dam sites will be especially devastating where watersheds close to the Chinese and Vietnam borders will make the catchment of each dam more accessible for environmental degradation (especially due to logging and poaching). Dams requiring resettlement from the reservoir basin are likely to make most of the residents and their descendants worse off. Most of those living downstream are likely to suffer the same fate, since their livelihood is likely to be harmed by the impact of the regularization of river flows on the valuable wetlands, on flood recession agriculture, on fishing, and on herding in the dry season. Tourism, an important source of income in Laos is also apt to suffer, when major rivers like the Nam Ou are no longer free flowing.

Then there is always the threat of dam collapse. On 23 July 2018, saddle dam D collapsed during the construction of the Xe Pian Xe Namnoy Dam. Downstream in Attapeu Province, up to 71 villagers died, a large but unknown number are missing and 6600 are displaced. A year later, compensation has been totally inadequate for the displaced to restore their former lifestyles. In one case, the land that was cleared was subsequently given to a Chinese company to grow bananas, and the resettlers, who had been growing rice on that land, were expected to work on the banana farm (International Rivers Network, 2019).

I have never been able to understand the rationale behind the government's lack of concern for the welfare of citizens being forced off their land, not just in connection with dams, but also when special economic zones are declared for industry or when the land of rural or urban citizens is allocated to private companies for plantations or urban development. Also destructive of local cultures is the government's lack of concern when better educated Lao-speaking immigrants further increase the pressure on resettlers' cultures when the government insists that they be consolidated as hamlets in consolidated villages.

Note

1. David McDowell, Elizabeth Mann (who replaced me) and Lee Talbot were the members of the report, while Rob Laking served as POE advisor and editor. He played a major role in pulling together the five pillar sections.

Disclosure statement

No potential conflict of interest was reported by the author.

References

Chamberlain, J. R. (2002). *Assessment of economic potentials and comparative advantages of the ethnic minority groups of Lao RDR*. Vientiane: Report Prepared for the Asian Development Bank.

Chellaney, B. (2019, August 2). Damming the Mekong Basin to environmental hell. *Project Syndicate*. Retrieved from https://www.project-syndicate.org/commentary/china-dams-mekong-basin-exacerbate-drought-by-brahma-chellaney-2019-08

International Rivers Network. (2019). *Reckless endangerment: Assessing responsibility for the Xe Pian-Xe Namnoy Dam collapse*. Retrieved from https://www.internationalrivers.org/resources/report-reckless-endangerment-assessing-responsibility-for-the-xe-pian-xe-namnoy-dam

Leslie, J. (2014, August 22). Large dams just are not worth the cost. *New York Times*. Retrieved from https://www.nytimes.com/2014/08/24/opinion/sunday/large-dams-just-arent-worth-the-cost.html

McDowell, D., Mann, E., & Talbot, L. M. (2018a). *Laos - Nam Theun 2 Multipurpose Project: Twenty-seventh report of the international environmental and social panel of experts (English)* (Panel of Experts; Report No. 27). Washington, DC: World Bank Group.

McDowell, D., Mann, E., & Talbot, L. M. (2018b). *Laos - Nam Theun 2 Multipurpose Hydro Project : Twenty-eighth report on the international environmental and social panel of experts (English)* (Panel of Experts; Report No. 28). Washington, DC: World Bank Group.

McDowell, D., Scudder, T., & Talbot, L. M. (2006a). *Laos - Nam Theun 2 Project: Ninth report of the international environmental and social panel of experts (English)* (Panel of Experts; Report No, 9). Washington, DC: World Bank.

McDowell, D., Scudder, T., & Talbot, L. M. (2006b). *Laos - Nam Theun 2 Hydropower Project: Tenth report of the international environmental and social panel of experts (English)* (Panel of Experts; Report No. 10). Washington, DC: World Bank.

McDowell, D., Scudder, T., & Talbot, L. M. (2010). *Laos - Nam Theun 2 Multipurpose Project: Seventeenth report of the international environmental and social panel of experts (English)* (Panel of Experts; Report No. 17). Washington, DC: World Bank.

McDowell, D., Scudder, T., & Talbot, L. M. (2013). *Laos - Nam Theun 2 multipurpose project: Report 21A and 21B of the international environmental and social panel of experts (English)* (Panel of Experts; Report No. 21). Washington, DC: World Bank.

McDowell, D., & Talbot, L. M. (2014). *Lao People's Democratic Republic Nam Theun 2 Multipurpose Project: Twenty-third report of the international and social panel of experts (English)* (Panel of Experts; Report No. 23). Washington, DC: World Bank Group.

Nam Theun 2 Hydroelectric Power Project Concession Agreement. (2005). *Consolidation. VOLUME 2A schedule 4 part 1: Social component (other than for Downstream Areas)*.

National Academy of Sciences, National Research Council. (1966). *Alternatives in water management*. Washington, DC: Publication 1408.

Scudder, T. (2019). *Large dams: Long term impacts on riverine communities and free flowing rivers*. Singapore: Springer.

Scudder, T., & Conelly, T. (1985). *Management systems for riverine fisheries*. Institute for Development Anthropology, for the Food and Agriculture Organization.

Scudder, T., & Talbot, L. M. (2003). *Sixth report of the international environmental and social panel of experts for the Nam Theun 2 hydro project*. Vientiane: Lao People's Democratic Republic.

Scudder, T., & Talbot, L. M. (2005). *Eighth report of the international environmental and social panel of experts for the Nam Theun 2 hydro project*. Vientiane: Lao People's Democratic Republic.

Scudder, T., Talbot, L. M., & Whitmore, T. C. (1998). *Third report of the international environmental and social panel of experts. Nam Theun 2 hydro project*. Vientiane: Lao People's Democratic Republic.

Scudder, T., Talbot, L. M., & Whitmore, T. C. (2001). *Fifth report of the international environmental and social panel of experts*. Vientiane: Ministry of Industry and Handicraft.

Shoemaker, B., & Robichaud, W. (Eds). (2018). *Dead in the water: Global lessons from the World Bank's model hydropower project in Laos*. University of Wisconsin Press.

World Bank. (2018). *Nam Theun 2 project overview*. Retrieved from https://www.worldbank.org/en/country/lao/brief/nam-theun-2-project-overview-and-update

What I learned from Asit Biswas about transboundary water, ethics, mentoring and, in general, how to be a better human being

Aaron T. Wolf

I grew up back and forth between California and the Middle East in the 1960s and 1970s, two regions where the link between water resources and seemingly intractable geopolitics was readily apparent to anyone paying even the least bit of attention. Like many post-'enlightenment' Westerners, I assumed that the most useful approach to helping resolve these twin challenges would be one rooted in rationality and, ideally, science. Surely if people had the right data, they would come together in harmony. So, after a meandering path through all manner of jobs and enrolment in a total of five universities over 11 years, I ended up with a master's degree focusing on hydrogeology and working for the US Geological Survey in Wisconsin, USA, trained and qualified to address complex hydropolitics. Or so I thought.

My first jolt out of complacency with science as *the* answer to politics came, ironically, in my first attempts to solve real-world problems.

Pretty Lake, Wisconsin is, in fact, quite a pretty lake in the rural southern part of the state, about an hour west of Milwaukee. But its level was dropping, and the people who lived along its banks were concerned about their views and their docks. Our mathematical models suggested that the drop in lake level was most probably caused by a nearby farmer's increased pumping of his well for irrigation; the well tapped the groundwater that fed the lake.

Triumphant in our science, we held a meeting with the property owners to share our findings. The first problem we encountered was that a vast majority of landowners simply weren't interested in our calculations. One said that he was sure that recent dredging had 'broken the plug' in the bottom of the lake, not a theory grounded in hydrology. Others asked whether we were 100% certain of our findings. Like responsible scientists, of course we weren't. The final problem came when someone asked what the solution was. At the time, in Wisconsin, there was no legal connection between groundwater and lake water, despite a clear hydrologic connection, and the farmer was not legally obligated to do anything at all for the property owners. The only solution was for them to talk through their differences and see whether they could find a mutually agreeable way forward.

As scientists, our job was done. And profoundly unsatisfying.

This was when it started to dawn on me that simply having the 'right' answers was not enough to bring people together; people had their ideas of how the world works, and no amount of data was necessarily going to change their minds. Moreover, it was clear that people are at the heart of *all* of these issues – they cause the problems and must likewise craft the solutions – and I had no training in people.

It was around then, as I was grappling with these gaps in my education, that an officemate back from an internship in Washington DC first mentioned the term 'environmental conflict resolution', a concept I'd never heard of but one that instantly resonated. Surely people are just systems like any other, but perhaps with greater uncertainties. And I was fine with uncertainties. (Groundwater science is rife with uncertainty. In another task, I had spent three months calculating that a plume of pesticides flowing underground towards a nearby municipal well would reach the well at some point between five years and 50,000 years from then. Again, the results were deeply unsatisfying to the residents who needed to figure out what to do about the problem.) Learn about the human system, combine it with understanding of the natural system, and the solutions would be unassailable.

That jolt – that people are actually at the centre of both conflicts and resolution – sent me back to school for a PhD focusing on policy analysis and conflict resolution; my dissertation was on the impact of water resources on the Arab–Israeli conflict. And that's how I met Asit Biswas in 1992.

Of course his name was already well known to me, as it is to anyone in the water profession. His *History of Hydrology* (Biswas, 1970) was and still is the seminal work in the field, despite being published back in 1970, and he has written or edited volumes of work on the cutting issues of the day for as long as I have known about him. Even in grad school, I knew that if I wanted to know about just about any topic in water policy, my first stop was to see what he had done in the field. Between his writings, bibliographies, and collections of cutting-edge authors he pulled together for his conferences and edited volumes, I could get fairly well grounded quite efficiently.

As luck would have it, my work on water and the Arab–Israeli conflict was coalescing just as the first rustlings of a potential dialogue between the parties were developing, and it was already clear that water would be one of the core issues to be addressed. The prevailing wisdom at the time was that water was an intense source of conflict between the riparians of the Jordan basin – all true – but my own work was focused rather on the history of both implicit and explicit cooperation across borders over water, and the potential for the shared resource to help facilitate hydro-political, and maybe even geopolitical, dialogue.

Asit saw a presentation on my PhD work at an International Water Resources Association (IWRA) meeting and apparently liked my approach, as he invited me to join the Middle East Water Commission, an IWRA-affiliated body he organized to help develop a strategy to address regional hydro-politics in parallel to the nascent formal Arab–Israeli peace talks.

In the years since, I can comfortably ascribe no small part of the trajectory of my career either to work that Asit directly supported, or to approaches that I learned from him.

- He helped guide publication of my dissertation (Wolf, 1995b) through the United Nations University.

- He led the Middle East Water Commission through its central study (Biswas, Kolars, Murakami, Waterbury, & Wolf, 1997; Middle East Water Commission, 1995) and presentations all over the world.
- He urged me to apply the approaches to hydro-politics that I had learned in work on the Jordan to other basins, first in the Middle East (Wolf, 1994), then in Asia (Wolf, 1995a) then worldwide.
- He sponsored the first Register of International River Basins, the first systematic delineation of transboundary basins since the mid-1970s (Wolf, Natharius, Danielson, Ward, & Pender, 1999), which became the foundation of the Transboundary Freshwater Dispute Database (https://transboundarywaters.science.oregonstate.edu). TFDD has since grown over the years, and now includes a computer compilation of 600 water-related treaties, negotiating notes and background material on case studies of conflict resolution, news files on cases of acute water-related conflict, and assessments of indigenous/traditional methods of water conflict resolution. With Asit's support, we just updated the Register of International River Basins (McCracken & Wolf, 2019), still the most complete and accurate list of its kind.
- Over the years, Asit has included me in a vast assortment of opportunities, working most recently on mega-trends for 2030 (McCracken, Peters, & Wolf, 2018).

In short, I owe no small part of my career to Asit's guidance and support. But none of this is what I wanted to write about.

I'm sure we could fill a small stadium with the professionals who owe major parts of their professional trajectories to Asit. The points that I actually wanted to make are not about a generous mentor and the careers he has launched – that's important for context, but he is too modest to allow that to be the focus here. The more important concentration is rather on the specific lessons I have learned from Asit over the years. Some are about water, some about academic work, but mostly they are about how to be a decent human being – attributes we could sorely use more of in the world today.

So over the course of our 27-year relationship, here are three key lessons I have learned and how I learned them.

First, people who are nice to grad students are genuinely nice people. Seriously. Watch any gathering in the water world, and see who gets the attention. The biggest crowds surround those with resources, such as reps of development banks and foundations. Then there are those who might help in other ways; maybe they can help with publications or access to grant programmes. Then the big names, and so on down the line. Grad students can't do anything for anyone, so anyone who is nice to them is doing it from the heart.

Asit included me at the highest levels simply because he thought the work was useful. That was true when I was a student, and it's been true over the years. And not just me – I've watched him support a veritable horde of up-and-comers, as long as the work held up. Conversely, he has no patience for those driven by ego or turf, nor those resting on long-expired laurels, no matter how important (or self-important) they are or claim to be.

Second, politics are important, but can't dictate the work. There is a moment I will always remember, when Asit put his own reputation behind this principle, in a very personal way. Of the five principals of the Middle East Water Commission, I was the

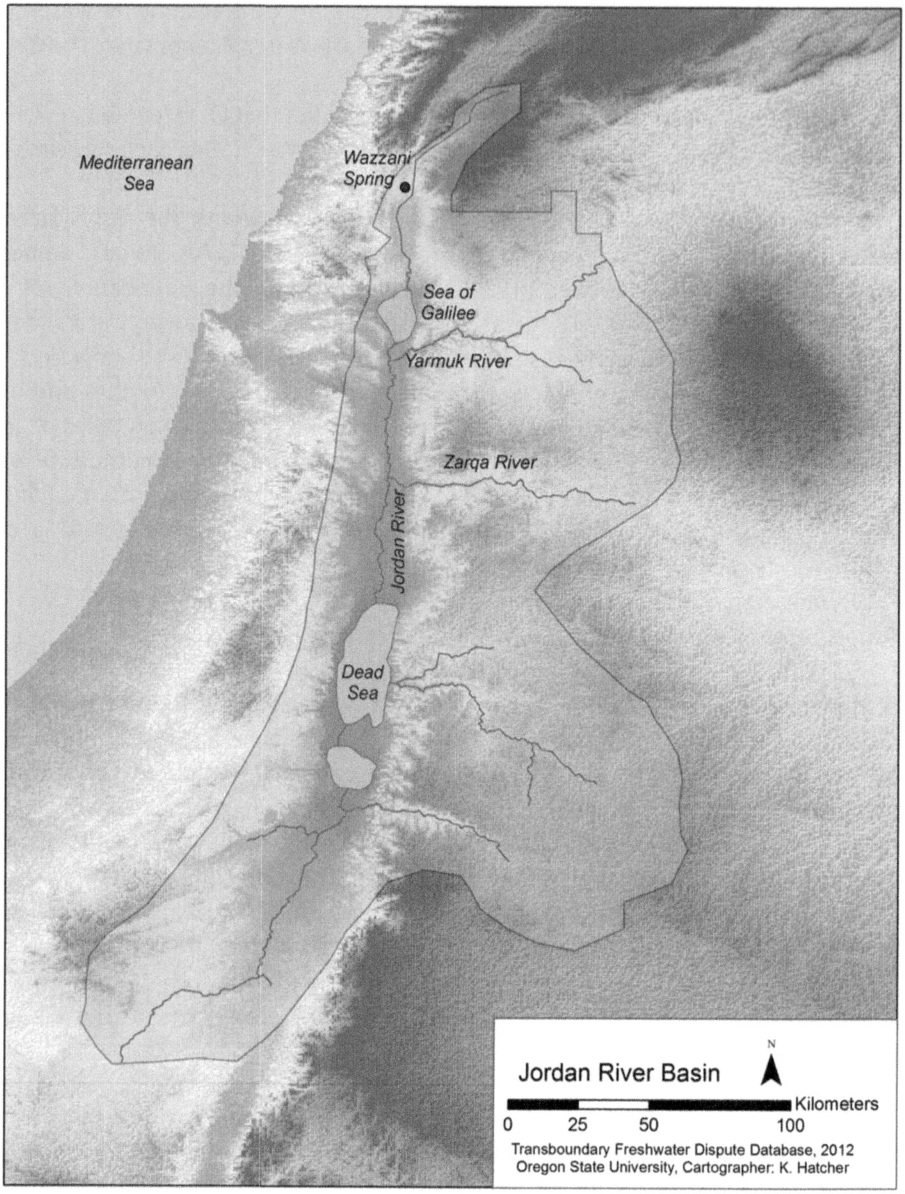

Figure 1. The Jordan River Basin.

only one with roots in the region – the others were eminent scholars in the field, all from the United States. As with just about everything related to the region, that point could easily have been politicized, if given the space. Indeed, when we presented our findings at a major international gathering of around 200 people, the first question was something like, 'I see Dr Wolf is a member of the commission. Shouldn't there be a member from X country for balance?'

As I started to stumble through a response, Asit eased me out of the way to take the mic: 'This is not the UN. We do our work based on quality, not on representation. If there is an issue with our results, we'd welcome your thoughts. Otherwise, your comment is absolutely irrelevant.' I sometimes wonder how different our world might look if more people had the fortitude, courage and generosity Asit showed at that moment.

And not only at that moment, but regularly, in ways both big and small. When there was an especially sensitive meeting on Middle Eastern water and there were some grumblings that representatives of countries with no relations with each other would be in the same room, I watched him craft a seating arrangement and flow of the workshop that showed his support for dialogue over posturing. Similarly, when I tried my own hand at crafting a workshop in his model, on the Salween basin, he made of a point of attending and contributing, simply to show support for my efforts through his presence.

Third, there is a world outside of academia. I know – for those of us inculcated within the boundaries of 'publish or perish', this is a hard one to swallow. But apparently it's not only true, it's important.

Over the years, I have watched how Asit approaches issues on the cutting edge, first identifying a topic, often years before it is popular, then bringing together a productive mix of scholars and practitioners to discuss it, then generating an edited volume that couples the bleeding edge of theory with its practical applications in the real world. While that would be enough for a stellar academic career, it's not enough to actually get the ideas out into the real world. So he then finds ways to make the material extremely accessible, either by making a deal with the publishers for affordability or by acquiring grant funding to purchase a number of the books for distribution, or both. Often, there are accompanying synthesis or executive summary documents to enhance accessibility even further. And finally, there may be an op-ed in a newspaper or magazine to guarantee even broader dissemination of the ideas.

Those of us entrenched in the university world will recognize that of the products mentioned above, there generally is an inverse relationship between the number of people who can access a format and the academic prestige associated with it. That's a shame; and we wonder why we have so little impact on the world around us. I think if I was going to synthesize, the key take-home from Asit would be, 'The work is paramount, but if we're really going to make the world a better place, don't forget the people.'

I happened to be in a meeting Asit was leading that coincided with his 75th birthday. For that occasion, the assembled group presented him with a map of the Jordan River Basin (Figure1). The image is so striking because the only boundaries shown are those of the watershed itself. Gone are the things that divide us: the political boundaries, the place names, the literal lines in the sand. All that remains are what unites us: surface water, groundwater, quality, quantity, the ecosystem in its entirety, and all the basin's inhabitants, all united by the flow of sustenance. This is how Asit has taught me and so many others to see the world.

The water world is a funny one. You don't get rich or famous in it, and we're often dealing with very unromantic topics. Like poop. And despite that, we have our share of prima donnas, blustery egos and empty figureheads. Then we have people like Asit – people of powerful intellect, generous spirit and unassailable character.

Happy birthday, Asit – the world is a better place, and I'm a better person, for your presence.

Disclosure statement

No potential conflict of interest was reported by the author.

References

Biswas, A., Kolars, J., Murakami, M., Waterbury, J., & Wolf, A. (1997). *Core and periphery: A comprehensive approach to Middle Eastern water*. Oxford: Oxford University Press.

Biswas, A. K. (1970). *History of hydrology*. Amsterdam: North-Holland Pub. Co.

McCracken, M., Peters, L. E. R., & Wolf, A. T. (2018). Megatrends in shared waters in 2030 and beyond. In A. K. Biswas, C. Tortajada, & P. Rohner (Eds.), *Assessing global water megatrends* (pp. 105–123). New York, NY: Springer.

McCracken, M., & Wolf, A. T. (2019, January 15). Updating the register of International River Basins of the world. *International Journal of Water Resources Development, 35*, 732–782. doi:10.1080/07900627.2019.1572497

Middle East Water Commission (A. Biswas, J. Kolars, M. Murakami, J. Waterbury, and A. Wolf). (1995, December). Observations regarding water sharing and management: An intensive analysis of the Jordan River Basin with reference to long-distance transfers. *International Journal of Water Resources Development, 11*(4).

Wolf, A. (1994). A hydropolitical history of the Nile, Jordan, and Euphrates River Basins. In A. Biswas (Ed.), *International waters of the Middle East*. Oxford: Oxford University Press.

Wolf, A. (1995a). The Asian Water Forum: Summary report. *Global Environmental Change: Human and Policy Dimensions, 5*(2).

Wolf, A. (1995b). *Hydropolitics along the Jordan River: The impact of scarce water resources on the Arab-Israeli conflict*. Tokyo: United Nations University Press.

Wolf, A., Natharius, J., Danielson, J., Ward, B., & Pender, J. (1999, December). International river basins of the world. *International Journal of Water Resources Development, 15*(4), 387–427. doi:10.1080/07900629948682

OPEN ACCESS

Water resilience and human life support - global outlook for the next half century

Malin Falkenmark

ABSTRACT

This article highlights green and blue water functions in the densely tied global water network, stabilizing the life support system and generating ecosystems and ecological services. Essential water challenges of the next half century are analyzed, identifying low-latitude dryland vulnerability and sharpening hydro-social water constraints. Attention is drawn to global warming, and the crucial roles of water and agriculture in stabilizing Holocene climate below a fatal warming of +2 °C or more. The article ends with a hydro-climatic, hydro-social and hydro-ecological outlook on how to principally navigate a resilient life support system stressed by climate change, population growth and increasing demands.

> Water permeates life on Earth. Water is essential as an enabler and sustainer both of life such as plants, animals, and humans, and of human civilization. The concern for this fundamental truth in fact increased after NASA's Mars missions. One of its conclusions was the urgent need to pay increased interest to the importance of the water cycle for life on this Planet – the only planet where water can exist in liquid form. (International Water Resources Association, 1991)

Introduction: Why?

Considering the global water situation towards the next half century, Rockström et al. (2014) stress that 'two giants collide – water demand from nine billion people and water impacts from a rapidly growing economy'. Ability to successfully approach this challenge will demand a broader water paradigm, connecting as essential components (1) green water in the soil with blue water in rivers and aquifers, and (2) land and water integration. A key strategy will be to build resilience and sustain rainfall, by *inter alia* sustaining forested areas as critical zones for moisture feedback. Stewardship of the landscape has to be seen as the core strategy. Water is not only the bloodstream of the biosphere, but also the key to resilience in social-ecological systems.

In this situation, a core question for the next generation to raise is how further future stresses, caused by ongoing climate change, continued population growth, increasing human demands and intensified land use change, will continue to disturb the life support system and how the interactions between water flows, water functions and roles, and

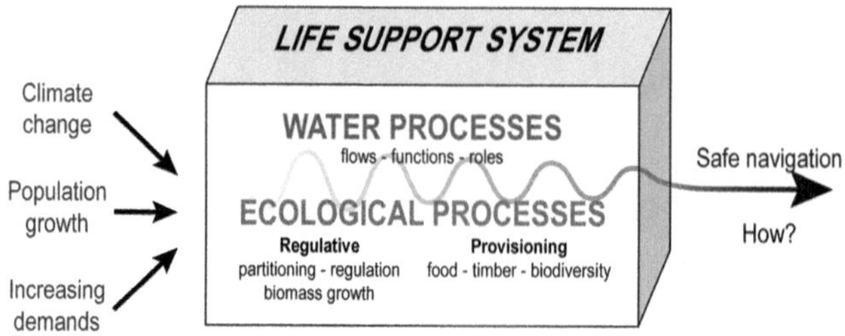

Figure 1. An expanded way to think about water as part of the life-supporting system. Diagram by the author.

relevant ecological processes like food production, timber production and biodiversity will be reflected in the life support system.

Critical questions worth focusing on, will be how to keep the planet in the present favourable Holocene-like conditions with a relatively stable climate, and how to achieve this by safe navigation of the life support system (Figure 1). What transformations will be needed? What shifts in governance approaches in terms of scope, scale, and speed will be required? *How* can that be done? And how closely will the UN's Sustainable Development Agenda reach this overarching goal?

The aim of this article is to identify some of the most essential components of the answers sought for the core questions raised in Figure 1. We will consider where the current understanding of the planet's biological playing field, of its many green and blue water functions and its different ecological processes, will lead. We will at the same time try to identify essential near-future constraints in both the green and the blue water realms. The time horizon will be the next half century.

Water: core of the life support system

Earth is the only planet in the solar system where liquid water makes life possible. The other planets are either too hot (like Venus) or too cold (like Mars). And while the energy transformations from ice to liquid and from liquid to vapour are essential for spreading solar heat across the surface of the Earth, one of the three core green water functions is to keep the Earth's temperature 30 °C warmer than it would be without H_2O as a key compound characterizing this planet. Water determines all processes on Earth of importance for human well-being, but is at the same time itself affected by all environmental processes influenced by human activities (Rockström et al., 2014).

Water's hidden roles and functions

As the core component of the global life support system, water is active in terms of having both water flows (playing different water roles) and water functions, together constituting the global bloodstream. In a recent article, Stockholm Resilience Centre scholars analyzed these hidden roles and core functions of water in the life support system (Falkenmark, Wang-Erlandsson, & Rockström, 2019). During circulation, water plays three roles: in its *controlling* role, it is a key in sustaining all life, generating ecosystem services and functions in both terrestrial and aquatic systems; in its *state* role, it is a victim of change, responding for example to land-use change and pollution; and in its *driving* role, it may cause social shocks by floods and droughts, or as a driver of conflict. These three roles exist simultaneously and interact dynamically.

There is also a dense interaction with the land through which water passes, together generating the life support system. Through this interaction, a set of water functions are active in transfer of human water uses and activities, as a rule causing water partitioning effects. There is a long series of such *core water functions*, active around the water cycle (Figure 2). The water-cycle circulation, together with the dense system interaction, stabilizes the life support system, making it water resilient.

Green water functions are three: *regulatory*, involving all the functions of soil moisture, evaporation and transpiration flows to regulate the Earth's energy balance and climate system through for instance carbon sequestration and water's ability as a greenhouse gas; *productive*, such as evaporation and transpiration to sustain food, biomass and bioenergy production; and *moisture feedback*, regulating the water cycle over land by evaporation. Water also has five different *blue water functions*: water for societal *supply*, available to be withdrawn; water as a *carrier* of nutrients and pollution, and for transport; water as *state*, involving the function of water masses and storages; the *productive* function, for irrigation

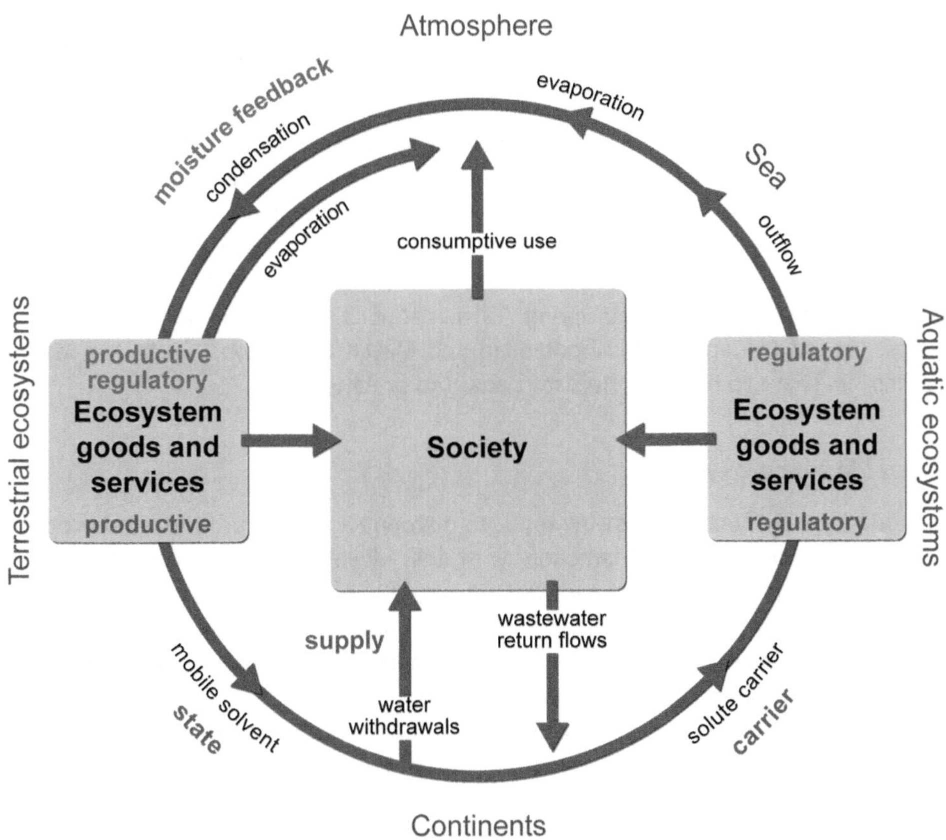

Figure 2. Water functions appear in many different positions in the water bloodstream. *Source*: Falkenmark et al. (2019).

to produce food, and water to sustain aquatic growth; and the *control* function, regulating the Earth's energy balance, sea levels and geological processes, such as subsidence.

Together, all these water flows, roles and core functions profoundly interact with the land system, forming a dense interactive network. This network constitutes the life support system of humanity, and is active through two kinds of ecosystem services: *regulating* ecosystem services, such as weather dynamics, albedo, carbon sequestration, land and aquatic habitats and water flow partitioning; and *provisioning* ecosystem services, such as provision of food, timber and energy. This intricate global system thus forms a densely tied water-related network, crucial for building the water resilience of ecosystems, and essential for the ability to generate ecosystem services.

Dense interaction with ecosystems

Human land-use activities tend to generate water partitioning phenomena, disturbing human roles and functions and contributing to a rich variety of typical ecosystem disturbances. Water flow alterations change water roles and functions, reflected in ecosystem degradation. Over time, such processes will modify ecosystems in a variety of ways. A rich archive of historical evidence shows that past land and water mismanagement has been degrading water functions (Falkenmark et al., 2019). The result is a long array of partial degradation in terms of severe ecosystem collapses and regime shifts. Desertification may develop after dryland crusting; groundwater rise and waterlogging may develop after alterations in the root zone; savannization may develop as a result of altered evapotranspiration reducing atmospheric water vapour and its condensation into new rainfall; monsoon change may develop in regions where large-scale irrigated agriculture has been increasing evapotranspiration; aquifer depletion may develop where groundwater withdrawals have been larger than natural groundwater recharge; and eutrophication may develop in systems overloaded with nutrients. Water-related societal problems may build up step by step, eroding water resilience. Recent cases are the Somalian drought, the Cape Town water crisis, and the Arab Spring / Syrian conflict. In the end societies may even collapse, as did the ancient Mesopotamian and Mayan civilizations. Such degradations humanity will have to live with, persist in, adapt to or transform.

Global life support system

Still, today, the dominant worldview tends to disconnect human progress and economic growth from fundamental interaction with the biosphere (Rockström et al., 2014; Rockström, Falkenmark, Lannerstad, & Karlberg, 2012). The sustainability agenda for humanity must urgently shift towards seeing people and nature as interdependent systems, in which much stronger emphasis is placed on managing water for social-ecological resilience and sustainability.

Thus, the twin objectives of global water resilience and human development require modernized water thinking, acknowledging that water is, as stressed by Rockström et al. (2014), the most important greenhouse gas and a prerequisite for all biomass growth. It sets the pace of global cycles of carbon, nitrogen and phosphorus; it is an agent of transportation and a solvent of chemicals; and it provides the basis for social-ecological resilience. The global life support system, the central role of water in both ecosystems and society, and the intricate linkages between the components make a system approach essential.

Awareness is required of the risk for global change in response to links between driving forces and potential tipping elements, of relevance for long-term land use planning. Such tipping elements may originate from three types of driving forces (Rockström et al., 2014): water-use driven (water crowding), land-use-change driven (food production, deforestation, afforestation), and climate driven (global warming, droughts, floods).

Without planetary stewardship for water resilience, it is difficult to see how the world can eradicate poverty and hunger, two of the Sustainable Development Goals. This makes understanding water's profound involvement in the interlinkages between societies, ecosystems and the Earth System (Folke, 2003; Rockström et al., 2012) essential. Water resilience, i.e. safeguarding a well-functioning water bloodstream, is a central prerequisite for global sustainability (Falkenmark et al., 2019). At the core of the life support system are the functions of both blue and the green water and the ecosystem services generated by their interaction with the land they pass through, in other words the water, land and ecosystem processes in landscapes. (Figure 3). Manoeuvring this system to achieve human well-being involves governance and management of its components and of the social transformations involved, to secure provision of ecological services and social-ecological resilience.

This system approach involves a switch from our past conceptualization of 'the environment' (Falkenmark, 2008) – a negative approach – to highlight its constructive components, i.e. the ecosystem services that form its core. Over time, the scale of water

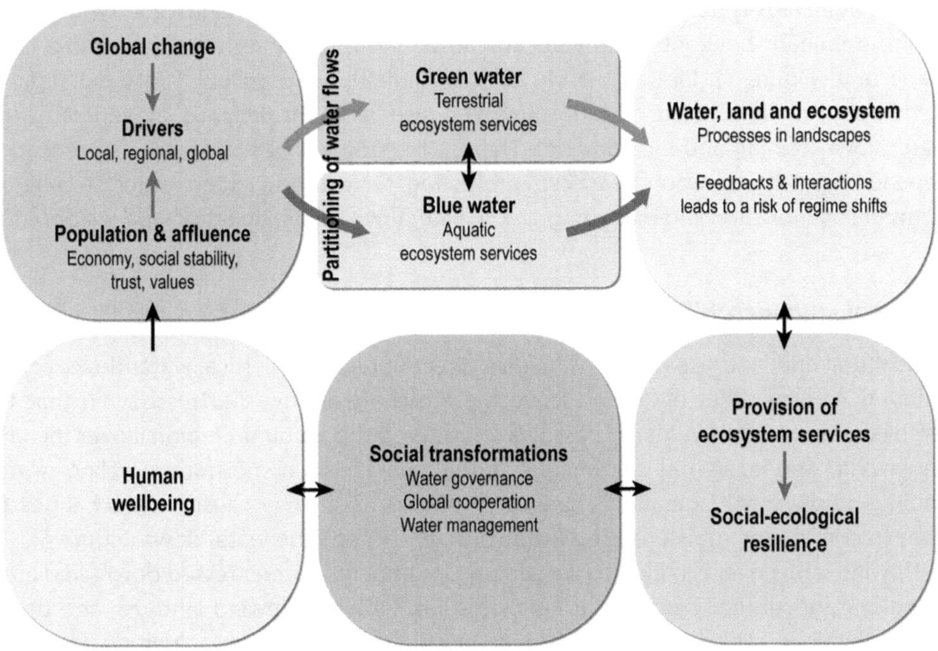

Figure 3. Interconnectedness of social drivers and processes in the landscape, where blue and green water interact with land and ecosystems in producing goods and services to secure human well-being. Adapted from Rockström et al. (2012).

impacts has increased with human activities such as withdrawals, land use change, air pollution and climate change (Rockström et al., 2014). Rainfall patterns, such as the monsoon, have changed. The function of large-scale biophysical systems, such as the tropical rainforests, has also changed.

In other words, the key is to shift from yesterday's focus on how to reduce the environmental impacts of human activities towards what is required to connect our societies with the biosphere supporting them. What is needed is a transition towards development of a safe, just, stable and resilient society within the biospheric playing field provided by the Earth System.

After this deep dive into the details of how water is active in generating ecosystems as an important component of generating resilience, we will now dive into two broad water-related problem areas: the giant task of learning to master the atmospheric water interaction of vast tropical drylands, inhabited by a rapidly expanding population of poor farmers; and the foreseeable challenge of securing household water supply in broad arid regions with multiplying populations.

Dryland water interaction with the atmosphere

Water-based categorization of landscape types

Agriculture is the largest water user on the planet, and the largest shaper of landscapes (Rockström et al., 2014). The two water functions involving the largest global amounts of water are both green: productive function (biomass) and moisture feedback (Falkenmark et al., 2019). In view of the global importance of arid lands for many millions of people, Weiskel et al. (2014) developed a water-related categorization of landscape types, based on the dominant horizontal and vertical inflows and outflows of water through a landscape unit (Figure 4). Input to landscapes is rainfall and/or inflow. In humid regions, landscapes are dominated by blue outflows (river flow), in drylands by vertical green water flows (rainfall and evaporation). There, development has to take a different form depending on green water practices, protecting or restoring green water storages in terms of soil moisture, and managing green water flow, i.e. precipitation and evaporation.

Sink region vulnerability

Agricultural and land use decisions involve direct impacts on vertical water flows, i.e. the amounts of water that enter and leave the atmosphere. Keys (2016) showed that the removal of vegetation in Mato Grosso, Brazil, altered the amount of rainfall over the land downwind, and even the seasonality of the rainfall. Such moisture-recycling-related findings imply that vegetation changes in one location may cause large changes far away in rainfall, soil moisture, crop production and even blue water flows (Figure 5).

Upwind land cover is critical to sustain precipitation in water-stressed downwind areas and allow agricultural production there. This link between upwind land use and downwind rainfall is especially relevant in drylands, where water is a limiting factor for agricultural production, since most rain evaporates before reaching a river, so that irrigation is difficult. Water-stressed areas are water constrained, and semiarid areas with aridity index P/EP (quotient between precipitation P and potential evaporation EP)

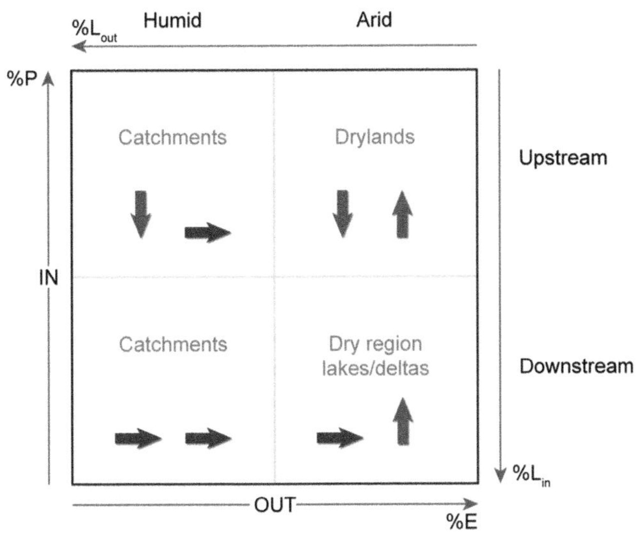

Figure 4. Categorization of hydroclimatic landscape situations based on composition of water inflow and outflow. Axes show percentage of vertical inflow and outflow components, respectively. P= precipitation; E = evaporation; L_{in} = river inflow; L_{out} = river outflow. Adapted from Weiskel et al. (2014).

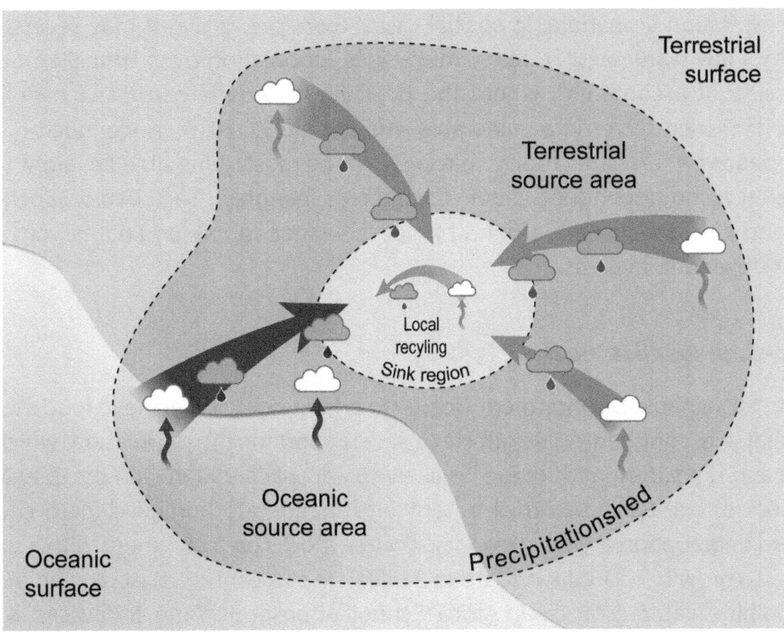

Figure 5. Precipitationshed and sink regions with rainfed agriculture. *Source*: Keys (2016).

less than 0.5 are therefore highly vulnerable to reductions in rainfall due to land use change. Keys et al. (2012) found that such water-constrained areas occupy 50% of the earth's land surface. Dryland rainfed agriculture is therefore particularly susceptible to even small changes in precipitation.

The concept of the precipitationshed indicates how upwind terrestrial evaporation *source* areas contribute moisture for precipitation to downwind *sink* regions. Keys (2016) identified seven terrestrial, water-constrained, recycling-dependent sink regions with 500–600 mm rainfall and vulnerable to upwind land use change. Many of these areas are also priority areas for global development. Two of Keys's seven cases have particular interest because of size and population: the Sahel and north and east China. In the western Sahel there is high local recycling and no absolute contribution from the nearby Sahara at present, but greater future evaporation in the Sahara might have large effect on precipitation in the Sahel. The precipitationshed is vast, containing 83 countries and more than 900 million people. The Chinese sink regions have the highest vulnerability of the seven regions, due to many potentially evaporation-altering land cover changes: expanded urbanization as well as irrigated cropland, deforestation in both East and South-East Asia and afforestation in northern China. They also have the largest populations, with eastern China exceeding 2 billion.

Keys's analysis suggests that the food security of some of the most water-constrained rainfed agricultural regions could be very sensitive to distant land use changes. Although until now Integrated Water Resource Management (IWRM) has been used primarily for holistic management of runoff (blue) resources, the importance of moisture feedback (green) would make IWRM appropriate for landscape management as well.

As a base for societal water supply, blue raw water, although harvested from river runoff or groundwater, basically originates from precipitation, which has its source in land evapotranspiration elsewhere. In special cases, therefore, drought may severely complicate a city's raw water supply. Many megacities (population over 10 million) are on the leeward side of a continent, where the prevailing winds have passed over land, and therefore find themselves in a vulnerable situation (Keys, 2016), since much of their raw water depends on terrestrial moisture recycling. The most vulnerable are eight terrestrial-moisture-recycling-dependent cities (including Shanghai, Sao Paolo, Buenos Aires, Karachi and Kinshasa), where around half of the water supply originates from precipitation over upwind land areas.

The arid-zone Achilles' heel

Achieving Sustainable Development Goal 2 (to end hunger and achieve food security) will require massive, continent-scale efforts to secure food for the population, which for only semiarid and dry sub-humid regions is likely to approach 900 million by 2030 (Figure 6). About 40% of sub-Saharan Africa is semi-arid or dry sub-humid; climate change and ecosystem degradation are creating major water shocks on a continent with a population projected to grow from 1 billion to up to 3 billion in this century. Based on an overview of green and blue water resources in Africa (Schuol, Abbaspour, Yang, Srinivasan, & Zehnder, 2008), and on the particular blue water geography in sub-Saharan Africa (Vörösmarty, Douglas, Green, & Revenga, 2005), it is not surprising that agriculture remains mostly rainfed. And as a consequence of the aridity, there is only limited irrigation – in the drylands, most rain evaporates before reaching a river – and most sub-Saharan agriculture is rainfed subsistence agriculture with very low yields.

The drought proneness seriously complicates crop production (Falkenmark & Rockström, 2006; Rockström & Falkenmark, 2000), both the interannual droughts, which

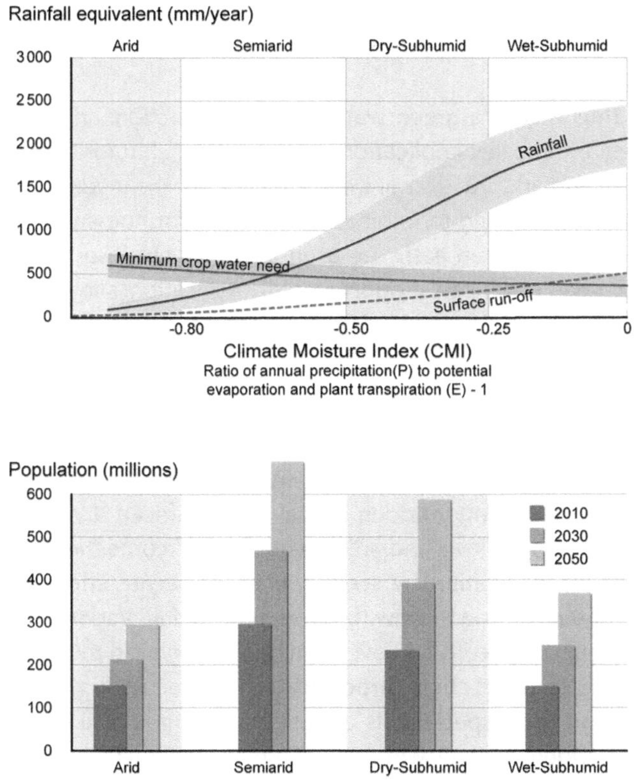

Figure 6. Hydroclimate and food production prospects in African savanna landscapes. Upper: Precipitation compared to crop water requirement ±1 standard deviation in arid, semiarid and sub-humid zones. Lower: population in 2010, 2030 and 2050. *Source*: Falkenmark and Rockström (2015).

are becoming both more serious and more frequent in response to the ongoing climate change, and the frequent dry spells, with many days or even weeks without any rain during the rainy season. During such dry spells roots are damaged, reducing their capacity to absorb green water for the production of crop biomass. As a consequence, yields become extremely low, typically of the order of only 1 t/ha out of a hydro-climatically possible yield of 7 t/ha (Garg, Karlberg, Barron, Wani, & Rockström, 2012).

In contrast to the irrigation-based Asian Green Revolution, a better idea to upgrade rainfed agriculture in dryland sub-Saharan Africa is a particular African Green Revolution (SIWI, 2016). An attractive possibility is to make better use of the rain by *vapour shift*, which helps the roots take up more of the infiltrated water in the soil and protects them from drought damage during dry spells. This can be done by small-scale supplementary irrigation during dry spells, with rainfall harvested during rainstorms and stored in small local dams. An African Green Revolution would thus involve three parallel green-water dimensions, combining blue water strategies with farming systems that operate on green water in rainfed systems (Bill and Melinda Gates Foundation, 2006; Dile, Karlberg, Temesgen, & Rockström, 2013) in a sustainable 'triply green revolution' (Rockström et al., 2014): maximized use of green water for radically increased production; adequate attention to protection of critical ecosystem services, increasing sustainability; and in the long term improving the ability of landscapes to safeguard water resilience, i.e. the capacity to regenerate rainfall by moisture feedback and wetness in landscapes for ecological functions.

'Triply green' thus means a green water, green production, and green sustainability revolution. There are three key implications of the vapour shift for overall water management (Keys & Falkenmark, 2019): minimal impacts on the hydrological environment means more water can be used for biomass production for human use; minimal reliance on blue water means more can easily be used for other purposes; and the vapour shift means that more green water can support crop diversification, allowing both subsistence food production and some cash-crop production for sale on market.

Vulnerability to upwind land use change

Development of large drought-prone regions with rain-dominated lands will be critical in the present poverty- and hunger-ridden global zones. African dryland developers have their focus on vertical water flows and are working to overcome the climatic challenge of limited and variable precipitation by seeking ways to secure effective rootzone water uptake through protective irrigation with harvested rainfall. Vapour shift is becoming a dominant component of agricultural development. Managers in more developed dryland regions have started to direct their vertical water flow focus on the origin of rainfall in terms in upwind land use, especially its dependence on land use changes there. Seven such recycling-dependent regions with only 500 mm of annual rainfall, including eastern China and the Sahel, are particularly vulnerable to upwind land use changes. A large part of the water supply of many megacities is also vulnerable to upwind land use changes (Keys et al., 2012).

Hydro-social perspective

Hidden challenges of the near future

With the increasing scale of socio-ecological drivers, blue water availability may rapidly change in response to land use change, local land use degradation, moisture feedback altering rainfall patterns, and in response to climate change. Oki and Kanae (2006) stressed that increasing population pressure is a growing challenge, and that more than two billion people live in highly water-stressed areas because of the uneven blue water distribution in time and space. Increasing population-driven water scarcity generates water crowding (Falkenmark & Widstrand, 1992; Kummu & Porkka, 2016), whereas economic development increases demand-driven water scarcity, so-called water stress. Climate change is expected to accelerate water circulation and therefore slow down the population-driven increase in water stress, but seasonality changes and increasingly severe extreme events may reduce this effect (Oki & Kanae, 2006). Figure 7(a) shows a blue water scarcity matrix, distinguishing between water stress (use-to-availability ratio) and water crowding (the inverse of per capita availability). The matrix identifies five different situations in terms of water use as related to water crowding and environmental priority/closed basins.

(a)

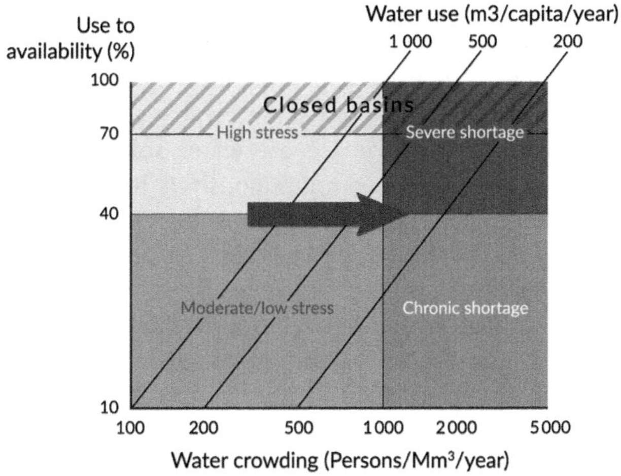

(b)

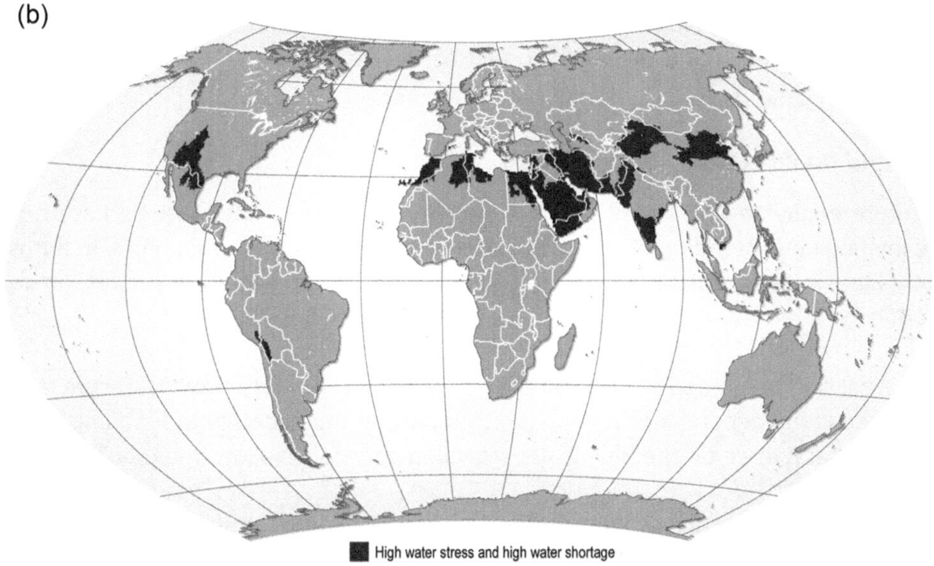

Figure 7. Water stress and scarcity. (a) Two modes of blue water scarcity. The vertical axis represents the water mobilization ratio: water accessible for use. The mobilization ratio reaches a peak at the amount necessary for aquatic ecosystem health (ecological flow, here 70%). The horizontal axis shows water crowding (people per million m^3/y of water flow), or the number of people jointly dependent on and polluting each unit of water. The large arrow indicates the effect of population growth. *Source*: Falkenmark, Jägerskog, & Schneider (2014). (b) Areas of both high water stress (use-to-availability above 40%) and chronic water shortage (water crowding beyond 1000 people per million m^3 per year) in 2000–2010. Adapted from Kummu and Porkka (2016).

In 2005, the most vulnerable situation, with more than 40% of the available water already in use, and more than 1000 people per million m^3 per year, included 1.13 billion people. The most critical geographical region in terms of this severe water shortage includes the Middle East and North Africa, and Central Asia (Figure 7(b)). These are also regions with transnational river basins and continuing population growth, driven by both high fertility and extended life expectancy (Kummu & Porkka, 2016).

The world therefore now finds itself in a situation where growing populations in many basins are approaching increasingly severe water constraints. More than 10 years ago, around 1 billion experienced severe water scarcity, and the increasing population pressure since then has been continuously reducing their possible water demand limit towards 200 m^3 per person per year – a level that Hillel Shuval, Israel, 20 years ago, considered the minimum for an industrialized country in a dry climate (Lundqvist & Gleick, 1997).

Such water-short basins have therefore been approaching a water use level where basin-scale economic planning will be urgently required for adaptation of the water supply to shrinking blue water availability. Basically, two types of water availability need to be balanced: water for food production (rainwater in the soil, green water) and water for municipal and industrial water supply (liquid, blue water). One pathway may be increasing reliance on green water in the soil for food production, improved by rainwater harvesting, and later increasing dependence on 'virtual water' (in food imports). As per capita availability shrinks further, a shift in thinking towards water reuse and desalination will be necessary.

Blue and green water sharing options

In future equitable and reasonable sharing in large river basins must be based on a preliminary understanding of the basic water resource constraints of a basin, in terms of both blue water constraints on water supply and green water constraints on food production:

- What degree of food security do the green water conditions provide: secure rainfed agriculture, dependence on irrigation support, or the necessity of food imports?
- To what degree do the blue water crowding constraints allow irrigation?

Some principal conclusions may be drawn by building on earlier work on water scarcity (Falkenmark & Xia, 2012). The answers to the two questions above can be derived from Figure 8(a), relating green and blue water availability. The next clarification needed refers to the blue water constraints within in the severe-shortage window, clarified in Figure 8(b), showing water allocation component as a function of blue water availability. Highest priority is given to municipal/industrial water supply, and second priority to protection of environmental flow (assumed to remain 30% of river flow). Irrigation withdrawal is possible only at higher availability levels and has to be maximized to limit consumptive water use (Rockström et al., 2012).

As mentioned, the region where water scarcity is most severe is the Middle East and North Africa, a global hot spot of unsustainable water use. Future water security options in that region have been analyzed by the World Bank (FAO/World Bank, 2018), considering reallocation of blue water from rural to urban users and from agriculture to industry.

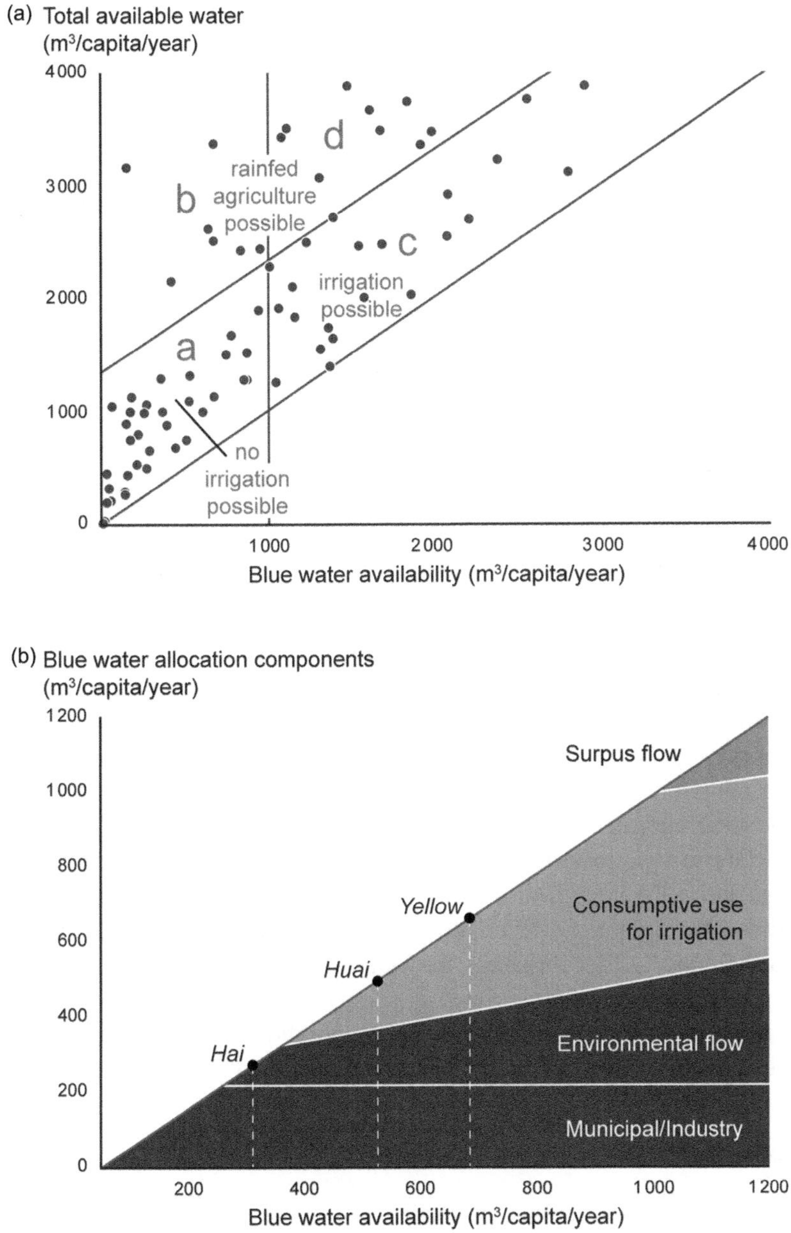

Figure 8. Food security and water supply. (a) Water availability constrains food security options. Enough green water for self-sufficient rainfed agriculture is available above the upper sloping line (areas *b* and *d*). Enough blue water for irrigation exists beyond the vertical line (area *c*). Inside area *a*, both green and blue water shortage implies dependence on food imports (adapted from Rockström, Karlberg, & Falkenmark, 2011). (b) Theoretically available water supply options, assuming 200 m^3 per person per year for municipal/industrial use, using the three Chinese rivers Hai, Huai, and Yellow (based on Falkenmark and Xia, 2012).

Water-scarcity-based vulnerability function

Intensifying water shortages in north-east China have vulnerability considerations, including analyses of the entire Hai River basin (Shi, Xia, Gippel, Chen, & Hong, 2017; Xia, Qiu, & Yuanyuan, 2012). The authors there introduce a water resources vulnerability function, dependent on the quotient of *sensitivity* and *adaptability*. The sensitivity of a water resources system is the sensitivity of annual runoff to precipitation change. Adaptability refers to adaptation strategies, integrated socio-economic capacity, and ability to tackle water stress (expressed as an exponential function of water stress [use-to-availability ratio], stress barrier, actual water crowding, and per capita water use). For the Hai basin analysis, vulnerability was rated from not fragile to extremely fragile, based on thresholds of water stress, water crowding and per capita water use in preparation for river basin agreements negotiations. For the very water-scarce Hai basin, the concept of 'water fragility' was tested through an index-based method, quantitatively evaluating water resources vulnerability and comparing different sub-basins (Shi et al., 2017).

Hydro-social water constraints now in view

Two perspectives have been highlighted in the approaching hydro-social water constraints which are expected to add complexity to water resources management in the coming half century. One is the ongoing population growth in water-constrained regions, especially those already developing high-level blue-water stress. There, long-term water supply planning – especially for mega-cities – will be essential for at least two central reasons: hydro-social constraints on sustainable development with safe municipal and industrial water supply; and implications of limits on irrigation possibilities. Implications of the importance of upstream–downstream cooperation have been illustrated both in the Middle East and North Africa and in the large rivers of north-east China (the Hai, Huai, and Yellow).

The other is the limitations originating in the origin of the rainfall that feeds the river basin and therefore further threatens the water resource. The large rivers in north-east China are examples of vulnerable rivers in a sink region, with a high proportion of their precipitation originating in upwind terrestrial evaporation in Siberia (Keys et al., 2012) and vulnerable to upwind use change in inner Asia (Gleeson et al., 2019).

Future outlook

Short overview

This article has clarified water's basic roles and functions in the life support system, not only as a generator of ecosystem services like food and energy, but also as a critical agent of change, for instance as a greenhouse gas, a regulator of temperature, and a victim of change through shocks related to global warming, like droughts and floods. Water is therefore a key in supporting life. On the continents, all its different functions and roles form one integrated framework with the land system. Water is also associated with shifts in social-ecological systems, as water functions cross tipping points. Recent research has also clarified the intense interaction between land and atmosphere, with profound implications for both plant growth (including food) and precipitation patterns, with their international dependence. The increased understanding of the importance of land use for water conditions, in terms of both water partitioning change (Keys et al., 2012) and the dependence of downwind rainfall on upwind land use, is a new dimension of fundamental importance, not only for future water planning, management and governance but also for long-term climate change mitigation.

Some current challenges and constraints regarding both green and blue water were also highlighted. The great population stress on drylands, especially in sub-Saharan Africa, makes food production a critical land use. The vulnerability of savanna landscapes to invisible water in the sky, i.e. rain and upwind evaporation rather than river flow, will have to be a new component in future dryland management. Vapour shift – turning large unproductive evaporation losses into productive transpiration –together with fertilization, will considerably increase crop yields, provided that root damage during dry spells can be avoided through supplementary irrigation, based on rainwater harvesting.

The world is rapidly approaching an era where water crowding will make technical shifts essential, avoiding throughflow as a basic philosophy for societal water supply. The land–atmosphere link makes mega-city water supply particularly vulnerable during drought periods. Water pollution abatement in highly polluted river systems, which is especially severe with high levels of water crowding, is an essential goal for water management.

How to navigate

After this short overview of water's crucial roles and functions in the life support system – the biological playing field for human activities – we will be seeking answers to the core question of this article: How to navigate to secure a sound and decent life for humanity in the next half century within the goals of the Paris Agreement, given further stresses on the life support system and the importance of securing a resilient water bloodstream that can secure safe land/water/ecosystem interaction. Safe navigation will depend on answering questions such as: What transformations will be needed? What shifts in governance approaches, in terms of scope, scale and speed, will be required? *How* can that be done? And how closely will the UN's Sustainable Development Agenda reach its overarching goal? Three perspectives will be essential: hydro-climatic, hydro-ecological, and hydro-social.

Future hydro-social stresses on the life support system will primarily originate from the combination of population growth, increasing water demands and foreseen climate change. Most population growth is expected to occur in Africa (Sturgis, 2014), where UN projections indicate that population might even quadruple before the end of this century (Gerland et al., 2014; United Nations, 2015). The rising demand will be policy dependent, but another 1 billion to 2 billion people may be expected in the coming half century, challenging the Sustainable Development Goals, which have been analyzed within the UN system (Vörösmarty et al., 2018).

Hydro-climatic management will have to be guided by the Paris Agreement to limit global warming to 1.5–2 °C, the amount seen as essential to avoid further tipping of the climate. Recent research in Earth System dynamics (Steffen et al., 2018) has clarified the risks involved in crossing the +2 °C limit; these results stress the fundamental importance of the Earth System remaining in the Holocene state. It is increasingly clear that allowing the global average temperature to rise by more than 2 °C might push the Earth System into even warmer conditions with a widely different biosphere. Even a 2 °C global warming might be enough to lock the climate onto a new Hothouse Earth era, with temperatures similar to those of several million years ago. The bio-geophysical processes involved would then be difficult or impossible to slow down or reverse. In other words, such a development would have catastrophic consequences for human civilization as we know it.

The risk of a Hothouse Earth scenario shows the importance of very conscious climate mitigation activities, making humanity planet stewards to keep the Earth System in Holocene conditions. In other words, mitigation will have to be a core component of navigation activities in the next half century. It will be not only essential but extremely urgent. And a core component of this urgent climate stabilization will be wise, water-resilient land use. In particular, agricultural production will be a characteristic land use activity to safeguard the Holocene climate. This will involve enhancing biosphere carbon sinks and increasing soil CO_2 uptake through intensified biomass production. Improved and expanded agricultural production will necessitate expanded control and management of freshwater functions.

Finally, a crucial component of hydro-ecological management will be adequate attention to the potential effects of land use change, especially on water flow, since the most visible manifestation of climate change will be seen in the hydrological lens: floods, droughts and sea-level rise. Also, green water phenomena will be linking land use and atmospheric water, and may trigger an under-studied interplay of ecological, biophysical and social feedbacks. As stressed by Rockström et al. (2014), 'The stability of fresh water flows has in the Holocene period played a fundamental role in enabling this human development.'

Many global and regional ecosystems are already approaching tipping points in terms of severe degradation of water, land and ecosystem services, threatening future human living conditions (Falkenmark et al., 2019). Tipping phenomena can be leading to erosion of water resilience and possibilities of ecosystem recovery, and can be water-related (groundwater collapse, river depletion), land use related (deforestation, land mismanagement, salinization) or climate change related (global warming, rainfall regime change, saltwater intrusion, sea level rise, sharpening droughts and floods) (Rockström et al., 2014).

The particular importance of the required climate stability of agricultural land use pinpoints the crucial involvement of the three green water functions. In the Holocene climate, water vapour is a powerful climate-regulating greenhouse gas, providing the basis for biomass growth, and thereby also regulating also carbon fluxes. One key strategy will be to sustain rainfall by treating forested areas as critical zones for moisture feedback. Research will be essential to clarify how to navigate in order to remain in the Holocene climate, by identifying available manoeuvring space, to secure the resilience of social-ecological systems.

This understanding has generated efforts, starting in the early 2000s, to identify the biospheric playing field of humanity in terms of finding a safe operating space for a set of key components. In the first-generation analysis of planetary freshwater boundaries (Rockström et al., 2014), the water boundary was developed by identifying maximum blue-water consumptive use, causing river depletion and undermining freshwater ecosystems.

A recent upgrade towards a second generation (Gleeson et al., 2019) was based on considering freshwater core functions in search of a set of sub-boundaries, which are now open for quantification of six sub-boundaries. Human activities in the landscape involve unavoidable water partitioning alteration, which suggests the question of at what stage such alterations are too large to allow Holocene conditions. Many water partitioning changes originate from land use change and therefore alteration of evapotranspiration (increasing food production), in other words increasing consumptive use.

A shift in thinking

Returning now to the question, where does the current more profound understanding of the close and tightly linked interaction between water and the life support system lead, and how can it be navigated? It will be critical to focus on what shifts will be needed in the management of the planet. Vital components of the navigation approach that is needed address both current problems, failures and oversights, and emerging long-term problems. Both land use and water use will be essential.

When it comes to blue water, attention is drawn to approaching water security problems, which call for awareness of increasing hydro-social fragility, foreseen from the expected combination of climate change, population growth and increasing water demand, especially in low-latitude regions. The increasing irrigation dependence that might follow from the rising importance of agriculture to balance temperature rise will further increase the stress on blue-water resources. Water pollution, as a large-scale hindrance to water usability, is another water management challenge of increasing importance for future socio-economic development and industrialization, especially in water-scarce regions with dense populations and therefore low access to dilution water.

Economic development and population growth have resulted in growing water scarcity, both demand-driven and population-driven (Gerland et al., 2014). The water crowding in the Middle East and North Africa and part of Central Asia will demand careful water use planning for social-economic development, taking an integrated approach to municipal and industrial water supply as opposed to irrigation needs. Special attention will be needed to secure mega-city water supplies.

A fundamental challenge will be hydro-climatic management, i.e. moderating temperature fluctuations to secure Holocene conditions in terms of remaining below 2 °C of global warming. In other words, attention to land use, and skilful attention to green water functions in terms of transpiration and energy flows, will be crucial. Reducing forest destruction will be essential, to reduce current net emissions from deforestation and land-use changes, today a sizable contribution to global CO_2 emissions. Wise land use is necessary, supporting subsurface carbon sequestration and CO_2 mitigation by safeguarding both sustainable management of tropical rainforests and water-secured agricultural development.

For hydro-ecological reasons, attention will also be needed to land use change and disturbance, and the possible risk of emergence of tipping-point situations, for instance from deforestation, which may complicate recovery (Runyan, D'Odorico, & Lawrence, 2012). Green water's increasingly dominant roles and functions in the life support system have deepened understanding of water's profound involvement in supporting terrestrial ecosystems. This represents a call for awareness of the core role that future land use change and therefore further water partitioning changes will have to play in moderating climate change. Land-use-oriented planning will be essential for regional food security.

The unfinished problems of mega-scale water pollution and the lack of successful approaches to overcoming other essential environmental problems imply the need to replace the increasingly outdated dichotomy between economic development and environmental protection. Constructive solutions are being sought in the ongoing planning for the Sustainable Development Goals (Vörösmarty et al., 2018), introducing a new ecosystem-based water security, by which all 17 of these goals can be addressed in a unitary way. A twenty-first-century approach to the world's water problems is currently under development, with water-related ecosystem services as a core concept, seeking responses to all the different Sustainable Development Goals in terms of a combination of nature-based components and technical components.

Final remarks

The missing answers for 'How to navigate?' will be built out of three groups of activities:

- *Hydro-climatic*: safeguarding the Holocene climate, relying on green water functions and therefore wise land use, supporting carbon sequestration and CO_2 mitigation by safeguarding sustainable management of tropical rainforests and water-secured agricultural development;
- *Hydro-social*: this has two parts. For water supply, modernizing and upgrading rural supply; expanding urban and industrial water supply in response to the enormous wave of mega-city development; constructively responding to groundwater depletion; recirculating and reusing wastewater; finding new technical approaches to high water stress and chronic water crowding; and producing new raw water through desalination. For water management, taking a practical and realistic approach with attention to basin scale, management complexity, and upstream–downstream relations.
- *Hydro-ecological*: developing the concepts of water-related ecosystem services and ecosystem-based water security; forest conservation and restoration; seeing the particular importance of agricultural production for global food security; launching a potential 'triply green revolution' in the vast drylands; and understanding sink area vulnerability to upwind land use changes.

Disclosure statement

No potential conflict of interest was reported by the author.

References

Bill and Melinda Gates Foundation. (2006). Retrieved from http://www.gatesfoundation.org/Media-Center/Press-Releases/2006/09/Foundations-Form-Alliance-to-Help-Spur-Green-Revolution-in-Africa

Dile, Y. T., Karlberg, L., Temesgen, M., & Rockström, J. (2013). The role of water harvesting to achieve sustainable agricultural intensification and resilience against water related shocks in sub-Saharan Africa. *Agriculture, Ecosystems & Environment*, *181*, 69–79. doi:10.1016/j.agee.2013.09.014

Falkenmark, M. (2008, March). Water and sustainability: A reappraisal. *Environment: Science and Policy for Sustainable Development*, *50*, 4–17. doi:10.3200/ENVT.50.2.4-17

Falkenmark, M., Jägerskog, A., & Schneider, K. (2014). Overcoming the land-water disconnect in water-scarce regions: Time for IWRM to go contemporary. *International Journal of Water Resources Development, 30*(3), 391–408. doi:10.1080/07900627.2014.897157

Falkenmark, M., & Rockström, J. (2006). The new blue and green water paradigm: Breaking new ground for water resources planning and management. *Journal of Water Resources Planning and Management, 132*, 129–132. ASCE/May/June 2006/129. doi:10.1061/(ASCE)0733-9496(2006)132:3(129)

Falkenmark, M., & Rockström, J. (2015). Double water blindness delaying sub-Saharan green revolution. In A. Jägerskog, T. J. Clausen, T. Holmgren, & K. Lexén (Eds.), *Water for development: charting a water wise path* (Vol. 35, pp. 64–69). Stockholm: Stockholm International Water Institute.

Falkenmark, M., Wang-Erlandsson, L., & Rockström, J. (2019). Understanding of water resilience in the Anthropocene. *Journal of Hydrology X, 2*, 100009. doi:10.1016/j.hydroa.2018.100009

Falkenmark, M., & Widstrand, C. (1992). Population and water resources: A delicate balance. *Population Bulletin, 47*(3), 1–36. Population Reference Bureau, Washington.

Falkenmark, M., & Xia, J. (2012). Urban water supply under expanding water scarcity. In T. A. Larsen, K. M. Udert, & J. Lienert (Eds.), *Wastewater treatment: Source separation and decentralization* (pp. 59–69). International Water Association.

FAO/World Bank. (2018). *Water management in fragile systems* (Discussion Paper). Cairo: Author.

Folke, C. (2003). Freshwater for resilience: A shift in thinking. *Philosophical Transactions of the Royal Society of London. Series B: Biological Sciences, 358*, 2027–2036. doi:10.1098/rstb.2003.1385

Garg, K., Karlberg, L., Barron, J., Wani, S. P., & Rockström, J. (2012). Assessing impacts of agricultural water interventions in the Kothapally watershed, Southern India. *Hydrological Processes, 26*(3), 387–404. doi:10.1002/hyp.8138

Gerland, P., Raftery, A. E., Evikova, H., Li, N., Gu, D., Spoorenberg, T., ... Wilmoth, J. (2014). World population stabilization unlikely this century. *Science, 346*(6206), 234–237. doi:10.1126/science.1257469

Gleeson, G., Erlandsson, L. W., Zipper, S., Porkka M., Jaramillo, F., Gerten, D., ... Famiglietti, J. S. (2019). The water planetary boundary: Interrogation and revision. EarthArXiv Preprints. doi:10.31223/osf.io/swhma

IWRA statement on water, environment, and development. (1991). *Water International, 16* (4).

Keys, P. W. (2016). *The precipitationshed: Concepts, methods, and applications* (PhD dissertation). Stockholm, Sweden.

Keys, P. W., & Falkenmark, M. (2019). Green water and African sustainability. *Food Security, 10*, 537–548. 2018. doi:10.1007/s12571-018-0790-7

Keys, P. W., van der Ent, R. J., Gordon, L. J., Hoff, H., Nikoli, R., & Savenije, H. H. G. (2012). Analyzing precipitationsheds to understand the vulnerability of rainfall dependent regions. *Biogeosciences*, (9), 733–746. doi:10.5194/bg-9-733-2012

Kummu, M., & Porkka, M. (2016, December). The world's road to water scarcity: Shortage and stress in the 20th century and pathways towards sustainability. *Scientific Reports*. doi:10.1038/srep38495

Lundqvist, J., & Gleick, P. (1997). *Sustaining our waters into the 21st century*. Stockholm: Stockholm Environment Institute.

Oki, T., & Kanae, S. (2006). Global hydrological cycles and world water resources. *Science, 313*, 1068–1072. doi:10.1126/science.1128845

Rockström, J., & Falkenmark, M. (2000). Semiarid crop production from a hydrological perspective: Gap between potential and actual yields. *Critical Reviews in Plant Sciences, 19*(4), 319–346. doi:10.1080/07352680091139259

Rockström, J., Falkenmark, M., Folke, C., Lannerstad, M., Barron, J., Enfors, E., ... Pahl-Wostl, C. (2014). *Water resilience for human prosperity*. Cambridge: Cambridge University Press.

Rockström, J., Falkenmark, M., Lannerstad, M., & Karlberg, L. (2012). The planetary water drama: Dual task of feeding humanity and curbing climate change. *Geophysical Research Letters, 39*. doi:10.1029/2012GL.051688

Rockström, J., Karlberg, L., & Falkenmark, M. (2011). Global food production in a water-constrained world: Exploring 'green' and 'blue' challenges and solutions. Ch. 7 in R. Quentin Grafton & K. Hussey (Eds.), *Water resources planning and management*. Cambridge University Press.

Runyan, C. W., D'Odorico, P., & Lawrence, D. (2012). Physical and biological feedbacks of deforestation. *Reviews of Geophysics, 50*(4), RG4006.

Schuol, J., Abbaspour, K. C., Yang, H., Srinivasan, R., & Zehnder, A. J. B. (2008). Modeling blue and green water availability in Africa. *Water Resources Research, 44*, 7. doi:10.1029/2007WR006609

Shi, W., Xia, J., Gippel, C. J., Chen, J., & Hong, S. (2017). Influence of disaster risk, exposure and water quality on vulnerability of surface water resources under a changing climate in the Haihe River basin. *Water International, 42*(4). doi:10.1080/02508060.2017.1301143

SIWI. (2016). Call for an African water revolution. In *Outcome from the Malin Falkenmark Symposium: A Triple Green Future for Humanity*. Stockholm: World Water Week.

Steffen, W., Rockström, J., Richardson, K., Lenton, T. M., Folke, C., Liverman, D., & Schellnhuber, H. J. (2018, August 14). Trajectories of the earth system in the Anthropocene. *PNAS, 115*(33), 8252–8259. doi:10.1073/pnas.1810141115

Sturgis, S. (2014). Africa's population will quadruple by 2100. What does that mean for its cities? *CityLab, The Atlantic*. Retrieved from http://www.citylab.com/design/2014/09/africas-population-will-quadruple-by-2100-what-does-that-mean-for-its-cities/380507/

United Nations. (2015). *Transforming our world: The 2030 Agenda for Sustainable Development*. New York: Author.

Vörösmarty, C. J., Douglas, E. M., Green, P. A., & Revenga, C. (2005). Geospatial indicators of emerging water stress: An application to Africa. *Ambio, 34*, 230–236. doi:10.1579/0044-7447-34.3.230

Vörösmarty, C. J., Osuna, V. R., Cak, A. D., Bhaduri, A., Bunn, S. E., Corsi, F., … Marcotullio, P. J. (2018). Ecosystem-based water security and the Sustainable Development Goals (SDGs). *AMBIO, 18*(4), 317–333.

Weiskel, P. K., Wolock, D. M., Zarriello, P. J., Vogel, R. M., Levin, S. B., & Lent, R. M. (2014). Hydroclimatic regimes: A distributed water-balance framework for hydrologic assessment, classification, and management. *Hydrology and Earth System Sciences, 18*(10), 3855–3872. doi:10.5194/hess-18-3855-2014

Xia, J., Qiu, B., & Yuanyuan, L. (2012). Water resources vulnerability and adaptive management in the Huang, Huai and Hai River basins of China. *Water International, 37*(5), 523–536. doi:10.1080/02508060.2012.724649

Adaptive and sustainable water management: from improved conceptual foundations to transformative change

Claudia Pahl-Wostl

ABSTRACT

Water resources management is far from being sustainable, despite decades of scholarly work to improve the conceptual foundations of water management practice. Arguments have been provided that paradigm shifts are needed towards more integrated and adaptive water management approaches. This article provides a critical reflection on the translation of such claims from discourse to practice. It reviews conceptual developments and discusses persistent challenges. Some developments that might trigger transformative change are highlighted. These include climate change, nexus approaches to integrated landscape management, and the role of indigenous communities. The article makes recommendations on how science can support mobilizing the transformative potential of these developments.

Introduction

Water is life, and there is no life without water. However, if one considers the state of the Earth's water resources one does not have the impression that human action is oriented towards this fundamental insight. Water resources management is far from being sustainable. Scarce water resources are overexploited in many parts of the world. Many people still lack access to basic water and sanitation services. Aquatic biodiversity is in serious decline. Despite decades of scholarly work and suggestions on how to improve the conceptual foundations, and despite ample experience of success and failure in water management practice, the trajectory of the state of water resources provides more reasons for concern than for optimism (United Nations, 2018; WWAP, 2019). In this article I want to discuss if and where one can observe transformative change in water management. First, I will review the major conceptual developments and discuss persistent challenges. Then I will discuss some promising developments that might facilitate transformative change.

To break the unsustainable trends and enhance sustainability, it has long been claimed that there is a need for paradigm shifts and changes in water management (Gleick, 2000, 2003; Pahl-Wostl, 2007). In a comprehensive review Pahl-Wostl et al. (2006) identified similarities in paradigm shifts advocated for water management by analyzing peer-reviewed articles and expert reports. The need for such paradigm shifts had been derived from perceived reasons for failure in prevailing water management practice. Recurring claims of change have included

- Participatory management and collaborative decision making
- Increased integration of issues and sectors
- Management of problem sources, not effects
- Decentralized and more flexible management approaches
- More attention to management of human behaviour through 'soft' measures
- Explicit inclusion of the environment in management goals
- Open and shared information sources (including linking science and decision making)
- Incorporation of iterative learning cycles into management processes.

At first sight it may be astonishing that some of the claims explicitly include the environment in water management goals. However, traditional water management had been the domain of engineering and focused on the provision of water-related services and the reduction of water-related risks to humans. As a consequence, water security for humans has often been achieved at the expense of water security for the environment (Nilsson, Reidy, Dynesius, & Revenga, 2005; Vörösmarty et al., 2010). In the long term, such management practices reduce the resilience of the social-ecological system as a whole. They are not sustainable from an economic, social or environmental perspective (Rockström et al., 2014). Claims of more integration of issues have paved the way for integrated river basin management and the search for systemic solutions. Searching for systemic solutions means taking into account the complexity of social-ecological systems and the uncertainties associated with their management, which requires more flexible and adaptive management approaches. The claims of change listed above highlight the need to include the often-neglected human dimension in water management. This means paying more attention to participatory approaches and social learning, and explicitly including human behaviour in the processes that need to be managed.

Developments in water governance and management: progress and persistent challenges

Pahl-Wostl, Jeffrey, Isendahl, and Brugnach (2011) how much these claims of paradigm shifts had already affected research and practice in the domain of water management. A bibliometric analysis showed the continued dominance of technical over social perspectives in scientific writings on water management. Publications in water-related science emphasized technology over governance. On the other hand, the number of publications on water management and governance with a social science focus increased from virtually none in 1999 to over 70 in 2009. How is the situation a decade later? Has research finally faced the challenge that many water-related problems have their origin in failed governance?

An updated bibliometric analysis of publications was undertaken using the SCOPUS database. The same search terms were used as those used by Pahl-Wostl et al. (2011). The term 'governance' was used to indicate a social science perspective. In contrast to 'water policy' or 'water management', 'governance' suggests a scholarly approach rooted in the social sciences. For example, 'water policy' is often used in articles that address engineering issues or decision support systems related to policy implementation. These articles deal with issues relevant to policy and governance, but they do not adopt a scholarly perspective rooted in the social sciences. The resulting data set records the number of publications in peer-reviewed journals in the search space 'articles and reviews' that included the defined search term in the abstract, title or keywords. Figure 1 shows the cumulative distribution of papers published since 1990. Table 1 shows the number of publications for selected years.

It is evident from Figure 1 that scholarly work on integration in water management has a longer tradition than work on adaptive management or governance. The distribution functions of papers in the latter domains are highly skewed. Table 1 shows that work on technology still dominates. It has even increased in recent years compared to work related to integration. This may be attributed to the increased interest in artificial intelligence and computer-based technology in water management. But it is also evident that work related to governance and on adaptive management has clearly taken off and developed into productive scholarly fields.

Has this productivity yet led to major breakthroughs and paradigm shifts in water management in science and practice? To address this question I will have a closer look at developments in recent years with respect to several key principles included in the claims of paradigm shifts: more integration, increased flexibility and learning, addressing the human dimension, and including the environment in management goals.

The discussion of the degree of adoption of a principle is organized according to four aspects:

- Adoption of the principle in water policies and regulatory frameworks
- Implementation of the principle in water management practice
- Outcomes that can be attributed to the implementation of the principle
- Impacts on water resource management goals that can be attributed to the implementation of the principle.

This exploratory assessment follows the diagnostic approach developed by Pahl-Wostl et al. (in review) for analyzing the performance of water governance and management systems.

Integration across sectors and issues

Due to the interconnecting nature of water it is hardly possible to deal with water problems in isolation or to solve water problems from within the water sector. For

Table 1. Number of papers published in selected year based on a bibliometric analysis with SCOPUS using different search terms, 1 December 2020 (see text for more details).

Year	'Water management' AND 'governance'	'Water management' AND 'adaptive'	'Water management' AND 'integrated'	'Water management' AND 'technology'
1997/98	2	5	73	78
2002/03	15	15	123	150
2007/08	57	33	295	346
2012/13	146	118	415	467
2017/18	209	200	587	928

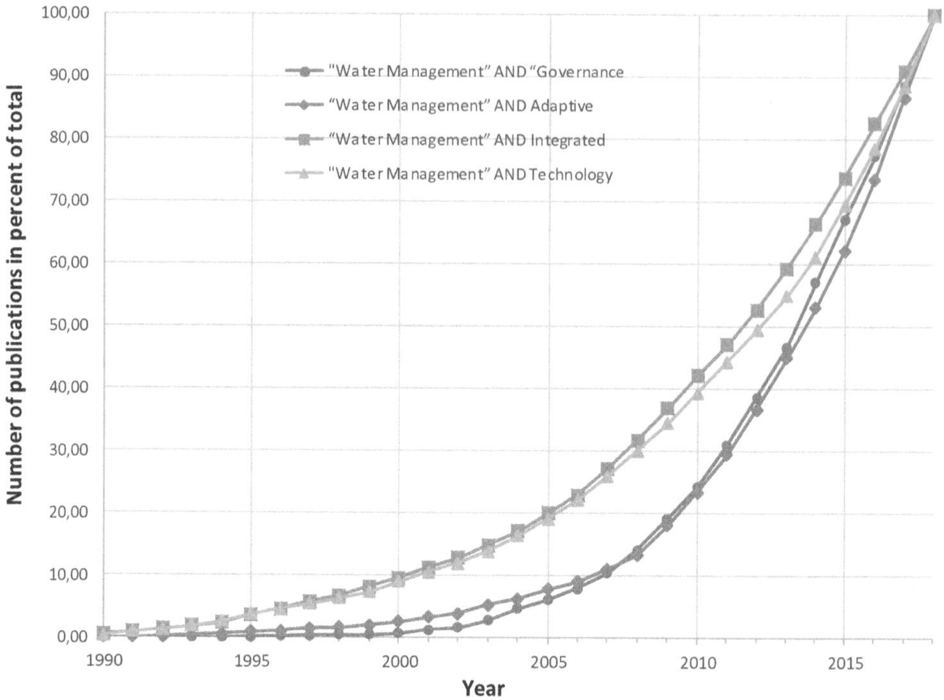

Figure 1. Cumulative distribution of papers published per year based on a bibliometric analysis with SCOPUS using different search terms, 1 December 2020 (see text for more details).

example, especially in water-scarce countries, most freshwater withdrawal is for agricultural water uses. Hence any sustainable allocation of scarce water resources needs to address agricultural and land use policies. IWRM (Integrated Water Resources Management) has been the key concept addressing integration as well as a sustainable approach to water management in general. The International Conference on Water and the Environment in Dublin in 1992 was a milestone event for stating the core elements of IWRM. At the UN Conference on Environment and Development in Rio de Janeiro in 1992, the governments of the world adopted Agenda 21 and with this committed to 'integrated management and development of water resources'. Since then IWRM has been broadly promoted in national and international policies arenas as a core guiding principle for water governance reform. Its continued popularity is reflected in the fact that Target 6.5 of Sustainable Development Goal (SDG) 6, the water goal, is dedicated to integrated water management: 'By 2030, implement integrated water resources management at all levels, including through transboundary cooperation as appropriate.'

According to a report commissioned by UN-Water, most countries had adopted IWRM principles in their laws and policies (UNEP, 2012). A report on SDG Target 6.5 came to a similar conclusion (UN Environment, 2018): 80% of countries had laid foundations for IWRM. Of those, the top 20% had generally achieved IWRM policy objectives, another 20% had implemented most elements of IWRM in long-term programmes, 40% had institutionalized most IWRM elements, and at the lower end, 20% had started to develop IWRM approaches. One might conclude that adoption of IWRM principles in water policies and regulatory frameworks is at an advanced state.

However, an emphasis on the adoption of principles in water policies without taking into account their effectiveness has been heavily criticized (Biswas, 2008; Giordano & Shah, 2014; Shah, 2016). According to these views, IWRM had become an end in itself rather than a means to achieve a goal, namely sustainable water management and greater water security. Indeed, implementation on the ground which would translate principles into management practice and ultimately into a better state of water resources and sustainable use of water services has been slow (Biswas, 2004; Jeffrey & Gearey, 2006; Medema, McIntosh, & Jeffrey, 2008; Schreiner, 2013; UN Environment, 2018). Adopting IWRM principles in laws and policies on paper does not overcome the lack of adherence to good governance principles, in particular low institutional capacity and corruption, in practice (Pahl-Wostl, Lebel, Knieper, & Nikitina, 2012). Large-scale infrastructural development may have become an end in itself, rather than a means to an end, fuelling rent-seeking by powerful elites and symbolizing state power in what may be called hydraulic bureaucracies (Molle, Mollinga, & Wester, 2009). 'Rent-seeking' refers to activities of actors to increase their own wealth without making a contribution to productivity by creating new wealth. One example would be corruption. It has become evident that the implementation of IWRM principles needs to take into account the prevailing conditions and the state of economic and institutional development of a country (Shah, 2016; UN Environment, 2018). The baseline assessment of Indicator 6.5.1 highlighted some implementation challenges (UN Environment, 2018):

- Efforts need to focus on advancing elements of IWRM implementation at subnational, basin and local levels (p. 20).
- Effectiveness of implementation of basin organizations needs major improvements. The capacity of these organizations needs to be increased in many countries to ensure they can effectively lead IWRM implementation (p. 37).
- Cross-sectoral coordination mechanisms are common but coordination in practice is weak (p. 56).

IWRM clearly has not yet achieved an integration of sectors and issues in dealing with water resource problems. This applies also to well-developed economies with high institutional capacity (Pahl-Wostl, 2019a). Measured by outcomes and impacts, IWRM's performance to date is weak. The concept of IWMR has clearly recognized the need for a more systematic approach. However, a water-centric approach has not led to effective cross-sectoral coordination and is a hurdle for sustainable water governance (de Loë & Patterson, 2017).

As a response to such deficits, in recent years the water–energy–food (WEF) nexus concept has been promoted in debates on business, policy and practice (Benson, Gain, & Rouillard, 2015; Hoff, 2011; Pahl-Wostl, 2019a). The concept was first promoted by business at the World Economic Forum in 2008, where water security became a central topic of global concern. Subsequent reports promoted a nexus approach (WEFWI, 2009, 2011). The World Economic Forum emphasizes threats and opportunities for business and sees market mechanisms and the green economy as effective and efficient solutions for dealing with resource scarcity across sectoral boundaries. The German government took the lead in promoting the WEF nexus concept in policy circles by organizing a conference, 'The Water-Energy-Food Security Nexus: Solutions for the Green Economy', in Bonn in 2011 (BMU, 2011; Hoff, 2011). But the idea was not taken up by the Rio+20 sustainability summit in formulating the SDG. The SDGs are formulated as 17 individual goals, but, in essence, they can only be achieved if interconnections are taken into account in policy formulation and implementation. As pointed out by Le Blanc (2015), the SDGs are a network of targets, where quite a few interconnections are already taken into consideration by targets referring to other goals. Each of the SDGs has a number of more specific targets that can be monitored by indicators. On the one hand, the explicit links between water, energy and food (SDGs 6, 7 and 2, respectively) via targets are not strong, far less than what the scientific community would have considered (Le Blanc, 2015). On the other hand, the central goals referred to by targets of other goals are sustainable consumption and production (SDG 12), reduction of inequality (SDG 10), ending poverty (SDG 1), and inclusive and sustainable economic growth (SDG 8). This suggests that policy priorities are not aligned with the priorities of scientists and vice versa, which may be important when framing new principles to guide transformative change in water governance.

Adaptive management: increase flexibility and foster learning

Adaptive management is one approach to increase the flexibility of management approaches and to foster learning. It explicitly recognizes uncertainty and the complexity of the systems to be managed and tries to overcome the limitations of natural resource management approaches that rely on prediction and control. Adaptive management was first developed and promoted in the context of ecosystem management (Holling, 1978; Walters, 1986). Management interventions have been perceived as experiments that generate new knowledge. Stated more broadly, adaptive management implies that management processes must be designed such that they support systematic and structured learning-by-doing. Originally the approach had a focus on the complexity of ecosystems and paid little attention to the complexity that is inherent in the human dimension of changing management practices (Lee, 1999). Such negligence was a major flaw and may also explain many failures of adaptive management projects (Allan & Curtis, 2005; Allen & Gunderson, 2011). But perceptions have changed, and more attention is now given to social learning and social capital as major outcomes of adaptive management processes (Allan & Watts, 2018; Collins & Ison, 2010; Wallis & Ison, 2011; Webb, Watts, Allan, & Conallin, 2018). However, increasing the flexibility of management approaches requires more than simply changing management processes. As highlighted by Pahl-Wostl (2007), adaptive water management requires an understanding and integrated design and major structural transformations of human-technology-environment systems to enable learning processes. The construction of large-scale infrastructure and associated sunk costs, for example, may severely limit options for learning and change. Or rigid regulations and formal use rights may hinder adaptation to changing resource conditions. In an adaptive paradigm, management goals and instruments are reviewed, negotiated, and if necessary reconstructed, to meet the needs of a changing world. But this puts great demands on the quality of governance processes. It must transparent who decides, on what kind of evidence, to change management goals and instruments (Pahl-Wostl et al., 2007).

European water policy has increasingly embraced more adaptive approaches. The European Water Framework Directive (WFD), for example, gives more flexibility to member states to tailor policy implementation to their national requirements and prescribes broad stakeholder participation. The WFD introduces cycles of six years for planning, implementation and monitoring of progress. Legal requirements thus provide an enabling environment and support an adaptive management approach. However, stakeholders have not been engaged broadly during implementation, and an adaptive management approach has hardly been adopted (Newig & Koontz, 2014; Voulvoulis, Arpon, & Giakoumis, 2017). Instead, member states used opportunities for adapting management goals to lower ambitions for environmental targets and delay implementation (Voulvoulis et al., 2017). But the increasing awareness of climate change may promote a transition towards more adaptive approaches that have been advocated by the corresponding guidance documents for WFD implementation (European Communities, 2009).

The most pronounced example of a paradigm shift taking place in practice towards more flexible and adaptive management approaches can observed in the transition to integrated flood management. Traditional flood management focuses on keeping the water out of the landscape through structural measures, such as dikes or reservoirs. It is a reactive approach, protecting human lives and assets that are exposed to flood risk when settling on former floodplains of rivers. In recent decades, one could note a progression towards more integrated approaches in flood management practice, such as moving from dike construction to increasing the storage of runoff in renaturalized or artificial wetlands, or acknowledging the need for risk prevention in land use policies (Moss & Monstadt, 2008). An integrated flood management paradigm argues that instead of destroying natural capital, preserving and/or restoring natural infrastructure is required to build adaptive capacity and reduce vulnerability to climate change impacts (Opperman et al., 2009; Smith & Barchiesi, 2009; WMO, 2009). The Netherlands is the country that is most advanced in implementing integrated flood management (Halbe, Knüppe, Knieper, & Pahl-Wostl, 2018; Mees, Driessen, & Runhaar, 2014; Pahl-Wostl, Becker, Sendzimir, & Knieper, 2013a). Climate change has impelled such transformative change. Yet, one cannot observe a similar kind of transformative change in dealing with droughts (Huntjens, Pahl-Wostl, & Grin, 2010; Pahl-Wostl, 2015a). The perception of the need for transformative change seems to differ between floods and droughts. The barriers to change inherent in prevailing land use practices, use rights, politics, power constellations and conflicts of interest seem to quite pronounced (Olivier, 2017; Rogers & St. Fleur, 2014; Ross & Connell, 2016).

In conclusion, one can clearly note more emphasis on adaptive and flexible management approaches, both in policy and in implementation. However, the example of the transition towards more adaptive and integrated flood management has shown that transformative change occurs on a decadal rather than annual time scale. It may thus be important to pay more attention to outcomes such as social learning and the development of institutional capacity to monitor progress of transformative change towards more adaptive approaches (Webb et al., 2018).

More attention to the human dimension and soft measures

The evolution over the past decades of principles guiding water policy shows a clear tendency to give more attention to the human dimension and soft measures (Pahl-Wostl, 2015d). In the 1960s and 1970s water policy worldwide was characterized by the strong role of central government and central regulation, in essence a hierarchical, top-down, command-and-control approach. This was in line with a technocratic approach and a focus on technical solutions. In the late 1980s and 1990s water policy increasingly emphasized principles of subsidiarity, decentralization and privatization, and the market became a key instrument for water management. The late 1990s and the 2000s saw an upsurge in participatory approaches. Central roles were delegated to community groups and water user associations, a shift that was especially noticeable in irrigation management. One could argue that this development corresponds to an increasing recognition of the human dimension. However, approaches have remained simplistic, not really addressing the complexity of social processes. Developments in water policy have seen changes in the role attributed to three major social agents: government, market/economy (production, consumption), and civil society/community (individual citizens and organized groups outside of government and market, i.e. public voice).

In the 1960s and 1970s, economic activities were blamed for water management problems. Government had the role of problem solver and service provider, acting in a hierarchical governance mode and pursing a command-and-control approach. Water governance and management were in the hands of bureaucrats and technicians. But later, government was seen as the reason for management problems. Lack of efficiency and effectiveness in governmental bureaucracies and rent-seeking by powerful elites were seen as reasons for the failure to deliver adequate water services and to address increasing water problems. Now the market economy was seen as the problem solver. However, such reform does not solve the systemic governance problems that initially had been a reason for reform (Brown & Cloke, 2004, 2005; Soliman & Cable, 2011): corruption, rent-seeking by powerful elites, and the dominance of informal institutions with goals that are often in conflict with sustainable resource management (Pahl-Wostl & Knieper, 2014). In a third phase, the 1990s and early 2000s, direct community involvement was supposed to make up for the failure of governments and markets. Civil society was assigned a leadership role in making progress towards more equitable, sustainable and effective resource governance.

Recent years have seen the emergence of diverse hybrid forms of governance typical of a more all-encompassing understanding of societal steering both from a descriptive and a normative perspective (Pahl-Wostl, 2019b). Modern water policy frameworks such as the European Water Framework and the Floods Directive embrace hybrid forms of policy instruments that combine hierarchical steering, market-based instruments and network-based, participatory approaches.

One can conclude that water policy and regulatory frameworks have increasingly embraced a broader understanding of the human dimension and have also promoted more soft measures. However, implementation problems are prevalent, and not only in developing countries. Understanding and addressing such implementation problems requires embracing a broader perspective on the human dimension and multilevel water governance. Such a perspective needs to address power and dominance of informal institutions (e.g. corruption) but also symbolic meanings, particularly regarding the relationship between humans and nature.

Explicitly including the environment in management goals

In their first global synthesis on understanding the interdependence of water security for humans and for ecosystems, Vörösmarty et al. (2010) showed that human water security was often achieved to the detriment of the environment. The construction of large-scale hydropower dams, for example, is in general disruptive of biodiversity and often harms local livelihoods. Such insights on dam construction are not new and have been a matter of controversy. But attempts to have global governance promote the adoption of guiding principles for dam construction have not been successful (Briscoe, 2010; Pahl-Wostl, Conca, Kramer, Maestu, & Schmidt, 2013b; Tilt, Braun, & He, 2009). Fuelled by the pressure to mitigate climate change, the hydropower boom continues, and an unprecedented number of dams are currently in the construction or planning phase (Grill et al., 2015; Winemiller et al., 2016; Zarfl, Lumsdon, Berlekamp, Tydecks, & Tockner, 2015). This is quite worrying given the impacts to be expected on aquatic ecosystems and associated livelihoods. In their comparative analyses of water governance, water management and environmental performance in various river basins, Knieper and Pahl-Wostl (2016) showed that the best predictor of a good environmental state is little human pressure. Water governance and management seem to mitigate environmental impacts but do not lead to a good state of the environment. Most modern water policies explicitly address environmental goals, but achieving these goals often conflicts with other water uses.

An example is the WFD, which came into force in 2000 (European Union, 2000). The WFD promotes an integrated management approach, with the explicit goal of achieving 'good' status for all European waters (surface waters and groundwater). Despite its innovative character, implementation of the WFD has also encountered obstacles. A major loophole has resulted in delays in the implementation process and stems from the fact that the WFD allows exemptions to the achievement of a good state for water bodies classified as heavily modified (Voulvoulis et al., 2017; Wolf, 2019). Exemptions can be sought for 'heavily modified water bodies' if the cost of improvement would be excessive, and it is ill-defined how 'excessive' is to be determined. Experience with the classifications of water bodies by member states shows that exemptions abound (Boeuf, Fritsch, & Martin-Ortega, 2016; European Environmental Bureau, 2010). Furthermore, a good state is particularly compromised by hydro-morphological and ecological indicators. The WFD classification revealed major ecological deficits in water quality. For example, while 88% of the surface water bodies in Germany have reached good chemical status, only 10% of them have good ecological status. As many as 34% are classified as poor, and 23% have bad ecological status (BMU, 2010). Only 18% are expected to achieve a good ecological status by 2021, the end of the first phase of WFD implementation. Quality improvements could largely be achieved by technical and often end-of-pipe measures, even when large investments (e.g. in wastewater treatment) were needed. Ecological improvements require more far-reaching transformations that involve decisions on water and land uses associated with considerable conflicts of interest. However, quality objectives are not always met. Germany has failed to meet the requirements for groundwater quality stated by the European Nitrate Directive. One major reason for this failure is the strong lobbying power of agricultural interest groups (Franz, Schlitz, & Schumacher, 2018; Pahl-Wostl, 2019a). A court case opened by the European Commission and the threat of high fines for lack of compliance with European policy has finally led to more stringent national legislation on the use of fertilizer in agriculture.

The recent Global Assessment Report on Biodiversity and Ecosystem Services of the Intergovernmental Science-Policy Platform on Biodiversity and Ecosystem Services concludes that the decline of biodiversity continues at rates unprecedented in human history and that freshwater ecosystems show the highest rate of decline (Díaz et al., 2019). And climate change is expected to aggravate this alarming situation (Knouft & Ficklin, 2017). Obviously, the trade-offs between human and environmental water security generated by prevailing water management and land use practices have not yet been overcome.

Despite undeniable progress and evolution towards more sophisticated environmental policies, water policy reformers cannot pride themselves on having achieved substantial breakthroughs in halting the deterioration of aquatic ecosystems. Here also, implementation problems prevail. Conflicts of interest between different water uses are often solved to the detriment of the environment. This experience casts doubt on the prospects for implementing an effective policy framework to bring about fundamental change. Improving ecological status requires a profound shift towards more holistic landscape management and significant transformations in institutional settings, actor networks, power constellations and in particular the symbolic dimension of the human–nature relationship.

Triggers for transformative change

Given all these persistent challenges and numerous obstacles to change, is there reason for optimism to believe that a transformation can be achieved? Transformative changes take time. In their analysis of transformation towards integrated and adaptive flood management, Pahl-Wostl et al. (2013a) showed that such change takes decades rather than years. Given the rapidly deteriorating state of the environment, a time scale of decades is obviously a matter of concern. Therefore, we have to ask if there are levers that might facilitate such change. I will elaborate on potential triggers for transformative change.

Severity of climate change and evidence of impacts

What has been called the 'global water crisis' is best described as a gradual decline of the state of water resources (Biswas, 1998; Srinivasan, Lambin, Gorelick, Thompson, & Rozelle, 2012; Vörösmarty, Pahl-Wostl, Bunn, & Lawford, 2013). Climate change has now increasingly exposed vulnerabilities and weaknesses in prevailing management practices. Yet, the response is lagging behind rather than anticipating. An example is the implementation of the WFD, which came into force in 2000. Initial guidance documents for the Common Implementation Strategy largely neglected uncertainties (Sigel, Klauser, & Pahl-Wostl, 2010). A guidance document on how to address climate change suggested an elaborate and comprehensive approach to addressing uncertainties in planning and decision, making largely embracing a paradigm shift towards adaptive management (European Communities, 2009). In contrast to the first implementation cycle, ending in 2015, climate-related threats and adaptation planning should now be incorporated in river basin management plans from the second planning cycle onwards. A recent assessment of WFD implementation concluded that most countries take now climate change into account in their river basin management plans (European Commission, 2019). Reference to climate change is mainly related to flood risks, which can also be explained by the influence of the European Flood Risk Directive and the joint implementation of the WFD. Drought received less attention, though, despite expectations of increasing extremes due to climate change (Füssel et al., 2017). And indeed, recent years have witnessed extreme water scarcity and reported conflicts on water, even in countries like Germany (Hänel, 2019). The Cape Town water crisis attracted world-wide attention. Despite knowledge of climate change impacts and expected water shortages, politics and governance failures seem to have been the causes of the lack of anticipatory action (Muller, 2017; Olivier, 2017; Zille, 2017). The extreme drought in California (2011–2017), with major social, economic and environmental impacts, was not entirely unexpected and may happen again (Rogers & St. Fleur, 2014; Ullrich et al., 2018).

Such crises can support transformative change. Recurring floods have been a major trigger of transformative change towards an integrated flood management paradigm (Pahl-Wostl et al., 2013a). But what are the conditions for recurrent crises to support long-term, reflected transformative change in the case of water scarcity, rather than short-sighted responses like the diversion of rivers or the shipping of icebergs?

Times of crisis are not necessarily times of reflection, but they are windows of opportunity for innovative approaches to enter mainstream policy. Such developments require effective interfaces for knowledge transfer between informal settings and formal policy processes (Pahl-Wostl et al., 2013a). Informal spaces are important to support the integration of knowledge and experimentation with innovative approaches. Vertical integration is important to involve actors from the implementation level in policy development and to support feedback from implementation to strategic goal setting and policy formulation. Leadership of individuals or groups is important for fomenting innovative ideas and realizing them in policy change. However, connections between learning and policy processes that hinge on individual actors are fragile if innovative approaches are not codified in formal institutions and widely shared practices (Pahl-Wostl, 2015c; Pahl-Wostl et al., 2013a).

Recommendations for science to support mobilizing the transformative potential

Scientific research needs to give more attention to implementation gaps and the identification of barriers to transformative change, such as institutional inertia, power constellations, and entrenched beliefs and practices. Crises may open windows of opportunity for change, and science needs to develop the capacity to make use of such opportunities.

Nexus approaches: towards integrated landscape governance and management

As discussed in the context of IWRM, the WEF nexus is a response to the evident failures of IWRM in supporting an integrated, cross-sectoral approach to water management. The WEF nexus argues for a reframing of the problem perspective from a sector-centric towards a more systemic view and more balanced negotiations of interests between sectors. It shifts the emphasis towards relationships and feedback between sectors, even if doing so does not yet solve the coordination challenge. But focussing on the often-neglected sectoral interfaces may trigger innovation. A systemic nexus narrative may break sectoral silo thinking (Pahl-Wostl, 2019a). Even when actors do not operate in silos but have opportunities to interact in platforms, resource governance and management strategies are still oriented towards individual sectors. What is required is that the WEF nexus not just become another element in the suite of 'universal remedies for good water governance' without real impact on policy and practice (Ingram, 2011).

The WEF nexus is indicative of a whole suite of nexus approaches to resource governance. Such development corresponds essentially to a move towards integrated landscape governance and management, where sustainable use of bundles of ecosystem services and the resilience of social-ecological systems as a whole would be promoted (Mouchet et al., 2014; Raudsepp-Hearne, Peterson, & Bennett, 2010). The ecosystem services concept may help operationalize and implement a systemic approach from a nexus perspective (Pahl-Wostl, 2019a). Ecosystem services may be perceived as an anthropocentric and utilitarian approach focusing on the economic valuation of nature's contribution to human well-being. However, as highlighted by Pahl-Wostl (2015b), a combination of different governance modes – markets, bureaucratic hierarchies and learning networks – is essential for the sustainable implementation of the ecosystem services concept. And at the same time, the ecosystem services concept could support and promote an integrated approach to governance – integrated in terms of connecting regulation, economic measures, deliberation and learning.

As argued by Pahl-Wostl (2015c), transformative change can be conceptualized as a multilevel and multi-loop process of social and societal learning. The success of the WEF nexus approach will thus depend on whether the concept becomes meaningful for different actors at different levels. For example, a WEF nexus approach might trigger new business models. If contextualized, it could become a narrative supporting collaboration and collaborative action towards an integrated landscape management approach. Narratives can act as glue for the formation of regional innovation networks (Ingram, Ingram, & Lejano, 2019; Ingram, Lejano, & Ingram, 2013).

Recommendations for science to support mobilizing the transformative potential

Science could and should become an active partner in regional innovation networks. Science can provide expert knowledge for evidence-based decision making and can facilitate processes of negotiation and learning. Scientific research should develop diagnostic approaches that allow teasing out which kind of lessons learned can be transferred and which kind of influence must be attributed to social, political, economic or environmental contexts.

The increasing influence and changing role of indigenous communities

In recent years, indigenous communities have started to influence water governance and management and change the symbolic dimension of human–environment relationships. Although not yet wide-spread, it might become a ground-breaking development in the future. Long marginalized in many countries, indigenous communities have in recent years been more successful in claiming legal titles and improving the appreciation for indigenous knowledge and worldviews (Curran, 2019; Tsatsaros, Wellman, Bohnet, Brodie, & Valentine, 2018). Such development has been supported by the Declaration on the

Rights of Indigenous Peoples and the Resolution on the Human Right to Water and Sanitation, adopted by the UN in 2007 and 2010, respectively.

In a landmark decision, the Supreme Court of Canada (2014) established Aboriginal land title for the Tsilhqot'in First Nation in British Columbia to guarantee their traditional access to land and water. This implies that exploitation activities such as logging or mining require prior consultation and permission from the original land holders. Another recent decision by the Canadian Federal Court of Appeal (2018) blocked a major oil pipeline project because First Nation groups had not been sufficiently consulted and environmental assessments had not been comprehensive enough. These court decisions strengthen the application of the principle of free, prior and informed consent for any development on ancestral land or exploitation of resources on indigenous territory. Another path-breaking example can be found in New Zealand, where the Whanganui River was given its own legal identity to recognize its importance as ancestor of the local Maori groups (Charpleix, 2018; Government of New Zealand, 2017). In October 2018 a Canadian national conference on environmental flow needs, 'Siwłkʷ (Water) For All – Our Responsibility', was organized in Kelowna, British Columbia (Jatel & Guy, 2018). The title included an Nsyilxcen word for 'water' (Nsyilxcen is the language of the Syilx people of the Okanagan) to reflect and respect that Syilx people made major contributions to the conference. A Syilx governance framework, *enowkinwixw* (four food chiefs), was used as an organizing principle of the conference to bring together indigenous and Western perspectives in an interactive format. Such formats are conducive to supporting triple-loop learning and building transformative knowledge. The Okanagan Basin Water Board, a co-organizer of the conference, is an example of an innovative institutional format to support integrated water management approaches and collaborative partnerships with First Nations (Melnychuk, Jatel, & Warwick Sears, 2017).

Although it is still a slow process, and success is still the exception rather than the rule, such developments hold much promise to catalyze transformative change in water governance and management. Indigenous communities transform water governance by introducing indigenous principles, methodologies and indigenous knowledge (Arsenault, Diver, McGregor, Witham, & Bourassa, 2018; Curran, 2019; Yates, Harris, & Wilson, 2017). Indigenous principles are rooted in a healthy environment and in general promote a holistic and integrated perspective on the environment. Human–nature relations are built on stewardship rather than ownership.

Arguing in favour of more recognition of indigenous knowledge and principles does not mean that such knowledge should be now valued higher than scientific knowledge and approaches. However, giving way to ontological pluralism and productive discourse is a way forward to foster innovation and transformative change. And the impact from indigenous communities has the potential to go far beyond place-based solutions that give more rights to currently underprivileged and marginalized groups.

Recommendations for science, and a greater role for first nations: to date research on the role of indigenous knowledge and community is quite fragmented. To develop a more holistic understanding more integrative research is required. Such research should integrate the epistemological dimension of indigenous knowledge, place-based approaches to local governance, and innovative legal principles from a multilevel governance perspective.

Conclusions

Exploratory assessment of whether claims of a paradigm shift have also led to transformative change in practice delivers rather sobering results. Compared to the increase in scholarly publications on related themes, the adoption of new principles in water management practice has been modest as of yet. Despite innovation in regulatory frameworks and water policies, implementation is weak. Transformative change in practice has been slow. Barriers are manifold and diverse. They exist in developed economies with high institutional capacity as much as in developing countries. System transformations – as required to realize a paradigm shift – operate over decades rather than years. Nevertheless, after decades of discourse, more action on the ground seems to be warranted. Science needs to take a more active role in solution-oriented action research to support the adoption of scholarly insights in practice and to improve the practical relevance of recommendations from scholarly work. Working towards building critical transformative capacity and supporting transformative change is an urgent and noble task for science, policy and practice alike.

Data availability statement

The data described in this article are openly available in the Open Science Framework at DOI:10.17605/OSF.IO/TPA6U.

Disclosure statement

No potential conflict of interest was reported by the author.

References

Allan, C., & Curtis, A. (2005). Nipped in the bud: Why regional scale adaptive management is not blooming. *Environmental Management*, *36*(3), 414–425. doi:10.1007/s00267-004-0244-1

Allan, C., & Watts, R. J. (2018). Revealing adaptive management of environmental flows. *Environmental Management*, *61*(3), 520–533. doi:10.1007/s00267-017-0931-3

Allen, C. R., & Gunderson, L. H. (2011). Pathology and failure in the design and implementation of adaptive management. *Journal of Environmental Management*, *92*(5), 1379–1384. doi:10.1016/j.jenvman.2010.10.063

Arsenault, R., Diver, S., McGregor, D., Witham, A., & Bourassa, C. (2018). Shifting the framework of Canadian water governance through indigenous research methods: Acknowledging the past with an eye on the future. *Water*, *10*(1), 49. doi:10.3390/w10010049

Benson, D., Gain, A. K., & Rouillard, J. J. (2015). Water governance in a comparative perspective: From IWRM to a 'Nexus' approach? *Water Alternatives*, *8*(1), 756–773.

Biswas, A. K. (1998). Deafness to global water crisis: Causes and risks. *AMBIO*, *27*(6), 492–493.

Biswas, A. K. (2004). Integrated water resources management: A reassessment. *Water International*, *29*(2), 248–256. doi:10.1080/02508060408691775

Biswas, A. K. (2008). Integrated water resources management: Is it working? *International Journal of Water Resources Development*, *24*(1), 5–22. doi:10.1080/07900620701871718

BMU. (2010). *Water framework directive: The way towards healthy waters. Results of the German river basin management plans 2009*. Berlin: Author.

BMU. (2011). *Messages from the Bonn2011 conference: The water, energy and food security nexus – solutions for a green economy*. Bonn: Author.

Boeuf, B., Fritsch, O., & Martin-Ortega, J. (2016). Undermining European environmental policy goals? The EU water framework directive and the politics of exemptions. *Water, 8*(9), 388. doi:10.3390/w8090388

Briscoe, J. (2010). Viewpoint. Overreach and response: The politics of the WCD and its aftermath. *Water Alternatives, 3*(2), 399–415.

Brown, E., & Cloke, J. (2004). Neoliberal reform, governance and corruption in the South: Assessing the international anti-corruption crusade. *Antipode, 36*(2), 272–294. doi:10.1111/j.1467-8330.2004.00406.x

Brown, E., & Cloke, J. (2005). Neoliberal reform, governance and corruption in Central America: Exploring the Nicaraguan case. *Political Geography, 24*(5), 601–630. doi:10.1016/j.polgeo.2005.01.008

Charpleix, L. (2018). The Whanganui River as Te Awa Tupua: Place-based law in a legally pluralistic society. *Geographical Journal, 184*(1), 19–30. doi:10.1111/geoj.12238

Collins, K. B., & Ison, R. L. (2010). Trusting emergence: Some experiences of learning about integrated catchment science with the environment agency of England and Wales. *Water Resources Management, 24*(4), 669–688. doi:10.1007/s11269-009-9464-8

Curran, D. (2019). Indigenous processes of consent: Repoliticizing water governance through legal pluralism. *Water, 11*(3), 571. doi:10.3390/w11030571

de Loë, R. C., & Patterson, J. J. (2017). Rethinking water governance: Moving beyond water-centric perspectives in a connected and changing world. *Natural Resources Journal, 57*(1), 75–100.

Díaz, S., Settele, J., ES, B., HT, N., Guèze, M., Agard, J., ... Zayas, C. N. (eds). (2019). *Summary for policymakers of the Global Assessment Report on Biodiversity and Ecosystem Services of the Intergovernmental Science-Policy Platform on Biodiversity and Ecosystem Services*. Bonn, Germany: IPBES secretariat.

European Commission. (2019). 'European overview: River basin management plans.' Accompanying 'Report from the Commission to the European Parliament and the Council: Implementation of the Water Framework Directive (2000/60/EC) and the Floods Directive (2007/60/EC)'. Brussels: Author.

European Communities. (2009). *Guidance document on River basin management in a changing climate: Guidance documents for the Common Implementation Strategy for the Water Framework Directive* (Vol. 204). Luxembourg: Author.

European Environmental Bureau. (2010). *10 years of the Water Framework Directive: A toothless tiger? A snapshot assessment of EU environmental ambitions*. Brussels: Author.

European Union. (2000). Directive 2000/60/EC of the European Parliament and of the Council of 23.10.00 establishing a framework for Community action in the field of water policy-EU Water Framework Directive (OJ L 327, 22.12.2000).

Federal Court of Appeal. (2018). *Tsleil-Waututh Nation v. Canada, 2018 FCA 153. 153*. Ottawa, Canada.

Franz, M., Schlitz, N., & Schumacher, K. P. (2018). Globalization and the water-energy-food nexus: Using the global production networks approach to analyze society-environment relations. *Environmental Science & Policy, 90*, 201–212. doi:10.1016/j.envsci.2017.12.004

Füssel, H.-M., Marx, A., Hildén, M., Bastrup-Birk, A., Louwagie, G., Wugt-Larsen, F., & Suk, J. (2017). *Climate change, impacts and vulnerability in Europe 2016*. Copenhagen: EEA Report European Environment Agency. doi:10.2800/534806

Giordano, M., & Shah, T. (2014). From IWRM back to integrated water resources management. *International Journal of Water Resources Development, 30*(3), 364–376. doi:10.1080/07900627.2013.851521

Gleick, P. (2000). The changing water paradigm: A look at twenty-first century water resources development. *Water International 25*(1), 127–138. doi:10.1080/02508060008686804

Gleick, P. (2003). Global freshwater resources: Soft-path solutions for the 21st century. *Science, 302*, 1524–1528. doi:10.1126/science.1089967

Government of New Zealand. (2017). *Te Awa Tupua (Whanganui River Claims Settlement) act 2017*. Christchurch, New Zealand.

Grill, G., Lehner, B., Lumsdon, A. E., MacDonald, G. K., Zarfl, C., & Reidy Liermann, C. (2015). An index-based framework for assessing patterns and trends in river fragmentation and flow regulation by

global dams at multiple scales. *Environmental Research Letters, 10*(1), 015001. doi:10.1088/1748-9326/10/1/015001
Halbe, J., Knüppe, K., Knieper, C., & Pahl-Wostl, C. (2018). Towards an integrated flood management approach to address trade-offs between ecosystem services: Insights from the Dutch and German Rhine, Hungarian Tisza, and Chinese Yangtze basins. *Journal of Hydrology, 559*, 984–994. doi:10.1016/j.jhydrol.2018.02.001
Hänel, L.. Germany facing risk of increased water shortages. *Deutsche Welle*. Retrieved January 28, 2020, from https://p.dw.com/p/3NWuA
Hoff, H. (2011). Understanding the nexus. Background paper for the Bonn 2011 Conference: The water, energy and food security nexus. Stockholm: Stockholm Environment Institute.
Holling, C. S. (ed.). (1978). *Adaptive environmental assessment and management*. New York: John Wiley and Sons.
Huntjens, P., Pahl-Wostl, C., & Grin, J. (2010). Climate change adaptation in European river basins. *Regional Environmental Change, 10*(4), 263–284. doi:10.1007/s10113-009-0108-6
Ingram, H. (2011). Beyond universal remedies for good water governance. In A. Garrido & H. Ingram (eds.), *Water for food in a changing world: Contributions from the Rosenberg International Forum on Water Policy* (pp. 241–261). Milton Park: Routledge.
Ingram, M., Ingram, H., & Lejano, R. (2019). Environmental action in the Anthropocene: The power of narrative-networks. *Journal of Environmental Policy & Planning, 21*(5), 492–503. doi:10.1080/1523908X.2015.1113513
Ingram, M., Lejano, R., & Ingram, H. (2013). *The power of narrative in environmental networks*. Cambridge, MA: MIT Press.
Jatel, N., & Guy, B. (2018). *Siwłkw (water) for all – Our responsibility. Environmental flow needs conference: Science, policy & practice, proceedings & outcomes*. Kelowna, British Columbia, Canada.
Jeffrey, P., & Gearey, M. (2006). Integrated water resources management: Lost on the road from ambition to realisation? *Water Science and Technology, 53*(1), 1–8. doi:10.2166/wst.2006.001
Knieper, C., & Pahl-Wostl, C. (2016). A comparative analysis of water governance, water management, and environmental performance in river basins. *Water Resources Management, 30*, 2161–2177. doi:10.1007/s11269-016-1276-z
Knouft, J. H., & Ficklin, D. L. (2017). The potential impacts of climate change on biodiversity in flowing freshwater systems. *Annual Review of Ecology, Evolution, and Systematics, 48*(1), 111–133. doi:10.1146/annurev-ecolsys-110316-022803
Le Blanc, D. (2015). *Towards integration at last? The Sustainable Development Goals as a network of targets* (DESA Working Paper) (Vol. 141). New York: Department of Economic & Social Affairs, United Nations.
Lee, K. N. (1999). Appraising adaptive management. *Ecology and Society, 3*(2). doi:10.5751/ES-00131-030203
Medema, W., McIntosh, B. S., & Jeffrey, P. J. (2008). From premise to practice: A critical assessment of integrated water resources management and adaptive management approaches in the water sector. *Ecology and Society, 13*(2), 29. doi:10.5751/ES-02611-130229
Mees, H. L. P., Driessen, P. P. J., & Runhaar, H. A. C. (2014). Legitimate adaptive flood risk governance beyond the dikes: The cases of Hamburg, Helsinki and Rotterdam. *Regional Environmental Change, 14*(2), 671–682. doi:10.1007/s10113-013-0527-2
Melnychuk, N., Jatel, N., & Warwick Sears, A. L. (2017). Integrated water resource management and British Columbia's Okanagan Basin water board. *International Journal of Water Resources Development, 33*(3), 408–425. doi:10.1080/07900627.2016.1214909
Molle, F., Mollinga, P. P., & Wester, P. (2009). Hydraulic bureaucracies and the hydraulic mission: Flows of water, flows of power. *Water Alternatives, 2*(3), 328-349.
Moss, T., & Monstadt, J. (2008). *Restoring floodplains in Europe*. London: IWA.
Mouchet, M. A., Lamarque, P., Martín-López, B., Crouzat, E., Gos, P., Byczek, C., & Lavorel, S. (2014). An interdisciplinary methodological guide for quantifying associations between ecosystem services. *Global Environmental Change, 28*, 298–308. doi:10.1016/j.gloenvcha.2014.07.012
Muller, M. (2017). Understanding Cape Town's water crisis. *Civil Engineering, 25*, 11–16.

Newig, J., & Koontz, T. M. (2014). Multi-level governance, policy implementation and participation: The EU's mandated participatory planning approach to implementing environmental policy. *Journal of European Public Policy, 21*(2), 248–267. doi:10.1080/13501763.2013.834070

Nilsson, C., Reidy, C. A., Dynesius, M., & Revenga, C. (2005). Fragmentation and flow regulation of the world's large river systems. *Science, 308*, 405–408. doi:10.1126/science.1107887

Olivier, D. W. (2017). Cape Town's water crisis: Driven by politics more than drought. *The Conversation*. Retrieved from https://theconversation.com/cape-towns-water-crisis-driven-by-politics-more-than-drought-88191

Opperman, J. J., Galloway, G. E., Fargione, J., Mount, J. F., Richter, B. D., & Secchi, S. (2009). Sustainable floodplain through large-scale reconnection to rivers. *Science, 326*, 1487–1488. doi:10.1126/science.1178256

Pahl-Wostl, C. (2007). Transition towards adaptive management of water facing climate and global change. *Water Resources Management, 21*(1), 49–62. doi:10.1007/s11269-006-9040-4

Pahl-Wostl, C. (2015a). Empirical analyses: From single case studies to comparative analyses. In *Water governance in the face of global change: From understanding to transformation* (pp. 203–248). Cham, Switzerland: Springer International.

Pahl-Wostl, C. (2015b). Shaping human-environment interactions. In *Water governance in the face of global change: From understanding to transformation* (pp. 125–158). Cham, Switzerland: Springer International.

Pahl-Wostl, C. (2015c). *Water governance in the face of global change: From understanding to transformation. Water governance: Concepts, methods and practice* (Vol. 1). Cham: Springer International. doi:10.1007/978-3-319-21855-7

Pahl-Wostl, C. (2015d). Water policy: From panaceas towards embracing complexity. In *Water governance in the face of global change: From understanding to transformation* (pp. 11–24). Cham, Switzerland: Springer International.

Pahl-Wostl, C. (2019a). Governance of the water-energy-food security nexus: A multi-level coordination challenge. *Environmental Science & Policy, 92*, 356–367. doi:10.1016/j.envsci.2017.07.017

Pahl-Wostl, C. (2019b). The role of governance modes and meta-governance in the transformation towards sustainable water governance. *Environmental Science & Policy, 91*, 6–16. doi:10.1016/j.envsci.2018.10.008

Pahl-Wostl, C., Becker, G., Sendzimir, J., & Knieper, C. (2013a). How multilevel societal learning processes facilitate transformative change: A comparative case study analysis on flood management. *Ecology and Society, 18*(4), 58. doi:10.5751/ES-05779-180458

Pahl-Wostl, C., Conca, K., Kramer, A., Maestu, J., & Schmidt, F. (2013b). Missing links in global water governance: A processes-oriented analysis. *Ecology and Society, 18*(2), 33. doi:10.5751/ES-05554-180233

Pahl-Wostl, C., Isendahl, N., Möllenkamp, S., Brugnach, M., Jeffrey, P. W. M., & Tessa de Vries, T. (2006). *Paradigms in water management*. Osnabrueck: European Commission.

Pahl-Wostl, C., Jeffrey, P., Isendahl, N., & Brugnach, M. (2011). Maturing the new water management paradigm: Progressing from aspiration to practice. *Water Resources Management, 25*(3), 837–856. doi:10.1007/s11269-010-9729-2

Pahl-Wostl, C., & Knieper, C. (2014). The capacity of water governance to deal with the climate change adaptation challenge: Using fuzzy set qualitative comparative analysis to distinguish between polycentric, fragmented and centralized regimes. *Global Environmental Change, 29*, 139–154. doi:10.1016/j.gloenvcha.2014.09.003

Pahl-Wostl, C., Knieper, C., Lukat, E., Meergans, F., Schoderer, M., Schütze, N., … Vidaurre, R. (in review). Enhancing the capacity of water governance to deal with complex management challenges: A framework of analysis.

Pahl-Wostl, C., Lebel, L., Knieper, C., & Nikitina, E. (2012). From applying panaceas to mastering complexity: Toward adaptive water governance in river basins. *Environmental Science and Policy, 23*, 24–34. doi:10.1016/j.envsci.2012.07.014

Pahl-Wostl, C., Sendzimir, J., Jeffrey, P., Aerts, J., Berkamp, G., & Cross, K. (2007). Managing change toward adaptive water management through social learning. *Ecology and Society, 12*(2), 30. Retrieved from http://www.ecologyandsociety.org/vol12/iss32/art30/10.5751/ES-02147-120230

Raudsepp-Hearne, C., Peterson, G. D., & Bennett, E. M. (2010). Ecosystem service bundles for analyzing tradeoffs in diverse landscapes. *Proceedings of the National Academy of Sciences, 107* (11), 5242–5247. doi:10.1073/pnas.0907284107

Rockström, J., Falkenmark, M., Folke, C., Lannerstad, M., Barron, J., Enfors, E., ... Pahl-Wostl, C. (2014). *Water resilience for human prosperity*. Cambridge: Cambridge University Press. doi:10.1017/CBO9781139162463

Rogers, P., & St. Fleur, N. (2014, July 7). California drought: Database shows big differences between water guzzlers and sippers. *San Jose Mercury News*.

Ross, A., & Connell, D. (2016). The evolution and performance of river basin management in the Murray-Darling Basin. *Ecology and Society, 21*(3). doi:10.5751/ES-08664-210329

Schreiner, B. (2013). Why has the South African National Water Act been so difficult to implement? *Water Alternatives, 6*(2), 239–245.

Shah, T. (2016). *Increasing water security: The key to implement the Sustainable Development Goals* (Background Papers) (Vol. 22). Stockholm: GWP.

Sigel, K., Klauser, B., & Pahl-Wostl, C. (2010). Conceptualising uncertainty in environmental decision-making: The example of the EU Water Framework Directive. *Ecological Economics, 69*, 502–510. doi:10.1016/j.ecolecon.2009.11.012

Smith, D. M., & Barchiesi, S. (2009). *Environment as infrastructure: Resilience to climate change impacts on water through investments in nature. Perspectives on water and climate change adaptation*. Gland, Switzerland: International Union for Conservation of Nature.

Soliman, H., & Cable, S. (2011). Sinking under the weight of corruption: Neoliberal reform, political accountability and justice. *Current Sociology, 59*(6), 735–753. doi:10.1177/0011392111419748

Srinivasan, V., Lambin, E. F., Gorelick, S. M., Thompson, B. H., & Rozelle, S. (2012). The nature and causes of the global water crisis: Syndromes from a meta-analysis of coupled human-water studies. *Water Resources Research, 48*(10). doi:10.1029/2011wr011087

Supreme Court of Canada. (2014). *Tsilhqot'in Nation v British Columbia. 2014 SCC 44*. Ottawa, Canada.

Tilt, B., Braun, Y., & He, D. (2009). Social impacts of large dam projects: A comparison of international case studies and implications for best practice. *Journal of Environmental Management, 90*, 249–257. doi:10.1016/j.jenvman.2008.07.030

Tsatsaros, J. H., Wellman, J. L., Bohnet, I. C., Brodie, J. E., & Valentine, P. (2018). Indigenous water governance in Australia: Comparisons with the United States and Canada. *Water, 10*(11), 1639. doi:10.3390/w10111639

Ullrich, P. A., Xu, Z., Rhoades, A. M., Dettinger, M. D., Mount, J. F., Jones, A. D., & Vahmani, P. (2018). California's drought of the future: A midcentury recreation of the exceptional conditions of 2012–2017. *Earth's Future, 6*(11), 1568–1587. doi:10.1029/2018EF001007

UN Environment. (2018). *Progress on integrated water resources management. Global baseline for SDG 6 indicator 6.5.1: Degree of IWRM implementation*. Nairobi, Kenya: United Nations Environment Programme.

UNEP. (2012). *The UN-Water status report on the application of integrated approaches to water resources management*. Kenia, Nairobi: United Nations Environment Programme.

United Nations. (2018). *Sustainable development goal 6 synthesis report 2018 on water and sanitation*. New York: Author.

Vörösmarty, C. J., McIntyre, P. B., Gessner, M. O., Dudgeon, D., Prusevich, A., Green, P., ... Davies, P. M. (2010). Global threats to human water security and river biodiversity. *Nature, 467*, 555–561. doi:10.1038/nature09440

Vörösmarty, C. J., Pahl-Wostl, C., Bunn, S., & Lawford, R. (2013). Global water, the Anthropocene and the transformation of science. *Current Opinion in Environmental Sustainability, 5*(6), 539–550. doi:10.1016/j.cosust.2013.10.005

Voulvoulis, N., Arpon, K. D., & Giakoumis, T. (2017). The EU Water Framework Directive: From great expectations to problems with implementation. *Science of the Total Environment, 575*, 358–366. doi:10.1016/j.scitotenv.2016.09.228

Wallis, P., & Ison, R. (2011). Appreciating institutional complexity in water governance dynamics: A case from the Murray-Darling Basin, Australia. *Water Resources Management, 25*, 4081–4097. doi:10.1007/s11269-011-9885-z

Walters, C. J. (1986). *Adaptive management of natural resources*. New York: MacMillan.

Webb, J. A., Watts, R. J., Allan, C., & Conallin, J. C. (2018). Adaptive management of environmental flows. *Environmental Management, 61*(3), 339–346. doi:10.1007/s00267-017-0981-6

WEFWI. (2009). *Managing our future water needs for agriculture, industry, human health and the environment.* World Economic Forum Water Initiative. Geneva, Switzerland: World Economic Forum.

WEFWI. (2011). *Water security: The water-food-energy-climate nexus*. World Economic Forum Water Initiative. Washington: Island Press.

Winemiller, K. O., McIntyre, P. B., Castello, L., Fluet-Chouinard, E., Giarrizzo, T., Nam, S., … Sáenz, L. (2016). Balancing hydropower and biodiversity in the Amazon, Congo, and Mekong. *Science, 351* (6269), 128–129. doi:10.1126/science.aac7082

WMO. (2009). *Integrated flood management concept paper*. Geneva, Switzerland: Author.

Wolf, C. (2019). *Wie viel ist streng genug? Ein Verfahrensvorschlag zur Festlegung des „bestmöglichen ökologischen Gewässerzustands" für Zielabsenkungen nach Art. 4.5 der EG-Wasserrahmenrichtlinie unter Berücksichtigung struktureller, funktionaler und ökosystemleistungsrelevanter Aspekte*. PhD thesis, Osnabrück University.

WWAP (UNESCO World Water Assessment Programme). (2019). *The United Nations world water development report 2019: Leaving no one behind*. Paris: UNESCO.

Yates, J. S., Harris, L. M., & Wilson, N. J. (2017). Multiple ontologies of water: Politics, conflict and implications for governance. *Environment and Planning D: Society and Space, 35*(5), 797–815. doi:10.1177/0263775817700395

Zarfl, C., Lumsdon, A. E., Berlekamp, J., Tydecks, L., & Tockner, K. (2015). A global boom in hydropower dam construction. *Aquatic Sciences, 77*(1), 161–170. doi:10.1007/s00027-014-0377-0

Zille, H. (2017, October 30). The Cape water crisis: FAQs and honest answers. *Daily Maverick*.

OPEN ACCESS

Economically challenged and water scarce: identification of global populations most vulnerable to water crises

Taikan Oki and Rose E. Quiocho

ABSTRACT

The best available high-resolution precipitation, GDP, available freshwater and withdrawal data sets are used in a combined global analysis of physical and economic water scarcity at 50 km resolution. We find that approximately 40.7 million people are living in areas with concurrent severe economic and water-scarcity constraints. These areas are mostly in semi-arid parts of Sub-Saharan Africa, the Middle East and Central Asia.

Introduction

Water is one of the most important resources in the world, if not the most important. Water is needed and used for practically everything, from household domestic use to industrial and agricultural production. Even though over 70% of the Earth's surface is covered by water, only a small fraction of Earth's water is viable for supply due to its great heterogeneity in space and time (Oki & Kanae, 2006). Water scarcity is broadly the consequence of the spatial distribution of population growth relative to available water resources (Kummu et al., 2016). More often than not, infrastructure to harvest and manage water supplies cannot keep up with the steadily growing demand. Varis, Biswas, Tortajada, and Lundqvist (2006) outlined the water management problems faced by several developing megacities around the world, citing unprecedented population growth and poor infrastructure planning as two of the common causes of water stress. To make things worse, climate change has altered natural hydrological patterns. There is a systematic increase in the variance of precipitation around the world over the last few decades; wet areas are becoming wetter, and dry and arid areas drier (Dore, 2005). Big cities all over the world are now experiencing recurring water shortages. Sao Paulo in Brazil, Jakarta in Indonesia, Bangalore in India and Cape Town in South Africa are just some of the cities that recently made international headlines due to water shortages.

By definition, water scarcity is a general state of water insufficiency. Water stress is defined as a state when certain threshold values are exceeded (Hanasaki, Yoshikawa, Pokhrel, & Kanae, 2018a). Water scarcity was further classified by Rijsberman (2006) into two different types: physical and economic. Physical water scarcity is the insufficiency or lack of water itself. This type of scarcity is often found in arid regions. Economic water scarcity is an insufficiency of water associated with lack of capacity to use water resources despite its availability or abundance. Economic water scarcity is often associated with inadequate infrastructure development and poor management, as well as cases of inequitable water allocation and access across economic levels. Access to safe drinking water tends to improve with economic growth. The achievement of the Millennium Development Goal for drinking water (Target 7-C) was associated with the rapid economic growth in China and India in 1990–2015 (Fukuda, Noda, & Oki, 2019).

Although supply and demand are the fundamental factors dictating water stress, economic forces interfere and alter the dynamics of these two. Standard of living changes water use behaviours; richer economies tend to use more water per capita. On the supply side, the capacity for building utility infrastructure also correlates with economic stature. Inter-basin transfers, groundwater extraction and seawater desalination are just some of the common alternatives to conventional water supply, which are all undeniably capital-intensive. Also, the urbanization process, along with the distribution and growth of population in megacities, is different in developed and developing economies (Biswas, 2004). Megacities in developing countries grow exponentially faster than their developed and industrialized counterparts. But the magnitude of economic development is concurrent with population growth only in industrialized cities, leaving developing cities behind (Varis et al., 2006). The importance of water resource management in alleviating water stress, especially in cases of economic water scarcity in developing countries, was highlighted by Biswas and Tortajada (2010a, 2010b). In their case study of Phnom Pehn, Cambodia, the drastic improvement in public access to water since institutional restructuring has demonstrated that effective leadership and governance can alleviate water scarcity (Biswas & Tortajada, 2010b).

Historically, water scarcity has been quantified by a multitude of indicators. Liu et al. (2017) provided a comprehensive summary of water stress indicators categorized into five classes. Among them, the indicators most widely used are the withdrawal-to-availability ratio, also commonly known as the withdrawal-to-water ratio (WWR), and availability per capita (APC). These indicators have their own respective classifications of scarcity levels. Hanasaki et al. (2018a) briefly discussed the development processes and the supporting evidence for these thresholds for both indicators, which were both primarily obtained empirically using several case studies and approximations.

Oki, Yano, and Hanasaki (2017) discussed the relationship among physical water scarcity expressed by APC, gross domestic product (GDP), and the export/import quantity of virtual water trade through major crops based on country-level analysis. They found that most of the net virtual water exporting countries have higher APC than the net virtual water importing countries, and moreover, there is no country with low APC and low GDP. The analysis suggests that a country can survive with little money provided that it has enough water to grow crops to feed itself, and even a water-scarce country can survive if it has the purchasing power to import necessary food from abroad or engineer additional water supply domestically. But countries facing both economic hardship and water scarcity cannot support their basic needs over the long term, so they do not exist in the contemporary world. This result implies that we need to consider both the physical and the economic water scarcity of a region to determine whether the region is truly in distress, with chronic water shortage.

In this study, we jointly analyze the physical and economic water scarcity of the world at 50 km resolution, in an extension of the precursor analysis by Oki et al. (2017). We illustrate the current state of global freshwater resources, and pinpoint the areas and populations at greatest risk of a water crisis.

Data

Table 1 summarizes the gridded data sets collected and used for this study, with particulars such as spatial resolution, units and variables. A brief explanation of the data sources and assumptions for each follows.

The GDP data set is from the Japan Center for Global Environmental Research, National Institute for Environmental Studies (Murakami & Yamagata, 2016). GDP was estimated by downscaling projected country population under different socio-economic pathways. SSP2 (the 'middle of the road' shared socioeconomic pathway) was used, in which the world population will peak early in the latter half of the twenty-first century (Takakura et al., 2019).

Climatological mean precipitation data are from Climatologies at High Resolution for the Earth Land Surface Areas (CHELSA; Karger et al., 2017). CHELSA is an organization hosted by the Swiss Federal Institute for Forest, Snow and Landscape Research WSL. The 0.01 × 0.01 degree data set was constructed using data from 1979 to 2013.

The gridded data sets of available freshwater and withdrawals were produced using the global hydrological model called H08 (Hanasaki et al., 2008, 2018a). This is a grid-cell-based model of global hydrology and world water resources, consisting of six submodels, including human interventions such as storage in and releases from artificial reservoirs and irrigation withdrawals, coupled with a crop growth model. The model was run in accordance with the ISIMIP2b protocol (Frieler et al., 2017). ISIMIP (the Inter-sectoral Impact Model Intercomparison Project, www.isimip.org) offers a framework and protocols for different modellers in projecting the impacts of climate change. Available freshwater was estimated as total runoff, the sum of surface and subsurface runoff components. Domestic, industrial and agricultural withdrawals were also obtained from the estimates of H08 (Hanasaki, Yoshikawa, Pokhel, & Kanae, 2018b). Net withdrawal was set to be the

Table 1. Data used in this study.

Parameter	Variable	Unit and Size	Source
GDP-PPP (0.5° × 0.5°)	GDP in 2020	USD billions per year	Murakami and Yamagata (2016)
Precipitation (0.01° × 0.01°)	Mean annual precipitation	mm/y	Karger et al. (2017)
Population (0.5° × 0.5°)	Population	capita per grid	Goldewijk, Beusen, Doelman, and Stehfest (2017)
Available freshwater (0.5° × 0.5°)	Total Runoff total (surface + subsurface)	$kg/m^2/s$	Hanasaki et al. (2018a)
Withdrawal rate (0.5° × 0.5°)	Net industrial water consumption Net domestic water withdrawal Net agricultural water withdrawal	$kg/m^2/s$	

sum of these three withdrawals. To be consistent, the population information provided for ISIMIP2b (Goldewijk et al., 2017) was also used. The precipitation information in ISIMIP2b is not from CHELSEA but based on various other sources.

Results

The distribution of population across the globe is uneven. A study by the United Nations found that the global urban population had exceeded the global rural population for the first time in 2007 (UNFPA, 2007). As of 2011, there were more than 3.6 billion people living in urban areas, and this number is projected to increase by another 2.6 billion by 2050 (UN, 2012).

Statistically, approximately 45% of earth's land is practically uninhabited, with less than one capita per square kilometre (Figure A1 in the online supplemental material). Sixty per cent of the world's 7.7 billion people live on only 9% of the land area.

Precipitation is concentrated in equatorial regions and coastal areas (Figure A2). The desert regions of North Africa and the Middle East are easily recognizable due to their low precipitation. People mostly live in areas with mean annual precipitation of 800–1600 mm/y, followed by 400–800 mm/y and 1600–3200 mm/y (Figure 1).

Figure 2 is based on the estimated global distribution of precipitation (Figure A2) cross-referenced with the global distribution of population (Figure A1) and shows the available precipitation water per capita per year. To avoid extreme magnification in the areas with very low population density, the minimum population density was set to one capita per square kilometre; areas with lower population density (indicated by grey shading) were excluded from further analysis.

Large areas in most of the continents have more than 20,000 m^3 per capita per year of available precipitation water (Figure A3), and only limited areas of Europe, South Asia, North Africa, the Middle East, South Asia and East Asia have less than 1000 m^3 per capita per year. The histogram is highest in the range of 2000–5000 m^3 per capita per year, followed by 1000–2000 m^3 per capita per year and 5000–10,000 m^3 per capita per year.

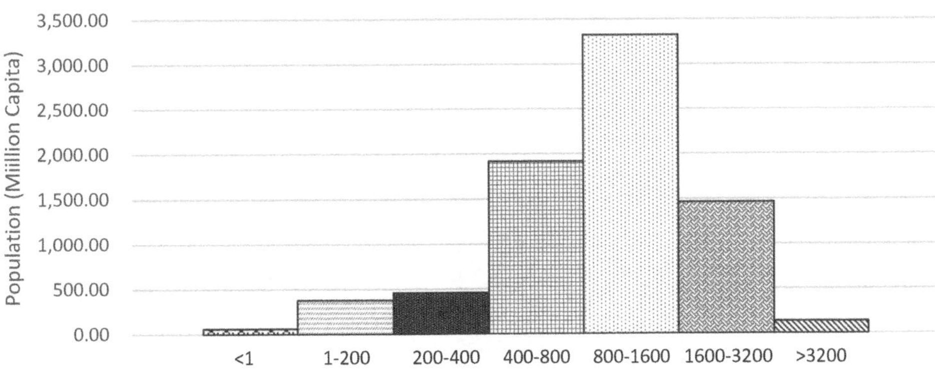

Figure 1. Histogram of population in terms of mean annual precipitation (mm/year).

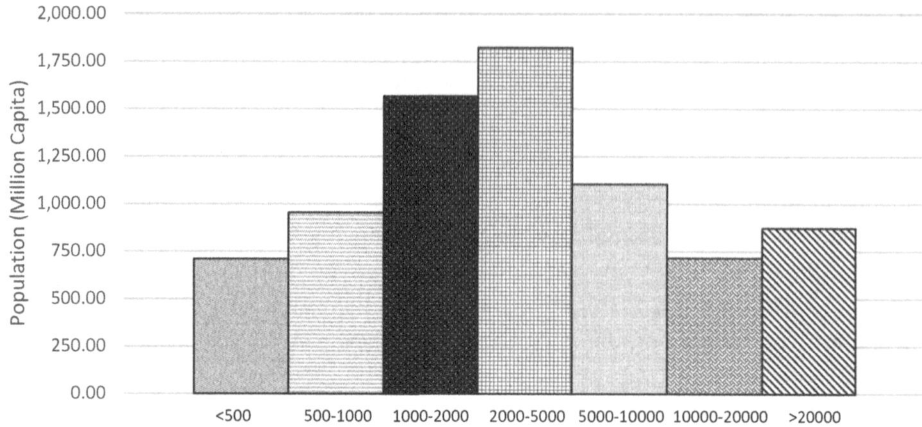

Figure 2. Histogram of population in terms of available precipitation water (m3/capita/year).

But more than 600 million people live in the other ranges. For example, more than 800 million live in areas with more than 20,000 m^3 per capita per year.

In general, available freshwater (Figure A4) is lower than precipitation (Figure A2). Of the more than 60,000 land grid boxes (excluding Antarctica), approximately 3000 have more runoff than precipitation, due to the runoff from additional irrigation water internally calculated in H08. The histogram of population in terms of annual runoff (Figure 3) is highest in the range of 1–200 mm/y, but similar for 200–400, 400–800 and 800–1600 mm/y. Due to the nonlinear conversion of precipitation into runoff, Figures 1 and 3 show different distributions.

The global distribution of available freshwater per capita is shown in Figure 4. As with Figure A3, a large fraction of Earth's land masses have more than 20,000 m^3 per capita per year of available freshwater. At the same time, semi-arid regions in Sub-Saharan Africa, large areas of Eastern Europe, and some parts of south-eastern China have less than 1000 m^3 per capita per year. Large tracts of northern and eastern Africa, the Middle East, West Asia and some parts of South and East Asia have

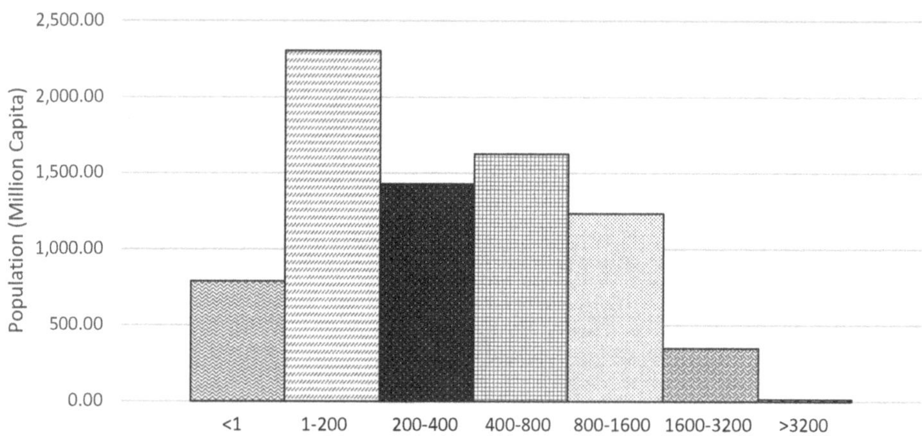

Figure 3. Histogram of population in terms of annual runoff (mm/year).

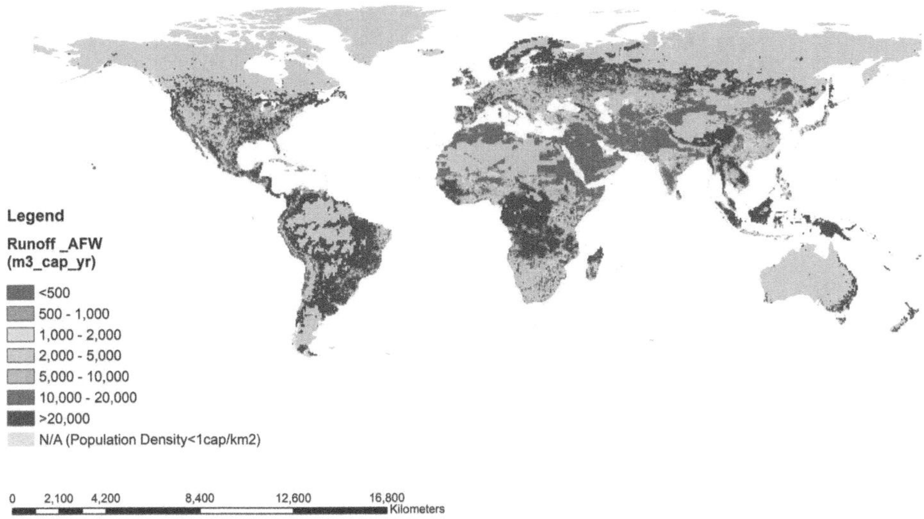

Figure 4. Spatial distribution of available freshwater (m^3/capita/year).

even less – under 500 m^3 per capita per year. Aproximately half of the world's population lives in areas in this category (Figure 5). Figures 3 and 5 suggest that population density tends to be higher in areas where more freshwater is available.

Based on these estimates, water-stress conditions can be inferred using the indicator and threshold values of Shiklomanov (1997) for available freshwater. Table 2 summarizes the ratio of population in each category of water scarcity assessed by APC, with available precipitation water per capita for comparison.

Water stress is fundamentally driven by two factors: supply and demand. Although water availability in terms of m^3 per capita per year, as summarized in Table 2, can provide a good estimate of water stress, this assumes that per capita demand is similar throughout the global population. But studies (FAO, 2016) have shown that per capita consumption varies across countries and regions, often affected by different factors, such as culture, climate and lifestyle (Akuoko-Asibey, Nkemdirim, & Draper, 1993; Khadam, 1988).

Withdrawal and consumption can be divided into several sectors. In this study, net withdrawal is taken to be the sum of agricultural, industrial and domestic water withdrawals. The spatial distribution of sectoral withdrawals is shown in Figures A5–A8 for agricultural, industrial, domestic and total withdrawals, respectively.

The global agricultural water requirement is the highest in these three sectors, with net annual requirements of 1607 km^3 (Figure A5). Despite being the largest component, the spatial distribution of irrigation withdrawal is highly concentrated in certain regions, such as southern and eastern Asia. With 1050 km^3/y, industrial withdrawal (Figure A6) comes in second. Domestic withdrawal is estimated as 377 km^3/y (Figure A7). Aggregating these sectoral withdrawals gives 3,034 km^3 global annual net withdrawals (Figure A8). Considering the population distribution, nearly 6 billion of the world's people use less water than 500 m^3 per capita per year (Figure 6).

It should be restated that some of the water withdrawals, particularly for agricultural and industrial water, are for external consumption in addition to local consumption, as expressed by the concept of 'virtual water trade' (Allan, 1998; Oki & Kanae, 2004).

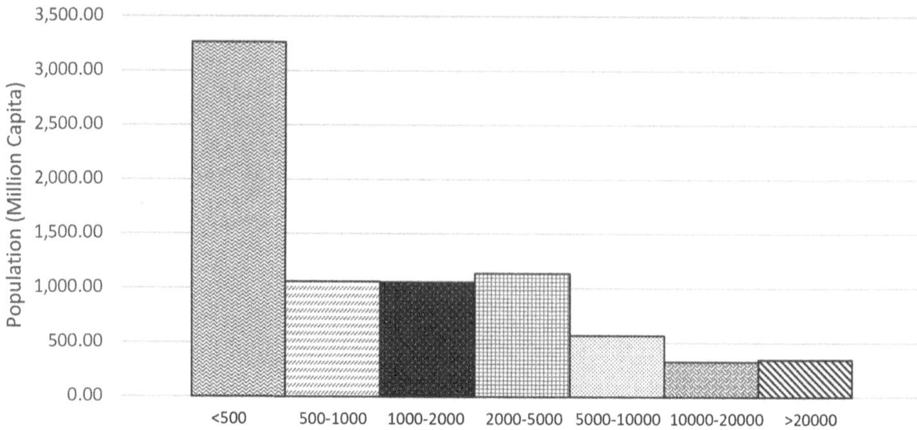

Figure 5. Histogram of population in terms of available freshwater (m^3/capita/year).

Table 2. Distribution of population by water availability.

		Population distribution (%)	
Availability (m^3 per capita per year)	Description	Rainwater	Freshwater
<500	Extremely low	9.2	42.2
500–1000		12.3	13.7
1,000–2,000	Very low	20.2	13.6
2,000–5,000	Low	23.6	14.7
>5,000	Average	34.8	15.9

Using the distribution of availability (Figure 4) and net total withdrawals (Figure A8), the unit-less indicator of water scarcity, WWR, can be estimated as

$$WWR = W/Q \tag{1}$$

where W is the annual water withdrawal and Q is the annual runoff/available freshwater. The geographical distribution of WWR is presented in Figure 7.

Raskin, Gleick, Kirshen, Pontius, and Strzepek (1997) suggest that when WWR is below 0.1, the region is classified as having no water stress, 0.1–0.2 is low water stress, 0.2–0.4 is moderate water stress, and over 0.4 is high water stress. Following this classification, the distribution of population with respect to water stress is summarized in Table 3 and Figure 8.

Although both APC (Table 2) and WWR (Table 3) are indicators intended to quantify water stress, they cannot be directly compared. If we compare the fraction of the most water stressed population, there is a considerable difference between these indicators. In Table 2, more than half of the world's population (55.9%, 4.3 billion) have extremely or catastrophically low water availability. But in Table 3, only 7.5% (582 million) are in high-water-stress conditions. This apparent discrepancy may be partly explained by the fact that return flow, or unconsumed water withdrawals that are returned to the natural system, are excluded from the analysis. Recall that net water withdrawal is considered in this study. Consequently, the water withdrawal in this study is much smaller than

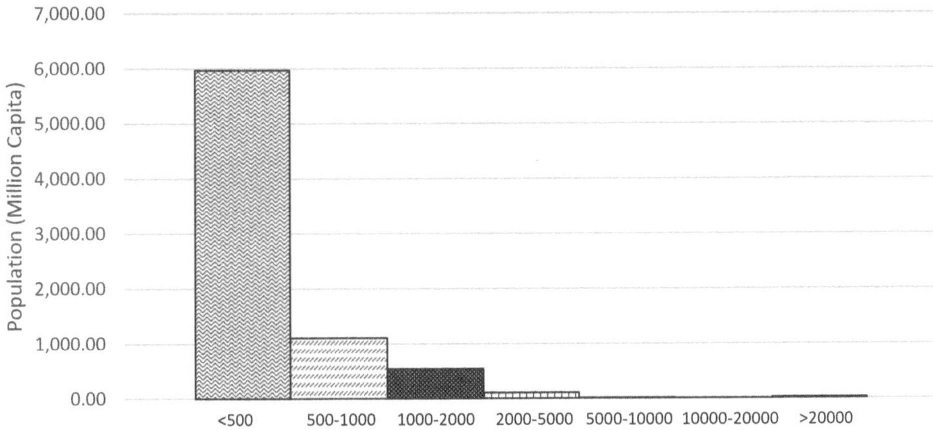

Figure 6. Histogram of population in terms of net total annual withdrawal (m^3/capita/year).

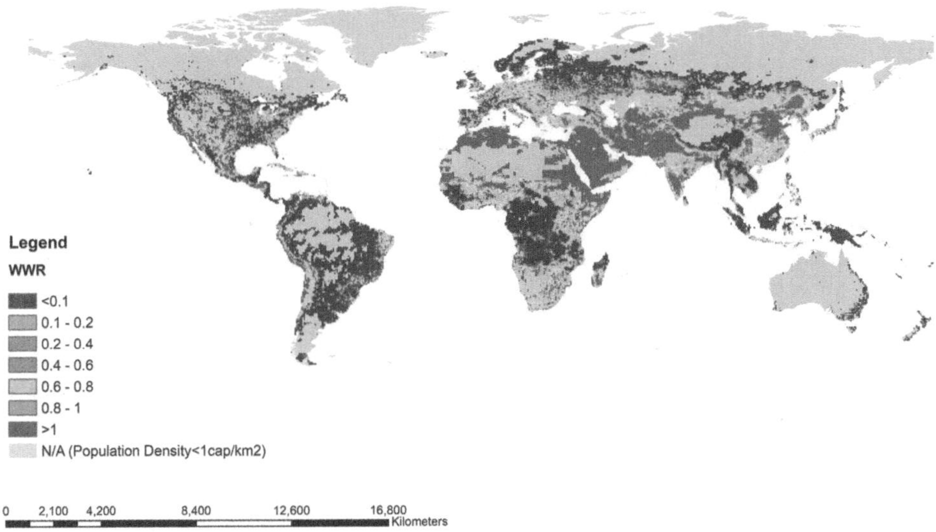

Figure 7. Spatial distribution of water stress represented by withdrawal-to-available-water ratio (WWR).

conventional water withdrawals, by approximately one-half for agricultural water withdrawals for example, and the WWR in Table 3 may be underestimated.

GDP is commonly used to quantify economic activity. Figure A9 shows the spatial distribution of GDP per capita (based on purchasing power parity, PPP) in USD in 2005.

Figure 9 is a scatter plot (log-log scale) of GDP-PPP per capita versus APC. The size of each circles indicates the population count. Oki et al. (2017) found that there are no countries that are both economically challenged and under water scarcity, as would be denoted by lying below the dashed thick line (connecting USD 10,000 of GDP-PPP per capita and 10,000 m^3 of available freshwater per capita per year). No country was found below the threshold line, but some 0.5° grid points do fall below that line in this study.

Table 3. Distribution of population by water stress.

Withdrawal-to-available-water ratio	Remarks	Population distribution (%)
<0.1	No water stress	81.8
0.1–0.2	Low water stress	6.2
0.2–0.4	Moderate water stress	4.6
>0.4	High water stress	7.5

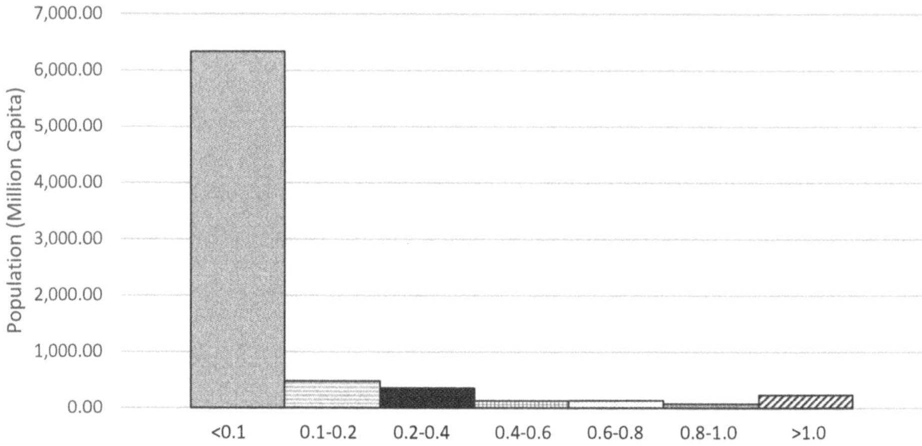

Figure 8. Histogram of population in terms of withdrawal-to-available-water ratio.

This could be caused by the heterogeneity of water and monetary resources within nations.

To check for consistency between the analysis of Oki et al. (2017) and our current study, the gridded data for water APC and GDP-PPP per capita were averaged in each nation (Figure 10). This is very similar to Oki et al.'s (2017) country-level analysis, and the population that is both economically challenged and water stressed can be only delineated in a finer-mesh analysis (Figure 9).

Finally, the grid boxes below the threshold line (connecting USD 10,000 of GDP-PPP per capita and 10,000 m^3 of available freshwater per capita per year), corresponding to regions with a perilous combination of low GDP per capita and water scarcity, are presented in Figure 11. Such areas are located in parts of northern and eastern Africa, the Middle East, West Asia, and central to north-eastern Asia. People in these regions are at great risk because they experience shortages of available freshwater to grow food, and also have difficulty purchasing food due to lack of economic power. Of the 40.7 million people living in these areas prone to water crises, approximately 10.2 million are living in areas with WWR of 0.4 or more, and 30.5 million in areas with WWR less than 0.4. These results suggest that more comprehensive assessments of water scarcity will be possible using multiple numerical indicators (Falkenmark, Lundqvist, & Widstrand, 1989).

There are identified grid boxes near Mexico City and Perth in Western Australia in Figure 11, as well. These could be due to the inconsistency between the downscaled population and GDP data used in this study, even though these regions are known to be

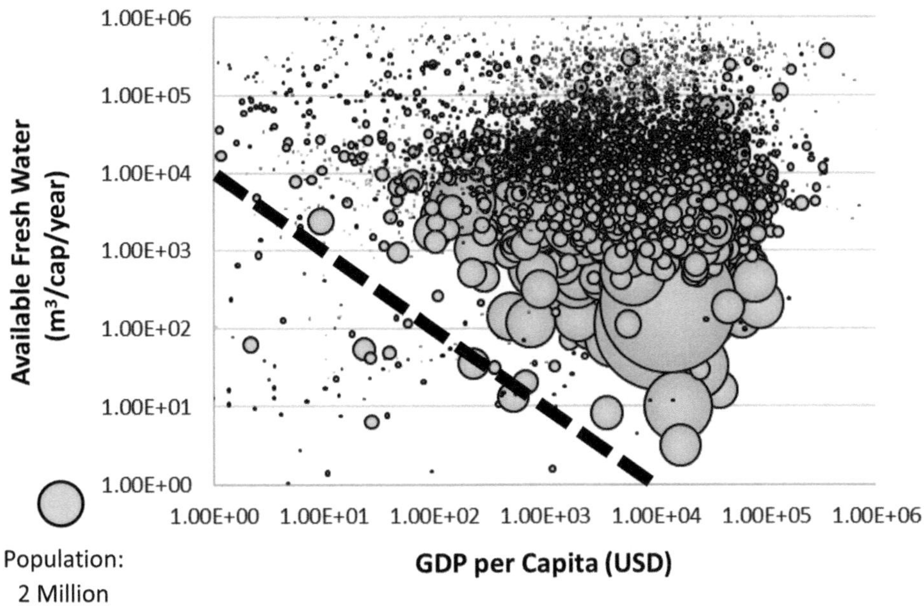

Figure 9. Scatter plot of water availability per capita and GDP-PPP per capita analyzed by 0.5° longitudinal and latitudinal grid boxes.

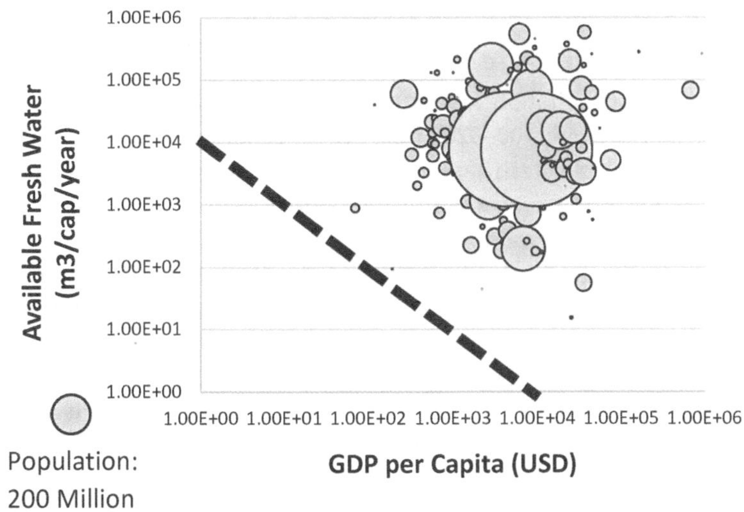

Figure 10. Scatter plot of water availability and GDP-PPP per capita by country-level analysis.

seriously water stressed; for example, a seawater desalination plant was built near Perth and started operation in 2006.

This study excludes the explicit considerations of various factors affecting physical water scarcity, such as seasonality, interannual variability, groundwater supplies, water quality and hydropower demands, which have been already considered in some

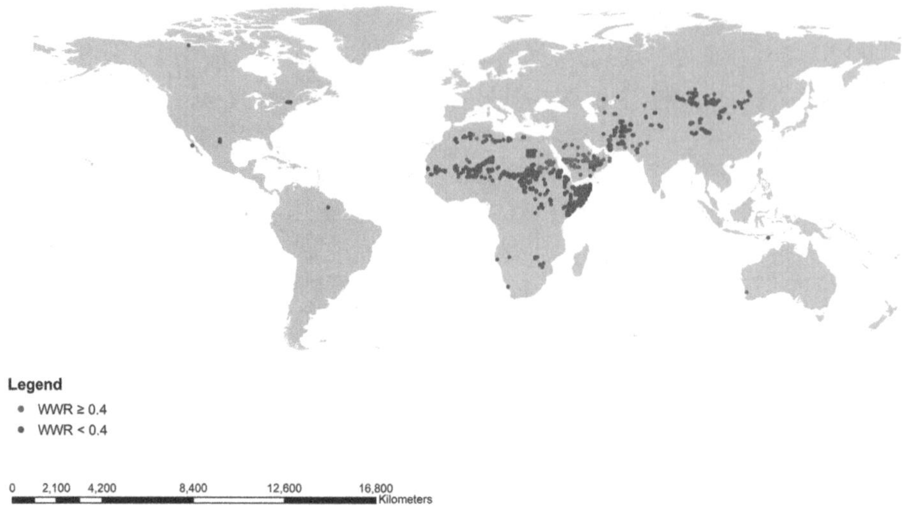

Figure 11. Longitudinal and latitudinal grid boxes (0.5° × 0.5°) showing areas below the threshold line of both economically poor and water-scarce.

pioneering studies (Hanasaki et al., 2018a; Wada et al., 2017). Further integration of socio-economic aspects in modern assessments of world water resources is expected.

Conclusion

Even though annual precipitation and annual runoff have high spatial heterogeneity, most people live in areas with 400–3200 mm/y of precipitation and less than 500 m^3 per capita per year of available freshwater. Net total annual withdrawal is also less than 500 m^3 per capita per year for nearly 6 billion people, and a similar number of people live in areas with a net withdrawal-to-availability ratio less than 0.1. Combined analysis of physical and economic water scarcity, for the first time ever, shows that some regions in the world, analyzed by 0.5° longitudinal and latitudinal grid boxes, are below the threshold line connecting the USD 10,000 per capita per year of GDP and 10,000 m^3 per capita per year of available freshwater recourses, and they are mostly in northern and eastern Africa, the Middle East, West Asia, and central to north-eastern Asia, with a total current combined population of approximately 40.7 million. People in such regions should have support from outside the region in the same nation, or from outside the nation, since they may have not enough water to grow food internally, and not enough purchasing power to compensate for water shortage by importing food.

These results depend on the spatial scale used in the analysis, as illustrated by Oki et al. (2001), and we would be able to differentiate more acute but limited areas of economically challenging and water-scarce regions from the majority of less water-scarce regions, if we had finer-scale information over the globe. But the proposed methodology to identify the regions with chronic water shortage due to economic and hydrological reasons should be useful to develop and implement countermeasures. Projections of future water crisis potential could be achieved by applying the approach used here to future GDP and water availability estimates (e.g. Ferguson, Pan, & Oki, 2018).

Acknowledgments

The authors thank Dr C. R. Ferguson of the University at Albany, SUNY, for his support to finalize the draft. The first author feels great honour and acknowledges Dr Asit Biswas for his generous offer to accept this work for his Festschrift, because Dr Biswas has been a mentor on the fundamental issues of how we should tackle and understand world water issues, and develop and propose policy-relevant solutions, for more than two decades, since the Next Generation Water Leaders programme, which Dr Biswas organized with the Nippon Foundation and prepared for the 2nd World Water Forum in 2000.

Disclosure statement

No potential conflict of interest was reported by the authors.

Funding

This work was supported by the Japan Society for the Promotion of Science [KAKENHI; 16H06291].

ORCID

Taikan Oki http://orcid.org/0000-0003-4067-4678
Rose E. Quiocho http://orcid.org/0000-0002-0167-9348

References

Akuoko-Asibey, A., Nkemdirim, L. C., & Draper, D. L. (1993). The impacts of climatic variables on seasonal water consumption in Calgary, Alberta. *Canadian Water Resources Journal/Revue canadienne des ressources hydriques*, *18*(2), 107–116. doi:10.4296/cwrj1802107

Allan, J. A. (1998). Virtual water: A strategic resource, global solution to regional deficits. *Groundwater*, *36*(4), 545–546. doi:10.1111/j.1745-6584.1998.tb02825.x

Biswas, A. (2004). Integrated Water Resources Management: A reassessment. A Water Forum contribution. *Water International*, *29*(2), 248–256. doi:10.1080/02508060408691775

Biswas, A., & Tortajada, C. (2010a). Future water governance: Problems and perspectives. *Water Resources Development*, *26*(2), 129–139. doi:10.1080/07900627.2010.488853

Biswas, A., & Tortajada, C. (2010b). Water supply of Phnom Penh: An example of good governance. *Water Resources Development*, *26*(2), 157–172. doi:10.1080/07900621003768859

Dore, M. (2005). Climate change and changes in global precipitation patterns: What do we know? *Environment International*, *31*(8), 1167–1181. doi:10.1016/j.envint.2005.03.004

Falkenmark, M., Lundqvist, J., & Widstrand, C. (1989). Macro-scale water scarcity requires micro-scale approaches: Aspects of vulnerability in semi-arid development. *Natural Resources Forum*, *13*(4), 258–267. doi:10.1111/narf.1989.13.issue-4

Ferguson, C. R., Pan, M., & Oki, T. (2018). The effect of global warming on future water availability: CMIP5 synthesis. *Water Resources Research*, *54*, 7791–7819. doi:10.1029/2018WR022792

Food and Agriculture Organization of the United Nations (FAO). (2016). AQUASTAT main database. Retrieved from http://www.fao.org/nr/water/aquastat/data/query/

Frieler, K., Lange, S., Piontek, F., Reyer, C. P. O., Schewe, J., Warszawski, L., … Yamagata, Y. (2017). Assessing the impacts of 1.5°C global warming: Simulation protocol of the Inter-Sectoral Impact Model Intercomparison Project (ISIMIP2b). *Geoscientific Model Development*, *10*, 4321–4345. doi:10.5194/gmd-10-4321-2017

Fukuda, S., Noda, K., & Oki, T. (2019). How global targets on drinking water were developed and achieved. *Nature Sustainability*, *2*, 429–434. doi:10.1038/s41893-019-0269-3

Goldewijk, K., Beusen, A., Doelman, J., & Stehfest, E. (2017). Anthropogenic land use estimates for the Holocene: HYDE 3.2. *Earth System Science Data, 9*, 927–953. doi:10.5194/essd-9-927-2017

Hanasaki, N., Kanae, S., Oki, T., Masuda, K., Motoya, K., Shirakawa, N., ... Tanaka, K. (2008). An integrated model for the assessment of global water resources, Part 2: Applications and assessments. *Hydrology and Earth System Sciences, 12*, 1027–1037. Retrieved from www.hydrol-earth-syst-sci.net/12/1027/2008/

Hanasaki, N., Yoshikawa, S., Pokhrel, Y., & Kanae, S. (2018a). A quantitative investigation of the thresholds for two conventional water scarcity indicators using a state-of-the-art global hydrological model with human activities. *Water Resources Research, 54*, 8279–8294. doi:10.1029/2018WR022931

Hanasaki, N., Yoshikawa, S., Pokhel, Y., & Kanae, S. (2018b). A global hydrological simulation to specify the sources of water used by humans. *Hydrology and Earth System Sciences, 22*, 789–817. doi:10.5194/hess-22-789-2018

Karger, D. N., Conrad, O., Böhner, J., Kawohl, T., Kreft, H., Soria-Auza, R. W., ... Kessler, M. (2017). Climatologies at high resolution for the earth's land surface areas. *Scientific Data, 4*, 170122. doi:10.1038/sdata.2017.122

Khadam, M. A. A. (1988). Factors influencing per capita water consumption in urban areas of developing countries and their implications for management, with special reference to the Khartoum metropolitan area. *Water International, 15*(5), 226–229. doi:10.1080/02508068808687095

Kummu, M., Guillaume, J. H. A., de Moel, H., Eisner, S., Ward, P. J., & de Moel, H. (2016). The world's road to water scarcity: Shortage and stress in the 20th century and pathways towards sustainability. *Scientific Reports, 6*, 38495. doi:10.1038/srep38495

Liu, J., Yang, H., Gosling, S. N., Kummu, M., Flörke, M., Pfister, S., ... Oki, T. (2017). Water scarcity assessments in the past, present, and future. *Earth's Future, 5*(6), 545–559. doi:10.1002/2016EF000518

Murakami, D., & Yamagata, Y. (2016). Estimation of gridded population and GDP scenarios with spatially explicit statistical downscaling. *ArXiv*. Retrieved from https://arxiv.org/abs/1610.09041

Oki, T., Agata, Y., Kanae, S., Sarushi, T., D., Y., & Musiake, K. (2001). Global assessment of current water resources using total runoff integrating pathways. *Hydrological Science-Journal-des Science Hydrologiques, 46*, 983–995. doi:10.1080/02626660109492890

Oki, T., & Kanae, S. (2004). Virtual water trade and world water resources. *Water Science and Technology, 49*(7), 203–209. doi:10.2166/wst.2004.0456

Oki, T., & Kanae, S. (2006). Global hydrological cycles and world water resources. *Science, 313*, 1068–1072. doi:10.1126/science.1128845

Oki, T., Yano, S., & Hanasaki, N. (2017). Economics of virtual water trade. *Environmental Research Letters, 12*, 044002. doi:10.1088/1748-9326/aa625f

Raskin, P., Gleick, P., Kirshen, P., Pontius, G., & Strzepek, K. (1997). Comprehensive assessment of the freshwater resources of the world. Stockholm, Sweden: Stockholm Environment Institute.

Rijsberman, F. R. (2006). Water scarcity: Fact or fiction? *Agricultural Water Management, 80*, 5–22. doi:10.1016/j.agwat.2005.07.001

Shiklomanov, I. A. (1997). *Assessment of water resources and water availability in the world* (pp. 88). Geneva: SEI and WMO.

Takakura, J., Fujimori, S., Hanasaki, N., Hasegawa, T., Hirabayashi, Y., Honda, Y., ... Hijioka, Y. (2019). Dependence of economic impacts of climate change on anthropogenically directed pathways. *Nature Climate Change, 9*, 737–741. doi:10.1038/s41558-019-0578-6

UNFPA. (2007). *State of world population 2007: Unleashing the potential of urban growth*. New York: UNFPA. doi:10.18356/fe74b223-en

United Nations (UN). (2012): *World urbanization prospects: The 2011 Revision*. New York: UN.

Varis, O., Biswas, A., Tortajada, C., & Lundqvist, J. (2006). Megacities and water management. *Water Resources Development, 22*(2), 377–394. doi:10.1080/07900620600684550

Wada, Y., Bierkens, M. F. P., de Roo, A., Dirmeyer, P. A., Famiglietti, J. S., Hanasaki, N., ... Wheater, H. (2017). Human-water interface in hydrological modeling: Current status and future directions. *Hydrology and Earth System Sciences, 21*, 4169–4193. doi:10.5194/hess-21-4169-2017

The status of the UN Watercourses Convention: does it still hold water?

Gabriel Eckstein

ABSTRACT

When the UN General Assembly adopted the Watercourses Convention in 1997, it was heralded as a major milestone in the evolution of international water law. Yet, more than 20 years later and five years since it came into force, enthusiasm for the instrument appears to have waned. Based on patterns in the UNGA vote and assorted ratifications, and statements of various delegates to the UN's International Law Committee, Sixth Committee and General Assembly, positions on the convention's text are explored to uncover possible reasons for its diminishing appeal. Other externalities are also considered in terms of the convention's viability.

Introduction

The Convention on the Law of the Non-navigational Uses of International Watercourses (Watercourses Convention) was adopted by the United Nations General Assembly (UNGA) on 21 May 1997 (Watercourses Convention, 1997), and went into force on 17 August 2014 (Schulz, 2014). Its drafting first began at the UN in early 1970 (G.A. Res. 2669, 1970, p. 127). It was conceptualized to articulate and codify the prevailing state practice in the area of international water law. The UN International Law Commission, which drafted the articles that eventually formed the basis of the convention, was tasked with addressing 'the law of the non-navigational uses of international watercourses with a view to its progressive development and codification' (UN GOAR, 1997, p. 2). Thus, the convention's principles and procedures were intended to reflect the rules, approaches, relations and best practices states usually imposed on themselves in the management of shared freshwater resources.

When the UNGA adopted the Watercourses Convention in 1997, it was heralded as a major milestone in the evolution of international water law, and a constructive and even progressive development for cross-border freshwater hydro-relations globally. The permanent representative of Mexico to the UN at the time, Ambassador Manuel Tello, said that it 'undoubtedly marks an important step in the progressive development and codification of international law' (p. 2). Even China, one of the three members who ultimately opposed the convention, stated that it believed 'the draft articles [on the law of the non-navigational uses of international watercourses] have laid a fairly good foundation for the formulation of an international convention' (p. 6).

Moreover, the fact that the convention was adopted by a significant majority of the UNGA –

103 in favour, three against, and 27 abstentions (p. 8) – indicated broad and robust support for what was then the only global instrument for the management of international watercourses. Stephen McCaffrey, a noted scholar and one of the special rapporteurs shepherding the process that eventually led to the convention, asserted that the vote 'suggests a sense among the overwhelming majority of delegation that the rules embodied in the convention are generally acceptable and, on the whole, reflect a reasonable balance between the interests of upstream and downstream states' (McCaffrey & Sinjela, 1998, p. 102).

But, despite the hopes and promises of the convention, nearly 50 years after its initial instigation at the UN, more than 20 years following its adoption by the UNGA, and over five years after it came into force, enthusiasm for that instrument appears to have waned. Although the convention is now in force for the states that have ratified it, it only attained that status after 17 years of slow progress, with the bare minimum of 35 required parties ratifying. Moreover, despite continued encouragement by various non-governmental and intergovernmental organizations, few new states seems poised to accede to the agreement. Since coming into force, only Palestine has joined the ranks of state parties.[1]

The purpose of this article is to examine the extent of support that nations have shown the convention and assess its continued sustainability. In so doing, the article does not reject the normative value of the convention or its relevance for many nations in their efforts to engage with their neighbours over transboundary freshwater resources. Rather, the article simply seeks to ascertain why so few nations have ratified the instrument. With this in mind, the article examines the support for the convention's drafted norms and procedures during its development, at its historic appearance on the global stage during the 1997 vote at the UNGA, and after, as nations ratified the instrument and eventually brought it into force. It also seeks to ascertain patterns in the 1997 vote and subsequent ratifications, and thereby uncover some of the possible reasons for the diminishing appeal of the instrument. Finally, this article considers other possible factors that may have reduced interest in the convention from the global community of nations.

Background to the Watercourses Convention

International water law is the result of an evolutionary process in legal doctrine related to the navigational and non-navigational uses of transboundary freshwater resources. Early civilizations are often described as *fluvial civilizations* because they settled along many of the world's major river basins, such as the Nile, Euphrates, Tigris, Indus, Amazon and Mississippi, and used the waters for irrigation and flood control, as well as for travel and transportation. Over time, many of these communities developed complex rules for the navigation, allocation and use of the waters. With the growth of travel and commerce, however, rules and procedures for navigation predominated over those for non-navigational uses, at least until the 1900s (McCaffrey, 2017).

Before the industrial revolution, legal doctrine emphasized ensuring continued transboundary water flow and preventing harm to neighbouring states, particularly as flow related to navigation (Teclaff, 1967). Both common law and civil law jurisdictions, for example, observed principles of freedom of navigation, maintaining navigability, and the right to impose duties and tariffs. But with the advent of industrialization and related expansion of populations and economies, greater demand for freshwater resources, especially for agricultural and industrial uses, propelled the non-navigational uses of transboundary watercourses into the forefront of national priorities. As a result, that movement engendered changes and innovations in state practices and interstate relations, and compelled the evolution of legal norms related to the use and management of freshwater resources in frontier regions (McCaffrey, 2017).

In the early years of industrial development, international water law was manifest primarily in the form of bilateral treaties, with few regional and no global agreements in existence. Typically, bordering countries would enter into agreements for the sharing of a river or lake in the context of defining political borders, managing floods, reallocating water for growing populations, and diverting river flow for agriculture and the newly developing industries. The development of the law, however, also resulted from various federal, states, and international cases concerning these same issues, most notably Kansas v. Colorado (1907); Wyoming v. Colorado (1922); Donauversinkung Case (Württemberg and Prussia v. Baden, 1927); Case Relating to the Territorial Jurisdiction of the International Commission of the River Oder (United Kingdom, Czechoslovakia, Denmark, France, Germany, Sweden v. Poland, 1929); Diversion of the Water From the Meuse (Netherlands v. Belgium, 1937); and Lake Lanoux Arbitration Case (Spain v. France, 1957).

Over the years, the large variety of issues and cases resulted in considerable incongruity among the laws on transboundary freshwater resources, especially where legal principles were devised or interpreted to fit specific state interests. As a result, various (and often irreconcilable) legal concepts emerged regarding allocating and sharing transboundary waters. These notions and modes of state practice varied from the self-centred perspectives of absolute territorial sovereignty (which says that states have the right to unrestrained use of all resources in their territories) and absolute territorial integrity (the opposing notion that lower riparians have the right to the continuous or natural flow of a river) (Tanzi & Arcari, 2001), to the more balanced and equitable viewpoint of limited (or restricted) territorial sovereignty (that states may use the waters flowing through their territory only to the extent that such use does not interfere with the reasonable utilization of other states), to the more holistic community-of-interests approach, which strives for optimal use and economic efficiency in the use and development of a transboundary water resource (McCaffrey, 2007).

In 1954, in an effort to bring uniformity and consistency to international water law, the International Law Association (ILA) began exploring the topic of 'inland water rights and obligations of the states' at its Edinburg Conference (Bogdanović, 2019, p. 30). After more than a decade of debate, the association produced its highly influential Helsinki Rules (International Law Association, 1966). Drafted as a comprehensive legal code for transboundary drainage basins, the Helsinki Rules included provisions on both the navigational and non-navigational uses of transboundary waters. But they have become best known for their non-navigational guidelines and are often regarded as the predecessor to the Watercourses Convention. Most notable of its provisions are Articles 4 and 5, which set forth the doctrine of 'equitable and reasonable share in the beneficial uses of an international drainage basin' (reconceptualized in the Watercourses Convention as 'equitable and reasonable utilization of an international watercourse'), and some of the geographical, hydrological, climatic, historical, social, economic and technical elements that may be used to effect the apportionment of benefits. The Helsinki Rules complemented this principle with articles providing that no category of use enjoyed any inherent preference over another (Article 6), that no state may reserve future uses for itself (Article 7), and that existing activities may be presumed equitable and reasonable unless established otherwise (Article 7).[2] Over the years, some of these principles were used as bases for negotiations by riparians over shared waters, and have played an important role in the development and codification of international water law, including in the context of the Watercourses Convention (Bogdanović, 2019).

Despite their great influence, the Helsinki Rules and related declarations are recognized only as unofficial and informal articulations of international water law. While the *raison d'être* of the ILA is the interpretation and codification of international law, it is a private non-governmental organization, without official status in the development of international law. Accordingly, the work of the ILA has always been regarded merely as aspirational in nature – goals to which we should aspire – and not as hard and fast rules of state conduct (Dellapenna, 1992).

Due to the lack of definitiveness, as well as growing tensions in various water-poor regions, in 1959 Bolivia proposed having the UN's secretary-general examine the legal issues relating to the utilization of international rivers (G.A. Res. 1401(XIV), 1959). In 1970, after some preliminary work by the secretary-general, the UNGA instructed the International Law Commission (ILC) to 'take up the study of the law of the non-navigational uses of international watercourses with a view to its progressive development and codification' (G.A. Res. 2669, 1970, p. 127). Between 1970 and 1994, the ILC amassed research from around the globe, drafted various proposed articles and standards, and produced 15 substantial reports on its progress. In 1994, it adopted a collection of principles in the form of the Draft Articles on the Law of the Non-navigational Uses of International Watercourses (Draft Articles), and the UNGA convened a working group to negotiate a convention on the basis of those drafts. In October 1996, and again in March and April 1997, the Sixth Committee of the UNGA convened as a working group of the whole to debate the draft text with a view towards producing a framework convention. On 21 May 1997, the final draft Watercourses Convention was brought to a vote before the UNGA, and adopted by a vote of 103 in favour, three against, and 26 abstentions (UN GAORUN GOAR, 1997).

The Watercourses Convention

That it took the ILC nearly 25 years to prepare the Draft Articles is just one indication of the complexity of the subject matter considered by the ILC and subsequently by the UNGA's Sixth Committee. It is in part a reflection of the great importance that states have given, and continue to give, to freshwater resources that cross international frontiers. It is also a function of the diverse geographic, political, climatic, economic and other factors that make each transboundary watercourse unique, and for which universal rules may be impracticable. Hilal Elver (2002, p. 185), a scholar and UN special rapporteur on the right to food, writes that 'the sharing of international rivers among riparians in different geographical regions is a problem of great magnitude, and its resolution demands much more than a single piece of international legislation'.

From the start of the process in 1970, the deliberations over the language, scope and purpose of the principles that were eventually included in the convention were contentious, and at times divisive. Three of the most contentious issues were the framework nature of the convention and its relationship to existing and future treaties, the relationship between the substantive rules of no significant harm and of equitable and reasonable utilization, and the dispute resolution mechanism.

While a consensus eventually was reached to allow adoption of the convention by the UNGA, many of the issues debated by the ILC, the Sixth Committee (serving as a working group of the whole), and the UNGA were never fully resolved. They continue to be sources of concern and hesitation for various states in their consideration of the rules and procedures outlined in the instrument.

The Watercourses Convention as a framework and its relationship to local and regional agreements

The convention was intended to serve as a framework agreement. In essence, it was designed to be flexible and open to a degree of interpretation, and to accommodate the development of more specific bilateral and multilateral agreements related to the use, management and protection of transboundary water resources. Accordingly, its preamble provides that the parties express 'the conviction that a framework convention will ensure the utilization, development, conservation, management and protection of international watercourses and the promotion of the optimal and sustainable utilization thereof for present and future generations'). It also explains that the convention takes 'into account the problems affecting many international watercourses resulting from, among other things, increasing demands and pollution'. It further acknowledges the 'special needs of developing countries' and 'the principles and recommendations ... in the Rio Declaration and Agenda 21'.

Despite this prefatory language explaining the need for a framework structure, during the UNGA vote on the draft convention, some states, including China, India and Turkey, voiced concerns that the aim of the international treaty had deviated from its framework design (UN Press Release, 1997). India, for example, which abstained from the final vote, emphasized that the instrument was intended to be 'a framework Convention that should not be prescriptive in nature. It should leave the watercourse States to evolve and implement mutually agreeable terms in respect of the particular international watercourses concerned.' 'Unfortunately', its representative asserted, 'in some of its provisions the present Convention has deviated from this agreed approach, and consequently it is not balanced enough to accommodate differing interests and promote wider acceptability of the Convention' (p. 9). Similarly, Turkey, which cast one of the three votes against, asserted, 'The draft Convention should have set forth only general principles and its application should have depended upon the drawing up of specific agreements which take into account the particular characteristics of the watercourses.... The draft Convention goes far beyond the scope of a framework convention' (p. 4).

More specifically, many countries questioned the relationship of the convention to existing and future local and regional treaties governing specific watercourses. As a framework agreement, the convention was designed with the explicit intent not to affect pre-existing agreements. However, its Articles 3.1 and 3.2 encouraged states to 'consider harmonizing' those earlier instruments with its 'basic principles', while Article 3.3 called on states to apply its principles in bilateral and regional agreements, and to 'adjust' those principles to the particular characteristics and uses of the watercourse that is the subject of the treaty.

The contradiction between the need to 'harmonize' existing treaties with the convention's principles, and the need in future agreements to 'adjust' the same principles to particular watercourse characteristics, was not lost on the members. India, for example, which abstained from the vote in the UNGA, remarked, 'Article 3 fails adequately to reflect the principle of freedom, autonomy and the right of States to conclude international agreements on international watercourses without being fettered by the present framework Convention' (UN GAOR, 1997, p. 9). Ethiopia, which also abstained, argued that adjusting the principles in future agreements 'will undermine the applicability of the Convention' and asserted that 'specific watercourse arrangements ... should be adjusted to the basic principles of the Convention not ... the other way around' (p. 10). While the Czech Republic voted in favour of the convention, it too expressed concerns that the convention is 'lacking [in] clarity and concision as to the relationship between existing and future particular agreements and the draft framework Convention itself' and concluded that 'the drafting appears to be unnecessarily complicated and could perhaps even be misleading in some cases' (p. 6).

More recently, the flexibility of the framework nature of the convention was highlighted as a source of ambiguity and confusion with respect to the ability of nations to understand the benefits and obligations of membership. Noted scholar Salman M.A. Salman (2007, p. 9) suggested that 'those interpretations and misconceptions no doubt contributed to the slow pace of the signing, ratification of, and accession to the Convention'.

Relationship between the rules of equitable and reasonable utilization and no significant harm

Undoubtedly, one of the most contentious issues arising during the Sixth Committee and UNGA deliberations concerned the scope and relationship of the substantive principles of equitable and reasonable utilization and of no significant harm. Many states, including many who voted in favour of the text, objected that in these articles the convention failed to establish the proper balance between the rights and obligations of upper and lower riparians. Article 5 provides that states 'shall in their respective territories utilize an international watercourse in an equitable and reasonable manner'. In sharp contrast, Article 7 provides that watercourse states 'shall ... take all appropriate measures to prevent the causing of significant harm to other watercourse States'. The unease voiced by concerned states focused on whether, when the two principles conflicted, one superseded the other. In other words, if a particular use is deemed equitable and reasonable, but results in significant harm, is it still lawful and permissible under the convention? Or, if a use is found not to cause significant harm but is deemed inequitable and/or unreasonable, is it still lawful and permissible?

Historically, downstream riparians have championed the principles of no significant harm for freshwater resources flowing through or adjacent to their jurisdiction. This position supported their claims for sustained flows from upper riparians in quantities equivalent or close to natural flows as a means of protecting their existing uses. In contrast, upstream riparians favoured the principle of equitable and reasonable utilization, as it gave them the right to utilize and benefit from the waters that flowed within or adjacent to their jurisdictions before they reached downstream riparians (Tanzi & Arcari, 2001). Both principles require states to consider the interests of other riparians in determining the application of these rules, as well as in their domestic water resources development plans. Both principles also benefited all watercourse riparians regardless of their geographic position on a river. For example, a downstream country could assert claims under the principle of equitable and reasonable utilization equally as an upper riparian, since use and benefits must be allotted equitably and reasonably throughout the basin, regardless of upstream or downstream status. Likewise, an upper riparian could benefit from the principle of no significant harm where a downstream user's conduct resulted in significant harm upstream, such as where a dam near a border causes upstream, cross-border flooding, or when a downstream riparian's claims of right detrimentally affect an upstream riparian's right to use the waters (Salman, 2010).

In any case, the questions before the Sixth Committee and the UNGA centred on the circumstances where the two principles conflict. Specifically, they related to the extent to which foreign interest had to be considered in evaluating a state's rights under both principles (equitable and reasonable utilization and no significant harm); whether foreign interests could override national interests; and whether either principle trumped the other.

These issues, however, were not new to the deliberations over the rules applicable to transboundary freshwater resources. In fact, they had surfaced years earlier during the ILC's deliberations and development of the Draft Articles. During the various formulations and drafts of the these two norms, the drafters seemed to engage in a constant tug-of-war (Meshel, 2018). Beginning in 1981, when the ILC's second special rapporteur, Stephen M. Schwebel, first attempted to formulate the basic principles of international water law, the ILC appeared to favour equitable and reasonable utilization, making the principle of 'no appreciable harm' (predecessor to the 'no significant harm' standard) subservient to that of equitable and reasonable use (Schwebel, 1982; Bourne, 1992). However, this approach reversed the following year when the third special rapporteur, Jens Evensen, elevated the principle of 'no appreciable harm' to the dominant position in the management of transboundary watercourses (Evensen, 1983; Bourne, 1992). And when Stephen McCaffrey succeeded Evensen as the fourth special rapporteur, he also wrestled with the two formulations, albeit favouring Schwebel's prioritization of the principle of equitable and reasonable utilization (Yearbook of the ILC, 1984 ; Yearbook of the ILC, 1985). Unsurprisingly, he found the ILC membership very divided on the matter (Yearbook of the ILC, 1987; Bourne, 1992). In fact, similar divisions over the relative importance of equitable utilization and no appreciable harm were evident in the Sixth Committee of the UNGA in 1988 when it discussed the first series of Draft Articles (UN GOAR, 1988), and in 1996 and 1997 when the Sixth Committee, serving as a working group of the whole, debated the final Draft Articles (Wouters, 1999).

As a result, the ILC revised the Draft Articles in 1994, and the Sixth Committee revised it again during its meetings in 1996 and 1997. When the dust settled, Article 7 provided that, 'where significant harm nevertheless is caused to another watercourse State, the States whose use causes such harm shall ... take all appropriate measures, *having due regard for the provisions of articles 5 and 6* ... to eliminate or mitigate such harm' (emphasis added). With this language, the principle of equitable and reasonable utilization appears to have been endorsed as the cornerstone principle of international water law, and recognized as superseding the principle of no significant harm (McCaffrey, 2007). Of the 64 nations that participated in the Working Group on this issue, the language was accepted by 38, while four (China, France, Tanzania and Turkey) voted against, and 22 others abstained (Wouters, 1999).

To some extent, this outcome might suggest that most of the states favoured a more conciliatory approach to the management and governance of transboundary watercourses (Wouters, 1997). But McCaffrey (1998, pp. 17, 22) argued that the new formulation constituted a valuable compromise: 'The final text is something like a basket of Halloween candy: there is something in it for everyone. No matter whether you are from equitable utilization or the no-harm school, you can claim at least partial victory.' Similarly, Ambassador Tello of Mexico asserted, 'The idea that the Convention provides an opportunity to compromise is supported by the sponsors' belief that this instrument will contribute to enhancing cooperation and communication among riparian States of international watercourses' (UN GOAR, 1997, p. 2).

Regardless, the adopted language overshadowed the considerable divergence in opinions and interpretations of the text during the deliberations. Some states argued that the language of the convention favoured the interests of downstream nations, either by prioritizing no significant harm or by diminishing the importance and effect of equitable and reasonable utilization. For example, the Tanzanian representative asserted that 'the delicate balance' between the two principles had been 'undone by the introduction in article 5 of the unspecified and unqualified reference to a demand' 'to take into account the interests of the watercourse States concerned' (UN GOAR, 1997, p. 3). And the delegate from France asserted, 'The Convention that has just been adopted is, in fact, clearly weighted in favour of the interests of downstream States. Thus, it seems unfortunately ill-suited to reducing the existing tensions in various geographic zones between States with international rivers flowing through them' (p. 8). Turkey argued, 'The draft Convention should clearly have established the primacy of the fundamental principles of equitable and reasonable utilization over the obligation not to cause significant harm. The present text is liable to create confusion as far as implementation of the whole Convention is concerned' (p. 5). More directly, Ethiopia asserted that 'the well-established right of equitable utilization in the Convention was the only reason and incentive for any upper riparian country in the position of Ethiopia to accept the Convention. In the absence of this clearly defined right, the Convention will mean very little to these countries. The rest of the Convention, in most cases, is tilted towards the lower riparian States and imposes obligations on upper riparian States which appear burdensome and difficult to meet, particularly by a developing country such as Ethiopia' (p. 10).

Yet, other states viewed the convention as favouring equitable and reasonable utilization, which they claimed benefitted upstream states at the expense of downstream nations. For example, the Argentinian representative said, 'A reordering of the articles in order to make … [no significant harm] the first principle of the future convention would be welcome. Only if no harm was caused could the utilization of a resource be acceptable' (UN GOAR, 1996c, p. 11). The delegate from Bangladesh asserted that 'any utilization that caused harm could not be equitable or reasonable' (UN GOAR, 1996d, p. 8), and the Brazilian representative stated that, although 'it would be desirable for both notions to be included, … if a choice had to be made, the no-harm rule must prevail' (UN GOAR, 1996c, p. 10). Egypt's representative stressed his understanding that the principle of equitable and reasonable utilization, as formulated in Article 5, does 'not affect the established principle of customary international law, as affirmed by the International Law Commission since its creation, that the exercise of one's rights should do no harm to others. This obligation dictates that the rights of others must not be affected with respect to the utilization of watercourses' (UN GOAR, 1997, p. 11).

In addition to the diverging opinions of nations from disparate geographies and economies, the International Court of Justice has sent mixed messages with regard to the relative status of the two principles under international law. In the 1997 *Gabcíkovo-Nagymaros* case between Hungary and Slovakia, the court asserted that 'Czechoslovakia, by ... depriving Hungary of its right to an equitable and reasonable share of the natural resources of the Danube ... failed to respect the proportionality which is required by international law' (Case Concerning the Gabcikovo-Nagymaros Project, 1997, para. 85). Surprisingly, the court never mentioned the principle of no significant harm, even though Hungary relied on it heavily in its pleadings. In contrast, in the 2010 *Pulp Mills* case between Argentina and Uruguay, the court asserted that every state is obligated to 'to use all the means at its disposal in order to avoid activities which take place in its territory, or in any area under its jurisdiction, causing significant damage to the environment of another State', and emphasized the obligations of every state 'to prevent any significant transboundary harm which might be caused by potentially harmful activities planned by either one of them' (Case Concerning Pulp Mills on the River Uruguay, 2010, paras. 101, 139). However, it only referenced equitable and reasonable utilization in the context of the allegations and in interpreting the regional treaty (paras. 55, 170, 171, 177, 266).

Not only is there tension between these two foundational principles, but their relationship is also ambiguous. According to Tamar Meshel (2018, pp. 63–64), 'Efforts to clarify the relationship between these two principles seem to continue, with no lasting consensus in sight.' She further asserts that 'the relationship between these two principles has been and remains inconsistent and controversial, hindering their ability to facilitate the resolution of transboundary water disputes' (pp. 57–58). Similarly, Ryan Stoa (2014, p. 1352) argues that that the two principles 'are ambiguously defined, inherently in tension with each other, and broad enough to provide states in conflict over water resources with reasonable arguments to support mutually incompatible positions'.

The dispute resolution mechanism

The controversy over the dispute resolution language in the draft convention centred on the extent to which the proposed mechanism should be compulsory for member states (Wouters, 1999). For example, Finland took the position that, because watercourse states may not always be able to achieve compromise, the draft articles should provide a system of compulsory third-party settlement (UN GOAR, 1996b). Finland's stance was supported by other nations, including Germany, Hungary and Syria (UN GOAR, 1996b). Likewise, Pakistan asserted that it 'favoured obligatory, binding, third-party settlement procedures', but that it was 'flexible as regards the choice between the International Court of Justice and arbitration'. It concluded, however, that the 'mechanism provided in the draft Convention – namely, fact-finding – is not binding on parties. It is therefore not acceptable to Pakistan' (UN GOAR, 1997, p. 5).

In contrast, the representative from India stated, 'In our view, any procedure for peaceful settlement of disputes should leave the parties to the dispute to choose freely, and by mutual consent, a procedure acceptable to them. My delegation is opposed to the imposition of any mandatory third-party dispute settlement procedure upon a State without its consent' (p. 9). Similarly, the representative from Israel noted that while 'States must settle their disputes peacefully ... the means of settling a dispute must be left to their agreement. The parties to a dispute must be allowed to choose the mechanism which is most appropriate for their specific needs and circumstances' (p. 11). More forcefully, the Chinese delegate asserted that 'the compulsory fact-finding dictated by the draft Convention goes against ... [Article 33 of the United Nations] Charter. The Chinese Government favours the settlement of all disputes by peaceful means, through consultations. We are not against fact-finding as an optional means of settlement, but we cannot agree to any mandatory means or procedures for the settlement of a dispute without the consent of the countries parties to the dispute' (p. 7).

Following continued debate, the final draft of 1997 recommended traditional provisions regarding negotiations and settlement of disputes by peaceful means, but also provided for compulsory fact-finding (p. 33). Within the Working Group, of the 62 nations that took part in these deliberations, only a slight majority of 33 voted in favour of the provision, with four opposed and 25 abstaining. As Patricia Wouters (1999, p. 313) noted, 'This closely divided voting (33 States for, 29 against or abstaining) highlights the extent of the discord among States on this delicate issue.'

Review of support for the Watercourses Convention

When the UNGA adopted the convention in 1997, it was lauded as a significant achievement for the governance of transboundary freshwater resources. Yet, while the actual votes supporting the convention appeared to overwhelm the negative votes – 103 voted in favour, with only Burundi, China and Turkey voting against – the numbers belie voting patterns that evidence the complexity of the subject matter, as well as the fragility of the coalition supporting the treaty. In addition, since that momentous occasion, support for the convention seems to have diminished considerably. By the end of the signature period, on 20 May 2000, only eight countries had become full parties to the convention, and another 10 had signed it. Since then, more than 22 years since the UNGA adopted the convention, the number of ratifications and accessions has only reached 36 (United Nations Treaty Collections, n.d.). And while three other nations – Paraguay, Venezuela, and Yemen – have signed it (in 1998, 1997 and 2000, respectively), indicating a future intent to abide by its terms, their failure to follow through with that intent over the past two decades makes it unlikely that these countries will formally ratify and implement it in the near future.

The following sections review some of the patterns that emerged from the vote at the UNGA and as evidenced by the existing membership of the convention. While certainly not definitive, these patterns may help interpret the status of the convention and its principles and procedures among the international community of nations.

Assessing the vote at the UNGA

The following analysis is based on a number of suppositions: a vote in favour indicated overall support by that nation for the convention and its text; a vote against indicated opposition either to the convention as a whole or to certain of its provisions, making qualified support or abstention untenable; abstention indicated that the state was either disinterested in the subject matter or dissatisfied with the text, but not enough to vote against; and recorded and unrecorded absences from the vote suggested that the state was disinterested in the subject matter of the vote or otherwise did not consider it a priority (Hayden 2010).

With this framework in mind, a review of the votes and official statements made when the convention was adopted by the UNGA on 21 May 1997 suggests that many states held, and may still hold, strong misgivings about the convention and its various provisions. In fact, the vote was not so clear-cut and does not fully support the long-touted argument that it showed a strong coalition in favour.

Of the 185 countries that were member states of the United Nations in 1997, 103 voted in favour of the convention, three voted against, and 27 abstained (see Table A1 in the Appendix). Another 33 were recorded formally as being absent from the vote, while 21 were not logged in the vote at all. On the positive side, the count might have been 106 in favour with 26 abstentions, because Belgium, which was recorded as abstaining, and Fiji and Nigeria, which were recorded as absent, later announced that they had intended to vote in favour (UN GOAR, 1997). On the negative side, the opposing vote might have been larger, but for diplomacy. Just prior to the vote, for example, the permanent representative to the UN for Tanzania indicated that his country intended to vote against because of serious concerns with the draft, though, in the final tally, Tanzania abstained (UN Press Release, 1997). It is unclear whether there were other nations who had intended to vote in favour or against but were swayed at the last minute.

But some states that voted in favour did so with considerable reservations. For example, the representative from the Czech Republic noted his country's 'serious concerns' with the language of the preamble and Articles 3, 5 and 7, and asserted that his nation's affirmative vote reflects 'more our firm and overriding attachment to the overall process of codification and progressive development of international law, rather than a strong conviction that the text of the draft Convention now before us is a fully satisfactory and balanced one which could not have been improved in some of its major aspects' (UN GOAR, 1997, p. 6).

The three states voting against were Burundi, China, and Turkey. All three are primarily upper-riparian states, and China and Turkey are engaged in controversial upstream hydro-projects. China has received significant criticism for constructing various dams in the upper reaches of the Mekong River (Bernstein, 2017; Sullivan, 2018), and Turkey has long been criticized by its downstream neighbours for its work on the Ataturk Dam and the Southeastern Anatolia Project, commonly known by its Turkish acronym, GAP (Hansen, 2018; Solomon & Pitel, 2018). Moreover, all three states are significant players in some of the world's major transboundary drainage basins: China controls the headwaters of the Mekong River; Turkey supplies the bulk of the water for the Araks, Euphrates and Tigris Rivers; and Burundi serves as the source of the White Nile River. These negative votes suggest a clear determination by these states to rely on the power of direct diplomacy rather than international law to resolve current and future disputes. In explaining his country's vote against, China's representative emphasized his country's preference for bilateral relations: 'The Chinese Government reserves the right to address the question of the non-navigational uses of international watercourses with its neighbours in a fair and reasonable manner and in accordance with relevant international practice and with bilateral watercourse agreements' (UN GOAR, 1997, p. 7). Burundi's vote is curious as it did not voice its opinions or dissent in the Working Group, and may not even have attended the group's deliberations (McCaffrey, 2007).

Of the 166 states recorded in the chronicles of the convention as voting, abstaining, or formally absent, 46 (28%) do not share freshwater resources with other states (Figure 1). These includes 29 island nations and 17 states with non-riparian geographies (no trans-boundary rivers or upstream/downstream characteristics). Of these, 36 participated in the vote, either by voting or abstaining. Of the 29 island states, 18 (62%) were present and participated in the vote, and of those, 17 voted in favour. Cuba was the sole island nation abstaining. Of the 17 non-riparian states, all voted in favour except Monaco and Panama, which abstained. Thus, 32 (91%) of the 35 island and non-riparian states present during the vote voted in favour (Figure 2). Given that these states have no national stake in transboundary waters, their vote could be presumed to be more of an intellectual exercise than a matter of state interests. Of course, it is also conceivable that the actions taken by some of these nations were motivated by political relations with states that do have transboundary water interests or concerns, especially those with active international investment and development activities.

Subtracting the 32 island and non-riparian states that voted in favour from the total of 103 leaves 71 states that presumably voted favourably because of particular national interests. Of these, 19 (27%) have lower or mostly lower riparian geographies, 44 (62%) both upper and lower, and 8 (11%) upper or mostly upper. Depending on the perspective taken, the vote could be described in terms of the 63 of the 71 countries (89%) with lower-riparian geographies (lower, mostly lower, and upper and lower), or the 52 of the 71 countries (73%) with upper-riparian geographies (upper, mostly upper, and upper and lower), that voted in favour. In either case, the numbers suggest that lower riparians favoured the text more than upper riparians. Khan (1997, p. 184) noted, 'The GA vote reveals a tendency of upstream riparian states not to vote for the adoption of the Convention', indicating that 'some states perceive a bias in favor of downstream nations'.

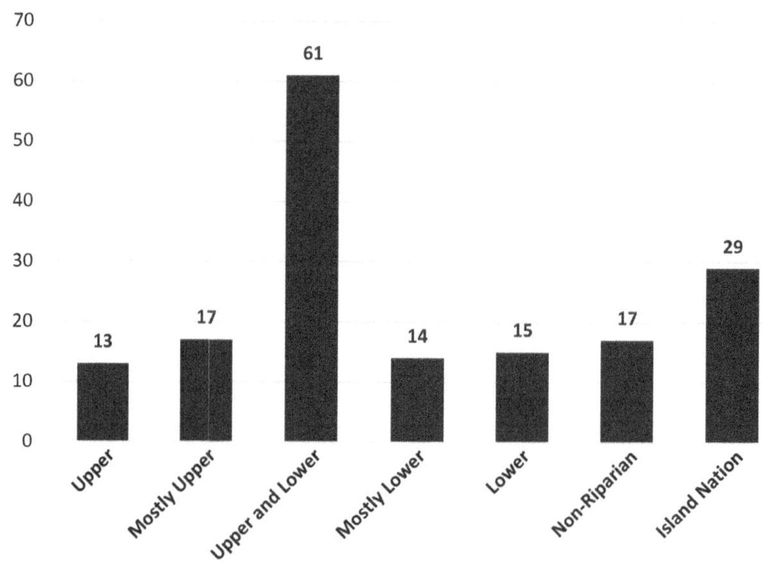

Figure 1. Count by riparian classification of nations voting on the Watercourses Convention at the UNGA in 1997.

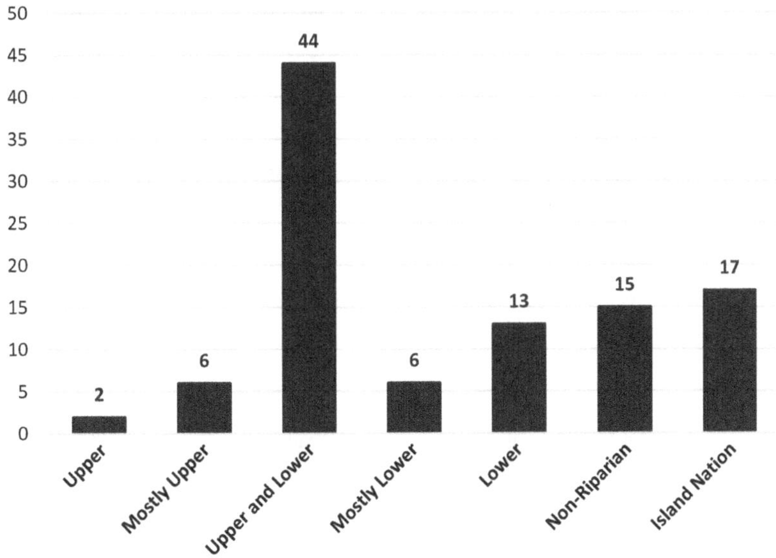

Figure 2. Count by riparian classification of nations that voted for the Watercourses Convention at the UNGA in 1997.

Also, given that the three votes against, and 17 of the 24 abstentions by nations with riparian geographies (i.e., excluding island nations and those with no riparian characteristics), were from states that have upper-riparian geographies (upper and lower, mostly upper, and upper), the vote may support the perception of bias claimed by several states, that the text favoured lower riparians and placed greater burdens on upper riparians in the context of future development. This viewpoint is a bit perplexing given that the principle of no significant harm (typically favoured by lower riparians) was made subservient to that of equitable and reasonable utilization (most often espoused by upper riparians). Nevertheless, perception typically equates with reality in the eye of the beholder.

Assessing the UNGA vote on the convention through the prism of the world's major international watercourses also offers insights. In general, consistency among riparians appears to have been the norm among the nations of Europe, North America and Southern Africa. In contrast, the vote amongst the riparians of international watercourses in North Africa, the Middle East, Central Asia, South Asia, East Asia and South America was much more erratic. In some cross-border watercourses, many riparian countries failed to participate in the vote at all, leaving unclear the status of the convention as it might apply to those water bodies (Table 1).

For example, some consistency was evident for the Danube River, where of the 10 riparians, seven voted in favour (Austria, Croatia Germany, Hungary, Romania, Slovakia, Ukraine), one abstained (Bulgaria), one was not a UN member at the time of the vote (Serbia), and one did not participate in the vote (Moldova). Similarly, for the Rhine River, while France abstained, and Switzerland was not a member of the UN at the time of the vote, the other four riparians (Austria, Germany, Liechtenstein, Netherlands) supported the convention.

Table 1. Votes of major watercourse riparians on the Watercourses Convention at the UNGA in 1997.

Transboundary Watercourse	For	Against	Abstained	Absent or unrecorded
Amazon River	Brazil, Guyana, Venezuela**		Bolivia, Columbia, Ecuador, Peru	
Amu Darya			Uzbekistan*	Afghanistan, Tajikistan, Turkmenistan
Brahmaputra River	India, Bangladesh	China		
Colorado River and Rio Grande	Mexico, United States			
Columbia River and Great Lakes	Canada, United States			
Danube River	Austria, Croatia, Germany*, Hungary*, Romania, Slovakia, Ukraine		Bulgaria	Moldova, Serbia
Ganges River	Bangladesh		India	
Indus River		China	Pakistan, India	
Limpopo River	Botswana, Mozambique, South Africa*			Zimbabwe
Mekong River	Cambodia, Lao PDR, Thailand, Vietnam*	China		Myanmar
Nile River	Kenya, Sudan	Burundi	Egypt, Ethiopia, Rwanda, Tanzania	DRC Congo, Eritrea, South Sudan, Uganda
Niger River			Mali (upper/lower)	Benin, Guinea, Niger*, Nigeria*
Orange River	Botswana, Lesotho, Namibia*, South Africa*			
Parana and Paraguay Rivers	Brazil		Argentina, Bolivia, Paraguay**	
Rhine River	Austria, Germany*, Liechtenstein, Netherlands*		France*	Switzerland
Syr Darya	Kazakhstan		Uzbekistan*	Kyrgyzstan, Tajikistan
Tigris and Euphrates Rivers	Syria*	Turkey		Iraq*
Uruguay Rivers	Brazil, Uruguay		Argentina	
Zambezi River	Angola, Botswana, Mozambique, Namibia, Zambia		Tanzania	Zimbabwe

Note: *denotes ratification; ** denotes signature but no ratification.

In the North American continent, which is composed of only three countries (Canada, Mexico and the United States), consistency was absolute, as all three voted in favour. Hence, all of the riparians of the Rio Grande, Colorado River, Columbia River, and the Great Lakes supported the convention.

Some consistency was also evident in Southern Africa. All three riparians of the Orange River (Lesotho, Namibia and South Africa) voted in favour; three of the four riparians of the Limpopo River (Botswana, Mozambique and South Africa) voted in favour, while Zimbabwe was absent; and five of the six riparians of the Zambezi River (Angola, Botswana, Mozambique, Namibia, Zambia) voted in favour, while Zimbabwe was absent.

Arguably, consistency *against the convention* could also be discerned for the Niger River, where four of the five riparians (Benin, Guinea, Niger and Nigeria) were absent, while Mali formally abstained. Similar assessments could be made for the Indus River, where China voted against and Pakistan and India abstained, as well as for the Amu Darya, where Uzbekistan abstained and Afghanistan, Tajikistan and Turkmenistan were absent.

In contrast, there was very little consistency for international watercourses in North Africa, the Middle East, Central Asia, South Asia, East Asia and South America:

- Nile River: Of the 11 riparian countries, only Kenya and Sudan voted in favour, while Burundi voted against; South Sudan did not exist at the time of the vote; and seven others abstained (DRC Congo, Eritrea, Ethiopia, Rwanda, Tanzania, Uganda, Egypt).
- Euphrates and Tigris Rivers: Turkey voted against, Syria for; Iraq was not recorded as participating.
- Syr Darya: Kazakhstan voted in favour, and Uzbekistan abstained, while Tajikistan was a formal absentee; Kyrgyzstan was not recorded as participating.
- Ganges River: Bangladesh voted in favour, and India abstained.
- Brahmaputra River: China voted against, while Bangladesh voted in favour, and India abstained.
- Mekong River: China voted against; Cambodia, Laos, Thailand and Vietnam voted in favour; and Myanmar was absent.
- Amazon River: Brazil, Guyana and Venezuela voted in favour, while Bolivia, Colombia, Ecuador and Peru abstained.
- Uruguay Rivers: Brazil and Uruguay voted in favour, and Argentina abstained.
- Parana and Paraguay Rivers: Brazil voted in favour, while Argentina, Bolivia and Paraguay abstained.

Assessing the 1997 UNGA vote from an economic income-level perspective offers additional insight into the voting patterns, albeit with less clarity in terms of how states voted. Of the 35 high-income nations that participated in the vote, 29 (83%) voted in favour, while six abstained. Of the 98 low, lower-middle and upper-middle-income countries (once known as 'developing nations') that participated, 74 (76%) voted in favour, three voted against, and 21 abstained. Of the five high-income island nations that participated, all voted in favour. Of the 12 low, lower-middle and upper-middle-income island nations, 11 (92%) voted in favour, and one abstained. Of the 15 non-riparian states that voted in favour, six (40%) were in the high-income category while nine were in the low, lower-middle and upper-middle income categories.

Overall, a number of inferences can be made from the UNGA vote. First, the vast majority (88%) of non-riparians recorded in the vote supported the convention at the time of its adoption by the UNGA. And countries identified as having lower, mostly lower, or both upper and lower riparian geographies strongly (75%) favoured the convention. Even taking out the few states designated as mostly lower (of which only 42% supported the convention), the remaining upper-and-lower and lower riparians together endorsed the convention by 70%. In contrast, almost half (47%) of the nations recorded in the vote and categorized as upper or mostly upper riparians voted against.

Considering income levels, the 36 high-income countries, like those of North America and Europe, significantly favoured the text (81%), regardless of their riparian situation. In contrast, states that opposed the text primarily included those with low, lower-middle and upper-middle income levels (historically labelled 'developing countries').

Considering geography, of the nations recorded in the vote, East Asia and the Pacific (71%), Europe and Central Asia (74%), the Middle East and North Africa (84%) and North America (100%) showed strong support for the convention (Figure 3). Latin America and the Caribbean (43%), South Asia (38%) and Sub-Saharan Africa (49%) seemed far less supportive. Breaking this down further, while 59% of island nations and 79% of European nations recorded in the vote supported the convention, only 25% of Central Asian countries did.

Particularly striking is the vote distribution in international watercourses that have been subject to ongoing disputes. On the Amu Darya, Syr Darya, Brahmaputra, Euphrates, Tigris, Ganges, Indus, Mekong, Jordan and Nile, 10 of the most politically sensitive transboundary rivers in the world, the pattern of votes in favour and against, as well as the abstentions and absences, evidenced the palpable tensions and sensitivities of the respective regions (Kahn, 1997). Even in more stable river basins, such as the Amazon, Paraná, Paraguay and Uruguay in South America, the divergent votes suggest that the instrument did little to assuage the disparate interests and priorities. Moreover, given that only 14 (36%) of the 39 riparians of these 14 significant international, cross-border waterways voted in favour, and only four have ratified it in the 22 years since the UNGA vote, it appears clear that the convention has not been effective in resolving disputes or anxieties over the utilization and management of international watercourses. Thus, the prognostication of scholars, like Asit Biswas, who wrote in 1999 (p. 439) that 'in all probability [the Watercourses Convention] will have very marginal impact on the resolution of conflicts', appears to have been borne out.

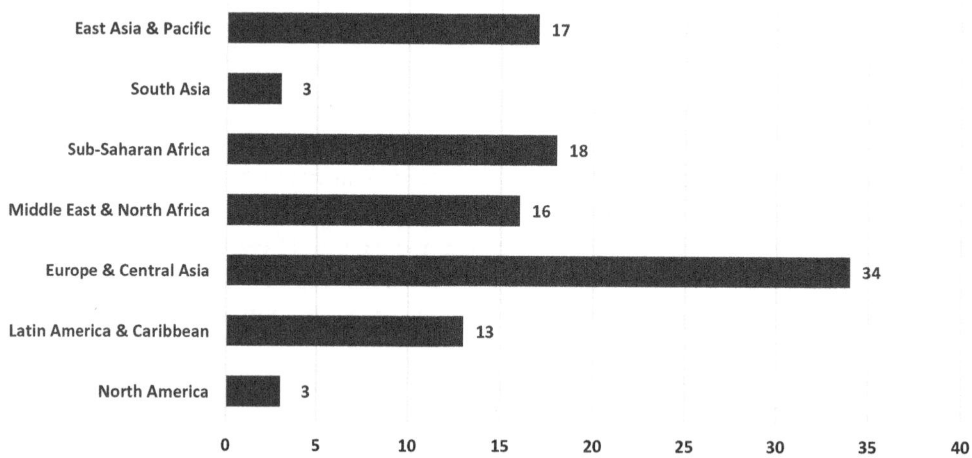

Figure 3. Number of countries by geographic region that voted for the Watercourses Convention at the UNGA in 1997.

Assessing the ratifications of the Watercourses Convention

Since the convention was adopted by the UNGA more than two decades ago, much has occurred in the world of water. In 2000, the member states of the UN agreed to establish the Millennium Development Goals for development progress, with a 2015 target to halve the number of people without sustainable access to safe drinking water and basic sanitation (Millennium Development Goals and Beyond 2015, n.d.) . This goal was actually achieved in 2010, five years ahead of schedule (UNICEF/WHO, 2012). In 2003, the UN founded UN-Water, an inter-agency platform to coordinate the efforts of UN entities and international organizations working on freshwater and sanitation issues (About United Nations Water, n.d.). In 2005, the UN declared 2005–2015 the International Decade for Action 'Water for Life' to prioritize water and sanitation development (International Decade for Action 'Water For Life' 2005-2015, n.d.). In 2010, the UNGA issued a declaration recognizing a human right to water and sanitation (G.A. Res. 64/292, 2010). In 2015, the UN member states established the Sustainable Development Goals as the successors to the Millennium Development Goals, including a specific target (Goal 6) prioritizing clean water and sanitation for all by 2030 (Sustainable Development Goals Knowledge Platform, n.d.) Between 1998 and 2018, the World Water Council (n.d.) held eight editions of the World Water Forum, the world's largest event on water, providing a unique platform for the water community and key decision makers to collaborate on and explore long-term solutions for pressing global water challenges. During this same period, the International Water Resources Association (n.d.) held seven World Water Congresses, bringing together scientists, policy makers and other stakeholders to advance water resources knowledge, policy and management worldwide. And between 1997 and 2007, more than 70 bilateral and regional treaties, directives, declarations and understandings were entered into by nations around the world over their cross-border freshwater resources (Program in Water Conflict Management and Transformation, n.d.).

In the midst of these activities and global achievements, the convention formally went into force on 17 August 2014, 90 days after Vietnam became the 35th nation to accede to it (Table 2). Long in coming, the convention's success had appeared promising, with the strong endorsement it deemed to receive at the UNGA in 1997. Yet, lacklustre support during its first 10 years brought the treaty's future into question. Between 1997 and 2007, 16 countries ratified the instrument (Finland 1998, Norway 1998, South Africa 1998, Syria 1998, Jordan 1999, Lebanon 1999, Hungary 2000, Sweden 2000, Iraq 2001, Namibia 2001, Netherlands 2001, Qatar 2002, Libya 2005, Portugal 2005, Germany 2007, Uzbekistan 2007) – less than half of the ratifications required to bring it into force – while another six signed it, signifying potential future ratification (Luxembourg 1997, Venezuela 1997, Côte d'Ivoire 1998, Paraguay 1998, Tunisia 2000, Yemen 2000 – of which only Tunisia 2009, Luxembourg 2012, and Côte d'Ivoire 2014 eventually submitted their ratifications).

Between 2008 and 2014, when the convention came into force, the ratification process somewhat accelerated. In those seven years, another 19 ratifications came through, bringing the total to 35 (Spain 2009, Tunisia 2009, Greece 2010, Guinea-Bissau 2010, Nigeria 2010, Burkina Faso 2011, France 2011, Morocco 2011, Benin 2012, Chad 2012, Denmark 2012, Italy 2012, Luxembourg 2012, Ireland 2013, Montenegro 2013, Niger 2013, United Kingdom 2013, Côte d'Ivoire 2014, and Vietnam 2014), the minimum needed to make the convention fully binding on its state parties. That resurgence was due, in large part, to the efforts of the World Wildlife Fund, which in 2006 added implementation of the convention to its advocacy agenda

Table 2. Member states of the UN Watercourses Convention.[3]

Country	Region	Riparian classification	1997 economic level by income	Convention sponsor	Recorded vote in 1997	Ratification date
Benin	Sub-Saharan Africa	Upper & Lower	Low		Absent	5 July 2012
Burkina Faso	Sub-Saharan Africa	Mostly Upper	Low		For	22 March 2011
Chad ‡	Sub-Saharan Africa	Mostly Lower	Low		Not recorded	26 September 2012
Côte d'Ivoire	Sub-Saharan Africa	Upper & Lower	Low		For	25 February 2014
Denmark ‡	Europe & Central Asia	Non-Riparian	High	Yes	For	30 April 2012
Finland ‡	Europe & Central Asia	Upper & Lower	High	Yes	For	23 January 1998
France ‡	Europe & Central Asia	Upper & Lower	High		Abstain	24 February 2011
Germany ‡	Europe & Central Asia	Upper & Lower	High	Yes	For	2 December 2010
Greece ‡	Europe & Central Asia	Upper & Lower	High	Yes	For	2 December 2010
Guinea Bissau	Sub-Saharan Africa	Lower	Low		Not recorded	19 May 2010
Hungary ‡	Europe & Central Asia	Upper & Lower	Upper middle	Yes	For	26 January 2000
Iraq	MENA	Lower	Lower middle		Not recorded	9 July 2001
Ireland	Europe & Central Asia	Upper & Lower	High		For	20 December 2013
Italy ‡	Europe & Central Asia	Lower	High	Yes	For	30 November 2012
Jordan	MENA	Upper & Lower	Lower middle	Yes	For	22 June 1999
Lebanon	MENA	Upper	Upper middle		Absent	25 May 1999
Libya	MENA	Non-Riparian	Upper middle		For	14 June 2005
Luxembourg ‡	Europe & Central Asia	Upper & Lower	High		For	8 June 2012
Montenegro ‡	Europe & Central Asia	Upper	N/A		Not recorded	24 September 2013
Morocco	MENA	Non-Riparian	Lower middle		For	13 April 2011
Namibia	Sub-Saharan Africa	Upper & Lower	Lower middle		For	29 August 2001
Netherlands ‡	Europe & Central Asia	Lower	High	Yes	For	9 January 2001
Nigeria	Sub-Saharan Africa	Upper & Lower	Low		Absent	27 September 2010
Niger	Sub-Saharan Africa	Upper & Lower	Low		Absent	20 February 2013
Norway ‡	Europe & Central Asia	Upper & Lower	High	Yes	For	30 September 1998
Palestine	MENA	Upper & Lower	Lower middle		Not a UN Member	2 January 2015
Portugal ‡	Europe & Central Asia	Mostly Lower	High	Yes	For	22 June 2005
Qatar	MENA	Non-Riparian	High		For	28 February 2002
Spain ‡	Europe & Central Asia	Upper	High		Abstain	24 September 2009
South Africa	Sub-Saharan Africa	Upper & Lower	Upper middle		For	26 October 1998
Sweden ‡	Europe & Central Asia	Mostly Lower	High	Yes	For	15 June 2000
Tunisia	MENA	Lower	Lower middle	Yes	For	22 April 2009
Uzbekistan ‡	Europe & Central Asia	Mostly Lower	Lower middle		Abstain	4 September 2007
UK ‡	Europe & Central Asia	Upper & Lower	High	Yes	For	13 December 2013
Vietnam	East Asia & Pacific	Lower	Low	Yes	For	19 May 2014

and made a considerable effort to work with various nations on the ratification process (Loures, Rieu-Clarke, Vercambre, & Witmer, 2015; World Wildlife Fund, n.d.). After 2014, however, international interest in the instrument subsided again, as only Palestine has become a state party.

The lack of more vibrant support for the convention may be perplexing when comparing the number of ratifications with the 103 nations that supported the convention in 1997. Only 23 nations, a mere 22% of those who voted in favour of the convention at the UNGA, have ratified it. And of the three nations that declared after the vote that they had intended to vote in favour, only one has since ratified it (Nigeria 2010). More puzzling still, of the 38 state sponsors that brought the convention before the UNGA (UN Press Release, 1997), only 14 have ratified it. Of those very nations who sought to champion and advocate this first-of-a-kind international instrument, only slightly more than a third followed through and ratified it.

Why states joined the convention, or declined to, may be difficult to discern simply by viewing a map, but Figure 4 does suggest certain geographic patterns. Of the 36 ratifications, nearly half (17 state parties) are in Europe and Central Asia. Sub-Saharan Africa and the Middle East and North Africa each have nine, while East Asia and the Pacific has only one. And there are no state parties to the convention from the entire American hemisphere.

While Venezuela and Paraguay were very early signatories, neither has moved towards full party status, and no other country in Latin America seems poised to join the convention. Likewise, Canada and the United States, which were quite involved in the ILC and the Sixth Committee during their deliberations, and which supported the convention in the UNGA vote in 1997, have shown little interest in becoming state parties. The latter nation's absence from the role of ratifying parties is particularly noteworthy given that four of the five special rapporteurs who guided and championed the development of the Draft Articles were Americans, whose election to and work on the ILC was ostensibly supported by the US government. The four American special rapporteurs were Richard D. Kearney, Stephen M. Schwebel, Stephen McCaffrey and Robert Rosenstock.

Status and fate of the Watercourses Convention

While adoption of the convention by the UNGA was a major achievement as the first global instrument to address the management of international watercourses, only a handful of nations – less than 19% of current UN member states – have taken the affirmative step of ratifying it. Moreover, many nations today seem uninterested or reluctant to join, and global interest in the instrument, its norms and its procedures has waned. As a result, scrutiny of the instrument's viability as well as its normative content is reasonable and justified.

As suggested above, although the 1997 vote indicated strong support for the fledgling instrument, the voting pattern masked long-held and deep-seated disagreements, as well as dissatisfaction with the convention's text among many of the member states. Various state representatives to the deliberations, as well as scholars, have even questioned whether the convention, actually presented the status of customary international law in the realm of transboundary watercourses, or whether it simply codified the outcome of negotiations.

For example, during the deliberations of the Sixth Committee, the delegate from the Czech Republic asserted that 'the framework convention represented a supplementary, progressive development of international law rather than a codification exercise' (UN GOAR, 1996a, p. 34).

Figure 4. Global map identifying the member states of the Watercourses Convention (as of 20 December 2019).

During the vote on the convention, Turkey asserted that 'the draft Convention goes far beyond the scope of a framework convention and … establishes a mechanism for planned measures. This has no basis in general and customary international law' (UN GOAR, 1997, p. 4). At that same meeting, Egypt stated that some of the convention's features 'are entirely new regulations that do not modify international customary law' and that 'the framework Convention does not prejudice in any way the legal weight and value of established customary law regarding the sharing of the waters of international watercourses and their non-navigational uses' (p. 10). More forcefully, France asserted that it 'views the negotiations that are concluding today as a relative failure, which is regrettable since, with a greater desire for compromise and the willingness of the Bureau to embark on serious negotiations, it certainly would have been possible to finalize a satisfactory text. As a substantive contribution to the legal system, we consider this to be insignificant, while it is a step backwards with regard to the methods for the codification of international law' (p. 9).

Charles Bourne (1997, pp. 230–31) asserted that 'whatever the content and intent of the Watercourses Convention, its chequered history prevents it from being taken as credible evidence of customary international law'. He added that given the 'substantial disagreement over the substantive articles of the Convention' in the ILC and Sixth Committee Working Group, 'it would seem to be impossible to argue successfully that the provisions of the Convention are accepted as customary law by the international community'. Aaron Schwabach (1997, p. 258) wrote, 'While the number of votes against the Convention was small, the significant number of abstentions and the misgivings expressed by some of the states voting in favor of the Convention indicate that the Convention, whatever else it may accomplish, does not codify the existing normative expectations of states.'

Since the UNGA adopted the convention, support for the instrument has been limited and insipid. Salman M.A. Salman (2007, p. 9) suggests that one reason for the sluggish progress of ratification is the misunderstanding of the norms contained in the instrument. For example, 'The perception by the upstream riparians that the Watercourses Convention is biased in favor of downstream riparians, and *vice versa*, is, no doubt, one of the main reasons for the stalling of the process of the signature and ratification, or accession to the Convention.' Salman also asserts that inaccurate interpretations have contributed to the slow pace of ratification, including those pertaining to rights and benefits under the notification provisions, the Watercourses Convention's effect on pre-existing agreements, the extent of obligations under the dispute settlement clauses, the scope and definition of 'watercourse state', and notions of sovereignty under international water law (pp. 9–12).

However, the misperceptions Salman points to may also be a function of a lack of understanding between the drafters of the convention and those responsible for interpreting and implementing the procedures, norms and duties contained in the agreement. The drafters, who were government representatives and legal experts, had to debate and negotiate over every word and concept in the convention. As suggested above, that process was far from easy and often required compromises that resulted in distinct understandings among some, but not all, of the delegates (Bourne, 1997, p. 228). Thus, for example, the Pakistani representative expressed concerns with the use of the term 'significant' in Article 7, asserting that it 'lacks precision and can become a bone of contention when one is considering the type of harm which should or should not be taken into account. One party's definition of 'significant' would be different from that of another. This could result in an impasse in any negotiation' (UN GOAR, 1997, p. 5). In contrast, the delegate from India lamented that Article 5 'was not drafted in clear and unambiguous terms' with regard to the rights of states to utilize the waters of an international watercourse (p. 9). And Spain's representative asserted that 'the wording of article 7 – "having due regard for provisions of article 5 and 6" – is not sufficiently explicit, and could give rise to friction and disputes when the Convention is implemented' (p. 12).

As a result, Biswas (1999, p. 439) asserts, 'One of the main problems with the proposed convention is that it is full of vague, broad and general terms, which can be defined, and in certain cases quantified, in a variety of different ways. Accordingly, expert advice can easily be "tailored" to legitimize each country's political views and demands.' Further, 'the Convention does not give any practical guidance to the negotiators and no operational assistance to the technical experts. It simply outlines a very broad, general framework, within which everything is considered to be relevant and important. It is likely to contribute to the generation of significant differences of opinion among the negotiators and technical experts as to how such general articles should be interpreted in operational terms.' Similarly, Ryan Stoa (2014, p. 1324) suggests that 'these principles can be used to support incompatible positions between upstream and downstream states, taking negotiations further away from an agreement'.

Regardless of whether Salman or Biswas and Stoa have correctly diagnosed the problem, both assessments indicate that the rules applicable to the use and management of transboundary watercourses are still not well developed or broadly understood, and therefore not fully appreciated, by the global community. Even if the challenge is a matter of misconstruing the scope, applicability, method of application, or interpretation of the rights and obligations of particular norms, the reality is that such misunderstandings can cause uncertainty and a lack of faith in the convention, and, as a result, a reluctance by states to endorse or comply with it.

Another possible explanation for the dwindling focus on the convention rests with the awkward situation created by the opening for global participation of the UNECE Convention on the Protection and Use of Transboundary Watercourses and International Lakes (Water Convention). While the Water Convention was crafted in 1992 for application within the pan-European region, in March 2016 it was formally expanded globally to allow all UN member states to accede to it. As a result, we now have a second global framework treaty for the use and management of transboundary freshwater resources. Currently, there are 43 parties to the Water Convention, including two from outside Europe, Chad and Senegal (United Nations Treaty Collections, n.d.) And at the eighth session of the Meeting of the Parties to the Water Convention, in Kazakhstan in October 2018, 20 more countries announced their intention to accede to it. Given the timing, it appears that the Water Convention is garnering attention at the expense of the UN Watercourses Convention.

While some aspects of the two conventions may be compatible, having two global regimes addressing the use and management of transboundary freshwater resources is politically inelegant and likely to cause confusion. Joining an international agreement creates commitments and responsibilities that should not be taken lightly, and states are rightly careful when assessing whether a particular treaty's regime comports with their priorities and values, the benefits are worthwhile, and they are willing to undertake the associated costs and obligations. As a result, states interested in committing to international legal norms for shared freshwater resources are likely to wonder why the UN has two apparently competing regimes. And even if they can be convinced that the two are compatible, they are still more likely to join only the one that best fits their particular interests, priorities and capacities.

Currently, only 17 countries (less than 9% of UN members) have joined both conventions, and, with the exception of Chad and Uzbekistan, all are found on the European continent. The full list is Chad, Denmark, Finland, France, Germany, Greece, Hungary, Italy, Luxembourg, Montenegro, Netherlands, Norway, Portugal, Spain, Sweden, United Kingdom and Uzbekistan.

Arguments for confusion and overlap can also be made with regard to the Draft Articles on the Law of Transboundary Aquifers, which also was crafted by the ILC and has been on the UNGA's agenda since 2008. While these norms are still in draft form and their status before the UNGA remains uncertain (Eckstein & Sindico, 2014), they do provide a regime for the use and management of transboundary groundwater resources that appears to compete, and in some cases conflict, with principles and procedures provided in both the UN Watercourses Convention and the UNECE Water Convention. Again, the situation could result in confusion among the world's nations as to which regime they should subscribe to, prompting awkwardness and inaction.

Conclusion

As the first global instrument to address the management of international watercourses, the UN Watercourses Convention was unquestionably a landmark achievement. It brought the world's nations together on an issue of critical importance and growing concern for nations in every transboundary basin: how to share and manage freshwater resources that traverse international political boundaries. Only a decade prior to the convention's adoption by the UNGA, Boutros Boutros-Ghali, then Egypt's minister of state for foreign affairs, bluntly remarked, 'The next war in the Middle East will be fought over water, not politics' (BBC News, 2003). Amidst water scarcity and ever-growing demand, the global community appeared to have charted a path towards cooperation.

Although Boutros-Ghali's prediction has yet come to pass, the full promise of the convention – to generate consensus and relieve tensions in the global community over one of life's most critical necessities – has also not been realized. When it was adopted in 1997, the convention was intended to reflect the prevailing rules and procedures recognized as customary law among nations. Yet, today, more than 20 years later, less than a fifth of the world's nations have become state parties, and only a small handful of these are in basins experiencing ongoing disputes. As a result, the current and future status of the convention appears uncertain.

Notes

1. While the state of Palestine is not a recognized nation and full member of the UNGA, on 29 October 2012, it received non-member observer status in the UN in accordance with Article 35, paragraph 2, of the UN Charter (G.A. Res. 67/19, 2012). According to an internal memorandum issued in 2012 by the UN's undersecretary-general for legal affairs, Palestine is 'able to become a party to any treaties that are open to "any State" or "all States" ("all States" formula treaties) deposited with the Secretary-General' (O'Brien, 2012).
2. The Helsinki Rules were later supplemented by the ILA through subsequent resolutions and reports: Articles on Flood Control, International Law Association, 1972; Resolution on the Protection of Water Resources and Water Installations in Times of Armed Conflict, 1976; Resolution on International Water Resources Administration, 1976; Regulation of the Flow of Water of International Watercourses, 1980; Articles on the Relationship between Water, Other Natural Resources and the Environment, 1980; Montreal Resolution on Pollution of the Waters in an International Drainage Basin, Report of the Sixtieth Conference of the International Law Association Held at Montreal, 1982; Complementary Rules Applicable to International Water Resources, Report of the Sixty-Second Conference of the International Law Association Held at Seoul, 1986; Seoul Rules on International Groundwaters, 1986; Rules on Cross-Media Pollution, 1994; Articles on Cross-Media Pollution Resulting from the Use of the Waters of an International Drainage Basin, 1996; and Articles on Private Law Remedies for Transboundary Damage in International Watercourses, 1996.

   In 2004, the ILA adopted its Berlin Rules on Water Resources, which were supposed to supersede all of the association's prior water-related rules and resolutions. However, due to disagreement over the scope and content of that report, the Berlin Rules have been controversial (Bogdanovic, Bourne, Burchi, & Wouters, 2004; Bogdanović, 2019).
3. See 'Notes for Table A1 and Table 2' at the end of this paper for criteria used to develop this table.

Acknowledgments

Special thanks to Courtney Gately, my research assistant and second-year law student at Texas A&M University School of Law, for invaluable research support and helping organize the data.

Disclosure statement

No potential conflict of interest was reported by the author.

Funding

This work was supported by the Texas A&M University School of Law.

References

Books, Chapters, Articles, Reports, and Stories

BBC News. (2003, June 10). *Talking point: Ask Boutros Boutros-Ghali*. Retrieved from http://news.bbc.co.uk/2/hi/talking_point/2951028.stm

Bernstein, R. (2017). China's Mekong plans threaten disaster for countries downstream. *Foreign Policy*. Retrieved from https://foreignpolicy.com/2017/09/27/chinas-mekong-plans-threaten-disaster-for-countries-downstream/

Biswas, A. K. (1999). Management of international waters: Opportunities and constraints. *International Journal of Water Resources Development, 15*(4): 429–441, doi: 10.1080/07900629948691

Bogdanović, S. (2019). The International Law Association Helsinki Rules: contribution to international water law. *Brill Research Perspectives: International Water Law, 3*(4): 1–110. doi:10.1163/9789004395480

Bogdanović, S., Bourne, C., Burchi, S., & Wouters, P. (2004). *Dissenting opinion, ILA Berlin conference 2004: Water Resources Committee report*. Retrieved from https://www.internationalwaterlaw.org/documents/intldocs/ILA/ILABerlinRulesDissent2004.pdf

Bourne, C. B. (1997). Comment: The primacy of the principle of equitable utilization in the 1997 Watercourses Convention. *Canadian Yearbook of International Law, 35*: 215–232 doi:10.1017/S0069005800006639

Bourne, C. B. (1992). The International Law Commission's draft articles on the law of international watercourses: Principles and planned measures. *Colorado Journal of International Environmental Law and Policy, 3*: 65–92

Dellapenna, J. (1992). Designing the legal structures of water management needed to fulfill the Israeli-Palestinian declaration of principles. *Palestine Yearbook of International Law, 7*(1): 63–103, doi: 10.1163/221161494x00055

Eckstein, G., & Sindico, F. (2014). The law of transboundary aquifers: Many ways of going forward, but only one way of standing still. *Review of European, Comparative & International Environmental Law, 23*(1): 32–42, doi: 10.1111/reel.12067

Elver, H. (2002). *Peaceful uses of international rivers: The Euphrates and Tigris Rivers dispute*. Ardsley, NY: Transnational.

Hansen, S. (2018, November). In Turkey, a power play will leave ancient towns underwater. *National Geographic*. Retrieved from https://www.nationalgeographic.com/magazine/2018/11/turkey-flooding-dams-displaced-antiquities-mesopotamia/

Hayden, G. M. (2010). Abstention: The unexpected power of withholding your vote. *Connecticut Law Review, 43*(2): 585–615.

International Law Association (1966). Helsinki rules on the uses of the waters of international rivers and comments. *Report of the Fifty-Second Conference*. London: ILA Publications.

International Water Resources Association. (n.d.). *Past Congresses*. Retrieved from https://www.iwra.org/pastcongresses/

Kahn, J. C. (1997). 1997 United Nations Convention on the Law of Non-navigational Uses of International Watercourses. *Colorado Journal of International Environmental Law and Policy, 9* (1997 Yearbook): 178–185.

Loures, F., Rieu-Clarke, A., Vercambre, M.L., & Witmer, L. (2015). *Everything you need to know about the UN Watercourses Convention*. World Wildlife Fund. Retrieved from https://www.gcint.org/wp-content/uploads/2015/09/UNWC.pdf

McCracken, M., & Wolf, A. T. (2019). Updating the Register of International River Basins of the World. *International Journal of Water Resources Development, 35*(5): 732–782, doi: 10.1080/07900627.2019.1572497

McCaffrey, S. C. (2017). The evolution of international law relating to transboundary waters. In A. Rieu-Clarke, A. Allen, & S. Hendry (Eds.), *Routledge handbook of water law and policy* (pp. 205–217), London: Routledge: 205–217.

McCaffrey, S. C. (2007). *The law of international watercourses*, 2nd ed. New York: Oxford University Press.

McCaffrey, S. C. (1998). The UN Convention on the Law of the Non-navigational Uses of International Watercourses: Prospects and pitfalls. In S. M. A. Salman & L. Boisson de Chazournes (Eds.), *International watercourses: enhancing cooperation and managing conflict: Proceedings of a World Bank Seminar* (pp. 17–28), World Bank Technical Paper No. 414. Washington, DC: World Bank. doi:10.1023/a:1022489017731

McCaffrey, S. C., & Sinjela, M. (1998). The 1997 United Nations Convention on International Watercourses. *American Journal of International Law, 91*: 97–107. doi:10.2307/2998069

Meshel, T. (2018). *International law and transboundary fresh water resources: A dispute resolution perspective* (Unpublished PhD dissertation), University of Toronto, Ontario.

O'Brien, P. (2012, December 21). *Interoffice memorandum: Issues related to General Assembly resolution 67/19 on the status of Palestine in the United Nations.* Retrieved from http://palestineun.org/wp-content/uploads/2013/08/012-UN-Memo-regarding-67-19.pdf

Program in Water Conflict Management and Transformation. (n.d.). *International Freshwater Treaties Database.* Oregon State University. Retrieved from https://transboundarywaters.science.oregonstate.edu/content/international-freshwater-treaties-database

Salman, S. M. A. (2007). The United Nations Watercourses Convention ten years later: Why has its entry into force proven difficult? *Water International, 32*(1): 1–15. doi: 10.1080/02508060708691962

Salman, S. M. A. (2010). Downstream riparians can also harm upstream riparians: The concept of foreclosure of future uses. *Water International, 35*(4): 350–364. doi: 10.1080/02508060.2010.508160

Schwabach, A. (1997). The United Nations Convention on the Law of Non-navigational Uses of International Watercourses, customary international law, and the interests of developing upper Riparians. *Texas International Law Journal, 33*, 257–279.

Schulz, A. (2014). UN Watercourses Convention to enter into force following 35th ratification. IISD Reporting Services. Retrieved from http://sdg.iisd.org/news/un-watercourses-convention-to-enter-into-force-following-35th-ratification/

Solomon, E., & Pitel, L. (2018). Why water is a growing faultline between Turkey and Iraq. *Financial Times.* Retrieved from https://www.ft.com/content/82ca2e3c-6369-11e8-90c2-9563a0613e56

Stoa, R. B. (2014). The United Nations Watercourses Convention on the dawn of entry into force. *Vanderbilt Journal of Transnational Law, 47*: 1321–1370.

Sullivan, M. (2018). China reshapes the vital Mekong River to power its expansion. *National Public Radio.* Retrieved from https://www.npr.org/2018/10/06/639280566/china-reshapes-the-vital-mekong-river-to-power-its-expansion

Tanzi, A., & Arcari, M. (2001). The United Nations *Convention on the Law of International Watercourses: A framework for sharing.* London: Kluwer Law International.

Teclaff, L. A. (1967). The *river basin in history and law.* The Hague: Martinus Nijhoff.

World Bank. (n.d.). *The World by Income and Region.* Retrieved from https://datahelpdesk.worldbank.org/knowledgebase/articles/906519-world-bank-country-and-lending-groups

World Water Council. (n.d.). *World Water Forum.* Retrieved from http://www.worldwatercouncil.org/en/world-water-forum

World Wildlife Fund. (n.d.). Tell global leaders to cooperate on fresh water. World Wildlife Fund. Retrieved from https://support.worldwildlife.org/site/Advocacy?cmd=display&page=UserAction&id=825

Wouters, P. (1999). The legal response to international water conflicts: The UN Watercourses Convention and beyond. *German Yearbook of International Law, 42*, 293–336.

Wouters, P. (1997). Editor's foreword: current status of international water law. In P. Wouters (Ed.), International *water law: Selected writings of professor* Charles B. Bourne (pp. xiii–xxvi), London: Kluwer Law International.

Cases

Case Concerning the Gabcikovo-Nagymaros Project. (1997). *Hungary v. Slovakia, Judgment, ICJ Reports*

Case Concerning Pulp Mills on the River Uruguay. (2010). *Argentina v. Uruguay, Judgment, ICJ Reports*

Case Relating to the Territorial Jurisdiction of the International Commission of the River Oder. (1929). *United Kingdom, Czechoslovakia, Denmark, France, Germany, Sweden v. Poland, P.C.I.J. Series A, No. 23, 1*

Diversion of the Water From the Meuse. (1937). *Netherlands v. Belguim, Series A/B, No. 70*. 4

Donauversinkung Case. (1927). Württemberg and Prussia v. Baden, *German Staatsgerichtshof, 18* June 1927

Kansas v. Colorado. (1907). 206 U. S. 46

Lake Lanoux Arbitration Case. (1957). *Spain v. France, Award of 16 November 1957, 24 Int'l L. Rep. 101*

Wyoming v. Colorado. (1922). *259 U.S. 419*

UN Treaties, Resolutions, Reports, and Websites

About United Nations Water. (n.d.). Retrieved from https://www.unwater.org/about-unwater/

Convention on the Law of the Non-Navigational Uses of International Watercourses. (1997). G.A. Res. 51/229, UN GOAR, 51st Sess., UN Doc. A/RES/51/229

Evensen, J. (1983). First report on the law of the non-navigational uses of international watercourses, Law of the non-navigational uses of international watercourses. Yearbook of the ILC, *II*(1), 155–194, Doc. A/CN.4/367

G.A. Res. 1401(XIV). (1959). UN GOAR, *14th Sess*. Retrieved from http://daccess-ods.un.org/access.nsf/Get?Open&DS=A/RES/1401(XIV)&Lang=E&Area=RESOLUTION

G.A. Res. 2669. (1970). UN GOAR, 25th Sess. Supp. No. 28, UN Doc. A/8202

G.A. Res. 64/292. (2010). 64th Sess., UN Doc. A/RES/64/292. Retrieved from https://www.un.org/en/ga/search/view_doc.asp?symbol=A/RES/64/292

G.A. Res. 67/19. (2012). 67th Sess., UN Doc. A/RES/67/19. Retrieved from https://undocs.org/A/RES/67/19 doi:10.1094/PDIS-11-11-0999-PDN

International Decade for Action 'Water For Life' 2005–2015. (n.d.). Retrieved from https://www.un.org/waterforlifedecade/

Millennium Development Goals and Beyond 2015. (n.d.). *Target 7.C*. Retrieved from https://www.un.org/millenniumgoals/environ.shtml

Schwebel, S. M. (1982). Third report on the law of the non-navigational uses of international watercourses, Law of the non-navigational uses of international watercourses. Yearbook of the ILC, *II*(1), 65–191, Doc. A/CN.4/348

Sustainable Development Goals Knowledge Platform. (n.d.). *Sustainable Development Goal 6: Ensure availability and sustainable management of water and sanitation for all*. Retrieved from https://sustainabledevelopment.un.org/sdg6

UN GOAR. (1988). 43rd Sess., Summary Record of the 30th Meeting, Sixth Committee, held on 4 November 1988, A/C.6/43/SR.30. Retrieved from https://www.un.org/ga/search/viewm_doc.asp?symbol=A/C.6/43/SR.30 doi:10.3168/jds.S0022-0302(88)79586-7

UN GOAR. (1996a). 51st Sess, Summary Record of the 12th Meeting, Sixth Committee, held on 7 October 1996, Distr. GENERAL A/C.6/51/SR.12. Retrieved from https://www.un.org/ga/search/view_doc.asp?symbol=a/c.6/51/sr.12

UN GOAR. (1996b). 51st Sess, Summary Record of the 20th Meeting, Sixth Committee, held on 14 October 1996, Distr. GENERAL A/C.6/51/SR.20. Retrieved from https://www.un.org/ga/search/viewm_doc.asp?symbol=a/c.6/51/sr.20

UN GOAR. (1996c). 51st Sess, Summary Record of the 16th Meeting, Sixth Committee, held on 9 October 1996, Distr. GENERAL A/C.6/51/SR.16. Retrieved from https://www.un.org/ga/search/view_doc.asp?symbol=a/c.6/51/sr.16

UN GOAR. (1996d). 51st Sess, Summary Record of the 15th Meeting, Sixth Committee, held on 8 October 1996, Distr. GENERAL A/C.6/51/SR.15. Retrieved from https://www.un.org/ga/search/view_doc.asp?symbol=a/c.6/51/sr.15

UN GOAR. (1997). 51st Sess., 99th plen. mtg., UN Doc. A/51/PV.99. Retrieved from https://undocs.org/en/A/51/PV.99

UN Press Release. (1997). General *assembly adopts convention on law of non-navigational uses of international watercourses*, GA/9248. Retrieved from https://www.internationalwaterlaw.org/documents/intldocs/convention_press.html

UNICEF/WHO. (2012). Millennium development goal drinking water target met, sanitation target still lagging far behind. 6 March 2012. Retrieved from https://www.who.int/mediacentre/news/releases/2012/drinking_water_20120306/en/ doi:10.1094/PDIS-11-11-0999-PDN

United Nations. (n.d.). Member States. Retrieved from https://www.un.org/en/member-states/

United Nations Treaty Collections. (n.d.). Convention on the protection and use of transboundary watercourses and international lakes. STATUS AS AT: 05-10-2019. Retrieved from https://treaties.un.org/Pages/ViewDetails.aspx?src=TREATY&mtdsg_no=XXVII-5&chapter=27&clang=_en

Yearbook of the ILC. (1984). Vol. I, Doc. A/CN.4/SER.A/1984. Retrieved from http://legal.un.org/ilc/publications/yearbooks/english/ilc_1984_v1.pdf

Yearbook of the ILC. (1987). Doc. A/CN.4/393, Vol. II, pt. 2. Retrieved from https://www.legal-tools.org/doc/760b39/pdf/

Appendix

Table A1. Relationship of UN Member States to the UN Watercourses Convention

Country	Region	Riparian Classification	1997 Economic Level by Income	Convention Sponsor	Record of Vote in 1997	Ratification Date
Afghanistan	South Asia	Upper	Low		Absent	
Albania ‡	Europe & Central Asia	Lower	Low		For	
Algeria	Middle East & North Africa	Non-Riparian	Low middle		For	
Andorra	Europe & Central Asia	Upper	High		Abstain	
Angola	Sub-Saharan Africa	Upper and Lower	Low		For	
Antigua and Barbuda	Latin America & Caribbean	Island Nation	Upper middle	Yes	For	
Argentina	Latin America & Caribbean	Mostly Lower	Upper middle		Abstain	
Armenia	Europe & Central Asia	Upper and Lower	Low		For	
Australia	East Asia & Pacific	Non-Riparian	High		For	
Austria ‡	Europe & Central Asia	Mostly Upper	High		For	
Azerbaijan ‡	Europe & Central Asia	Mostly Lower	Low		Abstain	
Bahamas	Latin America & Caribbean	Island Nation	High		Absent	
Bahrain	Middle East & North Africa	Island Nation	Upper middle		For	
Bangladesh	South Asia	Lower	Low	Yes	For	
Barbados	Latin America & Caribbean	Island Nation	Upper middle		Absent	
Belarus ‡	Europe & Central Asia	Upper and Lower	Low middle		For	
Belguim ‡	Europe & Central Asia	Upper and Lower	High		Abstain	
Belize	Latin America & Caribbean	Mostly Lower	Low middle		Absent	
Benin	Sub-Saharan Africa	Upper and Lower	Low		Absent	5 July 2012
Bhutan	South Asia	Mostly Upper	Low	Yes	Absent	
Bolivia	Latin America & Caribbean	Mostly Upper	Low middle		Abstain	
Bosnia and Herzegovina ‡	Europe & Central Asia	Upper and Lower	Low		Not recorded	
Botswana	Sub-Saharan Africa	Upper and Lower	Low middle		For	
Brazil	Latin America & Caribbean	Mostly Lower	Upper middle	Yes	For	
Brunei Darussalam	East Asia & Pacific	Non-Riparian	High		For	
Bulgaria ‡	Europe & Central Asia	Upper and Lower	Low middle		Abstain	
Burkina Faso	Sub-Saharan Africa	Mostly Upper	Low		For	22 March 2011
Burundi	Sub-Saharan Africa	Mostly Upper	Low		Against	
Cabo Verde (Cape Verde)	Sub-Saharan Africa	Island Nation	Low middle		Absent	
Cambodia	East Asia & Pacific	Upper and Lower	Low	Yes	For	
Cameroon	Sub-Saharan Africa	Mostly Upper	Low	Yes	For	
Canada	North America	Upper and Lower	High	Yes	For	
Central African Republic	Sub-Saharan Africa	Mostly Upper	Low		Not recorded	
Chad ‡	Sub-Saharan Africa	Mostly Lower	Low		Not recorded	26 September 2012
Chile	Latin America & Caribbean	Lower	Upper middle	Yes	For	
China	East Asia & Pacific	Mostly Upper	Low middle		Against	

Table A1. (Continued).

Country	Region	Riparian Classification	1997 Economic Level by Income	Convention Sponsor	Record of Vote in 1997	Ratification Date
Colombia	Latin America & Caribbean	Mostly Upper	Low middle		Abstain	
Comoros	Sub-Saharan Africa	Island Nation	Low		Absent	
Congo, Rep. of the	Sub-Saharan Africa	Upper and Lower	Low		Not recorded	
Costa Rica	Latin America & Caribbean	Upper and Lower	Low middle		For	
Côte d'Ivoire	Sub-Saharan Africa	Upper and Lower	Low		For	25 February 2014
Croatia ‡	Europe & Central Asia	Upper and Lower	Upper middle		For	
Cuba	Latin America & Caribbean	Island Nation	Low middle		Abstain	
Cyprus	Europe & Central Asia	Island Nation	High		For	
Czech Republic ‡	Europe & Central Asia	Upper	Upper middle		For	
Democratic Republic of the Congo (Zaire)	Sub-Saharan Africa	Upper and Lower	Low		Absent	
Denmark ‡	Europe & Central Asia	Non-Riparian	High	Yes	For	30 April 2012
Djibouti	Middle East & North Africa	Lower	Low middle		For	
Dominica	Latin America & Caribbean	Island Nation	Low middle		Not recorded	
Dominican Republic	Latin America & Caribbean	Upper	Low middle		Absent	
Ecuador	Latin America & Caribbean	Upper	Low middle		Abstain	
Egypt	Middle East & North Africa	Lower	Low middle		Abstain	
El Salvador	Latin America & Caribbean	Mostly Lower	Low middle		Absent	
Equatorial Guinea	Sub-Saharan Africa	Mostly Lower	Low middle		Not recorded	
Eritrea	Sub-Saharan Africa	Mostly Upper	Low		Absent	
Estonia ‡	Europe & Central Asia	Mostly Upper	Upper middle		For	
Eswatini (Swaziland)	Sub-Saharan Africa	Upper and Lower	Low middle		Absent	
Ethiopia	Sub-Saharan Africa	Upper	Low		Abstain	
Fiji	East Asia & Pacific	Island Nation	Low middle		Absent	
Finland ‡	Europe & Central Asia	Upper and Lower	High	Yes	For	23 January 1998
France ‡	Europe & Central Asia	Upper and Lower	High		Abstain	24 February 2011
Gabon	Sub-Saharan Africa	Lower	Upper middle		For	
Gambia, The	Sub-Saharan Africa	Lower	Low		Not recorded	
Georgia	Europe & Central Asia	Upper and Lower	Low middle		For	
Germany ‡	Europe & Central Asia	Upper and Lower	High	Yes	For	2 December 2010
Ghana	Sub-Saharan Africa	Mostly Lower	Low		Abstain	
Greece ‡	Europe & Central Asia	Upper and Lower	High	Yes	For	2 December 2010
Grenada	Latin America & Caribbean	Island Nation	Upper middle	Yes	Not recorded	
Guatemala	Latin America & Caribbean	Mostly Upper	Low middle		Abstain	
Guinea	Sub-Saharan Africa	Upper	Low		Absent	
Guinea-Bissau	Sub-Saharan Africa	Lower	Low		Not recorded	19 May 2010

(*Continued*)

Table A1. (Continued).

Country	Region	Riparian Classification	1997 Economic Level by Income	Convention Sponsor	Record of Vote in 1997	Ratification Date
Guyana	Latin America & Caribbean	Upper and Lower	Low middle		For	
Haiti	Latin America & Caribbean	Lower	Low		For	
Honduras	Latin America & Caribbean	Upper and Lower	Low	Yes	For	
Hungary ‡	Europe & Central Asia	Upper and Lower	Upper middle	Yes	For	26 January 2000
Iceland	Europe & Central Asia	Island Nation	High		For	
India	South Asia	Upper and Lower	Low		Abstain	
Indonesia	East Asia & Pacific	Non-Riparian	Low middle		For	
Iran	Middle East & North Africa	Upper and Lower	Low middle		For	
Iraq	Middle East & North Africa	Lower	Low middle		Not recorded	9 July 2001
Ireland	Europe & Central Asia	Upper and Lower	High		For	20 December 2013
Israel	Middle East & North Africa	Mostly Lower	High		Abstain	
Italy ‡	Europe & Central Asia	Lower	High	Yes	For	30 November 2012
Jamaica	Latin America & Caribbean	Island Nation	Low middle		For	
Japan	East Asia & Pacific	Island Nation	High	Yes	For	
Jordan	Middle East & North Africa	Upper and Lower	Low middle	Yes	For	22 June 1999
Kazakhstan ‡	Europe & Central Asia	Upper and Lower	Low middle		For	
Kenya	Sub-Saharan Africa	Upper and Lower	Low		For	
Kiribati	East Asia & Pacific	Island Nation	Low middle		Not UN Member	
Korea, Dem. People's Rep.	East Asia & Pacific	Upper and Lower	Low middle		Absent	
Korea, Rep.	East Asia & Pacific	Lower	High	Yes	For	
Kuwait	Middle East & North Africa	Non-Riparian	High		For	
Kyrgyzstan	Europe & Central Asia	Upper	Low		Not recorded	
Lao PDR	East Asia & Pacific	Upper and Lower	Low	Yes	For	
Latvia ‡	Europe & Central Asia	Lower	Low middle	Yes	For	
Lebanon	Middle East & North Africa	Upper	Upper middle		Absent	25 May 1999
Lesotho	Sub-Saharan Africa	Upper	Low		For	
Liberia	Sub-Saharan Africa	Mostly Lower	Low		For	
Libya	Middle East & North Africa	Non-Riparian	Upper middle		For	14 June 2005
Liechtenstein ‡	Europe & Central Asia	Upper and Lower	High	Yes	For	
Lithuania ‡	Europe & Central Asia	Upper and Lower	Low middle		For	
Luxembourg ‡	Europe & Central Asia	Upper and Lower	High		For	8 June 2012
Madagascar	Sub-Saharan Africa	Island Nation	Low		For	
Malawi	Sub-Saharan Africa	Mostly Upper	Low		For	
Malaysia	East Asia & Pacific	Non-Riparian	Upper middle	Yes	For	
Maldives	South Asia	Island Nation	Low middle		For	
Mali	Sub-Saharan Africa	Upper and Lower	Low		Abstain	
Malta	Middle East & North Africa	Island Nation	Upper middle		For	
Marshall Islands	East Asia & Pacific	Island Nation	Low middle		For	
Mauritania	Sub-Saharan Africa	Upper and Lower	Low		Absent	

(Continued)

Table A1. (Continued).

Country	Region	Riparian Classification	1997 Economic Level by Income	Convention Sponsor	Record of Vote in 1997	Ratification Date
Mauritius	Sub-Saharan Africa	Island Nation	Upper middle		For	
Mexico	Latin America & Caribbean	Upper and Lower	Upper middle	Yes	For	
Micronesia	East Asia & Pacific	Island Nation	Low middle		For	
Moldova ‡	Europe & Central Asia	Upper and Lower	Low		Not recorded	
Monaco	Europe & Central Asia	Non-Riparian	High		Abstain	
Mongolia	East Asia & Pacific	Upper	Low		Abstain	
Montenegro ‡	Europe & Central Asia	Upper	N/A		Not UN Member	24 September 2013
Morocco	Middle East & North Africa	Non-Riparian	Low middle		For	13 April 2011
Mozambique	Sub-Saharan Africa	Lower	Low		For	
Myanmar	East Asia & Pacific	Mostly Lower	Low		Absent	
Namibia	Sub-Saharan Africa	Upper and Lower	Low middle		For	29 August 2001
Nauru	East Asia & Pacific	Island Nation	N/A		Not UN Member	
Nepal	South Asia	Mostly Upper	Low	Yes	For	
Netherlands ‡	Europe & Central Asia	Lower	High	Yes	For	9 January 2001
New Zealand	East Asia & Pacific	Island Nation	High		For	
Nicaragua	Latin America & Caribbean	Upper and Lower	Low		Not recorded	
Niger	Sub-Saharan Africa	Upper and Lower	Low		Absent	20 February 2013
Nigeria	Sub-Saharan Africa	Upper and Lower	Low		Absent	27 September 2010
North Macedonia (Macedonia FYR) ‡	Europe & Central Asia	Mostly Upper	Low middle		Absent	
Norway ‡	Europe & Central Asia	Upper and Lower	High	Yes	For	30 September 1998
Oman	Middle East & North Africa	Non-Riparian	Upper middle		For	
Pakistan	South Asia	Lower	Low		Abstain	
Palau	East Asia & Pacific	Island Nation	Upper middle		Absent	
Palestine *	Middle East & North Africa	Upper and Lower	Low middle		Not UN Member	2 January 2015
Panama	Latin America & Caribbean	Non-Riparian	Low middle		Abstain	
Papua New Guinea	East Asia & Pacific	Non-Riparian	Low middle		For	
Paraguay	Latin America & Caribbean	Upper and Lower	Low middle		Abstain	
Peru	Latin America & Caribbean	Upper	Low middle		Abstain	
Philippines	East Asia & Pacific	Island Nation	Low middle		For	
Poland ‡	Europe & Central Asia	Upper and Lower	Upper middle		For	
Portugal ‡	Europe & Central Asia	Mostly Lower	High	Yes	For	22 June 2005
Qatar	Middle East & North Africa	Non-Riparian	High		For	28 February 2002
Romania ‡	Europe & Central Asia	Upper and Lower	Low middle	Yes	For	
Russian Federation ‡	Europe & Central Asia	Upper and Lower	Low middle		For	
Rwanda	Sub-Saharan Africa	Mostly Upper	Low		Abstain	

(*Continued*)

Table A1. (Continued).

Country	Region	Riparian Classification	1997 Economic Level by Income	Convention Sponsor	Record of Vote in 1997	Ratification Date
Samoa	East Asia & Pacific	Island Nation	Low middle		For	
San Marino	Europe & Central Asia	Upper and Lower	High		For	
São Tomé and Príncipe	Sub-Saharan Africa	Island Nation	Low		Not recorded	
Saudi Arabia	Middle East & North Africa	Non-Riparian	Upper middle		For	
Senegal ‡	Sub-Saharan Africa	Upper and Lower	Low		Absent	
Serbia ‡	Europe & Central Asia	Upper and Lower	N/A		Not UN Member	
Seychelles	Sub-Saharan Africa	Island Nation	Upper middle		Not recorded	
Sierra Leone	Sub-Saharan Africa	Mostly Lower	Low		For	
Singapore	East Asia & Pacific	Island Nation	High		For	
Slovak Republic ‡	Europe & Central Asia	Upper and Lower	Upper middle		For	
Slovenia ‡	Europe & Central Asia	Upper and Lower	High		For	
Solomon Islands	East Asia & Pacific	Island Nation	Low middle		Absent	
Somalia	Sub-Saharan Africa	Lower	Low		Not recorded	
South Africa	Sub-Saharan Africa	Upper and Lower	Upper middle		For	26 October 1998
South Sudan	Sub-Saharan Africa	Upper and Lower	N/A		Not UN Member	
Spain ‡	Europe & Central Asia	Upper	High		Abstain	24 September 2009
Sri Lanka	South Asia	Island Nation	Low middle		Absent	
St. Kitts and Nevis	Latin America & Caribbean	Island Nation	Upper middle		Absent	
St. Lucia	Latin America & Caribbean	Island Nation	Upper middle		Absent	
St. Vincent and the Grenadines	Latin America & Caribbean	Island Nation	Low middle		Absent	
Sudan	Sub-Saharan Africa	Upper and Lower	Low	Yes	For	
Suriname	Latin America & Caribbean	Upper and Lower	Low middle		For	
Sweden ‡	Europe & Central Asia	Mostly Lower	High	Yes	For	15 June 2000
Switzerland ‡	Europe & Central Asia	Mostly Upper	High		Not UN Member	
Syrian Arab Republic	Middle East & North Africa	Upper and Lower	Low middle	Yes	For	2 April 1998
Tajikistan	Europe & Central Asia	Upper and Lower	Low		Absent	
Thailand	East Asia & Pacific	Upper and Lower	Low middle		For	
Timor-Leste	East Asia & Pacific	Non-Riparian	N/A		Not UN Member	
Togo	Sub-Saharan Africa	Mostly Upper	Low		Not recorded	
Tonga	East Asia & Pacific	Island Nation	Low middle		Not UN Member	
Trinidad and Tobago	Latin America & Caribbean	Island Nation	Upper middle		For	
Tunisia	Middle East & North Africa	Lower	Low middle	Yes	For	22 April 2009
Turkey	Europe & Central Asia	Mostly Upper	Upper middle		Against	
Turkmenistan ‡	Europe & Central Asia	Upper and Lower	Low		Absent	
Tuvalu	East Asia & Pacific	Island Nation	N/A		Not UN Member	
Uganda	Sub-Saharan Africa	Mostly Upper	Low		Absent	
Ukraine ‡	Europe & Central Asia	Upper and Lower	Low middle		For	
United Arab Emirates	Middle East & North Africa	Non-Riparian	High		For	

(*Continued*)

Table A1. (Continued).

Country	Region	Riparian Classification	1997 Economic Level by Income	Convention Sponsor	Record of Vote in 1997	Ratification Date
United Kingdom of Great Britain and Northern Ireland ‡	Europe & Central Asia	Upper and Lower	High	Yes	For	13 December 2013
United Republic of Tanzania	Sub-Saharan Africa	Upper	Low		Abstain	
United States of America	North America	Upper and Lower	High	Yes	For	
Uruguay	Latin America & Caribbean	Upper and Lower	Upper middle	Yes	For	
Uzbekistan ‡	Europe & Central Asia	Mostly Lower	Low middle		Abstain	4 September 2007
Vanautu	East Asia & Pacific	Island Nation	Low middle		Not recorded	
Venezuela	Latin America & Caribbean	Mostly Lower	Upper middle	Yes	For	
Vietnam	East Asia & Pacific	Lower	Low	Yes	For	19 May 2014
Yemen	Middle East & North Africa	Non-Riparian	Low		For	
Zambia	Sub-Saharan Africa	Upper and Lower	Low		For	
Zimbabwe	Sub-Saharan Africa	Upper and Lower	Low		Absent	

Notes for Table A1 and Table 2

- Member states of the United Nations, as identified in United Nations (n.d.).
- Economic level and geographic location based on classifications in World Bank (n.d.).
- ‡ Denotes nations that are members of the UNECE Convention on the Protection and Use of Transboundary Watercourses and International Lakes.
- Palestine is included because its accession to the Watercourses Convention is recognized within the UN system as an accession by a 'state', as provided for in G.A. Res. 67/19 (2012); see also O'Brien (2012).
- *Riparian classification*. The rubric used here solely considers the upstream/downstream geographic relationships of nations. The term 'riparian' refers to a state through which a transboundary river or its major tributaries flow through or alongside. The rubric assigns five categories intentionally in general terms and considers each country's overall hydro-geography (it does not focus on a specific basin), using nations' transboundary river basins, derived primarily from McCracken & Wolf (2019). Google Earth was used as a supplement.
  - Upper: The country is a source of surface flows to one or more downstream nations, and receives comparatively minimal or no surface flows from other countries.
  - Mostly upper: The country is a substantial source of water through surface flows to one or more downstream nations, but also receives considerable surface flows from other countries.
  - Upper and lower: The country is a source of considerable surface flows to one or more downstream nations, and receives considerable surface flows from one or more countries, and/or has one or more contiguous rivers forming a significant portion of its border.
  - Mostly lower: The country receives substantial water through surface flows from one or more upstream nations, but is also a source of considerable surface flows for other countries.
  - Lower: The country receives surface flows from one or more upstream nations, and is not a source of (or provides comparatively minimal) surface flows to other countries.

Australian water decision making: are politicians performing?

James Horne

ABSTRACT
Australia has husbanded its water resources to deliver laudable environmental and economic outcomes. But a close examination reveals some areas where decisions have resulted in poor outcomes and unsatisfactory use of public funds. This article examines some of these decisions through four case studies in which I suggest that current water infrastructure governance arrangements should be improved, through compelling politicians to place a greater focus on delivering value for money from infrastructure investments. Delivering higher-quality water services to remote indigenous communities should also be accorded a much higher priority.

Compared with most other countries, Australia has husbanded its water resources to deliver laudable environmental and economic outcomes. In urban Australia (which accounts for around 90% of the population), water quality is of a high standard, safe, affordable and widely available. In the regulated rural water sector that supplies many irrigation communities, service delivery is relatively efficient, with established water markets ensuring that water moves to where it is valued most highly. With important exceptions, water use is monitored satisfactorily, and environmental interests have a significant seat at the decision-making table. In an international context, the Murray-Darling Basin (MDB) Plan, which covers around one million square kilometres, represents one of the first whole-of-basin attempts to halt the inexorable expansion of agricultural water use and to recognize the needs of the environment. Overall, water resource managers continue to strive for improved outcomes.

At some levels, this positive report card is not surprising: Australia is a rich, developed country, with a technically strong and largely corruption-free professional public sector at both state and national levels, and a political leadership that at times has been willing to support detailed economic reform, even if at times it is very slow to do so. Australia has a history of actively seeking to manage the impact of highly variable stream flows where that makes economic sense. Over the past decade, large water service providers in urban areas have become much more community focused, driven by independent economic regulators (see e.g. ACCC, 2019; IPART, 2019). And there has been an ongoing programme over the past decade to entrench more effective water markets, and better nation-wide access to better water information (Horne & Grafton, 2019). The literature on many aspects of the Australian water experience is both deep and broad (references in Grafton, Horne, & Wheeler, 2016; Horne, 2013, 2017a).

But while this is a noteworthy track record, it is far from perfect. There are many political decisions that have resulted in poor outcomes, particularly in the unsatisfactory use of investment capital. These decisions lead us to ask whether the role of politicians in contemporary water decision making needs to be reconsidered. Nearly everyone involved in water reform is playing politics, from governments to interest groups and the authors of so-called independent reports. Some might include even the recent South Australian Royal Commission into the MDB (South Australia, 2019). This article examines some of these decisions by the politicians and governments that oversee water management in Australia.

Four case studies illustrate issues around overt involvement by politicians and governments in important areas of water decision making. The first involves a spate of large-scale supply augmentation decisions in major urban areas. As traditional supply sources diminished rapidly during the Millennium Drought (1997–2009), governments turned to non-rainfall-dependent sources, especially desalination plants. The central question is why state governments (in four cases, with major financial assistance from the national government) involved themselves at all in these infrastructure decisions. Under normal circumstances most investment decisions have been made by state-owned corporatized water service operators. In aggregate, these political decisions were and remain very costly to the Australian community.

The second case study examines political involvement in how irrigation water is allocated and reallocated, and the associated compliance and enforcement, in the MDB, even after broad regulatory settings have been put in place. We ask whether the behaviour has been consistent with public commitments by governments to the MDB Plan and why relatively inefficient and costly water purchase methods have become the main vehicle for restoring the environment's access to water resources. Much of this involvement goes to questions around use of water between agriculture and the environment in individual states.

The third case study involves the poor level of water services in small indigenous communities in much of remote and very remote Australia, which has persisted over recent decades. It offers a stark contrast to the quality of service in major urban areas, covering 90% of the population. While this case study covers communities with barely 0.25% of the Australian population, clean water and sanitation services is important in overcoming indigenous disadvantage. The central question is why, despite apparent public support across the political spectrum (SCRGSP, 2016), upgrading water infrastructure in these communities has been both patchy and slow.

The fourth case study involves flood management, and the roles of different levels of government. The broad issue of managing infrastructure resilience is of critical forward-looking relevance, given that one of the key impacts of climate change will be greater incidence and severity of severe weather events, and associated flooding. We examine political involvement in land use planning, and its implications for flood management.

These four cases highlight the complex contribution of formal political decision making in some areas of water service management. They are areas that have periodically and individually been under the spotlight. Nonetheless, underperformance continues. In the context of this special issue celebrating the contribution of Professor Biswas, we seek to forthrightly lay bare some difficult issues relating to political roles in water decision making in Australia.

In the following sections, we undertake a brief desktop review of the four case studies in question. We then discuss whether changes in governance arrangements might help address the weaknesses illustrated by these case studies.

Large-scale urban water investments during the Millennium Drought

Work on desalination plants in Australia's five largest coastal capital cities commenced in the 2000s to bolster urban water security (Horne, 2018). All cities had experienced sharp declines in streamflow into their major water storages. The new plants added large climate-resilient capacity to urban water supply in each of the cities, totalling some 480 GL, or around 25% of their current urban water use. Three other large investment decisions made during this period also added significantly to capital city water supply capacity. They were augmentation of Canberra's water storages through a large new dam (around 76 GL), a new 75 GL pipeline to strengthen Melbourne's access to rural water supplies in an adjacent catchment, and a decision to construct Brisbane's Western Corridor Recycled Water Project (ACT Audit Office, 2015; Crase, Pawsey, & Cooper, 2014; Seqwater, 2014). All these decisions had one thing in common: they were made by the respective state or territory government in which the capital city was located (often with national government financial support), and not by the responsible water service provider which would normally make most investment decisions. At one level, given the size of each capital investment decision being contemplated, that might seem reasonable. However, given that state-owned corporatized water service providers were charged with delivering reliable water services and a return on equity, questions around the long-term cost versus benefits to the community were critical. Perth's two desalination plants provided a cost-effective approach to increase base load water supply in the aftermath of the collapse of streamflow to the established rainfed network of dams (Water Corporation, 2009, 2018). But there were major issues with all the remaining desalination plant processes, and with the Western Corridor Recycled Water Project (Carr, Marsden, & Jacob, 2012). An overview of the issues for these projects is set out in Table 1.

In each case, decisions were made during major water availability crises. But in each case the risk assessment involved not only an assessment of water supply risks but also an unacknowledged assessment of political risk. And the standards used in making these decisions were clearly very different. Many of these investments should not have been undertaken, at least at the scale selected. For example, in the case of the New South Wales (NSW) desalination plant, had the government followed the decision-making process it had in place, no plant would have been built beyond getting site preliminaries completed, and being prepared should the 'go' button need to be pressed at some time in the future. In South Australia (SA), there was no business case for Stage 2 to be built; a sensible business process the SA government had put in place for Stage 1 was derailed by a combination of a national government grant, Murray-Darling Basin politics and national/state first minister personalities (Wright, 2016). In Victoria, the construction of the Victorian desalination plant shifted the political risk by putting the project off budget, with the massive annual cost being borne by Melbourne water consumers for a small

Table 1. Underperforming large-scale urban water infrastructure investments.

Project	Decision	Decision maker	Benefit/cost study	Comment
Sydney Desalination Plant 2007	2007	NSW state government	None published	Political decision did not accord with state government's own rules. Had they been followed, it would not have been built. Only recently turned on.
Adelaide Desalination Stage 2	2009	SA state government, national government	None undertaken on business case to build Stage 2	Stage 1 made sense as a climate-independent water source and insurance policy, even if more expensive than some alternatives. Currently operating at minimum maintenance levels. Stage 2 was politically driven and should not have been built.
Melbourne Desalination Plant 2007	2007	Victorian state government	Feasibility study done; cheaper options were available	Annual cost of fully mothballed plant around $610m. A modular build would have been more cost-effective. Politicians were the driving force (every other major city was reacting to the Millennium drought).
Victorian North-South pipeline	2008	Victorian state government	The $750m pipeline project had, according to the Victorian government, a positive NPV	Following completion of the project and a change of government, the new state government decided that the pipeline should only be used in exceptional circumstances, making it effectively an extreme insurance policy for Melbourne. Had this been the original intention, it would never have been built.
Western Corridor Recycling Project	2007	Qld state government, national government	Business case undertaken but little rigour in estimating benefits; assessed as an insurance policy	Pricing of produced water determined six months after the decision to build. Relied on $408m national government grant. Now fully mothballed. Should not have been built.
Canberra Cotter Dam Expansion	2007	ACT territory government, national government	Yes, assessed as an insurance policy; initial cost estimate deficient	Has measurably increased the water security of the national capital. More cost-effective options were available, but they were judged politically unacceptable.

Sources: Horne (2018), plus author's comments

change in water security risk (Ben David, 2013; VAGO, 2013). Water security risks could have been well managed at much lower cost to the urban water consumer (Horne, 2018).

Water infrastructure investments and regulation making in the MDB

Politics and politicians have always been central in the collective decision making in the MDB (Horne, 2014, 2017a). Before 2007, detailed technical studies informed policy outcomes. The unanimous decision-making rule of the MDB Commission meant that any member government could veto a proposed course of action without a need to even argue a case. After the passage of the 2007 national Water Act, a new Basin Plan was put in place in 2012, and by 2014 a new environmental watering strategy and water trading rules were agreed. These were important reforms, with important implications for both irrigators and the environment.

But rather than taking actions to support their agreement to the MDB Basin Plan, politicians and governments continued to challenge aspects of the Water Act reforms. In 2015, at the national level, a limit was placed on the MDB market-based buybacks that had been occurring since 2007. Open tenders for on-market purchases ceased in 2016. These tenders had been the most cost-effective way of purchasing water for the environment (Grafton & Horne, 2014; Grafton et al., 2016; Zuo, Qiu, & Wheeler, 2019). Purchases under the buyback scheme virtually ceased in 2014 when the new conservative national government (which had promulgated the reforms in 2006–07 under different leadership) shifted focus from buy-backs to very expensive on-farm purchases and 'strategic purchases' (Australian Government, 2018). The on-farm purchases had been used from the outset in conjunction with market tenders, and could be seen as the price of getting the basin-wide water rebalancing project supported in the community, as the purchases effectively subsidized private on-farm infrastructure investment. But over time value-for-money use of public funds ceased to be a major consideration in public investment. While water purchases for the environment continued, they slowed dramatically.

While the veto power of an individual state government under the MDB Commission arrangements was much reduced with the formation of the MDB Authority, the role that was eventually agreed for the state ministers in the MDB Ministerial Council in the 2007 Water Act has provided ongoing opportunities to slow down the rebalancing of water to the environment. The acceptance of an 'adjustment mechanism' (MDBA, 2019a) in determining the overall quantity of water rights to be transferred to the environment in practice appears to be allowing a reduction in the amount of actual water that needed to be transferred to an environmental account. To date, it has materially slowed the rebalancing process. Half of the adjustment mechanism, which allows more water to transferred to the environment if there is an increase in on-farm water use efficiency, has rarely been mentioned, let alone used, illustrating the one-sided intent of governments and ministers.

NSW government actions on key issues, such as water allocation rules in catchment-specific water plans and compliance with and enforcement of those plans, is also undermining efforts to ensure water availability for the environment, and illustrates the emerging concern. In 2017, a high-profile TV documentary revealed major compliance and enforcement issues in the northern MDB in NSW (Horne, 2017b; Matthews, 2017). Seven governmental reviews that followed the airing of this documentary highlighted systemic problems in water administration in NSW. It is clear to anyone who has been involved in water administration that many of the key actions could only have occurred with at least tacit political support. Moreover, the NSW's 2012 Barwon-Darling water-sharing plan was clearly inconsistent with the Basin Plan (Natural Resources Commission, 2019). At the national level, there were completely inappropriate comments by the national water minister (who was also Australia's deputy prime minister), (Hannam, 2018), which highlight that poor political behaviour in NSW was not isolated.

At the subsequent MDB Ministerial Council Meeting, in December 2017,

> Ministers agreed that it was important that all Australians had confidence that the rules and regulations governing water use in the Murray–Darling Basin were being enforced and complied with. They acknowledged that this confidence had been eroded by allegations of theft of water and inadequate enforcement of the rules, particularly in the northern part of the Basin. (MDBA, 2017a)

But the political commitment to implement the legal intent of the 2007 Water Act and the MDB Plan still appears to be lacking, or at most tepid. For example, in 2018 the NSW water minister threatened that NSW would withdraw from the MDB Plan processes (Sullivan, 2019). The July 2019 MDBA report card on implementation of the plan provides further evidence: implementation of water resource planning, the sustainable diversion limit (SDL) adjustment mechanism and the northern basin initiative are all progressing more slowly than expected (MDBA, 2019b). There is ongoing concern that governments and individual politicians are not committed to ensure that policy is implemented effectively. Ministers have been at the forefront of decisions to weaken the operation of the Basin Plan and to undermine the process of rebalancing water use between environment and social and economic ends. These trade-offs are notoriously difficult to negotiate, and politicians and their governments have track records of doing their best to not implement actions they have previously agreed (see e.g. Horne, 2017a). For example, the national government's 'water grid' initiative, as outlined in public documents (e.g., McCormack, 2019) appears at odds with key elements of national water policy, and with the fundamental notion that in many places (including the MDB) water use has reached or exceeded a sustainable level. This approach undermines both transparency and certainty in decision making.

The implementation of the Basin Plan over its first six years in operation was effective in parts (for example, putting in place market and water trading rules), but in other parts quite unconvincing (such as rules applying to water allocations in NSW, and completion and implementation of effective and complying water resource plans in a timely fashion), in part reflecting inadequate state government political support. The independent panel review, set up *inter alia* to review compliance with the Basin Plan, suggests we should be 'less sanguine' about a number of states meeting their commitments (MDBA, 2017b). The MDBA July 2019 report card (2019b) on implementation suggests that progress in implementing the water resource plans continues to be very slow, with only one of 33 in place at the end of June 2019, the planned time for completion. The success of the Basin Plan will depend very much on the overall quality of these plans and how they are implemented. In June 2017 the Council of Australian Governments (COAG, 2017) reaffirmed its commitment to delivering the Basin Plan on time and in full, but it is already clear this will not occur.

It felt the need to do so again in August 2019 (COAG, 2019). Table 2 provides examples of how, since 2013, the political process has been used to slow efforts towards timely implementation of the Basin Plan.

These examples show that legislation and agreements between governments are simply not enough to get the job done. The mix of responsibilities has given both state governments and the national government opportunities to reduce their effective commitment to the Basin Plan, while still making public statements of that commitment. The core issue is not the Basin Plan per se but the commitment of political leaders to achieve the outcomes embedded in the plan – particularly the cost-effective reallocation of water

Table 2. Actions slowing implementation of the Basin Plan.

Issue	Comment
Tender-based 'buy-back' program to drive rebalancing water available for the environment	• The program spearheaded initial rebalancing, with 1094 LTAY held by the CEWH at the end of 2012, as the Basin Plan was put in place. This program was the most cost-effective and timely way to undertake the rebalancing. • In 2014, after a change in national government, water purchasing focus moved to infrastructure investments. • In 2015 the national government introduced a cap of 1500 GL on buybacks. But with the 'buy-back' progress effectively shut down, water purchased through this program remains at only 1227 GL LTAY. • **Political decisions led to mothballing the most efficient buy-back method, slowing water purchases for the environment**
Accreditation of new water resource plans	• 33 water resource plans required. Flagged in the 2007 Water Act, with timeline of June 2019 settled in 2012. • As of the end of June 2019, one accredited. • New commitment that key aspects be in place by June 2019. • **State political failure to commit to get the job done, despite over a decade (2007 Water Act) of notice. NSW underperformance stands out.**
Recovery of environmental water by June 2019	• As of the end of July 2019, 1952 GL held by CEWH, and around 160 GL held by state instrumentalities, compared to an initial overall target of 2750 GL. • **Reaching the target was slowed by national government and MDB Ministerial Council intervention.**
Efficacy of SDL adjustment mechanism constraints strategy	• Introduced in 2015 as a means on one hand to reduce demand for environmental water by increasing use efficiency, and to increase availability of environmental water by increasing agriculture efficiency. • Timeline for completion of projects: 2024. • Increasingly looks like a one-sided effort to reduce environmental water availability, and to slow reform. • Less than 1 GL has been recovered to date, but water recovery sought through 'supply contribution' has been set at 605 GL, pushing the recovery deadline out to 2024 – and even that timeline looks ambitious. • **Efficacy is not yet established.**
Compliance and enforcement	• Expectations are set out clearly in the Basin Plan. • The NSW state government has been exposed for moving in the opposite direction. • The 'no meter, no pump' approach is not in place in northern MDB as of March 2019. • **The jury is still out on state commitment to compliance and enforcement.**

Sources: Australian Government (2019); COAG (2019); Department of Agriculture and Water Resources (2019); MDBA (2019a, 2019b); author's comments. Notes: LTAY = long term average yield; CEWH = Commonwealth Environmental Water Holder.

to the environment, which requires efficient water purchasing programmes by the national government and effective compliance and enforcement of the plan by both state governments and the MDBA.

Closing the gap: rhetoric and water services to indigenous communities

In line with overall good urban water standards throughout Australia, small regional communities in most of Australia have reliable, safe water. But the exceptions are more numerous in remote and very remote communities, where many indigenous Australians live (Hall, Mott, & Hoy, 2018). The Productivity Commission's 2016 report on overcoming indigenous disadvantage states that the most recent new information on indicator 10.3 (access to clean water, functional sewerage and electricity services) is from 2006 (SCRGSP, 2016), suggesting that little priority is accorded to this area. The backlog of critical water- and sewerage-related infrastructure needed by remote indigenous communities in the Northern Territory (NT) was elsewhere estimated at $365m (IA, 2015), and little has changed since then. The question remains as to why these issues were not sorted out long ago (Fien & Charlesworth, 2012), particularly given the cross-party political support for 'overcoming indigenous disadvantage' on a range of social outcomes. The answer at some levels is more complex than it appears at first sight. The size of Australia and the spread of indigenous communities means one approach is not likely to fit all, and certainly the approaches taken by different governments to sorting out the problem are not fully consistent.

Table 3 aggregates data for 260 larger indigenous communities across northern and central Australia, covering four states and a territory. It covers around 80,000 inhabitants (around 0.25% of the Australian population) in communities that have garnered government attention (individual populations range from around 100 to over 4000). The size of communities clearly matters, as does remoteness, particularly in relation to standard operating and maintenance issues. History also matters. Many communities are only now starting to emerge from lengthy periods of neglect. There is also a question regarding the extent that the government should be responsible for very small communities, particularly those on now privately owned indigenous land, which in itself has delayed action.

The major government-owned water services corporations in the NT and South Australia now provide services to many of the larger indigenous communities in the two jurisdictions. Water quality and availability are still sub-par in some communities, but progress is being made through subsidized interventions (Power and Water Corporation, 2018; SA Water, 2019). The brake on progress in both cases is the speed at which both governments are prepared to tackle the investment backlog, and their ability to put in place operational and maintenance regimes that are resilient. Detailed involvement of communities in investment planning and maintenance is central to sustained progress. The NT's water service provider publishes detailed water quality reports, but the NT and Australian governments have been slow to underwrite sustained improvement in access to reliable, safe water.

In 2015, the Centre for Appropriate Technology Limited (CAT, 2016) undertook a detailed survey of community infrastructure in 400 small indigenous communities in the NT, including housing, electricity, water, sewerage and communications issues.

Table 3. Characteristics of water service arrangements for remote and very remote indigenous communities in Australia.

State*	Coverage	Recent Actions	Comment
Northern Territory	Under contract to NT government, NT Power and Water Corporation's not-for-profit subsidiary, Indigenous Essential Services (IES), provides water and wastewater services to 72 remote communities (38,000 customers) and 66 outstations; 95% of the water is from bores.	Smart water meters were installed at nine communities to focus on leak detection, substantially reducing water use. Focus on upgrading water quality to Australian Drinking Water Guidelines (ADWG).	Water quality improving but not yet fully meeting ADWGs. Infrastructure backlog remains. Heavily reliant on bores. Latest water quality report is from 2015–16. Housing program exposing inadequate water supply. Unfunded depreciation charge illustrates ongoing shortcomings.
Western Australia	Around 300 remote communities in total, with around 18,000 inhabitants. Around 90 of these communities (with around 11,000 inhabitants) are served under state government Remote Area Essential Services program. Focus is on larger indigenous communities.	Undertaking urgent infrastructure upgrades to address public health problems (hazardous chemicals, high nitrate and uranium concentrations, and water-borne diseases) and achieve compliance with ADWG. Focus on the Pilbara and Kimberly areas. Starting to use mobile apps. Strong indigenous involvement in delivery.	Instances of water quality below ADWG. Debate over the viability of very small communities and whether the public sector should be accountable for water quality and other service provision in those very small communities, which are on land owned by indigenous groups.
Queensland	Remote and very remote communities, including many island communities served in the main by the 16 indigenous councils (with around 21,000 inhabitants).	State-funded Indigenous Councils Critical Infrastructure Program ($120m over four years) addressing water and wastewater infrastructure deficiencies in the16 indigenous local councils.	Slow progress being made. Not all water facilities producing ADWG compliant outcomes. Reporting is often late, and data availability poor. Communities heavily reliant on state and federal funding grants.
South Australia	SA Water provides services to 21 remote Aboriginal communities, serving around 3000 inhabitants. Bores, rainwater and river sources, with mixture of desalination and UV treatments.	Increased number of communities covered by SA Water. National government has financed some capital works.	Compliant with AWDG but performance below metropolitan and country standards. Water quality shortfalls in communities recently added to responsibilities. Testing range more limited than in NT. No detailed survey of outcomes publicly available.
New South Wales	In 2008, the NSW Aboriginal Land Council entered into a partnership with the state government to provide joint recurrent funding for the operation, maintenance and monitoring of water and sewerage infrastructure in 62 eligible discrete Aboriginal communities across NSW, serving 6000 inhabitants. Many communities on the fringe of rural towns.	Agreements are negotiated between local ALCs and local councils to deliver services for the operation, maintenance and monitoring of water supply and sewerage services. As of February 2019, 42 communities had approved programmes to address backlogs in maintenance, special works and repairs. Twenty-one communities had water services on par with adjoining communities.	Overall, services appear to have improved, but no hard data from the first decade of operation of the Aboriginal Communities Water and Sewerage Program.

*The Australian government facilitated early stages of reform through the COAG Strategy on Water and Wastewater Services in Remote (including Indigenous) Communities. The program was funded ($52m) through the Australian government's Water for the Future programme. Grants were made to projects in all five areas.

Sources: Government of Western Australia (2018a, 2018b); Power and Water Corporation (2016, 2018); LGAQ (2019); Queensland Government (2019); SA Water (2019); WA Auditor General (2015); Water Corporation (2019); NSW Aboriginal Land Council (2019); author's comments.

These small homelands and outstations were home to around 5000 inhabitants on a regular basis. Table 4 shows significant issues in many of the small communities, but at a level that would be easily resolvable by a capital injection and closer ties between the service provider and the communities.

Available data do not allow us to chart progress in improving water quality across remote northern Australian indigenous communities in detail. But a high-level desktop analysis (Power and Water Corporation, 2016, 2018; CAT, 2016; Government of Western Australia, 2018a, 2018b; LGAQ, 2019 (including websites of listed communities); NSW Aboriginal Land Council, 2019; Queensland Government, 2019; SA Water, 2019; WA Auditor General, 2015; Water Corporation, 2019) suggests that

- Greater capital investment by governments in the most recent decade, by both national and state governments, has started to address the investment backlog to improve water quality (Australian Government, WA, NT, Qld and SA);
- Greater attention to outcomes, via greater monitoring (including remote monitoring) of performance, has commenced. There is an appreciation of the role that smart meters and software can play in keeping assets functioning as they should (WA, NT, SA);
- Greater involvement of indigenous workers in water service delivery is apparent (WA, NT, Qld and SA), but a nation-wide stocktake would make clear areas for joint actions;
- Overall, governments and political leaders have not given this matter the priority suggested by their rhetoric.

Safe water availability and improved sewerage services will improve health and educational outcomes (the latter through better school attendance). Community educational programs cost little and have potentially large gains. The unexplained question is why federal and state political leaders have not sought to put water quality and availability on the same footing as the rest of the community. More focus and greater resourcing are required, driven by political leadership. Use of smart meters could facilitate this transition. A spread of understanding around 'water wise' in schools, and linking water quality to health outcomes, will improve the prospect of long-term sustainability. A quid pro quo would be an upfront public investment in upgrading the capital stock and in ongoing training of indigenous maintenance operators. Such an upgrade could be undertaken on

Table 4. 2015 survey of Northern Territory small homelands and outstations.

401 homelands/outstations were surveyed.
290 were supplied by groundwater bores, and 40 piped by Power and Water from outside the community.
Resource agencies and Power and Water Corporation (the major NT water service provider) provide services to 93% of communities.
Total population: around 5000.
Bores are the key source of water, with only around 67% in good condition. 10% of properties are served by Power and Water pipeline reticulation. Water is carted to a small number of properties.
Around 15% of tanks inspected leaked or had damaged pipe fittings.
Around 25% had community water plans in place (largely put in place over a decade ago following national government investment).
Around 60% of water supplies were judged safe to drink and operate.
Around a quarter assisted with financing, and around half in actively managing operating and maintenance issues.

Source: Adapted from CAT (2016).

a stand-alone basis, but that seems unlikely given the parlous state of much remote indigenous housing stock.

Indigenous communities also have a role to play. Replacing 'free water' by paid services (a precondition of participation in the government-driven WA upgrading programme [Government of Western Australia, 2018b] should bring more attention to system faults and a behavioural shift towards valuing water.

Water-related disaster management: mitigation versus disaster relief

Australia regularly faces major storms and flood events. Damaging floods have affected large swathes of rural Australia, and many of its cities and towns have periodically experienced serious flooding, with all the associated disruption (Insurance Council of Australia, 2019; SGS Economics and Planning, 2016). Disaster management and recovery in Australia is the responsibility of individual states and territory governments in the first instance. The national government provides considerable financial assistance once an agreed financial cost threshold is reached. Both levels of government have spent heavily on disaster recovery efforts. Recovery processes are well established, and recovery funding substantial. Following widespread flooding in northern Australia in early 2019, this familiar pattern was repeated. In its 2019–20 budget, the national government foreshadowed establishment of a new emergency response fund, to provide assistance into the future (Parliament of the Commonwealth of Australia, 2019).

However, the same cannot be said of government investment in flood mitigation. While governments generally have provided generous assistance after a natural disaster, there has been little political and financial support to improve community resilience before the event. Governments spend about 3% of what they spend on post-disaster relief on disaster mitigation (PC, 2014b), despite a very strong case that greater government effort and involvement in mitigation would reduce the overall cost to the community (SGS Economics and Planning, 2016; Insurance Council of Australia, 2019; PC, 2014b). Australia has recently put in place a natural disaster risk reduction framework, which has identified investment strategies to reduce disaster risks over the period 2019–23 (National Resilience Taskforce, 2018), but funding to mitigate disaster risk, particularly flood risk, has been noticeably lacking. Why are governments so reluctant to spend on disaster mitigation programs, or put in place regulations that reduce future risk?

The first hurdle would appear to be a difficulty in having projects listed as priorities. Infrastructure Australia (IA, 2019) had only one risk-mitigation project on its February 2019 priority infrastructure list: the raising of the Warragamba dam wall and its link to the Hawkesbury Nepean Valley flood management strategy. A business case for this project is under development by the NSW government (WaterNSW, 2019). The Queensland Reconstruction Authority (2019) has also released a strategy document that will facilitate development of infrastructure proposals to respond to flood risks from possible extreme weather events in Queensland, *inter alia*.

The task of infrastructure bodies is to develop mitigation proposals that respond to risks of future flood events. A precursor in the case of floods is to understand whether a certain type of flood represents a once-in-20-years event or a once-in-100-years event, and how storm intensity is likely to change (Geoscience Australia, 2016). While impacts of climate change are apparently not showing up in data to 2013 (Handmer, Ladds, & Magee, 2018), we can expect that in many regions history will not be a good indicator of what to expect in the future. Basic science is key to underwriting good mitigation responses, but funding has been difficult to come by, in sharp contrast to how it has been set aside in the aftermath of many disasters, as noted above. Part of this antipathy reflects an ongoing struggle until recently to have the impacts of climate change adequately factored into the national policy debate, to the point that some key work has been left unfunded (Horne, 2018). Infrastructure Australia could immediately add funding flood risk information to the list of national infrastructure priorities.

But this provides only a partial explanation. State, territory and local governments are responsible for much of land use planning. Much of the flood-related damage arises directly from established land use approval processes. There is an ongoing tension between developers, who create risk by seeking to develop on the floodplain, and the public sector, insurance companies, households and businesses that must manage the risk after the initial development is approved. These processes have long been the subject of controversy. With a changing climate, poor historical land use decisions (like approving construction in flood zones) are in many cases made worse by, for example, elevated flood risk. Resolution of these issues is probably not possible. But it is clear that state, territory and local governments could use regulations to address future risk if they had access to up-to-date information to inform new approvals. How this information is used is another matter. Much depends on how risk-averse governments choose to be.

Dam management plans during floods are also critical. These activities also need to be based on the best information available. If climate change is materially changing flood risk, as it appears to be, this should be incorporated into flood management and dam management plans. Governments will need to ensure that the underlying data are based on the best science, and be forward looking. All of this sounds perfectly sensible, but the question is still how often these issues should be re-examined, and a clear articulation of the responsibility for funding and follow-through.

Australia's major urban water service providers (dominated by state government business enterprises) have all been actively engaged in climate risk management, and matters of storm and flood risk to their assets have largely been taken out of the political hands of the national and state governments (Horne, 2018). More difficult questions arise in the case of smaller water service providers. Once downscaling of climate models reaches a confidence level that provides actionable information, would this result in new responsibilities for state and local governments to acquit their duty of care? Is there a role for the national government in providing a database and modelling tools to ensure that all state and local governments can undertake consistent planning? Should Australia have national rules around use of flood zones? If probabilities of significant flooding have changed, how should legacy issues be managed? The implications are significant. COAG could play a role in this suite of issues, but states may object that issues around land use are constitutionally one of their core responsibilities. Under current administrative arrangements, politicians have a central role in understanding and funding the critical information requirement.

Discussion

Comments are regularly aired to the effect that Australia's infrastructure is inadequate, or there is a significant infrastructure deficit, or we need to spend more on it to drive economic growth, sustain high wages and underpin the richer society most Australians seek (Kaspura, 2016; Lowe, 2013; PC, 2014a; Turnbull, 2016). In some areas, such as transport, with increasing urban congestion, this may be true. But, as the case studies surveyed in this article illustrate in the water area, it is often not the availability of funding that is the issue but poor project selection resulting in poor value to the community for investments. Some infrastructure projects that are routinely ignored could easily be afforded if a number of less worthwhile projects had not been undertaken. A former Reserve Bank of Australia governor made it clear that how you choose projects is critically important, and that this needs to be appropriately arm's length from day-to-day politics (Stutchbury, Greber, & Maley, 2016). This section discusses proposals to improve the existing arrangements.

Divergent interests and poor infrastructure governance: improving transparency

The first case study, on large urban water supply augmentation, saw governments at the time being keen to be seen responding to an issue, rather than undertaking a careful analysis of the problem and following a set of criteria to determine the best value response (Horne, 2018). This is not surprising, as politicians generally seek to stay in power, rather than necessarily seeking to optimize national or state-based economic outcomes. While many of the desalination plants and Brisbane's large-scale Western Corridor Recycled Water Project (described in Table 1) are good examples of poor project selection, the ongoing Ord River irrigation project and the recently completed Broken Hill water pipeline underscore that they are not isolated cases (Dent & Ward, 2015; International Association of Hydrogeologists, 2018). Too many major water infrastructure decisions have delivered questionable value to the Australian public.

The fourth case study is similar in its outcome: political decision making is being driven by the wish to be seen to be acting when the community expects action, in the aftermath of a disaster. This event/response approach is followed even although it is well established that spending more on mitigation before the disaster will more than pay for itself after the disaster. The issue is a political unwillingness to provide budget funding to follow expert advice on infrastructure priorities to mitigate the impact of disasters such as floods.

These two case studies are a microcosm of the broader infrastructure debate. Governments at both the federal and state level started to grapple with project selection over a decade ago. At the national level, the government set up Infrastructure Australia in 2008, and strengthened its independence in 2014, to advise the government on key infrastructure priorities and the suitability of projects to be funded. There are now lists of worthy projects that have undergone benefit–cost analysis and business case development. But the major ongoing weakness is that neither major political party carefully follows the principles and processes that have been established. Governments continue to make infrastructure decisions and commitments to construct new infrastructure before undertaking a business case, including independent evaluation of costs and benefits. Some of these projects are not even mentioned on the extensive national priority project lists.

This is mirrored at the state level. Independent infrastructure advisors like Infrastructure NSW (established in 2011) and Infrastructure Victoria (established in 2015) appeared to be a step in the right direction, but the recommendations or approach embedded in the respective legislation is followed only when it is convenient, or across a range of projects the government determines. It is still regularly the case that basic information on major infrastructure projects is not transparently available, cannot be tested by non-government experts. In early 2019, for example, the NSW government announced the completion of a new 270 km water pipeline from the River Murray to Broken Hill, to improve the latter's urban water security. Prior to the release of the final business case in August 2019, after the completion of construction of the pipeline (NSW Department of Primary Industries, 2019), there was little information in the public domain as to how the NSW government arrived at its decision, including background technical reports. There were clear alternatives to the solution chosen, but there has been no discussion of them (International Association of Hydrogeologists, 2018). A more transparent process would have provided information on which a vigorous debate could have been conducted. Other states have not yet embraced even this level of independence, with infrastructure decisions generally a part of more closed cabinet processes.

The poor-value-for-money decisions identified in the first, second, and fourth case studies support the proposition that there should be deep concern about the processes followed in making these decisions, particularly in a world where all citizens are being implored to do more with less. No political party and no national or state government is immune from this criticism.

The question for the Australian community is whether it should accept these political decision-making processes any longer, or whether it is time to consider new processes. Are the governance arrangements in place to decide on what should be built adequate? That they are rarely followed by governments at the national or state level suggests that current arrangements are inadequate. One argument might be that in the overall scheme of things, our governments and politicians get most infrastructure decisions right, so we should accept the costs from the odd 'poor' decision in economic terms as one of the costs of democratic politics. The argument would be that we should accept these interventions up to a point, as politicians have a 'right' to be concerned about their interests even when from time to time they differ from those of the broader society. Those who take this view would probably say it has always been thus.

If the cost of poor decision making gets too large, the argument might run, society reacts by changing the governing political party. Of course, there are always many issues in election campaigns. Water issues are only high on the political agenda on limited occasions, such as in the latter stages of the Millennium drought (during 2006–07), and this may mean that significant issues with value for money or the viability of specific proposals go unnoticed and 'unpunished'. In the absence of governance reform, there is no reason to expect this to change. The most recent example is a campaign press release by the deputy prime minister during the 2019 national election suggesting that if the government won the election it would establish a new water authority to (among other things) build more dams and increase water availability for agriculture (McCormack, 2019). On the surface, it appears inconsistent with major aspects of current national water policy.

In a complex, very well-off society, with very short media attention spans, analysis and commentary quickly fall away in nearly every case. Occasionally, the opposition party may express a strong alternative opinion, and if elections bring a change of government, contracts or policies may be reversed. But this has rarely been the case in water infrastructure, and then it has been antithetic to the good use of prior investments or actions, as with the North-South Pipeline in Victoria (Melbourne Water, 2018).

Clearly, the water infrastructure projects discussed here are not without some merit and value to the community, but the opportunity cost and the actual ongoing costs can be very large. For example, if the Melbourne, Adelaide and Sydney desalination plant decisions (all undertaken without compelling business cases) had been left as technical augmentation decisions, the changes in project sizing and timing would have saved billions of dollars. This compels a comment that substantial public funds have been wasted on many projects with suboptimal social returns, as responses to political decisions to satisfy political needs rather than to boost water security or sustain economic performance. Under the current arrangements, these are 'legitimate' expenditures but at the same time quite puzzling in the context of discussion of improving the performance of the economy and the lack of funds to address, for example, water quality for remote indigenous communities (third case study). Eliminating unjustified infrastructure spending would allow other identified infrastructure priorities to be undertaken at a much earlier date, or allow existing services (such as urban water supply and sanitation services) to be provided at a much lower cost. This could be achieved by stronger requirements (backed by legislation) to be fulfilled before governments could commit to new projects.

Mandatory business case development and benefit–cost analysis

Establishing bipartisan political agreement to eschew making commitments to public funding of any water project prior to completion of a public business case, which includes professionally executed benefit–cost analysis, analysis of alternatives and stress testing of costs, would remove much of the poor performance identified in this article. This would make it more difficult for projects that are politically supported but otherwise of dubious value to society to be approved by the government.

Benefit–cost ratio requirements are not the whole answer, and on occasions can be misleading. In those cases, further analysis should be provided, with qualitative discussion of value. Many projects result in a net cost to society if only narrow direct costs and benefits are estimated. Projects relying on broader benefits should be subject to more intense scrutiny. The roll-out of the National Water Infrastructure Development Fund is a case where improved but far-from-perfect governance rules were put in place when it was announced. While commitments to specific projects were announced, commitments were subject to 'completion of business cases, final approvals and/or matching funding commitments from state governments' (National Water Grid Authority, 2019). For selected projects, public funds were provided for feasibility studies, which must demonstrate public value and adherence to the National Water Initiative. This approach provides improved transparency and takes examination of projects beyond vested interests pursuing noisy campaigns for specific projects, but it still remains to be seen how it is implemented in practice. Currently, at the national and state level, there are many infrastructure projects that are not referred to infrastructure advisory bodies until after decisions are announced. Government, through COAG, could strengthen existing arrangements by agreeing to project announcement rules overseen by auditors-general in all jurisdictions governing public-sector projects, requiring that no commitments be made to projects until a clear case of public value has been demonstrated, and other rules (such as adherence to the National Water Initiative) agreed in full.

Enhanced enforcement of rules rather than new decision makers?

The track record of governments and politicians actually implementing governance models they have agreed to implement on water infrastructure selection has been very patchy. There has been at best only partial application of its terms by state governments, although they are signatories to the National Water Initiative. Improving outcomes requires mandated approaches, such as the approach outlined above. For example, the rules could include

- A benefit–cost ratio greater than 1, using independent analysis. Any wider non-project benefits should be subject to transparent and detailed analysis.
- Full compliance with the National Water Initiative and the 2007 Water Act, the terms of which are clearly set out and open to transparent scrutiny. This should cover, for example, evidence of statutory water planning covering the project, water pricing consistent with full cost recovery, and clear evidence of environmental sustainability (COAG, 2004; Commonwealth of Australia, 2009; NRMMC, 2010). If subsidies are being proposed, their rationale needs to transparently documented.
- The national government should be required to be comfortable with the business case containing the above before it makes any financial contribution.

Reducing the role of politicians by entrenching the role of water regulators

A further question is whether there are additional areas where governments should entrust water infrastructure decisions to regulated service providers and the competition policy regulator. This tension is not new: in our political system we have a range of expert bodies, with a wide spectrum of varying independence from government, that provide advice to, and in some cases, make decisions on behalf of, the government. The Reserve Bank of Australia effectively makes decisions on monetary policy; the Australian Competition and Consumer Commission (at the national level) and independent competition policy providers make many decisions independent of the government in relation to many private and state-owned businesses (including water businesses); and experts administer many areas of government activities. For large urban water businesses, competition advice bodies such as the Independent Pricing and Regulatory Tribunal (IPART) in NSW and the Essential Services Commission (ESC) in Victoria now consider the case for supply augmentation as a part of determining the future revenue parameters of the regulated entity (see e.g. IPART, 2016, 2017). These are not decisions on which politicians have a comparative advantage. The form of supply augmentation would be left to price reviews. When these decisions are left to politicians, history suggests that the interest of the public is often ignored.

If governments announce commitments or pledges to construct or underwrite new infrastructure during election campaigns, or at other times, these promises should be tested after the election. This job could be entrusted either to the water service provider and regulator, as for most water infrastructure investment spending, or to the relevant infrastructure advisory body. This would help overcome a perplexing governance issue – the idea that election announcements have a status that means the public service should simply implement them as best it can, resulting in projects of dubious value being built. This approach challenges the view that winning elections confers authority on incoming governments to undertake economically or financially dubious projects that society can ill afford. The election 'commitment' and the election outcome should be only the first stages in a process to determine whether the project should be undertaken.

'Community standards' in remote indigenous communities

It is regularly posited that safe water supplies and effective sanitation for indigenous communities will assist greatly in delivering better health results in remote indigenous communities (Government of Western Australia, 2016; 2018a, 2018b; Power and Water Corporation, 2018; Rajapakse et al., 2018). But over the past two decades governments have been only half-hearted in addressing the issues raised in our third case study. Political rhetoric has dominated effective action. COAG should endorse the preparation of a business case immediately, with commitments to substantial new funding underwritten by national and state governments over five years (an indicative figure might be around $500 million), consequent on delivery of business cases, to deliver projects with good benefit–cost ratios. New ongoing revenue streams would come from introducing user payments for water and sanitation services, where this currently does not occur. The billions of dollars of poor investments in Cases 1 and 2 would have fully addressed the problems outlined in Case 3 many times over. Having a fixed timetable to achieve this outcome would put real pressure on all involved interests for action. Indigenous interests would need to be supportive with community education covering all that is necessary to sustain outcomes, including preparedness to pay for these services. The costs could be pegged to other costs (such as housing), but this would make clear the positive value of these services.

Currently the pace of upgrading water and sewerage service to remote communities is slow, and not commensurate with the stated public priority accorded to 'overcoming indigenous disadvantage'. Implementation of such a program would require a much-upgraded commitment by state water service providers, state governments, the national government, and communities (directly in relation to maintenance in particular and indirectly in relation to good hygiene practices). More than anything, it would require genuine political leadership.

Budget allocations and fit-for-purpose rules and information

The fourth case study poses specific issues around bringing budget funding by politicians closer to what might be characterized as 'society optimal'. At the national level, one approach would be to have Infrastructure Australia develop a short list of high-priority disaster mitigation projects. These would be funded jointly with the states, if the latter agree. The central aim is to give smaller projects a chance to compete against the very large transport projects that dominate existing lists, and to take such identification out of the hands of politicians and away from pressure from vested interests. In an era where flash flooding from extreme storm events is becoming a more regular occurrence, there is need for a greater national focus on land development rules. One element of the issue is examining the likely impact of changed weather patterns on existing structures, and management of new or heightened risks. Repurchasing private assets in some high-risk areas, as was done in Brisbane, is one approach to managing this issue (Brisbane City Council, 2016; Insurance Council of Australia, 2019). A second element is managing new land use developments in a manner consistent with societies' expectations. Regular updating of climate change risk (for example, updating information on 50- and 100-year flood zones) is one aspect of this issue. This requires adequate ongoing funding, which has not been available in recent years. The whole area of information and modelling (or soft infrastructure) requires more attention from infrastructure bodies and political leaders.

Conclusion

Australia's record on delivering good public policy outcomes in water is laudable, but increasingly in the face of climate change it should be striving to improve that performance. There is a real need to ensure that investments in water infrastructure achieve the best possible outcomes, not outcomes that address only or mainly political needs at the time decisions are made. This article questions whether the historic role of politicians in water decision making remains fit for purpose. It suggests that while changes have been introduced to improve decision making, further governance reforms are required. While not uniquely a water problem (similar problems arise in other sectors, particularly in transport infrastructure), it is very clear that current governance arrangements are not delivering the outcomes they should, and the problem in most cases is not primarily about funding adequacy. Stronger mandatory rules should be agreed by governments at COAG, and legislated at both state and national levels, to ensure that public expenditure on water infrastructure delivers better value for money to the community. Funding is an issue when the projects involve small, remote and dispersed indigenous communities not so able to make the noise used elsewhere to garner political support. Overcoming indigenous disadvantage can be given a major fillip by putting water services in remote communities on a par with the water services expected in urban Australia. The national government should agree to consider compelling projects directed at improving water services to remote indigenous communities under the Water Infrastructure Development Fund.

Disclosure statement

No potential conflict of interest was reported by the author.

References

ACCC (Australian Competition and Consumer Commission). (2019). *Water*. Retrieved from https://www.accc.gov.au/regulated-infrastructure/water

ACT Audit Office. (2015, June 24). *Enlarged cotter dam: cost and construction timing*. [Press release]. Australian Capital Territory, Canberra. Retrieved from https://www.audit.act.gov.au/__data/assets/pdf_file/0006/1179915/Media-release-Report-No-6-of-2015-Bulk-Water-Alliance.pdf

Australian Government. (2018). *Background information on significant Commonwealth strategic water purchases in 2017*. Retrieved from http://www.agriculture.gov.au/about/media-centre/on-the-record/background-significant-commonwealth-strategic-water-purchases-2017

Australian Government. (2019). *Environmental water holdings*. Retrieved from https://www.environment.gov.au/water/cewo/about/water-holdings

Ben David, R. (2013, July 29). *Paying for the Victorian desalination plant: A case study in regulatory ambiguity*. Paper presented at the Water 2013 Conference. Retrieved from https://www.esc.vic.gov.au/sites/default/files/documents/Paying-for-The-Victorian-Desalination-Plant.pdf

Brisbane City Council. (2016). *Brisbane's floodsmart future update 2016: Catchment floodplain management planning*. Retrieved from https://www.brisbane.qld.gov.au/sites/default/files/20161110-brisbanes-floodsmart-future-update.pdf

Carr, R., Marsden, J., & Jacob, P. (2012). *Case study: Governance, decision processes and pricing: Implications for potable water recycling. Case Study #1 (of 3): South East Queensland Western corridor recycled water project*. Retrieved from http://www.australianwaterrecycling.com.au/_literature_147772/Case_Study_1_%E2%80%93_Western_Corridor_Recycled_Water_Project

CAT (Centre for Appropriate Technology Ltd). (2016). *The Northern territory homelands and outstations assets and access review final report 2016*. Retrieved from https://static1.squarespace.com/static/5450868fe4b09b217330bb42/t/57f6f64746c3c4ab7345af96/1475802710933/Final-Master-HOAAR-Report-Oct2016-1.pdf

COAG (Council of Australian Governments). (2004). *Intergovernmental agreement on the National Water Initiative*. Canberra. Retrieved from https://web.archive.org/web/20090702031615/http://www.coag.gov.au/coag_meeting_outcomes/2004-06-25/index.cfm

COAG. (2017, June 9). *COAG meeting Communiqué* [Press release]. Retrieved from https://www.coag.gov.au/meeting-outcomes/coag-meeting-communique-9-june-2017

COAG. (2019). *Communiqué (Cairns – 9 August 2019)*. Cairns. Retrieved from https://www.coag.gov.au/sites/default/files/communique/coag-communique-august-9-2019.pdf

Commonwealth of Australia. (2009). Water Act 2007. Reprinted on 1 January 2009 (with amendments up to Act No. 139, 2008). Commonwealth of Australia.

Crase, L., Pawsey, N., & Cooper, B. (2014). The closure of Melbourne's North–South pipeline: A case of hydraulic autarky. *Economic Papers: A Journal of Applied Economics and Policy*, *33*(2), 115–122. doi:10.1111/1759-3441.12076

Dent, J., & Ward, M. B. (2015). *Food bowl or folly? The economics of irrigating Northern Australia*. Monash University Department of Economics Discussion Paper 02/15.

Department of Agriculture and Water Resources (2019, 8 July). Murray-darling basin plan. Canberra. Retrieved from http://www.agriculture.gov.au/water/mdb/basin-plan

Fien, J., & Charlesworth, E. (2012). Why isn't it solved? Factors affecting improvements in housing outcomes in remote Indigenous communities in Australia. *Habitat International*, *36*(1), 20–25. doi:10.1016/j.habitatint.2011.05.002

Geoscience Australia. (2016). *Australian rainfall and runoff*. Retrieved from http://arr.ga.gov.au

Government of Western Australia. (2016, July). *Resilient families, strong communities: A roadmap for regional and remote Aboriginal communities*. Perth. Retrieved from https://regionalservicesreform.wa.gov.au/sites/regionalservicesreform.wa.gov.au/files/pdfs/CS671_RSRU_RoadMapDocument_Web_v3.pdf

Government of Western Australia. (2018a). *Remote area essential services program*. Retrieved from http://www.drd.wa.gov.au/projects/Health/Pages/Remote-Area-Essential-Services-Program.aspx

Government of Western Australia. (2018b). *Essential and municipal services upgrade program*. Retrieved from https://regionalservicesreform.wa.gov.au/p/essential-and-municipal-services-upgrade-program

Grafton, R. Q., & Horne, J. (2014). Water markets in the Murray-Darling Basin. *Agricultural Water Management*, *145*, 61–71. doi:10.1016/j.agwat.2013.12.001

Grafton, R. Q., Horne, J., & Wheeler, S. A. (2016). On the marketisation of water: Evidence from the Murray-Darling Basin, Australia. *Water Resources Management*, *30*(3), 913–926. doi:10.1007/s11269-015-1199-0

Hall, N., Mott, S., & Hoy, W. (2018, November 21). Getting clean drinking water into remote Indigenous communities means overcoming city thinking. *The Conversation*. Retrieved from https://theconversation.com/getting-clean-drinking-water-into-remote-indigenous-communities-means-overcoming-city-thinking-106701

Handmer, J., Ladds, M., & Magee, L. (2018, April). Updating the costs of disasters in Australia. *Australian Journal of Emergency Management*. Retrieved from https://knowledge.aidr.org.au/media/5506/ajem-33-2-17.pdf

Hannam, P. (2018, August 28). Death certificate: Ex-water chief slams Barnaby Joyce's drought plan. *Sydney Morning Herald*. Retrieved from https://www.smh.com.au/environment/sustainability/death-certificate-ex-water-chief-slams-barnaby-joyce-s-drought-plan-20180828-p500an.html

Horne, J. (2013). Economic approaches to water management in Australia. *International Journal of Water Resources Development*, *29*(4), 526–543. doi:10.1080/07900627.2012.712336

Horne, J. (2014). The 2012 Murray-Darling Basin Plan: Issues to watch. *International Journal of Water Resources Development*, *30*(1), 152–163. doi:10.1080/07900627.2013.787833

Horne, J. (2017a). The politics of water reform and environmental sustainability in the Murray–Darling Basin. *Water International*, *42*(8), 1000–1021. doi:10.1080/02508060.2017.1412201

Horne, J. (2017b, December 15). *A low-water mark for the Murray-Darling Basin: Political commitment to the Basin Plan is long overdue*. Canberra: Policy Forum.

Horne, J. (2018). Resilience in major Australian cities: Assessing capacity and preparedness to respond to extreme weather events. *International Journal of Water Resources Development*, *34*(4), 632–651. doi:10.1080/07900627.2016.1244049

Horne, J., & Grafton, R.Q. (2019). The Australian water markets story – transformation incrementally. In J. Luetjens, M. Mintrom, & P. 't Hart (Eds.), *Successful public policy: Lessons from Australia and New Zealand*. Canberra: ANU Press.

IA (Infrastructure Australia). (2015, January). *Northern Australia Audit*. Infrastructure for a Developing North Report. Retrieved from https://www.infrastructureaustralia.gov.au/policy-publications/publications/Northern-Australia-Infrastructure-Audit.aspx

IA. (2019). *Infrastructure priority list*. Retrieved from https://www.infrastructureaustralia.gov.au/projects/infrastructure-priority-list.aspx#anc_ipl

Insurance Council of Australia. (2019). *Protecting communities against flood: Where is more work needed?* Retrieved from https://disasters.org.au/top20floodproneelectorates

International Association of Hydrogeologists. (2018, April 16). Submission by International Association of Hydrogeologists. To: Productivity Commission. On: Issues paper March 2018: Murray-Darling Basin Plan: Five-year assessment. Retrieved from: https://www.pc.gov.au/inquiries?query=&f.Topics%7CM=policy&sort=relevance&sort=date&sort=date&sort=date&sort=date&collection=productivity-commission-sub-web&f.Inquiry%7CT=murray-darling%20basin%20plan&f.Inquiries%20to%20show%7CH=completed&start_rank=111&sort=date

IPART (Independent Pricing and Regulatory Tribunal). (2016). *Prices for Sydney water corporation from 1 July 2016*. Retrieved from https://www.ipart.nsw.gov.au/files/sharedassets/website/shared-files/investigation-legislative-requirements-water-metropolitan-water-sydney-water-corporation-pricing-investigation-commencing-from-1-july-2016/fact_sheet_-_sydney_water_price_review_-_residential_customers_-_14_june_2016.pdf

IPART. (2017). *IPART submission to the productivity commission's issues paper on national water reform*. Retrieved from https://www.ipart.nsw.gov.au/files/sharedassets/website/shared-files/pricing-reviews-water-services-metro-water-water-pricing-tribunal-external-submissions/ipart-submission-to-the-productivity-commission-issues-paper-on-national-water-reform.pdf

IPART. (2019). *Water*. Retrieved from https://www.ipart.nsw.gov.au/Home/Industries/Water

Kaspura, A. (2016). *Engineers Australia infrastructure investment update 2016*. Canberra: Institution of Engineers Australia. Retrieved from http://newsroom.engineersaustralia.org.au/sites/default/files/resources/national_infrastructure_investment_report_0.pdf

LGAQ (Local Government Association of Queensland). (2019). Indigenous Councils. Retrieved from https://www.lgaq.asn.au/indigenous

Lowe, P. (2013). *Speech to the IARIW-UNSW conference on productivity measurement, drivers and trends, Sydney – 26 November 2013*. Retrieved from http://www.rba.gov.au/speeches/2013/sp-dg-261113.html

Matthews, K. (2017). *Independent investigation into NSW water management and compliance: Final report*. Sydney. Retrieved from: https://www.industry.nsw.gov.au/data/assets/pdf-file/0019/131905/Matthews-final-report-NSW-water-management-and-compliance.pdf

McCormack, M. (2019). *New era: Liberal and Nationals to deliver National Water Grid* [Press release]. Retrieved from https://www.michaelmccormack.com.au/media-releases/2019/4/30/new-era-liberal-amp-nationals-to-deliver-national-water-grid

MDBA (Murray-Darling Basin Authority). (2017a, December 19). *Communique: Murray–Darling Basin ministers meet in Albury*. Retrieved from https://www.mdba.gov.au/media/mr/communique-murray-darling-basin-ministers-meet-albury

MDBA. (2017b, November). *The Murray–Darling Basin water compliance review (Containing reports by the Murray–Darling Basin authority and the independent review panel)*. Retrieved from Canberra: https://www.mdba.gov.au/sites/default/files/pubs/MDB-Compliance-Review-Final-Report.pdf

MDBA. (2019a). *Sustainable diversion limit adjustment mechanism*. Retrieved from https://www.mdba.gov.au/basin-plan-roll-out/sustainable-diversion-limits/sdlam

MDBA. (2019b). *July 2019 report card*. Canberra: Author. Retrieved from https://www.mdba.gov.au/sites/default/files/pubs/MDBA%20July%202019%20Report%20Card_1.pdf

Melbourne Water. (2018, November). *North–South Pipeline*. Retrieved from https://www.melbournewater.com.au/community-and-education/about-our-water/water-supply/north-south-pipeline

National Resilience Taskforce. (2018). *National Disaster Risk Reduction Framework*. Canberra. Retrieved from https://www.homeaffairs.gov.au/emergency/files/national-disaster-risk-reduction-framework.pdf

National Water Grid Authority. (2019). *Water infrastructure projects*. Retrieved from https://www.nationalwatergrid.gov.au/nwi-development-fund/water-infrastructure-projects

Natural Resources Commission. (2019, September). *Final report. Review of the water sharing plan for the Barwon-Darling unregulated and alluvial water sources 2012*. Sydney. Retrieved from https://www.nrc.nsw.gov.au/announcements/news-bdwsp-final-report

NRMMC (Natural Resource Management Ministerial Council). (2010). *National Water Initiative pricing principles*. Retrieved from Canberra: http://www.agriculture.gov.au/water/policy/nwi/pricing-principles

NSW Aboriginal Lands Council. (2019). *Water and sewerage*. Aboriginal Communities Water and Sewerage Program. Retrieved from http://alc.org.au/nswalc-in-the-community/water-and-sewerage.aspx

NSW Department of Primary Industries. (2019). *Business case: Broken Hill long-term water supply solution, 31 March 2016 (first published August 2019)*. Sydney. Retrieved from https://drive.google.com/drive/folders/1DvuX3-7SEIN5rTeY2_p6_hLm73KpLMjo

Parliament of the Commonwealth of Australia. (2019). *Emergency Response Fund Bill 2019*. Canberra: Explanatory Memorandum. Retrieved from https://parlinfo.aph.gov.au/parlInfo/download/legislation/ems/r6390_ems_53e96fa8-8d78-471d-b6b5-266e4e93871a/upload_pdf/716910.pdf;fileType=application%2Fpdf

PC (Productivity Commission). (2014a). *Public infrastructure: Inquiry report no. 71*. Canberra. Retrieved from http://www.pc.gov.au/__data/assets/pdf_file/0003/137280/infrastructure-volume1.pdf

PC. (2014b). *Natural disaster funding arrangements volume 1 and 2*. Retrieved from Canberra: http://www.pc.gov.au/inquiries/completed/disaster-funding/report/disaster-funding-volume1.pdf

Power and Water Corporation. (2016). *Indigenous essential services drinking water quality report 2015-16*. Retrieved from Darwin: https://www.powerwater.com.au/__data/assets/pdf_file/0011/147359/Indigenous_Essential_Services_Drinking_Water_Quality_Report_2015-16.pdf

Power and Water Corporation. (2018). *Indigenous essential services annual report 2017-18*. Retrieved from https://www.powerwater.com.au/news_and_publications/reports/indigenous_essential_services_annual_reports

Queensland Government. (2019, *22 July*). Indigenous Councils Critical Infrastructure Program (ICCIP). Retrieved from: https://www.dlgrma.qld.gov.au/local-government/grants/indigenous-councils-critical-infrastructure-program.html

Queensland Reconstruction Authority. (2019). *Queensland Disaster Resilience Mitigation Investment Framework February 2019*. Brisbane. Retrieved from https://www.qra.qld.gov.au/sites/default/files/2019-01/queensland_disaster_resilience_mitigation_framework_-_february_2019.pdf

Rajapakse, J., Rainer-Smith, S., Millar, G. J., Grace, P., Hutton, A., Hoy, W., ... Hudson, B. (2018). Unsafe drinking water quality in remote Western Australian Aboriginal communities. *Geographical Research*. doi:10.1111/1745-5871.12308

SA Water. (2019). *Remote aboriginal communities*. Retrieved from https://www.sawater.com.au/community-and-environment/our-water-and-sewerage-systems/our-networks/regional-south-australia-water-supply/remote-communities

SCRGSP(Steering Committee for the Review of Government Service Provision). (2016). *Overcoming indigenous disadvantage: Key indicators 2016*. Canberra. Retrieved from: https://www.pc.gov.au/research/ongoing/overcoming-indigenous-disadvantage/2016/report-documents/oid-2016-overcoming-indigenous-disadvantage-key-indicators-2016-report.pdf

Seqwater. (2014). *Annual report 2013-14 for the Western Corridor Recycled Water Scheme: recycled water management plan*. Retrieved from https://www.seqwater.com.au/s3fs-public/PDF%20Documents/Annual%20Reports/Western%20Corridor%20Recycled%20Water%20Scheme%20%28WCRWS%29%20Annual%20Report%20to%20~%2014.pdf

SGS Economics and Planning. (2016, November). *At what cost? Mapping where natural perils impact on economic growth and communities*. Retrieved from https://www.iag.com.au/sites/default/files/Documents/Business%20sustainability/At%20what%20cost%20%20mapping%20where%20natural%20perils%20impact%20economic%20growth%20and%20communities.pdf

South Australia. (2019). *Murray-Darling Basin Royal Commission: Report*. Adelaide. Retrieved from: https://www.mdbrc.sa.gov.au/sites/default/files/murray-darling-basin-royal-commission-report.pdf?v=1548898371

Stutchbury, M., Greber, J., & Maley, K. (2016, September 7). RBA governor Glenn Stevens full exit interview. *Australian Financial Review*. Retrieved from http://www.afr.com/news/rba-interview-series/rba-governor-glenn-stevens-full-exit-interview-20160907-graws7

Sullivan, K. (2019). *ABC news: Murray-Darling Basin Plan 'untenable' says NSW, as inspector-general says more corruption wouldn't surprise*. Retrieved from https://www.abc.net.au/news/2019-08-05/murray-darling-basin-plan-untenable-says-nsw/11382396

Turnbull, M. (2016, February 17th). *Launch of the Infrastructure Australia Plan*. Brisbane. Retrieved from http://malcolmturnbull.com.au/media/launch-of-the-infrastructure-australia-plan-brisbane

VAGO (Victorian Auditor General's Office). (2013). *Auditor-general's report on the annual financial report of the State of Victoria, 2012–13*. Melbourne. Retrieved from https://www.audit.vic.gov.au/report/auditor-generals-report-annual-financial-report-state-victoria-2012-13?section=31029–5-public-private-partnerships&show-sections=1#5-public-private-partnerships

WA Auditor General. (2015). *Delivering essential services to remote aboriginal communities (Report 8, May 2015)*. Perth, Western Australia. Retrieved from https://audit.wa.gov.au/wp-content/uploads/2015/05/report2015_08-AbServices.pdf

Water Corporation. (2009). *Water forever: Towards climate resilience*. Retrieved from http://www.watercorporation.com.au/-/media/files/about-us/planning-for-the-future/water-forever-50-year-plan.pdf?la=en

Water Corporation. (2018). *Annual report 2018*. Perth. Retrieved from https://www.watercorporation.com.au/-/media/files/residential/about-us/our-performance/annual-report-2018/water%20corporation%202018%20annual%20report.pdf

Water Corporation. (2019). *Remote aboriginal communities get water service upgrade* [Media release]. Retrieved from https://www.watercorporation.com.au/about-us/news/media-statements/media-release/remote-aboriginal-communities—water-service-upgrade

WaterNSW. (2019). *Warragamba Dam raising*. Retrieved from https://www.waternsw.com.au/projects/greater-sydney/warragamba-dam-raising

Wright, J. (2016, April 12). *Oral reflections on SA desalination*. doi:10.1016/j.amjms.2015.11.019

Zuo, A., Qiu, F., & Wheeler, S. A. (2019). Examining volatility dynamics, spillovers and government water recovery in Murray-Darling Basin water markets. *Resource and Energy Economics, 58*, 101113. Retrieved from http://www.sciencedirect.com/science/article/pii/S0928765518304585

OPEN ACCESS

Rent-seeking behaviour and regulatory capture in the Murray-Darling Basin, Australia

R. Quentin Grafton and John Williams

ABSTRACT

We examine water governance in the Murray-Darling Basin using the frameworks of rent-seeking and regulatory capture. These frameworks are used to evaluate two government programmes intended to ensure an environmentally sustainable level of water diversions in the basin: targeted one-on-one purchases of water entitlements from designated sellers; and subsidies for irrigation infrastructure to increase irrigation efficiency. Deficiencies in delivering the stated environmental goals of both programmes, and questions about their 'value for money', are highlighted. Specific recommendations are provided about how to mitigate both rent-seeking and regulatory capture of water reform initiatives in large river basins.

Ministers and their senior officials share a common interest in success, which can lead to more influence for the Minister and the department, and improved prospects for its senior officers. They also share a basis for mutual antagonism towards the Minister's political opponents, whose criticisms may reflect on the department as well as the Minister. There is a natural human inclination for a subordinate to seek to give effect to the wishes of a superior, and policy can be sufficiently broad and elastic to allow public servants to exercise considerable discretion.

G. E. Fitzgerald (1989, p. 130), chair of the Commission of Inquiry into Possible Illegal Activities and Associated Police Misconduct

Introduction

A long-standing literature exists in relation to how non-state actors are able to influence, and even control, expenditures and priorities of states for their own particular benefit or interests (Buchanan & Tullock, 1962; Downs, 1957). This decision-making challenge exists not only in authoritarian states but also in well-established and high-functioning democracies.

In democracies, many political parties chose to identify with particular groups or interests (Hudson, 1995). The benefit of partisan identification by political parties is that it increases their likelihood of being elected to office through more votes, campaign funds or other assistance from their partisans. The benefit to partisan voters is that the self-identified parties that they support and influence, and that are elected into office, may provide them with favourable regulation, legislation, or pecuniary benefits through the tax and transfer system.

This political process of 'tit for tat' (Axelrod, 1980), whereby political parties reward their supporters, has a long history in democracies. Indeed, the process of 'buying' votes or securing support is most obvious in election promises or commitments (Congleton, 1989). This is because it is in the interest of political parties to 'signal', sometimes in coded language (Hindess, 2014), to their supporters the expected benefits of voting for them. One factor that prevents politics from degenerating into an orgy of self-interested, partisan policies is that electorally successful political parties typically need to win over multiple interests, as represented by the 'median voter' (Congleton & Bennett, 1995; Holcombe, 1989). Some voters, at least, also care about the national and public interest, and also good governance and competence, and this may supersede their immediate personal interests in how they vote.

A transparent comparison of the costs and benefits of public decision making, with consideration of who wins and who loses, is necessary to determine whether government decisions are in the public or national interest.[1] Indeed, a hallmark of good governance is that such evaluations are undertaken, at least for all larger programmes and projects, with clear and factual explanations as to why decisions are made, and who benefits. By contrast, a failure to provide transparent decision making creates opportunities for particular interests to influence government decision making that may benefit only a few, possibly at the expense of the many.

Here, we employ the concepts of *rent-seeking*, deliberate actions by particular interests to secure preferential treatment and/or pecuniary benefits from public decision making (Lambsdorff, 2002), and *regulatory capture*, decision making by public servants that favours particular and regulated interests (Stigler, 1971). Rent-seeking and regulatory capture are, respectively, the 'demand for' and the 'supply of' decision making intended to benefit particular interests rather than the broader, public interest.

We examine rent-seeking and regulatory capture in relation to water reform in one of the world's larger river basins by surface area and where the water policy and governance are claimed to be world leading: the Murray-Darling Basin (MDB) in Australia (Figure 1).[2] Recent water reform in the MDB began with the National Water Initiative, agreed to in 2004 by all state governments and the Australian government (Horne, 2017). The initiative had as a key objective to achieve sustainable water use in over-allocated or stressed water systems (Williams, 2017). In particular, the signatory governments committed 'to increase the productivity and efficiency of Australia's water use, the need to service rural and urban communities, and to ensure the health of river and groundwater systems by establishing clear pathways to return all systems to environmentally sustainable levels of extraction' (Council of Australian Governments, 2004, p. 1). Consistent with this intergovernmental agreement, the Australian government set aside A$ 3.1 billion for water entitlement purchases and also A$ 5.8 billion for water infrastructure investments (Grafton, 2010) intended to increase irrigation efficiency (Grafton et al., 2018; Grafton, 2019). Both programmes (purchases from willing sellers of their water entitlements and subsidies for irrigation infrastructure) were intended to ensure an environmentally sustainable level of water extractions in the MDB.

The first Australian government programme we review is the targeted one-on-one purchases from irrigators of water entitlements (long-term water rights) that occurred in

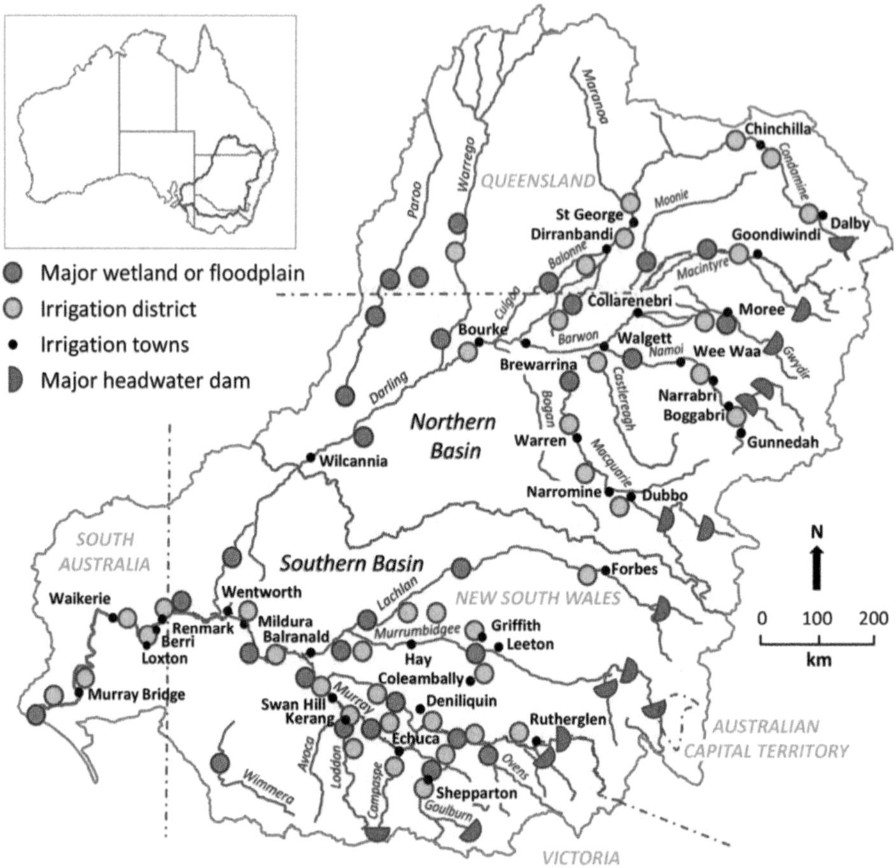

Figure 1. The Murray-Darling Basin, Australia: rivers, dams, floodplains, wetlands and irrigation districts.

Source: M. Colloff, personal communication, 18 June 2019.

2016 and 2017. Purchases targeted to a particular individual or entity replaced the use of open tenders in operation between 2008 and 2013. As with the previous open tender process, the stated goal of these purchases is to increase the water entitlements held by the Australian government for environmental purposes.

The second Australian government programme we examine is in relation to irrigation infrastructure subsidies. These subsidies had the same priority goal as targeted one-on-one purchases, 'to protect, restore and provide for the ecological values and ecosystem services of the Murray-Darling Basin' (Water Act, 2007, 3d (ii)), and were implemented by requiring recipients to provide a share (typically 50%) of the estimated 'water savings' to the Australian government in the form of water entitlements.

We provide evidence that rent-seeking behaviour and regulatory capture have affected public decisions with respect to both one-on-one targeted purchases of water entitlements and irrigation infrastructure subsidies in the MDB. We conclude with actions we contend would mitigate rent-seeking and regulatory capture in relation to irrigation water decision making by state actors in the MDB, and in general.

Rent-seeking behaviour and regulatory capture

The literature on rent-seeking originated with Kreuger (1974), who identified it as the actions of private individuals or entities who compete for the 'rents' or pecuniary returns that arise from quantitative restrictions imposed by government regulations, such as licences to import goods. Rent-seeking can be perfectly legal, and may even be a tax-deductible expenditure. For example, rent-seeking includes registered lobbying activities (Hogan, Murphy, & Chari, 2011). Rent-seeking may also be illegal, when public officials are bribed or coerced in some way.

Rent-seeking today is commonly understood to include a wide range of what may be called directly unproductive, profit-seeking activities (Bhagwati, 1982): actions undertaken by non-state actors to influence government decision making, including the disbursements of grants and subsidies and other budgetary assistance (Banks, 2013), for their pecuniary benefit. Rent-seeking may bring financial gain to rent-seekers and special interests (Tullock, 1989) but does not produce any goods or services. Thus, it reduces overall economic welfare. This welfare loss is exacerbated when rent-seeking results in welfare-distorting decisions by state actors (Anam, 1982) or increases inequality by reducing the progressivity of the tax and transfer system (Frijters & Foster, 2014).

In Australia, registered lobbying of the Australian government is a billion-dollar business (West, 2017) that exerts substantial influence on decision making (Wood & Griffiths, 2018). That lobbying continues, and is increasing, is evidence that rent-seeking has a positive expected return for lobbyists and those who hire them. There is also empirical evidence that lobbying and campaign contributions increase the likelihood of pecuniary benefits to individual entities or sectors. For instance, following the 2008 Global Financial Crisis, lobbying by financial institutions in the US in 2000–2007 was positively associated with higher likelihood of receiving federal bailout funds (Igan, Mishra, & Tressel, 2011). Witko (2011), again in the US, has shown that firms that contribute more money in the form of political contributions also receive more government contracts, although other factors, such as past contracting relationship and firm reputation, also increase the likelihood of receiving government contracts.

The term *regulatory capture* was used by Nobel laureate George Stigler in 1971, but it is also part of a broader literature in relation to public choice, regulation and how state actors make decisions (Clark & Lee, 2013; Gómez-Ibáñez, 2003). This literature shows that regulatory capture is more likely when the benefits of regulation are highly concentrated, because interested parties have a strong incentive to affect decision making or undertake 'entrepreneurial' politics (Wilson, 1980). As with rent-seeking, non-state actors who 'capture' politicians or public servants may not be acting illegally. Indeed, as noted by Thompson (1993, p. 369), actions whereby 'politicians take money from contributors to get elected, then do favors for them' are called 'mediated corruption'. This is a corruption of public decision making because it is mediated through the political process. Tit-for-tat actions between state and non-state actors are typically not illegal, because the gain that the politician or the political party receives in terms of votes or declared campaign funds does not represent a personal gain. Nevertheless, mediated corruption damages the democratic process because government decision making is influenced so as to direct benefits to particular interests even when this may be contrary to the broader, public interest.

One form of regulatory capture is 'revolving doors', whereby politicians or public servants, seeking to transition to alternative employment, provide special treatment or particular consideration to their future employer. This has been shown empirically in relation to 'transitioning' credit analysts at rating agencies, who have a higher likelihood of giving a more favourable rating to the firm that subsequently employs them than other firms (Cornaggia, Cornaggia, & Xia, 2016); and to examiners at the US Patent and Trademark Office, who give statistically significantly more patents to firms that subsequently employ them (Tabakovic & Wollmann, 2018). Both cases illustrate how regulatory capture can lower the quality of decision making and, if revealed, is likely to reduce trust in public institutions.

Another type of regulatory capture is when public servants are directed or 'advised' to make certain decisions, or to favour particular non-state actors, by their political masters and advisors. In some cases, this undue influence on public servants may come directly through non-state actors who have, or are perceived to have, the 'ear' of the minister or political decision makers. In other words, some non-state actors may have the ability to either advance or damage the careers of public servants. In turn, this affects how departments operate and their compliance and investigation processes. For instance, the inspector general for the Murray-Darling Basin has observed in relation to compliance with water regulations in the MDB that 'departments don't have the right structures in place to bring forward complaints' (Gribbin & Jasper, 2019).

Whatever its cause, regulatory capture means that decision making is unduly influenced by particular interests, possibly at the expense of the public interest. In the context of the MDB, Horne (2014) has observed that 'politics rather than scientific evidence is again playing a determining role' (p. 161) and that 'the role of politics ... can be as much about the exercising of power – of politicians, determining what best suits their interests – as weighing up economic, social and environmental considerations' (p. 1001).

Regulatory capture can occur when science is politicized or when there are 'industry supported scientists-*cum*-consultants whose credentials support their "hired gun" role in issue advocacy' (Pielke, 2007, p. 120). The problem arises when scientists use their credibility or prestige as 'stealth issue advocates' rather than acting as 'honest brokers' (Pielke, 2007). Such advocacy has been used to 'shut down' rather than 'open up' debate on water governance in the MDB, and in particular on the 2012 Basin Plan, which was legislated in the federal parliament in November 2012 and which has as its key goal to ensure environmentally sustainable levels of water extraction.

In our view, an example of Pielke's 'stealth advocacy' is a 19 July 2019 open letter, signed by 27 scientists, ostensibly in protest of an Australian Broadcasting Corporation television documentary that examined the very large public expenditures on irrigation infrastructure in the MDB. Several of the signatories of the open letter have declared interests with the Murray-Darling Basin Authority, which is responsible for implementing the 2012 Basin Plan (e.g., one is a member of its board, one is a former board member, and three are members of the authority's Advisory Committee on Social, Economic and Environmental Sciences). Consequently, there is the appearance that some of the signatories have used their scientific credentials to advocate policy that is supportive of the MDBA and of their own roles within the MDBA. In particular, the signatories say 'that the Basin Plan and the institutions implementing it are being unfairly maligned and that this is eroding public support for what we regard as generally sound public policy'. They also advocate a key position of the Australian government on water reform: that any substantial change to policy implementation should await a 'scheduled review of the Basin Plan in 2026' (Vertessy et al., 2019). On 1 September 2019, it was announced by the federal water minister that the lead signatory of the open letter would lead a '$20 million research program to increase knowledge around the Murray-Darling Basin', which would be administered by the Murray-Darling Basin Authority (Littleproud & Pasin, 2019).

Despite the statements in the open letter, there is already a large body of scientific evidence that the Basin Plan has so far failed to deliver environmental benefits at the basin scale, especially in terms of stream flows (Argent, 2017; Wentworth Group of Concerned Scientists, 2018, 2019). Low stream flows, due to excessive upstream irrigation extraction, were also identified by both the Australian Academy of Science (2019) and the New South Wales Natural Resources Commission (2019) as a key cause of the catastrophic decline in both water flows and water quality along the lower Darling River. Such declines in flow contributed to a massive fish kill along the Darling in January 2019 (Australian Academy of Science, 2019).

The 2012 Basin Plan has found to be failing by the Murray-Darling Basin Royal Commission, established by the state of South Australia. In particular, the commission identified important deficiencies in governance, compliance and enforcement, climate change, Aboriginal engagement, water diversions by irrigators on flood plains, groundwater monitoring and extraction, and public disclosure. The commission also observed ongoing failure to respond to policy problems and to improve the implementation of water reform in the MDB: 'The recent history – perhaps better called the politics – of the Basin is acutely framed by what may be called constraints that limit or discourage what may otherwise be regarded as beneficial change or improvements' (Murray-Darling Basin Royal Commission, 2019, p. 15).

In Australia, there is also evidence that regulatory capture may be widespread, going well beyond the water sector. For example, in a survey of over 2,200 respondents by Transparency International Australia and Griffith University in May and June 2018, two-thirds of respondents who self-identified as former Australian government public servants (245 respondents) claimed to have least once 'personally witnessed or suspected a government official or politician making a decision in favour of a business or individual who gave them political donations or support'. Of these, almost half had seen such decision making at least a few times, and almost one in five had seen it 'many times' (Transparency International Australia, 2018)

Corruption in the water sector

The 2008 *Global Corruption Report* by Transparency International focussed on the water sector in 35 countries. One of the report's foci was corruption in the irrigation sector. In India, for example, in relation to irrigation infrastructure contracts,

> [financial] 'leakages' were of the order of 30–45 per cent of approved amounts. Approved plans included costs that were overestimated by at least 15–25 per cent through the over-design of structures and misrepresentation of labour requirements, deceptions that then set the stage for the diversion of funds during implementation. (Lewis & Lenton, 2008, pp. 22–23)

More generally, corruption in the irrigation sector may include subsidy capture, whereby irrigators 'lobby governments to pay for projects that do not necessarily deliver net benefits to society, but that deliver a major subsidy to landowners' (Rijsberman, 2008, p. 69); corruption in the construction of irrigation infrastructure; and corruption in the maintenance and operation of irrigation structures.

Transparency International (2018) highlighted that the water sector, in general, is at high risk of corruption. This is because the capital-intensive and the public good nature of water infrastructure of the water sector, typically, means large and ongoing public expenditures. Water is governed by multiple agencies and government departments, making it difficult to identify lines of responsibility and authority and, thus, corrupt decision makers; the complex, technical nature of water projects makes it a challenge for non-specialists to identify corrupt practices; and also growing water scarcity, especially in arid and semi-arid regions, increases the payoffs from corruption for those able to increase their share of the available water. The losers of corruption in the water sector are typically the poor and marginalized, who have little or no influence or 'voice'. More generally, beyond the water sector, the general risks of corruption increase with the market power of providers of services to the public sector; the discretion of decision makers; and the lack of accountability and/or transparency in relation to decision making (Klitgaard, 1988).

While much of the corruption in the water sector occurs in low-income countries with limited public resources for audit, oversight, monitoring and compliance, it also includes high-income industrialized nations. Plummer (2008, p. 4), a respected governance and anti-corruption specialist, observed that 'in Europe, North America and Australia, corrupt practices involving or affecting water resources and services are not uncommon'. Repetto (1986) also highlights the widespread nature of rent-seeking in relation to public irrigation systems in the US. Despite the recognition of corruption in the water sector, Huppert (2013, p. 268) has observed a 'hear no evil, see no evil, speak no evil' approach to rent-seeking and regulatory capture by water professionals because 'pondering on issues of rent-seeking and corruption might impinge in unpleasant ways on the outcomes of projects and programmes they were involved in and hence on their personal ambitions and reputations'.

Plummer (2008, p. 6) identifies three forms of corruption in the water sector: petty corruption, in which a public servant extracts small bribes for particular favours; grand corruption, in which a small number of, usually senior, politicians or public servants receive payments 'under the table' for awarding contracts of large value to service providers; and state capture, in which 'decision-making process and enforcement of water policies are manipulated to favour the interests of a few influential water users or service providers at the expense of the broader public'. State capture, which is another term for regulatory capture, is most common in high-income countries, while petty and grand corruption are principally found in low- and middle-income countries.

Regulatory capture (or state capture) is difficult to identify, although there is evidence that it is common (Repetto, 1986).[3] In the MDB, for instance, through an ongoing water reform process (Hart, 2016), irrigators are the principal beneficiaries of infrastructure subsidy schemes that have cost, in public expenditures, some A$ 4 billion as of August 2019 (Australian Department of Agriculture and Water Resources, 2019a). On average, irrigators have received infrastructure subsidies worth A$ 400,000.[4] Such large payments, at the very least, suggest that irrigator lobbyists are able to direct much of the government benefits of water reform to irrigators. This perspective is supported by Marshall and Alexandra (2016, p. 689) who observe: 'One can only speculate on the degree to which irrigation lobbyists and hydraulic bureaucracies influenced specific policy decisions.'

The potential for regulatory capture in the MDB is highlighted by the former chief of the Australian Federal Police, who is examining links between political donations and the purchase of water entitlements from irrigators. In his view, reported in May 2019, there are undeclared conflicts of interest in relation to decision making about water programmes in the MDB. He notes, in particular, that

> if conflicts of interest aren't transparent, it could lead to corruption.... Water is now the value of gold. If you have corruption in other elements of society, if you have corruption in other areas of business, why wouldn't you have it here, when water is the same price of gold? (Middleton, 2019)

Further evidence of regulatory capture in the MDB stems from a 2017 media investigation of water theft in the northern MDB. In this investigation by the Australian Broadcasting Corporation, the most senior water official in the state government of New South Wales (NSW) at the time, the deputy director general of the NSW Department of Primary Industries, was recorded as offering to share allegedly classified documents with irrigators. He was also alleged to have resisted calls from investigators in his own department for a monitoring and compliance operation, even when there was evidence of water theft (Begley, 2017). This official was subsequently forced to resign. An independent investigation later found serious deficiencies in water administration and compliance. In particular, the independent investigator observed: 'increasing pressure from certain stakeholders to "water down" key reforms, including reforms to water metering and improving transparency of information about water usage' (Matthews, 2017, p. 1).

The extent of rent-seeking and regulatory capture in the MDB cannot be determined without a judicial inquiry that has the power to compel witnesses to testify under oath and to acquire documents. In the absence of such an inquiry, it is instructive to review the number of water-related meetings between non-state actors and NSW government ministers in 2014–2018 (Figure 2). Irrigation companies and industry, combined, accounted for over half of all ministerial meetings. The NSW Irrigation Council, a lobbyist and advocacy group, had more than 25. By contrast, many of the reported non-irrigation and non-industry entities had only one ministerial meeting in this four-year period. Combined, indigenous, catchment and environmental entities accounted for only about 20% of the total number of ministerial meetings given to irrigation and industry entities (Figure 2).

Additional evidence of regulatory capture is a business case undertaken by the New South Wales Department of Primary Industries (2016). It ignored the potential environmental costs and losses of cultural value associated with a major water supply project, but it highlighted the potential benefits of reduced environmental water recovery in the Northern MDB, which would provide economic benefits to upstream irrigators. Other evidence of regulatory capture includes a June 2019 review of the Barwon-Darling Water Sharing Plan in the Northern MDB by the New South Wales Natural Resources

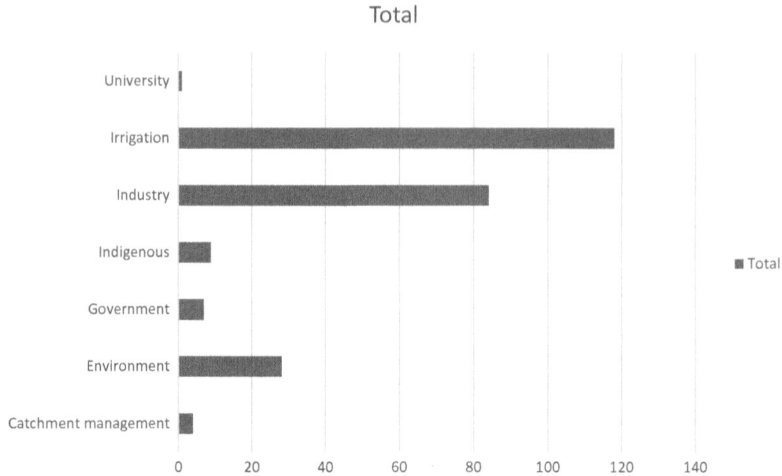

Figure 2. Number of water-related meetings with New South Wales government ministers, 2014–2018.
Source: Data sourced from Guardian Australia, '2019 NSW ministerial diary scrape output', https://docs.google.com/spreadsheets/d/1LXLwOL4CkBbNUTOg4shoKbN9mlUgFlb80tMsBp8-r3k

Commission (2019). The commission observed that for the Barwon-Darling region of northern NSW,

> changes to the water sharing rules in the Plan area have resulted in an increased allowance for extractive use at lower flow classes that are critical to the environment. These provisions benefit the economic interests of a few upstream users over the ecological and social needs of the many. (p. 1)

This water sharing plan, in force since 2012, is scheduled to continue until 2022, and while 'reduced inflows due to drought, upstream extraction, and climate change are all impacting the flows in the Barwon-Darling, the Plan provisions that allow increased access to low flows have resulted in poor ecological and social outcomes' (p. 8).

Targeted one-on-one purchases of water entitlements

In 2007, in the worst year of a decade-long drought that affected much of South-Eastern Australia, the Australian prime minister announced a A$ 10 billion funding package over 10 years to ensure the future of water security. This National Plan for Water Security, later called Water for the Future, had as a key objective 'putting the MDB back on a sustainable track, significantly improving the health of the rivers and wetlands of the Basin, and bringing substantial benefits to irrigators and the community alike' (Howard, 2019, p. 3).

Much of the allocated funds have notionally been spent on 'environmental water recovery' to increase stream and river flows in the MDB. Most of the funding for water recovery, or some A$ 4 billion (Australian Department of Agriculture and Water Resources, 2019a), has been directed to subsidies for water infrastructure, whereby the subsidy recipients provide to the Australian government water entitlements equal to about half of the estimated 'water savings'. To date, the Australian government claims it has acquired some 700 billion litres of water entitlements for the environment through water infrastructure subsidies, as measured by their long-term average yield.

Some A$ 2.5 billion has been spent on acquiring water entitlements from willing sellers (Grafton & Wheeler, 2018). As of 31 March 2019, the volume of water entitlements acquired by purchases from willing sellers was 1224 billion litres of surface water, as measured by the long-term average annual yield (Australian Department of Agriculture, 2019a). These water entitlements were purchased from willing sellers by the Australian government between 2008 and 2013 through a series of publicly announced open tenders. Irrigators who so wished had the opportunity to provide a closed bid for the volume and price of water entitlements they were prepared to sell to the government. Based on 'value for money', in relation to the reliability or the annual yield of the water entitlements to the price paid, and also to environmental needs in relation to how the purchased water entitlements were expected to be used, a purchase contract was offered to successful tenderers. In addition to comparing the value of money across competing bids in a tender, a well-developed market for water entitlements exists in the MDB (Grafton, Horne, & Wheeler, 2016) that gave the Australian government a benchmark in relation to value for money.

Following a federal election in August 2013, and a change in the Australian government, the open tendering for water entitlements was terminated in 2014. In 2015, the government imposed a legislative cap of 1500 billion litres on the volume of water entitlements that can be legally acquired by the government. Both actions were in response to concerns by some irrigators, and especially irrigation advocates and lobbyists (National Irrigators' Council, 2019), that the purchase of water entitlements for environmental purposes was undermining the socio-economic viability of irrigation communities.

In September 2015, the governing coalition replaced the prime minister and also combined the portfolios of agriculture and water into one department. The minister for the new Department of Agriculture and Water Resources was also the deputy prime minister. Shortly thereafter, the department initiated a series of one-on-one targeted purchases of water entitlements from particular sellers. By contrast to open tenders, these targeted one-on-one purchases of water entitlements had the support of the National Irrigators' Council (2019).

The ability of the government to discern value for money in targeted purchases of water entitlements is extremely limited, because there are no other offers for sale. Many of the details of these targeted purchases are deemed 'commercial in confidence' and thus not accessible to public scrutiny. What public details are available include the month of purchase, the total cost and location of the water entitlements, and the name of the seller (Australian Department of Agriculture, 2019b). The stated justification for adopting targeted purchases of water entitlements, rather than open tenders, is that they 'provide significant benefit, while minimising negative social and economic impacts' (Australian Department of Agriculture, 2019b).

In 2016–17 approximately A$ 150 million was spent by the Australian government on 10 separate targeted purchases of water entitlements. The one on which there is the most information relates to water entitlements sold at two properties (Kia Ora and Clyde) along the Condamine-Balonne catchment in southern Queensland, near the NSW border. These properties are owned by Eastern Australian Agriculture (EAA) which in turn has its holding company listed as Eastern Australia Irrigation (EAI). EAI has its registered head office in the tax haven of the Cayman Islands and was co-founded by the current federal minister for energy and emissions reduction.

In relation to the EAA purchase, the Australian Department of Agriculture spent A$ 78.9 million to acquire 28.7 billion litres of low-security water entitlements in the form of 'overland flow' – water that becomes accessible only when there is a flood that goes over the banks of the rivers and brings water onto the properties where the water entitlements are held. According to the department, the price paid of A$ 2745 per million litres represented 'a fair market value', and it 'undertook due diligence activities in investigating the proposal, including checking the validity of the licences on offer; and obtaining commercial water valuation advice, independent advice on the possible socio-economic impacts, and advice from the state government, the Murray-Darling Basin Authority and the CEWH'. The department also observed that, as a result of the targeted purchase of water entitlements from EAA, 'a large portion of the remaining [environmental] water recovery [under the 2012 Basin Plan] required for the Condamine-Balonne has been achieved with minimal impacts on employment and production' (Australian Department of Agriculture, 2019b).

Given the lack of details about the transaction, an order to produce documents was served on the Department of Agriculture by the Australian Senate. The relevant documents were made publicly available on 25 October 2018, although they were heavily redacted in relation to the price of comparable water entitlements (Parliament of Australia, 2018).

Important questions remain,[5] but the following facts are known.

- There is evidence that the initial communication to purchase water entitlements from EAA was initiated by the Department of Agriculture, although this is denied by the department (Slattery & Campbell, 2019a).
- EAA offered to sell some of its water entitlements to the Department of Agriculture prior to 2015, but these offers were declined.
- The average price paid for water entitlements in the MDB, and with higher long-term average yield, through the previous open tender process was A$ 2,000 per million litres (Grafton & Wheeler, 2018), 27% *less* than was paid to EAA.
- The settlement price of A$ 2745 per million litres paid to EAA was 25% *more* than the original sale price offered by EAA prior to the negotiations in 2017 with the Department of Agriculture (Slattery & Campbell, 2019a).
- The volumes of water attached to the overland flow water entitlements sold by EAA to the Department of Agriculture were, in part, determined by a business associate who has also acted as a consultant for EAA (Slattery & Campbell, 2019a).
- The profit from this transaction – the difference between the proceeds received by EAA and the value of the water entitlements that it sold –was A$ 52 million. By comparison, EAA's revenues from its farm operations in the financial years ending 30 June 2017 and 30 June 2018 were A$ 23.8 million and A$ 3.7 million, respectively (Australian Securities and Investments Commission, 2018). EAA also had negative assets (prior to the sale) of A$ 28.6 million, as of June 2017 (Chenoweth, 2019). The cumulative interest paid by EAA to EAI by 2018 was tens of millions, which suggests that EAA is 'unlikely to have paid cash tax' on the sale of its water entitlements, because the amount received would have been paid to EAI to cover its promissory and convertible notes to EAA (Chenoweth, 2019).

- A valuation of A$ 16 million for water storage on EAA properties was built into the purchase price paid by the government, but there is no agreement to store overland flows on the properties, nor has this storage yet been used by the government (Slattery & Campbell, 2019b).
- As of May 2019, most of the levees on the properties that are used to trap water during floods remain in place (The Project, 2019), though their removal was agreed as part of the purchase.
- The water entitlements acquired by this purchase are overland flows and thus are not secured from downstream users. Thus, downstream irrigators with their own water entitlements are able to divert the water recovered 'for the environment' by the government.

In sum, short of a judicial inquiry with witnesses testifying under oath, it is not possible to come to a definitive conclusion in terms of rent-seeking and regulatory capture regarding the targeted purchases of water entitlements from EAA. Nevertheless, the facts are: the purchase was an extraordinarily good deal for EAA in terms of the price paid per litre and also in comparison to the revenues from its farming operations; there has been little public transparency on this transaction, even after an order to produce documents from the Australian Senate; there is, at the very least, a perceived conflict of interest in relation to at least one person who undertook due diligence for or provided information used by the Australian government in relation to this purchase; and there is much uncertainty as to what increases in stream flows will be delivered to the designated downstream environmental sites as a result of the purchase of EAA's overland water flow entitlements.

Subsidies for irrigation efficiency

The redirection of water recovery from the direct purchase of water entitlements to irrigation infrastructure began in earnest in 2013 after the Liberal–National coalition government took office at the federal level. This change in how water recovery was implemented was supported by irrigator peak bodies which had previously questioned the need for water recovery for the environment (Horne, 2017, pp. 1010–1011), and which had expressed a strong preference for water infrastructure subsidies over the direct purchase of water entitlements from willing sellers through open tenders. The reprioritization from open tenders to irrigation infrastructure subsidies has been represented as a willingness by the Australian government 'to generate wealth transfers', noting that 'water users are highly likely to react to these signals and adopt new technology; but only after holding out for a subsidy' (Adamson & Loch, 2018, p. 99).

The almost exclusive focus on irrigation infrastructure for environmental water recovery after 2013 occurred even though 'irrigator preference for infrastructure expenditure over market-based expenditure (56% versus 44%, respectively) is less than what current budget allocations or stakeholder views recognize, suggesting the presence of rent-seeking in current arguments made by irrigation groups' (Loch et al., 2014, p. 403); and open tenders to acquire water entitlements for environmental water recovery are 'very positively regarded by those selling water into the market' (Horne, 2014, p. 157); and many irrigators identify themselves as willing to sell a portion of their water entitlements (Wheeler, Zuo, Bjornlund, & Lane-Miller, 2012); and there is publicly available evidence that water recovered for the environment through water infrastructure subsidies is neither cost-effective, nor a good value for the money (Horne, 2014, p. 159), but more than twice as expensive per litre than the direct purchase of water entitlements through open tenders (Crase and O'Keefe 209; Grafton, 2010). Importantly, the implementation of irrigation infrastructure subsidies by the Australian government ignored the explicit recommendation of one of its own agencies, the Productivity Commission (2010, p. 142): that irrigation infrastructure projects 'should only be approved where: (1) properly conducted cost–benefit analysis shows there to be net benefits (2) government contributions are commensurate with public benefits (excluding private benefits to irrigators)'.

Despite robust evidence that water infrastructure subsidies are likely to reduce return flows to groundwater and streams and rivers in the MDB (ACIL Tasman, 2003; CSIRO, 2005; Crase & O'Keefe, 2009; Productivity Commission, 2010; Young, Young, Hamilton, & Bright, 2002), also supported by international evidence (Batchelor et al., 2014; Food and Agriculture Organization of the United Nations, 2017; Grafton et al., 2018; Jensen, 2007; Perry, 2007; Qureshi, Grafton, Kirby, & Hanjra, 2011; Ward & Pulido-Velazquez, 2008), no systematic measurements at a project level were made of the effects on return flows of irrigation infrastructure subsidies. Further, 'no comprehensive benefit-cost analysis has been undertaken to confirm that the public benefits of these measures have exceeded the costs to taxpayers' (Productivity Commission, 2018, p. 97). Thus, despite the expenditure of A$ 4 billion on water infrastructure subsidies to date, there are no adequate or comprehensive irrigator-scale measurements of the net impact on stream flows (before and after the irrigation infrastructure upgrades) or the net public benefits.

In response to the uncertainty about the net effect on stream flows of water infrastructure subsidies, Williams and Grafton (2019) used the best available field water balance data to estimate the reduction in return flows of water to the environment as a result of irrigation infrastructure subsidies. They calculated that, in the MDB, the net change in stream and river flows is between a decrease of 140 billion litres and an increase of 280 billion litres. By comparison, a review commissioned by the MDBA found a reduction of 121 billion litres per year (Wang, Walker, & Horne, 2018). Using their own midpoint estimate, Williams and Grafton (2019) calculated that the net impact of the water infrastructure subsidies in the MDB is to increase stream flows by only 70 billion litres. The Australian government claims an impact of 700 billion litres (Grafton & Wheeler, 2018).

Notwithstanding the peer-reviewed evidence that irrigation infrastructure subsidies have contributed little towards an environmentally sustainable level of extraction in the MDB, and at great cost, additional water infrastructure subsidies were recommitted in April 2019 in the form of a National Water Grid (McCormack, 2019). In relation to existing and planned water infrastructure subsidies, the Australian deputy prime minister stated in May 2019: 'At the end of my political career, I want to be able to point to new dams, bigger weirs, more pipelines, they make so much difference at the local level' (quoted by Foley, 2019). This message of 'irrigators first' is echoed by the Australian minister of the environment, who stated in June 2019, in relation to the 2019 drought in the MDB, that 'sometimes the environment doesn't need all its water but farmers desperately do need water', and that in some cases 'there's water in the dams [holding environmental water] and there are crops that are dying and farmers with drought-affected stock that need hay' (quoted by Hasham, 2019).

In sum, the delivery of billions of dollars of irrigation infrastructure subsidies in the MDB appears to be a case of rent-seeking and regulatory capture, whereby taxpayer dollars are directed to the irrigation sector in the name of water reform. This is being done even though there exists a much more cost-effective and transparent method (direct purchase of water entitlements via open tenders) to deliver the same outcome; and though water infrastructure subsidies may have reduced rather than increased overall stream flows; and though some of the subsidies have involved the construction of private water storages and the automation of weirs and water metering that neither provide any 'water savings' nor increase irrigation efficiency (Australian Department of the Environment, 2014, Annexure A).

Conclusions

A large literature exists on the causes of corruption and ways to mitigate it. The water sector, especially the irrigation sector, is particularly prone to both rent-seeking and regulatory capture. Not all of these activities are illegal, and in democracies they occur through the political process, whereby political parties and their leaders can legally provide pecuniary benefits to their supporters via the tax and transfer system.

Using the water reforms in the Murray-Darling Basin, Australia, and in particular the billions of dollars allocated for water recovery for the environment, we examined the evidence for rent-seeking and regulatory capture. We find empirical evidence of both activities in this basin. We label this 'mediated corruption', because we do not suggest, nor do we imply, that there has been bribery or petty or grand corruption, such that decision makers have received direct personal, pecuniary benefits from their decisions. Instead, the government of the day has legally undertaken expenditures to benefit particular interests, *mediated* through the political process, even though this appears to be contrary to the stated goals of water reform, as per the Water Act 2007, and also best practice regulations agreed to by all Australian governments (Council of Australian Governments, 2007).

Transparency International (2008) provides four recommendations, including strengthening regulatory oversight of water management and much greater transparency in decision making, to mitigate corruption in its various forms in the water sector. In relation to the Murray-Darling Basin, and also in general, we highlight seven governance actions that we contend would reduce rent-seeking and regulatory capture in the irrigation water sector.

- Ensure timely, accessible and independently audited water accounts that include hydrological measurements and estimates of water consumption and return flows (Grafton & Williams, 2019).
- Establish an Integrity Commission (Brown et al., 2018) with judicial powers to compel witnesses to give testimony under oath and to acquire relevant documents on public expenditures.
- Require and make accessible transparent *before-and-after measurements* of the effects of water infrastructure subsidies on estimated and actual water savings (House of Representatives Standing Committee on Agriculture and Water Resources, 2017).

- Mandate that irrigators who divert water to irrigation provide a publicly available, annual water monitoring plan that outlines where the water is sourced from, and for what, when and how the diverted water is used, including water storages.
- Create a publicly accessible electronic register of recipients of individual infrastructure subsidies and government grants.
- Adopt easily accessible and searchable electronic registers, available in real time, of all meetings by ministers and their political advisors and senior public servants with non-governmental individuals and entities, as well as financial contributions to political parties.
- Prohibit third parties or contractors with any perceived or real conflicts of interest from performing 'due diligence' in relation to the spending of public funds; ideally, this should be done by public servants (Independent Commission against Corruption, 2018).

These seven actions will mitigate but not prevent either rent-seeking behaviour or regulatory capture. Other considerations also matter. For example, common law systems where legal decision making is based on 'common law' and precedents appear to provide a better check and balance on the executive and legislative parts of government than civil law systems (Gómez-Ibáñez, 2003). Freedom and democracy also matter, as does a free press.

Other factors may work in the opposite direction, to increase rent-seeking and regulatory capture. For instance, greater inequality of income and wealth may increase regulatory capture because it concentrates power in a smaller number of non-state actors. The longevity of the regulatory agencies and the term of appointment of the heads of such agencies, and who gets to make the appointments to these positions, also affect the vulnerability of agencies to regulatory capture.

In sum, rent-seeking and regulatory capture are influenced by multiple sectoral and also economy-wide social, cultural, economic and institutional factors. Understanding how to respond to these factors in different institutional settings is a critical first step in mitigating both rent-seeking and regulatory capture.

Notes

1. The Council of Australian Governments (2007, Appendix C) states: 'Decisions about the overall effectiveness of regulatory action should not be made on the basis only of its effect on particular groups in society. Public policy makers are expected to make judgments based on what is best for the community as a whole.'
2. The Australian Department of Agriculture (2019c) claims that 'Australia is at the leading edge in its approach to water resource management'. This view is shared by politicians inside and outside of government – for example, 'Australia is recognised as a world leader in water management' (Australian Securities and Investments Commission, 2018, p. 141) – and also by the CEO of the Murray-Darling Basin Authority: 'The Basin Plan is an achievement Australia should be proud of. Other countries look to our nation as having some of the best and most successful water management policies in the world' (Glyde, 2017).
3. Rijsberman (2008, p. 70) observes, in relation to the irrigation sector: 'Policy capture is difficult to prove, but the existence of powerful, politically well-connected large-scale farmers who manage to secure the bulk of irrigation subsidies in many countries makes policy capture a plausible premise.'

4. This is calculated by dividing the total Australian government subsidies for irrigation infrastructure to date, A$ 4 billion (Australian Department of Agriculture and Water Resources, 2019a), by the approximate number of irrigators in the MDB, 10,000 (Australian Bureau of Statistics, 2019), noting that not all irrigators have received such subsidies.
5. A summary of the connections across the various parties to the EAA sale of water entitlements is provided by West (2019), with further details given by Tee and Salt (2019). The federal minister for energy and emissions reduction has publicly stated that he ended all association with these companies before he entered parliament in 2013. He has also stated that neither he nor his family have received any benefits from the 2017 sale of water entitlements by EAA. The minister for water who approved the purchase of water entitlements from EAA in 2017 has also stated that he had no contact with any ministers in relation to this purchase.

Disclosure statement

No potential conflict of interest was reported by the authors.

References

ACIL Tasman. (2003). *Scope for water use efficiency savings as a source of water to meet increased environmental flows - Independent review. A report to the Murray Darling Basin Commission*, March 2003. Canberra, ACT: Author. Retrieved from https://www.mdba.gov.au/sites/default/files/archived/mdbc-tlm-reports/2080_Eflows_Scope_for_water_use_efficiency_savings_2003.pdf.

Adamson, D., & Loch, A. (2018). Achieving environmental flows where buyback is constrained. *Australian Journal of Agricultural and Resource Economics*, *62*, 83–102.

Anam, M. (1982). Distortion-triggered lobbying and welfare: A contribution to the theory of directly-unproductive profit-seeking activities. *Journal of International Economics*, *13*, 15–32.

Argent, R. M. (2017). *Australia: State of the environment 2016*. Inland water. Retrieved from https://soe.environemnt.gov.au/theme/inland-water

Australian Academy of Science. (2019). *Investigation of the causes of the mass fish kills in the Menindee region of NSW over the summer 2018–19*. Retrieved from https://www.science.org.au/files/userfiles/support/reports-and-plans/2019/academy-science-report-mass-fish-kills-digital.pdf

Australian Bureau of Statistics. (2019). *4618.0 - Water use on Australian farms, 2017–18*. Retrieved from http://www.abs.gov.au/ausstats/abs@.nsf/lookup/4618.0Media%20Release12017-18

Australian Department of Agriculture. (2019a). *Surface water recovery under the Basin plan as at 31 March 2019*. Retrieved from http://www.agriculture.gov.au/SiteCollectionDocuments/water/progress-recovery/surface-water-recovery.pdf

Australian Department of Agriculture. (2019b). *Background information on significant commonwealth strategic water purchases in 2017*. Retrieved from http://www.agriculture.gov.au/about/media-centre/on-the-record/background-significant-commonwealth-strategic-water-purchases-2017

Australian Department of Agriculture. (2019c). *Water management policy and legislation*. Retrieved from http://www.agriculture.gov.au/water/policy

Australian Department of Agriculture and Water Resources. (2019a). *Commonwealth water recovery (as at 30 November 2018) and expenditure in the Murray-Darling Basin (as at 30 November 2018)*. Personal communications, 11 January 2019.

Australian Department of the Environment. (2014). *Water recovery strategy for the Murray-Darling Basin*. Canberra, Australia. Retrieved from https://www.circleofblue.org/wp-content/uploads/2015/06/water-recovery-strategy-mdb2.pdf

Australian Securities and Investments Commission. (2018). *Copy of financial statements and reports of Eastern Australia Agriculture Pty Ltd*.

Axelrod, R. (1980). Effective choice in the prisoner's dilemma. *Journal of Conflict Resolution*, *24*(1), 3–25.

Banks, G. (2013). *Return of the rent-seeking society? Stan Kelly Lecture*. Economic Society of Australia. Retrieved from https://esavic.org.au/385/images/2013_GaryBanks.pdf

Batchelor, C., Reddy, V. R., Linstead, C., Dhar, M., Roy, S., & May, R. (2014). Do water-saving technologies improve environmental flows? *Journal of Hydrology, 518*, 140–149.

Begley, P. (2017, September 16). Top water bureaucrat Gavin Hanlon resigns after corruption allegations. *Sydney Morning Herald*. Retrieved from https://www.smh.com.au/national/nsw/top-water-bureaucrat-gavin-hanlon-resigns-after-corruption-allegations-20170916-gyiq7h.html

Bhagwati, J. N. (1982). Directly unproductive, profit-seeking (DUP) activities. *Journal of Political Economy, 90*, 988–1002.

Brown, A. J., Graycar, A., Kelly, K., Coghill, K., Prenzler, T., & Ransley, J. (2018). *A national integrity commission: Options for Australia*. Transparency International Australia. Retrieved from http://transparency.org.au/nic-options-for-australia/

Buchanan, J. M., & Tullock, G. (1962). The calculus of consent: The logical foundations of constitutional democracy. *Online Library of Liberty*. Retrieved from http://files.libertyfund.org/files/1063/Buchanan_0102-03_EBk_v6.0.pdf

Chenoweth, N. (2019, April 30). Eastern Australia agriculture's $80 million accounting triumph. *Australian Financial Review*. Retrieved from https://www.afr.com/rear-window/eastern-australia-agriculture-s-80-million-accounting-triumph-20190429-p51ics

Clark, J. R., & Lee, D. R. (2013). The impact of the calculus of consent. In D. R. Lee (Ed.), *Public choice, past and present: The legacy of James M. Buchanan and Gordon Tullock* (pp. 1–15). New York: Springer Science.

Congleton, R. D. (1989). Campaign finances and political platforms: The economics of political controversy. *Public Choice, 62*, 101–118.

Congleton, R. D., & Bennett, R. W. (1995). On the political economy of state highway expenditures: Some evidence of the relative performance of alternative public choice models. *Public Choice, 84*, 1–24.

Cornaggia, J., Cornaggia, K. J., & Xia, H. (2016). Revolving doors on Wall Street. *Journal of Financial Economics, 120*(2), 400–419.

Council of Australian Governments. (2004). *Intergovernmental agreement on a national water initiative*. Retrieved from https://www.pc.gov.au/inquiries/completed/water-reform/national-water-initiative-agreement-2004.pdf

Council of Australian Governments. (2007). *Best practice regulation: A guide for ministerial councils and national standard setting bodies*. Retrieved from https://www.pmc.gov.au/resource-centre/regulation/best-practice-regulation-guide-ministerial-councils-and-national-standard-setting-bodies#Appendix%20C

Crase, L., & O'Keefe, S. (2009). The paradox of national water savings: A critique of 'water for the future'. *Agenda, 16*(1), 45–60.

CSIRO. (2005). *Whole-of-catchment water and salt balance: Identifying potential water saving and management options in the Murrumbidgee catchment*. Canberra, Australia: Author. Retrieved from http://www.clw.csiro.au/publications/waterforahealthycountry/2005/WaterSaltBalance.pdf

Downs, A. (1957). An economic theory of political action in a democracy. *Journal of Political Economy, 65*(2), 135–150.

Fitzgerald, G. E. (1989). *Commission of inquiry into possible illegal activities and associated police misconduct*. Prepared for Queensland Minister for Police and Minister for Emergency Services and Administrative Services. Retrieved from https://www.ccc.qld.gov.au/publications/fitzgerald-inquiry-report

Foley, M. (2019, May 20). McCormack hails Nats 'new model' for stunning election win. *Mandura Mail*. Retrieved from https://www.mandurahmail.com.au/story/6133792/mccormack-hails-nats-new-model-for-stunning-election-win/?cs=9397

Food and Agriculture Organization of the United Nations. (2017). Does improved irrigation technology save water? A review of the evidence: Discussion paper on irrigation and sustainable water resources management in the Near East and North Africa, by C. J. Perry, P. Steduto, and F. Karajeh. Retrieved from http://www.fao.org/3/I7090EN/i7090en.pdf.

Frijters, P., & Foster, G. (2014). Rising inequality: A benign outgrowth of markets or a symptom of cancerous political favours? *Australian Economic Review, 48*(1), 67–75.

Glyde, P. (2017). The basin plan is working, but a century of damage cannot be repaired overnight. *Murray-Darling Basin Authority*. Retrieved from https://www.mdba.gov.au/media/mr/basin-plan-working-century-damage-cannot-be-repaired-overnight

Gómez-Ibáñez, J. A. (2003). *Regulating infrastructure monopoly, contracts, and discretion*. Boston, MA: Harvard University Press.

Grafton, R. Q. (2010). How to increase the cost-effectiveness of water reform and environmental flows in the Murray-Darling Basin. *Agenda, 17*(2), 17–40.

Grafton, R. Q. (2019). Policy review of water reform in the Murray-Darling Basin, Australia: The do's and do nots. *Australian Journal of Agricultural and Resource Economics, 63*(1), 116–141.

Grafton, R. Q., Horne, J., & Wheeler, S. (2016). On the marketisation of water: Evidence from the Murray-Darling Basin, Australia. *Water Resources Management, 30*(3), 913–926.

Grafton, R. Q., & Wheeler, S. (2018). Economics of water recovery in the Murray-Darling Basin. *Annual Review of Resource Economics, 10*, 487–510.

Grafton, R. Q., & Williams, J. (2019). Thirst for certainty: The urgent need for a water audit of the Murray-Darling Basin. *Farm Policy Journal 16*(2), 14–22.

Grafton, R. Q., Williams, J., Perry, C. J., Molle, F., Ringler, C., Steduto, P., … Allen, R. (2018). The paradox of irrigation efficiency. *Science, 361*(6404), 748–750.

Gribbin, C., & Jasper, C. (2019, September 3). Murray-Darling Basin corruption undermining faith in $13b plan. *ABC Rural News*. Retrieved from https://www.abc.net.au/news/rural/2019-09-03/mick-keelty-southern-basin-tour/11470352

Guardian Australia. 2019. *NSW ministerial diary scrape output*. Retrieved from https://docs.google.com/spreadsheets/d/1LXLwOL4CkBbNUTOg4shoKbN9mlUgFIb80tMsBp8-r3k

Hart, B. T. (2016). The Australian Murray-Darling Basin plan: Challenges in its implementation (part 1). *International Journal of Water Resources Development, 32*(6), 819–834.

Hasham, N. (2019, June 15). Environment minister floats 'lending' Murray Darling environmental water to farmers. *Sydney Morning Herald and The Age*. Retrieved from https://www.smh.com.au/politics/federal/environment-minister-floats-lending-murray-darling-environmental-water-to-farmers-20190614-p51xsf.html

Hindess, B. (2014). Whistling the dog. In J. Uhr & R. Walter (Eds.), *Studies in Australian political rhetoric* (pp. 143–153). Canberra: ANU Press.

Hogan, J., Murphy, G., & Chari, R. (2011). Regulating the influence game in Australia. *Australian Journal of Politics and History, 57*(1), 102–113.

Holcombe, R. G. (1989). The median voter model in public choice theory. *Public Choice, 61*, 115–125.

Horne, J. (2014). Policy brief: The 2012 Murray-Darling Basin plan – Issues to watch. *International Journal of Water Resources Development, 33*(1), 152–163.

Horne, J. (2017). The politics of water reform and environmental sustainability in the Murray-Darling Basin. *Water International, 42*(8), 1000–1021.

House of Representatives Standing Committee on Agriculture and Water Resources. (2017). *Making every drop count: Inquiry into water use efficiency programs in agriculture*. Retrieved from https://parlinfo.aph.gov.au/parlInfo/download/committees/reportrep/024116/toc_pdf/Makingeverydropcount.pdf

Howard, J. (2019, January 25). *A national plan for water security*. Retrieved from http://www.crcsi.com.au/assets/Resources/f21ceb9e-2258-4f40-9e11-50fa80ee940e.pdf

Hudson, J. (1995). Preferences, loyalty and party choice. *Public Choice, 82*, 325–340.

Huppert, W. (2013). Rent-seeking in agricultural water management: An intentionally neglected core dimension? *Water Alternatives, 6*, 265–275.

Igan, D., Mishra, P., & Tressel, T. (2011). *A fistful of dollars: Lobbying and the financial crisis* (Working Paper 17076) Cambridge, MA: National Bureau of Economic Research.

Independent Commission against Corruption. (2018). *Corruption and integrity in the NSW public sector: An assessment of current trends and events*. Retrieved from file:///E:/Users/Quentin%20Grafton/Downloads/Corruption-and-integrity-in-the-nsw-public-sector-an-assessment-of-current-trends-and-events_7Dec18.pdf

Jensen, M. E. (2007). Beyond irrigation efficiency. *Irrigation Science, 25*(3), 233–245.

Klitgaard, R. (1988). *Controlling corruption*. Berkeley: University of California Press.

Kreuger, A. O. (1974). The political economy of the rent-seeking society. *American Economic Review, 64*(3), 291–303.

Lambsdorff, J. G. (2002). Corruption and rent-seeking. *Public Choice, 113*, 97–125.

Lewis, K., & Lenton, R. (2008). Water Resources Management. Chapter 2 in *Global Corruption Report 2008: Corruption in the Water Sector*. Cambridge, UK: Cambridge University Press.

Littleproud, D., & Pasin, T. (2019, September 1). *$20m Basin research program increases security*. Minister for Water Resources, Drought, Rural Finance, Natural Disaster and Emergency Management. Retrieved from https://minister.agriculture.gov.au/littleproud/media-releases/20-million-basin-research-program-increases-security

Loch, A., Wheeler, S., Boxall, P., Hatton-Macdonald, D., Adamowicz, W. L., & Bjornlund, H. (2014). Irrigator preferences for water recovery budget expenditure in the Murray-Darling Basin, Australia. *Land Use Policy, 36*, 396–404.

Marshall, G. R., & Alexandra, J. (2016). Institutional path dependence and environmental water recovery in Australia's Murray-Darling Basin. *Water Alternatives, 9*, 679–703.

Matthews, K. (2017). *Independent investigation into NSW water management and compliance advice on implementation*. NSW Department of Industry. Retrieved from https://www.industry.nsw.gov.au/__data/assets/pdf_file/0019/131905/Matthews-final-report-NSW-water-management-and-compliance.pdf

McCormack, M. (2019). *New Era: Liberal & nationals to deliver national water grid*. Nationals for Regional Australia. Retrieved from https://www.michaelmccormack.com.au/media-releases/2019/4/30/new-era-liberal-amp-nationals-to-deliver-national-water-grid

Middleton, K. (27 April 2019), Keelty warns river 'ripe for corruption'. *Saturday Paper*. Retrieved from https://www.thesaturdaypaper.com.au/news/politics/2019/04/27/keelty-warns-river-ripe-corruption/15562872008055

Murray-Darling Basin Royal Commission. (2019). *Murray-Darling Basin royal commission report*. Retrieved from https://www.mdbrc.sa.gov.au/

National Irrigators' Council. (2019). *Submission 31 to senate environment and communications legislation committee Re: Inquiry into the water amendment (purchase limit repeal) bill 2019*. Retrieved from https://www.aph.gov.au/Parliamentary_Business/Committees/Senate/Environment_and_Communications/WaterAmendmentBill2019/Submissions

New South Wales Department of Primary Industries. (2016). *The final business case for the Broken Hill long-term water supply solution*. Retrieved from https://drive.google.com/drive/folders/1DvuX3-7SEIN5rTeY2_p6_hLm73KpLMjo

New South Wales Natural Resources Commission. (2019). *Final report review of the water sharing plan for the Barwon-Darling unregulated & alluvial water sources 2012*. Retrieved from https://www.nrc.nsw.gov.au/publications

Parliament of Australia. (2018). *Senate orders for production of documents—Environment—Murray-Darling Basin Plan—Water purchases—Order of 16 November 2017—Letter to the President of the senate from the minister for resources and Northern Australia (Senator Canavan), dated 25 October 2018, responding to the order, and attachments*. Retrieved from https://parlinfo.aph.gov.au/parlInfo/search/display/display.w3p;query=Id%3A%22publications%2Ftabledpapers%2Ffa585f8d-6f39-43ec-9e46-bef903173df5%22

Perry, C. (2007). Efficient irrigation; inefficient communication; flawed recommendations. *Irrigation and Drainage, 56*, 367–378.

Pielke, R. A., Jr. (2007). *The honest broker: Making sense of science in policy and politics*. Cambridge, UK: Cambridge University Press.

Plummer, J. (2008) Introducing water and corruption. Chapter 1 in *Global Corruption Report 2008: Corruption in the Water Sector*. Cambridge, UK: Cambridge University Press.

Productivity Commission. (2010). *Market mechanism for recovering water in the Murray-Darling Basin. Research report*. Canberra, Australia. Retrieved from https://www.pc.gov.au/inquiries/completed/murray-darling-water-recovery

Productivity Commission. (2018, August). Murray-Darling Basin Plan: Five-year assessment. *Draft Report*. Retrieved from https://www.pc.gov.au/inquiries/current/basin-plan/draft

The Project. (2019). *The Sunday Project 5 May 2019 (25 minutes to 36 minutes)*. Retrieved from https://tenplay.com.au/channel-ten/the-project/2019/5/5

Qureshi, M., Grafton, Q., Kirby, M., & Hanjra, M. (2011). Understanding irrigation water use efficiency at different scales for better policy reform: A case study of the Murray-Darling Basin, Australia. *Water Policy, 13*(1), 1–17.

Repetto, R. (1986). *Skimming the water: Rent-seeking and the performance of public irrigation systems* (Research Report No. 4). Washington, DC: World Resources Institute.

Rijsberman, F. (2008). Water for food. Chapter 4 In *Global Corruption Report 2008: Corruption in the Water Sector*. Cambridge, UK: Cambridge University Press.

Slattery, M., & Campbell, R. (2019a). *#Watermates: The buyers and sellers of Australia's most controversial water*. Canberra: Australia Institute. Retrieved from http://www.tai.org.au/content/watergate-s-water-mates-buyers-and-sellers-australia-s-most-controversial-water

Slattery, M., & Campbell, R. (2019b). *Debugging the Watergate Complex*. Canberra: Australia Institute. Retrieved from http://www.tai.org.au/sites/default/files/Debugging%20water%20gate%20%255bweb%255d.pdf

Stigler, G. J. (1971). The theory of economic regulation. *Bell Journal of Economics and Management Science, 2*, 3–21.

Tabakovic, H., & Wollmann, T. G. (2018). *From revolving doors to regulatory capture? Evidence from patent examiners* (Working Paper 24638). Cambridge, MA: National Bureau of Economic Research.

Tee, J., & Salt, R. (2019, June 4). *Watergate crew: The regatta of mates behind Australia's richest water deal*. Michael West. Retrieved from https://www.michaelwest.com.au/watergate-crew-the-regatta-of-mates-behind-australias-richest-water-deal/

Thompson, D. F. (1993). Mediated corruption: The case of the Keating five. *American Political Science Review, 87*(2), 369–381.

Transparency International. (2008). *Global corruption report 2008: Corruption in the water sector*. Cambridge, UK: Cambridge University Press.

Transparency International Australia. (2018). *Rising corruption concern drives support for federal integrity body: Global corruption barometer survey results*. Retrieved from http://transparency.org.au/tia/wp-content/uploads/2018/08/180820-Media-Release-Global-Corruption-Barometer-Griffith-University-TI-Australia.pdf

Tullock, G. (1989). *The economics of special privilege and rent seeking*. Dordrecht, The Netherlands: Kluwer Academic.

Vertessy, R., Stewardson, M., Wang, Q. J., Webb, A., Western, A., Nathan, R., … Dyer, F. (2019). *An open letter from scientists on the Murray-Darling Basin*. Ingenium. Retrieved from https://ingenium.eng.unimelb.edu.au/2019/07/19/an-open-letter-from-scientists-on-the-murray-darling-basin/

Wang, Q. J., Walker, G., & Horne, A. (2018). *Potential impacts of groundwater sustainable diversion limits and irrigation efficiency projects on river flow volume under the Murray-Darling Basin plan*. Report written for the Murray-Darling Basin Authority. Retrieved from https://www.mdba.gov.au/sites/default/files/pubs/Impacts-groundwater-andefficiency-programs-on-flows-October-2018.pdf

Ward, F. A., & Pulido-Velazquez, M. (2008). Water conservation in irrigation can increase water use. *Proceedings of the National Academy of Sciences, 105*(47), 18215–18220.

Wentworth Group of Concerned Scientists. (2018, April, 19), *Murray-Darling Basin plan: Five-year assessment*. Submission to the Productivity Commission Issues Paper. Retrieved from https://www.pc.gov.au/__data/assets/pdf_file/0006/227508/sub042-basin-plan.pdf.

Wentworth Group of Concerned Scientists. (2019). Water Flows in the *Murray-Darling Basin: Observed versus expected*. Summary Report. Retrieved from https://wentworthgroup.org/wp-content/uploads/2019/02/MDB-flows-summary.pdf

West, M. (2017). *Corporate lobbying a billion-dollar business*. Michael West. Retrieved from https://www.michaelwest.com.au/corporate-lobbying-a-billion-dollar-business/

West, M. (2019, April 21). *Barnaby Joyce, Angus Taylor, Australia and the Caribbean*. Michael West. Retrieved from https://www.michaelwest.com.au/barnaby-joyce-angus-taylor-australia-and-the-caribbean/

Wheeler, S., Zuo, A., Bjornlund, H., & Lane-Miller, C. (2012). Selling the farm silver? Understanding water sales to the Australian government. *Environmental and Resource Economics, 52*(1), 133–154.

Williams, J. (2017). Water reform in the Murray–Darling Basin: A challenge in complexity in balancing social, economic and environmental perspectives. *Journal and Proceedings of the Royal Society of New South Wales, 150*, 68–92. Retrieved from https://www.royalsoc.org.au/images/pdf/journal/150-1-Williams.pdf

Williams, J., & Grafton, R. Q. (2019). Missing in action: Possible effects of water recovery on stream and river flows in the Murray–Darling Basin, Australia. *Australasian Journal of Water Resources*. Retrieved from https://www.tandfonline.com/doi/full/10.1080/13241583.2019.1579965

Wilson, J. W. (1980). The politics of regulation. In J. Q. Wilson (Ed.), *The politics of regulation*. New York: Basic Books.

Witko, C. (2011). Campaign contributions, access, and government contracting. *Journal of Public Administration Research, 21*, 761–778.

Wood, D., & Griffiths, K. (2018). *Who's in the room? Access and influence in Australian politics* (Grattan Institute Report No. 2018–12). Retrieved from https://grattan.edu.au/wp-content/uploads/2018/09/908-Who-s-in-the-room-Access-and-influence-in-Australian-politics.pdf

Young, M., Young, D., Hamilton, A., & Bright, M. (2002, July). *A preliminary assessment of the economic and social implications of environmental flow scenarios for the Murray River System*. Report prepared for the Murray-Darling Basin Commission. Canberra, Australia. CSIRO Land and Water and PISA Rural Solutions.

Quenching the thirst of rapidly growing and water-insecure cities in sub-Saharan Africa

Madiodio Niasse and Olli Varis

ABSTRACT

It is in the water sector that Africa faces some of its more pressing challenges, which are exacerbated with the sprawl of megacities. The gap between water requirements and available water resources is widening. While the urbanization process is still accelerating, acute seasonal and chronic water shortages are already encountered in almost all major cities. Unless the direction is radically changed, sub-Saharan Africa is headed towards an urban water crisis of alarming proportions. Based on city experiences in Africa and comparison to those in India, we draw lessons and suggest response options for tackling urban water crisis risks in Africa.

Introduction

Severe water crises are becoming increasingly frequent on all continents: in Australia's east-coast cities, in the west and southwest of the US, in Mediterranean countries, in many parts of Asia (particularly in India's megacities – Delhi, Chennai, Bangalore, etc.), and perhaps most strikingly in Africa. Cape Town's unprecedented water shortage in 2017, a crisis referred to as Day Zero, was a dire warning to the world.

Experiencing the world's fastest population growth and urbanization (African Development Bank, 2018, 2019), with sprawling metropoles, Africa seems particularly vulnerable to water shortages, especially in the continent's largest cities. Many of them are already facing either seasonal or chronic water shortages. These include Bamako, Niamey and Harare, and also the cities in the wettest regions of the continent (Luanda and many others).

If the current trends persist and contemporary projections (see Hoornweg & Pope, 2014) are not totally wrong – in terms of demographic change, urban growth and climate change impacts on water – we can expect an urban water crisis of alarming proportions in sub-Saharan Africa in the decades to come.

Since urban water and development issues are highly complicated and context-specific, and a myriad of inconsistent views and argumentation prevail (Kumar, 2018), Tortajada and Biswas (2019) called for objective case studies of urban water management, to understand more broadly what has worked and what has not in various contexts of urban development. We examine the urbanization process in sub-Saharan Africa, starting from the root causes of the water crises threatening the continent's largest cities and conurbations. We analyze the key risks associated with severe and unresolved urban water crises: climate change, intensified competition, struggles for water, and possible knock-on effects related to peace and political stability. To improve our understanding of the urban water crisis risk in sub-Saharan Africa, we analyze the experiences of selected cities (in Africa and India) that are among the most vulnerable or are evolving towards widening water supply gaps. Building on the key findings and lessons from these city experiences, we propose an array of response options that could be considered to avoid, delay or minimize the risk of water crisis in the megacities of sub-Saharan Africa.

Magnitude of the water crisis in African megacities

Africa's urban water challenges are primarily related to the fast-growing population, and especially the pace at which urban areas are expanding. The world's population is growing by around 83 million people each year, and Africa contributes one-third of this growth, even though the continent has only 13% of the global population (United Nations, 2017). The population growth in African urban areas is even more spectacular.

Africa's demographic growth and rapid urbanization: a time bomb?

Sub-Saharan Africa's population is now growing by 28 million people per year (United Nations, 2017). The population is projected to double by 2053, triple by 2086 and grow four-fold by the end of the century. It will soon have a larger population than India (in 2028) and China (in 2026) (Figure 1). Whereas India's and China's population is projected to peak during this century (China in 2030 and India in 2070) and then begin to decline, sub-Saharan Africa's population growth will keep accelerating for several decades.

An increasing share of this massive growth will be urban. Although Africa today is the least urbanized of all continents, it has the fastest pace of urbanization (Muggah & Kilcullen, 2016). With an annual growth of almost 4%, Africa's urban population doubles every 20 years (Jacobsen, Webster, & Vairavamoorthy, 2012).

Along with Africa, China and South Asia dominate the urban growth, each contributing around 16 to 17 million urban residents per year (United Nations, 2017). But Africa's

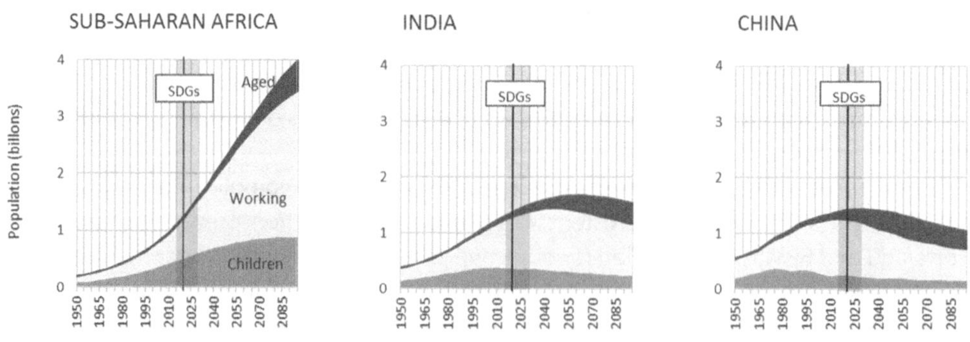

Figure 1. Population size of the main age groups in sub-Saharan Africa, India and China in 1950–2100 (United Nations, 2017).

outlook is different from the two other regions in the sense that its growth is projected to continue very rapidly for the rest of the century (United Nations, 2017), whereas in Asia (even in South Asia), the growth rate – despite being high now – will start to fall in the next three decades. Hutton and Varughese (2016) project that the urban population in sub-Saharan Africa will increase by 72% between 2015 (372 million) and 2030 (642 million), compared to 40% growth in South Asia.

Hoornweg and Pope (2014) analyzed the growth and development pathways of the world's 101 largest cities in this century. Using the shared socio-economic pathway scenarios (Arnell & Kram, 2010) and United Nations World Population Projections of 2011, they produced a matrix of scenarios for the development of population, urbanization, resource availability and scarcity, and economic growth. All scenarios include massive growth of these urban centres. By 2050, the largest megacities are projected to be in South Asia and Africa. In other continents, the size of cities and their growth rate are more modest. After 2050, Africa has the most massive growth.

India and Africa are almost the same size in terms of demography and economy (Table 1), although Africa has nine times the surface area. They are more or less equally represented in the list of the world's 101 largest cities (nine for Africa and seven for India). But by 2050, Africa is projected to almost triple its count on the list (to 25), while India's count is will still be 11 (Table 1).

The urban water crisis in Africa: contemporary threats and warning signs for the future

Urban water insecurity is a threat not only for the future but also for the present, which is shown by the soaring number of severe water shortages hitting several major African cities each year. In the last five years alone, cities in all sub-regions of the continent, both arid and humid, faced water deficits. We will mention a few cases, starting with Southern Africa. Harare and Bulawayo, Zimbabwe's two largest cities, faced severe water shortages in the first half of 2019, leading to drastic water rationing. During the same period, in neighbouring Mozambique, Maputo residents had access to tap water only on alternating days (Dontoh & Cohen, 2019).

In West Africa, we use two examples: Dakar (the coastal capital of Senegal) and Bouake (the second-largest city in Côte d'Ivoire, more than 200 km from the coast). With its satellite towns and villages, Dakar largely depends on Lake de Guiers, a tributary of the Senegal River, 250 km away (Cogels, Fraboulet-Jussila, & Varis, 2001). The city has severe

Table 1. Comparing Africa, India and China (population size, economy, present and future megacities).

	Africa	Sub-Saharan Africa	India	China
Population (thousands, 2018)	1,273,000	1,078,000	1,353,000	1,393,000
Total GDP (USD billions, 2018)	2321	1697	2726	13,608
GDP per capita (USD)	1823	1574	2014	9769
Number of cities in the largest 101 cities (more than 3.4 million residents) in 2010	9	6	7	15
Number of cities in the largest 101 cities (more than 5.7 million residents) in 2050	25	22	11	11

Population and GDP data from World Bank Data (https://data.worldbank.org/, accessed 15 August 2019); data for cities from Hoornweg and Pope (2014).

water deficits almost every year, including in April–July 2019, when tankers were used to supplement the failing utility-managed water distribution system. In 2018, Bouake faced a severe water shortage due to rainfall deficits and the shrinking Loka reservoir, which covers 70% of the city's water supply (Larcher, 2018). The government responded with massive water supplies from tankers and a decision to dig 44 boreholes, which can only be effective if the current trend in the dropping of groundwater tables is reversed.

In Eastern Africa, Nairobi (Kenya) illustrates the challenge of dealing with ever-expanding water demand. Nairobi's population swelled threefold from 1985 to 2010, leading to a 200% increase in urban water demand. It is no surprise that the city finds itself in frequent water crises, as in 2009, when water had to be rationed as a result of the city's main reservoir shrinking (Jacobsen et al., 2012). The city continues to grow rapidly, and water demand has increased by 30% since 2012. As a result of the widening gap between water demand and supply, water crisis management has become a permanent challenge for Nairobi, as for the whole of Kenya (Goswami, 2018).

Each of Africa's sub-regions is affected by urban water shortages, increasingly threatening the future of cities as dissimilar as Marrakech, Ouagadougou and Dar es Salaam, and even cities like Kampala and Kinshasa, which are on the shore of large water bodies – Lake Victoria and the Congo River, respectively. Throughout the continent, the gap between water demand and supply is widening, leading to crises each time a pronounced rainfall deficit occurs, which, in the current context of climate change, is more the rule than the exception.

To sum up, it is in the water sector that Africa faces one of its more pressing contemporary challenges, which is growing more difficult with the sprawl of large cities as we move to the future. Van de Bruggen, Borghgraef, and Vinckier (2009) estimate that for every urban citizen in sub-Saharan Africa in 1950, 53 more will have to be accommodated by 2050 and supplied with water. In a century, there will be more than a 50-fold increase in the urban population of sub-Saharan Africa. Along the same lines, Jacobsen et al. (2012) project that over the next 25 years the demand for water in Africa will almost quadruple, largely due to the anticipated dramatic growth in the urban population but also due to economic development, translating into industrial expansion, prosperity and a larger middle class. The challenge is not limited to Africa. Globally, it is anticipated that the number of urban dwellers living with seasonal water shortages will grow from about 500 million in 2000 to 1.9 billion by 2050 (World Bank, 2018). Large conurbations present additional water challenges of their own. They put enormous pressure on local sources and rapidly exhaust them, and hence require extensive, complex and onerous infrastructure such as dams and water transfer canals to transfer water over long distances.

The root causes of urban water crises

To improve the continent's preparedness for preventing and managing urban water crises, it is important to understand the causes of these crises. In this section, we analyze the causes of the currently observed urban water crises in sub-Saharan Africa from various angles: the pace, patterns and modalities of urbanization; the structure and spatial distribution of settlements; and the extent and soundness of investments in urban water infrastructure.

Soaring sub-Saharan Africa's urban population and sprawling cities

From a water-planning perspective, as well as for mobilization of finances and for physical construction and operation, the pace of urban sprawl is a serious challenge. In 2000 only two cities (Kinshasa and Lagos) exceeded 5 million, but two more exist today (Dar es Salaam and Luanda). By 2030, 15 sub-Saharan African cities are projected to host more than 5 million inhabitants: Addis Ababa, Nairobi, Antananarivo, Kampala, Dar es Salaam, Luanda, Douala, Yaounde, Kinshasa, Cape Town, Johannesburg, Abidjan, Abuja, Kano and Lagos. Of these, Dar es Salaam and Luanda are expected to exceed 10 million; and Kinshasa and Lagos, 20 million (UNDESA, 2018). Fast-growing cities tend to rapidly exhaust local natural resources, emptying the aquifers underneath and drying out lakes and reservoirs in their neighbourhood.

When patterns of urbanization influence the water stress risks of cities

The very process of urbanization and the pathways followed in city creation and urban growth play a major role in the water crisis we are witnessing today in many large African cities and conurbations. They explain why and how the location of the city was decided and the modalities and pace of urban growth. The location of a city – at the shore of a freshwater body, in a region with abundant aquifer reserves, or instead in a hard rocky environment far from surface waters – is a determining factor for a city's water stress and the available options to gain and preserve water security as the urban population expands.

Most of Africa's largest cities are former colonial capitals that maintained their status after independence. As colonial cities, they were created to serve as military barracks and economic entrepôts for trade (imports and exports). Often located along a coast and/or major rivers, many colonial capitals flourished as trading centres when they were administrative headquarters and hosted harbours linked to the countryside by railways (Coquery-Vidrovitch, 1991; Horvath, 1969; Thomas, 1970). As they became capitals of newly independent states, they consolidated their political, administrative, intellectual and economic roles. They received a large share of investments as symbols of the aspirations for modernity and affirmation of the national pride of newly independent states. As a result, they attracted more and more people to become the vast agglomerations they are today. Colonial centres were created with little or no consideration of the natural resource potentials and limitations of their locations. At present, we see a widening gap between the requirements of the cities they have become today and the natural endowment of their local environments, including physically available water resources.

Due to urbanization processes that failed to adopt an ecological approach (defined by Filani and Okafor, 2006, whereby the location of cities is decided in relation to their immediate physical environment), today many African cities are located in areas at risk of high water stress, for example Bamako, Lagos, Niamey, Ouagadougou and Dakar.

From the collapse of Africa's farming sector to the rural push to urban slums

Typically, cities grow through natural population growth, immigration, and/or the absorption of neighbouring cities and villages (Kasarda & Crenshaw, 1991). The natural or 'organic' growth of the population is and will remain very high, reflecting the high birth rate in sub-Saharan Africa, which applies to both urban and rural areas. In-migration (voluntary and involuntary) is what makes the difference for urban areas (Muggah & Kilcullen, 2016). Cities with high population growth from natural growth and in-migration, essentially from rural areas and smaller cities, will inexorably encroach on and convert neighbouring agricultural land and absorb surrounding settlements.

To understand the magnitude and nature of migration to African cities, it is important to place it in the context of Africa's particular development path. In the classic economic development path, growing agricultural production leads to wealth accumulation, which serves as the basis for industrial development (a secondary sector), which in turn boosts agricultural production through mechanization, both sectors feeding into the tertiary sector. Industrial development creates jobs and contributes to agricultural modernization, which frees labour from the agricultural sector that becomes available for generally urban-based secondary and tertiary activities. In such a development path, rural–urban migration takes place in a context where rural push coincides with urban pull (see Niva, Taka, & Varis, 2019).

Africa's trajectory is different. Despite the continent's considerable potential for agricultural expansion (including irrigation), the farming sector is ailing, which means low productivity, degrading soils and high vulnerability to fluctuating agricultural commodity prices and the vagaries of climate change (Bernstein, 1990; Evans, 2010). Impoverished and desperate farmers are fleeing rural areas in a massive rural exodus, and settling in the rapidly swelling slums of big cities (Moseley, Carney, & Becker, 2010). At the same time, the underdeveloped agriculture is unable to feed the expanding cities, which have to rely on food imports. This means that transfer of wealth out of the country (since the trade balance usually becomes strongly negative) and insufficient funds inhibit agricultural development. Comparing the factors behind rural out-migration to cities in China and Africa, Collier (2017) points out that in the former, rural migration was more a response to urban growth than to rural desperation, which is the case in Africa. This pattern of urban development has far-reaching impacts on urban water management and on the ability of African metropolitan areas to respond to water crisis risks.

This pattern of rural-to-urban migration results in what Filani and Okafor (2006) call the 'peasantization' of African cities, as new in-migrants tend to maintain their 'peasant-type' strategy to survive in their new urban environment.

And this contributes to the spectacular expansion of slums which accompanies the growth of major cities in sub-Saharan Africa. UN-Habitat (2006) defines a slum household as 'a group of individuals living under the same roof in an urban area who lack *one or more* of the following five conditions: durable housing, sufficient living area, access to improved water, access to sanitation, and secure land tenure titles'. It is estimated that more than 70% of sub-Saharan Africa's urban population lives in slums (Bahri, Brikké, & Vairavamoorthy, 2016; Dagdeviren & Robertson, 2011; Jacobsen et al., 2012; UN-Habitat, 2006). Thus, the urbanization process in sub-Saharan Africa has become virtually synonymous with slum growth (UN-Habitat, 2006).

This large proportion of informal settlements is highly relevant to urban water security in Africa. Access to tap water is very limited in slums. Slum dwellers find alternative solutions to their water needs by digging wells and using surface water ponds, which are often polluted because of the lack of sanitation and domestic waste treatment, resulting in high exposure to water-related diseases. The anarchy that often prevails in slums means a weak government presence, without the ability to enforce the law or to coordinate a response such as administering quotas for water allocation when it becomes necessary to apply drastic measures to limit urban water consumption.

Booming cities, flourishing water-intensive activities and lifestyles

Urbanization is accompanied by a boost in many water-intensive sectors and activities. As the population grows and becomes more urban, the need for food, energy, minerals, consumer goods, construction materials and other materials expands dramatically. Within their supply chains and life cycles (Hellweg & Milà I Canals, 2014; O'Rourke, 2014), they all have specific links to water. Urban areas also attract water-intensive industrial installations, which are increasingly located in special economic zones in the suburbs of megacities.

Also, urban metropoles typically host most of society's wealthiest segments and the middle class, whose water demand per capita often far exceeds the national average. In Asia's developing countries, per capita water use increases dramatically in households experiencing improvements in their living standards when introducing access to tap water facilities (Asian Development Bank, 2010). The same phenomenon is also seen in Africa (Dos Santos et al., 2017).

All of these factors, together with a swelling urban population, amplify the ever-expanding thirst of megacities in developing countries in general and in sub-Saharan Africa in particular.

The challenge of the water infrastructure gap

Infrastructure is essential in the development of societies (Muller, Biswas, Martin-Hurtado, & Tortajada, 2015). Investment gaps in water storage and ageing water infrastructure contribute significantly to Africa's water crisis, especially in the largest urban areas. But this investment gap is a global concern. Estimates of the investment needs vary significantly (see Barenjee & Morella, 2011; Foster & Briceño-Garmendia, 2010; Hutton & Varughese, 2016). According to Woetzel, Garemo, Mischke, Hjerpe, and Palter (2016), all infrastructure investment needs at the global level amounted to USD 2.5 trillion annually in 2013. This means that the cost of meeting the United Nations Sustainable Development Goals for 2030 would be on the order of USD 3.3 trillion per year. According to other estimates, the annual water infrastructure investment should be twice as much as the 2015 level of USD 236 billion (Hutton & Varughese, 2016). Substantial funds are necessary to close the water infrastructure gap. Nevertheless, when divided among the world's population of 7.7 billion in 2019, the sum becomes more comprehensible: from USD 30 to USD 60 per person annually.

In the African context, water infrastructure (water storage, water transfer schemes, wells and boreholes, water and wastewater treatment plants, sewer systems, etc.) typically covers only certain parts of urban areas – generally ignoring the slums, which as we have seen now take up the most area in most of the large African cities. Where water infrastructure exists (for example in the centres of former colonial cities), it tends to be old, obsolete and a source of important water losses (Bahri et al., 2016). Africa's water infrastructure gap is even more striking when examined using existing dams and water storage facilities. Of the world's 58,000 largest registered dams, only 2150 (4%) are in Africa, and most of the large African dams are in North Africa (20%) or between South Africa and Zimbabwe (63%). Water control is almost nonexistent in most of sub-Saharan Africa.

Water transfers from a water-abundant to a water-poor region – including cities facing water deficits – may be increasingly used in the future as discrepancies in water allocation widen due to climate change and evolving water demand. The highest water demand is concentrated in urban agglomerations and agricultural growth centres. Inter-basin water transfer schemes are more developed in Southern Africa (South Africa, Namibia and Botswana), but there are notable water transfer schemes in other parts of the continent. Among these, we can mention Libya's Great Man-Made River, a 3000 km network of underground pipes transferring water from the deep aquifers of the southern regions to the northern and coastal regions of the country for irrigation and water supply for Tripoli and other coastal cities. On the Atlantic coast, the cities of Dakar and Nouakchott receive most of their water from the Senegal River, through water transfer schemes of 250 and 170 km, respectively. For the future, the most ambitious inter-basin water transfer project is the Lake Chad Replenishment Project. It is a water transfer scheme 2400 km long, transferring about 50 billion cubic metres annually from the Ubangi River (in the Congo basin) to replenish Lake Chad (Lake Chad Basin Commission, 2016). The project has very ambitious targets in hydropower production and irrigation, but it will also benefit the cities of N'Djamena and Maiduguri and potentially the Komadugu-Yobe River basin, where Kano, Nigeria's second-largest city, is located.

Implications of protracted, unresolved urban water crises

The many impacts of the exponentially growing urban water demand in sub-Saharan Africa cannot all be covered here. We focus on two of these – the competition for water between rural and urban areas, and the intensification of water riots – and their possible implications in terms of social unrest, conflicts and political instability.

Competition within cities and between cities, the countryside and other sectors

Agriculture accounts for about 70% of global freshwater consumption. The high levels of water withdrawals in the agricultural sector are closely linked to irrigation activities. Despite the very low level of irrigation development in sub-Saharan Africa (less than 7% of cultivated land), agriculture still accounts for 80% of the region's water consumption, because the industrial sector is embryonic and household water use remains very low. Per capita freshwater availability (rainwater, surface water and groundwater) is estimated at 3967 m^3 per year for sub-Saharan Africa, which is far above the 'water scarcity' level of 1000 m^3/year per person and even the 'water stress' level of 1700 m^3/y per person (World Bank, 2019). The region is therefore rather water-rich. One might therefore expect limited competition for water between sectors, between regions within a country, between river basin reaches and between urban and rural areas. But in fact there are marked differences in water availability between sub-regions and between countries. In addition to North Africa, Southern Africa (Burundi, Ethiopia, Kenya, Rwanda, Tanzania, Uganda) is below the

1000 m^3 threshold, and so are many countries in Southern Africa and the Sudano-Sahelian region (such as Cape Verde and Burkina Faso). Evidently, the threshold values do not have much to do with water availability on the ground; what is essential is how well the water – a renewable resource – is managed (Biswas & Tortajada, 2019b).

Competition for water between urban and rural areas and between sectors is thus intense and soaring, especially in locations that are water-stressed or have a fast-growing population and economy. In fact, we are already observing that in some regions, substantial amounts of water are being drained from rural regions. A review by Garrick et al. (2019) covering 69 urban agglomerations served by 103 water reallocation projects, mostly in Asia and North America, found that in 2015 approximately 16 billion m^3 of water was transferred to urban regions through water transfer schemes of about 13,000 km in total length.

The already heavy reliance of urban areas on water transfers from rural areas is expected to continue to increase dramatically (Garrick et al., 2019). This is not only because of the expanding urban population but also because the largest share of the predicted growth of the industry and energy sectors will take place in urban and peri-urban areas.

If current urban development trends persist, along with the expansion of irrigated agriculture – which is unavoidable if the continent is to minimize the vulnerability of its food system to climate change – the competition between cities and the farming sector can be expected to intensify, especially if Africa experiences sustained economic growth.

Urban water demonstrations and riots intensify as the unmet water demand grows

Urban water demand is increasing rapidly in sub-Saharan Africa, especially in large cities. When government, municipalities and water utilities fail to make the necessary investment to meet the growing water demand, citizens take to the streets against water shortages and sometimes water tariffs, especially when the water supply is unreliable.

Using the Pacific Institute's (2019) database on water conflicts and while focusing on the types of water conflicts, and especially water riots and water-related demonstrations in sub-Saharan Africa in the last 10 years, we observed the following features.

- Most citizen protests regarding water service quality occur in urban areas, often in major cities and capital cities. Water riots and demonstrations have taken place in all sub-regions of sub-Saharan Africa: West Africa (Dakar, Bamako, Conakry, Abidjan, Lagos), Central Africa (Kinshasa), Eastern Africa (Nairobi, Dar es Salaam) and Southern Africa (multiple cities in South Africa, Bulawayo in Zimbabwe, Antananarivo).
- The demonstrations have so far generally been in the form of peaceful marches, but some involved burning tyres, throwing stones at security forces, and blocking main roads and highways, affecting urban mobility.
- Demonstrators complain of chronic water scarcity, untimely water cuts in water supply (sometimes with electricity blackouts), ineffective draining of excess rainwater, etc.
- The urban residents taking to the streets to organize marches and riots to complain of water service failures are from all types of neighbourhoods, although they tend to be predominantly from poor and populous neighbourhoods, especially slums.
- Their complaints are typically directed at the government in general, but in some cases, municipal authorities or water utilities are specifically targeted.

The question is how concerned we should be when seeing more and more urban residents expressing anger and organizing marches, which sometimes escalate into riots. For Almer, Laurent-Lucchetti, and Oechslin (2015), these riots are not always mere 'short-lived and local events'. Based on an analysis of a series of water-related conflicts, they observe that high-frequency and intensifying rioting can be warning signs of a build-up to 'major events like rebellions, political unrest and even revolutions'. This view is shared by a US Intelligence Community (2012) report: 'The lack of adequate water will be a destabilizing factor in some countries because they do not have the financial resources or technical ability to solve their internal water problems.' This report predicts that in the next decade, water shortages and inadequate government response to the challenge are likely to 'lead to social disruptions, pressure on national and local leaders, and potentially political instability'.

What can we learn from the current experiences in Africa?

Africa is diverse, with marked contextual differences between sub-regions and between countries. The FAO (2003) distinguishes between seven agro-ecological regions in the continent (Table 2). Based on their natural and per capita freshwater endowments, three of these regions (Central Africa, the Gulf of Guinea and the Indian Ocean) are 'wet regions'. Together they have 84% of the continent's total freshwater (combined rainwater, surface and groundwater resources), with per capita annual water availability ranging from 3400 m^3 to more than 12,000 m^3, which is far above the water scarcity and stress levels discussed above. The other four regions (North, Eastern and Southern Africa, as well as the Sudano-Sahelian region) are 'arid and semi-arid regions'. Together they account for 16% of the continent's total freshwater resources, with North and Southern Africa falling below the water scarcity limit.

We examine the experience of a large city in each of the semi-arid regions of sub-Saharan Africa: Dar es Salaam for East Africa, Dakar for the Sudano-Sahelian region, and Cape Town for Southern Africa. For the three wet regions, we take Kinshasa.

A feature common to these four cities is their rapid population growth over the last 70 years (1950 to 2020). During this period their combined population has increased 26-fold, ranging from Cape Town (which 'only' increased 7-fold) and Dakar (15-fold, not including the

Table 2. Marked differences in freshwater endowments among Africa's ecological sub-regions.

	Wetter regions			Arid and semi-arid regions				
	Central Africa	Gulf of Guinea	Indian Ocean	Eastern Africa	Southern Africa	Sudano-Sahel	Northern Africa	Africa
Freshwater avail., km^3/y*	1950	1025	345	262	309	374	135	3950
Share of Africa's freshwater	**49%**	**26%**	9%	7%	8%	9%	3%	100%
Total population (thousands)	153,644	296,843	28,459	283,137	145,169	172,029	195,492	1,274,772
Percentage of Africa's population**	12%	23%	2%	22%	11%	13%	15%	100%
Freshwater per capita (m^3)	**12,692**	**3452**	**12,123**	925	2126	2174	688	3099
Representative city		Kinshasa		Dar es Salaam	Cape Town	Dakar		

* From the UN (https://population.un.org/wpp/Download/Standard/Population/).
** FAO (2003).

conurbation) to the staggering cases of Kinshasa and Dar Salaam, which increased 71-fold and 90-fold, respectively. By 2030, their total population is projected to increase by 30%. Rapidly swelling population size is the primary driver of water demand and the widening urban water supply gap.

Experiences from wetter regions: Kinshasa (DR Congo)

Kinshasa's population grew from 200,000 in 1950 to 443,000 in 1960, when DR Congo became independent. Since then, the population has grown almost 30-fold and is projected to be over 22 million in 2030 (United Nations, 2018). Kinshasa depends on the Congo River for its water supply. This is Africa's second-longest river, after the Nile, and its mean annual discharge of 1320 km^3 is the world's second-biggest after the Amazon (van de Bruggen et al., 2009). This discharge represents about 20% of the projected 2030 global water demand of 6900 billion m^3. Thus, Kinshasa can be considered as having access to an unlimited amount of renewable freshwater – in addition to the annual rainfall of more than 1300 mm.

The paradox is that one-third of Kinshasa's residents are not connected to the city's drinking water network (Bahri et al., 2016), and the households with access to tap water suffer from water quality problems and frequent service disruptions, partly due to the ageing water infrastructure. Only 60% of the city's estimated water demand of 900,000 m^3 per day is covered (Ilemba & Nzitattira, 2019). Kinshasa is an archetype of a technical and governance-related water scarcity amid physical water abundance.

Experience in a semi-arid/sub-humid region: Dar es Salaam (Tanzania)

At the time of Tanzanian independence in the early 1960s, the city of Dar es Salaam had slightly more than 160,000 residents. The number grew to 850,000 in 1980 and 2.2 million in 2000, and today is over 6 or 7 million and projected to pass 10 million by 2030. Dar es Salaam is one of the fastest-growing cities in the world (5% annual growth).

The city has a sub-humid climate, with average annual rainfall of 1000 to 1300 mm. Four main rivers (Mpiji, Msimbazi, Kizinga and Mzinga) run across the city. But though it has abundant and diverse water resources, the city faces serious water challenges. The demand for drinking water is estimated at 533,000 m^3 per day, but only 245,000 m^3 per day is available in the city's water distribution network, of which 20% is lost due to the ageing water infrastructure and illegal water abstractions (Nganyanyuka, Martinez, Wesselink, Lungo, & Georgiado, 2014). No clear long-term, forward-looking strategy exists to address the widening water deficits (today 45% of the city water demand is not covered), and most city residents (especially slum dwellers) are on their own – they have to fend for themselves to cover their drinking water needs. The various water survival strategies include unregulated drilling of deep wells; installing water pumps and reserve tanks; buying water from private vendors, neighbours and even mosques; connecting illegally; and stealing water from the utility network (Nganyanyuka et al., 2014).

Experience in the arid and semi-arid Sahelian region: Dakar (Senegal)

Dakar is among the fastest-growing cities in West Africa and the Sahel region. From 400,000 people when Senegal gained independence in 1960, today Dakar (the greater

Dakar, including its eponymous administrative region) has more than 3 million inhabitants and is projected to grow to over 4.3 million by 2030 (United Nations, 2018). Dakar is in the southern margin of the Sahel region, and it used to receive about 600 mm in a normal rainfall year. Groundwater is rapidly dwindling due to the combined effects of increased aquifer abstraction, reduced recharge volumes (due to rainfall deficits) and excessive groundwater abstraction. Further groundwater withdrawals are constrained not only by dropping water tables but also by salt intrusion (Dasylva & Cosandey, 2005). An increasing proportion of freshwater supplies to Dakar (20% in the early 1990s, more than 50% today) is transferred from Lac de Guiers (a tributary of the Senegal River), 250 km away. Water losses are significant (about 20%) along the water pipe from Lac de Guiers and in the water distribution network in the city, largely due to the ageing water infrastructure: 1565 km (25% of the existing water conveyance network of 6145 km) is more than 30 years old (Japan International Cooperation Agency, 2014).

The 2011 Urban Water Master Plan projects water demand for greater Dakar to increase to 500,000 m^3 per day by 2030. In anticipation of this growing demand, important measures are being taken, including an additional water treatment plan and water pipe from Lake de Guiers and two water desalination plants (Japan International Cooperation Agency, 2014).

It remains to be seen whether these measures are enough. The demographic projections, and hence the forecasted water demand, seem too conservative. Moreover, the demographic effects of the creation of the Diamniadio urban centre (a quasi-new capital, less than 30 km from the Dakar city centre) are clearly not factored in. If the population of the conurbation of Dakar grows faster than predicted, which is highly probable, the objectives set for covering the medium-term water demand and the measures conceived to attain these objectives will be overtaken by the actual water demand even before the completion of these interventions.

Experience in semi-arid Southern Africa: Cape Town (South Africa)

Cape Town is South Africa's second-largest city. It had 600,000 inhabitants in 1950, passed 1 million by 1970, doubled in the following two decades, and doubled again in the three subsequent decades. From the current 4 million, the city is expected to reach 5.5 million by 2030. Since 1950, the population has increased seven-fold, which is a very fast pace, though much slower than Dakar (15-fold), Kinshasa (70-fold) and Dar es Salaam (90-fold).

While the 30-year average annual rainfall is over 800 mm, the city is experiencing a long-term decline, both in the number of rainy days and in the volume of recorded rainfall. In three consecutive years of severe rainfall deficits (2015–2017), the water level in the six dam reservoirs of the city shrank dramatically, especially in the first half of 2017 (Table 3). Water levels in the dams dropped below 30% of the reservoirs' capacity, triggering fears of a Day Zero, when the level fell below 13.5%. At this level, water supplies

Table 3. Variations in water volumes stored in Cape Town dams, 2015–2019 (City of Cape Town, 2019).

	Total capacity of six main dams	2015	2016	2017	2018	2019
Total water stored (million m^3)	898.22	566.51	465.33	250.78	509.88	847.90
Percentage	100%	63%	52%	28%	57%	72%

are depleted, and the water taps are turned off (Burls et al., 2019; City of Cape Town, 2019). In the Day Zero scenario, each city resident is entitled to 25 litres per day, to be distributed from water collection sites (Burls et al., 2019).

The city developed and implemented a comprehensive response to the challenge. First, it activated its disaster risk management plan (dated 2015), involving close monitoring of available water resources and water allocations. Second, drastic measures were taken to prevent (or at least delay) Day Zero. Safe drinking water was limited to 50 litres per person per day, water allocation for agriculture (a sector that ordinarily uses 60% of the water) was drastically reduced, and the use of potable water for non-essential purposes (such as watering lawns, filling swimming pools and washing cars) was banned. With the successful enforcement of these measures, Day Zero, initially predicted for 12 April, was moved to 9 July, and later postponed again.

The experience of Cape Town, which was feared to be the 'first city to run out of water in modern times' (Mulligan, 2018), is a dire warning about the magnitude of the water challenges facing megacities as a result of growing urban populations, changing lifestyles and climate change (Biswas & Tortajada, 2018). The way Cape Town responded to the challenges (despite imperfections noted here and there) is exemplary, from the resource-monitoring side, for the development of a clear disaster management response, the enactment of stringent restrictions, and the actual enforcement of measures taken.

India's urban water challenges: key features of relevance for sub-Saharan Africa

India is facing acute and frequent water shortages in its urban areas, especially in the major cities (Biswas & Tortajada, 2019a). The urban population is growing rapidly, with megacities continuing to sprawl. With a rapidly growing economy, the often water-thirsty industrial and energy sectors are developing, especially in urban and peri-urban areas. These factors, along with an expanding middle class, boost urban water demand. At the same time, the country is experiencing a drastic decline in groundwater resources, shrinking of surface waters and deficits in rainfall in the context of record high temperatures. Hence, the gap between urban water demand and supply is widening. NITI Aayog (2018), a renowned government think tank, predicts that 21 major cities, including New Delhi (the capital), Chennai, Bangalore and Hyderabad, may run out of water by 2020, affecting no less than 100 million people. Alarming voices warn of a growing 'national crisis' (Nagpal, 2019; NITI Aayog, 2018).

The urban water crisis in sub-Saharan Africa has clearly not yet reached the acute level we are seeing in India today. The current pace of population growth, the rapid urbanization, and the rise of megacities and expansion of slum populations in sub-Saharan Africa are all signs that the continent may be heading towards a major urban water crisis, at least on the scale of the current urban water nightmare in India.

What can we learn from India's experience that can serve sub-Saharan Africa to prevent, delay, mitigate and manage a major urban water crisis in the coming three to four decades? We consider three cities as examples to understand the magnitude and key features of India's water crises, which can then serve as a basis for discussing the potential lessons for Africa: India's capital city, Delhi; Bangalore, a major economic growth centre; and Chennai, a fast-growing megalopolis.

New Delhi. The population of the New Delhi city and conurbation (the Delhi region) has increased from 1.5 million in 1951 to more than 20 million today. Along the Yamuna River, the city was surrounded by hundreds of small lakes and ponds, through which underlying aquifers were seasonally recharged. But many of the lakes have dried out and been absorbed by the expanding city. The Yamuna's waters are highly polluted, while groundwater levels are dropping dramatically. To make things worse, from mid-2018 to mid-2019, the city experienced its driest year in 27 years while recording its highest-ever monthly temperature in June 2019 (Bhardwaj, 2019). As can be predicted in such a context, the fight for water is intensifying, exposing inequality between wealthy neighbourhoods and slums. Competition at all levels, using legal as well as illegal means, gives rise to corruption, with a more present 'water mafia' and proliferating 'water gangs' (Bhardwaj, 2019; Saikia, 2018). But despite the water scarcity and the extent of water pollution, little consideration and negligible investments are being made in water reuse and recycling.

Bangalore has grown even faster than Delhi. Known as India's Silicon Valley, the city's expansion is closely related to its attractiveness as India's information technology hub. Bangalore's population grew from 750,000 in 1950 to 1.6 million in 1970, reaching 4 million in 1990 and 6 million in 2001. Today's population of 12 million is expected to nearly double by 2030. Its freshwater sources are the Cauvery River (100 km away), groundwater, and local monsoon rain. A network of more than 160 small lakes in and around the city used to play the role of natural storage, also facilitating groundwater recharge. But most have been swallowed up by the expanding city, and the remaining ones have almost all dried out. The declining water table resulted from intensive groundwater abstraction (Banerji & Accheri, 2019). In response to increased water demand and declining water resource availability, numerous coping tactics are used. Private operators dig wells deeper and deeper to reach the falling water table. In some locations, wells can be 10 times deeper than a decade ago (Banerji & Accheri, 2019). Thousands of tank trucks distribute water in the city. Water prices tripled in 15 years; and in some areas, water can be 'auctioned to the highest bidders' (Dilip, Kapasi, & Talkhani, 2019).

Chennai's population grew from 1.4 million in 1951 to 2.4 million in 1971 and reached 3.8 million 20 years later (Sujatha & Janardhanam, 2014). Today the 10-million mark has been passed. With poor monsoon rainfall in 2018 and heat waves in the second quarter of 2019, Chennai is facing a severe water crisis. The four reservoirs that supply water to the city have almost entirely dried up. Groundwater levels have declined dramatically. In response to the water shortage, city residents had to resort to water distributed by public trucks and private water providers. Radical responses included trains loaded with water tanks bringing water to the city from wetter remote regions. In parallel, medium-term solutions are expected from the clearing and deepening of reservoirs, wells and canals (Karthikeyan & Gupta, 2019; Palanichamy, 2019).

Lessons learned and options for the future

The lessons presented here are essentially drawn from the experiences of large urban agglomerations in sub-Saharan Africa and India discussed in the previous sections. The emphasis on India's experiences is justified by many similarities in the contexts in Africa and India. Here are the key points from the Indian cities of New Delhi, Bangalore and Chennai that are potentially relevant to Africa.

- Those three cities are all fast-growing urban agglomerations, swelling demographically and expanding in area to swallow neighbouring small towns and cities. This is a pattern we see in many big cities in India, and in sub-Saharan Africa.
- Many concurrent trends contribute to the acute water scarcity facing all three megacities. Water needs are increasing dramatically due to population growth, higher per capita water use as the middle class expands, and greater water demand from the rapidly growing industry and energy sectors. These sectors are predominantly located in or near cities.
- On the supply side, the amount of water made available to urban dwellers is declining, or at best growing but more slowly than the demand (Biswas, 2016). Many factors hinder the urban water supply: ageing water infrastructure, resulting in the loss of massive quantities of water; surface water sources, like neighbouring lakes, rivers and man-made reservoirs, drying out; and water tables in aquifers falling deeper. All of these factors are linked to excessive and unsustainable water withdrawals.
- Spatially expanding cities disorganize and destroy natural aquatic ecosystems (networks of small rivers, lakes and ponds), impairing the hydrodynamics that enable regular groundwater recharge – let alone the fact that growing cities massively pollute both surface water and groundwater.
- Climate change is making things worse: in addition to monsoon rainfall deficits, average temperatures are reaching historic highs in many locations in the country.
- As the water supply gap widens, diverse and rapid-response alternatives (sometimes radical) are put into motion. These include digging deeper and deeper in the aquifers and importing water, even by train, from remote locations.
- Typically, an informal and messy water trade system is emerging to compensate for deficient government responses. Water vendors multiply, including water truck tankers collecting water by all means, from local deep aquifers and from remote locations. Water prices skyrocket in a water market marred by corruption and involving unregulated operators, local politicians, and organized crime gangs and mafia.
- Strikingly, limited attention is being paid to the treatment, recycling and reuse of the masses of wastewater generated by megacities.
- In reaction to the acute water crisis facing the country, especially many of the largest cities, the government of India has launched a comprehensive water security and water conservation campaign, Jal Shakti Abhiyan, targeting the country's most water-stressed districts (*Economic Times of India*, 2019). Key lines of action are water conservation and rainwater harvesting; renovation of traditional and other water bodies; water reuse for industrial and agricultural purposes and water recharge of wells and aquifers; watershed development; and intensive afforestation. The programme is ambitious, but it is too early to assess its effectiveness.

More general messages and recommendations based on the present analysis are collected in Table 4.

Table 4. Lessons learned from India and sub-Saharan Africa, and ways forward for preventing water crises in large urban agglomerations.

Early planning Anticipate and guide urban development, taking into account water resource availability and conservation.	Because action was not taken earlier, many options that could have helped address India's current urban water crises are no longer available. Territorial and urban planning could have prevented the formation of monster cities. Proper planning can prevent cities expanding in ways that profoundly disorganize the natural hydrodynamics in and around the city. Examples include Chennai and Bangalore, which have converted surface waters, such as lakes, ponds and other wetlands, into urban settlements (also Dakar to a large extent).
Long-term planning Use a long-term planning horizon with realistic estimates of the magnitude and growth of urban water demand.	Planning efforts – where they exist (e.g. Dakar) – tend to adopt short-to -medium-term planning horizons and to use overly conservative projections for the growth of water demand. By the time medium-term solutions are designed and implemented, the actual demand can be much greater than what the 'solutions' considered.
Risk preparedness Improve disaster risk preparedness, and pay due attention to water-related risks such as floods and droughts.	Given the current and predicted magnitude and frequency of extreme events (droughts, floods, storms), each city needs a disaster management plan entirely or partially focused on water. Without such a plan, with regularly updated information on the city's water resources, Cape Town's 2017 water crisis could have been worse. It is on the basis of this plan and the close monitoring of reservoir water levels that the city was able to identify the nature of the threats (including Day Zero, when the taps would be turned off) and deploy measures to delay and finally avoid the doomsday scenario.
Infrastructure Close the urban water infrastructure gap.	Investment in new water infrastructure and the renovation and refurbishing of existing structures need to grow to unprecedented scales to match the exceptional nature of the urban water challenge (African Development Bank, 2018). This applies to cities in both water-scarce and water-rich environments. Paradoxically, arid and semi-arid cities (Dakar and Cape Town) have invested more in water infrastructure (although still more could have been done) than water-abundant cities (Dar es Salaam and Kinshasa). Consequently, safe water is more available in water-scarce cities than in water-abundant cities. In both cases, massive infrastructure investment will be needed in the coming years. Given the widening gap between water supply and demand – in addition to the vulnerabilities associated with climate change – large-scale water infrastructure (such as large storage and large inter-basin transfer schemes) cannot be ruled out, although these should be planned with the highest standards, given their complexity and their large social and environmental impacts (Chan, Ruwanpura, & Brown, 2019).
Climate change Pay due consideration to climate change impacts on water resources.	Climate change and variability need to be factored into water investment strategies, including the choice and design of water infrastructure. Strategies need to cope with both seasonal and spatial variations in water availability (which are likely to grow as a result of climate change). Storage infrastructure needs to be designed not only to cover water needs for the year but also to cater to multi-year fluctuations in rainfall, surface water discharge and groundwater levels.
Water storage and banking Explore the possibility of applying 'water banking' principles in the management of saved excess water.	Investment in storage infrastructure and groundwater recharging schemes could be envisaged to store excess water from wet years and very rainy seasons to help offset water deficits in severely dry seasons and years. The saved water could be managed on the basis of the 'water banking' principles, whereby stored water is withdrawn by the 'banker' – the owner or manager of the saved water – whenever needed in subsequent years and transferred to supplement the water resources of the 'client' (the buyer) or for use by the banker in years of water shortages (World Bank, 2018).

(*Continued*)

Table 4. (Continued).

Wastewater treatment and reuse Invest in urban waste reclamation and reuse to increase urban water supply and serve industrial and agricultural sectors.	In the examples from both Africa and India, investment in urban water collection, water treatment and reuse has been minimal. This is a lost opportunity to address urban water crises and water challenges in general. Cities account for about 30% of global water use, a large part of which is disposed as wastewater (Dahan & Grijsen, 2017). Reclaiming more of this huge amount of water could contribute substantially to offsetting some of the non-drinking water uses. In Windhoek (Namibia), water reclamation supplies over 30% of the city's water use (World Bank, 2018). One of the major beneficiaries could be urban and peri-urban agriculture. The World Bank (2016) estimates that agriculture within a 20 km radius of urban centres covers more than 450 million hectares. Representing one-third of the world's agricultural land, urban and peri-urban agriculture contributes to the livelihood of 800 million urban residents (UNESCO, 2012). As it tends to be the primary victim of increased urban water demand, it is amply justified to transfer the treated wastewater back to peri-urban agriculture.
Diversification Diversify sources of water supply for cities.	Reliance on one dominant source of water (either surface water or aquifers) is a major source of vulnerability for cities, especially in the context of climate change. Rainfall deficits have direct impacts on local surface water and groundwater resources. Vulnerability resulting from limited sources of water is illustrated by the water crises in Cape Town. The city depends almost entirely on its six reservoirs. Similarly, the Indian cities of Delhi, Bangalore and Chennai have too little diversity in their water sources. Options for increasing and diversifying water supplies to cities include surface water storage, wells to draw water from aquifers, wastewater treatment and reuse, rainwater harvesting, artificial recharge of groundwater and desalination of sea water (Dahan & Grijsen, 2017). The latter is highly relevant, given that most of Africa's largest conurbations are in coastal areas. In its current Urban Water Masterplan, Dakar seems to be heading towards more diversified sources of water supply by investing massively in seawater treatment in addition to surface and groundwater.
Water demand management Enhance water demand management and raise water consciousness among urban residents.	Along with government and municipal authorities, who are expected to show great leadership qualities, ordinary citizens have a key role in preventing urban water crises and mitigating their impacts (Biswas & Hartley, 2019). Central and local governments are expected to put in place an enabling governance environment (the right legal and institutional framework and water institutions), upgrade and maintain the water infrastructure, closely monitor the resources and invest substantially in information-sharing and awareness-raising. As shown in the Cape Town water crisis, citizens' engagement, mobilization and cooperation with dedicated authorities is what really makes the difference. Citizens' commitment and water consciousness are paramount if efforts to promote water saving through water conservation and demand management (addressing leakages, promoting water demand management) are to succeed.
Externalities Enhance economic and social development.	Considerable enhancement in societal development and capacity, in the broadest sense, is needed. Everything possible should be done to make the current population projections too high. Education and economic development, accompanied by governance progress, should turn the ruralized, slum-dominated urban areas into more affluent societies, with balanced environmental and social development. In parallel, rural areas need a development boost along the same lines.

Conclusions

Africa today has the world's fastest population growth and pace of urbanization. This brings many challenges, including water supply and management for the continent's largest urban agglomerations. Africa's urban water problem is one of the continent's major challenges today and will only get larger in the decades to come. As experience shows, per capita freshwater use surges dramatically, especially in urban areas, as societies develop, industrialize and become more affluent, with an expanding middle class. All of these factors are currently at play in sub-Saharan Africa, especially in the many burgeoning metropolitan areas of the continent. At the same time, growing affluence often leads to increased awareness and political will to treat wastewater and take care of the environment, as well as to stabilize water consumption at a certain level. But these positive sides of development are conditional on improvements in education, from primary to vocational to the highest university education. Here, Africa stands today at the lowest level globally. Africa's upcoming economic structure and employment creation will depend largely on the education level of the population; and harnessing the opportunities of green growth, circular economy and the modern service sector would vastly improve its ability to enter the fourth industrial revolution in a timely manner.

Africa's current water problems cannot be fully grasped without taking into account some distinctive features and patterns of the urban trajectory of the continent. First, many African megacities are former colonial capital cities and centres created by colonial rulers to serve primarily as economic entrepôts, trade platforms, administrative centres and military barracks. Local freshwater availability in the medium and long term was given little consideration in the choice of these cities, most of which are along the coast. Second, the rapid urbanization of the continent is largely the result of the crisis in the agricultural sector. Impoverished and destitute farmers are fleeing to urban areas and in particular to informal urban settlements in slums, whose spectacular growth is part of the 'ruralization' of African cities. Third, investment in water infrastructure is lagging far behind the needs, while the existing infrastructure (sometimes dating back to the colonial era) is ageing and contributing to the high proportion of water leakages.

The urbanization process is still accelerating, and we already see acute seasonal and chronic water shortages and other water challenges in almost all of the continent's major cities, regardless of the ecological conditions and natural water endowments of the regions where they are located. These include cities as diverse as Dakar, Abidjan and Niamey in West Africa; Kinshasa and Luanda in Central Africa; Nairobi and Dar es Salaam in East Africa; and Harare, Maputo and Cape Town in Southern Africa. In these cities, water shortages amplify competition between urban and rural areas and within cities. Unresolved water shortages create room for emerging informal water markets and can trigger water riots and violent demonstrations. When they occur in capital cities, these riots can easily develop into major social disturbances that can threaten political stability. Day Zero in Cape Town in 2017 is a dire warning of how far an urban crisis can go and its potentially devastating effects on all urban and peri-urban life and activities.

To prevent, delay or mitigate major urban water crisis risks, Africa and especially sub-Saharan Africa must learn from the Cape Town experience and from other city experiences in the continent, as well as experiences abroad, such as in India. There, chronic and seasonal water shortages in most megacities have reached alarming levels, a phenomenon now considered a national crisis. Sub-Saharan Africa will be headed towards a worse scenario unless the necessary revisions are made in the continent's current urbanization trajectory.

Building on current experiences in Africa and India, we suggest that the following measures be considered, depending on the country and city contexts:

- Plan early to anticipate and guide urban development, taking into account water resource availability and conservation; and plan for the long term, without underestimating the real magnitude and growth rate of urban water demand.
- Close the urban water infrastructure gap, and improve the disaster risk preparedness of megacities, paying due attention to water-related risks such as floods and droughts in the context of changing climate conditions. Diversify sources of water for cities through conventional and non-conventional water supply solutions. In addition to increasing surface water storage and groundwater abstraction capacities, cities should consider options such as groundwater recharge, rainwater harvesting and seawater treatment.
- Invest in urban waste reclamation and reuse to increase urban water supply and serve the industrial and agriculture sectors, while exploring the possibility of applying 'water banking' principles in the management of saved water.
- Invest in communication and outreach targeting urban dwellers to raise awareness of water challenges and to create conditions for raising water consciousness among urban residents. Go boldly towards water demand management.
- Invest in societal development and capacity in the broadest sense. Everything possible should be done to make the current population projections too high. Education and economic development, together with governance progress, should turn the ruralized, slum-dominated urban areas into more affluent societies, with balanced environmental and social development. In parallel, rural areas need a development boost along the same lines. Africa clearly lags behind other continents, including most of Asia, in human development, economic progress and governance quality (Varis, Taka, & Kummu, 2019).

Today is the time to act. While the African urban population is projected to triple by 2050, it is anticipated that 'two-thirds of the urban space that Africa will have in 2050 does not yet exist and so must be built during the next 35 years' (Collier, 2017). This is indeed a challenge, but it is also an opportunity to correct the past mistakes that have piled up during the expansion of informal settlements, hindering efforts to improve the urban water infrastructure in Africa's rapidly growing cities.

Urban areas are centres of economic growth. The urban labour market is growing rapidly. The future of sub-Saharan Africa will be decided to a large extent in its urban areas. It is therefore critical to create the conditions for developing a healthy and economically attractive urban environment. Designing and implementing sustainable water solutions will contribute to creating friendly, dynamic, and socially and economically attractive cities.

Acknowledgments

The authors are deeply indebted to Professor Asit K. Biswas for pertinent, long-term inspiration on working with the toughest water issues of the planet. He has shown unique wisdom and courage in seeking solutions, often going beyond disciplinary ways and boldly challenging conventional approaches to create real impact and change problematic development paths in a meaningful way. The invaluable comments and stimulus to this article by Dr Cecilia Tortajada are highly appreciated, as always.

Disclosure statement

No potential conflict of interest was reported by the authors.

ORCID

Olli Varis http://orcid.org/0000-0001-9231-4549

References

African Development Bank. (2018). African economic outlook. Abidjan: Author.

African Development Bank. (2019). *African economic outlook*. Abidjan: Author.

Almer, C., Laurent-Lucchetti, J., & Oechslin, M. (2015). Water scarcity and rioting: Disaggregated evidence from sub-Saharan Africa (MPRA Paper No. 34487). Munich: Universität von München. Retrieved from https://mpra.ub.uni-muenchen.de/34487/

Arnell, N. W., & Kram, T. (2010). *A framework for a new generation of socioeconomic scenarios for climate change impact, adaptation, vulnerability, and mitigation research*. Boulder, CO: National Center for Atmospheric Research.

Asian Development Bank. (2010). *Key indicators for Asia for Asia and the Pacific 2010. Special chapter: The rise of Asia's middle class*. Manila: Author. Retrieved from https://www.adb.org/sites/default/files/publication/27726/key-indicators-2010.pdf

Bahri, A., Brikké, F., & Vairavamoorthy, K. (2016). Managing change to implement integrated urban water management in African cities. *Aquatic Procedia*, *6*, 3–14. doi:10.1016/j.aqpro.2016.06.002

Banerji, A., & Accheri, C. (2019). Running dry: India's booming 'silicon valley' faces dry times. Thomson Reuters Foundation. Retrieved from https://packages.trust.org/running-dry-india/index.html

Barenjee, S. G., & Morella, E. (2011). *Africa's water and sanitation infrastructure: Access, affordability, and alternatives*. Washington, DC: World Bank.

Bernstein, H. (1990). Agricultural 'modernisation' and the era of structural adjustment: Observations on sub-Saharan Africa. *Journal of Peasant Studies*, *18*(1), 3–35. doi:10.1080/03066159008438441

Bhardwaj, M. (2019, July 8). Drought-hit Delhi: The haves get limitless water, the poor fight for every drop. *Reuters*. Retrieved from http://www.thisisplace.org/i/?id=d30029e1-efe8-45bb-8d44-7911fd51cd17

Biswas, A. K. (2016, October 4). Water mismanagement In India: Why demand is a bigger problem than supply. Blog, *Huffington Post*.

Biswas, A. K., & Hartley, C. (2019, July 9). Public awareness key to curbing pollution. *China Daily*.

Biswas, A. K., & Tortajada, C. (2018, February 28). Managing urban waters in Africa: Challenges ahead. *Business Times*.

Biswas, A. K., & Tortajada, C. (2019a). India's water future. In V. D. Reddy, K. V. Rao, & K. R. Krishna (Eds.), *Insights on global challenges and opportunities for the century ahead* (pp. 169–175). Hyderabad, India: Osmania University.

Biswas, A. K., & Tortajada, C. (2019b). Water crisis and water wars: Myths and realities. *International Journal of Water Resources Development*, *35*(5), 727–731. doi:10.1080/07900627.2019.1636502

Burls, N. J., Blamey, R. C., Cash, B. A., Swenson, E. T., Fahad, A., Bopape, M.-J. M., … Reason, C. J. C. (2019). The Cape Town "Day Zero" drought and Hadley cell expansion. *Npj Climate and Atmospheric Science*, *2*(1), 27. doi:10.1038/s41612-019-0084-6

Chan, L., Ruwanpura, K. N., & Brown, B. D. (2019). Environmental neglect: Other casualties of post-war infrastructure development. *Geoforum, 105*, 63–66. doi:10.1016/j.geoforum.2019.07.010

City of Cape Town. (2019, July 29). *Dam levels report*. Cape Town: Author. Retrieved from http://resource.capetown.gov.za/documentcentre/Documents/City%20research%20reports%20and%20review/damlevels.pdf.

Cogels, F.-X., Fraboulet-Jussila, S., & Varis, O. (2001). Multipurpose use and water quality challenges in Lac de Guiers (Senegal). *Water Science and Technology, 44*(6), 35–46. doi:10.2166/wst.2001.0335

Collier, P. (2017). African urbanization: An analytic policy guide. *Oxford Review of Economic Policy, 33* (3), 405–437. doi:10.1093/oxrep/grx031

Coquery-Vidrovitch, C. (1991). The process of urbanization in Africa (from the origins to the beginning of independence). *African Studies Review, 34*(12), 1–98. doi:10.2307/524256

Dagdeviren, H., & Robertson, S. A. (2011). Access to water in the slums of Sub-Saharan Africa. *Development Policy Review, 29*(4), 485–505. doi:10.1111/j.1467-7679.2011.00543.x

Dahan, S., & Grijsen, J. (2017). *Managing urban water scarcity in Morocco*. Washington, DC: World Bank.

Dasylva, S., & Cosandey, C. (2005). L'exploitation de la nappe des sables quaternaires pour l'alimentation en eau potable de Dakar: Une offre compromise par l'insuffisance de la recharge pluviométrique. *Géocarrefour, 80*(4). Retrieved from http://journals.openedition.org/geocarrefour/1385

Dilip, V., Kapasi, P., & Talkhani, R. (2019, July 1). On verge of acute water crisis, Bengaluru may turn uninhabitable in next few years, warn experts. *News18*. Retrieved from https://www.news18.com/news/india/on-verge-of-acute-water-crisis-bengaluru-may-turn-uninhabitable-in-next-few-years-warn-experts-2130111.html

Dontoh, E., & Cohen, M. (2019, March 18). Africa's booming cities are running out of water. *Bloomberg*. Retrieved from https://www.bloomberg.com/news/articles/2019-03-18/africa-is-running-out-of-water-as-cities-see-populations-boom

Dos Santos, S., Adams, E., Neville, G., Wada, Y., de Sherbinin, A., Mullin Bernhardt, E., & Adamo, S. B. (2017). Urban growth and water access in sub-Saharan Africa: Progress, challenges, and emerging research directions. *Science of the Total Environment, 607–608*, 497–508. doi:10.1016/j.scitotenv.2017.06.157

Economic Times of India (2019, July 1). 'Jal Shakti Abhiyan': Government launches water conservation campaign. Retrieved from https://m.economictimes.com/news/politics-and-nation/jal-shakti-abhiyan-government-launches-water-conservation-campaign/articleshow/70027058.cms. See also the government webpage for the Jai Shakti Abhiyan campaign (https://indiawater.gov.in/jsa/JSA/Home.aspx).

Evans, A. (2010). *Globalization and scarcity: Multilateralism for a world with limits*. New York: Center on International Cooperation. Retrieved from http://www.globaldashboard.org/wp-content/uploads/Globalization-and-Scarcity.pdf

FAO. (2003). *Review of world's water resources by country*. Rome: Food and Agricultural Organization of the United Nations. Retrieved from http://www.fao.org/tempref/agl/AGLW/ESPIM/CD-ROM/documents/5C_e.pdf

Filani, M. O., & Okafor, S. I. (eds). (2006). *Foundations for urban development in Africa: The legacy of Akin Mabogunje*. Washington, DC: Cities Alliance/UN-Habitat.

Foster, V., & Briceño-Garmendia, C. (Eds.). (2010). *Africa's infrastructure: A time for transformation*. Washington, DC: World Bank.

Garrick, D., De Stefano, L., Yu, W., Jorgensen, I., O'Donnell, E., Turley, L., … Punjabi, B. (2019). Rural water for thirsty cities: A systematic review of water reallocation from rural to urban regions. *Environmental Research Letters. 14*, 043003. doi:10.1088/1748-9326/ab0db7

Goswami, S. (2018, March 22). Nairobi's water crisis likely to continue till 2026 [Blog post]. *DownToEarth*. Retrieved from https://www.downtoearth.org.in/news/water/nairobi-is-likely-to-continue-rationing-water-till-2026-59983

Hellweg, S., & Milà I Canals, L. (2014). Emerging approaches, challenges and opportunities in life cycle assessment. *Science, 344*(6188), 1109–1113. doi:10.1126/science.1248361

Hoornweg, D., & Pope, K. (2014). *Socioeconomic pathways and regional distribution of the world's 101 largest cities*. Toronto: University of Ontario.

Horvath, R. J. (1969). In search of a theory of urbanization. Notes of the colonial city. *East Lake Geographers, 5*, 69–82.

Hutton, G., & Varughese, M. (2016). *The costs of meeting the 2030 Sustainable Development Goal targets on drinking water, sanitation, and hygiene*. Washington, DC: World Bank, Water and Sanitation Programme.

Ilemba, T. L., & Nzitattira, E. S. (2019). Kinshasa. In UNESCO-IHP (Ed.), *Water, megacities and global change: Portraits of 16 emblematic cities of the world* (pp. 54–57). Paris: UNESCO.

Jacobsen, M., Webster, M., & Vairavamoorthy, K. (Eds.). (2012). *The future of water in African cities: Why waste water? Directions in development*. Washington, DC: World Bank. doi:10.1596/978-0-8213-9721-3.

Japan International Cooperation Agency. (2014). *Mission de Collecte d'Informations pour l'Approvisionnement en Eau de la Région de Dakar*. Dakar: Author. Retrieved from http://open_jicareport.jica.go.jp/pdf/12148581.pdf

Karthikeyan, D., & Gupta, S. (2019, June 22). *'I'm scared for my daughter': Life in India's first city that's almost out of water*. Chennai: Cable News Network CNN.

Kasarda, J. D., & Crenshaw, E. M. (1991). Third world urbanization: Dimensions, theories, and determinants. *Annual Review of Sociology, 17*, 467–501. doi:10.1146/annurev.so.17.080191.002343

Kumar, M. D. (2018). Water management in India: The multiplicity of views and solutions. *International Journal of Water Resources Development, 34*(1), 1–15. doi:10.1080/07900627.2017.1351333

Lake Chad Basin Commission. (2016). *Inter basin water transfer project: Signing of a memorandum of understanding between LCBC and powerChina International Group Limited*. N'djamena: Author. Retrieved from http://www.cblt.org/en/news/inter-basin-water-transfer-project-signing-memorandum-understanding-between-lcbc-and-PowerChina

Larcher, L. (2018, April 20). À Bouaké, en Côte d'Ivoire, plus d'un million d'habitants n'ont plus d'eau; La deuxième ville de Côte d'Ivoire est frappée par une pénurie sans précédent. *La Croix*. Retrieved from https://www.la-croix.com/Monde/Afrique/A-Bouake-Cote-dIvoire-dun-million-dhabitants-nont-deau-2018-04-20-1200933386

Moseley, W. G., Carney, J., & Becker, L. (2010, March 30). Neoliberal policy, rural livelihoods, and urban food security in West Africa: A comparative study of The Gambia, Côte d'Ivoire, and Mali. *PNAS, 107*(13), 5774–5779. doi:10.1073/pnas.0905717107

Muggah, R., & Kilcullen, D. (2016). These are Africa's fastest-growing cities – And they'll make or break the continent. *World Economic Forum for Africa*. https://www.weforum.org/agenda/2016/05/africa-biggest-cities-fragility/

Muller, M., Biswas, A., Martin-Hurtado, M., & Tortajada, C. (2015). Built infrastructure is essential. *Science, 349*(6248), 585–586. doi:10.1126/science.aac7606

Mulligan, G. (2018, January 12). Will Cape Town be the first city to run out of water? *BBC News*. Retrieved from: https://www.bbc.com/news/business-42626790

Nagpal, A. (2019, June 27). Delhi is running out of water, and it is everybody's problem. *The Wire*. Retrieved from https://thewire.in/urban/delhi-water-crisis-problem

Nganyanyuka, K., Martinez, J., Wesselink, A., Lungo, J. H., & Georgiado, Y. (2014). Accessing water services in Dar es Salaam: Are we counting what counts? *Habitat International, 44*, 358–366. doi:10.1016/j.habitatint.2014.07.003

NITI Aayog. (2018). *Composite water management index: A tool for water management*. New Delhi: National Institute for Transforming India (NITI) Aayog. Retrieved from https://niti.gov.in/writereaddata/files/document_publication/2018-05-18-Water-Index-Report_vS8-compressed.pdf

Niva, V., Taka, M., & Varis, O. (2019). Rural-urban migration and the growth of informal settlements: A socio-ecological system conceptualization with insights through a 'water lens'. *Sustainability, 11*, 3487. doi:10.3390/su11123487

O'Rourke, D. (2014). The science of sustainable supply chains. *Science, 344*(6188), 1124–1127. doi:10.1126/science.1248526

Pacific Institute. (2019). *World's water/conflict database (updated January 2019)*. Oakland: Author. Retrieved from http://www.worldwater.org/conflict/list/

Palanichamy, R. B. (2019). *How does a flood-prone city run out of water? Inside Chennai's 'day zero' crisis* [Blog post] Washington, DC: World Resources Institute. Retrieved from: https://www.wri.org/blog/2019/06/how-does-flood-prone-city-run-out-water-inside-chennai-day-zero-crisis

Saikia, G. (2018, June 17). In Delhi's Sangam Vihar, fight over water claims another life [Blogpost]. *Newsbytes*. Retrieved from https://www.newsbytesapp.com/timeline/India/25192/114282/delhi-s-water-starved-locality-a-hotbed-of-criminal-gangs

Sujatha, P., & Janardhanam, P. V. S. (2014). Population growth: Trends, projections, future plans and development. *International Journal of Humanities and Social Science Invention*, *3*(8), 30–42.

Thomas, B. E. (1970). On the growth of African cities. *African Studies Review*, *12*(1), 1–8. doi:10.2307/523678

Tortajada, C., & Biswas, A. K. (2019). Objective case studies of successful urban water management. *International Journal of Water Resources Development*, *35*(4), 547–550. doi:10.1080/07900627.2019.1613766

UNDESA. (2018). *The world's cities in 2018: Data booklet*. New York: Author.

UNESCO. (2012). World water development report 4: Managing water report under uncertainty and risk. Paris: Author. doi:10.1094/PDIS-11-11-0999-PDN

UN-Habitat. (2006). *State of the world's cities 2006/7*. London: Earthscan.

United Nations. (2017). *World population prospects: The 2017 revision*. New York: Author.

United Nations. (2018). *World urbanization prospects: The 2018 revision*. New York: Author.

US Intelligence Community. (2012). *Global water security US Intelligence Community Assessment (ICA) 2012-08*. Washington, DC: Federal Government of the United States. Retrieved from https://www.dni.gov/files/documents/Special%20Report_ICA%20Global%20Water%20Security.pdf

van de Bruggen, B., Borghgraef, K., & Vinckier, C. (2009). Causes of water supply problems in urbanised regions in developing countries. *Water Resources Management*, *24*(9), 1885–1902. doi:10.1007/s11269-009-9529-8

Varis, O., Taka, M., & Kummu, M. (2019). The planet's stressed river basins: Too much pressure or too little adaptive capacity? *Future Earth*, *7*, 1118–1135. doi:10.1029/2019EF001239

Woetzel, J., Garemo, N., Mischke, J., Hjerpe, M., & Palter, R. (2016). *Bridging global infrastructure gaps*. Brussels: McKinsey Global Institute.

World Bank. (2016). *High and dry: Water, climate change, and the economy*. Washington, DC: Author.

World Bank. (2018). *Water scarce cities: Thriving in a finite world*. Washington, DC: Author.

World Bank. (2019). *World Development Indicators*. Washington, DC: Author.

Sustainability of water and energy use for food production based on optimal allocation of agricultural irrigation water

Mo Li and Vijay P. Singh

ABSTRACT

Food security is inextricably linked with water and energy use in irrigated agriculture. This article develops an optimization model to evaluate the sustainability of water and energy use for food production, and the coordination among water, energy and carbon footprints. A case study of Heping Irrigation District, China, demonstrates the applicability of the model. We find that 87.47, 86.12, and 83.67 million m^3 of irrigation water allocation are sustainable for high, normal, and low flow levels, respectively, considering economic, social and environmental benefits. The structure of surface water and groundwater allocation remains consistent for different subareas.

Introduction

Water, food and energy constitute a resource base that is vital for sustainable development. Irrigation production and food security are inextricably linked to water and energy use (Li et al., 2019b). As the largest consumer of freshwater resources, irrigated agriculture plays a critical role in socio-economic well-being worldwide, and significantly affects the sustainability of water use, energy use, and food production. This raises a question as to how irrigation water can be used and how it will affect economic, social and environmental development.

It is well known that water crises are occurring too frequently in many places because of continuing population growth and rapid socio-economic development. Of all water users, irrigated agriculture consumes approximately 70% of available freshwater resources in the world (Galán-Martín, Vaskan, Antón, Esteller, & Guillén-Gosálbez, 2017). The troubling reality is that the availability of water for agricultural irrigation is decreasing, because water demand for the domestic, industrial, energy production, ecological and environmental sectors is on the rise. It is particularly troubling in arid and semi-arid regions. Meanwhile, inappropriate management of agricultural irrigation is one of the main reasons for excessive wastage of irrigation water. We have to allocate and use the available irrigation water in an efficient and optimal way.

In recent years, a growing number of scholars and policy makers have proposed agricultural irrigation strategies using optimization techniques, such as dynamic programming, linear programming, non-linear programming, multi-objective programming and intelligence algorithms, and combinations of these (Li et al., 2019a; Li, Fu, Singh, & Liu, 2018; Ren, Li, & Zhang, 2019; Singh, 2014; Zhang, Zhang, Guo, Liu, & Guo, 2018). Allocation of irrigation water is complex because it involves many elements, for example multiple water resources, including surface water, groundwater, wastewater, and water diversion, various regions and crops, different crop growth stages, and different irrigation methods (Kumar & Singh, 2007; Singh, 2012). Changes in these elements cause changes in strategies for the allocation of irrigation water, and thus affect socio-economic development and eco-environmental protection (Tan, Zhang, & Li, 2017). Therefore, optimal allocation of irrigation water in time and space, considering multiple water resources, is needed to help policy makers narrow the gap between water supply and demand, while promoting economic performance.

Policy makers have increasingly recognized that sound management of agricultural irrigation requires more than simple crop cultivation commensurate with hydrological processes. It also needs to evaluate the effect of irrigation water allocation strategies on other correlated components in irrigated agriculture to promote sustainable development (Lalehzari, Boroomand Nasab, Moazed, & Haghighi, 2016; Zhao, Li, Guo, Zhang, & Tan, 2017). In an agricultural system, water, food and energy are linked, in that irrigation contributes to food production, while food production consumes water and energy. Energy is needed for water collection, pumping, irrigation and drainage, while water is used in generating energy. Also, energy availability restricts some farm practices for food production, such as the use of fertilizer, pesticides, agricultural machinery and agricultural films. In turn, food production consumes energy and contributes to biomass energy (Finley & Seiber, 2014; Li, Fu, Singh, Liu, & Li, 2019c; Ringler, Bhaduri, & Lawford, 2013; Tian et al., 2018). The nexus approach allows us to analyze the complex linkages among resources and their use, and therefore the concept of the water-food-energy nexus (WFEN), introduced by Hoff (2011), comes into play.

Several indices have been reported in the literature with the aim to operationalize the WFEN approach, for example water footprint (WF), carbon footprint (CF) and ecological footprint (de Vito, Portoghese, Pagano, Fratino, & Vurro, 2017). However, few studies have evaluated them, considering the optimal allocation of irrigation water. Hence, there is an increasing need for a tool to rationally allocate irrigation water and evaluate how the allocation strategies affect the sustainability of water use, energy use and food production, considering their interrelationships in irrigated agriculture.

The objective of this article therefore is to develop an optimization-evaluation model to evaluate the sustainability of water use, energy use and food production, based on the optimal allocation of agricultural irrigation water. The article entails several elements: (1) development of a non-linear optimization model for allocating irrigation water in time and space; (2) development of a system for evaluating the sustainability of water use, energy use and food production, considering irrigation WF, energy footprint (EF) and CF; and (3) assessment of the sustainability of water and energy use, and food production for irrigated agriculture, based on their degree of coordination. The model is tested by application to Heping Irrigation District (HID) in north-east China, an important demonstration area for rice planting in the country. Policies and suggestions for sustainable irrigation water use in the district are proposed. This study provides insights for local policy makers for effective and sustainable management of agricultural irrigation water.

Study area

Location and climate

HID is the largest irrigation area in Qing'an County, Heilongjiang Province, China, ranging in latitude from 46°04′ to 47°04′ N and in longitude from 127°20′ to 127°49′ E, and has a large trunk canal (the Heping Trunk) and 18 lateral canals. It contains three subareas: Lishantun subarea in the upper reaches of the Heping Trunk, Anbanghe subarea in the middle reaches, and Zhengwenju subarea in the lower reaches. Its climate is temperate semi-arid and semi-humid continental monsoon, with obvious characteristics of seasonal weather. The annual average temperature is 1.7 °C, and the highest temperature is 36.7 °C. The average effective accumulated temperature and sunshine duration are 2518 °C and 2577 h, respectively. The average frost-free period is 128 days, with the longest being 150 days and the shortest, 114 days. Annual average precipitation and evaporation are around 545 mm and 665 mm, respectively, and precipitation is concentrated in June, July and August (Liu, Guo, Li, & Zheng, 2019).

Water resources management

The Hulan, Lalinqing and Anbang Rivers (the Lalinqing and the Anbang are tributaries of the Hulan) pass through HID, with a total land area of 15.2 thousand ha. They are the sources of surface water supply where irrigation is under gravity and surface water is the main water source for agricultural irrigation. Recently, because of spreading irrigation area, surface water supply is insufficient to meet the irrigation requirement. Therefore, groundwater is being used as a supplementary water source to guarantee crop yield. Surface water and groundwater are being used conjunctively as the one of the main methods for irrigation (Fu, Xiao, Cui, Liu, & Li, 2017). As one of the irrigation experimental bases for rice, mainly because of its high quality and potential for high economic return, more than 95% of the total land in the district is used for growing rice (Li, Fu, Singh, Ma, & Liu, 2017). Hence, most of the water supply is used to irrigate rice, and the government aims to improve the yield of rice and enhance economic gains, while ensuring water conservation to achieve 'water-saving and production increase', which is the requirement for agricultural development in Heilongjiang Province. Hence, optimization of irrigation water is necessary.

In irrigation water allocation, economy and natural resources are interrelated. For example, more allocated water will result in higher yield and thus improve farmer's living standards. Moreover, on the background of sustainable agricultural development, policy makers are required to make decisions for irrigation in a sustainable and efficient way. Therefore, the following questions should be considered by policy makers: (1) How to handle water use contradictions among different subareas and different growth stages of rice (including tillering, elongation, heading and milk)? (2) How to effectively allocate the limited available water, including canal water, groundwater and precipitation? (3) How do irrigation water allocation schemes affect food production, greenhouse gas emissions, and energy consumption? (4) Are optimal water allocation schemes sustainable from the perspective of WFEN? Here, in response to these questions, an optimization-evaluation model is developed.

Materials and method

Optimization model for agricultural irrigation water allocation

The objective of maximizing crop yield and consequent benefits of agricultural irrigation water allocation is usually considered in an optimization model (Nguyen, Ascough II, Maier, Dandy, & Andales, 2017). Higher crop yield not only promotes agricultural economy but also implies social benefit, because higher yield usually generates more income and thus improves the living standard of farmers. The crop water production function (CWPF), which is capable of reflecting the relationship between crop yield and evapotranspiration (ET), is usually used to express this objective quantitatively, and is also an effective tool for irrigation policy making in water-scarcity situations (Tong & Guo, 2013). There are two types of CWPF; one describes the relationship between crop yield and ET during the whole crop growth period, while the other focuses on each crop growth stage. Generally, CWPF for different crop growth stages can depict crop growth more distinctly and guide irrigation water allocation more precisely, because crop yield depends not only on the ET during the whole crop growth process but also on the distribution of water in different stages of crop growth. CWPF for different crop growth stages can use addition or multiplication models; the Jensen (1968) multiplication model, which is commonly used and is one of the representative models for CWPF, was used in this study. The objective was to maximize net economic benefit, based on the Jensen multiplication model, expressed as:

$$\max F = \sum_{i=1}^{I} P_i\left(A_i^s + A_i^g\right) \cdot Y_i^{\max} \prod_{t=1}^{T}\left(\frac{ET_{it}}{ET_{it}^{\max}}\right)^{\lambda_{it}} - \sum_{i=1}^{I}\sum_{t=1}^{T}\left(\frac{C^s A_i^s I_{it}^s}{\eta^s} + \frac{C^g A_i^g I_{it}^g}{\eta^g}\right) - \sum_{i=1}^{I} C_i\left(A_i^s + A_i^g\right) \tag{1}$$

where i is the index of subarea; t is the index of growth stage; s is the superscript for surface water irrigation; g is the superscript for groundwater irrigation; F is the objective function of maximizing net economic benefit; P_i is the crop price of subarea i (in Yuan; 6.5 yuan = USD 1); A_i^s and A_i^g are the surface water and groundwater irrigation areas of subarea i, respectively (ha); $Y_i^{\max}$ is the maximum yield of subarea i (kg/ha); ET_{it} is the actual crop evapotranspiration of subarea i in growth stage t (m^3/ha); $ET_{it}^{\max}$ is the maximum crop evapotranspiration of subarea i in growth stage t (m^3/ha); λ_{it} is the water sensitivity index of subarea i in growth stage t; C^s and C^g are the costs of surface water and groundwater utilization, respectively (yuan/m^3); I_{it}^s and I_{it}^g are the net surface water amount and groundwater irrigation amount of subarea i in growth stage t, respectively (m^3/ha), and they are decision variables; η^s and η^g are the water utilization coefficients for surface water and groundwater, respectively; C_i is the cost of planting for subarea i (yuan/ha); and in Equation (1), $Y_i^{max}\prod_{t=1}^{T}\left(ET_{it}/ET_{it}^{max}\right)^{\lambda_{it}}$ represents the actual yield of subarea i.

In Equation (1), ET_{it} for rice can be expressed as

$$ET_{it} = h_{it} - h_{i(t+1)} + EP_{it} + I_{it}^{s} + I_{it}^{g} - S_{it} - D_{it} \quad \forall i, t \tag{2}$$

where h_{it} and $h_{i(t+1)}$ are the depth of the surface layer of subarea i in the growth stage t and in the growth stage t+1, respectively (m^3/ha); EP_{it} is the effective precipitation of subarea i in growth stage t (m^3/ha); S_{it} is the seepage amount of subarea i in growth stage t (m^3/ha); and D_{it} is the drainage amount of subarea i in growth stage t (m^3/ha).

To optimally allocate limited water resources to rice in different growth stages in different subareas, this objective function should be subjected to certain constraints. Five major sets of constraints are included: (1) surface water and groundwater availability constraint to ensure that irrigation water is allocated within the limits of total water availability (Equations (3–5)); (2) water balance constraint to guarantee allocation continuity (Equation (6)); (3) water demand constraint to guarantee the water requirement for crop growth (Equation (7)); (4) electricity availability constraint to restrict electricity consumption for water collection (Equation (8)); and (5) maximum water allocation constraint to avoid water waste (Equation (9)). Non-negativity constraints are also included (Equation (10)).

$$A_i^s I_{it}^s/\eta^s \leq WS_{it}^s + R_{i(t-1)} \quad \forall i, t \tag{3}$$

$$\sum_{t=1}^{T} WS_{it}^s \leq TW_i^s \quad \forall i \tag{4}$$

$$\sum_{i=1}^{I}\sum_{t=1}^{T} A_i^g I_{it}^g/\eta^g \leq TW^g \tag{5}$$

$$R_{i(t-1)} = R_{i(t-2)} + WS_{it}^s - A_i^s \cdot I_{i(t-1)}^s/\eta^s \quad \forall i, t \tag{6}$$

$$\sum_{t=1}^{T}\left(A_i^s I_{it}^s/\eta^s + A_i^g I_{it}^g/\eta^g\right) \geq IR_i \quad \forall i \tag{7}$$

$$\frac{H^s}{102 \times 3.6 \times \mu^s}\sum_{i=1}^{I}\sum_{t=1}^{T}\left(A_i^s I_{it}^s/\eta^s\right) + \frac{H^g}{102 \times 3.6 \times \mu^g}\sum_{i=1}^{I}\sum_{t=1}^{T}\left(A_i^g I_{it}^g/\eta^g\right) \leq E \tag{8}$$

$$\sum_{i=1}^{I}\left(A_i^s I_{it}^s/\eta^s + A_i^g I_{it}^g/\eta^g\right) \leq I_t^{max} \quad \forall t \tag{9}$$

$$I_{it}^s \geq 0, \quad I_{it}^g \geq 0, \quad WS_{it}^s \geq 0, \quad R_{it} \geq 0 \quad \forall i, t \tag{10}$$

where WS_{it}^s is the surface water supply for subarea i in the growth stage t (m^3), and it is a decision variable; R_{it} is the remaining water of subarea i in the growth stage t (m^3); TW_i^s is the total surface water supply of subarea i (m^3); TW^g is the total groundwater supply (m^3); IR_i is the irrigation requirement of subarea i (m^3); H^s and H^g are the heads for surface water abstraction and groundwater pumping, respectively (m); E is the electricity available for irrigation water collection (kWh); and I_t^{max} is the maximum irrigation amount in growth stage t (m^3).

Indices for water use, energy use and carbon emission

To evaluate the sustainability of water and energy use, and food production in an irrigated agricultural system, an index-based methodology can be used, based on the optimal strategies of agricultural irrigation water resource allocation. Key elements that characterize the related irrigation water use patterns and irrigation practices should be considered. In particular, water and energy consumption are considered the main determinants of crop production. Three indices, WF, EF and CF, are introduced to reflect water use, energy use, food production and their connections, and thus allow policy makers to estimate the specific configurations of irrigation water, cropping pattern, water source and farming practices. WF aims to quantify water consumption along the entire production chain of products, processes and businesses within nations or catchments (Hoekstra, Aldaya, Chapagain, & Mekonnen, 2011). In an irrigated agricultural system, WF refers to the volume of water required to produce a certain crop yield (Le Roux, van der Laan, Vahrmeijer, Bristow, & Annandale, 2017). WF in an irrigated agricultural system is the sum of the WFs of blue water, green water, and grey water over the crop's whole growing process (Xiao et al., 2019) (Table 1).

Table 1. Description of WF, EF and CF.

Item	**Equation and parameter interpretation**
Water footprint (WF)	$WF = WF_{green} + WF_{blue} + WF_{grey}$
	where WF_{green}, WF_{blue} and WF_{grey} are the green water footprint, blue water footprint and grey water footprint, respectively (m^3/kg).
	$WF_{green} = \frac{10ET_{green}}{Y}$, $WF_{blue} = \frac{10ET_{blue}}{Y}$
	where ET_{green} and ET_{blue} are the evapotranspiration for green water and blue water, respectively, (mm); Y is the crop yield per unit area (kg/ha) and can be obtained from the optimization model.
	$ET_{green} = \min(ET_c, P_{eff})$, $ET_{blue} = \max(0, ET_c - P_{eff})$
	where P_{eff} is the effective precipitation during the whole crop growth stage (mm) and can be estimated by the method of USDA SCS.
	$P_{eff} = \begin{cases} P(125 - 0.6P)/125 & P \leq 250/3 \\ 125/3 + 0.1P & P > 250/3 \end{cases}$
	where P is the precipitation during a period of 10 days (mm).
	$WF_{grey} = \frac{(AR \times \alpha)/((C_{max} - C_{nat}))}{Y}$
	where AR is the amount of nitrogen applied per unit area (kg/ha); α is the leaching coefficient rate; C_{max} is the maximum allowable nitrate concentration; and C_{nat} is the natural nitrate background concentration, generally taken as 0.
Energy footprint (EF)	$EF = EF_{sur} + EF_{gro}$
	where EF_{sur}, EF_{gro} are the EF for surface water and groundwater abstraction, respectively (kW·h/kg).
	$EF_{sur} = \frac{H_{sur}}{102 \times \eta_{sur} \times 3.6} \times \frac{Q_{sur}}{Y}$, $EF_{gro} = \frac{H_{gro}}{102 \times \eta_{gro} \times 3.6} \times \frac{Q_{gro}}{Y}$
	where H_{sur}, H_{gro} are the hydraulic heads related to surface and groundwater system, respectively (m); Q_{sur}, Q_{gro} are the irrigation quota for surface water and groundwater, respectively (m^3/ha).
Carbon footprint (CF)	$CF = \frac{CE}{Y}$
	where CE is the carbon emission from crop production (kg CO_2 eq per hectare).
	$CE = E_{CO_2} + E_{N_2O} \times 298 + E_{CH_4} \times 25 + E_{CO_2-SB}$
	where E_{CO_2} is the direct emission of CO_2 (kg CO_2 eq per hectare); E_{N_2O}, E_{CH_4} are the emissions of N_2O and CH_4, respectively (kg/ha); E_{CO_2-SB} is equivalent CO_2 emission from crop straw burning (kg CO_2 eq per hectare); and 298 and 25 are the conversion coefficients of N_2O and CH_4, respectively.

The EF for irrigation considers the energy requirement from source to field, and it strongly depends on the specific water source as well as the characteristics of conveyance, distribution and irrigation systems, considering water losses and operational pressures. Generally, EF in an irrigated agricultural system is the sum of EF of surface water and that of groundwater in the crop growing process, and can be expressed as energy consumption per unit yield related to surface water or groundwater abstraction (Table 1).

CF is defined as the total emission of greenhouse gases (in carbon equivalent) from a product across its life cycle (Wu, Hu, & Mo, 2013). In an irrigated agricultural system, it can be expressed as the ratio of carbon emission from crop production and yield (kg CO_2 eq per kg; see Table 1). Carbon emissions have four main parts: direct emission of CO_2, emission of N_2O, emission of CH_4, and an equivalent CO_2 emission from crop straw burning. Direct emission of CO_2 is mainly caused by the use of fertilizers, pesticides, agricultural films, diesel used by agricultural machinery, and electricity used for irrigation in the cropland. N_2O emission includes the N_2O gas and ammonia volatilization produced by nitrification-denitrification from the fertilizer in the soil, and the potential greenhouse effect caused by nitrogen leaching. Emission of CH_4 in the field is mainly from rice paddy. Equivalent CO_2 emission from crop straw burning consists of greenhouse gases such as NO_x, CH_4 and NH_3. For details, see Chen (2018).

The interconnected water, food and energy subsystems compose the WFEN. WF, EF and CF are the three important indices that can reflect the linkages between these subsystems, based on the optimal irrigation strategies and the corresponding crop yield. The sustainability assessment of water use, energy use and food production can not only support sustainable development of an irrigated agricultural system but also reflect, to some extent, the performance of irrigation water allocation strategies. Coordination degree (CD), which is a measure of the synchronization, cooperation and complementation among subsystems and indicates the system's state of coordination or balance, can be adopted to evaluate sustainability (Wang, Fang, Cheng, & Wang, 2013). CD is based on synergy theory, which can be used to study the self-organization of subsystems or elements. We consider the study object (WFEN) as a compound system that is constituted by subsystems or elements (WF, EF, and CF), and the subsystems are correlative, making the whole system produce a holistic effect, which is quantitatively reflected by the CD, expressed as

$$CD = \sqrt{B \cdot C} \tag{11}$$

where B is the degree of coupling of subsystems and C is the comprehensive index of the system. If there are three subsystems, then C can be expressed as

$$B = \left\{ \frac{f(x)g(x)h(x)}{[f(x) + g(x) + h(x)]/3} \right\}^k \tag{12}$$

$$C = \alpha f(x) + \beta g(x) + \gamma h(x) \tag{13}$$

where $f(x)$, $g(x)$ and $h(x)$ are the utility values of the three subsystems, and k is the adjustment coefficient; α, β and γ are the weights of the subsystems; and $\alpha+\beta+\gamma=1$. In this study, WF, EF and CF represent the three subsystems. CD ranges from 0 to 1, and the larger the value, the better the cooperativity of the system.

Irrigation water resources allocation in the Heping Irrigation District

Relationship between water allocation and water demand

Flow levels depend on random variations in water supply and precipitation. This necessitates different irrigation water allocation schemes corresponding to different flow levels, such as wet, normal and dry. In this study, the division into different flow levels was based on empirical frequencies that were calculated according to the long-series runoff data, giving 25%, 50% and 75%, for high, normal, and dry flow levels, respectively. The variation of water supply and precipitation is shown in Table 2. Based on the optimization model, the irrigation water was allocated as illustrated in Figure 1. Flow levels significantly affected water allocation schemes, which is natural, that is, the irrigation water allocation amount for a higher flow level is higher because of the greater surface water supply and precipitation at higher flow levels. Accurate prediction of the flow level is needed when planning irrigation water to provide policy makers reasonable water allocation strategies.

With normal and dry flow levels, water shortages generally existed, especially in the milk stage, because in this stage water supply decreased, while water demand increased. Water allocation in the tillering and elongation stages was much higher than that in the heading and milk stages. These results are based on the corresponding sensitive indices, which were 0.46 for the tillering stage, 0.58 for elongation, 0.14 for heading, and 0.07 for milk. More sensitive indices meant more water was needed. The tillering and elongation stages were the irrigation peaks, which contributed the most to the irrigation effect. Although surface water and groundwater were used conjunctively, water shortages still existed in all three subareas (Lishantun, Anbanghe and Zhengwenju). To fully satisfy the water demand, water diversion from adjacent regions with sufficient water resources might be an efficient way, subject to cost–benefit analysis.

Table 2. Water supply and precipitation.

Item	Subarea/growth period	Flow level		
		Wet	Normal	Dry
Surface water supply (10^4 m^3)	Lishantun	1234.80	1102.81	972.63
	Anbanghe	1209.55	1079.13	930.08
	Zhengwenju	1603.45	1410.75	1277.98
Precipitation (m^3/ha)	Tillering stage	940.03	831.09	644.42
	Elongation stage	628.35	563.00	476.95
	Heading stage	460.79	412.86	349.76
	Milk stage	685.90	554.12	482.89

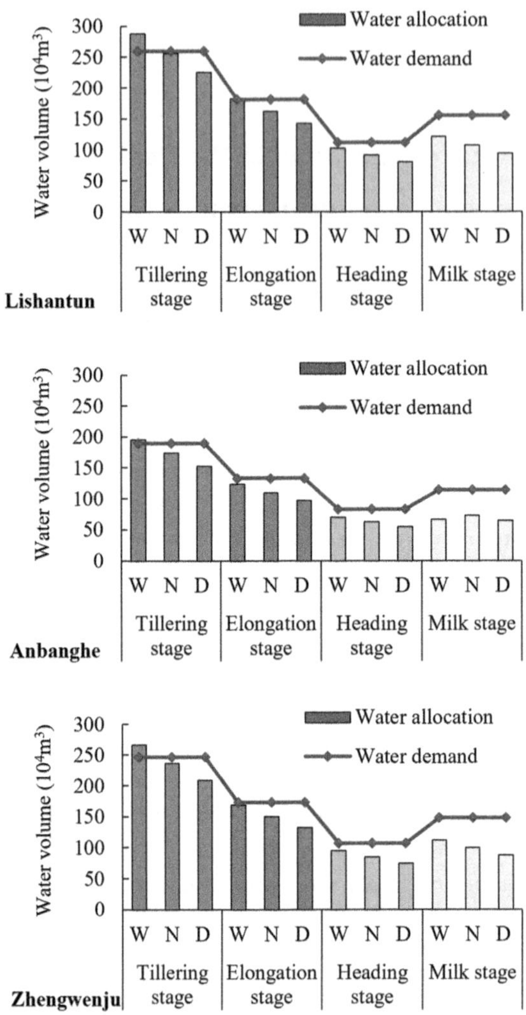

Figure 1. Water allocation in Heping Irrigation District.

Conjunctive use of surface water and groundwater

To alleviate water shortages in HID, surface water and groundwater were conjunctively optimized. Figure 2 provides the joint allocation schemes for both surface water and groundwater. The total water allocation was the largest in wet flow level and the smallest in dry flow level. However, the allocation percentages for the three subareas changed little: from 38% to 39% for Lishantun and from 25% to 26% for Anbanghe, and stable at 36% for Zhengwenju. This finding provided guidance for policy makers: if the water supply was known, water could be easily allocated. Such results indicate that the attention in water resources management might be on predicting water supply, considering natural conditions and human activities. Based on planning, only Lishantun was

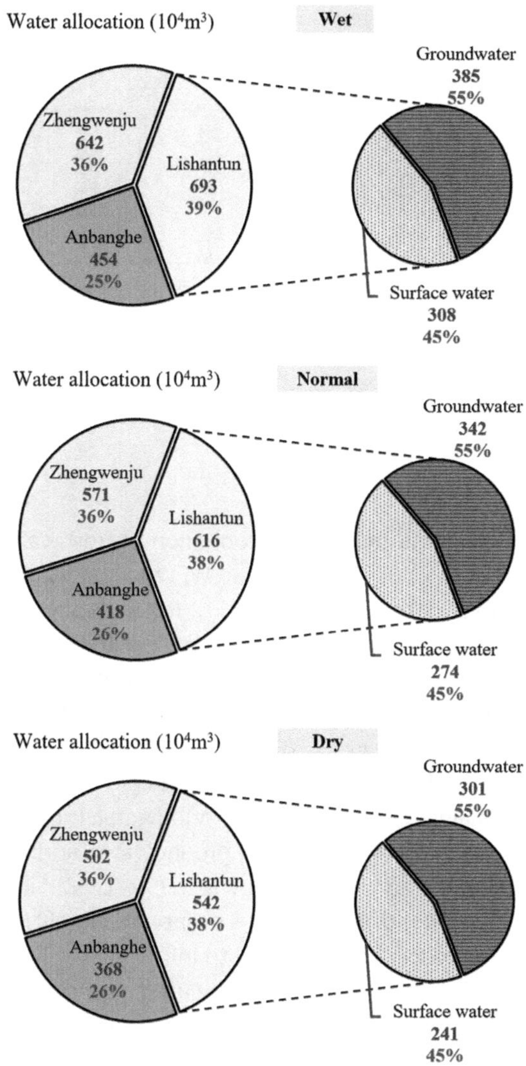

Figure 2. Conjunctive use of surface water and groundwater.

allocated both surface water and groundwater. Optimal results showed that for Lishantun, the ratio of groundwater and surface water utilization was 11:7.

Effects of water allocation on water use, energy use and food production in HID

The optimal allocation of irrigation water resources schemes directly affected the performance of water use, energy use and food production, which can be seen in the WF, EF and CF indices.

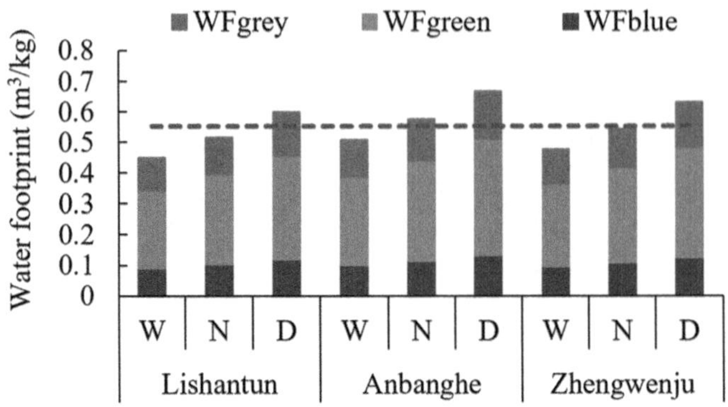

Figure 3. Water footprint.

Water footprint

WF is an indicator of direct and indirect appropriation of freshwater resources, including both consumptive water use (blue WF and green WF) and the water required to assimilate pollution (grey WF) (Mekonnen & Hoekstra, 2011). Figure 3 shows the WF for the three subareas under different flow levels, including blue WF, green WF and grey WF. Green water accounted for 57% of the total water consumption, grey water for 24%, and blue water for 19%. Both green and blue water contributed to food production. Green water refers to water stored in the unsaturated zone of soil and available for evapotranspiration by crops (Johansson, Fader, Seaquist, & Nicholas, 2016). Blue water can be defined as water above and below the ground: mainly rivers, lakes and groundwater. It can be divided into renewable water sources, such as runoff and shallow groundwater, and non-renewable sources, such as fossil groundwater and glacier meltwater (Su, Li, & Singh, 2014). Taking full advantage of green water would promote the economic benefit of irrigated agriculture, because blue water has a direct cost attributed to infrastructure requirements as well as a high opportunity cost, while green water cannot be used by socio-economic sectors (Konar, Dalin, Hanasaki, Rinaldo, & Rodriguez-Iturbe, 2012). The green water utilization rate for rice production was 74.4%, indicating that water use efficiency was relatively high. Pollution of water directly affected environmental sustainability and public health; moreover, it increased the competition for freshwater (Vörösmarty et al., 2010). Therefore, grey WF was also important part analyzing water utilization conditions. The grey WF for the three subareas was about the same, at about 0.11, 0.13 and 0.15 in wet, normal and dry flow, respectively. It was clear that the smallest WF occurred in wet flow, and the largest in dry flow. This was mainly because in dry flow the water supply was smaller, leading to a smaller crop yield. For the three subareas, the WF for Lishantun was the lowest, and for Anbanghe the highest, due to their different rice yields. The average WF was 0.5526.

Energy footprint

The EF was related to energy used for surface water abstraction, groundwater pumping and drainage, and the results of calculations for EF for irrigation are illustrated in Figure 4. For Lishantun subarea, the EF involved both surface water and groundwater, because it

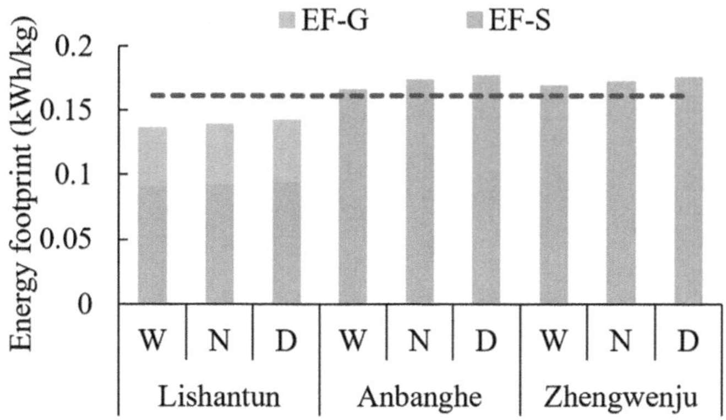

Figure 4. Energy footprint.

was irrigated by both surface water and groundwater. For this subarea, the EF for surface water accounted for 67%, while for groundwater it was 33%. The lift of the pumping station for surface water was 90 m, and the efficiency of pumping station was taken as 0.5. Then, based on the method of de Vito et al. (2017), the energy demand per cubic metre of water from surface water could be obtained. According to the method of Daccache, Ciurana, Rodriguez Diaz, and Knox (2014), one can get the energy demand per cubic metre of water from groundwater. The parameters for calculating it were pump efficiency of 0.8, motor efficiency of 0.4, and water table depth of 5 m; nominal operating pressure and head loss were assumed to be 20 m, and 20% of the nominal operating pressure was assumed to offset friction losses. Computation showed that the energy demand per cubic metre of water from surface water was higher than that from groundwater for Lishantun subarea. Also, the surface irrigation quota was higher than the groundwater irrigation quota. These led to a higher energy demand per unit area when using surface water compared with groundwater. So the EF for surface water was higher than the EF for groundwater, and the average EF was 0.161. It was clear that EF for Lishantun was below average, while Anbanghe and Zhengwenju were above average. Higher EF usually corresponded to lower profitability, if the energy demand was kept consistent. There was no significant change in EF under different flow levels. This indicated that EF was not sensitive to crop yield but was influenced by the comprehensive effects of crop yield and irrigation quota, both of which were varying with flow levels.

Carbon footprint

CF was another important index that could reflect irrigation water amount and crop production. Four parts contributed to the CF (Figure 5): direct emission of CO_2 (CF-C), emission of N_2O (CF-N_2O), emission of CH_4 (CF-CH_4), and an equivalent CO_2 emission from crop straw burning (CF-CSB). It was clear that CF-N_2O and CF-CSB were negligible. So it was mainly the direct emission of CO_2 and the emission of CH_4 that contributed to CF. Larger CF usually represented larger environmental impacts. The use of fertilizer, pesticides, agricultural film and diesel (used for agricultural machinery) and electricity use for irrigation contributed to the direct emission of CO_2, and of these, fertilizer

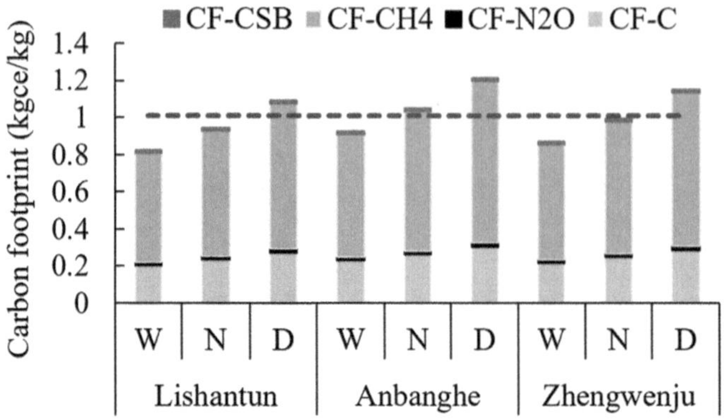

Figure 5. Carbon footprint.

accounted for 43% of all the farming practices. Therefore, increasing fertilizer efficiency was beneficial not only for higher economic gains but also helped reduce environment pollution. The main crop was rice, leading to significant CH_4 emissions. For CF, the changes were dramatic between different flow levels, indicating that CF was sensitive to irrigation water amount. The differences in CF between subareas were not large. The average CF under all the scenarios was 1.01.

Degree of coordination of water, energy use and food production

Comparative analysis of the three indices allowed us to underline the specific impacts and trade-offs related to irrigation practices. Based on the values of WF, EF and CF, the CD of water use, energy use and food production was calculated, which could link the three indices together and could reflect, to some extent, the sustainability of WFEN. CD was based on the coupling factor (Table 3) and the weights of the three indices. In general, the range of the adjustment coefficient, i.e., *k* in Equation (12), was [2, 5] (Hua, Liu, & Li, 2018), and it was set to 2 in this study. Many approaches that are based on synergy theory can be adopted to assess the interrelation between water use, energy use and food production. In this study, CD was chosen because of its high efficiency in calculation. In this study, two scenarios were used in calculating CD. Scenario 1 took the three indices as equally important, while Scenario 2 put more emphasis on CF, which was directly related to environmental impacts (Table 3). For Scenario 1, all the values of CD were between 0.2 and 0.3, indicating that the WFEN was in the state of moderate imbalance (the category system for WFEN coordination can be seen in Appendix 1). In Scenario 2, CD for Lishantun subarea was between 0.3 and 0.4, representing mild

Table 3. Coupling factor of the water-food-energy nexus.

	Coupling factor			Coordination degree (Scenario 1)			Coordination degree (Scenario 2)		
Sub-area	Wet	Normal	Dry	Wet	Normal	Dry	Wet	Normal	Dry
Lishantun	0.24	0.20	0.16	0.33	0.32	0.32	0.38	0.37	0.36
Anbanghe	0.26	0.23	0.20	0.37	0.37	0.36	0.42	0.43	0.42
Zhengwenju	0.29	0.25	0.21	0.38	0.38	0.37	0.44	0.43	0.42

imbalance, while the CD for the Anbanghe and Zhengwenju subareas was between 0.4 and 0.5, in the state of slight imbalance. The WFEN was in a state of imbalance based on WF, EF and CF, but when the environmental impact was paid more attention, the harmony of the nexus improved. This was because the values of WF, EF and CF were based on the optimal irrigation water allocation, with the aim of emphasizing economic benefit only. This would bring more environmental pollution, because usually, economic benefit and environmental protection were contradictory. The changes in CD with different flow levels were not obvious, indicating that the harmony of WFEN was not sensitive to the changes of external environment, especially of hydrological elements.

Discussion and policy implications

This study optimized irrigation water for rice in different subareas of HID in different growth stages, including tillering, elongation, heading, and milk. Wet, normal and dry flow levels were considered to investigate how the changes in hydrological elements affected irrigation strategies, and to give policy makers more alternatives for irrigation water allocation in response to different possible scenarios. The irrigation water was optimized focusing on economic benefit, that is, re-allocating limited water resources (both surface water and groundwater) to achieve the maximum net economic benefit, considering the restrictions of water availability, water balance, water demand, water allocation threshold and electricity availability. The water allocation for the three subareas was robust, because the water allocation structure remained almost the same under different flow levels: about 38% for Lishantun, 26% for Aanbanghe and for 36% for Zhengwenju, at all flow levels. The ratio of surface to groundwater was 11:9 for Lishantun subarea for any flow level. Although the water allocation percentages remained stable, the specific quantities changed, based on the inflow volume. Thus, accurate forecasting of the inflow volume appeared to be particularly important, because it would help policy makers make quick decisions on irrigation water allocation. Lishantun subarea is a combined well/canal subarea, with the ratio of surface water to groundwater utilization being 7:11. This result was obtained considering the actual exploitable groundwater capacity. Although the limited available water was optimized, which alleviated water shortages to some extent, water demand was still not satisfied. Optimizing irrigation water from the perspective of management was only one aspect of improving profit and efficiency of irrigation. Engineering measures, such as water diversion, increase of canal lining rate, and lifting efficiency, were also indispensable.

For an irrigation district, irrigation patterns directly affect crop yield, energy consumption and greenhouse gas emissions. Accordingly, the sustainability of water and energy use and food production was evaluated. This evaluation served two purposes: first, to assess how the optimal irrigation resources allocation schemes affected the performance of WFEN; and second, to quantitatively evaluate the harmony of WFEN, based on CD. Three important indices associated with WFEN, WF, EF and CF, were chosen and estimated, because they could reflect the correlation among water use, energy use and food production, as well as social and environmental impacts. Specifically, CF could directly reflect the environmental impact in the form of carbon emission. Larger values of CF meant more environmental issues in terms of greenhouse gas emissions. Grey water footprint could also reflect environmental impact because it was related to fertilizer usage. Blue and green water footprints could reflect economic and social impacts to some extent. A larger value of green water footprint was desired because the efficient use of green water for food production could reduce the use of blue water, which could be transferred to other water consumers (e.g., industrial, domestic and environmental). This would promote economic growth, social stability and ecological environment improvement. Larger WF usually corresponded to higher CF, both of which were sensitive to water consumption. However, EF had no significant changes. Economic and environmental benefits were contradictory and should be balanced as much as possible by reducing blue WF and CF. Accurate prediction of water availability was of vital importance due to the high sensitivity of comprehensive economic and environmental benefits to different flow levels. Increasing the utilization efficiency of water resources and farming practices (especially fertilizer use) was a potential way to improve the cooperativity of water and energy use, and food production.

The maximum net economic benefits through irrigation were 2.1, 1.8, and 1.5×10^8 yuan for wet, normal and dry flow, respectively. This would lead to irrigation water resources allocation strategies that tended to allocate as much water as possible, with the water utilization structure adjusted among different subareas, different crop growth periods, and different types of water supply at the same time. This might cause larger environmental pollution, because usually more water means more energy use and more farmland drainage, thus generating more air and water pollution. Compared with the consideration of economic benefit under normal flow levels, if the social objective was considered, i.e., to guarantee the equilibrium allocation of water resources among different subareas as much as possible (expressed as Gini coefficient), crop production would decrease by 4.7%, net economic benefits by 5.7%, and the optimum level of extraction of water by 2%. If environmental objectives are quantified as carbon emission, crop production would decrease by 19.1%, net economic benefits by 22.6%, and the optimum level of extraction of water by 17%. If water for economic benefit is given priority, then there would be 20% more carbon emissions compared with the water allocation strategy considering the environmental objective. However, in all these cases, the Gini coefficient was around 0.2, representing the relative average level. This indicated that the social effect was not sensitive to changes in agricultural irrigation water allocation amounts, and the economic and environmental objectives were contradictory. This provides policy makers a sense of agricultural irrigation water allocation strategies on the basis of priorities. From the farmers' angle, the economic objective should be given priority, because this could improve their lives. Generally, farmers care more about their income from increasing food production, and are not concerned about how increasing food production impacts environmental and social development. Both environment-based and society-based water resources strategies reduced economic benefit and led to underutilized water, but the usage of water and energy resources could be better balanced. From the perspective of policy makers for a region, the consciousness of environmental protection and seeking a balance between economic development and environmental protection might contribute to the stability and robustness of water and energy use, and food production.

If policy makers treat the economic, environmental and social benefits equally, total water resources allocation was 87.47 million m^3 for high flow, 86.12 million m^3 for normal flow, and 83.67 million m^3 for dry flow. Such water allocation strategies would help policy makers manage agricultural irrigation water in a more sustainable way. Also, increasing the efficiency of water use, energy use and farming practices, including the use of fertilizer, pesticides, agro-machinery engineering, and agricultural films, is important to reduce blue and grey WF, EF and CF. In other words, such measures could help promote food production as well as reduce agricultural pollution. To do that, raising awareness of the efficient use of these resources to avoid waste is important, but is not enough. Policy makers have to solve problems fundamentally, for example, adopting a policy of 'stepped water price' for irrigation water resources, energetically popularizing technology for integrated control of water and fertilization, and implementing ID cards to strictly control water and energy consumption in every field.

Conclusion

This article optimized agricultural irrigation water for rice in HID from an economic perspective, and assessed the sustainability of WEFN to help policy makers gain insights into (1) how irrigation water schemes for both surface water and groundwater supplies can be adjusted in response to different inflow volumes; (2) how irrigation activities affect crop yield, energy consumption and greenhouse gas emissions; and (3) the multi-dimensional sustainability of WFEN. To achieve these goals, this article developed an optimization-evaluation approach, in which a nonlinear optimization model was established to optimize agricultural irrigation water, and an index-based method based on the concept of 'footprint' was used to evaluate the sustainability of water use, energy use and food production. The optimization and evaluation modules are based on input–output relationships. Water shortages exist in HID, and the approach developed here can help policy makers adjust current irrigation patterns to be more profitable and efficient, and thus mitigate water shortages. This article focused on generating agricultural irrigation water allocation strategies from an economic point of view; if environmental and social impacts are considered, food production will decrease by 4.7% and 19.1%, respectively, and the corresponding economic benefits will decrease by 5.7% and 22.6%, respectively. The approach is portable and can be extended into a decision support system for the efficient and sustainable development of irrigation water resources, which may help policy makers make quick decisions on irrigation management.

Disclosure statement

No potential conflict of interest was reported by the authors.

Funding

This work was supported by the Natural Science Foundation of Heilongjiang Province of China [E2018004]; and the Heilongjiang Postdoctoral Science Foundation [LBH-Z18019].

References

Chen, X. H. (2018). *Resource and environmental costs of cropping structure change in China* (Doctoral dissertation). China Agricultural University, Beijing.

Daccache, A., Ciurana, J. S., Rodriguez Diaz, J. A., & Knox, J. W. (2014). Water and energy footprint of irrigated agriculture in the Mediterranean region. *Environmental Research Letters*, *9*(12), 124014. doi:10.1088/1748-9326/9/12/124014

De Vito, R., Portoghese, I., Pagano, A., Fratino, U., & Vurro, M. (2017). An index-based approach for the sustainability assessment of irrigation practice based on the water-energy-food nexus framework. *Advances in Water Resources, 110*, 423–436. doi:10.1016/j.advwatres.2017.10.027

Finley, J. W., & Seiber, J. N. (2014). The nexus of food, energy and water. *Journal of Agricultural and Food Chemistry, 62*(27), 6255–6262. doi:10.1021/jf501496r

Fu, Q., Xiao, Y. Y., Cui, S., Liu, D., & Li, T. X. (2017). Multi-water resources optimal allocation of irrigation district based on fuzzy multi-objective programming. *Transactions of the Chinese Society for Agricultural Machinery, 48*(7), 222–227. (in Chinese with English abstract).

Galán-Martín, Á., Vaskan, P., Antón, A., Esteller, L. J., & Guillén-Gosálbez, G. (2017). Multi-objective optimization of rainfed and irrigated agricultural areas considering production and environmental criteria: A case study of wheat production in Spain. *Journal of Cleaner Production, 140* (Part 2), 816–830. doi:10.1016/j.jclepro.2016.06.099

Hoekstra, A. Y., Aldaya, M. M., Chapagain, A. K., & Mekonnen, M. M. (2011). *The water footprint assessment manual: Setting the global standard*. London, UK: Routledge.

Hoff, H. (2011). Understanding the nexus. Background paper for the Bonn 2011 Nexus conference: The water, energy and food security nexus. Stockholm Environment Institute.

Hua, J., Liu, X., & Li, J. J. (2018). Evaluation of coordination degree of water conservancy project system and "economy-social-water ecology" complex system in Henan Province. *Journal of Economics of Water Resources, 36*(5), 1–6. (in Chinese with English abstract).

Jensen, M. E. (1968). Water consumption by agricultural plants. In T. T. Kozlowski (Ed.), *Water deficits and plant growth* (Vol. 2, pp. 1–22). New York: Academic Press.

Johansson, E. L., Fader, M., Seaquist, J. W., & Nicholas, K. A. (2016). Green and blue water demand from large-scale land acquisitions in Africa. *Proceedings of the National Academy of Sciences of the United States of America, 113*(41), 11471–11476. doi:10.1073/pnas.1524741113

Konar, M., Dalin, C., Hanasaki, N., Rinaldo, A., & Rodriguez-Iturbe, I. (2012). Temporal dynamics of blue and green virtual water trade networks. *Water Resources Research, 48*, W07509. doi:10.1029/2012WR011959

Kumar, M. D., & Singh, O. P. (2007). *Groundwater management: Physical, institutional and policy alternatives*. New Delhi: Sage Publications.

Lalehzari, R., Boroomand Nasab, S., Moazed, H., & Haghighi, A. (2016). Multiobjective management of water allocation to sustainable irrigation planning and optimal cropping pattern. *Journal of Irrigation and Drainage Engineering, 142*(1), 05015008. doi:10.1061/(ASCE)IR.1943-4774.0000933

Le Roux, B., van der Laan, M., Vahrmeijer, T., Bristow, K. L., & Annandale, J. G. (2017). Establishing and testing a catchment water footprint framework to inform sustainable irrigation water use for an aquifer under stress. *Science of the Total Environment, 599–600*, 1119–1128. doi:10.1016/j.scitotenv.2017.04.170

Li, M., Fu, Q., Guo, P., Singh, V. P., Zhang, C. L., & Yang, G. Q. (2019a). Stochastic multi-objective decision making for sustainable irrigation in a changing environment. *Journal of Cleaner Production, 223*(20), 928–945. doi:10.1016/j.jclepro.2019.03.183

Li, M., Fu, Q., Singh, V. P., Ji, Y., Liu, D., Zhang, C. L., & Li, T. (2019b). An optimal modelling approach for managing agricultural water-energy-food nexus under uncertainty. *Science of the Total Environment, 651*, 1416–1434. doi:10.1016/j.scitotenv.2018.09.291

Li, M., Fu, Q., Singh, V. P., & Liu, D. (2018). An interval multi-objective programming model for irrigation water allocation under uncertainty. *Agricultural Water Management, 196*, 24–36. doi:10.1016/j.agwat.2017.10.016

Li, M., Fu, Q., Singh, V. P., Liu, D., & Li, T. X. (2019c). Stochastic multi-objective modeling for optimization of water-food-energy nexus of irrigated agriculture. *Advances in Water Resources, 127*, 209–224. doi:10.1016/j.advwatres.2019.03.015

Li, M., Fu, Q., Singh, V. P., Ma, M. W., & Liu, X. (2017). An intuitionistic fuzzy multi-objective non-linear programming model for sustainable irrigation water allocation under the combination of dry and wet conditions. *Journal of Hydrology, 555*, 80–94. doi:10.1016/j.jhydrol.2017.09.055

Liu, X., Guo, P., Li, F. H., & Zheng, W. S. (2019). Optimization of planning structure in irrigated district considering water footprint under uncertainty. *Journal of Cleaner Production*, *210*(10), 1270–1280. doi:10.1016/j.jclepro.2018.10.339

Mekonnen, M. M., & Hoekstra, A. Y. (2011). The green, blue and grey water footprint of crops and derived crop products. *Hydrology and Earth System Sciences*, *15*, 1577–1600. doi:10.5194/hess-15-1577-2011

Nguyen, D. C. H., Ascough II, J. C., Maier, H. R., Dandy, G. C., & Andales, A. A. (2017). Optimization of irrigation scheduling using ant colony algorithms and an advanced cropping system model. *Environmental Modelling & Software*, *97*, 32–45. doi:10.1016/j.envsoft.2017.07.002

Ren, C. F., Li, Z. H., & Zhang, H. B. (2019). Integrated multi-objective stochastic fuzzy programming and AHP method for agricultural water and land optimization allocation under multiple uncertainties. *Journal of Cleaner Production*, *210*, 12–24. doi:10.1016/j.jclepro.2018.10.348

Ringler, C., Bhaduri, A., & Lawford, R. (2013). The nexus across water, energy, land and food (WELF): Potential for improved resource use efficiency? *Current Opinion in Environmental Sustainability*, *5* (6), 617–624. doi:10.1016/j.cosust.2013.11.002

Singh, A. (2012). Optimal allocation of resources for the maximization of net agricultural return. *Journal of Irrigation and Drainage Engineering*, *138*(9), 830–836. doi:10.1061/(ASCE)IR.1943-4774.0000474

Singh, A. (2014). Irrigation planning and management through optimization modelling. *Water Resources Management*, *28*(1), 1–14. doi:10.1007/s11269-013-0469-y

Su, X. L., Li, J. F., & Singh, V. P. (2014). Optimal allocation of agricultural water resources based on virtual water subdivision in Shiyang River basin. *Water Resources Management*, *28*, 2243–2257. doi:10.1007/s11269-014-0611-5

Tan, Q., Zhang, S., & Li, R. (2017). Optimal use of agricultural water and land resources through reconfiguring crop planting structure under socioeconomic and ecological objectives. *Water*, *9* (7), 488. doi:10.3390/w9070488

Tian, H., Lu, C., Pan, S., Yang, J., Miao, R., Ren, W., … Reilly, J. (2018). Optimizing resource use efficiencies in the food-energy-water nexus for sustainable agriculture: From conceptual model to decision support system. *Current Opinion in Environmental Sustainability*, *33*, 104–113. doi:10.1016/j.cosust.2018.04.003

Tong, F., & Guo, P. (2013). Simulation and optimization for crop water allocation based on crop water production functions and climate factor under uncertainty. *Applied Mathematical Modelling*, *37*(14–15), 7708–7716. doi:10.1016/j.apm.2013.03.018

Vövösmarty, C. J., McIntyre, P. B., Gessner, M. O., Dudgeon, D., Prusevich, A., Green, P., … Davies, P. M. (2010). Global threats to human water security and river biodiversity. *Nature*, *467*(7315), 555–561. doi:10.1038/nature09440

Wang, Z. B., Fang, C. L., Cheng, S. W., & Wang, J. (2013). Evolution of coordination degree of eco-economic system and early-warning in the Yangtze River Delta. *Journal of Geographical Sciences*, *23*(1), 147–162. doi:10.1007/s11442-013-1000-3

Wu, X. M., Hu, S., & Mo, S. J. (2013). Carbon footprint model for evaluating the global warming impact of food transport refrigeration systems. *Journal of Cleaner Production*, *54*, 115–124. doi:10.1016/j.jclepro.2013.04.045

Xiao, G. M., Zhao, Z. C., Liang, L., Meng, F. Q., Wu, W. L., & Guo, Y. (2019). Improving nitrogen and water use efficiency in a wheat-maize rotation system in the North China Plain using optimized farming practices. *Agricultural Water Management*, *212*, 172–180. doi:10.1016/j.agwat.2018.09.011

Zhang, C. L., Zhang, F., Guo, S. S., Liu, X., & Guo, P. (2018). Inexact nonlinear improved fuzzy chance-constrained programming model for irrigation water management under uncertainty. *Journal of Hydrology*, *556*, 397–408. doi:10.1016/j.jhydrol.2017.11.011

Zhao, J. M., Li, M., Guo, P., Zhang, C. L., & Tan, Q. (2017). Agricultural water productivity oriented water resources allocation based on the coordination of multiple factors. *Water*, *9*(7), 490. doi:10.3390/w9070490

Appendix 1

The category system of coordination type of the WFEN.

Level	Coordination degree	Score standard
V1	High imbalance	0 ~ 0.1
V2	Serious imbalance	0.1 ~ 0.2
V3	Moderate imbalance	0.2 ~ 0.3
V4	Mild imbalance	0.3 ~ 0.4
V5	Slight imbalance	0.4 ~ 0.5
V6	Narrow balance	0.5 ~ 0.6
V7	Mild balance	0.6 ~ 0.7
V8	Moderate balance	0.7 ~ 0.8
V9	Well balance	0.8 ~ 0.9
V10	High balance	0.9 ~ 1.0

Appendix 2

Abbreviation of proper noun

Abbreviation	Full name
CD	Coordination degree
CF	Carbon footprint
CWPF	Crop water production function
EF	Energy footprint
ET	Evapotranspiration
HID	Heping Irrigation District
WF	Water footprint
WFEN	Water-food-energy nexus

Rethinking on the methodology for assessing global water and food challenges

M. Dinesh Kumar, Nitin Bassi and O. P. Singh

ABSTRACT

The article delinks food security challenges from the challenge of supplying water to meet the needs of the industrial, livestock, domestic and environmental sectors to analyze the food security and water management challenges of individual nations. For this, three indices are developed: the water adequacy index, water-land index and water-land-pasture index. Their values are computed for 172 countries. The analysis suggests that the criteria for assessing the magnitude of food insecurity and water scarcity problems should include agricultural land, particularly cultivated land and pastureland, along with renewable water.

Introduction

Water is needed for human and animal consumption, for growing food, feed and fodder; for a myriad of functions – manufacturing processes, power generation, and finally, the environment.[1] Per global projections, food, fodder and feed production will continue to consume the most water for many decades to come (Alexandratos & Bruinsma, 2012). Availability of agricultural land is one major factor in agricultural production (Alexandratos & Bruinsma, 2012; Food and Agriculture Organization of the United Nations [FAO], 2011; Helfand & Levine, 2004; Kumar, Bassi, Singh, Ganguly, & Chattopadhyay, 2017; Kumar & Singh, 2005; Zhao, Hubacek, Feng, Sun, & Liu, 2019). Yet, the challenges of meeting the water needs of the domestic, urban, industrial and environmental sectors and that of growing food, feed and fodder are all generally lumped under water management challenges. Hence, the challenges of meeting future food production and water supply needs at the global, regional and national levels are viewed from the perspective of water.

Global water scarcity maps have been generated comparing renewable water supplies in different regions with estimates of aggregate water demand for all the above-mentioned sectors in those regions, and support inferences about the nature of water scarcity, i.e. whether it is physical or economic (Seckler, Amarasinghe, Molden, de Silva, & Barker, 1998), and the degree of scarcity, i.e. whether it is 'absolute water scarcity' or 'water scarcity' or 'water stress' facing a country or a region (Falkenmark, 1989).The inferences are then used to predict whether a region or country will face water shortage for food production, economic growth or even basic survival needs. The physical water scarcity index, which is widely used to indicate the sufficiency of water for economic production and basic survival needs in a region, based only on per capita renewable water resources, is a good example (Falkenmark, 1989, 1997). This approach is highly water-centric (Kumar et al., 2017; Zhao et al., 2019).

As a result there is a skewed understanding of the nature of water and food challenges that will be faced by the world in future (Kumar & Singh, 2005). For instance, estimates of aggregate demand of water for various future needs above renewable supplies for any given region eventually led to the conclusion that such regions will face water scarcity (Kummu et al., 2016; Mancosu, Snyder, Kyriakakis, & Spano, 2015; Rijsberman, 2006; Seckler et al., 1998). An index that captures water use versus water availability, the 'criticality ratio', was derived by Raskin, Smith, and Salt (1997). On this approach, a country is water-scarce if annual withdrawals are 20–40% of annual supply, and severely water-scarce if they exceed 40% (While, 2014). Such an approach does not factor in the differences in the quantum of water required to produce a kilogram of food-grain or other agricultural produce between different climatic settings, say between the hot and arid tropics and cold or temperate regions. Nevertheless, predictions of future water scarcity are made by juxtaposing such figures with population projections, and such predictions have become the basis for 'doomsday' prophecies.

But a distorted view of the food security scenario of a country is obtained when the food security challenge is assessed purely from the perspective of renewable water resources or water use. Such a distorted view produces complacency among the water-rich nations that they can be food-secure, and unwanted pessimism for water-scarce nations that they cannot produce enough food. The point is that for food security, access to arable land is equally or even more important, and therefore this factor should be integrated with other considerations in national food and water policy making. In the same manner, it is dangerous to assess the water management challenges of nations based solely on renewable water availability and aggregate demand for water (Jia, Long, & Liu, 2017; Zhao et al., 2019). While most of the aggregate demand for water comes from food production (de Fraiture & Wichelns, 2010; Hanjra & Qureshi, 2010; Kumar & Singh, 2005), an important determinant of effective water availability for the same is access to water in the soil profile (Bodner, Nakhforoosh, & Kaul, 2015; Rockström et al., 2009). Conversely, the demand for water from the agriculture sector will increase with the area of cultivated land per capita, and this can induce water scarcity, even with moderately high per capita renewable water resources. Yet, irrigation water availability is often used to indicate food security challenges, ignoring the contribution of land (Beddington, 2010; Falkenmark, 1997; Mancosu et al., 2015).

Such methodological drawbacks also lead to erroneous conclusions about the magnitude of water scarcity and food insecurity in various countries and regions within countries (While, 2014). Often, future food demand is translated into equivalent future water demand, which is then compared to usable water supplies (Kummu et al., 2016; Mancosu et al., 2015). If the latter exceeds the former, suggestions are made to increase the utilization of the available water and improve access to water (see e.g. Mukherji, Shah, & Banerjee, 2012; Namara et al., 2010; Rosegrant, Ringler, & Zhu, 2009), completely ignoring the critical question of whether enough land is available to produce food using this water. Ideally, what need to be assessed are: the maximum amount of water the available arable land in the region can absorb for irrigation under the highest possible intensity of land use for crop production; the maximum production possible under the scenario of most intense land use; and the amount of food that has to be imported (given the likely future deficit) from other regions that have surplus land (Kumar et al., 2017).

This new paradigm for analyzing food and water challenges, which integrates arable land as a key variable for estimating both the supply of and demand for water for agricultural production, and production of food and other agricultural commodities, will compel us to revisit the estimates of future food production requirements for regions or countries that have excess arable land. Obviously, in addition to meeting their own demand, such regions and countries will also have to produce surplus for export to regions that are land-scarce. The estimation of future water demand for agriculture in such regions should therefore include the quantum of surplus food for export to the neighbouring food-insecure regions or countries that are potential buyers of these agricultural commodities, even if the countries with excess arable land are water-scarce (Kumar et al., 2017). This is quite contrary to the conventional wisdom of suggesting that such regions import food to reduce their water footprint (Allan, 1997; Hoekstra, 2003), which does not take into account the fact that water-rich regions often lack enough arable land to produce food even for their own needs, due to high population density. The new paradigm will also force us to revisit the estimates of future water requirements for various uses in regions that with a severe shortage of arable land.

Such a paradigm would add a new dimension to the global debate on national and regional food and water policy by bringing out very clearly the type of interdependence that exists or is likely to develop in future between countries, and between regions within countries, for achieving water and food security, in the form of international and interregional water transfer and international and interregional food trade.

In this article, we assess the nature of the challenge facing different countries, i.e. whether it is related to food security or water (supply and demand) management. We also analyze the scope for improving food security and water supply in the countries that are confronting food insecurity and water shortage today, by examining the current level of utilization of water in the soil profile for agricultural production, blue water for water supplies and agricultural production, cultivation of cropland for overall agricultural production, and use of pastureland for dairy production.

Approach and methodology

The basic premise of the analysis and arguments presented in this article is that water abundance (or water richness) by itself does not enable a country to have enough agricultural production to achieve food security and a surplus for export. What is required is enough cultivable land, supported by enough usable water resources to meet the crop water requirement of the available land, for the entire crop growing season. This means that there is an optimum level of water availability for a given amount of cultivable land to achieve the highest agricultural output. However, even with optimum water availability, what proportion of that cultivable land gets cultivated and how much of the water gets used up depend on the aggregate per capita land availability compared to that required to meet the domestic consumption needs and export potential of the agricultural produce. That said, any increase in water availability up to this level would help crop production.

If renewable water availability goes above that level, it does not increase crop production but only creates a water surplus, and the surplus water can be made available for domestic purposes, livestock watering and industrial production.

To this effect, we derived a 'water adequacy index', which indicates to what extent the current water availability meets the maximum crop water requirement of the available cultivable (arable) land for an assumed crop-growing period of 300 days. It is estimated by dividing the total renewable water availability by the product of total cultivable land and annual ET_0:

$$WAI = AWR/(CA \times ET_0 \times 300) \tag{1}$$

where ET_0 is the average daily evapotranspiration for the country as a whole; CA is the cultivated area in ha. However, the maximum value of the index is 1, and accordingly the values are adjusted. These values indicate the water adequacy for likely future needs when the cultivated area increases and becomes equal to the cultivable area. If the index is greater than 1, it is taken as 1.

Our water adequacy index is distinctly different from the 'index of drinking water adequacy', which is a tool designed to assess and benchmark the performance of countries in providing *adequate drinking water* to their citizens. The latter index was developed to provide a robust indicator for monitoring access to drinking water of adequate quantity and quality (Rao & Mingxuan, 2010), whereas our water adequacy index is about the adequacy of the water resources in a region or country to bring the cultivated land under intensive crop cultivation.

If the water adequacy index is less than 1, it is modified by dividing it by the fraction of the cultivable land that is actually under cultivation (as shown in Table S1, column I/column G, presented in column R, in the online supplemental data at https://doi.org/10.1080/07900627.2019.1707071), to reflect the current water needs. If the original water adequacy index is 0.5, and if only two-thirds of the arable land is under cultivation, the modified water adequacy index becomes 0.75. But again, if the index for any country exceeds 1, it has to be adjusted to 1, the maximum possible value.

The modified water adequacy index is multiplied by per capita cultivated area (in ha) to derive a new index, the 'water-land index' (Kumar et al., 2017). This captures the agricultural production potential of a country. Computed values range from zero (Sao Tome and Principe) to 2.056 (Australia).

Milk production, an important part of food and nutritional security, is a water-intensive farming activity, and an important component of the farm economy in many regions around the world. In addition to the drinking water use, a significant amount of water is indirectly used by dairy animals in the form of water embedded in the (green and dry) fodder and feed; this indirect use is several times greater than drinking water consumption. The intensity of water use for dairy production depends on the climate, which heavily influences the water needed to produce the feed and fodder (Sultana, Uddin, Ridoutt, & Peters, 2014).

Since milk production is dependent also on biomass (grass) production along with by-products from cultivated land, to understand the effect of the same in milk production, a pastureland index was derived by multiplying the amount of pastureland (in ha) per capita and a coefficient, which represents the quality of the pastureland in terms of primary productivity. The coefficient is used to simulate the variation in the quality of pastureland across countries in terms of primary productivity; it is based on rainfall, reference evapotranspiration and overall climate (tropical or temperate). Up to 300 mm of rainfall, the coefficient is the same as that of the rainfall in metres. Beyond 300 mm of annual precipitation, the coefficient is only a fraction of the rainfall, with the value increasing with more uniform pattern of occurrence: higher where the rainfall is high, reference ET is low, and the climate is cold or temperate; and vice versa for low-rainfall regions with high aridity and a tropical climate. The coefficient chosen for the analysis varied from 0.05 for Saudi Arabia, UAE, Bahrain and Qatar to 1.7 for New Zealand (Kumar et al., 2017).

The sum of the multiple of the modified water adequacy ratio and available cultivated land per capita, and pastureland index is the 'composite water-land-pasture index' (Kumar et al., 2017).

These three indices were used to assess the comparative situation of 153 countries around the world in terms of self-sufficiency to meet future water needs, and agricultural production potential, including milk production potential. The computed values of the last two indices for the individual countries are used as independent variables in statistical models to explore how far they could predict the agricultural production and milk production potential of the countries, thereby testing the robustness of the indices. Based on the nature of relationship shown by the model, different typologies of countries were established in terms of their characteristics, defined by water adequacy index and water-land index, and the consequent implications for water security and food security.

Irrigation potential utilization was estimated as a ratio of the total amount of irrigation water withdrawal (m^3 per capita) against the total amount required to irrigate the cultivated land for 300 days per year. Then, based on the current level of utilization of agricultural land for crop production, the extent of withdrawal of renewable water from the natural system and the current level of utilization of irrigation potential, inferences are drawn with regard to the steps these countries need to take to deal with future water scarcity and food insecurity.

The analysis used global data sets for total population, geographical area, agricultural land, cultivated land, area under permanent crops and area under pasture (ha) for the group of 172 countries, from FAO (fao.org/faostat/en/#data), along with milk production from different types of livestock and dairy animals; annual irrigation water withdrawal volumes by a group of 155 countries and irrigation potential utilization in percentage terms (also from fao.org/faostat/en/#data); estimates of green water use by a group of 155 countries, from Kumar and Singh (2005); and data on virtual water export/import by a group of 155 countries, available from Hoekstra and Chapagain and Hoekstra (2003). The original data sets obtained from various sources and the estimates of various indices derived from them are presented in column A to AF of Table S1 (in the supplemental online data).

The tenuous link between 'renewable water' and cultivated land

The nexus between land and water, which define the food security and water management challenges, was not appreciated in the past (Kumar, Sivamohan, & Narayanamoorthy, 2012). This nexus operates in two ways. First, even if a region does not have enough renewable water, the availability of certain amount of cropland (cultivated land and pastureland) ensures the use of water in the soil profile, available from precipitation, which can be used by the crop (Rockström et al., 2009) Second, even if a region is highly water-rich (say owing to excessive precipitation), without enough cultivable land, the water cannot be used for crop production, making the region food-insecure (FAO, 2011; Kumar et al., 2012). There are many such regions around the world (FAO, 2011).

We analyzed the data on per capita renewable water availability and per capita cropped land (agricultural land) in 150 countries (Table S1). The former ranges from 8 m^3 per year to 582,190 m^3 per year; the latter, from 0.0028 ha to 2.094 ha. Figure 1 show the data as a chart. One can see that there is no relationship between the two variables. (A two-sample paired *T* test confirms this.) Many countries with abundant renewable water resources (per capita) have little agricultural land (per capita). On the other hand, many countries with plenty of agricultural land (per capita) have very limited water resources (Kumar et al., 2017).

Very few countries are well-endowed with both renewable water resources and cultivable (agricultural) land. They are very unlikely to face any problems related to water and food, if other factors of production such as labour, machinery, irrigation infrastructure and crop and water-use technologies are available. Now we consider how the positioning of a country *vis-à-vis* access to renewable water resources (including water from precipitation available in the soil) and agricultural land affect land and water utilization for crop production, food security and water available for the environment. Land utilization is analyzed in terms of the percentage of agricultural land under crop production, and water utilization in terms of extent of water diversion from the hydrological system (Kumar et al., 2017).

If a country has abundant utilizable and renewable water resources (say more than 20,000 m^3 per capita per year), and enough agricultural land to feed its population, it will

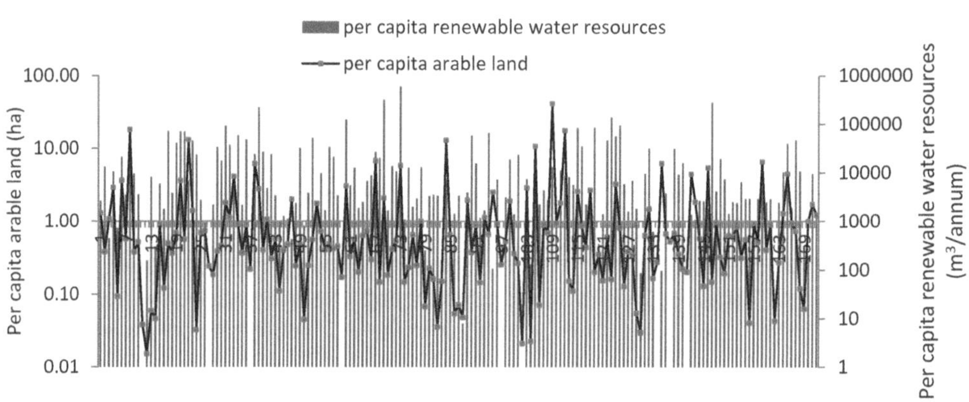

Figure 1. Per capita renewable water resources and arable land in different countries.

try to bring all that land under cultivation to meet its food consumption needs (Cambodia, Vietnam and South Korea are examples). Such countries may still have a lot of renewable water flowing into the natural sink, or into neighbouring countries (Kumar et al., 2017).

But, in a water-rich country, if more agricultural land is available than is required to produce crops for domestic needs, it is likely that much of that land will remain uncultivated. Yet, the country might produce surplus food and other crops for export. The result is that a lot of renewable water remains untapped. Nevertheless, the situation of a good portion of the land lying uncultivated can also occur when the renewable water available is less than would be required to bring all the land under cultivation, but more than would be required to feed the population (as in Australia, where there is 24 ha per capita of agricultural land). If the agricultural land is too little (like in Bangladesh or Indonesia), the country will try to intensify land use, but might still have food shortage, while a lot of water will be available as untapped runoff or groundwater. However, wealthy nations like Japan will import food, and leave the agricultural land fallow or convert it into pastureland (Kumar et al., 2017).

On the other hand, if a country has very little renewable blue water (less than would be needed to produce agricultural commodities) due to low precipitation and high aridity, but has a large amount of agricultural land, it will try to use all of it for irrigated production, while also using the available soil moisture optimally through rainfed production by choosing the right season and areas. In the process, it might also mine the fossil water (like many MENA (Middle East and North Africa) countries, plus Pakistan, Iran, Iraq and Afghanistan). In this case, due to water shortage there will still be a lot of cultivable land left uncultivated in the form of pasture, though such land have offer low productivity (Kumar et al., 2017).

If both renewable water resources and cultivable land are limited, the country or region will try to use all its renewable blue water, along with water in the soil profile, to increase cropping intensity by going for irrigated crops after harvesting rainfed crops. In such a situation, there will be less water left in the natural system, and there will be too little land left uncultivated. Such cases will be encountered in very arid regions that receive very little precipitation. The western and north-western parts of India are examples.

Therefore, in countries with an excess of renewable water resources, even if the area of land available for cultivation is large (though this is not often the case), the utilization of water for agricultural production and the needs of other sectors will be relatively low. It will be limited to what is required for producing food and other agricultural commodities for the domestic population and meeting domestic and manufacturing water needs, plus some water to produce surplus agricultural commodities for export. This is because of the costs involved in harnessing that additional water, with uncertain benefits from using that. It should be kept in mind that some countries refrain from using their potential land and water resources due to the economic burden of agriculture production, as most countries allocate a substantial share of their budget to protect their agriculture with input and output subsidies. The converse would be true for countries with very limited renewable water resources. This is evident in Figure 2: effective/actual renewable water resources determine the extent of water utilization to the extent of 65%. Hence, one of the major reasons many countries are able to leave a lot of water in the hydrological system for nature is that they have plenty of renewable water resources in per capita terms (Kumar et al., 2017).

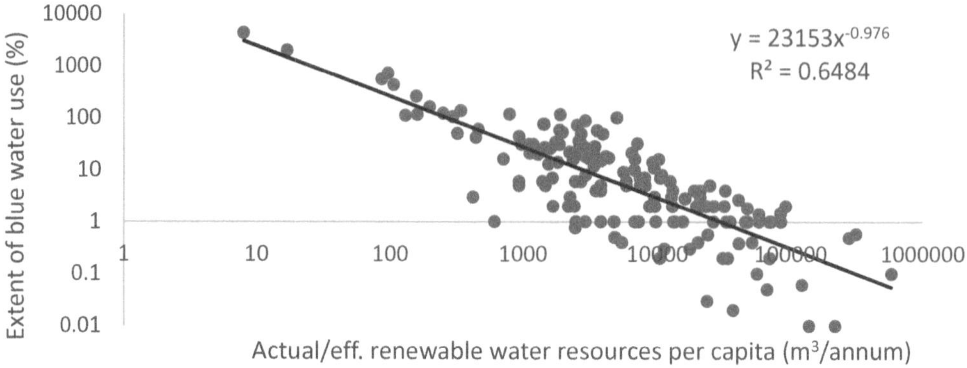

Figure 2. Bblue water withdrawal versus effective/actual per capita renewable water resources.

On the other hand, in countries with an excess of cultivable land, even if usable water resources are plentiful (which again is rare), not all the land will be put under cultivation. To a large extent, the land area that is put under cultivation will be decided by the domestic demand for food grains and other agricultural commodities (oil seeds, vegetables, fruits, fibre, fodder and fuel-wood) and to a different extent by the international demand for agricultural commodities and domestic policies on agricultural commodity trade. There are two reasons for the latter not becoming a major determining factor. There are many players in the global agricultural commodity trade, and the international agricultural commodity market can be highly sensitive to global agricultural outputs, which is determined by domestic production surplus. Hence, as per capita cultivable land increases, the proportion of the agricultural land that is under cultivation will keep declining, as depicted in Figure 3; R^2 is 0.31, and the relationship is significant at the 95% confidence level (Kumar et al., 2017).

But there are countries which have ample cultivable land and usable water resources but are facing food shortages owing to very little area being under crop production, and little of the water resources being tapped for irrigation. The extent of infrastructure development to improve water supplies is also very low in these countries (Kumar et al., 2017). Several countries in Africa, especially in eastern Africa, are in this category (African Union, 2014; Kumar, Saleth, Foster, Niranjan, & Sivamohan, 2016). There is large amount of water flowing out of these countries into the downstream countries – from Ethiopia through the Blue Nile into Egypt. As the governance in these countries improves, the extent of water utilization will increase, and so will the chances for expansion of cultivated land, with the provision of irrigation facilities (Kumar et al., 2017).

Which countries have plenty of water for future crop production?

Kumar and Singh (2005) found that net 'virtual water' export through agricultural commodities from a country (Hoekstra & Hung, 2003) is a direct function of gross cropped area, and explained this relation using the concept of 'effective agricultural water withdrawal', the sum of irrigation water withdrawal and water use from the soil profile, which increased linearly with per capita gross cropped area. Verma, Kampman, van der Zaag,

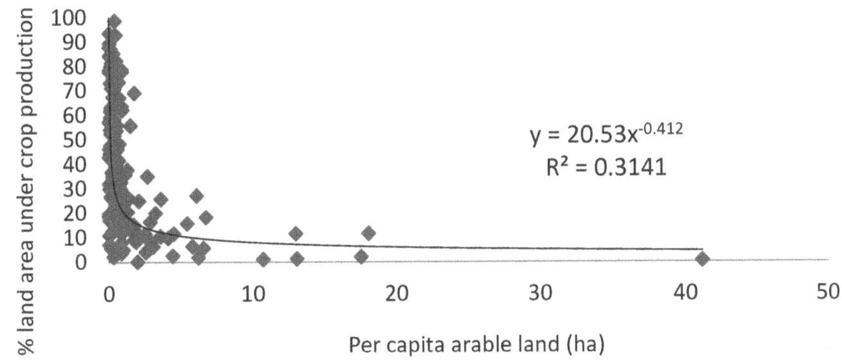

Figure 3. Percentage of land area under crop versus per capita arable land.

and Hoekstra (2009), who analyzed virtual water trade between provinces of India, corroborated the finding. Kumar and Singh (2005) also developed a framework according to which a country with a large amount of agricultural land and enough water to bring it under crop production has the greatest advantage in terms of producing agricultural surplus and exports. However, another country that has the same amount of water as the first one, but very little agricultural land, will not enjoy the same advantage. But a third country, with less renewable (blue) water, but the same amount of agricultural land as the first country, will be better off than the second country, in terms of agricultural production. Thus, beyond a certain point, having much more water than what would be needed to bring all the cultivated land under intensive production does not help in securing food self-sufficiency.

Our water-land index captures two important dimensions of the agricultural production potential of a country: adequacy of water to bring the available cultivated land under intensive irrigation (water adequacy index) for 300 days in a year, and the total amount of cultivated land per capita. The water-land index varies from zero for the Solomon Islands to 2.056 for Australia. Regression between water-land index and per capita virtual water exports showed a linear relationship, with R^2 of 0.55 (Figure 4). The relationship is significant at the 95% confidence level. A higher water-land index means greater agricultural surplus after domestic consumption, and a lower index means a production deficit for domestic consumption needs. This strong relation means that the water-land index is robust enough to capture the agricultural production potential of a country (Kumar et al., 2017).

There are 22 countries with enough renewable water resources (water adequacy index of 1), which could be used to expand cultivated land by tapping unused irrigation potential to boost agricultural production: Argentina, Belie, Benin, Bolivia, Brazil, Myanmar, Canada, Finland, France, Guatemala, Hungary, Lithuania, Nicaragua, Paraguay, Romania, Sweden, Thailand, USA and Uruguay (Table S2). They are not doing so for several reasons. Some of them are marginal quality of the land available for future harvest, high cost of production, and the need to tap additional export markets due to insufficient domestic demand for the produce. These are countries which have an excess of renewable water in per capita terms and a smaller fraction of their agricultural land under cultivation, leaving the remaining land under permanent crops and pasture. Essentially,

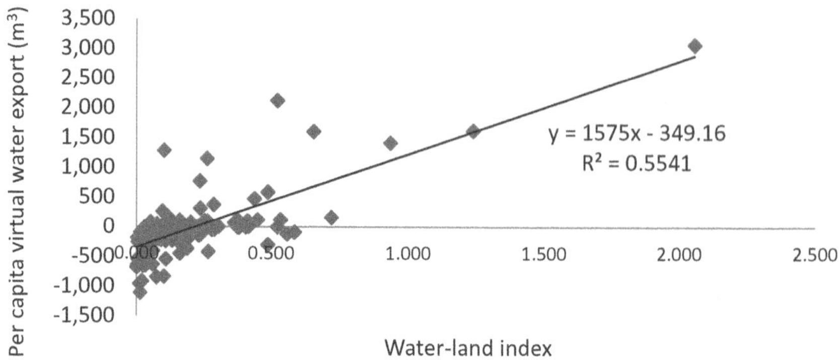

Figure 4. Virtual water export versus water-land index.

these are also most likely to be countries with a large amount of agricultural land in per capita terms (ranging from 0.49 for the US to 1.24 for Canada), if we go by the model presented in Figure 3. Their water-land index ranges from 0.104 for Guatemala to 1.239 for Canada. So, by merely bringing a small portion of this agricultural land under cultivation, they are able to meet their needs for export as well as domestic consumption.

This is in contrast to countries like India, which have utilized nearly 90% of the agricultural land for (temporary) crop cultivation, in spite of the very small extent of agricultural land per capita, resulting in excessive anthropogenic pressure on land. Future population growth in these countries is likely to result in expansion of cultivated land, but not in all cases, as population growth is either nil or negative in many of these countries that are developed.

Now, there are 39 countries which do not have enough renewable water resources to bring all the cultivated land under irrigated production. Their per capita cultivated land area is in the range of 0.003 (Kuwait) and 2.069 (Australia). Their water adequacy index is less than 1 (Table S3). This means that even if all the utilizable water were harnessed and diverted for irrigation, it would not be enough to meet the irrigation demand of the entire cultivated area. The low water adequacy index is also a reflection of the abundance of cultivated land and high irrigation water demand. It is important to know how many of these countries are producing enough food, and if not, whether there is possibility of increasing agricultural production (Kumar et al., 2017).

For this, we looked at the current level of utilization of irrigation potential in these countries. Of them, 12 countries use a small fraction of their irrigation potential: Australia, Denmark, Burkina Faso, Sudan, Ukraine, Cuba, Moldova, Nigeria, Malawi, Uganda, Zimbabwe and Afghanistan. Even with a small volume of blue water, they are able to produce surplus agricultural output by tapping soil water and remain virtual water exporters, as they have much agricultural land per capita. If they expand irrigation, they can increase greatly their production. But their ability to trade these agricultural commodities globally depends largely on the cost of production and international market trends. All other countries (27 of them) are net importers of virtual water.

Among these 39 countries without enough renewable water resources, there are seven countries whose water use far exceeds their renewable water availability; they are able to do so by mining fossil groundwater: Jordan, Kuwait, Libya, Israel, Qatar, Yemen and

Pakistan. Yet, they are heavily dependent on virtual water imports. Irrigation expansion is not possible in those countries because surface and groundwater resources are already over-exploited, rainfall is very low, and too little productive land is left uncultivated. But the data suggest that in 20 of these 39 countries irrigation expansion through infrastructure development is possible and also needed to boost agricultural production, as their current utilization of irrigation potential is low and they are also dependent on agricultural commodity imports: Algeria, Armenia, Barbados, Bulgaria, Cuba, Eritrea, Ethiopia, Iran, India, Kenya, Mali, Malta, Morocco, Niger, Rwanda, Senegal, South Africa, Tanzania, Togo and Tunisia (Kumar et al., 2017).

Now there is a third category of countries, 69 in total, which have a water adequacy ratio greater than 1, and therefore taken as 1 (see Table S4) per our methodology. In some cases, the high water adequacy ratio is because those countries have very little cultivated land, and not because they have abundant renewable water resources. As a matter of fact, only four of these 69 countries have more than 0.5 ha of cultivated land per capita, and 29 have less than 0.10 ha. Due to the severe water shortage, some (Bahrain, Oman, etc.) have a small portion of their agricultural land under cultivation with temporary crops. Nevertheless, many others (Bangladesh, Jamaica, El Salvador, Dominican Republic, etc.) have a large amount of renewable water but very limited agricultural land and cultivated land. What makes them different from countries such as the United States, Argentina, Brazil and Canada, which have abundant cultivated land and abundant water resources, is that they have disproportionately less arable land than water resources. This reduces their water-land index. And as a result, they are virtual water importing countries. Their irrigation potential utilization, estimated as a ratio of the total amount of irrigation water withdrawal (m^3 per capita) to the total amount required to irrigate the cultivated land for nearly 300 days in a year and expressed in percentage terms, ranges from as low as 0.1% to as high as 451% (Kumar et al., 2017).

As evident from the above description, there are a few countries which actually divert more water than what is required by the reported cultivated land: Bahrain, Bangladesh, Ecuador, Egypt, Japan, Oman, Suriname, Tajikistan and Uzbekistan. This excessive diversion could be because the actual water diversion for irrigation is much higher than the consumptive water use we have estimated on the basis of average ET; or because some countries are using perennial crops, due to which the total ET requirement of crops would be higher than what we have considered, which is for only 300 days. Regarding the first point, for crops like paddy, a large amount of water is applied to the field to inundate it, which is far in excess of the crop ET requirements. In certain cases, a lot of water is required in hyper-arid climatic conditions for the non-beneficial consumptive use of water such as barren soil evaporation. Yet they are dependent on food imports. Unless crop yields increase substantially, there is no way these countries can become food self-sufficient.

As Table S4 shows, 60 of these 69 countries are not fully utilizing their irrigation potential, and thereby remain net importers of agricultural commodities. Many are developing countries with limited economic power and want to boost their agricultural production. These countries can invest more in water resources development for irrigation intensification and thus become self-sufficient in agriculture, depending on the cost of water resources development and on the productivity of the land which is under cultivation. However, cropping to cover 300 days of the year is not easy. In any case, many of the developed countries in this list (such as Germany and Italy) are not in a position to expand or intensify irrigation, due to scarcity of labour and the high cost of production of crops. Also, in many countries in Northern Europe and in North America, the land is covered by snow for several months of the year, limiting intensive crop production (Kumar et al., 2017).

Linkage between agricultural land, cultivated land and milk production

From the foregoing discussion, it is clear that having plenty of renewable water does not guarantee large agricultural production; nor does having plenty of cultivable land guarantee large-scale agricultural production. Some countries (for instance, Kazakhstan and Mongolia) have much land classified as agricultural land, but it is of poor quality, and at best is suitable for grazing (in Mongolia, even the pastureland is of poor quality, capable of producing grasses only for four months of the year). Therefore, what matters is the amount land that is cultivated (Kumar et al., 2017) with adequate inputs of water and nutrients. Without water to irrigate and nutrients to reinforce the soils, such marginal lands cannot produce much biomass, due to poor crop yields. But globally, such lands are used extensively for livestock production and dairy farming (Kumar et al., 2017). Dairy farming, which contributes to food and nutritional security, is a water-intensive activity involving direct use of water by animals for drinking, plus indirect use of water for the feed and fodder they consume. The former is small fraction of the total water consumption. The latter involves the use of biomass from cultivated and grazing land, along with water, labour and other inputs (Sultana et al., 2014), and therefore captures the use of the available cultivable land and usable water.

The interaction between renewable water resources and cultivated land and between precipitation and pasturelands to produce biomass outputs is through a complex web, with climate as the backdrop. The amount of water required to irrigate a unit area of cropland (for intensive cropping to cover the whole year) is determined by the effective precipitation and climate. The climate determines the ET, and effective precipitation decides the amount of irrigation, for a given crop ET. If enough water is available to irrigate the cropped land, the aggregate production depends on the total amount of cropped land. If this is not available, the productivity per unit crop area declines. If more water is available than is required to irrigate the crop, it will not lead to increased production but increase the water available for ecological uses. The climate also influences farming to a great extent by allowing or disallowing certain types of crops and dairy animals and their varieties in an area (Kumar et al., 2017).

Pastureland availability, along with the cultivated land area and the intensity of cultivation, determines the amount of dairy output. Very importantly, in any country, the expansion of cropped land is at the cost of pastureland, as the amount of agricultural land is either static or shrinking over time, with urbanization, industrialization and more built-up area (Jayne, Anriquez, & Collier, 2013). As Figure 3 indicates, several countries with much per capita cultivable land have much pastureland, and vice versa. India is an example. The average per capita pastureland in India is as little as 0.0085 ha. In the United States it is 0.795 ha, nearly 100 times as much. The productivity of pastureland is a function of climate and precipitation. Year-round precipitation ensures high productivity of pastureland with grasses if the climate is moderate (Kumar et al., 2017).

The best production system that illustrates this complex web of interactions is dairy production (Paulsen, 2013). Dairy animals live on grazing in pastureland, stock feeding (of grasses of other fodder crops either from pastureland or from cropland), or both (Capstaff & Miller, 2018; O'Mara, 2012). To test the hypothesis about this complex web of interactions (illustrated above), a composite index incorporating the water-land index and the pastureland index was used.

The coefficient used in the pastureland index is determined on the basis of the total annual precipitation and the average daily evapotranspiration, to give a composite index of milk production capability. Higher rainfall and lower ET_0 raise the value of the coefficient. The highest value of the coefficient is 1.7 (for New Zealand), and the lowest value is 0.05 for hyper-arid and desert countries (UAE, Saudi Arabia, Kuwait, Bahrain, Qatar, Yemen, Egypt, Oman, Libya, Algeria) with very low rainfall (200 mm or less). A large coefficient indicates better primary productivity of the pastureland to produce biomass.

However, the full influence of climate in deciding the milk production potential of a region cannot be captured in this composite index. The climate largely determines what kind of dairy animals are suitable for a region or locality. For instance, a cold climate is very suitable for high-yielding breeds of cows (which are found in Northern, Central and Eastern Europe, the Americas and New Zealand); the hot and arid tropics are not suitable for these animals. Buffaloes are adapted to both hot/arid and hot/humid tropical climates and are seen in India, Pakistan, China, Nepal, Bangladesh, Afghanistan, Iran, Iraq and some of the countries in Africa and Latin America.

A regression is run between per capita milk production and the composite water-land-pasture index. The composite index ranged from 0.002 to 2.50. Per capita milk production is the total milk yield from cows, buffaloes, goat, sheep and camels in 2013. The regression produces an R^2 of 0.64, which means that the composite index explains milk production to the extent of 64%, and the relationship is significant at the 95% confidence level. This means that the index is realistic. When regression was run on the computed composite index, with the water adequacy index merely a function of the renewable water, no relationship emerged. This once again validates our assumptions in estimating the water adequacy index of the water-land index.

Per capita milk production increases linearly with increase in the composite index (Figure 5). However, two trend lines clearly emerge, a steep one and a mild one. Most countries on the steep gradient are developed countries, with a cold and temperate climate. Most of the countries on the mild gradient are developing countries, with a hot tropical climate. The difference in productivity is mainly due to the difference in climate, which influences the production potential of the land and production technologies, and dairy production practices.

The countries on the steeper gradient, which we call the technical efficiency frontier, generally have higher milk production efficiency. This might be due to (1) favourable climatic conditions (high humidity, low temperature and higher incident solar energy), leading to production of more biomass with less transpiration, resulting in higher crop/fodder/grass yields and physical productivity of water; (2) adoption of certain high-yielding varieties of cows, such as Holstein Friesian and Jersey, which are better suited to cold and temperate climates; and (3) high energy conversion ratios due to stock

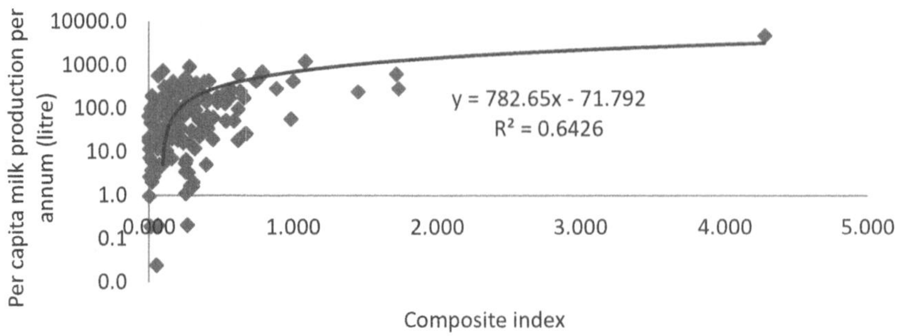

Figure 5. Milk production per capita versus water-land-pasture (composite) index.

feeding of animals. A closer look at the regression shows that India, whose composite index is a mere 0.113, has per capita milk production of 113 kg/y, though the value predicted by the model is only 16.3 kg/y per capita. Therefore, India is on the technical efficiency frontier, with production seven times greater than the potential predicted by the model. On the other hand, New Zealand, whose composite index is 4.25, produces 4836 kg/y, just 50% more than the value predicted by the model (3254 kg/y). Therefore, India remains a great performer in dairy production in spite of its unfavourable production environment of climate, rainfall, pastureland availability and amount of cultivated land. The model could be strengthened by taking climate into account (Kumar et al., 2017).

Findings and conclusions

The article has analyzed the food security and water management challenges facing the world by delinking the food security challenges from the challenges of managing water supplies. This is based on the premises that assessing food security purely from a water resources perspective gives a distorted view of the food security challenges facing a country (Alexandratos & Bruinsma, 2012; FAO, 2011; Kumar et al., 2017; Kumar & Singh, 2005; Rockström et al., 2009), and that assessing water management challenges purely from the point of view of renewable water availability also can be misleading (Kumar et al., 2017; Kumar & Singh, 2005).

The composite water-land index developed for this study captures the adequacy of water to bring all the cultivated land under irrigated production (the water adequacy index, whose maximum value is 1) and the amount of cultivated land per capita (ha). We also derived a composite index, which combines the water-land index, thus computed, and the amount of good pastureland (pastureland per capita × pastureland coefficient) available for grazing and grass production to predict the maximum per capita milk production in different countries. Then, we assessed water adequacy; estimated the water-land index; and estimated the composite index of water, cultivated land and pastureland to simulate the milk production potential in per capita terms for 152 countries, using global data sets.

The analysis shows that per capita agricultural land availability is important in determining how much of their agricultural land is used by countries for cultivation and how much is left as permanent pastures, when plenty of water is available. While the first (cultivated land) determines crop outputs, both the first and the second (pastureland) influence dairy production (Kumar et al., 2017). Earlier studies provides sufficient indications of this effect (Alexandratos & Bruinsma, 2012; FAO, 2011; Kumar & Singh, 2005; Verma et al., 2009; Zhao et al., 2019). Countries with much per capita agricultural land use a small proportion of that land for production of temporary crops, leaving most as pastureland for grazing and fodder production (FAO, 2011; Kumar et al., 2017). The analysis also shows that certain countries are able to leave a large proportion of the blue water in their territory in the natural hydrological system as ecological flows, merely because they have more renewable water resources higher than are required to bring all the cultivated land under intensive cropping (Kumar et al., 2017).

The modelling of virtual water trade, a proxy variable for a country's deficit/surplus in agricultural production (Kumar & Singh, 2005; Paulsen, 2013), for 152 countries across the world, using the water-land index and per capita virtual water export, showed that the water-land index could be a significant variable explaining virtual water trade. When the water-land index increased, the agricultural export from the country increased linearly. The composite index consisting of the water adequacy index, per capita cultivated land, per capita pastureland and richness coefficient for the pastureland together explained 64% of the milk production potential of countries (in per capita terms).

Further, availability of large amount of renewable water resources per capita does not mean enough water to irrigate all the cultivated land if per capita cultivated land is large. The water adequacy ratio can also be less than 1, and in such cases the country can face severe water shortages, as the situation in Australia illustrates (Barrett, 2019). Yet, this does not constrain agricultural production, as the country produces a large surplus for export (Qureshi, Hanjra, & Ward, 2013). And, as the situation of 10 countries illustrates, the availability of copious renewable water resources, enough to bring all the cultivated land under irrigated production (water adequacy ratio greater than 1), and its full utilization, also does not guarantee food self-sufficiency, unless it is complemented by enough arable land. Dependence on food imports increases for those water-rich countries with less utilization of irrigation potential.

In sum, in assessing the magnitude of food security and water management challenges we have to factor in the role of agricultural land, particularly cultivated land. When this is done, we have four categories of countries: countries with plenty of renewable water and cultivated land, with both water and food self-sufficiency; countries with plenty of renewable water resources, but a disproportionately larger area of cultivated land, resulting in low water adequacy but a food surplus, despite occasional water shortages; countries with enough cultivated land but not enough water, facing different degrees of water shortages and food self-insufficiency; and countries with high 'water adequacy' – usually because of plenty of renewable water and little cultivated land per capita, but in some cases because of less area of cultivated land than the available water can bring under intensive production, combined with low water availability – but mostly dependent on food imports. The availability of rich pastureland along with cultivated land significantly influences milk production, an important component of food and nutritional security (Kumar et al., 2017).

Around 60 countries belong to the fourth category, with large unused irrigation potential that could be tapped to increase cropping intensity. They could reduce their food imports, but some of them (especially in Europe) will not due to labour scarcity, high production cost and ecological factors. On the other hand, around 20 water-scarce countries belong to the third category (mostly in sub-Saharan Africa), having poor water adequacy for crop production but also having varying quantities of water still unutilized, which could be harnessed to increase irrigation (Kumar et al., 2017). Investment in water resources development would improve their food security (Alexandratos & Bruinsma, 2012).

Grassland availability has a major role in production of milk and meat (Capstaff & Miller, 2018; O'Mara, 2012). Modelling of per capita milk production against the composite index of water adequacy, cultivated land and pastureland shows that the index is a significant variable explaining the milk production in a country. The composite index ranged from 0.003 in Kuwait, Bahrain, United Arab Emirates and Sao Tome and Principe to 4.275 in New Zealand. The composite index explained 61% of the variation in per capita milk production, with a linear relation (Kumar et al., 2017).

To conclude, historically, analyses of water scarcity and food security challenges confronting nations around the world have treated them as a single challenge, using simplistic considerations of renewable water availability and extent of withdrawal of renewable (blue) water from the natural system (Falkenmark, 1997; Kummu et al., 2016; Raskin et al., 1997). Such skewed analyses ignore the role of access to agricultural land, particularly cultivated land (Zhao et al., 2019), which increases the access to water in the soil profile for crop production, thereby reducing the demand for blue water in agriculture, in determining the agricultural production potential of a country, while increasing the overall agricultural production potential (Kumar & Singh, 2005). On the other hand, the extent of good pastureland reduces the cultivated area needed to support production of fodder and feed for dairy animals (Kumar et al., 2017).

The regions with plenty of cultivated land per capita and enough water to cover all the land under intensive production will have a comparative advantage in producing agricultural surplus for export (FAO, 2011; Verma et al., 2009; Zhao et al., 2019). They are followed by countries (39 in number) with plenty of per capita cultivated land but a relatively low water adequacy index. Countries (69 in number) that are water-rich but have little cultivated land in per capita terms will not have problems related to water supply but might depend on food imports to meet domestic consumption needs. But there are many countries in the second and third categories (20 of the 39, and 60 of the 69, respectively), which need to and can increase their production through increasing the utilization of irrigation water.

Overall, the parameters we found to have a significant impact on water supply and overall water demand, and crop and dairy production potential of countries are water adequacy ratio (which considers renewable water resources, cultivated land, climate and crop growing period); per capita cultivated land; and the pastureland index (considering per capita pastureland and the pastureland coefficient). There is a need to develop quantitative indicators to assess the water supply and food security situation of individual countries using these parameters.

Note

1. This article is derived from an occasional paper by Kumar et al. (2017).

Disclosure statement

No potential conflict of interest was reported by the authors.

References

African Union. (2014, July 14–18). *African Union Programme for Infrastructure Development in Africa (PIDA): Addressing the infrastructure gap in Africa, to speed up regional integration*. Seventh conference of African ministers in charge of integration, Swaziland.

Alexandratos, N., & Bruinsma, J. (2012, June). *World agriculture towards 2030/50: The 2012 revision* (ESA Working Paper No. 12-03). Rome: Agricultural Economics Development Division, Food and Agriculture Organization of the United Nations.

Allan, J. A. (1997). *'Virtual water': A long-term solution for water short Middle Eastern economies?* Occasional paper no. 3. London, UK: School of Oriental and African Studies, University of London.

Barrett, J. (2019, September 28). Drought hit Australian towns prepare for 'unimaginable' water crisis. *Environment*. Retrieved from https://www.reuters.com/article/us-australia-drought/drought-hit-australian-towns-prepare-for-unimaginable-water-crisis-idUSKBN1WC2EP

Beddington, J. (2010, January 12). Food security: Contributions from science to a new and greener revolution. *Philosophical Transactions of the Royal Society B: Biological Sciences, 365*(1537), 61–71. doi:10.1098/rstb.2009.0201

Bodner, G., Nakhforoosh, A., & Kaul, H.-P. (2015). Management of crop water under drought: A review. *Agronomy for Sustainable Development, 35*(2), 401–442.

Capstaff, N., & Miller, A. (2018). Improving the yield and nutritional quality of forage crops. *Frontiers in Plant Science, 9*, 535. doi:10.3389/fpls.2018.00535

Chapagain, A. K., & Hoekstra, A. Y. (2003). *Virtual water flows between nations in relation to trade in livestock and livestock products* (Value of Water Research Report Series No. 13). Delft, Netherlands: UNESCO-IHE Institute for Water Education.

de Fraiture, C., & Wichelns, D. (2010). Satisfying future water demands for agriculture. *Agricultural Water Management, 97*, 502–511. doi:10.1016/j.agwat.2009.08.008

Falkenmark, M. (1989). The massive water scarcity now threatening Africa: Why isn't it being addressed? *Ambio, 18*(2), 112–118.

Falkenmark, M. (1997). Meeting water requirements of an expanding world population. *Philosophical Transactions of the Royal Society of London, Series B: Biological Sciences, 352*, 929–936. doi:10.1098/rstb.1997.0072

Food and Agriculture Organization of the United Nations. (2011). *The state of the world's land and water resources for food and agriculture: Managing systems at risk*. New York: Earthscan and FAO.

Hanjra, M. A., & Qureshi, M. E. (2010). Global water crisis and future food security in an era of climate change. *Food Policy, 35*(5), 365–377. doi:10.1016/j.foodpol.2010.05.006

Helfand, S. M., & Levine, E. S. (2004). Farm size and the determinants of productive efficiency in the Brazilian Center-West. *Agricultural Economics, 31*(2–3), 241–249. doi:10.1111/agec.2004.31.issue-2-3

Hoekstra, A. Y. (2003). Virtual water: An introduction. In A. Y. Hoekstra (ed.), *Virtual water trade: Proceedings of the international expert meeting on virtual water trade*, 2002, 12–13 December. Delft, the Netherlands: IHE Delft.

Hoekstra, A. Y., & Hung, P. Q. (2003). Virtual water trade: A quantification of virtual water flows between nations in relation to international crop trade. In A. Y. Hoekstra (Ed.), *Virtual water trade: Proceedings of the international expert meeting on virtual water trade* (Value of Water Research Report series No. 12). Delft, the Netherlands: IHE.

Jayne, T. A., Anriquez, G., & Collier, E. (2013, February 27). African agriculture toward 2030: Changes in urbanization and agricultural land dynamics and their implications for CGIAR research. Paper presented at ISPC Foresight meeting, January 24–25, 2013, Boston, MA.

Jia, S., Long, Q., & Liu, W. (2017). The fallacious strategy of virtual water trade. *International Journal of Water Resources Development, 33*(2), 340–347. doi:10.1080/07900627.2016.1180591

Kumar, M. D., Bassi, N., Singh, O. P., Ganguly, A., & Chattopadhyay, S. (2017, June) *Assessing global water and food challenges: Time to rethink on methods* (Occasional Paper No. 12). Hyderabad, India: Institute for Resource Analysis and Policy.

Kumar, M. D., Saleth, R. M., Foster, J. D., Niranjan, V., & Sivamohan, M. V. K. (2016). Water, human development, inclusive growth, and poverty alleviation: International perspectives. In

M. D. Kumar, A. J. James, & Y. Kabir (Eds.), *Rural water systems for multiple uses and livelihood security* (pp. 3–22). Amsterdam: Elsevier.

Kumar, M. D., & Singh, O. P. (2005). Virtual water in global food and water policy making: Is there a need for rethinking? *Water Resources Management, 19*(6), 759–789. doi:10.1007/s11269-005-3278-0

Kumar, M. D., Sivamohan, M. V. K., & Narayanamoorthy, A. (2012). The food security challenge of the food-land-water nexus in India. *Food Security, 4*(4), 539–556. doi:10.1007/s12571-012-0204-1

Kummu, M., Guillaume, J. H. A., de Moel, H., Eisner, S., Flörke, M., Porkka, M., … War, P. J. (2016). *The world's road to water scarcity: Shortage and stress in the 20th century and pathways towards sustainability*. Scientific Report 6, 38495. doi:10.1038/srep38495

Mancosu, N., Snyder, R. L., Kyriakakis, G., & Spano, D. (2015). Water scarcity and future challenges for food production. *Water, 7*, 975–992. doi:10.3390/w7030975

Mukherji, A., Shah, T., & Banerjee, P. S. (2012). Kick-starting a second green revolution in Bengal. *Economic and Political Weekly, 47*(18), 27–30.

Namara, R. E., Hanjra, M. A., Castillo, G. E., Ravnborg, H. M., Smith, L., & Van Koppen, B. (2010). Agricultural water management and poverty linkages. *Agricultural Water Management, 97*(4), 520–527. doi:10.1016/j.agwat.2009.05.007

O'Mara, F. P. (2012). The role of grasslands in food security and climate change. *Annals of Botany, 110* (6), 1263–1270. doi:10.1093/aob/mcs209

Paulsen, A. (2013). *Virtual water: A useful concept for informing land use in New Zealand*. Dissertation, Master of Environmental Policy. Lincoln University, Canterbury, New Zealand.

Qureshi, M. E., Hanjra, M. A., & Ward, J. (2013). Impact of water scarcity in Australia on global food security in an era of climate change. *Food Policy, 38*, 136–145. doi:10.1016/j.foodpol.2012.11.003

Rao, B., & Mingxuan, F. (2010). Introduction and motivation. In J. Seetharaman & R. Bhanoji (Eds.), *Index of drinking water adequacy: International and intra-national explorations*. Singapore: NUS Press, Ridge Books.

Raskin, I., Smith, R. D., & Salt, D. E. (1997). Phytoremediation of metals: Using plants to remove pollutants from the environment. *Current Opinion in Biotechnology, 8*, 221–226. doi:10.1016/S0958-1669(97)80106-1

Rijsberman, F. R. (2006). Water scarcity: Fact or fiction? *Agricultural Water Management, 80*(1–3), 5–22. doi:10.1016/j.agwat.2005.07.001

Rockström, J., Falkenmark, M., Karlberg, L., Hoff, H., Rost, S., & Gerten, D. (2009). Future water availability for global food production: The potential of green water for increasing resilience to global change. *Water Resources Research, 45*(7), 16. doi:10.1029/2007WR006767

Rosegrant, M. W., Ringler, C., & Zhu, T. (2009). Water for agriculture: Maintaining food security under growing scarcity. *Annual Review of Environment and Resources, 34*, 205–222. doi:10.1146/annurev.environ.030308.090351

Seckler, D., Amarasinghe, U., Molden, D., de Silva, R., & Barker, R. (1998). *World water demand and supply, 1990 to 2025: Scenarios and issues* (Research Report 19). Colombo, Sri Lanka: International Water Management Institute.

Sultana, M., Uddin, M. M., Ridoutt, B. G., & Peters, K. J. (2014). Comparison of water use in global milk production for different typical farms. *Agricultural Systems, 129*, 9–21. doi:10.1016/j.agsy.2014.05.002

Verma, S., Kampman, D. A., van der Zaag, P., & Hoekstra, A. (2009). Going against the flow: A critical analysis of inter-state virtual water trade in the context of India's National River Linking Program. *Physics and Chemistry of the Earth, 34*, 261–269. doi:10.1016/j.pce.2008.05.002

While, C. (2014). Understanding water scarcity: Definitions and measurements. In R. Q. Grafton, P. Wyrwoll, C. White, & D. Allendes (Eds.), *Global water: Issues and insights* (pp. 161–165). Canberra, Australia: ANU Press, Australian National University.

Zhao, D., Hubacek, K., Feng, K., Sun, L., & Liu, J. (2019, April 15). Explaining virtual water trade: A spatial-temporal analysis of the comparative advantage of land, labor and water in China. *Water Research, 153*, 304–314. doi:10.1016/j.watres.2019.01.025

Index

For Product Safety Concerns and Information please contact our EU representative GPSR@taylorandfrancis.com Taylor & Francis Verlag GmbH, Kaufingerstraße 24, 80331 München, Germany

Batch number: 10726294

Printed by Printforce, the Netherlands